Fundamentals of Insurance

The Irwin Series in Financial Planning and Insurance

Consulting Editor Jerry S. Rosenbloom University of Pennsylvania

Fundamentals of Insurance

ROBERT I. MEHR

Professor of Finance
University of Illinois at Urbana-Champaign

ASSISTED BY

SUSAN L. WAGNER, MS

JOHN R. SULGA, MBA

Both Graduate Assistants in Finance
University of Illinois at Urbana-Champaign

1983

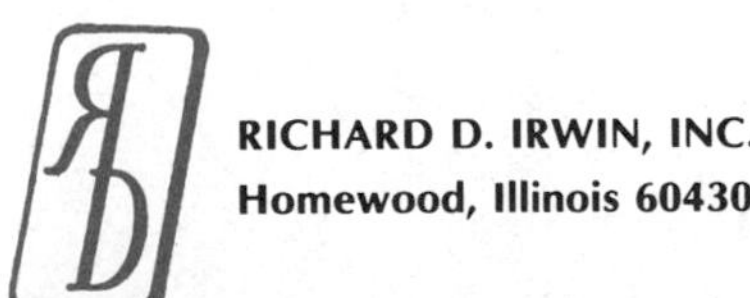

RICHARD D. IRWIN, INC.
Homewood, Illinois 60430

ISBN 0-256-02625-4
Library of Congress Catalog Card No. 82–82520

Printed in the United States of America

1 2 3 4 5 6 7 8 9 0 K 0 9 8 7 6 5 4 3

Dedication

This book is dedicated to my academic progeny—the following group of past and present graduate students who transformed my work at the University of Illinois from a daily routine to a delightful experience, enhancing my life immeasurably. Over the past 35 years we have challenged each other with open minds as both professor and student should in a community of scholars if minds are to expand and learning is to be intellectually enriching and enjoyable. I am proud of them all and look forward to more of the same. Most of the students are now teaching at other universities and building academic families of their own. I wish for them as much happiness from their students as they have given to me.

Barnie E. Abelle
Sadi A. Assaf
William M. Beckemeier
Robert T. Boling
Charles Carlyle
James J. Chastain
Dongsae Cho
Stephen P. D'Arcy
William R. Desollar II
Mark S. Dorfman
James R. Eck
Gary J. Eldred
Campbell K. Evans
Frank L. Gile
Sandra G. Gustavson
Scott E. Harrington
Leslie A. Hearn
Bob A. Hedges
Han Bin Kang
Bruce S. Kaplan
Kenneth F. Kennedy
William V. Kessner
David R. Klock
Joan A. Krueger
Keith McVicker
Brian A. Montigney
Arlynn W. Nelson
Terry L. Rose
Jeffrey L. Shade
Mack H. Shumate
Peter F. Steger
Fred G. Stubbs
John R. Sulga
Susan L. Wagner
Melvin D. Williams
Jay A. Yager

A Prefatory Letter

Robert I. Mehr
101 W. Windsor Road Apt. 1102
Urbana, Illinois 61801

January 1983

Dear Reader:

Edward Gibbon in *The History of the Decline and Fall of the Roman Empire* observed that one Roman had 62,000 books and 22 acknowledged concubines. Seneca philosophized that "Since you cannot read all the books which you possess, it is enough to possess only as many as you can read." One purpose of this letter is to explain why this book is one you can read and thus one you should possess. As for concubines, I have no advice to offer and I am truly sorry.

Before giving you the reasons for possessing this book, I must tell you a story about its development. Originally the publishers asked for an essentials of insurance text. What they wanted was a short, simplified version of my *Principles of Insurance* text written with Professor Cammack. That book was born in 1952 and is now in its seventh edition (1980). I expect the eighth edition to be published on schedule. So what happened to the essentials text? Really nothing, because I soon found that few people agree on what is essential.

After much agonizing over the issue, I decided that no one can determine what is essential per se. The answer seems to depend on the interests of students, teachers and on course objectives. Fortunately for education, these interests do not have to coincide. This text has been designed with this thought in mind. The prenatal name *essentials* was changed to the broader given name *fundamentals* while retaining the family name *insurance.* Too bad you missed the christening ceremony—it would have done justice to royalty!

Now that we are on the subject of royalty, let's digress for a moment. James Boswell in *The Life of Samuel Johnson LL.D* said, "No man but a blockhead ever wrote except for money." Do you know that until 1709 authors had no legal right to a royalty on the sale of their books? The first statute in the world that gave them this right was an Act, Statute 8 Anne, *c* 19. Such writers as the university wits (Christopher Marlowe, George Peele, John Lyly, Thomas Lodge, Robert Greene and Thomas Nashe), Geoffrey Chaucer and Francis Bacon all published before 1709. Would you call them blockheads?

In contrast to Boswell's curious statement, the possibility of royalties is not a consideration in the writing of this book. My goals are multifaceted, and all of them are for your benefit. Your desire to learn and the fulfillment of this desire are the rewards—two powerful forces.

Let's get back to the objectives of the text rather than my personal goals. Despite the abandonment of the proposed title, the objectives remain unaffected. The challenge is how to achieve them. I want to help you build a foundation of insurance knowledge that you will find useful regardless of whether you are an undergraduate at any institution of higher education or studying on your own. In this case *useful* means learning sufficient basic elements of the subject so that you can deal with insurance as buyers, sellers, concerned citizens, company employees or regulators. To reach this goal requires a second objective: An introductory text that encompasses all concepts and practices that could be considered essential to any one of these interest groups.

So what is the challenge I face? Several insurance scholars reviewed the text as it developed, and they all wanted additional concepts discussed; rarely did they suggest deletions. When a deletion was suggested, it was usually a discussion that another reader wanted expanded. Yet all wanted the size of the book reduced! Such is the life of an author. If I didn't enjoy writing so much, I would look upon it as George Orwell did in *England Your England:* "Writing a book is a horrible, exhausting struggle, like a long bout of some painful illness." Now if experts can't agree on what is essential, how can a beginning student make this determination? I have lived with this discipline so long that I think everything about it is essential. I know this is wrong, but if I had to make a selection, it would not be the same as your instructor's.

When you learn more about the subject, you will develop your own ideas about what is essential. So for most readers, this text will include some "nonessential" essentials. That is why the book is called *Fundamentals.* All that is essential is fundamental, but all that is fundamental is not essential. The important quality of the book is its breadth which makes it possible for you to learn about the concepts and practices that *you* find interesting, particularly as you expand your interest in the subject. Forcing people to learn what they do not want to know is as foolish as feeding them what they don't want to eat. Why feed people broccoli, for example, when the only good thing you can say about it is that it has no bones.

In writing about *Paradise Lost,* Samuel Johnson said, "it is a book that the reader admires and lays down, and forgets to take up again. Its perusal is a duty rather than a pleasure." I want this book to be a pleasure to read so that you can enjoy your learning experience. That is really the overriding objective.

As I have been writing in the basic principles field over 30 years, it is impossible to write a new book without some repetition of ideas from past writings. But this text has been structured with the appeal directed toward special interests, special likes and special dislikes. Individuality not standardization is the theme. The book could be viewed as *A Variation on a Theme of Mehr and Cammack.* However, it is written with a different emphasis and new concepts that further distinguish it as a separate book without plugging the slot reserved for the *Principles of Insurance* in the scheme of insurance education.

The recognition of the inequality of individuality is the principal means used to help this text meet its objectives. It is divided into eight parts and each part includes two or more chapters. The chapters are divided into articles, sections, stanzas and verses with the headings plainly marked in the margin of the text. The parts are clearly described, the chapter objectives are stated and the titles of the chapter components are distinctly identified. Each part, chapter and segment stands on its own. Entire parts, whole chapters and parts of chapters can be skipped without interfering with the continuity of the text. For example, Part Five, Employee Benefit Plans, can be eliminated or Chapter 18, Social Insurance, included in Part Five can be omitted. If some but not all of Chapter 17 (Retirement Plans) in Part Five is of interest, segments of that chapter can be ignored: the funding issue, taxation and/or special types of retirement plans can be disregarded. The book has been written and organized to cater to many appetites. In this regard, I think of myself as a cafeteria dietitian providing a wide selection of food for thought. No one is expected to select all items on display in a cafeteria on the first visit!

The text contains a number of innerscripts judiciously interspersed throughout the book. These innerscripts, akin to postscripts except for their location, are another technique used to permit selection because they can be skipped. They provide information that falls into one of three classes: interesting but not essential (frills), amusing but can be skipped (thrills) and too difficult for an elementary text (chills). The chapter summaries and questions also can be helpful in selecting subject matter of interest.

The extensive glossary at the end of the book prepared by Irving Finston should be helpful. Words included in the glossary are printed in boldfaced type in the text and in lightface in the innerscripts. The use of the index with the glossary is helpful in locating the pages in the text where these concepts are discussed more fully, and thus could be of additional aid in selecting material for study.

Professor Sanford Halperin has prepared a student's manual for this text to help you learn, understand and retain as much as you can from your assignment. The manual could be especially valuable at some later time if you need help in studying segments of the text that have not been assigned.

Let's chat a moment about the publisher. Sometimes authors regard publishers as scheming, deceitful tightwads. The poet Thomas Campbell, who clamored for the founding of London University, in toasting Napoleon at an authors' dinner said, "to Napoleon! I agree with you that Napoleon is a tyrant, a monster, the sworn foe of our nation. But, gentlemen—he once shot a publisher!" In *Summaries of Thought:* "Authors," Christian

Bovee wrote: "There is probably no hell for authors in the next world—they suffer so much from critics and publishers in this." We'll get back to critics, but as for publishers, this book is among the first to be published by Richard D. Irwin, Inc., in 1983, its golden anniversary year. I am especially proud to have a book published by Dick Irwin during this important year for him. I suspect writers who criticize publishers have never had the pleasure of working with Richard D. Irwin. My relationship with Dick goes back more than 30 years. "It is with publishers as with wives: one always wants somebody else's." Not me, I have the best of both!

As for critics, some of the more complimentary remarks made about them are that they are legless people who teach running; they know the way but can't drive; they are people who seek to grow important at small expense and they are hot, envious, noisy, proud and, furthermore, they waste paper. Some of the less complimentary remarks are unprintable, at least in this prefatory letter. But I like critics and welcome their comments when they are helpful. Everyone's work can be improved by the suggestions of competent critics. You are not only invited but urged to write me about any aspects of this text that you believe can make it more palatable.

I thank Jerry Rosenbloom, Irving Finston and Chris Prestopino for their valuable comments on an early draft of the manuscript. Most of the comments were helpful. I thank editor Bonnie Smothers for her sincere dedication toward creating an innovative book. I am grateful to Irving Finston for preparing the glossary and to the two students (Susan Wagner and John Sulga) whose names appear on the title page. Finally, I thank my wife, Margaret, for her help in offering suggestions on many (it seems like all) aspects of this book and her tireless effort in proofreading. (She reads proofs like she reads the hundreds of catalogs that come our way, except in the catalogs she overlooks price! All that I owe, I owe because of my wife.) Seriously, we all owe this special person a great deal, for I could not have made it through the final stages of this project without her dedication.

In closing, I believe you will agree that this book is handsome and beautifully designed. It should be one you will want to keep not only for its practical value but for its beauty. "No furniture is so charming as books, even if you never open them or read a single word." Perhaps you will want to redecorate your living room, with this book as the focal point on your coffee table. So take care of it.

Cordially,

Robert I. Mehr

Robert I. Mehr

Contents

PART ONE THE NATURE OF RISK AND INSURANCE: AN INTRODUCTION

1. A prelude to the study of insurance 4

How to Proceed 6
The Burden of Financial Loss 6
Shifting the Burden by Law 7
Insurance and the Burden of Loss 7
The Insurance Business 8
The Insurer 8
The Insured 8
The Contract 9
Underwriting and Rating 9
Finance 9
Public Control 9
Fields of Insurance 10
Private Insurance 10
Government Insurance 11
Insurance and Society 12
Innerscript: Origins of Insurance 12
Social Values of Insurance 14
Social Costs of Insurance 16
Social Responsibility 17

2. Risk and insurance 20

Basic Definitions 21
Chance of Loss 21
Definition of Risk 22
Innerscript: Loss Predictability 22
Peril 24
Hazard 25
Loss 26
Risk and Risk Bearing 26
Social Cost of Risk 26
Methods of Handling Risk 27
Innerscript: Sinking Funds 28
Insurance as a Device for Handling Risk 32
Definition of Insurance 32
Indemnity 33
The Law of Large Numbers 33
Criteria of an Insurable Exposure 34

PART TWO RISK MANAGEMENT AND RISK ANALYSIS

3. Risk management and risk analysis: Life and property exposures 42

Managing Risk 43
Types of Risks 43
Objectives of Risk Management 44
The Risk Management Process 44
Achieving the Risk Management Goal 44
The Risk Manager's Functions in Buying and Administering Insurance 46
Risk Analysis: Life and Property Exposures 47
Life and Health Exposures for the Family 47
Final Expenses 47
Adjustment Income 47
Mortgage or Rent Fund 48
Family Period Income 48
Life Income for the Surviving Spouse 48
Education Fund 49
Emergency Fund 49
Medical Expenses 49
Retirement Income 49
Life and Health Exposures for the Business Firm 49
Loss of Key Employees 50
Loss of Owner 50
The Employee Benefit Plan Exposure 52
Property Exposures for the Family 52
Loss of the Property Itself 52
Loss of Use and Extra Expense 53
Property Exposures for the Business Firm 53
Loss of the Property 53
Loss of Use and Extra Expense 53

4. Risk analysis: Liability exposures 56

The Nature of Law 57
Sources of the Law 57
Classifications of the Law 58
Legal Liability 58
Torts 59
Innerscript: The Reasonable Man 62
Liability Arising from Negligence 64
Essential Elements of a Negligent Act 65

Innerscript: Standard of Care Owed by Owners and Tenants 65
Innerscript: *Sine Qua Non* and Proximate Cause 68
Defenses in a Negligence Action 68
Statutory Modifications of the Common Law of Negligence 70
Liability Imposed by Contract 71
Liability Assumed under Contract 72
Breach of an Implied Warranty 72
Dual Liability Exposures: Torts and Contracts 72
Products Liability 72
Professional Liability 73
Examples of Tort Liability Hazards 73
Personal Liability Exposures 73
Business Liability Exposures 74

PART THREE THE INSURANCE CONTRACT AND ITS INTERPRETATION

5. The insurance contract 80

The Insurance Contract Defined 81
The Formation of the Contract 82
The Application 82
The Binder 83
Essential Elements of an Insurance Contract 84
Agreement—Offer and Acceptance 84
Competent Parties 85
Legal Purpose 86
Consideration 86
Characteristics of the Insurance Contract 86
Aleatory Contract 86
Contract of Adhesion 87
Unilateral Contract 88
Conditional Contract 88
Utmost Good Faith 88
Personal Contract 91
Principle of Indemnity 91
Innerscript: Borderline Cases 93
Innerscript: Subrogation Clauses 94
Agents and Brokers 96
Creation of an Agency Relationship 96
The Power and Authority of the Agent 96
Responsibility of Principles 97
Brokers as Agents 97
Remedies 98
Waiver and Estoppel 98
Rescission 99
Reformation 100

6. How to read a policy—Some directions 104

The Insurance Policy 106
The Policy Form 106
A Procedure for Analyzing Insurance Coverage 107
Defining the Perils Covered 107
Specified Perils and All-Risk Contracts 108
Interpreting the Peril 108
Limitations on the Peril 108
The Doctrine of Proximate Cause 109
Defining the Property Covered 110
Defining the Losses Covered 110
Defining the Persons Covered 110
Innerscript: Assignment 111
Defining the Locations Covered 112
Defining the Time of Coverage 112
Term of the Policy 112
Hour of Inception 113
Effect of Policy Period 113
Cancellation 113
Defining the Hazards That Suspend or Exclude Coverage 114
The Policyowner's Duties after a Loss 115
Notice of Loss 115
Protection of Property 116
Inventory 117
Evidence 117
Proof of Loss 117
Assistance and Cooperation 118
Appraisal 118
Settlement Options 119
Replacement Option 119
Abandonment and Salvage 119
Pair or Set 119
Settlement Options in Life Insurance 120
Settlement Options in Health Insurance 120
Relations with Third Parties 120
Time Limit for Bringing Suits 120
Innerscript: Physical Damage and Liability Policies 120
Time Limit for Paying Claims 121

7. Further directions for reading a policy 124

Amount of Insurable Interest 125
Actual Cash Value 125
Innerscript: Replacement Cost Refined 126
Actual Cash Value and Liability Insurance 127
Actual Cash Value in Life and Health Insurance 127
Exceptions to the Actual Cash Value Limitation 128

Policy Face or Limits 128
Types of Policy Limits 129
Restoration and Nonreduction of Amounts of Insurance 130
Other Insurance 131
Types of Other-Insurance Clauses 131
Coinsurance 132
Innerscript: Theory behind Coinsurance 133
Deductible Clauses 135
Types of Deductibles 136

8. An analysis of the homeowners policy 138

The Homeowners Series 139
"Readable" Forms 139
Homeowners Series Endorsements 139
Insurance for Mobile Homes 140
Defining the Perils Covered in the HO–3 141
Defining the Property Covered 143
Defining the Types of Losses Covered 143
Defining the Persons Covered 145
Innerscript: Assignments 145
Defining the Locations Covered 146
Defining the Period of Coverage 147
Defining the Hazards That Exclude or Suspend Coverage 147
Limitations on the Amount of Recovery 148
The Policyowner's Duties after a Loss 148
Settlement Options 150
Time Limits: Suits and Claims Payment 150

9. An analysis of the personal auto policy 154

Defining the Perils Covered 155
Interpreting the Perils 156
Defining the Property Covered 157
Defining the Types of Losses Covered 158
Defining the Persons Covered 159
Innerscript: No-Benefit-to-Bailee Clause 160
Determining the Locations Covered 160
Defining the Period of Coverage 160
Defining the Hazards That Exclude or Suspend Coverage 161
Limitations on the Amount of Recovery 163
The Policyowner's Duties after a Loss 163
Settlement Options 163
Innerscript: An Emerging Development for Total Losses 163
Time Limits: Suits and Claims Payment 164
Variations among the PAP, FAP, and SAP 165

PART FOUR PROPERTY AND LIABILITY INSURANCE COVERAGES

10 Fire and marine coverage 172

Fire Insurance Coverage 173
Innerscript: Background on Fire Insurers 173
The Standard Fire Insurance Policy 174
Analysis of the Standard Fire Policy 175
Forms Used with the Standard Fire Policy 176
Forms Providing Commercial Coverages 178
Forms Increasing Perils Covered 180
Forms Covering Additional Losses 182
Innerscript: Demolition Insurance 183
Allied Lines 186
Differences in Conditions Insurance 187
Tailored Forms 187
Marine Insurance Coverage 187
Ocean Marine Insurance 187
Classification of Policies 187
The Ocean Marine Policy 189
Inland Marine Insurance 191
Domestic Shipments 191
Instrumentalities of Transportation and Communication 193
Property Floater Policies 193
Bailee Forms 194
Yacht and Motorboat Insurance 195

11. Liability coverages 198

Liability Insurance Policies 199
General Liability Program 199
Personal Liability Forms 200
Professional Liability Forms 200
Basic Business Liability Forms 201
Endorsements and Separate Policies 202
Innerscript: Coverages in Broad Form CGL Endorsement 205
Automobile Liability 207
Personal Auto Insurance 207
Innerscript: Auto Rating 208
Business Auto Insurance 209
Compensating Victims of Automobile Accidents 211
Workers' Compensation and Employers' Liability 213
Historical Development 214
Organization of the U.S. Workers' Compensation Program 215
Workers' Compensation Insurance Policies 216

Second-Injury Funds 217
Direction of Workers' Compensation Laws 217

12. Crime, surety, miscellaneous and multiple-line coverages 222

Crime Coverages 223
Crime Coverages for Individuals 223
Crime Coverages for Business 224
Federal Crime Program 227
Bonding 227
The Nature of Bonding 228
Fidelity Bond Coverages 228
Innerscript: Additional 3D Coverages and the Advantages of the 3D 231
Surety Bond Coverages 232
Miscellaneous Coverages 234
Comprehensive Glass Insurance 234
Boiler and Machinery Insurance 234
Credit Insurance 235
Accounts Receivable Insurance 235
Valuable Papers and Records Insurance 235
Title Insurance 236
Innerscript: Municipal Bond Insurance Association (MBIA) and Mutual Fund Insurance 236
Aviation Insurance 236
Multiple-Line Insurance 237
Multiple-Line Programs 237
Special Multi-Peril Program 238
Businessowners Program 239
Miscellaneous Multiple-Line Coverages 240

PART FIVE LIFE AND HEALTH INSURANCE

13. Life insurance and annuities 246

Broad Classifications of Life Insurance Policies 247
Policy Dividends 247
Life Insurance Cash Values 248
Types of Life Insurance 250
Term Insurance 250
Endowment Insurance 252
Whole Life Insurance 252
Universal Life Insurance 255
Special-Purpose Policies 256
The Family Income Policy 256
The Family Maintenance Policy 257
Multiple-Protection Policies 257
Mortgage Protection Policies 257
The Family Policy 257
Joint Life Policy 258
Preferred Risk 258
Guaranteed Insurability Agreements 258
Variable Life Insurance 259
The Adjustable Life Policy 259
Index-Linked Policies 259
Deposit Term 259
Other Special Policies 259
Classes of Life Insurance 260
Ordinary Life Insurance 260
Industrial Life Insurance 260
Group Life Insurance 260
Life Insurance Riders 261
Disability Income Rider 261
Accidental Death Rider 261
Waiver of Premium 261
Payor-Benefit Rider 261
Cost-of-Living Rider 261
Annuities 262
The Annuity Principle 262
Classification of Annuities 262
Special Annuity Policies 264
Innerscript: Recent Trends in Life Insurance 267

14. The life insurance contract 272

Decisions by the Policyowner 273
Beneficiary Designations 273
Ownership 273
Policy Options 273
Other Policy Provisions 277
Provisions Required by State Law 277
Permissible Provisions 278
Other General Provisions 279
Third-Party Rights in Life Insurance 279
Innerscript: Creditors Rights in Life Insurance Examined 280

15. Health insurance 284

Types of Health Insurance Coverages 285
Nature of the Peril 285
Type of Losses Covered 286
Basis of Loss Payments 286
Breadth-of-Benefit Provisions 287
Underwriting Standards 288
The Health Insurance Contract 289
Guideposts for Buying Health Insurance 289
Points to Consider When Comparing Health Insurance Policies 289
Use of the Guideposts 295

PART SIX EMPLOYEE BENEFIT PLANS: PUBLIC AND PRIVATE

16. Employee benefit plans: Group life, group health and other group insurance plans 300

Reasons for Using Employee Benefit Plans 302
Group Insurance 302
Distinguishing Features of Group Insurance 302
Group Insurance Principles 304
Group Life Insurance 305
State Regulation 305
Standard Provisions for Group Life Policies 306
Types of Group Life Insurance Coverage 308
Innerscript: Regulations Applicable to Group Ordinary 309
Innerscript: Rationale for and Reaction to SIBI Plans 310
Group Health Insurance 313
State Regulation 313
Group Health and Individual Health Contracts 313
Types of Coverages 314
Franchise (Wholesale) Health Insurance 314
Blanket Health Policies 314
Group Credit Health Insurance 314
Administrative Service Only Group Insurance (ASO) 315
Cost of Group Health Insurance 315
Innerscript: Funding Benefits Through an Internal Revenue Code (IRC) 501(c)9 Trust 315
Decisions in Establishing Employee Benefit Plans: Group Life and Health 316
Contributory or Noncontributory 316
Specifying Coverages for Life and Health Benefit Plans 318
Other Group Plans 323
Group Property and Liability Insurance 323
Prepaid Legal Insurance 325

17. Employee benefit plans: Retirement plans 330

Funding Issues 331
The Concept of a Fully Funded Plan 332
Defined Benefit versus Defined Contribution Plans 332
Innerscript: Funding Standards—Variances and Exceptions 335
Actuarial Cost Methods 336
Accrued Benefit Cost Method 336
Projected Benefit Cost Method 336
Advantages of Funding 340
Funding Agencies 340
Trust Fund Plans 340
Insured Plans 340
Termination of Plans 343
Basic Decisions in Establishing Retirement Plans 343
Eligibility of Coverage 343
Eligibility for Benefits 344
Benefit Levels 344
Types of Benefits 347
Funding the Benefits 348
Innerscript: Income Taxation of Benefits—Qualified Pension and Profit-Sharing Plans 349
Plan Termination Insurance 353
Fiduciary Responsibilities 353
Disclosure 354
Special Retirement Plans 354
Individual Retirement Account 354
Self-Employment (Keogh) Retirement Plan 354
Tax-Sheltered Annuity (TSA) 355
Employee Stock Ownership Plans (ESOP and PAYSOP) 355
TEFRA and Retirement Plans 357
Innerscript: Taxation of Joint and Survivorship Annuities 358

18. Social insurance 364

The Nature of a Social Insurance System 365
Definition of Social Insurance 365
Kinds of Social Insurance in the United States 366
Innerscript: The Need for Social Insurance 366
Old-Age, Survivors, Disability and Health Insurance (OASDHI) 368
Innerscript: Public-Assistance Programs 368
The Insurance Coverage 369
Innerscript: A Summary Illustration of a PIA Computation 377
The Social Security Leviathan 385
Social Security and Politics—Siamese Twins 385
Brief History of the Social Security System 385
Current Financial Status of the Social Security System 387
Reasons for Problems 387

Unemployment Compensation 388
Coverage Provisions 389
Benefits 389
Eligibility for Benefits 389
Financing 390
Temporary Disability Income Benefit Plans 390
Finance 391
Eligibility 391
Benefits 391
The Future of Temporary Disability Laws 391
National Health Insurance (NHI) 392
Basic Principles for a NHI Plan 392
Three Basic NHI Proposals 392
Solutions 393
Appendix: Average Monthly Wage Calculation for the Social Security Primary Insurance Amount 394

PART SEVEN ORGANIZATION AND ADMINISTRATION OF INSURERS

19. Types of insurers 400

A Preview 401
Motives for Formation 401
Similarities and Differences 401
Unincorporated Proprietary Insurers 402
Lloyd's of London 402
Innerscript: Lloyd's of London: Defense Insurance against a Takeover Battle 406
American Lloyds 407
Incorporated Proprietary Insurers 408
Consumer-Type Cooperative Insurers 408
Reciprocal Insurance Exchanges 408
Mutual Companies 410
Producers' Cooperatives 413
Medical and Hospital Service Plans 413
Health Maintenance Organizations 414
Governmental Insurers 414
Federal Insurers 414
State Insurers 415
Special Contributions of Governmental Insurers 415

20. Management organization and functions: Marketing, claims and loss control 418

Management Organization 419
Departmentalization 419
Marketing Insurance Company Products 421
Sales Organizations 421
Producers 423
Claims Administration 425
The Mechanics of Loss Adjustment 425
Difficulties Encountered by the Adjuster 427
Examples of Loss-Adjustment Problems 427
Loss Control 429
Cooperative Efforts of Insurers in Loss Control 429
Individual Efforts of Insurers in Loss Control 430
Loss Control and the Firm 431
Cooperative Organizations 431
Why Cooperate? 431
Ratemaking Organizations 432
Innerscript: Other Association Functions, Underwriting Associations and Public Relations 433
Company Fleets 434

21. Underwriting and pricing insurance 438

Underwriting Insurance 439
Select or Be Selected Against 439
Profitable Distribution of Exposures 440
Who Is the Underwriter? 440
The Agent as Underwriter 440
Insurer Underwriting Departments 441
The Underwriting Process 441
Preselection 441
Postselection 443
Retention 443
Line Limits in Life Insurance 444
Line Limits in Property and Liability Insurance 444
Reinsurance 444
Types of Reinsurance 444
Innerscript: Proportional and Nonproportional Reinsurance 445
Reasons for Reinsurance 447
Special Problems of Underwriting 447
Moral Hazard 448
Conflict between Underwriting and Production 448
Innerscript: Conflict between Underwriter and Agent—A Sing Along 448
Governmental Pressures on Underwriting 450
Pricing Insurance 450
Principles of Ratemaking 450
Types of Ratemaking 451
Examples of Underwriting and Pricing of Insurance 453
Underwriting and Rating of Fire Insurance 453
Innerscript: The Universal Mercantile System Illustrated 455
Underwriting and Pricing of Life Insurance 456

22. Financial structure 466

Assets of Insurers 467
Valuation of Assets 469
Regulation of Insurers' Investments 469
Reserves of Property and Liability Insurers 470
Unearned Premium Reserve 470
Loss Reserves 471
Voluntary Reserves 472
Reserves of Life Insurers: The Policy Reserve 472
The Nature of the Policy Reserve 473
Reserve Computation 474
Overconservatism in Computing Policy Reserves 477
Innerscript: A Welcome Innovation—Flexible Standard Valuation and Nonforfeiture Laws 477
Other Reserve Accounts 478
Earned Surplus of Property-Liability Insurers 479
Underwriting Profit 479
Investment Profit 481
Property and Liability Insurer Profitability 481
Profitability of Life Insurers 482
Earned Surplus of Life Insurers 482
Policy Dividends 484
Financial Reporting 485

PART EIGHT THE PUBLIC AND INSURANCE: REGULATORS AND CONSUMERS

23. Regulation of the insurance business 490

Objectives of Regulation 491
A Business Affected with a Public Interest 491
Innerscript: The Changing Concept of Public Interest 491
Regulation and Competition 492
Other Reasons for Regulation 493
Regulatory Goals 494
Methods of Regulation 494
Legislative Control 494
Judicial Control 495
Administrative Control 495
The National Association of Insurance Commissioners 495
Self-Regulation 496
The History of Regulation in the United States 496
Regulation by Charter 496
State Insurance Departments 496
Paul v. *Virginia* 496
The South-Eastern Underwriters Association Case 497
Public Law 15 498
Developments after Public Law 15 498
Federal Regulatory Issues and Public Law 15 499
State versus Federal Regulation 500
What Is Regulated? 501
Financial Regulation 501
Product Regulation 506
Regulation of Business Methods 506
Innerscript: Taxation of Insurance Companies 508

24. How to buy insurance 512

Self-Insurance 513
Principles of Commercial Insurance Buying 514
The Large-Loss Principle 514
Graduation of Insurance Coverages 514
Innerscript: The Loss That Could Never Happen 515
Integrated Insurance Planning 516
Choosing among Coverages: Personal Insurance Needs 517
The Life and Health Insurance Programming Process 517
Executor Fund 518
Mortgage or Rent Fund 519
Adjustment Income 519
Family Period Income 519
Lifetime Income for the Spouse 520
Education Insurance 521
Emergency Fund 521
Retirement Insurance Needs 521
Family Insurance Needs 522
Caution: Inflation Ahead? 523
Property and Liability Insurance Planning 523
Motor Vehicle Coverage 524
Choosing among Coverages: Business Insurance Needs 524
Property and Liability Insurance 524
Business Life and Health Insurance 525
Innerscript: Policy Standardization 526
Choosing the Agent 528
Innerscript: The Story of Poor Herman and His Bevy of Agents 530
Selecting the Insurer 530
General Considerations 530
Factors in Insurers' Finances 531
Services to the Policyholder 532
Costs of the Insurance 532
Concluding Remarks 535

GLOSSARY 539

APPENDIXES 551

1. Policy Declarations Page 552
2. Standard Fire Policy 553
3. Homeowners 3 Policy 555
4. Personal Auto Policy 567
5. Whole Life Insurance Policy 580
6. Major Medical and Disability (Recovery) Income Policies 594
7. A Mathematical Note 604

INDEX 607

Fundamentals of Insurance

PART ONE THE NATURE OF RISK AND INSURANCE: AN INTRODUCTION

The fundamental objective of insurance is to provide a means for offsetting the burden of financial loss. Part One consists of two chapters. Chapter 1 gives an overview of insurance including its purpose and how that purpose is accomplished, the business of insurance and how it is organized and how insurance affects society. It provides a miniature, and hopefully refreshing, summary of the text. This bird's-eye view of insurance is followed in Chapter 2 by an explanation of fundamental concepts relating to risk and risk bearing including the methods of dealing with risk. Of the methods dealing with risk, insurance is the most important and thus has grown and flourished as a risk-bearing institution. Chapter 2 examines the theoretical concept of insurance as a device for reducing risk and sharing losses through the use of the law of large numbers. In that discussion, the criteria for an insurable exposure are examined to explain why some exposures are insurable while others are not insurable.

CHAPTER

1 A prelude to the study of insurance

John Thoeming/Richard D. Irwin

CHAPTER OBJECTIVES

1. **To identify the primary purpose of insurance.**
2. **To explain how and why the law may shift the burden of loss from one person to another.**
3. **To describe the nature of insurers and insureds.**
4. **To introduce the functions that must be performed in operating an insurance company.**
5. **To outline the fields of insurance.**
6. **To compare and contrast the social values and social costs of insurance.**

Pascal (1623–62) is credited with proposing the modern theory of probability. Also in 1642, when he was 19, he invented a calculating machine. While the theory of probability is important to the concept of insurance and the calculating machine is valuable to insurance company operations, more significant at this point is Pascal's observation: "The last thing that we discover in writing a book is to know what to put at the beginning." A logical approach is to introduce the subject in a manner that attracts the reader.

All readers of this text will have heard of insurance and most of them will have at least a superficial acquaintance with it. Thus the task is clear. As Samuel Johnson (1709–84) noted: "The two most engaging powers of an author are to make new things familiar, and familiar things new." These are the objectives here.

Insurance affects everyone. Few people could own homes, drive cars, attain adequate medical attention and provide financial security for their families without it. By providing the means to help people accomplish these goals and many others, insurance helps improve the quality of life. These truths will be self-evident as the reader becomes absorbed in this text.

The often repeated sayings, "Ignorance is bliss" and "What you don't know won't hurt you," do not apply to insurance. Few people know and understand the essentials of insurance. So if ignorance is bliss, why are not more people happy with their insurers? People would fare better by embracing the idea that "What you don't know won't help you much either." The lack of consumer knowledge about insurance results in numerous mistakes in insurance planning. (Many of these mistakes would be avoided if buyers could rely on the expertise of insurance personnel. Unfortunately just as in many other businesses, some salespersons and their backup people are not always qualified to serve the consumer nor are they dedicated to the consumer's interests.)

Many consumers face common problems and make the same mistakes when buying insurance. In particular a number of gaps and overlaps can occur in insurance plans unless the buyer is well informed about the protection needed and the coverage various policies provide. For example, purchasing insurance to cover loss or destruction of a residence could create a gap. Individuals might buy a policy to protect themselves against loss to or destruction of their houses by fire or other causes and overlook the loss that occurs while their houses are repaired or reconstructed, forcing the owners to pay the mounting costs of living in substitute accommodations.

As another example, when purchasing cars on the installment plan buyers may be exposed to a major gap in auto insurance. The lender (e.g., a bank or credit union) requires that the automobile be pledged as security for the loan. Unless the buyer owns insurance covering damage to the car the security for the loan is unreliable. Therefore physical damage insurance is required before the loan is made. After purchasing auto physical damage insurance car buyers may be lulled into believing they have protected themselves from any losses connected with car ownership. But a serious coverage gap exists if protection is not bought against liability claims for injury to someone's person or property. Even in states that require auto liability coverage either directly or indirectly, lax enforcement of these laws might allow a person to drive unprotected against liability claims.

Persons can create overlaps in insurance coverage by buying several policies covering the same loss exposure from one or more insurers. The result is that buyers often pay for coverage that they might not collect when a loss occurs. "Other insurance clauses" in policies usually limit total payments to the amount of the loss regardless of the number of policies or amount of insurance owned. This practice reduces the possibility that insureds might profit from a loss. While gaps in coverage can be costly in the event of a loss, overlaps are costly whether or not a loss occurs.

These are but a few of the questions that plague insurance buyers. To handle these and other insurance questions intelligently consumers must learn the appropriate answers. One purpose of this text is to prepare insurance buyers to deal effectively with insurers and their representatives. An equally important objective is to help those in the insurance business understand their responsibilities and relationships to other people in the organization. This latter objective helps insurance personnel improve their service to consumers as well as achieve greater enjoyment from their work.

HOW TO PROCEED

What is insurance? Why is it so hard to obtain and sometimes even harder to keep? The task is to help unravel this mystery.

The difficulty with insurance is that the student needs to know everything at once. Similar to a circle, a clear starting point is lacking. In geometry one can begin with a few axioms and postulates and proceed to build the whole apparatus. In history one can start at the beginning or at any intermediate point and proceed through any desired period. But what is needed in insurance is comprehensive knowledge of the subject in advance.

Because of the impossibility of a "chugalug" approach to learning insurance, the subject must be learned one sip at a time while the reader gradually develops a taste for the fundamentals of insurance. But for full enjoyment it must be taken in small sips. Like brandy, to intensify the total experience derived from its consumption one should savor the aroma while engaged in this delightful sip-by-sip operation. In the remainder of the chapter the reader is exposed to the aroma and given the opportunity to acquire a taste for insurance from a rapid whirl around the insurance world.

The Burden of Financial Loss

When Russia's first spaceship (Sputnik) began its tumble toward earth a man in Arizona, fearing damage to his luxurious house and its expensive contents, purchased an insurance policy to protect himself against loss in the event that the craft through a computer error smashed his property. Relief from the burden of financial loss caused by falling spaceships or, more likely, by such mundane perils as fire, auto accident, sickness and "premature" death, usually is primary when thinking about insurance. Other important aspects of insurance must be noted, but examining the problem of the burden of financial loss is a good way to begin.

Newspapers relate stories about financial losses. A 25-year-old father dies leaving a wife and three small children. Terrorists blow up a $40 million Boeing 747. Three men steal an armored car containing $2.2 million from the loading bay of a New York bank. Fire burns a new house. An automobile seriously injures a pedestrian.

Who bears the financial losses? Who must now support the widow and her three children? Who will replace the Boeing 747? What is the source of recovery for the stolen funds? How will the money be provided to rebuild the house? Where will the funds be obtained to offset the cost of medical expenses and loss of work time of the injured pedestrian? Usually, in the absence of legal remedies, contractual arrangements or cooperative efforts of friends and neighbors, these losses are allowed to remain where they fall, i.e., on the widow and children, the airline, the bank, the homeowner and the pedestrian.

Shifting the Burden by Law

If the loss is caused by negligence of another, it might be shifted by society through common law to the responsible person. If the young father dies as a result of alleged malpractice by the physician, the loss might be shifted to the doctor. If the house is burned by a fire carelessly set by a neighbor, the loss might be shifted to that person. If the pedestrian is injured by a reckless driver or a defective automobile, the loss might be shifted to the motorist or the car manufacturer. *Might be shifted* is used for two reasons: (1) fault must be proved to the court's satisfaction and (2) if fault is proved, the guilty party must have the resources to pay the damages.

Where society believes common-law allocation of loss is not in the public interest, it has passed laws to redistribute the loss. For example, workers' compensation laws charge losses from industrial accidents to employers, without regard to fault. In addition, the laws require employers to guarantee the availability of funds for these losses. If the death of the 25-year-old father resulted from an industrial accident, the loss would be shifted in part to the employer.

In some jurisdictions no-fault laws governing auto accident reparations have shifted the burden of financial loss from the responsible party to the injured party. In these states injured parties must look to their own insurers for compensation for economic loss rather than to the alleged negligent party. This system permits the injured individual to avoid lengthy and expensive court litigation to determine who is at fault and therefore who must pay the damages.

Social security laws have been passed to redistribute income losses resulting from unemployment, disability, old age and death. If the 25-year-old father was employed in covered employment, the loss would be partly shifted to the social security fund. If the pedestrian was a worker in one of the six jurisdictions requiring compensation for nonoccupational disability, the loss would be shifted in part to that fund.

Insurance and the Burden of Loss

Whether the burden of the loss remains where it falls or is shifted by law, that loss may cause someone financial difficulty. The owner whose property is destroyed or damaged or the family whose income is interrupted by death, disability or forced retirement of the breadwinner is likely to suffer a severe financial loss. A person who becomes legally liable to someone else for bodily injury or property damage can suffer disastrous financial consequences.

Family and business units exposed to serious property, income and liability losses seek methods to offset these losses. One effective solution is a private contractual arrangement allocating the burden of individual losses to members of a selected group who are exposed to similar losses. These loss-sharing arrangements are called **insurance policies.**

THE INSURANCE BUSINESS

While the principle of insurance is simple, its application is complex, involving many skills.

The Insurer

First, organizations known as **insurers,** must be formed to administer insurance plans. They may be corporations, partnerships or syndicates of individual underwriters. The safe operation of the insurance principle depends upon a large number of policyowners who are acquired by most insurers through sales representatives. These representatives, known as the "field force," are either employees or independent agents. Acquiring, training, supervising and compensating a field force require the services of sales management experts.

The Insured

An insurance transaction requires one or more insureds. An insured is anyone protected by the policy from financial loss.

Who is insured by a life insurance policy? Is it the person upon whose life the insurance is written (called the subject) or the person who collects the policy proceeds when the subject dies (called the beneficiary)? Who is insured by a fire insurance policy? Is it the owner of the house covered by the insurance or the lender who holds the mortgage? Who is insured by a liability policy? Is it the policyowner who by negligently injuring others is ordered to pay damages or the injured person to whom damages are paid? The insured in life insurance is the policy beneficiary. The insured in fire insurance is the house owner *and* the lender if the lender is named in the policy. The insured in liability insurance is either the policyowner or the person to whom damages are paid, or both.

An example may be helpful to clarify who is insured in liability insurance. Al Zucker owns a liability policy with a limit of $500,000 for bodily injury. Lena Wu sues him for damages and is awarded $400,000. Is Al or Lena the insured?

Under earlier liability insurance policies the insurer promised to *reimburse* policyowners for damages they were legally obligated to pay because of a negligent act. Suppose Al is able to pay Lena only $25,000 in damages. Al's loss would be $25,000 and his liability insurer would reimburse him for that amount. In this event Al is the insured.

Under most *current* liability policies the insurer agrees to pay *on behalf of the policyowner* damages the policyowner is required to pay for a negligent act. Here the insurer would pay Lena $400,000. Because Lena collects $375,000 more than she otherwise would have received, she is clearly an insured. Al also is an insured because without the policy his loss would have been $25,000.

Al's bankruptcy or insolvency does not relieve the insurer of its obligation to pay Lena. Thus liability policies are called **third party coverages.**

Confusion and vagueness surround the word **insured.** Therefore more explicit terms, such as **policyowner, subject, beneficiary, claimants** and so on are preferred. However, the insurance industry is less concerned about precision here than in other matters. It uses the term *insured* indiscriminately to mean the person or property covered by the policy. For simplicity, this text occasionally but reluctantly follows common industry usage.

The Contract

Insurers deal primarily in promises described in legal documents known as **contracts.** Insurance contracts define circumstances under which the insurer will pay and the amount to be paid. Lawyers are involved in preparing contracts and handling disputes over their interpretation. The latter function often requires aid from the courts.

Developing an insurance contract is not solely a matter of drafting a legal instrument. An intensive analysis of economic and technical considerations is needed to determine not only the kinds of insurance to be written but also the rates and restrictions to be applied. These **underwriting decisions** are made by specialists, such as engineers, statisticians, physicians, meterologists and economists. An analysis of insuring agreements, limitations, exclusions and conditions is important in understanding insurance coverage.

Underwriting and Rating

The success of a cooperative plan like insurance requires an equitable distribution of cost among participants. Underwriters classify and rate each loss exposure to maintain a semblance of equity toward policyowners. If Roger Mesznik, a local merchant, wants to protect himself from financial loss due to burglary, he will be charged a rate comparable to the exposure. The premium will vary directly with the probability of the occurrence of the loss and its probable severity.

Although a large number of policyowners is essential to the operation of the insurance principle, insurers may be unable to insure all applicants. Safe operation of the plan requires skill in the selection of applicants. Underwriters must know when to refuse applications. They must restrict the amount of liability assumed on exposures in some areas and on some properties. Highly concentrated exposures run counter to sound underwriting principles. Refusal to accept an application also can be based on the physical nature of the property or the moral character of its owner.

Finance

Insurers collect and accumulate funds from their policyowners in advance of claim payments. Some claims (e.g., liability insurance claims) require many years to settle. Consequently the nature of insurance requires handling and investing large sums of money by persons skilled in investment analysis. Insurance as a major financial institution has a significant effect on the economy.

Public Control

Because insurance has been held to be "affected with a public interest" (See Chapter 23) it is subject to a greater degree of public control than most other businesses. Nearly all aspects of insurance are regulated, starting with the formation of insurers and ending with their liquidation. Individual states establish criteria and standards for policy provisions, rates, expense limitations, valuation of assets and liabilities, investment of funds and the qualifications of sales representatives. Regulation is more complete and sometimes more complicated for some forms of insurance than others. Also, the extent and quality of regulation varies from state to state and over time.

FIELDS OF INSURANCE

Insurance may be divided into several branches. The broadest division is between private and government.

Private Insurance

Once upon a time the private insurance business in the United States was separated into three branches: life, fire and marine, and casualty and surety. Most states chartered insurers to write coverage only in one of these branches. For a long time many insurance experts doubted the wisdom of such strict division of the business. They insisted that only life insurance be a separate operation. A classification that labeled some coverages fire lines and other closely related ones casualty lines seemed ridiculous. Automobile insurance, for example, was split between fire insurers (for physical damage) and casualty insurers (for liability). Collision coverage could be written by either type of insurer.

Agitation against this artificial classification finally resulted in legislation passed by the states in the late 1940s and early 1950s providing for full multiple-line underwriting powers for fire and casualty insurers. As a result all states (Ohio completed the list in 1955) have passed legislation allowing an individual insurer to write both fire and casualty insurance. Multiple-line underwriting powers, however, do not extend to life insurance except in 13 states that had never required separation of underwriting powers. The former classification of fire, marine, casualty and surety is not dead, as some insurers still restrict operations to one field. Before multiple-line underwriting was allowed, homeowners and businessowners had to have separate policies for fire insurance and liability insurance. Separate policies also were written for theft insurance and a host of other coverages.

Multiple-line underwriting allows insurers to design special policy forms to cover in one policy the major property and liability exposures of particular customers e.g., homeowners and businessowners. The advent of multiple-line insurers reduced the classification of private insurance from three to two major branches: life and property-liability. Health insurance may be written by either life insurers or property-liability insurers.

Life insurance

Life insurers write three types of coverages: life insurance, annuities and health insurance. Life insurance provides money upon the death of the insured to pay death expenses and to continue an income for survivors. Annuities are the reverse of life insurance. They liquidate an estate under an arrangement that guarantees the annuitant an income for life. Health insurance provides money for payment of medical expenses caused by accident or illness and protects the insured against loss of income resulting from disability.

Property and liability insurance

Coverage written by property and liability insurers may be divided into five types: (1) physical damage or loss, (2) loss of income and extra expenses resulting from physical damage to property, (3) liability, (4) health and (5) surety. Physical damage or loss coverage protects the insured against loss of or damage to owned property. Examples are financial protection against direct loss from fire, windstorm and theft. Loss of income and extra expense coverage protects insureds against income loss and extra expense incurred because of damage to their property or property of others. Liability coverage protects the insured against third-party claims for bodily injury or property damage caused by negligence or imposed by statute or contract. Automobile liability, workers' compensation and contractual liability insurance are examples of this type of coverage. Health coverage written by property-liability insurers is the same as that written by life insurers. Suretyship coverage is a means whereby parties may offer a financial guarantee of their honesty or of their performance under a contract or agreement. Fidelity, construction and bail bonds are examples of this type of coverage.

Government Insurance

Government insurance is written by federal and state agencies and may be voluntary or compulsory.

Voluntary government insurance

Voluntary government insurance plans written by the federal government include crop insurance, military personnel life insurance, bank-deposit insurance, savings and loan insurance, securities investor protection insurance (for cash and security balances held with participating brokers), crime insurance, mortgage and property improvement loan insurance, supplemental medicare insurance for the aged written with basic social security medicare, insurance against foreign expropriation of a limited class of U.S.-owned companies (those with new or substantially increased investments in developing countries) and backup programs written in cooperation with private insurers for coverage against perils of flood and riot in qualified areas and for writing of surety bonds for small minority contractors. Voluntary insurance plans written by one or more state governments include hail, life (Wisconsin), title, auto (Maryland), medical malpractice and workers' compensation.

Compulsory government insurance

Government insurance coverage required of the masses generally is called "social insurance" and is written both by federal and state governments. The federal social insurance program, popularly known as social security, offers income coverage for qualified survivors of deceased covered workers, disability and retirement income coverage for qualified workers and their dependents and medical care coverage for qualified persons upon reaching age 65. Pension termination insurance is another form of compulsory federal coverage. New federal insurance plans continue to be proposed and discussed. For example, national health insurance has been closely scrutinized for many years.

Social insurance plans administered by state governments include coverage for unemployment benefits. Compulsory nonoccupational health insurance is required in five states and in Puerto Rico and six states operate monopolistic state funds (no private insurance allowed) for workers' compensation. Twelve states operate workers' compensation funds that compete with private insurance.

Although workers' compensation insurance is required in most states, the coverage can be written by private insurers. In those states where automobile liability insurance is required of car owners, the insurance also is written by private insurers.

INSURANCE AND SOCIETY

The contributions of insurance to society are significant, although not without their costs. On balance, however, the gains outweigh the costs. The rise of England as a great trading nation and at the same time as a nation with exceptional insurance facilities was no coincidence. A trader who sent a shipload of finished goods to colonial America to exchange for raw materials might have remained content with domestic trade had there been no ocean marine insurance available in the coffeehouses of London.

INNERSCRIPT: ORIGINS OF INSURANCE

A rebellion by traveling salesmen may be given credit for the origin of the first real contracts of insurance. The story begins about 5,000 years ago in the Tigris-Euphrates Valley. The Babylonians had expanded industry to the point where they needed both a wider market for their goods and a wider source of raw materials than nearby areas provided. The local industrialists at first sent their slaves, brothers-in-law or other representatives into the surrounding countryside on short trading excursions. These representatives had no share in the profits (or losses) of these trips and acted only as servants of the businessmen.

As business improved a wider outlet for products was required. The slaves and brothers-in-law no longer were adequate to the task. Traveling salesmen entered the scene. The businessman made arrangements with the salesmen to sell and buy goods throughout the known world. A Babylonian businessman would not trust his goods and money to a traveling salesman without assurance of that trader's honesty anymore than a Chicago business owner would today. The businessman required the salesman to pledge his property, wife and children as security.

In return for the "loan" of the money and goods, the salesman paid the businessman half the profits of the trip. This arrangement proved satisfactory. To be sure, an occasional salesman, preferring life abroad with the goods and money to life in Babylon with his wife, would abscond with the loan and leave his unfortunate(?) wife to the mercy of the businessman. The trouble arose from the nature of the ethical codes of peoples in the foreign lands. Thieves abounded in the nations in which the salesman traveled. To make matters worse, these peoples considered piracy a more honorable way of making a living than trading. Thus many honest salesmen lost merchandise and were forced to forfeit their pledged security through no fault of their own. As trade extended into less civilized areas the problem of robbers became greater and finally intolerable to the salesmen.

When the salesmen rebelled insurance entered the picture. The businessmen needed the salesmen as much as the salesmen needed them. They reached a compromise: they retained the former system with the additional provision that in the event the caravan

(*continued*)

was pillaged the salesman would be freed from debt if he was innocent of conspiracy or negligence. The practice spread to Phoenicia where the principle was applied to all kinds of shipping and from there throughout the ancient world.

Bottomry and respondentia contracts

Greek bottomry contracts developed from this Babylonian idea. If a Greek shipowner wanted to go on a voyage to bring cargo from a foreign land, he would borrow the necessary money by pledging the ship as collateral. The contract provided that if the ship failed to return to port intact the lender would have no claim against the shipowner.

This type of contract became common throughout maritime countries. Sometimes the cargo was pledged instead of the ship under a type of contract called respondentia. The interest charged on these contracts included a sum in addition to that normally charged for the loan to compensate the lender for insuring the safety of the voyage. This additional amount logically was called a premium, and to this day the consideration paid for insurance is still referred to as a premium.

To bring lenders and borrowers together an exchange was established at Athens to assist in making bottomry loans. This institution may well have been the world's first insurance exchange. In its manner of operation it was not unlike Lloyd's of London. Not only did the exchange simplify placing of bottomry contracts but it collected and disseminated all kinds of shipping information for the use of merchants, shipowners and other interested persons.

The beginning of life insurance

No one knows just when life insurance was first written. It is known that retirement insurance of a sort was available in Babylonia. Under Babylonian law a person could adopt a son, rear him and depend on him for support during retirement.

In early Greece many religious sects had certain devotees whose function was the care and custody of a temple belonging to the group. Quite secondary to this religious interest, these temple societies collected monthly subscriptions from other devotees. In return each member was assured a decent burial according to the rites of the particular group as well as some funds to pay the immediate cash needs of survivors. If a member fell behind in monthly premiums, fines were levied. If a person died while in default, the burial was not provided. At least one of the temple societies allowed members to borrow money under certain circumstances, thus providing an early instance of policy loans.

The Romans took over from Greece her arts, literature, philosophy and the idea of religious societies furnishing burial insurance and funds for the most pressing post-burial necessities of the de-

(continued)

ceased's family. The Romans, however, began to place less emphasis on the religious element and opened societies to the general public. They developed a special society for soldiers that provided death benefits and pensions for disability or old age.

Although insurance had its origins in the ancient world, the development of insurance forms known today did not begin until the 14th century. Beginning with the chartering of an insurance company in Flanders in 1310, the insurance industry and policy forms began to take on a modern appearance.

During the Middle Ages the guilds continued to cover lives in a manner similar to the Roman burial societies. The guilds were organizations of persons associated in trade or industry. They were not formed for religious purposes. In addition to providing burial insurance, the guilds accumulated insurance funds that were used to pay other losses. The perils of fire, robbery and livestock mortality were among those commonly covered. Loss payments were restricted. For example, no one who burned his own house could receive payment from the guild. One English guild refused to pay fire losses for persons guilty of "lust, dice-playing and gluttony." The Middle Ages provide at least one instance of nonmutual, all-risk property insurance. In the 13th century the merchants of Flanders each year attended a fair held at the abbey at Messines. Each trader attending the fair had to pay a fee and, in return, was guaranteed the safety of his goods.

Insurance exchanges

Marine insurance was written at least as early as the 14th century. Early marine policies were not written by companies but by merchants who wrote insurance as a side line. Because the merchants of Lombardy, an Italian province, wrote much of the business, the earliest policies written on English ships were in the Italian language. These merchants conducted their business through agents who had the power to make binding insurance contracts. In London the chief location of these brokers came to be known as "Lombard Street" because of the large number of Lombard merchants with marine insurance offices there.

When it became obvious that insurance was a full-time business, the merchants who were replaced by full-time insurance underwriters organized groups for writing insurance and spreading information pertinent to their business. The coffeehouses of London provided a logical meeting place for these insurers. There they could spend a pleasant morning and conduct their business at the same time. (Lloyd's of London is discussed in Chapter 19.)

Social Values of Insurance

Insurance plays an important role in approaching an optimum allocation of resources. The effect is the same as that attempted through legislation designed to restrict monopoly in that insurance eliminates one of the barriers to establishing a business. If an individual planning to invest in a grocery business found that fire insurance was unavailable, the person might change plans and invest in another business where insurance is available. Other investors might do the same. The resulting reluctance to invest in grocery stores would mean higher prices through higher sales margins for the few willing to take the risk.

One of the influences that interferes with the smooth function of competition is imperfect knowledge. To the extent that insurance eliminates the uncertainty of financial losses resulting from a given set of causes, it increases knowledge, thus decreasing one of the obstacles to competition.

Insurers through loss-prevention activities also contribute to the economy by decreasing the chance of loss. Insurers not only maintain large engineering staffs to determine why accidents occur and how to prevent them but they also support safety research, medical research and health education.

An important value of insurance is its indemnity function. Many family and business units are able to continue intact because a loss is offset in full or in part by insurance funds. Thus insurance contributes to social and business stability.

Insurance is of primary importance as the basis of the credit system. Becky may trust her friend Irma to repay the $200 she lent her last payday. Undoubtedly, Irma will pay if she lives and continues to work. However, if she dies or becomes disabled, Irma's life and disability income insurance can protect her creditor. The same principle applies to loans made on the security of property. What good is an ironclad mortgage to a banker if a fire occurs and the building is not covered by fire insurance? The mortgagee would be in no better position than if the money was loaned on the signature of the borrower.

Insurance also alleviates concerns about personal loss exposures. The accomplishment of life insurance in relieving mental anguish is immeasurable. Parents have deep-seated fears that they may die before building financial security for their family. Life insurance banishes that worry by providing funds to keep the family together until the children are grown and to pay the surviving spouse a lifetime income. Annuities for the aged perform a similar service.

Insurance is a useful device to solve complex social problems. Compensating victims of industrial accidents is handled by compulsory workers' compensation insurance; and indemnifying innocent automobile accident victims is met to some extent by financial responsibility laws under which most people comply by furnishing evidence of ownership of automobile liability insurance. Social insurance is used to help solve the financial problems of unemployment, old age, disability, death and medical care for the aged.

Insurers play an active role in finance, influencing the investment and financial markets of the world. Insurers fund the growth of basic industries and engage in financing government projects. Some insurers no longer restrict their activities exclusively to insurance. They argue that they are in the "financial planning" business, and this view has led them to activities that can be described only as extracurricular (or extra-insurance). Some have become part of conglomerate corporations or have created conglomerates themselves. They have organized or bought mutual funds, real estate investment trusts, financial consulting services and investment brokerage firms. This book ignores these activities and limits itself to insurance only.

In 1967, nearly 175 life insurers pledged $1 billion for investment in urban ghetto areas that previously did not qualify for loans from most financial institutions. This program was known as I-CAP (Inner-City Capital Investment Program). Although retaining control over the distribution of these funds, the insurers were subject to guidelines that made the following eligible for loans: (1) projects not ordinarily financed by life insurers because of the "risk" or location involved, (2) housing and residential projects providing improved living space for low- and moderate-income families now living in blighted urban areas and (3) businesses offering new job opportunities or medical community services for people living in the inner city.

After investing most of the first billion, in 1969 the life insurers pledged another billion. These funds have been loaned to ghetto residents to finance many projects, including factories, apartments, hospitals, office buildings, job-creating enterprises, shopping centers and single-family dwellings. One large insurer pledging approximately 35 percent of the total commitment reported a default rate of about 15 percent of the funds at the end of 1974. This rate, believed to be typical for the industry, is about double the average experience.

One of the early problems life insurers faced in investing these funds was their inability to find property insurers willing to write coverage against physical damage to the structures pledged as security for mortgage loans. This problem was partially solved by an industry-government-sponsored facility known as the FAIR plan (fair access to insurance requirements).

Social Costs of Insurance

The social costs of insurance should not be overlooked. Not all premiums paid by policyowners are used to pay losses. For example, during the 70s capital-stock property insurers incurred annual losses ranging from 66 to 79 percent of annual premiums *earned.* About 78 percent of the annual income of life insurers is used to pay current or future claims of policyowners. Expenses of capital-stock property insurers for the same decade ranged from 27 to 30 percent of annual premiums *written.*[1] Life insurers' operating expenses have ranged from about 16 to 18 percent of annual income.[2] The seemingly greater efficiency of life insurers is misleading. Life insurers experience a lower percentage of operating expenses to income because of their higher investment income. Life insurers are more than insurance institutions. They function also as savings intermediaries.

The difference between premiums earned and losses paid is used to compensate those who either work in insurance or provide it with operating capital, supplies and space. Some funds are used in loss-prevention activity and for building surpluses for future use in expanding the operations or strengthening the company. Nearly 2 million people are required to operate the industry.[3] The business also uses land and capital resources. The tying up of these resources is part of the social cost of insurance. The net social cost of capital used in insurance, however, is reduced because the assets offsetting the large reserves insurers must maintain are invested in other industries and services.

Insurance is the cause of many fraudulent losses. Insurers are the victims of arson, murder and suicide claims. Willful destruction of lives and property to collect insurance proceeds is a cost of insurance to society. Insurance also

---

[1] See Chapter 22 for (1) the distinction between premiums written and premiums earned and (2) an explanation of why losses are related to earned premiums and expenses are related to written premiums.

[2] Data cited in this paragraph are found in the *Life Insurance Fact Book,* published by the American Council of Life Insurance, 1850 K Street, N.W., Washington, D.C. 20006; *Insurance Facts,* published by the Insurance Information Institute, 110 Williams Street, New York, N.Y. 10038 and the U.S. Department of Commerce, Social and Economic Statistics Administration, Bureau of Economic Analysis. For relatively current data see the latest edition of these sources.

[3] Ibid.

may reduce the incentive to protect property against loss. The reduction of this incentive may be responsible for losses that otherwise would have been prevented. In addition, because payment for certain services generally is made by a third party, the insurer interferes with normal cost control mechanisms between consumer and provider. For example, increases in the cost of medical care have been caused, in part, because the consumer does not have to pay directly for much of the service but simply passes the bill on to the insurer.

Social Responsibility

Even though the business is said to be "affected with the public interest," the exact meaning of this concept is not clear. Some observers believe that insurance should be regulated in the same way as railroads and public utilities. Others favor increased competition in the business. Although the exact role of insurers in solving social problems is in dispute, clearly these problems will not solve themselves. If the industry does not aid in the solution of those problems for which it has both the expertise and the opportunity, the federal government surely will, and not always in a manner attractive to the insurance business.

The objectives of the insurance industry conform closely with many social goals. Achieving a high degree of loss predictability by reducing social unrest, minimizing the chance of unexpected loss, lessening damage from catastrophes and encouraging loss prevention all provide useful social functions in addition to stabilizing insurers' profitability.

SUMMARY

1. Insurance contracts are loss-sharing agreements made to reduce the financial burden of losses arising from specific kinds of exposures.
2. Insurers primarily are business organizations formed to administer insurance plans.
3. Insureds are the persons reimbursed for their losses by insurers. The use of the word *insured* may create confusion. Thus, more explicit terms like *policyowner, subject, beneficiary* and *claimant* are preferred. For simplicity, this text occasionally adopts the common industry usage of the word *insured* to mean the person or property covered by the policy.
4. Operation of the insurance business requires the use of many specialists to draft contracts, determine underwriting standards and establish premium rates. Persons skilled in investment analysis are also needed.
5. The origins of insurance date back to the Babylonians, Greek shipowners, religious societies, the medieval guilds and the coffeehouses of London.
6. Insurance is "affected with the public interest" and consequently subject to government regulation mostly by the states. The two broad divisions of insurance are private and government. Private insurance is divided into life and property-liability insurance. Government insurance is written by federal and state agencies and may be voluntary or compulsory.
7. Social values of insurance include its role in: affecting a favorable allocation of resources, loss-prevention activities, loss indemnification, providing security for credit, eliminating worry and providing a channel for investable funds.

8. Social contributions are not without cost. A large part of the premiums is used to pay expenses of operation. Insurance employs substantial amounts of labor, capital and land. Insurance is the cause of a number of fraudulent losses. It is also responsible in some cases for losses induced by carelessness because insurance may eliminate one's incentive to protect against or control losses once they occur.
9. Societal changes have many implications for insurance and insurers. While it is not clear how far social responsibility of business should extend, the thought is that insurance should assume greater responsibility than most other businesses.

REVIEW QUESTIONS

1. Statutes have been passed to redistribute loss where the common-law loss allocation is considered socially deficient. Cite two types of loss situations in which the common-law solution is considered socially inadequate.
2. Name the specialists needed to make underwriting decisions for private insurers. Explain why each is needed.
3. A fast-food chain has three identical units located in three areas. One outlet is charged a higher premium for the same amount of crime coverage than another, and the third was denied crime insurance by the same insurer. What factors might account for this disparity?
4. What are the social costs of insurance? On what grounds does the text conclude that the social values outweigh the social costs?
5. Distinguish the major types of coverage written by property-liability insurers from those written by life insurers.
6. Explain why homeowners and businessowners policies were not written 30 years ago.
7. What are the social values of insurance for:
   a. Businessowners?
   b. Mortgagees (banks, savings and loan companies and so on)?
   c. New ventures?
   d. Investment markets?
   e. Widows and widowers?
   f. Children?
   g. Employees?
8. How does buying an insurance policy relate to making an investment in the U.S. economy?
9. The purpose of insurance is to shift the financial burden of loss. What forms of government insurance are available to accomplish this purpose? What groups of insurance buyers or taxpayers are ultimately responsible for financing government insurance plans?
10. Do government insurance plans ever compete with private insurance?
11. Are the states and the federal government involved in insurance other than as suppliers?
12. What is a bottomry contract? What effect has it had on current insurance terminology?

CHAPTER

2 Risk and insurance

John Thoeming/Richard D. Irwin

CHAPTER OBJECTIVES

1. **To define such essential terms as chance of loss, risk, degree of risk, peril, hazard and loss.**
2. **To explain the social cost of risk.**
3. **To describe the methods of handling risk.**
4. **To develop a definition of insurance.**
5. **To show how the law of large numbers is a basis for insurance.**
6. **To list the criteria for an insurable exposure.**

Insurance is purchased to offset the risk resulting from perils that expose a person to loss. Note the term risk. What does it mean? **Risk, hazard** and **chance of loss** are often used interchangeably. The assignment of precise meanings to these terms will help in the understanding of insurance.

BASIC DEFINITIONS

Such terms as *chance of loss, risk, peril, hazard* and *loss* not only have several connotations outside the business but also are subject to varying usage within the business. Such variations can be a source of misunderstanding to the beginning student.[1]

Chance of Loss

Chance of loss is the long-run relative frequency of a loss. Chance of loss is best expressed as a fraction or a percentage. It indicates the probable number and severity of losses from a given number of exposures. Expressed as a fraction, the probable number of losses is the numerator and the number of loss exposures is the denominator. If a person flips a coin for a cup of coffee, the chance of loss is one half, or 50 percent. If a prize is offered for drawing a white ball from a box that contains nine black balls and one white, the chance of loss is 9/10, or 90 percent.

In these cases chance of loss is easy to understand and measure. But what about exposure to loss by fire, windstorm and other perils? Here one cannot rely solely on logic; instead, a mass of statistical data must be collected. For example, to determine the probability of loss or damage to a house by fire all possible statistics must be collected concerning fires on comparable houses. These statistics must include the number of fires in a given time and the number of houses exposed to fire losses during that period. If 100 out of 100,000 similar houses have burned, the chance of loss or damage to one of these houses by fire during any equivalent period will be 100/100,000, or 0.1 percent. This figure gives only the **loss frequency.** For insurance the **loss-severity** figures are more important. Suppose the houses not including the land were worth $60,000 each, making a total value of $6 billion, and the total value of the losses was $3 million (most losses were partial). The chance of loss in terms of severity would be 3 million/6 billion, or 0.05 percent. The pure insurance cost (i.e., without

[1] Occasional lapses into the jargon of the insurance agent are found in later chapters where, for example, the word *risk* is used to mean the property or person covered by a policy.

allowance for expenses, profits or contingencies) then would be 5 cents for each $100 of exposure, or $30 for each house.

The same principle is used in determining the chance of death at any given age. If 65 out of 1,000 people alive at age 75 die before reaching age 76, the chance of death during their 75th year can be expressed as 65/1,000 or 6.5 percent. Because death is permanent and total, loss-frequency and loss-severity statistics produce the same results.

Chance of loss is important in insurance as a basis for setting rates. A reasonable degree of accuracy in measuring loss probabilities is necessary if adequate, equitable and nonexcessive insurance rates are to be developed. Furthermore, chance of loss affects the decision concerning how risk should be handled. If the chance of loss is "relatively high," risk avoidance or risk assumption coupled with a major loss-prevention effort appears to be the most efficient method of dealing with risk. If the chance of loss is infinitesimal, the best approach may be to ignore the risk.

Definition of Risk

Risk is a concept with several meanings depending on the context and the scientific discipline in which it is used. Using the term loosely, the concept of risk means exposure to adversity or danger. Mathematicians are interested in the behavior of phenomena and define risk as the degree of dispersion of values around the mean. The larger the degree of dispersion, the greater is the risk. Behavioral scientists rarely define risk because to them the concept has several meanings related to how people behave.

Here the interest lies in a definition of risk that facilitates communication and risk analysis in the study of insurance. That definition is a simple one: *risk is uncertainty concerning loss.* It contains two concepts: uncertainty and loss. While both concepts are important to insurance, risk is the uncertainty and not the loss, the cause of loss or the chance of loss. The basic function of insurance is to handle risk. Defining risk as uncertainty considers effectively the question of how insurance deals with it. Attention is limited to *pure* rather than to *speculative* risk and is confined to risk from the viewpoint of the insured—not the insurer. Pure risk can produce loss only, while speculative risk can result in either gain or loss. To illustrate: If lightning strikes a house, the result is loss; but if the lightning bypasses the house, the homeowner does not gain, that is, his or her financial position is not improved. However, if a person buys 100 shares of stock in the Good Life Insurance Company, that investor becomes exposed to a speculative risk. If the insurer is profitable the investor gains. Otherwise the investor loses. Taking speculative risks can make the investor either richer or poorer. (At the end of this section, an operational definition of risk for the insurer is considered.)

INNERSCRIPT: LOSS PREDICTABILITY

Assume that the chance of loss by fire to a store is 1 in 1,000. If a person owns one store the loss cannot be predicted. Either it will or will not burn. No basis for predicting the outcome exists,

so the owner is faced with complete uncertainty even though the chance of loss is low. Suppose the person owns a chain of 1,000 similar stores. Now at least one store can be expected to burn because the probability of loss is 1 in 1,000. But even here no assurance can be given that actual losses will equal expected losses. Because the outcome still is uncertain, risk remains. If two stores burn, actual loss exceeds expected loss by 100 percent. However, the loss of one more store represents only 0.1 percent of the exposure.

But suppose the person owns 100,000 stores. Then 100 stores can be expected to burn. If as many as 10 more burn, the actual loss exceeds the expected loss by only 10 percent or 0.01 percent of the exposure. The large number of stores improves loss predictability; that is, it reduces the probable margin of error in predicted results. Thus, with 100,000 stores the degree of risk is reduced; yet the chance of loss still remains 1 in 1,000. The risk is not entirely eliminated, however, because of the ever-present probability that losses will not occur as predicted.

Degree of risk

The accuracy with which losses can be predicted is the measure of degree of risk. The degree of risk is measured by probable variation of actual experience from expected experience. The lower the probable percentage of variation the smaller the risk. This percentage variation decreases as the number of exposures increases. Assume that over time on the average 1 out of 100 trucks is damaged by collision each year. If 10,000 trucks are covered by insurance, the expected number of trucks damaged in any given year is 100. Assume that losses over this period have varied between 80 and 120, so the variation above and below the expected is 20. Consequently, with 10,000 trucks the area of uncertainty is 20/100, or 20 percent. If the number of covered trucks increases a hundredfold from 10,000 to 1 million the expected damage becomes 10,000 trucks. However, according to statistical theory, the variation will be only tenfold, not one hundredfold. Therefore the expected number of damaged trucks will vary between 9,800 and 10,200.[2] The relative area of uncertainty then is 200/10,000, or only 2 percent, rather than 20 percent as before.

If it is known that an event will or will not occur, no uncertainty and hence no risk is involved. The inability to predict accurately the course of future events is the essence of risk. And as events become more predictable risk is reduced.

[2] The sampling error rises only by an amount equal to the square root of the increase in the number of exposures. Thus if the number of exposures increases a hundredfold (from 10,000 to 1 million) the sampling error increases only tenfold (in this example from 20 to 200). Do not worry yourself or your instructor as to why, but if you are truly interested, see any statistical textbook for further discussion of concepts relating to standard error in sampling.

Risk is reduced (1) when the loss range from its expected value remains the same while the loss probability decreases or (2) when the loss probability remains the same while the loss range from its expected value is reduced. For example, risk is reduced if the probability that the loss will fall within 2 percent of its expected value is increased from 90 to 95 percent or if the probability remains at 90 percent while the loss range from its expected value is reduced from 2 to 1 percent.

Chance of loss versus degree of risk

The distinction between chance of loss and degree of risk is clarified by a simple illustration. Assume that A and B represent two groups of exposures to loss. The chance of loss in each group is 10 out of 1,000 (1 percent). In group A over a period of years annual losses varied from 3 to 18, whereas in group B losses varied from 8 to 12. The annual experience is more stable for group B. Therefore, losses are more predictable because of the low degree of variability. The more predictable the loss, the less is the degree of risk. So notwithstanding an equal chance of loss (1 percent), the degree of risk is less for group B. The degree of risk is in part a function of the probability distribution of losses over time.

Risk makes insurance both desirable and possible. If a loss is certain to occur, insurance could not be obtained. No insurer could write it at commercially feasible rates. If a loss is certain not to occur, insurance also would not be written. No one would buy it. The owners of a house located on a river bank where flood damage occurs three years out of four would be eager to buy flood insurance, if offered. The owners of houses on a nearby hill would not buy the insurance because floods cannot cause them damage. Insurance thrives because people do not know what will happen to their property or to their personal earning power in the future. They prefer a small certain cost that can be budgeted (the insurance premium) to an uncertain but potentially large loss that may not be budgeted.

Unlike the insured, the *insurer* is exposed to *speculative risk* in that the value of actual claims incurred may be higher or lower than that projected in the rate structure. If they are higher the insurer loses; if they are lower the insurer gains. Risk for the insurer, therefore, is defined as the exposure to fluctuations between actual claims incurred and those expected.

Peril

A peril is the cause of a loss. People are subject to loss or damage from many perils. Typical perils are fire, windstorm, explosion, collision, premature death, accidents and sickness, negligence and crime. Causes of loss often are loosely called risks. Correctly, risk is the uncertainty about the occurrence of the event that creates the loss, while the peril is the loss-producing agent. Perils that expose property and income to loss must be studied by prospective insureds and their agents and brokers so if insurance protection is purchased the appropriate coverage can be arranged.

Hazard

Behind the ostensible cause of loss (peril) is hazard. The fire in the garage is the peril, but the pile of oily rags on the garage floor is the cause of the fire and thus the basic cause of loss. Further investigation would reveal that poor housekeeping is the fundamental cause. Yet, for insurance purposes, fire is the basic cause of the loss and is the peril against which the fire policy is written.

Hazard is defined as a condition that may create or increase the chance of loss from a given peril. Carelessness, poor housekeeping, bad highways, unguarded machines and dangerous employments are examples of hazards, as they increase chance of loss.

Two types of hazards are important to insurers: physical and moral. *Physical hazard* is a material condition increasing chance of loss. The production of gunpowder in a building is a physical hazard increasing chance of loss by fire or explosion. *Moral hazard* is an individual characteristic of the insured that increases the probability of loss. For example, dishonest insureds increase arson losses. Another form of moral hazard is indifference to loss. This condition is sometimes called *morale hazard* in insurance textbooks, but this subtle differentiation is rarely made in insurance underwriting. For example, carelessness in safekeeping property increases the chance of loss by theft. Moral hazard arises when insureds induce or fake a loss to collect on their policies as well as when the insured fails to protect property from loss because it is covered by insurance.

Insurers must review hazards when applications for insurance are submitted. If the hazards exceed those contemplated in the rate schedule, the insurer generally rejects the application, restricts the coverage or increases the premium. Insurers are interested in loss-prevention activities, so they study hazards to discover methods of reducing or eliminating losses.

Insurance buyers must be able to recognize hazards that can cause loss and isolate those to be covered by insurance. Hazards can be handled intelligently only through a systematic study of them. For example, if the risk manager of a firm decides to purchase adequate coverage for the liability exposure (a wise decision) but overlooks the elevator and products hazards, a financial shock can be expected when a liability suit results from one of these hazards.[3]

Loss

Loss is an unintentional decline in or disappearance of value. The adjective *unintentional* is an essential part of the definition. If a college student gives his girlfriend a diamond ring he has certainly parted with something of value; but he probably would not admit (at least at this stage of the game) that he has suffered a loss. Most medical and hospital care expenses are considered losses, although their payment is not unintentional. The occurrence (accident or illness) generating them usually is unintentional.

Loss does not necessarily imply the loss of a physical article. The owner of common stock, for example, has a paper loss if its market price declines, yet the certificate remains intact. Technical obsolescence is another loss that does not result from physical damage. Large desk calculating machines have lost some value because of progressively less expensive electronic pocket calculators. Losses caused by changing conditions of the market are called speculative losses and generally are not insurable because they do not meet some of the criteria for insurable exposures, explained later.

Pure losses include those where a physical article is damaged or destroyed,

[3] See Chapter 21 for an additional discussion of physical and moral hazards.

those caused by disability and death, those caused by outliving one's income and those resulting from liability suits. These losses generally are insurable. Losses resulting from destruction of property may be of three types: loss of the article, loss of its income or use until the article can be replaced and extra expenses incurred because of the loss. If a house is destroyed by fire, the owner not only has lost the house but also must pay rent elsewhere until it is rebuilt. If the homeowner had rented a room to another person the rental income also is lost. If the family moves to a motel or must spend several hundred dollars to remove the debris of the house from the street following the fire, substantial extra expenses are incurred. Insurance should be planned to cover these three types of property and income losses.

Suppose a fire caused by burning leaves spreads to a neighbor's house. The neighbor may bring suit against the leaf burner, charging negligence. The defendant will incur the defense cost of the legal action and if found guilty will be obligated to pay the damages awarded by the court. These losses also require insurance protection.

RISK AND RISK BEARING

Risk involves social as well as individual cost. Therefore both society and individuals are interested in how it may be handled.

Social Cost of Risk

Because most persons are risk averters, risk creates a social cost by retarding economic progress. The cost of risk is apart from the cost of replacing destroyed or damaged property and is usually recognizable only on close analysis.

Risk discourages investors and affects the allocation of resources. Many resources are used in industries where risk is slight, while fewer are used in industries exposed to a high degree of risk. The result is that resource allocation is not maximized for society. If risk were eliminated, some resources eventually would move from industries formerly exposed to a lower degree of risk to those formerly subject to a higher degree of risk, thus maximizing resource allocation. The effect of risk on the economy is the same as that of socially undesirable monopolies. Both similarly affect production and prices by discouraging production and restricting supply, thus leading to high prices. The social cost of risk is its effect on the allocation of resources. Uncertainty discourages the production of goods and services, and this lack of production is a measure of the social cost of risk. That cost is not the loss of capital resulting from the occurrence of an uncertain event. The cost of that loss is *in addition* to the cost of risk.

Some areas of economic activity are deemed so important to society that the government intervenes in the risk process. When the risk is so great that it totally discourages needed capital investment, the government may, through legislation, reduce the amount of risk to encourage investment. For example, the Price-Anderson Act limits the aggregate liability resulting from a nuclear accident to a maximum of $560 million. By limiting the maximum loss, the amount of risk is reduced to an "acceptable" level. This limitation has resulted in increased investment in nuclear energy. Another example of government involvement to reduce the amount at risk is the Swine Flu Vaccine Program of 1976. To encourage drug manufacturers to produce the vaccine, the government, by legislation, assumed the liability for settling and paying all claims resulting from mass immunization, reserving the right to proceed against the drug manufacturers only in cases of negligence or breach of contract with the government. This action removed the responsibility for the drug manufacturers of settling the many nuisance claims that recently tend to develop in this type of program. By reducing the amount of risk, the government encouraged additional investments in these endeavors.

Chance of loss also can exert an influence on economic activity. A high chance of a severe loss discourages business activity irrespective of the degree of risk.

Methods of Handling Risk

Jawaharlal Nehru once wrote: "People avoid action often because they are afraid of the consequences, for action means risk and danger." He added that while these results seem frightening from a distance, they are not so terrifying upon close scrutiny. Often risk "is a pleasant companion, adding to the zest and delight of life." Most people, however, do not regard risk so kindly and seek to cope with it efficiently. Risk is universal, present in all things, all lives, inherent in being. The concept of a person free from all risk is as theoretical as the concept of perfection. What can be done about risk? Methods of dealing with risk may be classified under six headings: (1) risk may be avoided, (2) risk may be retained, (3) hazard may be reduced, (4) loss may be reduced, (5) risk may be shifted and (6) risk may be reduced.

Risk may be avoided

To quote an old chestnut: "There is a way—but it's not much fun." The British humor magazine *Punch* once published "Advice to a Young Man Who Is about to Marry." The advice consisted of a single word: *DON'T!* A couple can avoid the risk of a fire loss to their house by selling the house or burning it to the ground. The uncertainty of the date of death can be avoided by judicious use of a knife or gun. Truly, it is not much fun.

Often alternatives are available for handling risk that cannot be avoided. For example, upon graduation from the university Phyllis Klock is offered two jobs: one a salaried position in the home office of a property and liability insurer, the other a commission-paying connection with a local general insurance agency. Phyllis believes she would enjoy the work in the agency more, but does not know if the earnings would be adequately rewarding during the years required to become established. Although not so promising for the future nor so challenging, the salaried position in the home office does offer a regular income. Phyllis must make a choice. Her decision rests on how she appraises the relative attractiveness of the two opportunities. Everyone does not measure the undesirability of risk bearing equally. When the reluctance to accept risk is so great it cannot be counterbalanced by possible gains from risky action, the risk should be avoided. Avoidance is possible, however, only if that choice is possible. If the risk cannot be avoided it must be handled some other way.

Risk may be retained

Those who bear their own risks (as all must do to an important degree) must be prepared to withstand not only the risk but also the loss. The retention of risk often is the path of least resistance in meeting uncertainty. Risk may be retained out of ignorance. For example, owning a house creates risk of loss from many sources: fire, windstorm, explosion and so on. The homeowner can insure against loss from all these perils and yet not be fully protected against risk. Financial loss may be suffered because of legal liability for persons injured on the premises. Failure to insure against this liability exposure may be a result of unawareness rather than a conscious risk-retention decision.

Risks are also retained out of inertia. A couple may realize the family faces risk of loss of income should the breadwinner die prematurely and that the family cannot assume this risk. Yet they delay buying life insurance until pressured by an agent.

Risks are retained also if no other way is possible. A person might want to insure the risk of death, but if his or her occupation is racing motorcycles, insurance may be unattainable. Risk retention, however, may be the result of positive action. Many instances are found where retention is the most economical solution to the risk problem. Operators of truck lines frequently have oral tilts with highway regulatory authorities. Tests indicate weights exceeding certain limits produce an extra-heavy strain on highways, so laws of most states limit trucks to specified axle-weight loads. Some truckers frequently carry weights far in excess of the limit. They are aware of the law but are taking a calculated risk. Excessive loads are so much more profitable that truckers find it economical to haul illegal loads and pay the fine when they are caught. Risk also is retained if the loss exposure is too small to be of concern. For example, students are forever losing pens and pencils, but these inexpensive losses can be replaced without financial burden.

If the maximum loss is small and losses are frequent, they can be handled on a current basis without funding. If the losses are irregular and too large to be absorbed when they occur, some funding might be required. The purpose of the fund is to spread the losses over time. The cost is borne by a steady series of small payments to the fund although the loss occurs infrequently for large amounts. Difficulties arise in this method because losses may occur more often than expected or before the fund is sufficient to pay for them; also management might not keep the fund intact for its designated purpose.

INNERSCRIPT: SINKING FUNDS

Business executives sometimes accumulate sinking funds to meet uncertainty in the erroneous belief that they are operating scientifically. Assume the manager of a store that has escaped fire losses casts covetous eyes at the firm's annual fire insurance bill. The manager is loss-prevention conscious, conducts monthly fire drills and is never out of arm's reach of a fire extinguisher. So the decision is made to "self-insure" the fire loss exposure. Instead of renewing the insurance, the premiums are put in a new account, "Fire Self-Insurance Fund." (As is soon explained, the term *self-insurance* is used incorrectly here.) One evening when the manager has locked up the extinguisher for the night, a hungry rat, who is new in the building and has missed the fire drills, gnaws into the casing of an electric line causing a short circuit, which, before morning, starts a fire that cannot be extinguished. The loss is $500,000 to be offset by a fund of $3,500. What then is the effectiveness of the so-called self-insurance fund?

This observation does not imply that self-insurance is impossible. Suppose this store was one unit of a national chain with hun-

dreds of similar stores. The chain could probably predict its fire losses within reasonable limits and thus self-insure its risk. The principal objection is that, even with its hundreds of units, the company will not have the broad basis for predicting losses available even to a medium-sized fire insurer. A particularly unfavorable year may exhaust the insurance fund before all losses have been replaced. See Chapter 24 for further discussion of self-insurance and the conditions under which it may be desirable.

Sometimes insurance is impossible to buy because insurers are either unable or unwilling to write the coverage. In these instances the accumulation of a sinking fund is the best way to handle the problem. The motorcycle racer who cannot buy life insurance can set aside a large portion of winnings to create a life insurance fund, that, if luck holds, may be sizable before the last race is lost.

The hazard may be reduced

Efforts may be made to reduce the hazard. If metal conduits had been used in constructing the rat's adopted self-insured store building, the rat could not have gnawed the wiring and started a fire. Well-defined safety precautions reduce accidents. Recent progress in medical science has accomplished much in eliminating or controlling diseases greatly feared a generation ago. Much loss-prevention research is conducted or financed by insurers. For example, Underwriters' Laboratories, Inc., was originally established by midwestern fire insurers to test materials, devices and processes against fire hazards.[4]

The cost of losses is an important factor and is distinguishable from the cost or risk. The cost of risk is the before-the-loss evaluation of the cost of uncertainty about losses. For example, the cost of risk is equated with loss-control expenditures and necessary periodic contributions to a fund to pay losses. Budgeting for the before-the-loss cost of risk can reduce the cost of loss because a prepared for loss generally costs less than an unprepared for loss. The cost of loss is the after-the-fact evaluation of the loss. Thus the building of a fund is a cost of risk. That cost primarily is the opportunity cost of holding liquid funds. When the fund is used to pay for a loss, that expenditure is the cost of loss. That cost is likely to be less because funds are available immediately to offset it.

Risk managers have important duties in controlling losses. Loss control requires a variety of trained specialists, e.g., loss control engineers, accountancy systems analysts, attorneys and others. The risk manager's most important loss control task is to motivate management personnel to control losses. In several insurance lines (e.g., boiler and machinery) the coverage offers important loss-control services. When some risks are retained rather than insured, loss-control services must be provided by the business in-house and/or outside consultants.

Losses may be reduced

Action may be taken to minimize a loss if one occurs. The chance of loss is not eliminated, but its severity is reduced. Fire extinguishers or automatic sprinklers throughout a factory do not change the likelihood of a fire but do curtail its

[4] Underwriters' Laboratories, Inc., is now an independent self-supporting organization.

spread. Periodic medical examinations may not reduce the chance of heart disease; however, regular doctor visits can result in recommendations and treatment that may diminish or cure existing physical problems. Hazard reduction and loss minimization often are coexistent aims and are usually found together. Thus a physical checkup not only will reduce the loss from disease but the doctor's recommendation may also reduce the hazard. An automatic traffic signal at an intersection of two heavily traveled highways will lower the accident frequency rate. At the same time, it reduces the severity rate because the signal usually slows traffic. The result is that, although collisions may still occur, both the impact and resulting damage is less.

Risk may be shifted

Hedging, subcontracting, surety bonding, incorporation and insurance are examples of methods of shifting risk to another party.

Hedging is making commitments on both sides of a transaction so the risks offset each other. A simple illustration is a betting transaction: an overenthusiastic sophomore bets five dollars that the home team will win its game Saturday. During the week preceding the game, the student's enthusiasm wanes in the light of cold, hard realism concerning the home team's chances. One way to offset the risk is to shift it to someone else. So a naive freshman full of school spirit is enticed to bet five dollars on the home team with the sophomore taking the opponent. Now, with offsetting bets, the sophomore will break even regardless of which team wins.

In legitimate business the activities of a grain elevator operator offers an example of hedging. The operator buys grain from farmers for shipment to a central market. Each farmer receives the price prevailing the day the grain is purchased although it will not be shipped for some time. When the grain arrives at the central market prices may have dropped, so the elevator operator cannot sell the grain for a price high enough to cover the amount paid the farmer plus the handling cost. However, prices may be up the day the grain arrives; then a speculative profit is made. But at the time of purchase no one knows what the price of the grain will be on arrival at the central market.

The elevator operator does not retain the unexpected gain or loss resulting from the risk of price changes; the risk is shifted to the grain speculator who buys and sells "futures," that is, makes contracts to buy or sell grain at a given time in the future at a specified price.

Subcontracting is another method of shifting risk. A general contractor is building a dormitory at an agreed-upon price. Subcontracts are let for various operations—for instance, plumbing, electrical wiring and roofing—all at fixed prices. Although the general contractor still has residual liability for the job, portions of the risk of increasing costs have been shifted to the subcontractors. If the price of bathroom fixtures or electrical conduits rises the subcontractors must bear their proportionate share.

Hold harmless agreements allow liability risks to be shifted. One party agrees to assume the legal obligations of another in a lawsuit for damages to third parties arising from specified operations. For example, a contractor agrees to hold the project owner harmless from liability if a third person is injured during the building of a shopping center. (The project owner does not avoid liability and must pay if the contractor fails to honor the hold harmless agreement.)

Surety bonding is a three-party agreement in which a bonding company (the surety) and the principal (e.g., a contractor) promise an obligee (for whom the work is to be done) a specified performance. Under a surety bond (contract) the surety must answer for the default of the principal. The general contractor for a school dormitory must furnish a surety bond to the school authorities guaranteeing that the dormitory will be built as specified and within the time agreed upon. If the contractor is unable to finish by that time, the bonding company might be obligated to make daily payments of specified amounts to the school until the contractor has fulfilled the obligation. If the contractor cannot complete the building, the surety is obligated to pay the necessary additional costs to have another contractor finish it.

Incorporation is another method of shifting risk. The corporation has been defined as "an ingenious device for obtaining individual profit without individual responsibility." The stockholders, if their shares of stock are fully paid, have no liability. Their losses are limited to their investment in the stock. In an unincorporated business the owners are the ultimate risk bearers in the event business assets are insufficient to pay all claims. In the corporation, because of limited liability, risk is shifted to creditors.

Insurance is the most common method for shifting risk. By purchasing insurance, the insured shifts the financial consequences of loss to the insurer. If a loss occurs the insured is reimbursed by the insurer for the loss subject to the terms of the policy.

Risk may be reduced

In the previous examples methods for retaining or shifting risk were explained. These methods attempt to cushion the loss or transfer it to someone else.

Even loss-prevention activities do not reduce risk unless the chance of loss is reduced to zero—an unlikely event. In fact, loss-prevention activities may increase risk. For example, if the chance of loss is reduced to an infinitesimal level enough loss exposures to give sufficient credibility to the meager loss statistics might be impossible. The methods discussed in this section succeed in reducing the degree of risk.

Large-scale business is a method of reducing risk. A person who has erected a telephone pole for the sole purpose of supporting a television antenna will lose this entertainment source if lightning strikes the pole. The degree of risk is high even though the chance of loss is low but this small chance of loss does not decrease the uncertainty. AT&T with its millions of widely scattered poles, does not have this high degree of risk because it can predict within an acceptable range the number of poles that will be lost each year through lightning—as well as through termites, motorists and those who "borrow" a pole to use as a base for a television antenna.

Many kinds of managerial controls tend to reduce risk. Materials-control systems, audits and other accounting controls and process and product inspection plans improve prediction and hence reduce risk.

From an individual point of view, insurance can be considered a method of shifting risk. However, insurance also is a method for reducing risk. Insurers are willing to assume the risk because with a large number of exposures the number of losses becomes more predictable. For instance, a couple owning a home knows that some houses will burn but are uncertain as to whether their house will burn. They also are uncertain about the loss they will suffer if a fire does occur. They cannot set up an adequate sinking fund for these losses because that method is unsuitable for only one piece of property. They could buy 9,999 other houses so their loss would be more predictable, but most homeowners would consider this solution neither sensible nor practical. They can achieve the same end by combining their risk with the risks of thousands of other homeowners through an insurer. When risks are combined, losses become more predictable and risk is reduced. All members of the group then know the amount of their share of the loss. They can budget for this small fixed amount, knowing this charge limits the direct cost by a fire.

Life insurance is comparable. "Nothing more certain than death; nothing more uncertain than the hour of death." The possibility that even the healthiest person may die this year is always present, but whether the possibility will become a reality is unknown. By combining the death risk of one person with that of many the uncertainty of financial loss can be eliminated. Each individual's share of the cost can be determined and spread equitably among the members of the group.

INSURANCE AS A DEVICE FOR HANDLING RISK

The real nature of insurance is often confused. The word *insurance* sometimes is applied to a fund accumulated to meet uncertain losses. For example, a specialty shop dealing in seasonal goods must charge more early in the season to build up funds to cover the possibility of loss at the end of the season when prices must be reduced below cost for quick sale. An accumulation of funds to meet uncertain losses is not sufficient to qualify as insurance.

A transfer of risk often is called insurance. A store selling television sets promises to service the set for one year without additional charge and to replace the picture tube should the glories of television prove too much for its delicate wiring. This agreement, loosely referred to as an "insurance policy," is simply one that transfers risk, and risk transfer is insufficient for an economic or legal definition of insurance. If it were sufficient then insurance regulation would extend to a host of commercial promises for which the insurance regulating system was not designed.

Definition of Insurance

An adequate definition of insurance must include *either* the accumulation of a fund *or* the transference of risk but not necessarily both. In addition it must include a combination of a large number of separate, independent exposure units having the same common risk characteristics into an interrelated group.

Insurance may be defined as a device for reducing risk by combining a sufficient number of exposure units to make their individual losses collectively predictable. The predictable loss is then shared proportionately by all units in the combination.

These exposure units include both an entity (for example, one automobile, one house or one business) and a time unit (for example, one year). Commonly, insurance involves spreading losses over more than one entity within one unit of time. However, insurance also can involve spreading losses of one entity over a long enough time to increase the predictability of loss. This technique of spreading losses for a single entity over a long time span is known as self-insurance. The question of whether that technique should be called insurance has caused considerable controversy within academic circles, the accounting profession and in Internal Revenue Service rulings. That issue is tangential to the discussion at this point. The important characteristics of the concept of insurance as used in this text is that *uncertainty is reduced* and that *losses are shared or distributed* among the exposure units.

Insurance allows the individual insured to substitute a small, definite cost (the premium) for a large but uncertain loss (not to exceed the amount of the insurance) under an arrangement whereby the fortunate many who escape loss will help compensate the unfortunate few who suffer loss. Even if no loss materializes, insurance helps to eliminate any anxiety the insured might have about a potential loss. Insurance, therefore, provides the insured not only postloss but also preloss utility.

Indemnity

With some notable exceptions discussed in Chapter 7 the purpose of an insurance contract is to provide indemnity. Webster defines indemnity as "compensation or remuneration for loss or injury sustained." Thus to prevent the insured from obtaining unjust enrichment, insurance policies limit payments to the amount of the loss subject to policy limits. For example, if an insured has a $100,000 fire policy covering a house worth $80,000 and sells it during the policy term, nothing will be paid if the house is destroyed by fire, because no loss is suffered by the insured. If the house is destroyed before it is sold, the insured can collect only $80,000, because that is the amount of the loss. Indemnity is the only legitimate use for insurance; otherwise insurance would be a gambling instrument and contrary to public policy.

Insurance may be distinguished from gambling. In gambling the risk is created by the transaction; in insurance the risk is reduced by the transaction. For example, no chance of loss is created at the racetrack until a bet has been placed, but the risk of loss of property by fire or windstorm is present until reduced or eliminated by insurance. Therefore gambling and insurance are opposites: one creates risk, the other reduces it.

The Law of Large Numbers

To repeat, insurance reduces risk. At first glance it may seem strange that a combination of individual risks would result in the reduction of total risk. The principle that explains this phenomenon is called the "law of large numbers," sometimes loosely termed the *law of averages* or the *law of probability.*[5] However, it is only a part of the subject of probability, which is not a law but a field of mathematics.

In the 17th century European mathematicians were constructing crude mortality tables. From these investigations they discovered that the percentage of male and female deaths among each year's births tended toward a constant, if sufficient numbers of births were tabulated. In the 19th century Simeon Denis Poisson named this principle the "law of large numbers." This law is based on the regularity of events. What seems random occurrence in the individual happening appears so because of insufficient or incomplete knowledge of what is expected. A simple statement of the law of large numbers is as follows: the greater the number of exposures, the more nearly will the actual results obtained approach the probable result expected with an infinite number of exposures. Thus if a coin is flipped a sufficiently large number of times the results of the trials will approach half heads and half tails—the theoretical probability if the coin is flipped an infinite number of times.

Events that seem the result of chance occur with surprising regularity as the number of observations increase. A car races around a corner one July 4th.

[5] Called the "law of great numbers" by our British cousins. The economist John Maynard Keynes suggested a more accurate term would be the *stability of statistical frequencies.*

A tire blows and the car crashes, killing the driver. If the car had been moving slowly and its tires were in good condition, the accident might not have happened. It seems impossible to have predicted this particular acccident, yet the National Safety Council predicts within a small margin of error how many motorists will die in accidents over the July 4th holiday. Even more accurate is the Safety Council's estimates of yearly accidental deaths, because the larger the number of exposures to loss the closer the results will be to the underlying probability.

Similarly, insurers with statistics on millions of lives can make a close forecast of the number of deaths in a given period; the longer the period, the greater accuracy. The prediction of the number of persons in a college class who will die during the year probably would be far from accurate. The prediction on the basis of enrollment in a large university would show a moderate degree of accuracy. And the prediction of deaths in all U.S. colleges and universities would have a high degree of accuracy.

The law of large numbers is the basis of insurance. Under this law the impossibility of predicting a happening in an individual case is replaced by the demonstrable ability to forecast collective losses from a large number of cases. Insurers note that every year a given number of dwellings burn or a particular number of deaths occur. If a small group of cases were isolated, a wide variation between actual loss experienced and average loss expected might be found. Insurers within their financial limits use the benefits of the law of large numbers by insuring the largest possible number of acceptable exposure units to facilitate loss forecasting. In addition insurers want the units spread widely to minimize deviation from underlying probabilities occurring when the units are concentrated in one location.

Insurance does not completely eliminate risk because achieving an infinite number of exposure units is impossible. Some deviation of actual from expected results can be anticipated. Furthermore, statistics on which predictions are based are not perfect. Even if they were, tomorrow's losses will not necessarily conform to yesterday's because so many dynamic elements are involved. The possibility of the presence of moral hazards also may interfere with loss prediction.

Criteria of an Insurable Exposure

Considering that insurance seems such a logical method of handling risk, why not combine all uncertainties in one big pool and rid the world of most risk? The limiting factor is that several broad criteria must be considered before attempting to operate a successful insurance plan: (1) a large group of homogeneous exposure units *must* be involved, (2) the loss produced by the peril should be definite, (3) the occurrence of the loss in the individual cases should be accidental or fortuitous, (4) the potential loss should be large enough to cause hardship, (5) the cost of the insurance should be economically feasible, (6) the chance of loss should be calculable and (7) the peril must be unlikely to produce loss to a great many insured units at one time.

Among these criteria a few are essential while most are only requisite. The difference between essential and requisite is the importance of the characteristic to the concept of insurance. If a criterion of insurability is deemed essential, insurance is impossible without it. A requisite provides one means to an end, but others are available. If a criterion of insurability is considered a requisite, insurance is possible without it by substituting some other characteristic. Those characteristics considered essential and those considered requisite depend on the rigidity of the definition of insurance. It has been suggested that the rigidity of the definition be sufficiently relaxed so that none of the criteria is essential or requisite. The assertion is made that an insurable exposure is one for which insurance can be purchased and that in turn is a function of the knowledge and persuasiveness of the broker and the knowledge, imagination and courage of the insurer rather than a list of criteria for insurability. However, to support precise thinking, a rigid definition of insurance is used in this text. Accordingly, not every contract written by an insurer is one of insurance even though it is called insurance. For the purpose of this text the essential criteria in the foregoing list are (1) and (7). The others are considered requisites. The rationale becomes apparent as the discussion develops.

1. A large group of homogeneous exposure units

To predict probable loss through the law of large numbers it is *essential* that a large number of similar though not necessarily identical units be exposed to the same peril. Large numbers in this context means numbers sufficient to make losses predictable within ranges compatible to insurers. A fire insurer cannot operate with a population of only 25 or 50 houses to insure. With so few exposures, the difference between losses experienced and those expected probably will be excessive. Insurance is impractical when the probable deviation from predicted loss is so large that a reasonable addition to the premium to offset the risk increases insurance rates to levels unattractive to buyers. In life insurance many persons are needed in each age, health and occupational classification. To accommodate this essential criterion risk classifications for insurance are frequently broad.

2. Definite loss

The loss should be difficult to counterfeit. Death, perhaps, comes closest to perfection in meeting this requisite. In sickness insurance, claims personnel sometimes find it difficult to determine if a loss has occurred. During the depression of the 1930s sickness claims rose sharply. Persons unable to find jobs either worried themselves sick or faked illness in order to collect benefits. During this period a common observation was that while a covered accidental injury was indeed needed to collect under an accident policy, no illness was needed to collect under a sickness policy. The policy itself was sufficient because illness could be falsely claimed without fear of detection. Inability to recognize fraudulent claims was in part responsible for the receivership of several insurers writing disability insurance covering sickness during the 1920s and 1930s. Disability income insurance contracts are subject to stricter underwriting standards today because of that adverse experience. Coverage is more liberal for disability resulting from accident than from sickness partly because accidental injury is more easily confirmed than illness.

3. Accidental loss

Although some losses are expected for the group, specific individual losses themselves should be unexpected, that is, fortuitous. Ideally the loss should be beyond the control of the insured. Under mercantile theft insurance normal (anticipated) shoplifting losses are included. In credit insurance bad debt losses that are normal for the trade are not covered. Unless (or until) medical researchers find a way to prolong life forever, everyone is certain to die. The uncertainty involved in life insurance is the time of death.

4. Large loss

The peril covered should be capable of producing a loss so large the insured could not bear it without economic distress. Insurance against breakage of shoestrings is unknown. The loss involved is so small that it is not worth the time, effort and expense to enter into an insurance contract to indemnify the loss.

This example is a *reductio ad absurdum,* but it illustrates the principle. Nevertheless insurance often is written to cover small losses because unsophisticated insurance buyers want these losses covered in their policies. Insurance for losses that can be absorbed is uneconomical because the insurance premium includes not only the loss cost but also an expense margin.

5. Economically feasible cost

To be insurable the chance of loss should be small. The cost of the policy consists of the pure premium (amount needed for claims) and the expense addition. If the chance of loss is much above 40 percent the policy cost will exceed the amount the insurer must pay under the contract. For example, a life insurer could issue a $1,000 policy on a man aged 99. However, the pure premium (about $980) plus an amount for expenses would increase the total premium to more than the policy amount. For insurance to be attractive for the consumer the coverage must exceed the premium. The amount by which the coverage must exceed the premium depends on the degree of the individual's risk aversion. The chance of loss involving small damage to autos by collision is so high that collision policies usually are written to exclude at least the first $100 of loss, often more, e.g., $250.

6. Chance of loss should be calculable

Some probabilities of loss can be determined by logic alone, for example, the probabilities in a flip of a coin. Others must be determined empirically, that is, by a tabulation of experience with a projection of that experience into the future. Most types of insurance probabilities are determined empirically. Some chances of loss, however, cannot be determined either by logic or from experience. Unemployment is an example because it occurs with such irregularity that no one as yet has succeeded in determining its future incidence. If no statistics on the chance of loss are available, the degree of accuracy in loss prediction is low in spite of a large number of exposures. Nevertheless, insurers rely heavily on subjective probabilities in estimating the chance of loss especially for new exposures and for some old ones.

The essential criterion of a large number of homogeneous exposure units and the requisite of a measurable chance of loss are violated by insurance for such loss exposures as the fingers of a pianist or the pitching arm of a baseball player. These types of policies are not true insurance. They are transfers of risk from the insured to the insurer but do not combine exposures to reduce risk.

7. The loss must not occur to a large number of insureds at the same time

No insurer can afford to insure a type of loss likely to happen to a large percentage of those exposed to it. A large percentage as used in this context means one so high a single occurrence could force well-managed insurers and their reinsurers into (or close to the brink of) insolvency. Life insurers write coverage against death, even though all policyowners will die eventually. Its premium rates and asset accumulations are calculated to pay claims as they mature without causing the insurer financial hardship. If *all* policyowners of a life insurer should die prematurely, it would be insolvent just as a fire insurer would whose policyowners all lost their houses by fire.

Unemployment insurance written by private insurers violates this essential criterion. Individuals with secure jobs (other than on the colleges campuses where many professors are tenured, where are these secure jobs in this world of fast-changing technology?) would be poor prospects for unemployment insurance. Prospective customers would be only those insecure in their employment, many of whom would lose their jobs during a recession. Through insurance the unfortunate few who lose are indemnified by the fortunate many who escape loss. If the many suffer the loss the few will prove inadequate to indemnify them properly except at an uneconomic premium. To guard against catastrophic losses, fire insurers for instance seek a wide distribution of exposures and apply underwriting standards prohibiting concentrations of business in small sections of a city. They also exclude from coverage losses caused by war, thus relieving them of this particular danger of catastrophic loss. Life insurers often insert war clauses in new policies when war seems imminent.

The criteria of insurability are not always followed rigidly. Coverage is written in violation of one or more of them. Insurers write policies for small amounts; they write insurance for which no adequate statistics are available for scientific ratemaking; they write contracts when the chance of loss is high or the exposure is catastrophic; they write coverage where the loss is not accidental; and they cover losses that are not definite in time, amount and place. These criteria must be viewed as the optimum to achieve rather than characteristics to be met in every instance. Note that these criteria apply mostly to private insurance. Because social insurance is often compulsory and frequently subsidized (see Chapter 18), these criteria are inappropriate.

SUMMARY

1. An understanding of the definitions of terms that have both analytical and communicative value in studying insurance is important.
   - *a.* *Chance of loss.* The long-run relative frequency of a loss, best expressed as the probable number and severity of losses from a given amount of exposures.
   - *b.* *Risk.* Uncertainty concerning loss.
   - *c.* *Degree of risk.* The probable variation of actual experience from expected experience.
   - *d.* *Peril.* The cause of the loss.
   - *e.* *Hazard.* A condition that may create or increase the chance of loss.
   - *f.* *Loss.* An unintentional decline in value resulting from a contingency.

2. Economic fear, which causes an uneconomic allocation of resources, is the real cost of risk to society. Insurance eliminates or reduces this fear thus helping to optimize resource allocation.

3. Six basic methods are available for the management of risk:
   - *a.* The *risk* may be *avoided.*
   - *b.* The *risk* may be *retained.*
   - *c.* The *hazard* may be *reduced.*
   - *d.* The *loss* may be *reduced.*
   - *e.* The *risk* and consequently, the *loss* may be *transferred.*
   - *f.* The *risk* may be *reduced.*

4. The cost of risk and the cost of loss are distinguishable. Risk managers must be prepared to deal with both costs.

5. The foundation of insurance is based on loss prediction and loss sharing. It assumes a calculable chance of loss and a combination of loss exposures to permit a reasonably accurate prediction. The predicted loss is shared proportionately by all members of the group.

6. Indemnity (compensation for actual losses incurred) is the principal function of most property insurance contracts.

7. A number of criteria must be considered in determining the insurability of a loss exposure. Two of these criteria are essential while the others are only requisite. These criteria are:
   a. There must be a large number of homogeneous exposure units.
   b. The loss should be definite in amount, time and place.
   c. The loss should be accidental.
   d. The peril should be capable of producing a loss large enough to have serious adverse financial effects on the insured, otherwise the insurance would not be economically attractive.
   e. The chance of loss should be small enough so the insurance cost will not be prohibitive.
   f. The chance of loss should be calculable to permit the insurer to devise a premium scale sufficient to pay losses and expenses as they occur.
   g. The loss must not happen to a great many insureds at the same time, because a catastrophic loss may cause insolvency for an insurer. Criteria (*a*) and (*g*) are essential.

REVIEW QUESTIONS

1. Distinguish chance of loss from degree of risk. What is the relationship between a hazard and a specific peril?
2. Aside from the moral hazard, what other type of hazard is important to insurers? Distinguish between the two types of hazard.
3. Distinguish between the six methods of dealing with risk by giving an example of each. Explain with examples how more than one method may (or should) be used simultaneously in handling the same risk.
4. Explain the difference between an essential criterion and a requisite criterion of insurability. What criteria are essential? Why? Select two of the other criteria and explain why they are requisite rather than essential.
5. Why are insurers less likely to insure a homeowner against loss from flood damage than loss from a tornado?
6. Explain the different kinds of losses that might occur.
7. When should risks be retained rather than insured?
8. Are sinking funds insurance?
9. When is the use of sinking funds appropriate in dealing with risks?
10. Define insurance and explain how that definition relates to the law of large numbers.
11. Distinguish between pure and speculative risk.
12. Why would an insurer reject a proposal to cover the expected profits from manufacturing and merchandising a new product line?
13. Distinguish between the cost of risk and the cost of loss.
14. Develop a set of circumstances that would cause a risk manager to avoid a risk.

PART TWO RISK MANAGEMENT AND RISK ANALYSIS

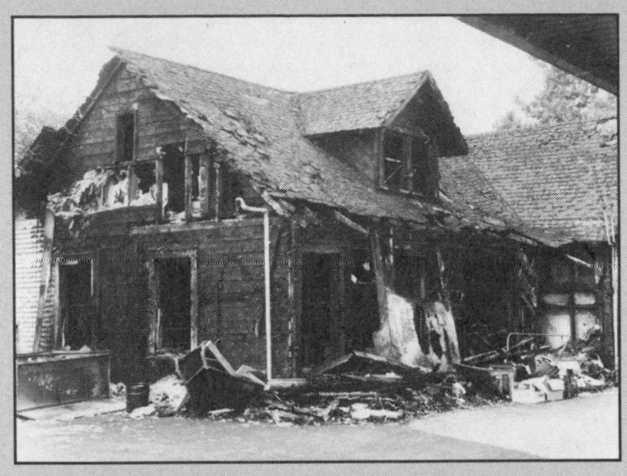

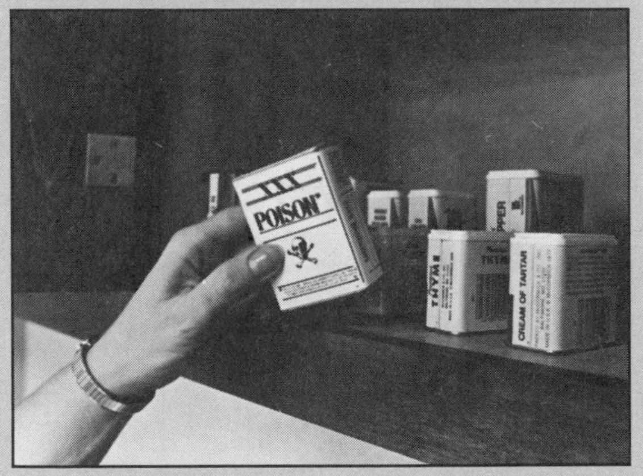

Part One established a foundation for the study of insurance and risk management. Important concepts relating to both risk and insurance were discussed. Definitions of insurance and risk were developed to show how insurance deals with the two important aspects of risk: uncertainty and loss. Through insurance, uncertainty (risk) is reduced and losses are shared. Other methods of dealing with risk were also examined in Part One.

Part Two consisting of two chapters (3 and 4) comes to grips with basic issues of managing risks—primarily pure risks (those that offer only a chance of loss) rather than speculative risks (those that offer a chance of gain as well as a chance of loss). Chapter 3 considers the overall risk management objective: an efficient preloss arrangement for an effective postloss balance between needed and available resources to meet family and business financial goals. The risk management process is outlined and explained step-by-step with special emphasis given to the risk manager's functions in buying and administering insurance.

For risk managers to perform their jobs effectively, they must engage in risk analysis. Chapter 3 defines risk analysis as it relates to life, health and property loss exposures of families and businesses. Family and business liability loss exposures are identified and explained in Chapter 4. Part Two suggests the depth and breadth of knowledge (legal, engineering, financial, accounting, insurance and so on) needed by risk managers to perform their functions successfully.

CHAPTER

3 Risk management and risk analysis: Life and property exposures

Courtesy of Bernice Davis

CHAPTER OBJECTIVES

1. **To describe the risk management process.**
2. **To identify the risk manager's role in buying and administering insurance.**
3. **To point out the possible life and health loss exposures for families and businesses.**
4. **To indicate the possible property loss exposures for families and businesses.**

In one sense, the history of risk management began with the dawn of civilization. Long before women's lib, when primitive man had his mate sleep nearer the mouth of their cave so the noise of her being attacked by a saber-toothed tiger would give him time to grab a firebrand and make his escape, he was engaging in a rudimentary form of risk management. Today's liberated women rightfully would refuse to cooperate with this male chauvinistic behavior.

The modern history of risk management originated with the organization in 1931 of the insurance section of the American Management Association. In the 1930s the person in charge of purchasing insurance for a company was usually called "the insurance buyer." The title later became "insurance manager." The term *risk manager* is of recent origin, and the responsibilities of the job have grown. Risk managers must be skilled and effective or be relegated to a subordinate role. The Risk and Insurance Management Society, Inc. (RIMS) seeks to upgrade the professional standards of risk managers through conferences, seminars and publications. RIMS has local chapters throughout the country.

MANAGING RISK

Risk has been defined in this text as uncertainty about loss and may be classified as pure and speculative.

Types of Risks

The risk manager's primary concern is pure risk, a risk category other personnel in most businesses ignore. Pure risk offers no opportunity of gain, only an exposure to loss. Speculative risk offers the opportunity for both gain and loss and interests risk managers only to the extent that it can influence pure risk management decisions. When exposures to speculative risks are large the risk manager may deal more conservatively with pure risks because financial resources are limited. Losses from both types of risks draw upon the same pool of financial resources. Consequently, when speculative risk is large the risk manager must concentrate more than ever on reducing the possible adverse effects and exposure to pure risk. Less pure risk can be retained when speculative risk is a major factor. In these situations pure risk rather than speculative risk offers the best promise of efficient control. Controlling speculative risk involves major capital expenditures designed to diversify products, territories, customers and so on. However, pure risk is subject to less expensive loss-control techniques. Furthermore, unlike speculative risk, pure risk is insurable.

Three important observations can be made in comparing pure risk with speculative risk: (1) both pure and speculative risks involve uncertainty, but in pure risk the uncertainty relates only to the occurrence of a loss—no chance for profit is present; (2) although statistical analysis is useful in dealing with either type of risk, pure risk is more adaptable to pooling and loss sharing and (3) firms may suffer losses from speculative risks that result in social gain. While competition is the life of trade it can be the death of an individual firm. Although the development of new products and technologies helps society, it can adversely affect companies with heavy investment in old products or techniques. If a firm incurs losses from pure risk society loses. When assets are destroyed total national output (and net worth) is reduced. This observation does not always hold, however. Some losses produce social improvements (e.g., when a dilapidated tenement burns and is replaced by new housing society gains from improved living conditions).

Objectives of Risk Management

The objective of risk management is to make the most *efficient* preloss arrangement for an *effective* postloss balance between needed and available resources to assure continuation of the family or business. Implied in this objective is management of resources through loss prevention and control programs.

Two basic rules of risk management are: the size of potential losses must have a reasonable relationship to resources of the loss bearer and the benefits of assuming the risk must be related to its cost. These rules advise risk takers not to risk more than they can afford to lose, to consider the odds and not to risk a lot for a little.

THE RISK MANAGEMENT PROCESS

The risk management process requires setting and achieving the goal of maintaining a sufficient cash flow to enable families or businesses to meet their objectives with the minimum of interruption following a loss. For example, when part of a plant is damaged its revenue cycle is disrupted. Manufacturing halts, inventories are depleted, sales revenues decline and the company's market share falls. These developments place a severe hardship on the business unless risk management practices are designed to maintain the flow of funds as though no interruption occurred.

Achieving the Risk Management Goal

The steps for achieving the risk management goal are to: (1) discover the risk problems, (2) consider the methods available to solve the problems and choose the most efficient ones, (3) implement the decision and (4) evaluate the results.

These four steps can be translated into three basic responsibilities of the risk manager to (1) identify and evaluate the firm's exposure to losses from pure risk, (2) select what appears to be the optimum methods of handling these exposures and (3) verify on a continuing basis that these methods are indeed optimum and efficiently used.

Identifying and evaluating exposure to loss

The risk manager must determine pure risk in three broad areas: life and health exposures, property exposures and liability exposures. Exposure to loss from pure risk falls into six categories: physical damage to assets; fraud and criminal violence; adverse judgments at law; damage to property of others (e.g., a major supplier or a major customer); death and disability of family members, key employees of a business or businessowners and death, disability, medical and retirement benefits promised under employee benefit plans.

For property exposures measuring loss potential includes surveying possible damages to the property itself and loss of use of the property including additional expenses from business interruptions. Identifying and measuring loss potential from liability exposures appears to be the most complicated. Professional risk managers are aware of large liability loss exposures; but so many liability hazards exist (both old and new) that some escape notice. Even for detected exposures, no estimate of the maximum loss potential can be made with confidence. For life and health exposures, measuring loss potential includes surveying the resources needed in the event of disability or death of key personnel and owners and reviewing the promises made under employee benefit plans for death, disability, medical care and retirement income benefits.

Organizing the search. Discovery and evaluation of loss exposures require knowledge about assets, income and activities of the family or business. The risk manager has several available sources of information.

Financial records (the balance sheet and income statement) are an important source of information for risk analysis. A systematic study of each asset owned will help locate loss exposures. Pertinent questions should be asked about physical assets: their location, their replacement cost, perils and hazards to which they are exposed and loss-control devices available for their protection. Questions about sources of income and expense items help reveal and measure loss exposures not otherwise detected.

Risk analysis information can be developed from a systematic *physical inspection* of the premises plus a study of all *contracts* entered (e.g., leases, sales, purchase and employment agreements). Usually an exposure guide will direct attention to facts required for a thorough risk analysis. Risk managers can tailor "fact finders" to fit their particular operations or can adapt one of those published by insurance companies or service organizations.

Organizing the information. How information is to be used controls how it is to be organized. Risk analysis information is used in making risk management decisions. Because insurance is the most common method of handling pure risk, most risk managers organize their information to produce data needed for underwriting and rating loss exposures. Broadly conceived, the data must be organized to analyze types of losses, potential amounts of losses, rates of loss, perils that can cause loss and hazards that increase the chance of loss.

Selecting optimum methods of dealing with exposures

Once the risk manager has identified and evaluated exposures to pure losses, he or she must select the optimum method of dealing with them. The risk manager must decide how to reduce postloss resources required (loss prevention and control) and determine the most efficient postloss financing. In making these decisions the techniques selected must balance costs and benefits. In measuring costs and benefits of a risk management tool, the cost is determined by the amount of the outlay; the benefit is measured by the loss to be averted if the outlays are made.

Resources available for offsetting losses are: (1) resources within the family or business unit, (2) credit resources and (3) claims against others arising from the loss. In this last category are claims against those who by statutory or common law are legally responsible to pay the loss. Also included are claims against those to whom the risk has been transferred by contract. Insurance is in the latter class and in many instances proves to be the most efficient preloss arrangement for the postloss resources needed. The criteria for measuring the desirability of postloss resources are adequacy, reliability and cost. The risk manager must measure the preloss arrangements for postloss resources against these criteria.

Using optimum methods efficiently

After the risk manager has decided which loss exposures will be covered and how to cover them the problem remains to assure that the arrangements are handled efficiently. Effective administration of the risk management department is essential in successfully executing risk management policy. Loss prevention and control programs should be administered conscientiously. No risk should be accepted or retained in violation of company risk management policy or because of ignorance or carelessness. Risk planning should always be reevaluated in view of any change in the company's financial position.

To perform effectively a risk manager must communicate intelligently with statisticians, lawyers, engineers, accountants, financial managers, personnel managers and other management specialists. Many risk managers prepare themselves to meet the challenge through the Institute of America's risk management diploma course and the many seminars conducted by the American Management Association and the Risk and Insurance Management Society. Large insurance brokerage firms and various universities operate risk management seminars. Usually the risk management program is built around commercial insurance.

The Risk Manager's Functions in Buying and Administering Insurance

After making the decision to use insurance as a tool the risk manager's duties are to (1) develop specifications for coverage and arrange contracts that meet them; (2) establish criteria and standards for qualifying insurers and their representatives, then select from among those eligible; (3) buy insurance at the lowest possible prices compatible with services desired and (4) use insurers', brokers' and agents' services effectively during the policy period.[1]

Developing specifications for the coverage

In many policies the coverage is standardized by law, custom or intercompany agreement, but even with the most rigid policy some flexibility may be obtained through standard policy riders. Two important reasons for the risk manager to develop specifications are to clarify the coverage needed in the policy and to cover gaps by a different policy or by some other risk management technique. Coverage differs in many types of policies, and the trend seems to be away from standardization.[2] Special contracts often are tailored specifically to the desires of the risk manager.

Establishing criteria for insurers and agents

Having established specifications for coverage the risk manager must select the insurer and the agent best equipped to write the coverage. The insurer's claims-settlement philosophy and financial standing are important considerations. Often extra-insurance factors affect the decision (e.g., an insurance agent who is a relative of the president or an insurer who is an important customer). Also, loss prevention and risk analysis service might be important factors.

Buying insurance—at what price?

Insurance pricing is a complicated matter,[3] making a fair price difficult to determine. Shopping among reliable agents and insurers is necessary to find the best

[1] Chapter 24 includes suggestions on insurance buying.

[2] Today one hardly dares talk about *a* standard automobile policy let alone *the* standard automobile policy!

[3] See Chapter 21.

buy. Complete understanding between the risk manager and the insurer regarding contract and service specifications is vital in the bargaining process. Many risk managers invite bids based on clearly stated specifications, and sometimes the cost of insurance can be cut by omitting several services. In some circumstances the risk manager may not want insurance coverage but only one or more special services the insurer has to offer (e.g., loss control, risk analysis or claims administration). In this event, an administrative services only (ASO) contract will be used where only the special services sought are provided.

To assure a peaceful night's sleep, some risk managers believe that good risk management policy dictates staying with an old and trusted insurance relationship even at higher cost rather than shifting to a different and untried insurer or agent. Convenience, protection of markets for hard-to-place coverage and a sound risk management program often are reasons for maintaining the status quo.

RISK ANALYSIS: LIFE AND PROPERTY EXPOSURES

Risk analysis is the process of locating loss exposures, measuring the amount of losses that can result from these exposures, estimating the probability that losses will occur and evaluating the exposures to determine actions necessary to meet family or business risk management objectives. Risk analysis is not simple. The risk manager's success depends on awareness of the types of information needed, knowledge of how to acquire this information and an understanding of how to use it. The job of risk analysis is keyed to three basic issues: (1) loss causes, (2) postloss resources needed to continue effective operations and (3) the most efficient methods to obtain or reduce the amount of needed postloss resources. The discussion of risk analysis in this text is divided into life and property exposures (the subject of the remainder of this chapter) and liability exposures (Chapter 4).

LIFE AND HEALTH EXPOSURES FOR THE FAMILY

Families are exposed to losses due to premature death and disability. Additionally, a family must plan for its retirement needs.

Final Expenses

Dying is expensive. To put it bluntly, someone must be paid to dispose of the body. In most cases, doctors' bills, hospital and nursing expenses and other medical expenses will accumulate. The spouse will also be left with other bills, e.g., charge accounts, bank loans, utility bills, accrued taxes, cost of estate administration and death taxes. The death of any member of the family will cost money, but the major nonmedical expenses usually will be associated with the death of the husband or wife. When an estate is large, an estate-planning problem may exist. Federal and state death taxes may be a source of a substantial loss in some estates. Although the federal Economic Recovery Tax Act of 1981 eliminates the estate tax on property passed to a surviving spouse, the estate of the survivor may face a large death tax liability.

Adjustment Income

Even if spouses are skillful money managers they may not be able to reduce expenditures immediately when the breadwinner dies. In the event of disability the family will be even less able to cut expenses instantly. First, disabilities create many extra costs, such as special foods and household help that cannot be covered by medical insurance. Second, because disability rarely seems as final as death, the family may continue with its present budget assuming the breadwinner will be at work again. The idea may persist for months while savings are exhausted and debts are incurred to maintain the usual standard of living. And cutting costs over time is easier than cutting them overnight. An immediate budget cut will add to the psychological strain already suffered because of the tragedy. The family must recognize the problem of reducing the standard of living following the loss of the breadwinner's income and if possible arrange to provide an adjustment income.

Mortgage or Rent Fund

If the income of the family is lost due to disability or death, plans must be made for paying housing costs, i.e., mortgage or rent payments, property taxes and home maintenance expenses.

Family Period Income

The years before the children are self-supporting usually are the financially burdensome ones. The children's need for parental care and guidance during preschool years may inhibit a parent from entering the labor market. Therefore family financial programs should provide sufficient income to allow the surviving spouse to stay at home or to provide a qualified person to care for the children.[4] The problem of budgeting for family income after the death of a breadwinner has been eased by social security.

Continuing the assumption that only one member of the husband-wife team earns an income to support the family, the death of the "nonearning" member can cause financial loss to that family. For example, income taxes for the surviving spouse will increase because (1) the advantages of income splitting no longer will be available and (2) the progressive income tax will place the survivor in a much higher tax bracket. Furthermore, the home managing services of the deceased spouse will have to be replaced (including the care of any surviving dependent children), perhaps at considerable expense.

Life Income for the Surviving Spouse

After the children are grown, the surviving spouse will still need income. Social security benefits are suspended from the time the youngest child reaches age 16 until the surviving spouse reaches age 60. Income will also be needed for family support in case a breadwinner is disabled. The surviving spouse may be able to find employment. However, work for an older person is not found easily—especially for those who have not worked for many years. If a breadwinner is disabled, the spouse's full-time attention might be required at home. Although grown children can contribute to the support of the family, this burden should be avoided if possible. Also, the spouse probably would not want to accept help from the children, so the family risk manager should plan for the spouse to have a minimum income for life after the children are grown.

---

[4] The cost of hiring a person is partly deductible from taxable income (for federal income tax but rarely for state or municipal income taxes). However, the deduction will offset only a small part of the cost for those in low or middle tax brackets.

Education Fund

The importance of financing college educations for children in the event of the death or disability of the breadwinner will vary among families. Whether the interests and abilities of the children will lie in a college education is difficult to predict. Whether or not the parents expect their children to attend college will influence the family risk manager in the decision concerning an education fund. Often it is too early to know the answer when the planning must be initiated.

Emergency Fund

No matter how well the risk manager has provided for the expenses of a family following a loss, unforeseeable events or "emergencies" requiring the outlay of cash could occur. Thus the risk manager should consider making provisions for such contingencies.

Medical Expenses

Many of the foregoing loss exposures deal with the income loss of the breadwinner resulting from disability or death. In addition, injury or sickness of any family member can create medical expenses that represent a large loss potential. When a life is threatened, few people weigh the cost of medical care in seeking treatment. Highly paid specialists will be consulted, if necessary, and concern about payment will be postponed. To perform the task adequately, the family risk manager should understand this psychology and make suitable arrangements for the loss exposure.

Retirement Income

Some people do not look forward to the day when they can "quit work and take it easy." They find that after 40 years or so their job has become not only a vocation but also an avocation. Even when employees do not want to quit work, business (or their health) forces them to retire. Compulsory retirement before age 70, with some exceptions, is now prohibited by federal law—but plans for a retirement income must still be made.

Planning for income in old age is difficult. The increasing standard of living (luxuries become necessities), the continued growth of superselling that caters to one's weaknesses, progressive income taxation and lack of investment expertise all tend to restrict funds that can be accumulated for old age. Social security and employee retirement plans provide a large part of the retirement income for an increasing number of people. But the average person finds that some or all of accumulated capital must be liquidated to generate the desired retirement income. The capital must be withdrawn systematically, however, so that the retiree is not left without an income. Ideally, the retiree and the capital fund committed for retirement income should expire simultaneously.

Four needs are important in retirement:

1. An income sufficient for the retired person to live comfortably.
2. An estate clearance fund whenever a person dies. (Arrangements made for this fund should be continued beyond retirement.)
3. Adequate provisions for medical expenses.
4. Sufficient income for the survivor when the retired spouse dies.

LIFE AND HEALTH EXPOSURES FOR THE BUSINESS FIRM

Businesses are composed of people. Most of them occasionally become sick, and all eventually die. The risk manager should study the firm's possible loss exposures from disability and death and from commitments under employee benefit plans.

Loss of Key Employees

Reduced revenues and increased expenses may result from the disability or death of such key personnel as a top salesperson or department manager. The replacement of these key employees probably will involve losses in efficiency and extra expenses for training replacements. The risk manager must analyze these potential business losses.

Loss of Owner

Businesses are owned by persons seeking a profitable return on their investment. Often the owners supply not only capital but also time and talents. Thus a risk manager must be aware of any loss that may develop when an owner dies or becomes disabled.

The sole proprietorship exposure

Over 90 percent of the business units in the United States are sole proprietorships. The sole proprietorship makes no legal distinction between the personal and the business estate. The debts of the business are the debts of the estate. The sole proprietor's estate does not pass to the heirs until all creditors (business and personal) have been paid.

When a sole proprietor dies or becomes disabled, a decision must be made to continue the business, sell it or liquidate it. In sole proprietorships, the owners usually are the active managers and key employees. If they become disabled or die, someone must be hired to replace them, thus reducing net income. Also, revenues may decline because the proprietor was responsible for much of the business's success.

Consequently the risk manager has to make *preloss* arrangements: upon death the proprietor's general estate must be protected against the debts of the business; and plans for a prospective buyer of the business should be made. Sometimes a buyer can be found in advance through a binding buy-and-sell agreement with a key employee interested in owning the business. In this event, the key employee agrees to buy and the sole proprietor authorizes the estate to sell at a price set by formula. For example, the formula could be six times average annual earnings for the past five years. If the owner becomes disabled a buyer is not necessary unless the disability is permanent, but an additional employee may be needed. Furthermore, during the disability period earnings may decline. Therefore the risk manager must prepare for these loss exposures.

The partnership exposure

The legal relationship between partners is a personal one. Each is fully responsible for the business acts and debts of all others. If one partner withdraws from the firm, the partnership is terminated. It must then be either liquidated or reorganized and the withdrawing partner compensated. If the partner's disability causes the withdrawal, the firm's resources will be severely strained—especially if the partner was a key employee. Although financial resources are strained, the partners may want to continue the disabled partner's income at the same level. If a partner is permanently disabled, the firm may find it advantageous to buy that partner's interest. But the partnership is not legally compelled to liquidate or reorganize.

The partner's interest may also be terminated by death. In that event, the law requires that the partnership be terminated or reorganized. (The issues involved in a choice between liquidation and reorganization are similar regardless of whether the choice arises from a partner's disability or death.)

In the event the partnership is liquidated, the *assets* of the business may be sold and the net proceeds divided proportionally among the surviving partners and heirs. This solution rarely will prove satisfactory. First, liquidation nearly always results in loss. Second, the surviving partners are out of a job. In some cases, it may be possible to sell the business intact rather than liquidate its assets. A firm sold as a "going concern" rarely results in a loss. Furthermore the sale often can be arranged to provide continuing employment for the surviving partners. The buyer can be either a local competitor or a large national expanding conglomerate.

If the firm is to be continued and reorganized rather than liquidated, four options are available to the heirs and surviving partners:

1. The heirs of the deceased's interest may become partners in the new partnership.
2. The heirs may sell the deceased's interest to an outside party.
3. The heirs may buy the surviving partners' interests.
4. The surviving partners may buy the deceased's interest from the heirs.

For the first two alternatives, the law requires the consent of the surviving partners.

Usually the most satisfactory alternative is for the surviving partners to buy out the heirs. However, two problems arise with this alternative: (1) setting the price and (2) finding the money to finance the purchase. The price can be set in a mutually binding buy-and-sell agreement among the partners while all are alive and in equal bargaining positions. The agreement specifies either a set price for the share of each partner or, more commonly, a valuation formula to be applied when the partner dies. If the price specified is paid to the heirs at the partner's death, the surviving partners can then organize as a new partnership and continue the business.

The risk manager of a partnership should be aware of its legal problems in order to deal properly with its life and health exposures. If the partners have a buy-and-sell agreement, the risk manager also must arrange the funding of that agreement.

The close corporation exposure

The close (or "closed") corporation is one where the stock is closely held by a few individuals and not offered for public sale. Usually the stockholders are company employees with a relationship similar to a partnership. In fact, the close corporation is often called an "incorporated partnership."

If an employee stockholder becomes disabled, the same problems arise as with a disabled partner. If the disability is permanent, either the other stockholders or the corporation itself (if legally permitted) may buy the disabled stockholder's shares. The risk manager must plan for available funds to make the purchase.

When a shareholder dies, the corporation's existence is not affected. Although the law protects the partners from an unwanted partner, similar protection is not granted to surviving stockholders because the heirs have legal ownership of the deceased's shares. Furthermore, if they can find a buyer they may sell the shares even to a competitor. Retaining the shares of the deceased may prove unsatisfactory both to the survivors and to the heirs. Stock in a close corporation generally is considered a poor investment for minority stockholders, especially when they are not also employees. Because the surviving shareholders are usually employees, they believe that corporation profits are primarily the result of their efforts. They may resent sharing profits with nonproductive shareholders and use profits to expand the business or to increase their salaries. While minority stockholders have rights and can demand an accounting to determine if excessive salaries are paid or if an excessive amount of profits is reinvested in the business, an investment that leads to bickering, personal recriminations and even legal action is not a sound one for the heirs.

A good solution to the problem of disposing of a deceased stockholder's shares is for the surviving stockholders (or the corporation if legally permitted) to buy them. The disposal problems are the same as those for deceased partners: determining the price and finding the money to pay it. The risk manager must review the various solutions and use the most efficient ones.

The Employee Benefit Plan Exposure

Employee benefit plans play a major role in employee financial security (see Chapters 16 and 17). When employers grant employees death, disability, medical care and retirement income benefits, they accept a life and health loss exposure. Risk managers (or employee benefit plan managers) must look at the many ways to fund these benefits and to control their costs. New funding and loss control techniques are constantly sought and introduced to manage the employee benefit plan exposure as efficiently as possible. Because of the increasing cost and the major effect of employee benefit plans on business profits, risk managers are forced to keep abreast of new developments in this field and introduce those that best fit their firm's objectives.

PROPERTY EXPOSURES FOR THE FAMILY

Three types of property value loss exposures can be identified: loss of property, loss of its use and extra expenses. The family risk manager must identify and consider a wide variety of perils.

Loss of the Property Itself

Families must know the extent and location of their property. Householders may have property stored in the garage, at another person's home, at a summer cottage or in a commercial warehouse. The perils to which the property is exposed must be determined. Dwellings may be subject to losses resulting from fire, windstorm, hail, explosion, smoke damage, glass breakage, water damage, sprinkler leakage, riot damage, malicious damage, damage by aircraft and other vehicles, earthquake damage and other perils. Personal property is exposed to the additional perils of burglary, theft, misplacement, disappearance, temperature changes, breakage, spotting, collision and others. No perils that could cause a serious loss should be ignored.

Loss to the property may be either direct or indirect and may be on or off premises. The measurement of potential property losses from a single event requires the family risk manager to consider all these possibilities. Direct loss or damage may occur on the premises to dwellings and their contents. Direct loss also may occur to neighboring dwellings, power lines or personal property damaged by falling trees or walls on the premises. Indirect or consequential loss may result from temperature or humidity changes that damage property. For example, power interruption caused by lightning may damage food stored in a home freezer. The food may be spoiled to the point where even university dorms would refuse it (students will readily understand the severity of the spoilage!). Consequential damage can occur from the destruction of part of a pair or set. A fire destroys the pants, but the coat is not damaged. The value of a pantless suit coat is significantly reduced.

Loss of Use and Extra Expense

The typical family exposure to loss of use is additional living expenses arising from destruction of the family dwelling until it can be restored. The family may have to live in an expensive motel and pay higher food and transportation costs. If the owner had a room rented to a student, the rental income would also be lost. Other loss-of-use exposures are possible. Suppose that Cleora and her husband are raising tomatoes in their yard to sell at a roadside stand. If the neighborhood children (seeking smashing entertainment) snatch the tomatoes to fling at passersby the couple will have little or no produce to market, and hence will suffer an income loss. People who perform services in their homes (such as laundry or catering for parties) are exposed to loss of income if their homes are damaged by a fire or other perils.

PROPERTY EXPOSURES FOR THE BUSINESS FIRM

Professional risk managers face problems similar to those for families but generally on a larger scale.

Loss of the Property

Risk managers must be aware of all company property and its location. They need to consider when title passes on incoming or outgoing goods, whether any goods are stored or processed off premises, where money, securities and other valuables are kept, how they are moved to and from the bank, whether vehicles are always stored in a central garage or sometimes elsewhere. In listing properties, interests other than those of the tenant or owner should be considered. Among these interests are those of mortgagees, merchandisers using installment plans and bailees. (A bailee is one holding property for another.) Direct damage to business property, equipment, machinery, stock and other personal property can be caused by the numerous perils mentioned earlier.

Loss of Use and Extra Expense

Damage to business property can cause several identifiable losses. For example, rental revenues may be lost if property rented to others is damaged. The value of a long-term lease with rental payments below current market values are destroyed if the lease is terminated following a major fire. Profits on finished goods are lost if these goods are destroyed. Income is lost if the business suspends or terminates operations after a fire.

These loss exposures can be important. For example, a cap and gown company lost a large share of its profits when the garments burned just prior to commencement. The MGM Grand Hotel in Las Vegas lost about $63 million when it was closed until July 29, 1981, following a major fire on November 21, 1980. (The property loss was an estimated $215 million.) These types of losses are not unusual; yet many risk managers consider direct damage without planning for loss of use. Losses caused by business interruption are a major consideration in risk analysis. Sometimes income losses arise from the destruction of property not owned or used by the firm. These loss exposures may include damage to plants belonging to those who supply the business with raw materials, parts, fuel and power. They may also result from damage to premises belonging to customers and to their customers' customers (and perhaps even to their customers' customers' customers and so on!).

Closely allied to loss of use is the extra expense caused by a peril. A major fire on a college campus may force the school to close a full term. If the college decides to continue operating, using more expensive facilities, the loss will be the increased cost of operations rather than a decrease in revenues. Newspapers that experience fires often continue operation at increased costs because they believe a temporary closing would cause former readers to become permanently interested in a competing paper. A major extra expense can result from liability exposures. These exposures are discussed in the next chapter, but it can be noted here that the MGM Grand Hotel fire killed 84 and injured about 700 people, producing about 3,000 claims for damages. More than 2,000 of these claims were settled out of court for an undisclosed amount. Two attorneys, however, reported that they settled 204 claims for more than $15 million. When the final claim is paid the liability loss might exceed the direct property loss and even the combined direct and business interruption losses.

SUMMARY

1. Risk is classified into two categories: pure and speculative. Pure risk, the primary concern of the risk manager, can produce loss only. Speculative risk can create loss or gain. Speculative risk is of interest only to the extent that it influences pure risk management decisions.

2. The objective of risk management is to develop an efficient preloss plan for an effective postloss balance between resources needed and those available.

3. Risk analysis is the process of: (*a*) locating loss exposures and measuring the loss they can produce, (*b*) estimating loss probability and (*c*) evaluating loss exposures to determine the most efficient method to protect against them.

4. The risk manager's functions will often be focused on insurance and require:
   a. Developing specifications for the desired coverage.
   b. Creating a set of criteria and minimum standards for qualifying insurers and their representatives.
   c. Selecting insurers and representatives from among those eligible.
   d. Purchasing insurance at the lowest possible price compatible with the coverage and services desired.

5. Risk management for the family requires plans for handling needs after the death or disability of a family member. Some of the needs include cash for final expenses, adjustment income, mortgage or rent fund, income during the family period, income for the surviving spouse after the children are grown, education fund, money for emergencies, cash for expenses attributable to the death of a spouse and funds for medical expenses and retirement income.

6. In locating and measuring a business firm's loss exposures, the risk manager should conduct a physical inspection of the premises, study all company contracts and examine all financial information and supporting records.

7. Businesses must protect themselves from revenue losses or increased expenses caused by disability, death or resignation of key employees.

8. Sole proprietorships, partnerships and closely held corporations must be concerned with arrangements to transfer ownership after the death or disability of a proprietor, partner or shareholder.

9. Risk managers must select the most efficient methods to fund and control employee benefit plan exposures in keeping with company policy.
10. A family is exposed to three types of property value losses: (1) loss of the property itself, (2) loss of its use and (3) extra expenses that arise when the property is damaged or destroyed.
11. A business is exposed to the same types of property value losses as a family. However, loss of use is a more serious loss exposure for a business than for a family.

REVIEW QUESTIONS

1. Distinguish between pure and speculative risk. "The insured's risk is pure risk." "The risk assumed by the insurer is speculative." Explain why you agree or disagree with these statements.
2. What is the function of risk analysis? Upon what does successful risk analysis depend? What is a major loss exposure facing a person as a sole proprietor, partner or stockholder in a close corporation?
3. Explain the term *final expenses.* What types of income losses and expenses are incurred when a family member dies?
4. Explain four loss-of-use property exposures.
5. How do property exposures in a family differ from those in a business? How do life and health exposures in a family differ from those in a business? Explain.
6. How is risk analysis information organized?
7. Why is retirement planning difficult?
8. What are four major retirement needs?
9. How important is family risk analysis?
10. How important is business risk analysis?

CHAPTER

4 Risk analysis: Liability exposures

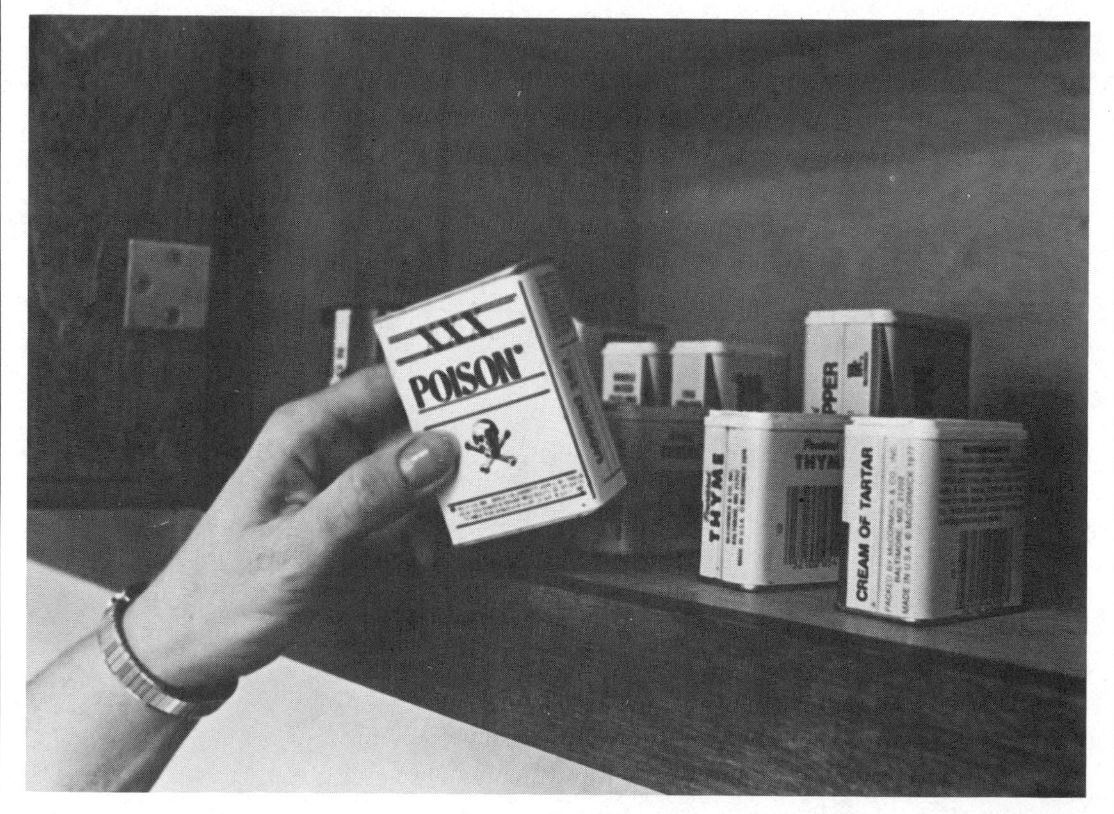

John Thoeming/Richard D. Irwin

CHAPTER OBJECTIVES

1. **To classify the nature and sources of law.**
2. **To identify and describe the three legal bases for tort liability exposures.**
3. **To point out the defenses available in various types of tort actions.**
4. **To explain statutory modifications of the common law of negligence.**
5. **To examine liability exposures commonly imposed by contract.**
6. **To show how several types of liability exposures may be based either on a tort or a breach of an implied warranty.**
7. **To list several types of tort liability hazards faced by families and businesses.**

In Greece a widow preparing a funeral banquet made a mistake that has played a pivotal part in many old slapstick film comedies: she accidentally added the wrong ingredient to the cake. But unlike in the old movies the mistake involved insect poison, not alum. Instead of a humorous puckering among the mourners the result was sudden death to nearly 50 of them. In a Chicago suburb a car suddenly went out of control and hit a bevy of teenagers crossing the street. Four were killed immediately; others suffered permanent injury.

These losses can be compensated in several ways. If the Greek widow's victims had life insurance, insurers would compensate for the deaths. Similarly in the Chicago incident, life and health insurance would offset much of the losses. However, another route to compensation may be available. If the widow or the driver of the car had been **negligent** in their actions they could be sued for damages.

THE NATURE OF LAW

"The law is sort of a hocus-pocus science that smiles in your face while it picks your pocket; and the glorious uncertainty of it is of more use to the professors than the justice of it." The law, with all of its hocus-pocus and glorious uncertainty may be defined as the principles and regulations established by legislation or court decisions. The law plays a major role in determining how losses are to be compensated, i.e., who should bear the financial consequences. Thus some knowledge of the law is important to an understanding of liability exposures.[1]

American law is based on British common law modified by statutes and court interpretations. The law can be classified by rights of prosecution. A right may be either public (government), private (the injured party) or both. The government prosecutes under criminal law, but the injured parties bring suits under civil law.

Sources of the Law

Statutory law is written law established by the legislative body and incorporated in a formal document. Together all these formal documents are called a code,

[1] These concepts are also useful in understanding the insurance contract discussed in Chapter 5.

and an insurance code is a collection of existing laws primarily governing insurance regulation. Each state has its own insurance code. Similarly each state has its own workers' compensation laws governing benefits to work-accident victims or their dependents regardless of fault.

A body of law known as **common law** (often called case law) has been established by court decisions. Common law evolved from 12th-century England and reflects what judges over hundreds of years considered to be just. In the United States today the common law is composed of appellate court decisions and that part of English law reflecting local public policy. In any legal dispute the court applies the written law (constitutional or statutory) if any; otherwise the common law applies.

Common law is based on the principle that previous court decisions provide precedents to be followed in subsequent cases involving essentially the same facts and the same question of law. This principle is called the doctrine of *stare decisis.* Although common law provides stability many observers believe that justice is better served by creating rather than following precedents. A number of forces can contribute to reversing a precedent, e.g., a change in court personnel, a change in public attitudes or the belief that such precedent was in error.

Questions of law arise when neither an applicable statute nor previous court decisions apply. The court must then render a decision based on an unwritten system of law composed of general rules, court opinions on other issues and those principles from English law consistent with local public policy. Decisions in these cases then may be used as precedents. Laws governing liability exposures are primarily embodied in common law and have been shaped by court decisions rather than by statutes.

Classifications of the Law

Because **criminal law** deals with actions harmful to the public, the government is responsible for enforcing the law and punishing its offenders. Criminal offenses have a wide range, including major felonies (premeditated murder) and minor misdemeanors (failure to feed the parking meter, premeditated or not). The basis for criminal law is always statutory.

Under **civil law** the injured victim, not the government, has the responsibility for deciding to prosecute the wrongdoer.[2] Private rights are protected by civil law that provides remedies for contract violations and damages for injuries caused by the wrongful actions of others. While civil law primarily is based on common law and court decisions, the role of statutory law here is increasing in importance. (See Figure 4–1.)

Under some circumstances a person may violate both criminal and civil law and be subject to prosecution both by the government and the injured party. For example, an intoxicated driver who injures another person may be subject to both criminal and civil actions.

LEGAL LIABILITY

Liability exposures often result in large losses. In 1975 a Maryland court awarded damages amounting to $12.1 million in a case involving the brutal rape and murder of a young mother. The award included $11.1 million in punitive damages

[2] The term *civil law* is used here to distinguish civil law from criminal law. The concept of civil law is also used to distinguish civil law (as used in Louisiana) from common law (as used in nearly all other states).

FIGURE 4–1 **Right of Prosecution** (A Classification of the Law)

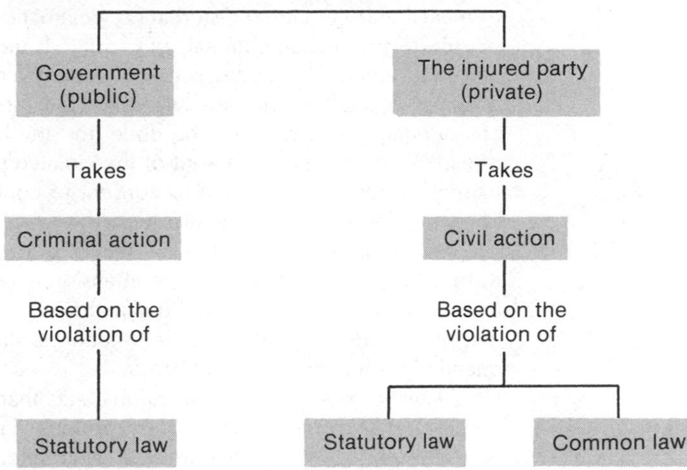

assessed because the defendant, a New York-based real estate conglomerate, had lulled the tenants of the building where the rape occurred into a false sense of security about the safety of the building.

Punitive damages are awards to plaintiffs in excess of compensatory damages (full compensation for injuries sustained) and are made to punish the defendant and discourage others from engaging in conduct causing injuries. Defective products have produced large liability settlements. In 1978 a large arms manufacturer agreed to pay $6.8 million to a man who became paraplegic after one of its rifles discharged when he pushed the safety to the "off" position. A business or family may find itself subject to liability claims from a variety of sources, some of them surprising.

The legal bases for liability exposures are torts and contracts. A **tort** is a wrongful act committed by one person against another that may result in a civil action. The common law, with some statutory modifications noted later, provides the basis for legal action. The wrongful act must cause bodily injury, property damage or personal injury. Personal injuries include a number of wrongs (e.g., defamation, false arrest, mental distress) that differ from bodily injury. Liability imposed by contract may be assumed under a contract or arise from a breach of an expressed or implied warranty.

Torts

Tort claims arise from (1) intentional interference, (2) liability without fault and (3) negligence. Most tort claims are based on negligence.

Intentional torts

An act resulting in an injury to another may be an intentional tort whether or not the intention is to benefit or harm. Unless the actor's conduct is "privileged," the consequences may be liability for an intentional tort. (Defenses based on privileges are discussed later in this chapter.)

Intentional interference with the person. Intentional torts may be classified as (1) intentional interference with the person and (2) intentional interference with the property of others. Examples of the former are battery, assault, infliction of mental and emotional disturbance, defamation and false imprisonment.

Battery is the intentional, unpermitted and unprivileged contact with the person of others. It includes contact with anything connected or associated with others, e.g., clothes they are wearing, cars they are driving or packages they are carrying. No harm need be done nor any hostility intended. Only absence of expressed or implied consent of the violated person is necessary to constitute battery. A person is assumed to consent to contact customary in everyday life. Thus, a friendly grasp of the arm would not be battery.

Assault is an attempt at or a threat of physical violence to another. It differs from battery. Assault involves apprehension over threatened contact; battery requires contact. Intent to carry out a threat is not a factor in assault; a belief that the threat may materialize into action is sufficient. Assault and battery frequently accompany one another.

Liability may arise from intentional acts that cause someone severe and extreme *mental or emotional distress.* Serious illness resulting from distress often is necessary to qualify for damages. A creditor, for example, who repeatedly harasses a debtor causing the debtor to have a nervous breakdown, can be held liable for inflicting emotional distress.

Defamation involves actions that injure another's reputation. Defamatory acts may be either libel (written) or slander (oral). New forms of communication have affected the distinction between libel and slander. The distinction is based on the permanence of the form or its potential harm with the more permanent or harmful forms considered libelous. To be actionable (1) the defamatory statements must be intentionally or negligently communicated to *someone other than the defamed party* and (2) they must be reasonably understood by the third party. Libel and slander law differs substantially among jurisdictions and is characterized by inconsistency and confusion.

The intentional restraint of another's freedom of movement may impose liability for **false imprisonment.** The restraint must be intended but does not have to be malicious. Thus, even if the actor believes the restraint is necessary for the good of the person restrained, the actor may be liable for false imprisonment. Furthermore, the restraint need not be physical but may consist of threats of force that intimidate another into compliance.

Malicious prosecution (knowingly instituting groundless civil or criminal action against another party) is often confused with false imprisonment. Sufficient grounds for damages based on malicious prosecution require the plaintiff to show that (1) in the questioned proceedings no probable cause existed for the action and (2) the court decided the case in his or her favor. Recovery usually is limited to the attorney's fees and costs incurred in defending the groundless action and any special injuries to the plaintiff (e.g., damage to his or her professional reputation). Suits against malicious prosecution are increasing in number as irate physicians retaliate after winning an unwarranted medical malpractice suit.

Intentional interference with property. Trespass to real or personal property and conversion are examples of actionable intentional interference with property.

Trespass to real property is the wrongful entry on the land of another or failure to remove property from another's land. Trespass includes invasion of the area above and below the land as well as the surface of the land. Trespass to personal property is the intentional interference with its possession or physical condition without legal justification. An innocent mistake is no defense against liability. However, proof of damage is usually required to establish liability for *any* trespass to *personal property* and for an *unknowing* trespass to *real property.* Willful trespass to *real property* requires no proof of damage to establish liability.

Conversion is the wrongful disposition and detention of the personal property of others. Conversion differs from trespass in that prior to the conversion the converter is legally justified in possessing the property. Examples of conversion are: (1) taking possession of goods to exercise control adverse to the owner; (2) depriving the owner of control through an unauthorized transfer of goods, as in the misdelivery of a TV set from the repair shop; (3) refusing to surrender goods to one who has a right to them and (4) using the goods in defiance of the owners, e.g., driving a car an owner left at the garage to be washed. Tort law dealing with conversion gives wronged persons a cause of action in a civil court to recover their property values.

Privilege

An individual will not be held liable for an intentional tort if the conduct is privileged. Privilege has many meanings. In the context here, privilege is a legal freedom for a person to act in a given manner. Whether the conduct of an individual is privileged depends on the circumstances and the court attitude. Persons have no advance assurance that their conduct is privileged and not subject to tort liability. Common types of privilege are mistakes, consent and protective acts.

Mistakes are privileged under limited conditions. An act may be privileged if the actor moves quickly to protect a right believed to be endangered even if the party is mistaken. Thus a person may be privileged to use force as a defense whether or not the defense was necessary. Certain acts are privileged if the actor reasonably infers the *consent* of the alleged aggrieved party. For example, a person is privileged to kiss the lips offered and consequently could not be held liable for battery even if the offerer is displeased with the results. Persons are privileged to use reasonable force as a protective act to prevent interference with their property or person or to defend others who have privilege to defend themselves. The jury decides what is reasonable force. Shooting a child who is stealing a bicycle would not be considered reasonable. Shooting a rapist during the rape probably would be deemed reasonable force and thus privileged. Suppose Linda Smith, noticing someone stealing her excellent *Fundamentals of Insurance* textbook (this one), grabs the thief and threatens a thrashing unless the text is returned. She would not be liable for false imprisonment, assault or battery because the act was privileged.

Absolute liability

Liability without fault (often called absolute or strict liability) is imposed when public policy demands a person be held liable for injury to others even though the injury may be neither intentionally nor negligently inflicted. This type of liability exposure arises from three sources: (1) dangerous instruments (e.g., explosives or wild animals), (2) extra-hazardous operations (e.g., blasting and mining) and (3) defective products (unsafe products). Of the three sources, families generally are affected mostly by the dangerous instruments exposure and businesses are affected mostly by the defective products exposure.

Many families keep domestic animals on their premises. If these animals are dangerous, their owners are exposed to liability without fault. A sign warning "DANGER—BAD DOG" is a dead giveaway! A number of families are exposed to absolute liability by keeping firearms. The rationale for absolute liability for dangerous instruments is they create an unreasonable hazard to others; the same rationale applies to the extra-hazardous operations exposure.

Liability without fault is most commonly applied to products liability. Manufacturers and merchandisers are held liable for injuries caused by defective products they sell, regardless of fault or negligence. But the claimant must prove the product defective and that the defect made the product unreasonably dangerous. The claimant must also prove that the defect existed at the time of sale and was the proximate cause of the injury. Furthermore, proof must be established that the product was used for its intended purpose. If the injured party proves these facts, the defendant is held "strictly" liable (without regard to fault or negligence). Thus strict liability is not absolute for the products liability exposure. Strict liability is only one basis for collecting damages for defective products. Other bases are discussed later in this chapter.

Liability without fault is not restricted to common law. Strict liability has been created by statutes. For example, states have passed laws making employers strictly liable to employees for work-related injuries and diseases. Several states have laws imposing strict liability on aircraft owners for injuries they cause others by operating the aircraft. A number of states have laws that make sellers of alcoholic beverages strictly liable under certain circumstances for injuries to others resulting from the illegal sale of intoxicating drinks.

Negligence

Everyone is exposed to loss arising from negligence. The law imposes an obligation on all persons to use prudence in their actions so others will not suffer bodily injury or property damage. Failure to do so gives the injured party a right of action against the wrongdoer (tort-feasor) for damages.

Negligence is the act of an unreasonable and imprudent person. Often it results from carelessness or thoughtlessness, but it may be due to forgetfulness, bad temper, ignorance, bad judgment or stupidity. Negligence never involves intent. A husband who deliberately runs over his wife and her boyfriend as they leave a tavern is guilty of battery, not negligence (although leaving his wife with time on her hands and the opportunity to meet other men may be negligence). But the husband, who, in his haste to reach the tavern before departure of the couple, runs a red light and hits a stranger is guilty of negligence. The standard "reasonableness" is based on what society expects of the individual. The conduct must be reasonable in view of the risk involved.

INNERSCRIPT: THE REASONABLE MAN

How a negligence case is decided depends on the definition of a "reasonable man." "Reasonable men" are those who meet the required standard of conduct. That standard is not always clear. If the judge believes the standard of care owed is clear, he or she will decide if negligence has occurred. Where the judge recognizes room for disagreement (often the case), that decision will be left to the jury. (If the court holds that a negligent act has been

committed, the amount of damages to be awarded will be determined by the jury.)

A. P. Herbert, a British humorist, poet and long-time independent member of Parliament for Oxford, discusses the reasonable man:

> **He is one who invariably looks where he is going, and is careful to examine the immediate foreground before he executes a leap or a bound; who neither star-gazes nor is lost in meditation when approaching trap-doors or the margin of a dock; who never mounts a moving omnibus and does not alight from any car while the train is in motion; who investigates exhaustively the bona fides of every mendicant before distributing alms, and will inform himself of the history and habits of a dog before administering a caress; who believes no gossip, nor repeats it, without firm basis for believing it to be true; who never drives his ball till those in front of him have definitely vacated the putting-green which is his own objective; who never from one year's end to another makes an excessive demand upon his wife, his neighbours, his servants, his ox, or his ass; who in the way of business looks only for the narrow margin of profit which 12 men such as himself would reckon to be "fair," and contemplates his fellow merchants, their agents, and their goods, with that degree of suspicion and distrust which the law deems admirable; who never swears, gambles, or loses his temper, who uses nothing except in moderation, and even while he flogs his child is meditating only on the golden mean. Devoid, in short, of any human weakness, with not one single saving vice, sans prejudice, procrastination, ill-nature, avarice, and absence of mind, as careful for his own safety as he is for that of others, this excellent but odious creature stands like a monument in our Courts of Justice, vainly appealing to his fellow citizens to order their lives after his own example.[3]**

Herbert goes on to point out "that in all that mass of authorities which bears upon this branch of the law there is no single mention of a reasonable woman." The assumption is made that the term *man* **encompasses the whole human race and thus includes women.**

The reasonable man is assumed to have the minimum perception, memory, experience and information common to the community and to have normal intelligence and mental capacity. A lesser standard of care is expected of the legally insane, children and those who are senile. Persons engaged in a trade or profession are expected to have the basic knowledge necessary to practice in their community.

Presumed negligence. In a negligence case the burden of proof that the defendant failed to exercise the reasonable care of a "prudent man" is ordinarily on the plaintiff (claimant). However, if the facts justify a reasonable inference of negligence the courts may decide to lift that burden by applying the common

[3] A. P. Herbert, *Misleading Cases in Common Law* (London, 1930), pp. 12 ff.

law doctrine of ***res ipsa loquitor*** ("the thing speaks for itself"). Under this doctrine a legally sufficient case of negligence can be established and referred to the jury if (1) the plaintiff's injury was caused by the defective object, (2) the injury could not have occurred without the defendant's negligence and (3) the object causing the injury was controlled by the defendant. These conditions establish **presumed negligence.**

The doctrine of presumed negligence applies when an accident causes an injury preventable by the use of care and safety inspections, if the person responsible for the accident (the defendant) is knowledgeable about the accident's cause and if the plaintiff (the injured party) is otherwise unable to establish proof of negligence. Presumed negligence has been applied in a number of cases: injuries where no witnesses are available, railroad or aviation injuries, medical malpractice claims and damages from defective products. Products liability cases appear to be difficult ones in which to apply *res ipsa loquitor* because the claimant, not the defendant, controls the product. However, the courts have held the defendant to be in control of the product if it has not been changed since leaving the manufacturer. Thus, for example, the consumer was awarded damages when a defective refrigerator froze the hand of a homemaker, knocked her unconscious and caused serious electrical shock. However, the courts are not consistent. When the fork supporting the front wheel of a rented three-wheel golf cart collapsed, the cart stopped suddenly, ejecting the golfer and causing him injury. He sued the golf club using *res ipsa loquitor.* The court decided for the defendant in this case, stating that under *res ipsa loquitor* the instrument causing injury must be in the control of the defendant.

When negligence is presumed the plaintiff must not be guilty of contributory negligence. The circumstances of the accident must unquestionably point to negligence as its cause. If the accident could be caused by any other means the doctrine is inapplicable. If some other physical reason for the injury can be established the doctrine does not apply. Similarly, if the accident results from causes beyond the control of the defendant no presumed negligence exists. Any accident resulting from a third person's involvement or from any physical or mechanical actions is also excluded. In summary, presumed negligence requires the defendant's behavior to be the sole cause of the accident.

Imputed negligence. **Imputed negligence** (*vicarious liability*) makes one person responsible for negligent acts of others. For example, employers are often held liable for the negligence of their employees. (Employees are also liable for damages from their own negligence.) If an employer uses independent contractors whose employees negligently cause injury, that employer is liable if it provides faulty instructions or tools. Similarly, liability is imputed to landlords whose tenants cause injury from a negligent act. Automobile owners may be liable for negligent acts committed when their cars are driven by another person. In summary, although presumed negligence may not apply if a third person is involved in the negligent act, imputed negligence extends to third persons not directly involved, e.g., employers, landlords, parents, auto owners, tavern owners and others.

LIABILITY ARISING FROM NEGLIGENCE

Allegations of negligence present major issues in tort liability. Important ones are (1) the essential elements of a negligent act, (2) defenses in a negligent action and (3) statutory modifications of the common law of negligence.

Essential Elements of a Negligent Act

Four elements of a negligent act are essential before a court will award damages: (1) a legal duty to protect the injured party; (2) a breach of that duty; (3) an injury to the claimant's person, property, legal rights or reputation and (4) a reasonably close causal relationship between the breach of duty and the claimant's injury.

A legal duty to protect the injured party

A station wagon slowly sinks into the Ohio River. The driver, with great difficulty, crawls from inside the vehicle to its roof. People on the bank listen to the motorist's pleas for help indicating an inability to swim! The onlookers stand mute as the victim drowns. Have the relatives of the drowned victim a cause of action against these observers? Suppose the Olympic swimming team is on the bank; would the victim's survivors have a valid case against them? The law is clear. For a successful suit a duty to exercise a particular standard of care toward the victim is essential.

The law does not impose on anyone the obligation to aid another in distress and may even penalize a Good Samaritan. Because Rich Porter, a poor swimmer, jumped into the water to aid a drowning child, Dawn Kelly, a good swimmer, refrained. Had Rich not made the attempt Dawn would have made the rescue. If Rich failed in his rescue attempt he might be sued by the decedent's family. If the child were drowning in a swimming pool, the owner, the operator *and* the lifeguard who had been ogling scantily clad swimmers might be held liable for the drowning.

To whom duty is owed is a complicated question. The answer varies with changing social conditions, the relative abilities of the parties to bear the losses, the desire to encourage greater care and so on. Whether a duty was owed the injured party and whether that duty was breached is decided by the courts. The judge decides questions of law and the jury questions of fact. Unfortunately, negligence cases usually are not divisible into two such neat compartments and juries are not experts. The prevalence of unwarranted verdicts and awards has led some members of the bar to call for the abolition of jury trials in negligence cases. A character in a popular novel puts the matter nicely:

> Did Levine have a lawyer? A specialist in accident cases? If not, he recommended Coniff, on Court Street. Coniff the *Goniff.* Out of a cracked sidewalk, a rusty nail, a cigarette burn, a piece of bad wiring, he mounted claims for thousands. Let two A&P shopping carts collide and a son went through medical school.[4]

Often awards allegedly are made on the basis of ability to pay (i.e., the size of the insurance policy available) or other extralegal grounds. Some members of the bar question whether abolition of jury trials would solve the problem and argue that serious reform of the judiciary is also necessary.

INNERSCRIPT: STANDARD OF CARE OWED BY OWNERS AND TENANTS

The standard of care owed by owners or tenants to persons entering their property depends on the intent of the entry. A person

(*continued*)

---

[4] Wallace Markfield, *To an Early Grave* (New York: Simon & Schuster, 1964).

may enter as a trespasser, licensee or invitee. For each a different degree of care is required. The standard of care owed trespassers is less than ordinary (that owed to the general public), except for an attractive nuisance. **An attractive nuisance is any novel device particularly enticing to children, e.g., an unusual piece of machinery or a swimming pool. Owners and tenants are required to warn or protect children who may be attracted to these potentially dangerous devices. Defenses available are that the child was old enough to perceive the danger or that the device was common to the locality and therefore not novel.**

In many states the doctrine of attractive nuisance has been replaced by Section 339 of the *Restatement of Torts (Second)*.[5] **Under this statute the owners or tenants are held liable for injuries to trespassing children under the following conditions: (1) they maintain a condition on their property that may be reasonably expected to attract children incapable of perceiving the hazards and (2) the condition provides the owner or tenant small benefit compared to the risk involved for young children. One defense is that the owner or tenant could not reasonably be expected to know the condition would attract children and be unreasonably hazardous to them. Another defense is that the condition provides benefits that far outweigh the dangers involved.**

With the adult trespasser the owner or tenant need only avoid deliberate injury. A burglar tried to break into a vacant Iowa farmhouse and was greeted with a blast from a shotgun set to hit anyone opening the door. The Iowa court awarded more than $50,000 damages to this trespasser. A higher court sustained the judgment. The standard of care required for licensees (those on the premises with permission but for their own benefit, e.g., to use the phone) is less than ordinary but greater than that owed a trespasser. The standard of care required for invitees (persons on the premises for the benefit of the owner or tenant) is greater than that owed trespassers and licensees and varies according to the status of the invitee.

If the invitees are social guests, the standard of care required is less than if they are on the premises for the exclusive benefit of the owner or tenant (for example, a friend repairing the TV set gratis). Courts decide what constitutes ordinary care and the gradations of care required, and they seem to believe that the prudent persons of today are more careful than their grandparents. The result is that an increasing standard of care is expected.

Two states (California and Hawaii) consider it illogical to allow the conduct of a reasonable person to depend on the legal status

---

[5] *The Restatement of Torts (Second)* is a text written by the American Law Institute and adopted upon its completion on May 22, 1964. It is a revision from *The Restatement of Torts (First)*, adopted in 1939, and summarizes the laws and court decisions concerning tort cases. Its objectives are not only to update tort rulings but also to clarify ambiguous statements and correct misinterpretations.

of the injured party. Thus they no longer consider the distinctions among trespasser, licensee and invitee in determining the required standard of care. Still the majority opinion is that reasonableness and fairness require a lesser degree of care toward trespassers than toward licensees and invitees. But courts change their views to reflect changing attitudes, so the present position might not continue.

Breach of that duty

The plaintiff must show not only that the alleged tort-feasor had a duty to the injured person but also that the duty was breached. A trial judge may conclude that the defendant performed that duty and dismiss the case. However, the facts are usually nebulous. So questions concerning breach of duty nearly always are decided by jurors.

Injury must be suffered by the claimant

For a successful suit, the injury must result from a breach of duty. The injury may be property damage, bodily injury, loss of income, pain and suffering. The general rule is that mental disturbance is not an injury unless accompanied by physical harm. Thus a person who suffers a heart attack while seeing a child hit by a train would have no cause of action against the railroad. But if the heart attack occurs after physical involvement in an accident, the court decision would probably be different. This rule has been modified in several cases. A California court awarded a mother damages for emotional illness resulting from viewing her son shortly after he was injured by a negligently caused explosion.[6] The bystander's right to damages is a limited one, usually requiring (1) the plaintiff to be near the scene of the occurrence, (2) the event to cause a direct emotional impact and (3) the plaintiff and victim to have a close relationship.

Reasonably close causal relationship

The final essential is a reasonably close causal relationship between the breach of duty and the claimant's injury. The breach of duty must be a **proximate cause** of the injury. While the court decides questions of proximate cause, its interpretation may be unpredictable. Because any act may be said to have its origins in the beginning of time, the question is at what point in the chain of events leading to the loss will the court conclude a cause is proximate. A homeowner burns leaves in the yard. A strong wind begins and the fire spreads, destroying a neighbor's house. Is the leaf burner liable for the house next door? Suppose the fire spreads to destroy the entire block?

During World War I the powder magazine on Black Tom Island in New York harbor exploded. Concussion damage was suffered in a 25- to 30-mile radius. Was the federal government liable for these losses? In saying "no" New York courts are alone in holding that the consequences must be quite close in time and space to establish liability. The leaf burner is responsible for burning the adjacent house but is absolved from liability if additional houses are destroyed. (In Kansas liability is limited to within four miles of the fire.) In all other courts remoteness in time and space are important but not decisive factors in determining liability. Substantive statements about whether an act will be deemed the proximate cause of an injury are difficult to make. In most cases the decision will be based on numerous variables rather than on clear-cut rules.

[6] *Archibald* v. *Braverman,* 79 Cal. Rptr. 723 (4 Dist. 1969)

INNERSCRIPT: *SINE QUA NON* AND PROXIMATE CAUSE

In many cases the problem of causation can be handled by the *sine qua non* **(without which not) rule. Under this rule a person's conduct is not held to be the cause of a loss that would have occurred anyway. For example, the Minnesota Supreme Court found that a train's failure to give bell and whistle signals for a crossing was not the proximate cause of a collision between the train and an approaching auto because the auto struck the 68th car of the train. When the rule** *sine qua non* **is not applicable, other factors must be considered. Furthermore,** *sine qua non* **does not mean liability will always be automatic if the injury occurred from the defendant's actions. Other factors are considered before holding an action the proximate cause of the loss.**

A person will be held liable for all direct consequences stemming from a breach of duty even though no reasonable person would have expected the results. Sometimes an intervening cause is present, and if that cause is unforeseen courts will usually find the defendant not liable. In the leaf-burning incident, if the wind was calm when the fire was set, a sudden windstorm scattering leaves and setting fire to other houses probably would not cause the homeowner to be liable. An ordinary wind sufficient to spread the fire to the neighbor's house would not excuse the leaf burner from liability.

In *Palsgraf* v. *Long Island Railroad,* **a New Yorker bound for Rockaway Beach was on the platform when a train headed for another destination pulled in. Two men ran to catch this train. One reached it safely although the train was moving. The other, carrying a package, jumped aboard the car but teetered on the edge of the steps as if he were about to fall. A train guard held the door open and reached to pull him in while a platform guard pushed him from behind. During this action the package containing fireworks fell and exploded. The explosion upset scales (a weighing instrument—not fish, musical or salary scales) on the platform many feet away. The plaintiff still waiting for the Rockaway Beach train was struck by the falling scales. She brought suit against the railroad.**

Justice Benjamin N. Cardozo, speaking for the New York Court of Appeals, denied the claim because the conduct of the defendant's guard was not negligent relative to the plaintiff. The court concluded that the guard had no reason to know the package was dangerous. Therefore the plaintiff's rights were not violated. This decision has been accepted in section 430 of the *Restatement of Torts (Second).* But many courts in similar situations have awarded damages on grounds that the causal connection was sufficient.

Defenses in a Negligence Action

An injured person may prove all four elements of a negligent act and still not be awarded damages. Several successful defenses are available to the defendant. The two principal ones are contributory negligence and assumption of risk.

Assumption of risk argues that the plaintiff by consenting either expressly or by implication to relieve the defendant of the duty to protect had accepted the risk of injury. The risk may be assumed by written agreement, e.g., leases signed by apartment renters. The lease may waive the tenant's right of action against the landlord and require the tenant to assume liability to others that normally would be the landlord's responsibility. Thus Ms. Finston may agree that if her guest trips on a broom left in the hall by the janitor, she, rather than the landlord, will be liable for any injuries.

The more troublesome cases arise in the absence of a written agreement. Bill Beckemeier and Joan Krueger are wrestling. Joan slams Bill to the mat breaking Bill's nose. Does Bill have a cause of action against Joan? No, the presumption is assumption of risk. Suppose that Bill picks up Joan and throws her off the mat onto a spectator's lap! Does the spectator have a cause of action against Bill? Again the answer is no. Justice Cardoza, in rejecting a similar claim wrote: "The timorous may stay at home."

The defendant in a negligence action may use **contributory negligence** as a defense. If the plaintiff is also negligent and that negligent action contributed to the loss, he or she may be denied recovery. Contributory negligence does not relieve the defendant of duty to the plaintiff. Instead, it denies the plaintiff recovery if both parties are at fault.

The first case of contributory negligence, *Butterfield* v. *Forrester,* was tried in 1809.[7] Forrester was repairing his house and had used a pole to block part of the public highway, leaving a passageway on the far side. Butterfield left a pub at dusk and, riding fast, hit the pole and was seriously injured. The judge instructed the jury that "if a person riding with reasonable and ordinary care could have seen and avoided the obstruction; and if they were satisfied that the plaintiff was riding along the street extremely hard, and without ordinary care, they should find a verdict for the defendant." The jury so found.

Two widely used variations of the contributory negligence rule are **comparative negligence** and **last clear chance.** Under comparative negligence the court (often the jury) attempts to scale the verdict according to the comparative degrees of negligence of the parties. Thirty-six states have comparative negligence laws.

The most widespread modification of contributory negligence is the last clear chance doctrine accepted in some form by many courts. It originated in *Davies* v. *Mann,* tried in England in 1842. The plaintiff had fettered his ass on the public highway where it was hit by a buggy driven by the defendant. The jury found for the plaintiff's servant and returned a verdict for 40 shillings (the good old days—$9.50 for an ass). The judge asked the jury to ignore that the animal was on the highway illegally and said that if they

> were of the opinion that it was caused by the fault of the defendant's servant in driving . . . at a smartish pace, the mere fact of putting the ass upon the road would not bar the plaintiff of his action. . . . Were this not so, a man might justify purposely running against a carriage going on the wrong side of the road.

The last clear chance doctrine is most acceptable to the courts when the negligent party (the defendant) is able to prove the injured party (the plaintiff) had the *last clear chance* to avoid the accident. The last clear chance doctrine states that the defendant with the last clear chance to avoid the accident is guilty of contributory negligence by failure to take advantage of that chance. Where both plaintiff and defendant were inattentive, the doctrine does not apply.

---

[7] 103 Eng. Rep. 926 (KB 1809).

Role of the jury

The jury often plays a crucial role in negligence cases as illustrated by *Rush* v. *Commercial Realty Company.*[8] The Commercial Realty Company owned the house where Mrs. Rush lived and the adjacent house. The landlord provided a detached privy for the use of both houses. While using this privy Mrs. Rush allegedly fell nine feet through a trapdoor in the floor into the accumulation at the bottom and was extricated by use of a ladder. The defendant denied the existence of a pit and claimed the floor was only nine inches above ground. This alleged fact, like several other features of the case, presented a disputed question for the jury. The judge noted the jury had found the facts to be favorable for Mrs. Rush, as follows:

> The argument for a nonsuit or for a direction must be restricted to the questions of contributory negligence and assumption of risk. In dealing with these, it should be observed that Mrs. Rush had no choice, when impelled by the calls of nature, but to use the facilities placed at her disposal by the landlord, to wit, a privy with a trap door in the floor, poorly maintained. We hardly think this was the assumption of a risk; she was not required to leave the premises and go elsewhere. Whether it was contributory negligence to step on a floor, which she testified was in bad order, was a question for the jury to solve according to its finding of the conditions and her knowledge of them, or what she should have known of them; it does not seem to be a court question.

Statutory Modifications of the Common Law of Negligence

The common law of negligence has been modified by statute. The last clear chance or comparative negligence doctrines have been embodied in the statutes of several states. The liability of employers for injuries to their employees has been modified as discussed in Chapter 11. Other statutory modifications include those relating to automobile liability and survival and wrongful death.

Automobile liability

The law covering liability toward others in the use of automobiles has moved in two directions in the United States. It has become stricter concerning the operator's liability to those hit by the automobile. However, for injuries suffered by guests in the car the law has moved toward relaxing the operator's liability.

France, West Germany, Great Britain, Sweden, Switzerland, Italy and the Netherlands have partially extended the auto operator's liability to bodily injury losses without regard to fault. All seven countries provide payment of medical expenses and wage losses to victims of automobile accidents on a prompt no-fault basis while maintaining the driver's responsibility for damages negligently inflicted on vehicles and other property.[9] This type of legislation has its advocates in the United States, and in recent years the question of the uncompensated or poorly compensated accident victim has received much attention. Some concerned persons advocate the extension of the no-fault principle to property damage as well as to bodily injury. As of mid-1982, 14 states had no-fault laws in effect that restrict law suits. For example, Massachusetts adopted a modified no-fault insurance plan that eliminates most liability claims under $2,000 and provides coverage for medical expenses and lost wages. In addition, eight states have enacted add-on no-fault coverage to tort liability law, usually in the form

---

[8] 7 N.J. Misc R. 337, 145A 476-App & E 927 (7); Land & Ten 168 (11), 169 (11).

[9] Weiner Pfennigstorf, *Compensation of Auto Accidents Victims in Europe* (Chicago: American Insurance Mutual Alliance, 1972).

of compulsory personal injury protection. These states place no restrictions on tort liability.

Thirteen states have laws (12 by statute and 1 by case) modifying the common-law rule that the automobile operator has the duty to use reasonable care for protecting a guest. Under *common law,* the driver is required to tell the guest about any defects in the car. (Strict enforcement of this principle might result in a lost evening before the recital of a car's defects could be concluded!) Under *guest statutes* the guest (one who neither pays for the ride nor serves the host in any fashion) is due a lesser standard of care than the common law requires. The driver is not liable unless guilty of "gross negligence," "willful," "wanton" and/or "reckless" action. The purpose of these statutes primarily is to protect insurers from suits arising from collusion between the operator and the guest and to protect the operator from ingratitude on the part of the guest.

At the beginning of 1970, 28 states had guest statutes. By the early 1980s that number was reduced to 13. What happened to these statutes in the 15 states that no longer have them? Seven were ruled unconstitutional by state supreme courts and eight were repealed, some after adverse lower court decisions. Supreme courts in California, Idaho, Michigan, Nevada, New Mexico, North Dakota, Ohio and Wyoming ruled guest statutes unconstitutional under the Equal Protection Clause of the U.S. Constitution (the 14th Amendment). Guest statutes appear destined to become a matter of history, leaving no effective method of preventing collusion between driver and passenger, at the expense of the automobile liability premium-paying public.

About one fourth of the states have modified the common-law rule of negligence to hold the owner of a vehicle liable for negligent use by another person, provided that use was within the scope of the permission granted. Dan Anderson lends Norma Larsen his new Mercedes to rush her overdue book to the library. On the way Norma hits a motor scooter operated by Joey Jessee and breaks his arm. These statutes make Dan, the owner of the car, liable for Joey's injury. Had Joey been injured while Norma was deviating from her library route to buy a pizza, Dan would not be liable because the car was not being used within the scope of the permission granted. (See earlier discussion of imputed negligence.)

Survival and wrongful death

A basic principle of the common law of negligence was that only the injured person had a right of action against the wrongdoer and this right died with the injured person. The death of the wrongdoer also terminated any action, bringing forth the advice that when a motorist hits a pedestrian who is still wiggling, back up for another try!

Today all states have statutes providing a remedy for wrongful death. Most of these statutes provide that in the event of a wrongful death the survivors have a new right of action against the wrongdoer. Many states limited the amount of recovery to $5,000 for a single wrongful death. As time passed and inflation continued, this amount was raised. Today only seven states limit the recovery (generally from $35,000 to $75,000). These limits apply only to a wrongful death action. Survivors may also seek awards for loss of income, loss of consortium (the services of the spouse) and other related losses.

LIABILITY IMPOSED BY CONTRACT

An individual or business may be subject to liability imposed by contract. This liability may be either assumed explicitly or arise from a breach of an implied warranty.

Liability Assumed under Contract

A person may contract to assume in whole or in part the liability of another. When students sign leases for apartments, they may agree to assume the landlord's liability for negligence imposed by common law. These risk-shifting clauses in a lease is standard practice. However, failure of the tenant to honor the agreement does not free the landlord of liability. A business firm may assume liability of others under railroad switch track agreements, contracts to supply goods or services to others or required municipal permits.

Breach of an Implied Warranty

In the preceding section, liability assumed under contract is a risk-transfer device only, rather than an additional exposure. Breach of an implied warranty, however, is a separate form of liability based on contract law. Under contract law proof of negligence is not required for damages. The plaintiff need only prove that an implied promise was not fulfilled. Two common liability exposures for breach of warranty emanate from the manufacture and sale of products and from the practice of professional services.

DUAL LIABILITY EXPOSURES: TORTS AND CONTRACTS

Liability for defective products and professional malpractice may be based either on a tort or breach of an implied warranty. Legal action(s) taken by the plaintiff will be determined by the trends in contract and tort law.

Products Liability

A person injured by a defective product may bring suit for breach of an implied warranty. Two implied warranties are **merchantability** and **fitness for a particular purpose.** The warranties are for the buyer's protection and apply even if the seller is ignorant of the defect. The Uniform Commercial Code requires that to be merchantable, goods must (1) be fit for the purposes intended, (2) be adequately packaged and labeled and (3) conform to the promises and statements made on the package or label.[10] The warranty of fitness is in effect if the seller has reason to know (1) the intended use of the product and (2) that the customer relies on the seller's expertise to provide goods suitable for this intended use.

Historically, the principle of **privity of contract** prevented direct action by a consumer against a manufacturer of a defective product. The principle of privity allowed only a party to the contract to bring action for its breach. Because many manufacturers sell to consumers through wholesalers and retailers, the privity requirement gave the consumer recourse only against the retailer. But the privity requirement has undergone a gradual erosion. Consumers in most states can now sue the manufacturer of a defective product for breach of implied warranty.

In addition, a person injured by a defective product has two causes of action in tort: negligence and liability without fault (strict liability). An injured party in a negligence suit must prove that the seller or manufacturer failed to exercise the standard of care required in producing or handling the product. Strict liability eliminates the necessity to prove negligence. The extension of strict liability to products liability has significantly increased the products liability exposure of

[10] The Uniform Commercial Code was promulgated in 1951 by the National Conference of Commissioners on Uniform State Laws and the American Law Institute with the endorsement of the American Bar Association. The Code was eventually adopted in all states except Louisiana.

manufacturers and sellers. Under strict liability, the injured person need only prove (1) a defect in the product made the product unreasonably dangerous, (2) the defect existed when leaving the defendant's possession, (3) the defect was the proximate cause of the injury and (4) the use of the product was reasonable. With the advent of strict liability, actions for breach of contract and negligence are becoming less important. As in other liability cases, court decisions establishing the requisites for a successful products liability action vary among jurisdictions.

Professional Liability

Physicians, attorneys, accountants, beauticians and other professional persons or skilled tradespersons may be held liable for breach of an implied warranty to render the agreed-upon service. Professionals are held liable with much greater frequency and for increasing amounts of damages for failure to exercise reasonable (sometimes more stringent) care.[11] This development has drastically increased the cost of liability insurance for professionals, especially physicians. How to solve the problem of the increasing frequency and severity of professional liability claims continues to be a controversy.

EXAMPLES OF TORT LIABILITY HAZARDS

Family risk managers should be concerned with all tort exposures, but their primary emphasis is liability resulting from negligence. Risk managers for businesses also must be aware of and plan for all tort exposures, but they should be most concerned with strict liability, liability arising from negligence and liability imposed by contract.

The interest of risk managers in the tort exposure is twofold: (1) the loss exposure caused by a potential tort action against their families or companies and (2) the opportunity to collect for a loss through tort actions against others. Tort actions, therefore, not only are important sources of losses but also provide major postloss resources.

Personal Liability Exposures

Individuals must be aware of hazards that increase the chance of liability losses. Sidewalks, stairways, freshly waxed floors and unsecured rugs increase the chance of loss from liability exposures. For example, an icy sidewalk may or may not present a liability hazard to owners or tenants. The general rule is that owners or tenants are not obligated to remove ice from their sidewalks resulting from natural causes but may be held liable for injuries if a fall on a slippery sidewalk is the result of accumulated ice caused by a condition of the owners' or tenants' property, e.g., gutter leakage.

As noted, the same standard of care is not owed by the owner or tenant to trespassers, invitees or licensees except in a few states. However, the individual does not know before an accident the standard of care that will be expected by the court. Thus the classification of trespasser, invitee and licensee is of little use in studying liability hazards except for obvious attractive nuisance cases.

Optimists believe that bonds of friendship prevent close companions from filing tort suits against them. However, in the words of one expert on liability

[11] Professionals, especially physicians, are increasingly held for conduct standards above that normally expected, leaving the professionals in a quandary as to what is reasonable performance.

hazards, "When injury results, friendship is strained; when an attorney is retained, it wanes; and when those who are involved go to court, it ceases to exist."[12] If this observation applies to friends, what about others? Those participating in sports, driving automobiles, running the rumor mills and engaging in any other activity are exposed to liability claims. The liability exposure is capable of springing many unpleasant surprises.

Business Liability Exposures

Property owned or rented by the business or for which the business has responsibility can be the source of liability claims. Liability also may result from injuries caused by business operations. If an injury occurs from an employee's negligence, the employer may be held liable to the injured person. In a California case a salesperson involved in an accident while driving to a company meeting was held to be acting as an employee and the employer was held liable for the $10,000 judgment even though the car was owned by the employee. Employers also are exposed to liability under workers' compensation laws for injuries to employees.

For laundries, dry cleaners, warehouses, repair establishments and other businesses that handle customers' goods deposited with them the liability is not absolute. Losses for which bailees are not responsible are those caused by "acts of God," e.g., tornadoes. But many businesses dealing with consumers realize that sound business practice dictates reimbursing customers for losses regardless of legal responsibility to retain customers' goodwill.

Tavern owners and operators are exposed to the "dramshop" hazard. Many states have dramshop laws making the seller of alcoholic beverages liable for bodily injury and property damage caused by persons under the influence of alcohol consumed in their establishment. They may also be held liable for the wrongful death or injury of the intoxicated person and in some jurisdictions for loss of consortium damages to the decedent's spouse. Owners and operators of taverns should become familiar with the dramshop act as interpreted by the courts in their jurisdiction to identify this exposure.

A business should be aware of its exposure to large losses from the products recall hazard. Once a products liability claim has arisen from the use of a defective product and often before such a claim occurs, a manufacturer is required to recall all products that might contain defects in order to prevent any (or additional) injury to the public.

This miniscule survey of liability hazards is intended solely to provide a few examples of exposures that may increase the chance of liability loss. A comprehensive discussion of liability hazards would require a textbook of its own.

SUMMARY

1. The legal codes in the United States, the individual states and local entities are based on the statutes passed by Congress, state legislatures and municipalities and on British Common Law.
2. Common law is based on precedents—previous court decisions.
3. Liability risks result from torts (wrongful acts) or breach of contracts.

---

[12] Reginald W. Spell, *Public Liability Hazards* (Indianapolis, Ind.: Rough Notes Co., 1941), p. 228.

4. Torts arise from:
   a. Intentional interference.
   b. Liability without fault.
   c. Negligence.

5. Intentional torts may be committed against persons or property. Intentional torts committed against persons are:
   a. Assault.
   b. Battery.
   c. Defamation—libel/slander.
   d. Mental distress.
   e. False imprisonment.
   f. Malicious prosecution.

   Intentional torts committed against property are:
   a. Trespass.
   b. Conversion.

6. Legal defenses against intentional torts are:
   a. Privilege.
   b. Mistakes.
   c. Consent.
   d. Protective acts.

7. Liability without fault (often called absolute or strict liability) imposes liability regardless of negligence or intentions. It applies to dangerous instruments, extra hazardous operations and defective products.

8. Strict liability is not limited to common law. States have statutes imposing strict liability, e.g., workers' compensation laws. Strict liability implies violation of two warranties:
   a. Merchantability.
   b. Product was fit for its intended use.

9. Negligence is liability that results from failure to act as a "prudent man." The standard of care due from a prudent man differs for trespassers, licensees and invitees.

10. Two forms of negligence are implied by circumstances surrounding the act that caused injury:
   a. Presumed negligence: when the instrument that caused the injury was under the complete control of the defendant and the injury would not have resulted unless the instrument was used negligently.
   b. Imputed negligence (vicarious liability): when the act that caused the injury was indirectly controlled by the defendant (e.g., employers, landlords and automobile owners might be held liable for the acts of others).

11. The essentials of a negligent act are:
   a. A duty to protect the injured person.
   b. Breach of that duty.
   c. Injury to a person or property.
   d. A reasonably close causal relationship between the breach of duty and the injury.

12. Defenses against liability from negligence are:
   a. *Sine qua non*—the injury would have happened anyway.
   b. Assumption of risk.

c. Contributory negligence.
d. Comparative negligence.
e. Last clear chance.
f. Guest statutes.

13. Consumers injured by defective products have three courses of action:
a. Strict liability.
b. Negligence.
c. Breach of contract.

14. In strict liability cases the injured person must prove:
a. The defect made the product unreasonably dangerous.
b. The defect existed at the time of sale.
c. The defect caused the injury.
d. The product was used in the manner and for the purpose intended by the manufacturer.

REVIEW QUESTIONS

1. What are two sources of liability?

2. Define the following terms:
a. Intentional torts.
b. Liability without fault.
c. Negligence.

3. Name a legal defense for each of the following intentional torts:
a. Assault.
b. Battery.
c. Defamation—libel/slander.
d. False imprisonment.

4. What is the standard of care owed trespassers? Does it differ from that owed licensees or invitees?

5. If you are injured and seek to claim damages for negligence, what must you prove to have a valid case?

6. If you are sued for negligence, what are your possible defenses? Explain.

7. What three legal courses of action are available to consumers who are injured by defective products?

8. If the injured consumer (in Question 7) chooses to sue based on strict liability, what four conditions must he or she prove in court?

9. What is mental distress? Who can sue for damages from mental distress?

10. The common law principle that the "right of action" dies with the injured party has been replaced by state statutes that provide remedy for wrongful death. What kinds of losses are survivors entitled to receive?

11. What are the Uniform Commercial Code requirements for a merchantable product?

12. Under what circumstances might the court apply the common law doctrine of presumed negligence? Imputed negligence?

PART THREE THE INSURANCE CONTRACT AND ITS INTERPRETATION

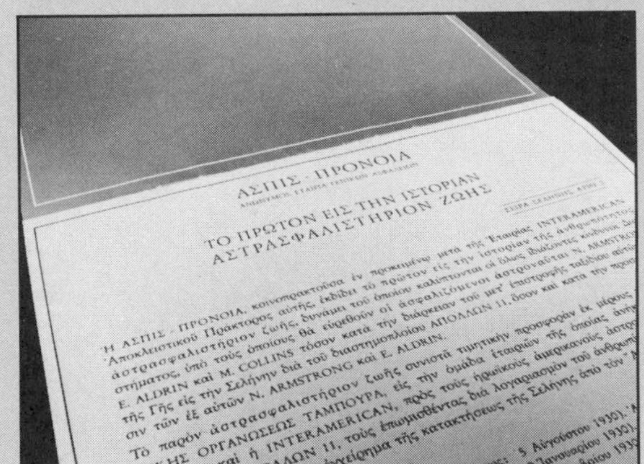

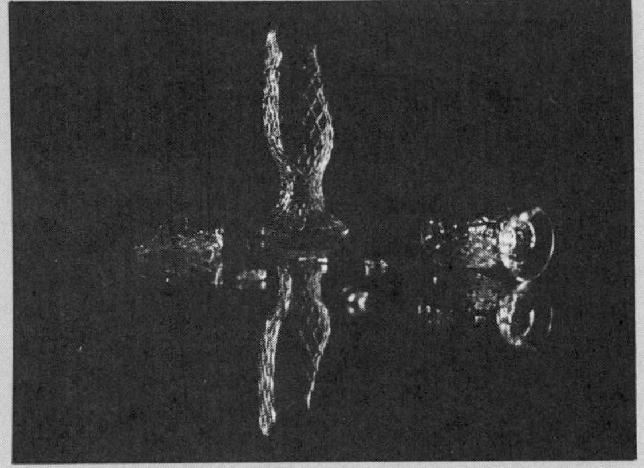

The first four chapters of this book examined the concepts of insurance, risk and risk management. Various methods of handling risk were identified and discussed. The risk management process, including risk analysis, was explained.

Risk management deals with two fundamental functions: loss financing and loss control. This text is concerned primarily with loss financing. Given that insurance is the cornerstone of most risk management loss financing programs, focus throughout the remainder of the text is on insurance. To learn about other loss financing techniques and about loss control, additional specialized texts are required. Knowledge of insurance is the first step toward becoming a qualified risk manager. Therefore, attention at this point is shifted primarily to insurance beginning with the study of the insurance contract and its interpretation.

Part Three includes five chapters designed to explain the law as it applies to the insurance contract, develop a procedure for analyzing the coverage provided by insurance policies and demonstrate how this procedure is applied in analyzing the two most important personal insurance policies: the homeowners policy and the personal auto policy. The purpose of the analysis is to apply the technique for reading policies rather than to explain homeowners and automobile insurance per se. Insurance coverage for dwellings, their contents and autos is discussed in Chapters 10, 11 and 12. The discussion in Part Three on how to read a policy focuses on determining (1) the coverage offered, (2) the amount that will be paid in event of the loss and (3) the conditions that must be met to collect the amount due following a loss.

CHAPTER

5 The insurance contract

John Thoeming/Richard D. Irwin

CHAPTER OBJECTIVES

1. **To explain the instruments used in forming an insurance contract.**
2. **To examine the essential elements of an insurance contract.**
3. **To identify the distinguishing characteristics of an insurance contract.**
4. **To define legal concepts important to the understanding and interpretation of insurance contracts: warranties, representations, concealment, indemnity, insurable interest and subrogation.**
5. **To point out and clarify the nature, power and authority of agents and brokers and the principal's responsibility in insurance marketing.**
6. **To distinguish among the legal and equitable remedies available for resolving disputes among parties to an insurance contract: waiver, estoppel, rescission and reformation.**

Knowledge of the law is important to both family and business risk managers. How the law affects loss exposures is explained in Chapter 4. The law also governs one of the major techniques for dealing with loss exposures—loss transfer by insurance.

An insurance policy is a legal contract establishing the rights and duties of policyowners and insurers. Although the policy is a complete document, reference to statutes and court decisions may be necessary for its interpretation. In this chapter the legal requirements for an insurance contract are presented first. Then the many ways that these contracts have been modified by statutes and case law are discussed.

THE INSURANCE CONTRACT DEFINED

Because so many dissimilar contracts are classified as insurance, no short, precise definition of insurance contracts is acceptable. Yet a broad, general definition would include contractual arrangements that are not insurance. One definition is:

> Insurance is a financial arrangement where one party agrees to compensate another for a loss if it results from occurrence of a specified event.

While neat and seemingly appropriate, this definition fails to exclude contracts that are not insurance. For example, consider a nonrenewable service contract where the manufacturer or dealer agrees to maintain merchandise and replace parts for a specified period. Although this type of agreement provides compensation to another for a loss subject to the occurrence of a specified event, the contract is *not* insurance because it excludes loss by external causes, e.g., fire and theft.

Insurance and noninsurance must be differentiated because an activity classified as insurance becomes subject to insurance regulation. In addition, the rights of parties in an insurance contract are determined by common law and statutes peculiar to insurance. Finally, because corporations operate under charters that limit their activities, any firm writing insurance without the necessary charter and licenses will be committing an *ultra vires* (beyond the authority) act.

A Philadelphia newspaper publisher fell afoul of the legal distinction between permitted and prohibited corporate acts by advertising payment of a given sum to the heirs of anyone killed while possessing a copy of its paper. In a test case the court decided this promise was an insurance contract. Rather than trying to obtain a charter as a life insurer, the publisher discontinued the offer.

The difficulty in developing a short but accurate definition of insurance was recognized by the court:

> Necessarily, in defining insurance in a single sentence, only the most general terms can be used, and any general definition must be extended to cover the ever-changing phases in which the subject is presented to the public.[1]

A study of court decisions on definitions of insurance contracts leaves one with a lack of direction. Yet to expect anything else is to fall victim to the "fallacy of legal certainty—that sure, certain, and consistent results can be projected when a legal problem arises. . . ."[2]

With the understanding that no short definition can be completely accurate, the definition of insurance developed in Chapter 2 is acceptable:

> Insurance is defined as a device for reducing risk by combining a sufficient number of exposure units to make their individual losses collectively predictable. The predictable loss is then shared proportionately by all units in the combination.

THE FORMATION OF THE CONTRACT

Two basic instruments used in insurance transactions are (1) the application and (2) the binder.

The Application

Technically the function of an insurance agent is to solicit prospects to apply for insurance (and in some cases find an insurer to write the coverage) rather than offer insurance for sale. In life, health, hail, livestock and credit insurance, the application must be in writing on forms supplied by insurers. Applications for property and liability insurance may be either oral or written. Historically, property and liability insurance applications have been oral and informal, especially for personal lines (e.g., auto and homeowners insurance). Many of these contracts are still made with oral applications although the trend is to use standardized model application forms.

A written application states the kind and amount of insurance requested, the premium to be paid and detailed information about the loss exposure. Some applications include a notice that agents do not have the authority to modify the terms of the application or of the policy. The information in the application is used chiefly for underwriting and identification. Although some applications for insurance may have no legal consequences in contract formation, they do contain a number of statements that affect the contract after it is made. In life and health insurance, the application is made a part of the contract because

---

[1] *State* v. *Hogan,* 1899, 8 N.D. 301, 78 N.W. 1051, 45 L.R.A. 166, 73 Am. St. Rep. 759.

[2] Herbert S. Denenberg, "The Legal Definition of Insurance," *The Journal of Insurance,* September 1963, p. 325.

most states prohibit insurers from using statements of the insured in contesting a claim unless these statements are part of the written contract.

Declarations are informational statements about the exposures to be covered and usually form the basis for decisions on the issuance and rating of the insurance. In some types of insurance, the declarations are included in a written application attached to the policy; but where a written application is not required a declarations schedule is in the policy and becomes part of the contract when accepted. See Appendix 1 for a specimen declaration page.

The information in the declarations is supplied by the insured or the broker. Declarations include the name of the insured, location of the exposure, type of business and other pertinent facts. In personal auto insurance, for example, the declarations include information about the covered automobile: make, model, year, body type, list price, date purchased, use, distance traveled to work and the principal area where the car is driven (urban, suburban or rural). The declarations also inquire into specific driver characteristics, e.g., occupation, driving record and, where permitted, age and sex.

The Binder

A binder is a temporary contract, pending issuance of the policy. Binders may be either written or oral. The disadvantage of an oral contract is the difficulty of proving its existence. Nevertheless, oral binders often precede their written confirmation. In many types of coverage, insurance takes effect when the agent convinces the prospect of the need for insurance. When the prospect says, "I want it" and the agent says, "You have it!" a legal oral binder has been executed—subject to such other legal contract requirements as consideration, legal purpose, meeting of the minds and so on. Immediately upon creating an oral binder, the agent should record when the binder is made, the terms of its coverage and the parties involved. To reduce the possibility of disputes, the oral binder should be followed by a written one if a delay occurs in issuing the policy. A written binder is especially important where policies are not standardized. Only a written binder can provide clear-cut evidence of an understanding by both parties of the insurance coverage, its amount, its premium and the insurer(s) acceptance of the risk. When policies are standardized, the courts assume that the binder conforms to standard policy provisions.

Generally, property insurance agents have the power to bind the insurer and issue the policy. However, for certain coverages insurers ask their agents to delay writing the policy until the insurers have inspected the exposure to see if it meets underwriting standards. Workers' compensation and steam boiler exposures are examples of lines where a delay may occur in issuing the policy. Some exposures require investigation of the applicant's moral character and financial status. When other underwriting factors are favorable, insurers are generally willing to be bound temporarily while the investigation is conducted. To control expenses insurers are unwilling to issue the policy until they know they will accept the applicant.

Binders generally are not used by life insurers because life insurance sales representatives are soliciting agents and not contract-writing agents. Because life insurance policies are noncancellable, insurers want applications approved in the home office before writing policies. Most insurers are unwilling to be bound even temporarily by an agent.

Binders may offer unscrupulous people free insurance. An agent may bind an insurance contract, and when the policy is issued the buyer may refuse it if no losses have occurred. The client is legally obligated to pay the premium for the covered period; but agents seldom ask for payment. Instead, they cancel the policy back to its inception date. Through a series of binders one after the other, a scheming person can have free insurance until the plot is uncovered.

Agents may also be guilty of binder abuse. Sometimes they issue oral binders when they have no binding authority, or they mislead applicants into thinking coverage begins before the effective date. Insurance buyers, therefore, must be sure agents have immediate binding authority.

ESSENTIAL ELEMENTS OF AN INSURANCE CONTRACT

Knowledge of the legal form and the conditions for valid contracts as applied to insurance is useful to both buyers and sellers to prevent unpleasant surprises.

Agreement—Offer and Acceptance

Agreement consists of an offer made by one party and acceptance by another. An insurance offer is made by the buyer when submitting an application. Rarely does the insurer make the offer. An exception is found in life insurance. The insurer may make an offer if the first premium is not sent with the application.

In many forms of insurance the application might be oral. A couple deciding to insure against loss of their house by fire may apply by telephone. When the homeowners request the insurance, the policy is effective immediately upon the agent's acceptance. Offer and acceptance are completed because the agent has the power to bind the insurer.

In contrast, the life insurance application is always in writing. The life agent usually does not have binding power, so the insurance cannot become effective when the application is submitted. For the application to be an offer, it must be accompanied by the first premium. In return, the agent gives the customer a conditional receipt.

The most common conditional receipt provides that the face amount of the policy will be paid before the policy is issued if, at the date of the application (or medical examination, if one is required), the applicant met the insurer's requirements for insurability. To illustrate: Marc Steer applies for a $10,000 policy that requires no medical examination. He pays the premium for the first year and leaves the agent's office. Thinking the elevator has arrived, he steps into the elevator shaft and tumbles 32 stories to his death. If the insurer would have approved Marc for life insurance (except for the technicality that he is now dead), the insurer would pay the face amount of the policy.

Under a second type of conditional receipt, protection begins when the application and other accompanying documents have been approved at the home office. This type of conditional receipt is more restrictive—it offers no protection for the time between the filing of the application and its approval. Had Marc been given this form of conditional receipt, his 32-story fall would have produced no insurance benefits—though Marc was in the best of health before being shafted.

In 1965 a New Jersey court ruled that if the premium accompanies the life insurance application, the policy is in effect from that moment until the applicant is notified of rejection.[3] This ruling means that if the premium is paid with an application, the subject has life insurance immediately regardless of the underwriting standards of the insurer. This ruling places greater underwriting responsibil-

[3] 208 A.(2d) 638 (1965). The California Supreme Court made a similar ruling.

ity on the agent. The ruling expresses an increasing though minority view of what these courts consider just and equitable. If the premium does not accompany the application, the insurer has only an invitation to make an offer by issuing the policy. The offer is accepted when the policy is delivered to the applicant (if healthy) and the premium is paid.

Silence on the part of the offeree ordinarily does not mean acceptance. In most jurisdictions, silence is rejection, but some jurisdictions hold insurers negligent (and subject to damages) for failure to act on an application within a reasonable time. (But the majority opinion holds that the policyowner must cancel the coverage within a reasonable time after receiving a renewal policy. Otherwise the delay is interpreted as acceptance; and the policyowner is liable for the premium for the period covered.) When buying life insurance, the applicant should pay the first premium to take advantage of the protection given by the conditional receipt.

Competent Parties

Insurance contracts to be valid must be made by competent parties. Two problems arise with insureds: minors and the mentally incompetent. Only one problem could develop with insurers: have they complied with the necessary regulations to permit them to write the insurance?

Minors

A contract made by a minor with an insurer is voidable at the minor's option. However the insurer must honor the contract unless disaffirmed by the minor. The minor may disaffirm after reaching majority. The disaffirmation must occur within a reasonable time and before committing an act constituting ratification of the contract (i.e., conduct indicating approval or satisfaction with the contract). No reason for disaffirming need be given.

An exception to the general rule applies to contracts made for necessaries. These obligations may not be disaffirmed because the law holds minors (the law calls them infants) responsible for *the reasonable value* of necessaries furnished them. Because insurance has not generally been considered a necessity for minors, insurance contracts can be disaffirmed by a minor. Most courts hold that, upon disaffirming the contract, the minor is entitled to a return of all premiums paid without deducting the value of the insurance protection received for the time the policy was in force.

Necessaries are whatever is needed (measured by age and position in life) for the minor's subsistence (e.g., food, clothing, shelter, medical service, education and even an auto if needed to earn a living). Necessaries are distinguished from necessities in that the latter is considered the basic minimum *essential for existence.*

Many states have enacted statutes that reduce the age at which contracts for life and health insurance bind minors. These statutes usually apply only to minors contracting for insurance on their own lives for the benefit of their father, mother, husband, wife, child, brother or sister. The reduced ages range from 14½ to 16, with 14½ the most common.

Mentally incompetent

A person officially declared insane is not legally competent and may not make a valid insurance contract or any other contract. A contract made with a mentally incompetent person not yet officially declared incompetent is voidable at that person's option. The test of insanity is the ability to understand the nature of the transaction. The rigid application of this test to insurance buyers might expand the numbers eligible for admission to mental institutions.

Insurers

The insurer also must have the legal capacity to contract. For the corporate insurer this capacity is expressed in its charter or articles of incorporation. Where agreements made with legally incompetent insurers are void by statute, the insurer is held liable only for a return of premiums. The corporate officers responsible for the *ultra vires* act are subject to personal liability under the contract. Most courts uphold the insured's agreement with a legally incompetent insurer if the agreement was made by the insured in good faith and without knowledge of the insurer's incompetency. The insured cannot be expected to know whether the insurer has complied with the regulations for legal competency. If an otherwise competent insurer writes insurance contracts in a state without complying with that state's laws, it is bound by these contracts but its responsible officers are subject to penalties.

Legal Purpose

Not only do courts refuse to enforce a contract with an illegal purpose, but they also refuse to enforce an insurance contract that promotes results contrary to the public interest. Thus insurance written against arrest of a safecracker while attempting a burglary would be illegal and unenforceable. No valid contract can be made to cover goods held illegally. The illegality of an enterprise does not prohibit covering articles that do not enter directly into the illegal aspect of the business. Valid fire insurance may be bought on furniture in an illegal gambling house, although insurance covering the croupier's equipment might be questionable. After much legal wrangling, the courts held that fire insurance can be written on furniture in a house of prostitution.

Consideration

No contract is valid unless each party gives value or assumes some obligation to the other. Insurance contracts often state that the insured's consideration is "the provisions and stipulations herein and of the premium specified." This statement does not mean the premiums must be paid before the policy is effective. Most property and liability policies are in force before premium payments are received. The promise to pay is the consideration. The insurer's consideration is the promise to pay if a covered loss occurs.

CHARACTERISTICS OF THE INSURANCE CONTRACT

Certain characteristics are peculiar to insurance contracts or are found in few contracts other than insurance.

Aleatory Contract

Contracts may be either **commutative** or **aleatory.** Most contracts are commutative: each party gives up goods or services presumed to be of equal value. The insurance contract, however, is aleatory: the contracting parties realize that the dollar amount to be exchanged will not be equal. If a loss is suffered, a much larger amount may be received from the insurer than was paid in premiums, and if no loss is suffered (the more likely outcome), nothing will be paid. The distinguishing feature of an aleatory contract is the presence of chance. This characteristic does not mean that the buyer pays more or less than the insurance is worth or that the insurer collects more or less than the anticipated amount needed to conduct its business. The insurer expects to collect enough in premiums to pay its claims and expenses.

Contract of Adhesion

In contrast to a bargaining contract, the insurance contract usually is a contract of **adhesion.** The agreement is usually prepared by lawyers, representatives of the insurer or perhaps by state regulatory bodies and offered to the prospective insured on a take it or leave it basis. The typical applicant can make no counterproposal or suggest that the insurer alter a provision or change a word. However, insureds may have their coverage altered within limits by standard endorsements or riders; but they must select their coverage from standard policies and forms provided by the insurer. This characteristic of the contract benefits the insured if the contract becomes a subject of litigation. Courts rule that because the insurer drew up the contract any ambiguity in it must be interpreted in favor of the insured. This principle has resulted in long, explicit and seemingly repetitious policy exclusions.

For example, the exclusions for liability coverage in a homeowners policy were hastily revised after the following case was tested. A young boy picked the lock on a sleek aircraft to take it on a flight. Because he was not a trained pilot (or even an untrained one!) his takeoff attempt ended in a crash causing a total loss to the plane. The young boy was an ''insured'' under his parents' homeowners policy (see Chapter 8). That policy covers personal liability claims subject to specific exclusions. One exclusion eliminated coverage if the property causing the damage was in the care, custody or control of the insured. The family's insurer said no coverage was available because the plane was in the control of the insured. However, the court ruled that the insurer was obligated under the policy because the young man was clearly not in control of the aircraft. Otherwise, the crash would never have occurred. Consequently, the insurer added the following words to this exclusion: ''or as to which the insured is for any purpose exercising physical control.''

The rule of interpreting ambiguity in favor of the policyowner has deep historical roots. On June 18, 1536, Richard Martin, a marine underwriter whose principal place of business was the Old Drury Ale House in London, suggested to some of his underwriting companions that they might extend their business to include insuring human life. He had in mind one of their fellow drinking companions, William Gybbons (described as a ''hail-fellow-well-met sort of individual, robicund of jowl, healthy of person, and apparently destined to live the full biblical 'three score and ten' ''). Martin, with confidence in his judgment elevated either by a series of lucky underwritings or the ale, proposed to insure the life of Gybbons for 12 months in an amount of $2,000 for a premium of about $80. Fifteen underwriters joined in the proposal. Gybbons accepted, and, as fate would have it, died on May 29, 1537.

Martin and his associates were so upset by their bad selection that they decided to contest the claim. Their plea to the court was that in insuring Gybbons for ''a period of 12 months,'' they had in mind that the contract was to run for a period of 12 lunar months of 28 days each. Thus, the policy had expired on May 20. The court was not impressed with this argument and ordered the claim to be paid. To this day, courts have rigorously held to this principle of interpreting any ambiguity in a contract against the underwriters.

Unilateral Contract

Contracts may be **bilateral** or **unilateral.** An exchange of a promise for a promise is bilateral whereas an exchange of an act for a promise is unilateral. In general the insurance contract is unilateral. After the insured has paid the premium only the insurer is exposed to a legally enforceable promise. Except in assessment policies, the insured has made no legally enforceable promises and cannot be held for breach of contract.[4]

Conditional Contract

The insurance contract is **conditional,** requiring the insured to meet specified conditions in order to collect for losses. These conditions are not legally enforceable. A breached condition only makes the insurance uncollectible. Under the fire insurance contract, the insurer promises to indemnify the insured for losses caused by fire. The insured is subject to several conditions concerning filing proofs of loss but is under no legal obligation to do so. However, a proof of loss must be filed for the insured to collect. On the other hand the fire insurer can be forced by law to keep its promise to pay indemnity if the insured has met all the contract conditions. Insureds are under no obligation to continue premium payments if they discontinue the policy. Premium payments must be made only for protection before the date of cancellations.

Utmost Good Faith

Most ordinary contracts are bona fide or **good-faith contracts.** Insurance contracts, however, are contracts *uberrimae fidei,* or contracts of utmost good faith. The greatest degree of good faith is needed in the negotiations before the insurance contract is issued. Insurers rely on information furnished by prospective buyers in deciding whether to write the insurance and the premium to charge. If the information is false or incomplete the insurer may be able to avoid the contract on one of three grounds: warranty violation, misrepresentation or concealment (see Figure 5–1).

Warranties

An insurance **warranty** stipulates that a particular statement in the policy about the subject of the insurance is true. Thus, in a theft insurance contract if the insured agrees to keep the doors locked while the house is unattended that promise is a warranty. If the insured states in the policy that a watchdog is used, that statement also is a warranty. Noncompliance with a warranty, or a falsely warranted statement, furnishes grounds for the insurer to avoid the contract. A warranty is presumed to be material.[5] To avoid the contract the insurer need prove only that a warranty has been violated. Although the actual conditions may be more favorable to the insurer than those warranted, a breached warranty still gives ground for avoidance.

Two types of warranties are **promissory** and **affirmative.** A promissory warranty states that a fact is presently true and will continue to be true. The affirmative warranty states that a fact is true but makes no statement about the future. If an insured obtains a special rate for fire insurance because of the installation of an automatic sprinkler system, that system must be kept in good working order throughout the life of the contract. If a fire occurs and the sprinkler system was not in good order, the insurer can avoid the claim because the warranty would

[4] A few insurers known as assessment companies reserve the right to assess policyowners additional premiums under specified circumstances. See Chapter 19.

[5] A statement is considered to be material if it affects the insurer's underwriting and rating decision.

FIGURE 5–1

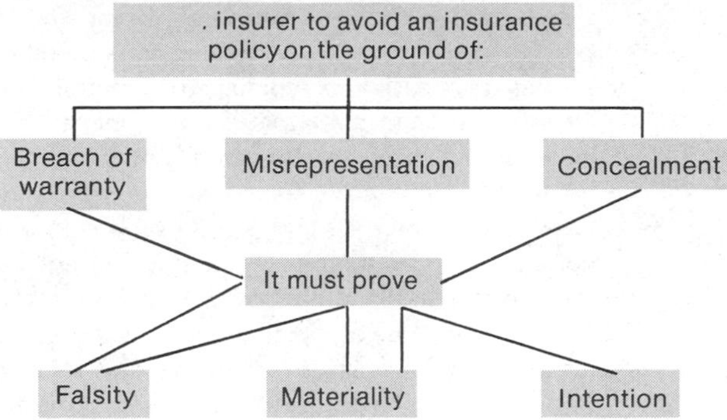

be held to be promissory. In the absence of clear proof that a warranty is intended to be promissory, the courts will construe it to be an affirmative warranty.

Generally a warranty must be written and made a part of the contract either by attaching it to the policy or by a specific reference to it in the policy. An exception is in marine insurance where three warranties not written in the contract are implied: (1) the ship is seaworthy; (2) it moves on the customary course between the ports named and (3) it is used for a legal purpose. Deviation is permitted only to avoid storms or for errands of mercy. Because the shipper usually has no knowledge of the ship that will carry the goods, these warranties are generally removed by the insurer from cargo policies.

The common-law doctrine of warranty has been softened by the courts' refusal to consider as warranties immaterial statements not formally warranted. For a statement to be formally warranted it must be introduced by the words *it is warranted that* or *provided that.* Otherwise the statement is considered informal and not a warranty.

The doctrine of warranties is further softened in most jurisdictions by liberal interpretations. Most courts interpret warranties liberally where a literal application shows only a superficial breach affecting the risk insignificantly. For example, an insured warranted that a security guard would always be on duty. Suppose a reliable guard left the premises to use the "John/Jill" next door because the home-based facilities were temporarily out of order. A literal interpretation of this warranty would allow the insurer to avoid the insurance contract; a liberal interpretation would preserve the insurance coverage.

Representations

Representations, as distinguished from warranties, are not a part of the contract but are statements made by the applicant to the insurer in the process of obtaining a policy. Representations may be oral or included in a written application. Oral representations, however, are difficult to prove.

Unlike the warranty, no presumption is made that a representation is material. If the contract becomes a subject of litigation the insurer has the burden of proving the materiality of a representation. The insurer must show that if the truth had been known the policy would not have been issued. Therefore, representations need be false *and* material to furnish grounds for rescission.

A second difference is that although warranties must be absolutely true any representation dealing with the applicant's belief, intention or opinion need only be substantially true. Unless given fraudulently, opinions cannot be used by the insurer as a basis for avoiding the contract regardless of their materiality. For example, an applicant writes in an application for life insurance that no change in employment is contemplated. Suppose that at the same time his wife was buying two one-way tickets to Africa where she decided (without his knowledge) they would open a safari business. The insurer will not be able to avoid the contract because the representation was not fraudulent.

An increasing number of court decisions tend to blur the distinction between misrepresentation of opinion and misrepresentation of fact by ruling that the insured's duty is performed by making representations "to the best of his (or her) knowledge and belief." These decisions are especially prevalent in disputes involving life insurance. They are accomplished principally by interpreting representations as statements of opinion rather than statements of fact where the slightest doubt exists.

Concealment

Concealment is the failure to disclose known facts when obligated to do so. Because insurance is a contract of utmost good faith, the insured must reveal to the insurer every fact material to the contract, subject to several qualifying conditions: the insured must be aware of the fact, know it is material and understand that the insurer has no knowledge of it.[6] In addition, deceiving of the insurer must be the motive for silence. Consequently an insurer is not permitted to avoid the contract unless the fact concealed not only was obviously material but also was concealed by the insured with intent to defraud. Furthermore, courts place the burden of proof on the insurer.

Even if the insured knows a fact to be material, failure to disclose it does not always constitute fraud. The insured is under no obligation to disclose facts of common knowledge or facts that the insurer is expected to know. If a singles' bar near a college campus is known as a hangout for unruly students, its insurer probably would not be successful in an attempt to avoid a claim for a fire loss on the grounds that the proprietor did not reveal that these students were the principal customers. Finally, the motive for silence may be solely that of protecting the applicant's reputation and not one of deceiving the insurer. The courts in some cases have accepted that there are certain matters that gentlefolks should not be expected to talk about regardless of their materiality to the risk.

Statutory modification

In many states a softening of the warranty and misrepresentation doctrines developed from judicial interpretation and statute. Under one type of statute, the **entire-contract statute,** the policy and the application attached to it shall constitute the entire contract between the parties. These statutes are found in many states but are usually limited to life and health insurance. Their effect is to prevent the insurer from using the insured's misrepresentations as grounds for avoiding the policy unless these representations are written in an application as a part of the policy.

Statements written in an application and incorporated into the policy become warranties. To relieve the insured of the adverse effects of the stricter interpretation of warranties over representations, statutes require that all statements made by

[6] These three qualifying conditions apply only to nonmarine insurance. In the United States, marine insurance adheres to the strict interpretation that failure to reveal a material fact, whether or not with intent to defraud, will give grounds for avoidance.

the insured in the application shall be deemed representations and not warranties. Most of these statutes apply to life insurance only or are restricted to life and health insurance. Their effect is to require the insurer to prove the materiality and falseness of statements when seeking to avoid a policy on breach of warranty grounds.

In a few states the common law has been modified by statute so that no breach of warranty or misrepresentation can be used to avoid a contract unless the violation caused or contributed to the loss or increased the hazard. Thus if the applicant says her mother died at age 98 from overexertion on the dance floor when she really died of cancer at age 53, the insurer cannot use this statement to deny a claim if the insured's subsequent death was caused by colliding mopeds. (In California the American common law of concealment is modified by a statute making concealment, intentional or unintentional, grounds for avoidance of the contract.)[7]

Personal Contract

The **property insurance contract** is as personal as a wedding contract. Both the insured and the insurer rely on utmost good faith in the character, conduct and credit of each other in negotiating the contract. Although in common parlance a certain piece of property is spoken of as "insured" the property owner, not the property, is insured. The insurance is not attached to the property and does not pass with it to a new purchaser without approval from the insurer. However, a life insurance policy is not a personal contract. A new owner of a life insurance policy does not affect the risk. Therefore, all or some of its benefits may be transferred without the permission of the insurer. Once a loss has occurred, an insurance contract of any type becomes solely a money claim and therefore is freely transferable.

Principle of Indemnity

Property and liability insurance contracts in general are contracts of **indemnity;** they provide for compensating the insured only for the amount of the loss or damage. One problem in applying the indemnity principle is measuring the exact amount of compensation that will avoid profit or loss from the event insured against.

Because the value of a human life cannot be measured, life insurance policies are not contracts of indemnity but contracts to pay the face amount of the policy upon the subject's death.

Health insurance may be written as an indemnity contract, particularly for medical care. Group health insurance contracts (see Chapter 16) contain coordination-of-benefits clauses that prevent insureds from collecting more than their losses. However, the lack of coordinated benefits among individual health insurance policies allows insureds double dipping, i.e., collecting from more than one insurer for the same loss. Furthermore, when a person is injured by the negligent act of another, the injured person may collect twice for the same loss: (1) from the health insurer and (2) from the person causing the injury (assuming a successful tort action).

In property insurance the indemnity principle may be defeated by the use of valued policies that provide payment of a specified amount for a total loss. Many policies covering objects of art are written on a valued-policy basis. While

[7] Vol. 42, sec. 330, Annotated Calif. Codes.

valued policies in fire insurance are illegal in most states, some states have valued-policy laws requiring an insurer to pay the face amount of the policy for a *total loss of real property* regardless of its actual cash value at the time of the loss.

Two important doctrines arise from the principle of indemnity: insurable interest and subrogation.

Insurable interest

The principle of **insurable interest** is basic to the structure of insurance. In property insurance an exposure to a financial loss must exist to create an insurable interest. The law requires an insurable interest so that insurance policies are neither gambling devices nor tools in the hands of those who would profit by deliberately destroying the property of others. In life insurance an insurable interest is any reasonable expectation of financial loss caused by the death of the person whose life is insured.

Insurable interest in property insurance

Anyone owning a house, furniture or an auto has an insurable interest in that property. Less obvious are insurable interests based on other relationships. An expectation of benefit from the continued existence of property is sufficient to support an insurable interest if the expectation is based on a legal right. A mortgagee has an insurable interest in the property pledged as security for a debt. A TV mechanic holding a lien on a television set while awaiting payment for charges has an insurable interest in the set. Possession may give the holder of goods an insurable interest. Thus, a bailee has an insurable interest (called a representative interest) in goods left in its care and custody. One who buys stolen goods in good faith has an insurable interest in those articles. A business has an insurable interest in profits it could lose if another person's property, e.g., the plant of a principal supplier or of a customer, is damaged. The insurable interest is in its own profits and not in its customer's or supplier's plant.

Legal liability from a tort or a breached contract exposes an individual or firm to loss. Therefore, the person or business has an insurable interest in protecting its assets from claims of others.

Legally, the insurable interest need be present only at the time of the loss. However, insurers have underwriting rules that prohibit writing policies if an insurable interest does not exist or if it is apparent that none will develop in the near future. In those instances where insurance is bought before acquiring the property, e.g., insurance covering furniture to be bought for a new home, the insurer will indemnify the named insured if an insurable interest exists at the time of the loss.

The amount of the insurable interest is generally measurable and usually sets a maximum limit the insured can collect following a loss. A $125,000 policy covering the insured's $110,000 house is valid because ownership satisfies the insurable interest requirement. But the maximum amount the insured can be paid following a loss is $110,000.

Insurable interest in life insurance

A person has an insurable interest in the life of another if a financial benefit is expected from the continuation of that life. This expectation need not have a legal basis as in property insurance. Thus, a *general* creditor has an insurable interest in the life of the debtor but not in any specific property of the debtor.

The doctrine of insurable interest does not apply when a person buys a policy on his or her own life. Although others may suffer a loss from the death of the insured, the deceased is in no position to incur a financial loss or, indeed, a loss of any kind.

To understand insurable interest in life insurance, three terms are useful: **subject, owner** and **beneficiary.** The subject is the person whose death causes the policy's proceeds to be payable. The owner is the one who has the authority to exercise all rights in the policy, e.g., the right to receive policy dividends, assign the policy, surrender the policy, change the policy's beneficiary and execute a policy loan. The owner usually is the purchaser of the policy. The beneficiary is the person entitled to the policy's proceeds. All three parties or any two parties can be the same person.

To illustrate: when Mike Carrington buys insurance on his own life and names himself (that is, his estate) beneficiary he is the subject, owner and beneficiary. If he retains all incidents of ownership but names his creditor, Walter Wagner beneficiary, he is both owner and subject. If he buys insurance on the life of his debtor Frank Murphy and names himself beneficiary he is both owner and beneficiary. If he buys insurance on the life of his employee, Ray Albert, and names Ray's estate beneficiary but retains the incidents of ownership, Ray is the subject and the beneficiary of the insurance. And if Mike buys insurance on the life of his father, names his mother beneficiary and retains the incidents of ownership the subject, owner and beneficiary are three different people. *The rule of insurable interest is that either the owner or the beneficiary must have an insurable interest in (or actually be) the subject of the insurance.* So Mike may buy insurance on the life of anyone and name a third person as beneficiary if either Mike or the beneficiary has an insurable interest in the subject. The rule is called the subject-owner-beneficiary rule, or the SOB rule.

At one time courts held that insurable interest in life insurance occurred only when the policy buyer could prove a monetary interest in the continued life of the subject. The widely accepted principle now is that closeness of blood or legal relationship creates a sufficient presumption of insurable interest without requiring proof of financial ties.

INNERSCRIPT: BORDERLINE CASES

What about love and affection without a close blood relationship—two gay men or women, for example, or a close blood relationship without love and affection such as Cain and Abel? Are these relationships sufficient in themselves to support an insurable interest? The courts have not answered this question, but logic suggests (1) love and affection between nonrelated persons would be insufficient and (2) a close blood relationship without love and affection would also be insufficient. An actual or factual expectation of an economic benefit from the continuation of the life of the insured would appear to be necessary in these relationships.

Although one person has an insurable interest in the life of another, the prospective buyer is not allowed to buy insurance on that person's life without the subject's consent. Exceptions are made in some jurisdictions that allow spouses to buy insurance on the lives of each other without the consent of the covered person, and a parent to buy insurance on the lives of minor children without their consent.

Insurable interest is required only at the inception of the policy; it is not required at the time the policy matures. Generally the amount of insurable interest is impossible to measure in life insurance. Furthermore, life insurance policies are not contracts of indemnity. So the law holds that the amount of interest is unimportant and has no relationship to the amount payable under the policy. If an insurable interest is present when the policy is issued, the contract will be honored for its face amount. The one exception is life insurance bought by a creditor on the life of a debtor. In most jurisdictions the face amount of the insurance must bear a reasonable relationship to the size of the debt when the policy is written. What is reasonable is a matter for the courts. The courts have been liberal in allowing amounts that exceed the debt so the creditor would have adequate insurance to offset the unpaid principal, the insurance premiums paid and the interest on both the debt and the accumulated premiums.

Subrogation

Most insurance policies provide that the insurer can require the insured to assign all rights of recovery against another party who caused the loss for the amount the insurer paid the insured for the loss. This requirement is called **subrogation.** If a loss is caused by the insured's own negligence subrogation does not apply. The right of subrogation gives the insurer only the right of action held by the insured. Even the bar association president would find it difficult to convince insureds to bring suit against themselves.

To permit the insured to collect the proceeds of a policy from the insurer and to collect again from the person responsible for the loss would be contrary to the principle of indemnity. Suppose that Wi Saeng-Kim crashes into April Klein's parked automobile one morning when he is rushing his daughter to a Little League game. If Saeng-Kim pays April's loss in full she may not collect from her insurer. On the other hand, if April applies to her insurer for indemnity under her collision policy she will not be allowed to retain Saeng-Kim's payment except for the amount not paid by her insurer, the deductible for example. However, April's insurer will be entitled to payment from Saeng-Kim for the amount it paid under April's policy.

If insurers were not allowed subrogation rights, either (1) insureds could collect twice for the same loss or (2) tortfeasors could escape liability to pay a loss for which they are responsible. Neither alternative is in the public interest. A reasonable solution is to allow the insurer to collect from the wrongdoer under the right of subrogation.

INNERSCRIPT: SUBROGATION CLAUSES

Subrogation is a right in equity independent of the contract. A basic legal principle (other than in life and health insurance) is that the insurer who pays a claim to an insured is entitled to all the insured's legal and equitable rights of action against responsible third parties. However, where applicable, insurers include a subrogation clause in their policies stating that the insurer can require

an assignment of recovery rights from the insured any party responsible for the loss. The purpose of the clause is to discourage the insured from signing away an important right that would accrue to the insurer; subrogation cannot give the insurer any right the insured no longer has. According to the subrogation clause if the insured waives the subrogation right after the insurance contract becomes effective the right to receive indemnity from the insurer also is waived.

Many policies contain subrogation clauses although subrogation claims are not so frequent in liability as in property coverages. In liability insurance the opportunity for subrogation arises when the insured is held liable for the negligence of another. For example, if an employer is held liable for an accident involving an employee who is using the family automobile, the employer's nonownership automobile liability insurer will pay the loss and then proceed against the employee's insurer for reimbursement. A workers' compensation insurer can proceed against a third party who negligently causes injury to a covered employee.

Life and most health insurance contracts do not include subrogation clauses because these policies are not contracts of indemnity. A widow can collect the proceeds from the insurance on her husband's life and retain the benefits from a judgment against the culprit who caused his death. The reason is the court's belief that setting dollar limits on the value of a human life is impossible. Subrogation does not apply in disability income insurance because no accurate method has been developed to determine the monetary value of pain and suffering or the loss of personal services of an individual to other family members. (In bodily liability cases the courts are forced to establish these values but no one believes them to be accurate or even realistic.) The insured, therefore, is allowed to retain both the insurance and the amount collected through legal processes. Furthermore, courts usually hold that large policy limits do not cause insureds to bring about losses deliberately through intentionally inflicted disability. Insurance underwriters disagree. Many well-documented cases of malingering, fake illnesses and self-inflicted injuries among insureds are on record. Therefore underwriters attempt to limit amounts policyowners can collect from disability income insurance to "reasonable" economic losses by limiting the insurance that they will write to those amounts and by including other-insurance clauses in their policies to limit double recovery.

Although no logical basis appears for omitting subrogation clauses from medical expense policies, some insurers do not include them. However, recognizing that medical expense insurance should be written on an indemnity basis as a cost-control measure, an increasing number of insurers are including subrogation clauses in medical expense coverage.

AGENTS AND BROKERS

For the most part, insurance marketing is conducted by agents. An insurance agent is anyone authorized by an insurer to solicit, create, modify or terminate insurance contracts. Also involved in marketing are insurance brokers. An insurance broker solicits and negotiates contracts of insurance for an insured and is the agent of the insured, not of the insurer.

Creation of an Agency Relationship

An agency relationship may be established between principals (e.g., insurers) and agents by mutual assent. This assent usually but not always is given in an express agreement known as an agency contract. However, mutual assent can be reached after a transaction has occurred by one party sanctioning the actions of another, creating an **agency by ratification.** For example, Bob Bray appears to Tony Clements to be acting as an agent for the Antique Car Insurance Company and writes a policy for Tony covering his Maxwell. If it has full knowledge of the facts, the Antique Car Insurance Company may ratify Bob's act either expressly or by conduct that implies ratification. The result is a legal contract that binds all parties.

While an agency relationship between principal and agent usually is created only with the principal's agreement or ratification, special circumstances are construed to deny the principal the right to claim that no agency relationship existed. These circumstances establish a **presumptive agency** based on estoppel—a legal restraint placed on involved parties (in this case insurers) to prevent them from contradicting a previous assertion, act or lack of action (silence) that induces others (in this case insurers) to perform in a manner detrimental to their interest, thus giving legal recognition to the adage, "actions speak louder than words." If the insurer's behavior causes a reasonable person to believe that a particular individual is an agent of the company (e.g., a student uses a sample from a policy kit provided by an insurer to bind it to an insurance contract), a court is likely to hold that a presumption of agency exists. The insurer, therefore, would be prevented from denying a claim on the grounds that no agency relationship had been created.

The Power and Authority of the Agent

Agents' powers rest primarily on the authority granted in the agency contract. However, power to bind the principal extends beyond the contractual authority specifically granted.

Insurance agents have three kinds of authority. First, the agent has the **stipulated** or **expressed authority** given by the terms of the contract with the insurer. The insurer specifies types of insureds, types of coverage and the amount of insurance that may be written.

Second, the agent has **implied authority.** The law gives agents that power the public reasonably may believe them to have. If the public is reasonable in believing an agent has the power to perform some particular act, then the law gives the agent the power. The assumption that a life insurance agent has the right to accept the initial premium with the application is reasonable. Therefore if a life insurer for any reason does not specifically empower an agent to accept the first premium the agent would be granted that right through the doctrine of implied authority. Even if the agency contract stated specifically that the agent was not empowered to collect the first premium, the courts would hold that applicants could pay their initial premiums to the agent unless this restriction had been communicated to every applicant. In disputed issues what is reasonable for the public to believe is decided by the court, not by the policyowner or the insurer, and is resolved on the basis of actions necessary and customary for agents.

Apparent authority goes beyond expressed and implied authority. If agents without expressed or implied authority lead a buyer to believe they have power to bind the insurer, the courts may hold that apparent authority exists. Two conditions must be met to establish apparent authority: (1) the insurer makes no effort to prevent the agent from overstepping his or her authority (in many instances the insurer acquiesces by acting as though the agent has authority) and (2) the buyer has no way of knowing that the agent has overstepped his or her authority. To illustrate, assume that agent Meriden Elizabeth has been told by her company not to write auto insurance on drivers under 25 years of age. Nevertheless she writes auto insurance for an 18-year-old sophomore. By accepting the premium the insurer acquiesces, thus giving the agent power to write auto policies for 18-year-olds.

Responsibility of Principles

Acts of the insurance agent operating within the scope of expressed, implied or apparent authority are viewed as acts of the insurer. The law considers the agent and the insurer as one and the same. Consequently the insurer is legally responsible for the actions of its agents while performing their prescribed duties even if agents make fraudulent assertions unknown to or unauthorized by the insurer. While the insurer may limit the agent's authority and these limitations are binding on the agent, they are not always binding on third parties. Third parties may rely on a "normal" agency relationship. Therefore "unreasonable" limitations on the agent's authority are not binding on insureds unless effectively communicated to them. The court will determine what is "unreasonable and normal" in disputed cases.

Knowledge of the agent is presumed to be knowledge of the insurer. Any factor pertaining to the risk known by the agent is presumed to be known by the insurer. If the insurer's agent knows the applicant's health is seriously impaired by drug abuse, the insurer is presumed to have that knowledge regardless of whether the agent has communicated it. If the insurer issues the policy it is prevented from asserting drug addiction as grounds for challenging the validity of the contract. Insurers have attempted to neutralize this rule of agency law by providing that only statements made in the policy application or declarations are considered knowledge of the insurer, but courts have been in conflict on the validity of these disclaimers.

Brokers as Agents

The broker is an agent of the insured and may bind only the insured; knowledge, actions and assertions of brokers acting within their authority remain with them and their clients and do not extend to insurers.

Unlike payment to the agent, payment of premiums to the broker is not payment to the insurer unless provided by statutes. In some states the broker is made an agent of the insurer for collecting premiums. Also, some states make anyone who solicits insurance and creates a policy the insurer's agent. Insurance buyers, insurers and brokers need to be informed of state law to determine the circumstances that create an agency relationship.

REMEDIES

Remedies have been developed by statutes and legal precedent to apply when disputes arise among parties to insurance contracts regarding rights and obligations. These remedies may be broadly classified as **legal** and **equitable.** The doctrines of waiver and estoppel are important common-law (legal) remedies. Rescission and reformation are important equitable remedies.

Waiver and estoppel provide remedies against unfair consequences of strict adherence to terms of the contract. Liberal interpretation of documents by the courts also provides a legal remedy. If the court considers the language either inconsistent or ambiguous it may reform the contract to reflect the parties' intentions. The application of these legal remedies, however, is limited by the parol evidence rule, discussed later. When an adequate legal remedy is unavailable an effort can be made to achieve justice by a suit in equity. Maxims (principles of conduct) rather than rules of law are used in determining equitable remedies. Decisions in equity are based on natural justice and moral rather than legal rights.

Cases involving legal remedies are decided by juries while suits in equity usually are tried without jury. The belief is that compared to judges, juries are harsher on insurers and are more easily deceived by dishonest policyowners. Therefore insurers are more comfortable in suits in equity than in suits involving legal remedies. Conversely, insureds are more secure seeking legal rather than equitable remedies.

Waiver and Estoppel

Waiver is the relinquishment of a contractual right either directly, indirectly, intentionally or unintentionally. For example, an insurer normally requires payment of the next policy premium prior to renewal. If an insurer mistakenly or otherwise sends an insured a revised declarations page for a new policy period, the insurer waives the right to deny renewal. Thus if the insurer waives this right, as in the foregoing example, the doctrine of **estoppel** would prevent the insurer from successfully asserting that because the premium had not been paid prior to renewal, the policy had not been renewed.

Questions of waiver and estoppel arise largely in matters involving the relationship of agent and policyowner. Sometimes an applicant for a policy will inform the agent of some condition that would seem to be a breach of the policy at its inception. For example, a prospect for auto insurance may indicate that she regularly drives coemployees to work, charges them each a fare and profits from this arrangement. The agent explains that the practice is permissible; or perhaps the agent says nothing, issues the policy and collects the premium.

A loss occurs while the insured is driving to work. When the adjuster learns about the small-scale taxi service and files a report with the home office, the insurer probably will deny liability based on the exclusion "to any automobile while used as a public or livery conveyance." If the insured goes to court, in most jurisdictions the insurer will be forced to pay the claim. These courts rule that the agent's action constituted a waiver of the livery conveyance exclusion and the insurer cannot disclaim liability.

Insureds, however, must not place too much reliance on the courts' leniency in circumstances involving alleged waivers. In judging whether a particular action or inaction constitutes a waiver the courts usually consider a number of questions. Was the insurer or its agent expressing an informal opinion or making a formal statement of fact? Did the agent have the authority to create the alleged waiver? Would the conduct of the insured have been different had there been no reliance on the agent's or the insurer's behavior? How important is the default giving rise to the waiver defense? The answers are not always black and white, and when they are gray different courts will render conflicting decisions.

Parol evidence rule

The **parol** (oral) **evidence rule** places important limitations on the operation of waiver and estoppel by disallowing any evidence that the terms of the policy are other than those written in the contract. The parol evidence rule applies only to contract terms and specifically only to statements made *before* the formal contract is created. For example, a fire insurance policy is issued to cover farm equipment and automobiles at three locations. The face amount of the policy was written for $76,000 with a limit of coverage of $35,000 at the first location, $1,000 at the second and $40,000 at the third. A monthly report was required to show the values at each location. *After* the policy was issued the agent informed the insured that regardless of the limits shown in the policy loss would be settled on the basis of the values shown for each location in the monthly report. The insured had a $60,000 loss at the first location. The asset values shown on the monthly report at the location just before the fire were $60,000. The insured asked $60,000 indemnity. The insurer offered only $35,000, the policy limit at that location. The court said:

> It is well-settled law that an oral agreement cannot vary the terms and provisions of a written contract. It is also well settled that a policy provision to the effect that an agent is not empowered to alter the terms of a policy contract is binding. However, neither of these rules applies here. As a general agent of the insurer, the agent had authority to issue oral binders. His statements to the president of the insured equipment company constituted an oral binder; hence, a new contract was brought into existence and the suit is under such new contract.

The insured was paid $60,000.[8]

Waiver provisions

Many policies include "waiver" or "change" clauses. Insurers are represented by many eager agents who occasionally promise coverage not contemplated by the contract or waive conditions important to the insurer. As a result the previously mentioned waiver clause is inserted in policies for the insurers' protection. For example, the contract clause in a life insurance policy includes the words "only the president, a vice president, or the secretary of the company has authority to alter this contract or to waive any of its provisions." The legal interpretation of the waiver clause is unclear. Although the Supreme Court has held the waiver clause valid, conflicting court decisions are difficult to reconcile.

Oral (parol) waivers may be made prior to, or at the inception of, a contract or after the policy has been issued. Some courts hold that parol waivers made by agents before the contract is issued are not effective. Others hold them binding on the insurers under the theory that the insured did not know the agent's authority was limited and had no reason to believe the agent was acting beyond granted authority.

Rescission

If evidence shows that one party causes another to enter into a contract by fraud or misrepresentation of a material fact, the wronged party may seek the equitable remedy of **rescission**—that is, to have the contract declared void from its inception. To take advantage of this remedy the injured party must act as

[8] *Federal Mutual Implement and Hardware Company* v. *Fairfax Equipment Company,* 261 F.2d 207, U.S. App., 10th Cir., Okla.

soon as the wrong becomes apparent and must return whatever was received under the contract.

Reformation

An important equitable remedy is a suit for **reformation** of the contract. In these suits the parol evidence rule does not apply. Where proof is conclusive that a prior agreement between the insured and the insurer had been reached that—either by mistake on both sides or by a mistake on one and fraud on the other—does not appear in the written contract, the court will correct the mistake by reforming the contract to express the original intention of both parties.

Reformation also can be used by the insurer to rectify mistakes in the policy made in favor of the policyowner. For example, Mr. Hunt and the agent intended to cover a house known as the Byrd Hill dwelling. Instead, the policy was written incorrectly to cover a second house owned by Hunt. The second house burned and Hunt decided to take advantage of the mistake in the policy. The court, however, ordered the policy reformed to conform to the parties' intentions.

SUMMARY

1. An insurance policy is a legal contract establishing the rights and duties of the policyowner and the insurer.
2. Two legal instruments are essential in forming insurance contracts: (1) the application and (2) the binder.
3. Oral applications are customary in property-liability insurance. Therefore, policies require declarations to provide information about the risk.
4. Binders are not used in life insurance because life agents are not contract-writing agents (they do not have power to bind the insurer).
5. To create an insurance contract an offer and acceptance must be made by competent parties for a legal purpose and valuable consideration.
6. The insurance contract is aleatory; it involves an unequal exchange of values between insurer and insured.
7. The insurance contract is a contract of adhesion; the insurer sets the policy terms and the buyer agrees to them without modification.
8. The insurance contract is unilateral; after the premium is paid, only the insurer is obligated to act.
9. The insurance contract is conditional; the insured cannot collect unless he or she meets certain conditions. These conditions are not legally enforceable.
10. The insurance contract is a contract of utmost good faith; an insurer who writes a policy relies on the applicant's honesty. Any false information may be grounds for avoiding the contract.
11. A warranty is a stipulation in the policy that a given statement about the subject of the insurance is true. If the insured makes a false warranty, the insurer is not obligated to pay for a loss.
12. Warranties are promissory and affirmative. Promissory warranties state a fact is true and will continue to be true. Affirmative warranties state a fact is true but make no statement about the future.

13. Breached warranties are always material and are grounds for avoiding a contract.
14. Representations are not part of the contract and are not presumed to be material. They are either oral or written and need only be substantially true.
15. Concealment is failure to disclose material facts when obligated to do so. To be grounds for avoiding a contract; the facts concealed must be material, the buyer must know the insurer is unaware of the facts and the intention is to deceive the insurer.
16. Property-liability policies are contracts of indemnity; life insurance policies are not contracts of indemnity but contracts to pay the face amount of the insurance.
17. Insurable interest is present when there is exposure to a financial loss.
18. In life insurance the policyowner or beneficiary must have an insurable interest in the subject (unless the subject is either the owner or beneficiary).
19. Subrogation is the insurer's right to recover damages from a third party. Subrogation prevents insureds from collecting twice for the same loss. The subrogation clause requires the insured to assign subrogation rights to the insurer.
20. An agency relationship is created by:
    a. An explicit agreement in the contract.
    b. An agency by ratification: the insurer approves an agent's action thereby binding itself to the contract.
    c. A presumptive agency: when a reasonable person would believe the agent has the power to act for the insurer in a given matter.
21. Agents have the authority expressed in their contract and the implied and apparent authority determined by law.
22. The law considers the agent and the insurer one and the same. Therefore knowledge of the agent is knowledge of the insurer.
23. Unless provided by statutes brokers cannot bind the insurer. Brokers act as agents for the insured.
24. Legal remedies to insurance contracts are waiver and estoppel. Equitable remedies are reformation and rescission.
25. Legal remedies involve jury trials in courts of law. Equitable remedies are tried by judges in courts of equity.
26. Waiver is the giving up of a legal right. Estoppel prevents an insurer from using a waived right to assert a claim on the insured.
27. The parol evidence rule applies to statements made before the formal contract is created and prevents using any such oral evidence to avoid the contract. Oral evidence is anything not written in the contract.
28. Rescission declares a contract void from its inception.
29. Reformation changes the contract to express each party's original intentions.

REVIEW QUESTIONS

1. Why is a precise definition of an insurance contract so difficult to develop?
2. What policy instruments are necessary to form an insurance contract?
3. Are insurance applications oral or written?
4. What is a binder? Why are binders generally not used by life insurance agents?
5. What four elements are essential to form an insurance contract?
6. Explain the following characteristics of an insurance contract:
   a. Aleatory.
   b. Contract of adhesion.
   c. Unilateral.
   d. Conditional.
   e. Utmost good faith.
7. What is a warranty? Explain four different kinds of warranties.
8. What grounds can an insurer invoke to avoid a policy? Explain.
9. What is the subject-owner-beneficiary rule?
10. How is an agency relationship created?
11. What three kinds of authority do agents have?
12. What are legal remedies in insurance? Explain.
13. What are equitable remedies in insurance? Explain.
14. Explain parol evidence. What is the parol evidence rule?
15. Explain the concepts of insurable interest, indemnity and subrogation.

CHAPTER

6 How to read a policy—Some directions

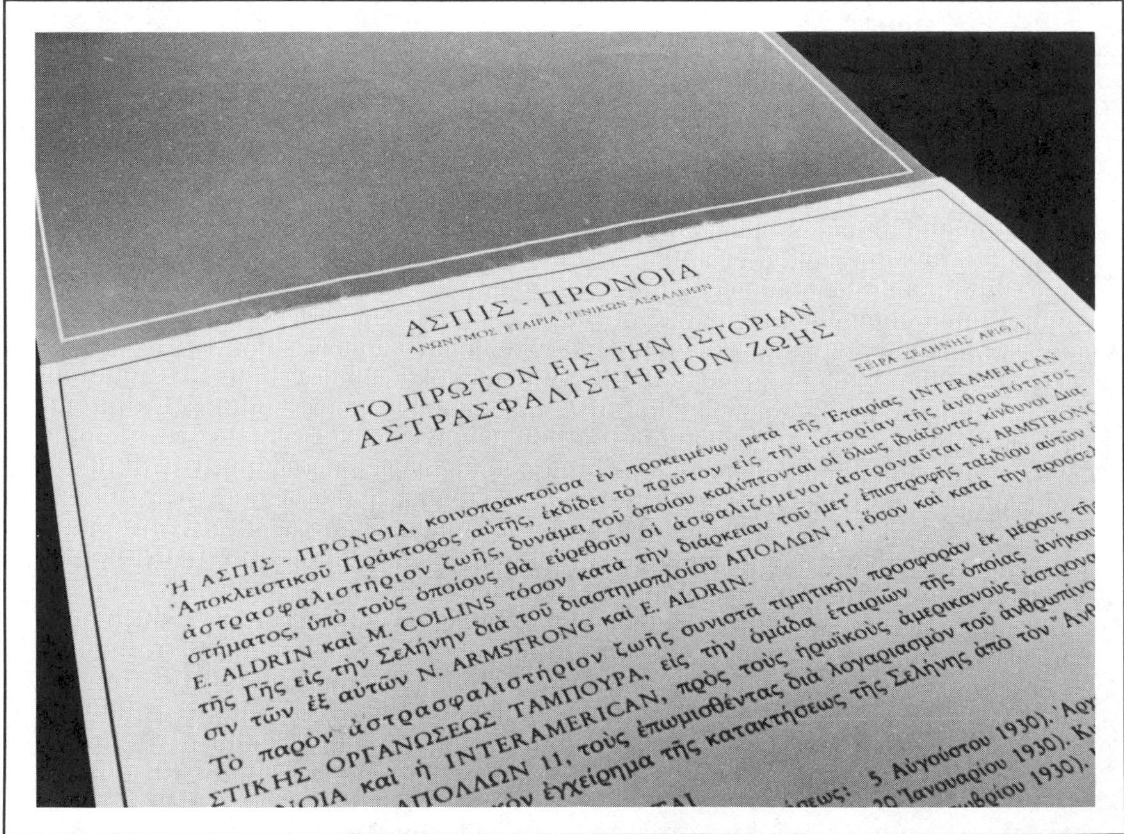

John Thoeming/Richard D. Irwin

CHAPTER OBJECTIVES

1. **To examine the components of an insurance policy: declarations, insuring agreements, exclusions, conditions and endorsements (or riders).**
2. **To develop a procedure for analyzing insurance coverages.**
3. **To explain the issues to be resolved in identifying covered perils.**
4. **To show how policies define the property and losses covered.**
5. **To point out how policies specify the persons covered and the locations covered.**
6. **To indicate how policies designate the duration of coverage and stipulate the covered hazards.**
7. **To describe the policyowner's duties following a loss and the time limits imposed on policyowners for filing suits and on insurers for paying claims.**

Because the insurer is obligated to pay the insured only under circumstances specified in the policy, the policyowner must know the answers to three fundamental questions: "What events are covered?" "How do I get it?" and "How much am I going to get?" The first two questions are discussed in this chapter. The third is considered in Chapter 7.

The answers are in the policy.[1] Even so, owners seldom read their insurance contracts until a loss occurs and often not then. Because losses are few compared with the policies written an insurance contract may be the nation's number one "unread" best seller. As a result a policyowner's first realization that insurance does not cover "everything" comes with notification that a claim has been denied. At this point the policyowner might be advised by "friends" that "what insurance companies give you in big print, they take away in small print."[2] However, if the disappointed policyowner had been forewarned to read the policy both the policyowner and the insurer would benefit: fewer dissatisfied claimants and a better reputation for the insurance industry.

---

[1] The reader would find it helpful to refer to specimen policy forms in the study and discussion of this and the next four chapters. A separate copy of the policy rather than bits and pieces is preferable for discussion of particular clauses because it creates a feel for the contract that cannot be obtained from an isolated clause or by the awkward procedure of referring to policies reproduced in the Appendix. Nevertheless the Homeowners 3 special form and the personal auto policy are reproduced in Appendixes 3 and 4 of this text.

A *Policy Kit for Students of Insurance* is published by the Alliance of American Insurers, 20 N. Wacker, Chicago, Ill. 60606. Another kit is assembled and distributed by the Insurance Information Institute, 110 William Street, New York, N.Y. 10038. The kit published by the Alliance of American Insurers is especially useful because it contains a number of different policies that can be helpful in studying Chapters 10, 11, 12, 14 and 15. The kit prepared by the Insurance Information Institute contains fewer policies but is useful because it permits students to eliminate the annoying and time-consuming problem of flipping back to the Appendix. It is also sufficient for an elementary course, particularly at the junior college level.

[2] The saying is false. Most states have laws providing that "conditions" and "exclusions" must be in type at least as large as statements of coverage or, in certain cases, in larger type or even in boldface type.

THE INSURANCE POLICY

An insurance policy is the contract between the policyowner and the insurer. It may be a short, uncomplicated agreement like the limited-coverage accident policy newspapers offer with subscriptions or a long, complex document with agreements insuring properties throughout the world. Regardless of length and complexity the policy defines the rights and duties of the contracting parties.

The Policy Form

Insurance policies all have the same components: declarations, insuring agreements, exclusions and conditions. Many policies also have endorsements or riders.

Declarations

Declarations are descriptive material relating to subjects covered, persons insured, premiums charged, period of coverage, policy limits and warranties or promises made by the insured regarding the nature and control of the hazard. Declarations are discussed in Chapter 5.

Insuring agreements

The insuring agreements broadly define coverages in an insurance policy. For example, in most liability policies these agreements cover claims arising from the insured's negligence. They promise to defend any liability suit brought against the insured if the coverage applies.

The definitions of important policy terms may also be found in insuring agreements. In the new readable *Personal Auto Policy* developed by the Insurance Services Office (ISO) a section is devoted to definitions, e.g., "your covered auto," "trailer," "family member," "occupying," "covered person," "uninsured motor vehicle" and "collision." When used in the policy these terms appear in boldface type.

Exclusions

Exclusions reduce the broad coverage provided in the insuring agreements. When reading their policies policyowners soon find that some of what the insurer gave in the insuring agreements, it hath taken away in the exclusions. Insurers modify insuring agreements to: (1) facilitate management of physical and moral hazard, (2) eliminate duplicate coverage in other policies the policyowner may have, (3) eliminate coverage not needed by the typical policyowner even though important to some, (4) eliminate uninsurable exposures and (5) eliminate specialized coverage that the insurer is not qualified to offer or that requires special underwriting and rating more conveniently handled under other contracts. The positive effect of exclusions is to lower the price of insurance.

Conditions

The ground rules of the transaction are stated in the conditions that control the insurer's liability for covered losses by imposing obligations on the policyowner and insurer. Typical conditions are those related to the policyowner's duties and obligations after a loss, other insurance, subrogation, assignment, cancellation and optional settlements. These conditions and others are discussed later in this and in the next chapter.

Endorsements and riders

Standard or printed policies often do not suit a particular need. To remedy the problem, these policies can often be modified by adding special provisions. In life insurance these provisions are generally called **riders;** in property and liability insurance they are usually called **endorsements.** Endorsements and riders are used to complete a contract, alter coverages to meet particular needs and change policies in effect.

A PROCEDURE FOR ANALYZING INSURANCE COVERAGE

The main purpose of this chapter is to give the reader a procedure to use in analyzing the coverage under *any* insurance policy. The *procedure,* rather than the specific details, is the important consideration. It is used to analyze in depth a homeowners policy (HO) in Chapter 8 and the personal auto policy (PAP) in Chapter 9. These two policies are usually the most relevant to college students. Every student belongs to a household and drives a car (or so it seems when a professor tries to cross the street).

For nearly 30 years a series of contracts designated as homeowners policies (HO–1 to HO–8) has proved popular with insurance buyers. The homeowners series provides coverage in two sections: section I covers the real and personal property of the insured; section II provides comprehensive personal liability coverage. The personal auto policy provides broad coverage on autos owned by the family and also protects the family members against liability claims from the use of autos. In no-fault states the personal auto policy includes personal injury protection (PIP).

To determine the protection a policy offers, a systematic approach is useful. Seven questions must be answered to learn if a given event is covered.

1. Is the peril covered?
2. Is the property covered?
3. Is the type of loss covered?
4. Is the person covered?
5. Is the location covered?
6. Is the time period covered?
7. Are there hazards that exclude or suspend coverage?

If the answer is "no" to *any* of these questions the event is not covered. Finding the answers requires a thorough reading of the policy. In some policies coverage may appear to be found only to be lost by a subsequent exclusion. However, one should not stop at this point because the coverage may be reinstated by a supplementary coverage clause, an endorsement or rider or by an exclusion to an exclusion found later in the policy (all so very simple, isn't it?).

In addition, four other questions are important to the policyowner in analyzing a policy.

1. What are the policyowner's duties after a loss?
2. What are the insurer's options in settling a loss?
3. What are the time limits for the policyowner to bring suit against the insurer?
4. What are the time limits for the insurer to pay a claim?

These two groups of questions are discussed in this chapter. A final question, the amount of coverage, is the subject of the next chapter.

DEFINING THE PERILS COVERED

Determining if a peril is covered requires policyowners to check the policy to see whether it is a specified peril or an all-risk contract. When perils are named (either as covered or not covered) their meaning must be defined. Furthermore, limitations on covered perils have to be identified. Finally, the question of whether the peril is the proximate cause of the loss needs to be resolved.

Specified Perils and All-Risk Contracts

Peril is defined as the cause of loss. Typical insurable perils are fire, windstorm, explosion, burglary, negligence, collision, accident, sickness and death. Policies may cover one or more perils. Policies that name the perils covered are called **specified perils contracts** while those that cover all perils except those specifically excluded are called **all-risk contracts.**

Interpreting the Peril

In addition to knowing by name the covered perils the insured must know what the perils mean. What are the meanings of the words **fire, collision, riot, accident** and **smoke?** The insurance meaning may differ from everyday usage.

The principal source of information is the policy. Definitions are given for key terms in the homeowners policies and the personal auto policy. In contrast the fire policy contains no definition of terms—not even a definition of fire. For the meaning of terms not defined in the policy policyowners must look either to statutory provisions or court decisions.

Consider the story of the person who bought a box of expensive cigars, insured them against loss by fire, smoked them and then filed a claim with the fire insurer. The insurer denied the claim and the case went to court. Legend has it that the judge ordered the insurer to pay the claim because the cigars were destroyed by fire. The insurer paid the claim and had the insured jailed for arson. This storybook insured could not have collected because of an old court ruling.

Long ago the courts decided that the policy meaning of *fire* is restricted to one that is hostile or unfriendly, that is, one that has left its intended receptacle. A friendly fire is one located where it should be—a fireplace, stove or at the end of a cigar. But if a friendly fire leaps from the fireplace onto a table where a box of cigars is located the fire becomes unfriendly and any fire damage is covered by the fire policy.

For there to be a fire—either friendly or unfriendly—sufficiently rapid combustion must occur to cause ignition. The combustion of a fallen tree in the forest (decay) and the combustion of an iron stake in the ground (rust) are not sufficiently rapid to cause ignition and consequently are not perils covered by the fire policy. A flame or glow is required.[3]

What is the peril under the riot and civil commotion coverage? The contract does not define a riot. Instead the coverage depends on the state law. In one state, for example, riot is defined as an act (unlawful or lawful) committed with force or violence by two or more persons against the person or property of another.[4] Most states have similar laws, except that many require that at least three persons be involved. Even with a legal definition it is not always clear if a riot has occurred. When the court decides the issue the burden of proof is on the insured.

Limitations on the Peril

After a person identifies the covered perils and their meanings the next step is to determine the extent of the coverage against these perils. The coverage may

---

[3] Some insurers pay claims for cigarette burns even though an unfriendly flame is difficult to prove. Insurers also have been liberal in other borderline cases.

[4] Note that *riot* requires the unlawful act to be with force or violence. Courts have held that the damage caused by a group of people does not constitute a riot unless accompanied by force or violence. An unruly crowd of college students who cause damage to the student union building while protesting the construction of a nuclear power plant may be construed to be committing a riotous act.

be limited to specific circumstances. For example, neither all fire nor all smoke damage losses are covered in the homeowners policy although these perils are included as covered perils. Restricted coverage for the smoke peril in the homeowners policy is limited to sudden and accidental damage from smoke, excluding smoke from agricultural smudging or industrial operations. Also, HO policies exclude losses from the insured's neglect to use all reasonable means to protect property when endangered by a covered peril. Consider the case of Howard Ross, who was airing his wife's $10,000 fur coat on his clothesline. While watching the coat Ross noticed that the tortilla parlor next door was on fire. Fascinated by fires, he went for his camera. Upon returning he found the coat destroyed by the fire. Ross's HO insurer denied coverage because Ross failed to protect property endangered by an otherwise covered peril.

The Doctrine of Proximate Cause

The **proximate cause** of a loss is the efficient cause. The proximate cause is not necessarily the cause nearest to the destruction either in time or place but the cause that was responsible for the loss through an unbroken chain of events.

For a loss to be covered the insured peril must be either the proximate cause or be within the chain of events that links the proximate cause to the loss. Assume a pile of oily rags catches on fire in a building covered only by a fire policy. While the damage by the fire is minimal the smoke and water damage is severe. Because the fire was the proximate cause of the loss the insured can collect under his or her fire policy for the smoke and water damage even though those perils were not listed in the policy. The rule is that insureds can collect for some portion of a loss if they have a policy covering *any* of the "causes" of the loss from the proximate to the immediate cause. So when a loss occurs the insured is advised to look back as far as possible (to Adam and Eve if necessary) to find a covered peril that may be a proximate cause of the loss.

Proximate cause in property insurance

Problems involving the doctrine of proximate cause arise most often in property insurance. Most of the discussion has centered on interpretation of the fire policy. Fire fighters are called to put out a fire in a neighbor's house. Through error the fire fighters smash their way into your house. Will your fire policy cover this damage? Yes, say the courts. The hostile fire next door was the proximate cause of the loss. Suppose that on the way to put out the fire in your neighbor's house the fire truck sideswiped your car parked down the street. Is the hostile fire the proximate cause? No, say the courts. Where is the line to be drawn? The courts draw it somewhere between the smashed house next door and the car down the street. Exactly where is their decision.

How remote the fire can be and yet be covered by the fire policy is shown by the landmark case of *Lynn Gas and Electric Company* v. *Meriden Fire Insurance Company*. A fire in a wire tower in a remote part of the building caused a short in electrical wiring, making a machine run too fast, which in turn broke a belt, leaving a flywheel spinning freely. The flywheel flew off its moorings, extensively damaging the machinery and building. The court held the small fire in the distant tower to be the proximate cause of the loss and the insurer had to pay.

Proximate cause in life and health insurance

In life insurance the doctrine of proximate cause has little significance. With the exception of suicide within the policy's first year or two (and the occasional war and aviation restrictions), life insurance covers any cause of death.

In health insurance the doctrine of proximate cause has more significance. A problem arises when the policy contains a requirement that the loss must be "independent of all other causes" or "not contributed to by any other cause." Suppose that an 80-year-old person with severe rheumatism owns an accident policy. While crossing a street the octogenarian, unable to outrun a motorcycle, suffers a broken leg. If the insured had been 20 and healthy the accident might not have happened. Yet the courts invariably rule the accident to be the proximate cause of the injury and ignore age and health factors, stating that "A policy of insurance is not accepted with the thought that the coverage is to be restricted to an Apollo or a Hercules." In an attempt to avoid the **judicial risk** many accident policies require that the accident be the *sole* cause of loss for benefit payments.

DEFINING THE PROPERTY COVERED

Insurance contracts do not cover all the insured's property. They usually define the property protected. Property covered, like perils, may be defined comprehensively or on a specified property basis.

Homeowners policies provide examples both of specified and comprehensive property coverage. To be covered, real property (e.g., the dwelling) must be specified. Personal property is covered on a comprehensive basis, the policy stating that all household and personal property incidental or usual to the occupancy of the dwelling and owned or used by any insured is covered with certain exceptions. (Property exclusions are inappropriate in life and health insurance except, in the latter, for false teeth, artificial limbs and so on.)

DEFINING THE LOSSES COVERED

Losses can be classified as (1) direct: the physical loss of the property; (2) indirect: (*a*) loss of net income caused by the inability to use the damaged property, (*b*) spoilage loss arising from specific perils, e.g., temperature and humidity changes and (*c*) loss of a part of a set or pair (losses *b* and *c* are often referred to as **consequential losses**) and (3) extra-expense losses, like the cost of defending a liability suit and the expenses incurred in obtaining the use of temporary facilities until damaged property is restored. Many policies cover direct losses only; others cover some forms of indirect losses and extra expenses.

In life insurance defining losses covered is simple. The insurer pays the face amount upon the death of the insured. Health insurance contracts may be written to cover medical, surgical and hospital expenses and disability income losses.

In studying the coverage provided by a contract the insured must not overlook the importance of needed and available coverage for indirect and extra expense losses because these losses can damage the financial position of an individual or a business. Business-interruption losses (discussed in Chapter 3) often are more severe than direct losses causing the interruption.

DEFINING THE PERSONS COVERED

Some policies cover only named insureds and their representatives. Representatives include the insured's executors or heirs and receivers in bankruptcy. Other policies, as noted in Chapters 8 and 9, cover persons in addition to named insureds and their representatives. The need to extend the coverage to additional persons is best illustrated by coverage of the interests of mortgagees.

A mortgagee (holder of a mortgage on a piece of property as security for a loan) has an insurable interest in the mortgaged property and can buy insurance to protect that interest. However, a mortgage clause is included in policies bought by a mortgagor (property owner who has borrowed the money and pledged the property to the mortgagee for collateral) to protect the mortgagee. This clause assures that the mortgagee will be indemnified up to the amount of the unpaid mortgage loan. Thus only one policy is necessary to cover two interests.

Under life insurance contracts the insurer agrees to pay the beneficiary upon the death of the named insured. Any number of persons may be beneficiaries. Health insurance policies providing disability income have only one named insured. Health policies covering medical expenses may be written with one named insured, but most frequently are written to cover all immediate family members including the named insured, spouse and all dependent children. The dependency period is usually limited to a maximum age, although some policies modify this limit for students or the mentally or physically incompetent.

INNERSCRIPT: ASSIGNMENT

Policyowners usually have the right to assign (transfer) to other persons some or all the rights they hold on their policies. However, assignment clauses in the policy may place restrictions on the right of assignment. **For some policies written consent of the insurer is required for a valid assignment; for others only notice to the insurer is necessary. Some policies prohibit assignment; others permit assignment freely. Credit insurance is an example of a policy that is not assignable. However, by agreement, proceeds may be payable to a bank, a trust company or some other payee on behalf of the insured. By custom some ocean marine insurance contracts covering cargo are freely assignable because the cargo usually is outside the custody of the insured. Therefore allowing free assignment of cargo policies probably does not increase the moral hazard.**

An assignment of a policy may or may not create a new contract. If the insured transfers ownership of both the covered property and the insurance, no interest is retained in either the property or the insurance. If the insurer agrees to the assignment the majority opinion is that a new contract, subject to the old terms, has been created between the insurer and the assignee and that any prior actions of the assignor cannot affect it, e.g., unpaid premiums.

If the policy is assigned as security for a debt the insured retains an interest in both the property and insurance. The insured is in possession and control of the property and in case of loss may collect insurance proceeds in excess of the amount due the creditor. This type of assignment does not create a new contract. The rights of the assignee are the same as those of the assignor. Both prior

(*continued*)

and subsequent actions of the assignor may invalidate the policy.

Assignment clauses apply only to assignments before a loss. After a loss the policy represents a right of action that may be assigned by the insured without the consent of the insurer. This type of assignment cannot increase the moral hazard. The loss has occurred and the claim is due. The assignment changes only the payee. When the loss is partial only that part of the policy covering the loss may be assigned without consent.

DEFINING THE LOCATIONS COVERED

Insurers limit locations covered. Some policies cover one location only; others include several. In some policies protection is restricted to the United States and Canada; in others coverage is limited to the Western Hemisphere. Some provide worldwide protection.

Protection under a life insurance policy usually is worldwide, although some policies exclude travel in various areas for an initial period. Thus the beneficiary usually may collect no matter where the insured might die. Health insurance policies usually are also worldwide.

DEFINING THE TIME OF COVERAGE

Although many insurance policies are written for one year, some policies are written for longer or shorter periods. Other policies—life insurance for example—may be written for an indefinite duration.

Term of the Policy

One-year policies, called **annual policies,** are written at the basic rate. Property and liability insurance policies written for more than a year, called **term policies,** often are written at a discount. Policy rules and rate manuals indicate which policies may be written for periods longer than a year. Various available budget plans allow policyowners to take advantage of term premiums without making large initial outlays.

Policies written for less than one year, called **short-rate** or **short-term** policies, often are written at higher rates. Auto insurance is an exception. Many insurers write six-month policies and quote semiannual rates to allow for semiannual rate increases when justified and to decrease the unearned premium reserve and thus the drain on surplus (see Chapter 22).

When an insured cancels a policy during its term the premium refund is based on a short-rate table, often printed in the policy. These rates apply to the expired portion of the coverage. Under a typical fire policy, for example, six months' coverage costs 60 percent of the annual premium. In many motorcycle policies the rates are "shorter" and no refund is paid if the policy has been in force at least six months.

Two reasons account for the higher premium on short-term policies. (1) If the expensive acquisition cost is spread over less than a year, the premium must be larger for each day of insurance. (2) Policies for short periods are likely to coincide with the time when the loss exposure is greatest. Therefore a higher daily rate should be charged for protection. If the policy were in force for the year, good experience periods might offset bad ones. Averaging experience under short-term policies might be impossible.

Life insurance is written for an indefinite duration, paying death benefits when the subject reaches age 100 (called whole life policies), or for specified terms, e.g., 1 year, 10 years or to the subject's age 65 (called **term insurance** policies). Health insurance policies usually are written on an annual basis.

Hour of Inception

Most policies run from 12:01 A.M. standard time at the building's premises on the date of inception to 12:01 A.M. standard time at the building's premises on the date of expiration. Note that the governing time zone is the one associated with the building's premises. For example, Teri Biachi loses her clothing in a Los Angeles fire that commenced at 11:00 P.M. Pacific Standard Time on the day before her policy expired. Her residence premises is in Illinois where she bought the policy and there the time was 1:00 A.M. Because the contract had expired in Illinois at 12:01 A.M. (it had expired in Los Angeles at 10:01 P.M.), no coverage was provided. The standard fire policy is from noon to noon.

Effect of Policy Period

Most policies require only that the *onset* of the damage occur during the policy period. This requirement applies not only to direct damage coverage but also to loss-of-use and extra-expense coverage. If Cleora's dwelling catches fire at 11:55 P.M. on the day her policy expires, all insured loss or damage from that fire is covered regardless of the fire's duration. If the home catches fire at 11:55 P.M., however, on the day before her policy is effective, no loss or damage from that fire is covered even though the fire fighters finally extinguish the blaze at 6:30 A.M. on the day the policy is effective.

All life and most health policies written on a continuing basis include a grace period to pay renewal premiums. Protection continues for 31 days after the end of the policy period. Any loss during the grace period is a valid claim.

Cancellation

Most property and liability contracts give both the insurer and policyowner the right to cancel the policy upon written notice before its expiration date. For the policyowner cancellation may be immediate or upon some specified date. The insurer, however, cannot cancel the policy immediately but is required to give the policyowner a minimum number of days before the effective cancellation date. Advance notice by the insurer is required to allow the policyowner time to negotiate for other insurance to take effect at date of cancellation and to prevent an unscrupulous insurer from cancelling the policy when a loss is about to occur.

When the insurer cancels the policy the premium will be refunded on a pro rata basis. If the policyowner cancels, the returned premium is based on a short-rate table and is less than a full pro rata refund. For example, if the annual premium is $480 and the policy is cancelled by the insurer after two months the policyowner is refunded $400 (10/12 of $480). But if the policyowner cancels the policy the short-rate refund is only $350.40.

Cancellation clauses are included in insurance for several reasons. First, these clauses are necessary to give insurers some control over the risk after the contract is written. Circumstances may change or conditions may be discovered that make a risk undesirable. The ability to postselect is important to insurers, allowing them to select "out" as well as "in." The cancellation clause is particularly valuable when an insurer wants to discontinue writing a particular kind of insurance, withdraw from a geographic area or retire from the business. The cancellation clause is also useful when an agent wants the insurer to terminate a policy for nonpayment of premium. Generally insurers do not have to give a reason for cancelling a policy. They do not have to give a reason for rejecting an application either. However, statutes and administrative rulings in many states require insurers to give reasons for cancellation (and nonrenewal), particularly for personal auto insurance.

Insureds also find cancellation clauses useful. If Walter Primeaux sells his auto he no longer needs auto insurance. He can terminate his policy and collect a premium refund. The insured does not need to give a reason for cancellation.

Because a person cannot ordinarily enter and break an agreement at will cancellation clauses are important; they give a legal procedure for discontinuing a contract when either party finds it no longer advantageous. Without a cancellation clause both parties must perform unless the contract is terminated by mutual agreement.

The cancellation privilege is not included in some policies because the time factor is important. Rain insurance would be nearly worthless if the insurer could cancel when rain was predicted. If the forecast is for clear weather, to allow the insured to cancel and collect a refund would also be inequitable. Similarly, neither the insured nor the insurer has a cancellation right in life insurance. The insured, however, may terminate the policy at the end of any premium period by ignoring the next premium within the 31-day grace period. In absence of fraud the insurer cannot terminate a life insurance policy. Nonpayment of premium is not a sufficient cause for an insurer to cancel a life insurance policy if that policy has enough cash value to continue it in force under one of the nonforfeiture options (see Chapter 14). A life insurance policy would be worthless if the insurer could cancel the policy when the insured's health became seriously impaired. Some health policies are both noncancellable and guaranteed renewable (see Chapter 15).

DEFINING THE HAZARDS THAT SUSPEND OR EXCLUDE COVERAGE

Insurance policies may have provisions designed to suspend coverage when the hazard is increased beyond that provided by the premium. These provisions, which help the insurer control risk, usually are *while* clauses, i.e., they suspend coverage while the hazard is increased. When the hazard is reduced coverage is restored. Occasionally, *if* clauses are found, voiding the policy if certain conditions are present. A new policy is then necessary to restore coverage. Finally, policies may specify particular hazards that are excluded from coverage.

The standard fire policy includes several conditions that suspend or restrict the insurance. Some of them may be eliminated by endorsements often without requiring a premium increase. Examples of while clauses in the fire contract are those dealing with increases in the hazard or with vacancy and unoccupancy. An unoccupied or vacant building may be more hazardous than one in use. A vacant building is one without furnishings; an unoccupied building is furnished but untenanted. The standard fire policy states that the insurer is not liable for loss occurring while the hazard is increased within the insured's control or knowledge or while the building is vacant or unoccupied more than 60 consecutive days. Concealment and misrepresentation are the only *if* conditions for voidance in the standard fire policy. These clauses state the policy will be void if the insured has willfully concealed or misrepresented any material fact or circumstance whether before or after a loss.

A fire policy covers fire and lightning. If the policyowner stores heavy explosives in the basement and lightning damages the roof of the building, the coverage under the fire policy is suspended although the loss is not connected with the increase in hazard. Assume the explosives are removed and that the policyowner lights firecrackers in the basement. The policy would cover even though the hazard was temporarily increased. The courts interpret increase-in-hazard condition to mean a substantial and permanent change in the premises or in their use. Customary and minor hazard increases are not within the meaning of the condition. The policy however, may be endorsed to allow certain substantial or permanent hazard increases.

As noted in Chapters 8 and 9 some named hazards are specifically excluded by the policy, e.g., the nuclear hazard in the homeowners policy and the use of an auto as a taxi in the personal auto policy.

THE POLICYOWNER'S DUTIES AFTER A LOSS

Insurance policies include a number of provisions dealing with loss settlement. Among these are (1) notice of loss, (2) protection of property, (3) inventory, (4) evidence, (5) proof of loss, (6) assistance and cooperation and (7) appraisal. Not every insurance contract includes each provision. For example, life insurance policies have just two—proof of loss and settlement options.

Notice of Loss

Many insurance policies require policyowners to give immediate written notice to the insurer of any loss. Others require notice "as soon as practicable." These clauses differ also as to time limits and method of notification.

The purpose of **immediate notice** is to allow investigation of a loss while it is still recent. Delay gives the insured an opportunity to eliminate valuable evidence. Immediate notice also allows the insurer the opportunity to suggest measures to protect property from further loss. The meaning of immediate notice is not literal. Courts have interpreted "immediate" to be as soon as reasonably possible. What is reasonable depends on the facts and how the court views them.

Many policies require **notice as soon as practicable** rather than immediate notice. Although a fine line is drawn between the two, courts have interpreted as soon as practicable even more liberally than immediate notice. As soon as practicable means whatever is practical relative to all the facts.

In some policies interpreting *immediate* and *practicable* is avoided by use of specific time limits. For example, the hail policy requires notice within 48 hours. Health insurance requires written notice to the insurer within 20 days after the loss or as soon thereafter as reasonably possible. Because time limits for filing notice of loss vary, the policyowner must read the policy to determine its limit. The safest procedure is to give notice the day the loss occurs or as soon as possible thereafter.

Some policies require written notice but this requirement may be waived by the insurer or its agents. If an oral notice is given an agent and the agent accepts it and initiates loss investigation, the written notice requirement is held to have been waived. Furthermore, when the insurer acts upon a loss it is estopped from avoiding liability by claiming lack of notice.

Notice may be mailed rather than delivered in person. Notice also may be given to the insurer at its home office or to a duly authorized agent. Crime insurance policies require that the police also be notified as soon as practical. For a credit card loss, notice must be given to both the bank and the insurer.

Notice provisions in liability policies

Two notice clauses apply to liability coverages. One deals with **notice of accident** (written notice as soon as practicable containing such specified information as the circumstances of the accident and the identity of the injured party and available witnesses). The other deals with **notice of claim or suit** (the immediate forwarding of all claims or suits initiated by the injured party).

The insurer needs the loss information immediately to assemble the facts necessary to handle the case. Undue delay makes it difficult to find witnesses who remember (or care to remember) the accident details. The notice clause also reduces the moral hazard in cases of collusion between policyowners and third parties. Furthermore, it may allow insurers to avoid suit by offering prompt settlement to injured persons. Failure to comply with these notice clauses is interpreted by the insurer to mean that the policyowner has elected to assume liability for defense costs and judgments for third-party claims. But in the absence of suspicious circumstances or flagrant violations insurers will perform despite delays in notice or other failures by policyowners to comply with policy provisions. Nevertheless, wise insureds comply with policy terms rather than rely on the insurer's goodwill.

Protection of Property

Another group of provisions deals with the protection of property after a loss. Some policies require policyowners to make reasonable and necessary repairs to protect property from further damage. In addition the policyowner may be required to separate and put in order damaged and undamaged personal property.

Although it is not always explicitly stated, most property insurance policies require the insurer to bear all reasonable expenses incurred to protect covered property from further damage. Indemnifying policyowners for expenses to save property from further loss affects insurers in much the same way as indemnifying them for property that would otherwise have been damaged. The preservation expenses will likely be less than the amount of the loss avoided.

The purpose of the protection provision is to minimize losses. If policyowners fail to comply with this condition the insurer is not relieved of all liability but only liability for losses resulting from the policyowner's failure to protect the property. However, the amount of loss not covered is not often clear-cut. Neither is the amount of effort policyowners must make to protect property from further damage. These questions are usually left to the courts. To avoid controversy insurance adjusters often assume the task of preventing further loss.

Courts have relieved the insurer of all liability when policyowners willfully neglect to protect property from further loss. To be safe, insured persons should care for property after a loss just as they would if they were uninsured. When they take reasonable steps to protect covered property the insurer pays for all reasonable expenses plus indemnity for losses incurred up to the limits of the policy.

Inventory

Some policies require policyowners to prepare an inventory of damaged personal property showing in detail the quantity, description, actual cash value and amount of loss. All bills, receipts and related documents substantiating the figures must be attached. Policyowners may not be able to comply with the detailed inventory requirements prescribed in the HO, especially when the evidence has been damaged. Therefore only reasonable compliance with the inventory provisions is necessary. In addition some policies require policyowners to furnish a complete inventory of the destroyed, damaged and undamaged property. An inventory of undamaged goods is required, as a rule, only if the policy contains a coinsurance clause to enable the adjuster to determine the value of the property relative to the amount of insurance. (Coinsurance is discussed in Chapter 7.)

Regardless of the inventory clause, policyowners should maintain a complete inventory of property. Some insurance agents furnish inventory forms for homeowners. Policyowners with adequate inventory records are in a favorable position to deal with loss adjusters. These records should be kept in a fireproof safe.

Evidence

Insurance contracts have provisions to help insurers determine the validity of a claim. For example, the HO provides that policyowners "exhibit the damaged property as often as we reasonably require and submit to examination under oath." Policyowners must have ample notice of an examination, indicating the time, place and names of the examiners. If policyowners during the examination answer material questions falsely and fraudulently the policy may be voided. If asked to produce books of account, bills and so on and these items are unavailable, policyowners are excused because they cannot be expected to comply with impossible provisions. If evidence is purposely destroyed the contract may be voided. Insurers must be reasonable in the use of these conditions.

No evidence clause is needed for liability claims. The judgment awarded by the court is sufficient proof. Medical payments coverage requires the injured person or a representative to furnish reasonably obtainable information about the accident and injury and to authorize the insurer to obtain medical reports and records as soon as practicable. The injured person must submit to physical examination by physicians selected by the insurer when and as often as the insurer may reasonably require. These provisions provide the insurer an opportunity to protect itself against false claims. The insurer's right to examine the claimant when and as often as it may reasonably require is necessary because claimants could easily fake disability in order to enjoy a paid vacation.

Proof of Loss

Insurers require proof of loss in various ways that are often expressed in the policy. Under some policies policyowners are required to furnish a signed and sworn statement to the insurer within 60 days after the insurer requests it.[5] The statement provides the insurer with facts necessary to reach an equitable loss adjustment. If policyowners fraudulently make a false and material statement the policy is voided. However, if the courts find the discrepancy to be an honest mistake, policyowners are excused and the policy covers. Proof-of-loss statements usually include the following items designed to determine the insurer's liability:

[5] For the purposes of the lay person, "sworn statements" can be read to mean "notarized affidavits" that are sworn to and not at.

1. *The time and cause of loss.* This information (interpreted to mean to the best of the policyowner's knowledge or belief) is used to determine if the loss occurred during the policy period and if coverage is provided for the particular cause of the loss.

2. *The interest of the policyowner and all others in the property and all encumbrances on the property.* This information establishes the policyowner's insurable interest and the extent of third party interests in the loss.

3. *Other insurance that may cover the loss.* This information is necessary because the liability of the insurer may be reduced if other insurance covers the loss.

4. *Specifications of any property damage and detailed estimates for repair of the damage.* This information is necessary to determine the replacement cost of a damaged building and the actual cash value (and in some policies the replacement cost) of any damaged personal property.

5. *Receipts for extra expenses incurred and records supporting fair rental value losses, if any.* This information enables the insurer to determine its liability under these loss-of-use coverages.

6. *Receipts for medical expenses.* These receipts are necessary for health insurers and liability insurers under medical payments coverage.

In summary, proof-of-loss clauses vary as to the time limit for filing notice and the information required. Policyowners should read and comply with the proof-of-loss requirements in their policies. Fortunately, insurers generally furnish proof-of-loss forms that show the information required.

Assistance and Cooperation

Provisions requiring cooperation between the insurer and policyowner in dealing with other parties after a loss are most often included in crime and liability policies. Liability insurers need the cooperation of policyowners in defending suits because they are usually essential witnesses. Insurers are unwilling to defend uncooperative policyowners. When dealing with third parties, policyowners are expected to behave as though they had no insurance. Policyowners are reimbursed for out-of-pocket expenses incurred at the insurer's request and are generally given limited reimbursement for loss of earnings while attending hearings or cooperating with the insurer in other matters relating to the claim.

Because voluntary payments might be construed as an admission of liability and interfere with the insurer's defense of policyowners, liability policies include a clause that permits insurers to deny the insured reimbursement for voluntary payments made to injured victims. However, reimbursements are made for first-aid expenses because immediate first aid attention may reduce the amount of loss.

A typical clause in crime insurance requires policyowners making a claim to take legal action at the insurer's request and expense to secure recovery of the property and the arrest and prosecution of the offenders.

Appraisal

Most property insurance contracts have an appraisal clause that applies when policyowners and insurers fail to agree on the amount of liability. If the insurer denies liability the claimant is free to sue immediately. But if the amount of loss is disputed the claimant may sue immediately *only* if the insurer refuses to arbitrate the differences; otherwise the claimant must fulfill the appraisal clause provisions. The appraisal clause provides that the insured and the insurer each appoint appraisers, who select a third appraiser called an umpire. Together they determine the amount of loss. The appraisers are paid by the parties selecting them and the expenses of the umpire are shared equally. If the insured or the insurer is not satisfied with the appraisers' decision either may sue. But it must be shown that an inequitable award resulted from fraud or error. The courts, however, give strong weight to the appraisers' values. The burden of proof in setting aside the appraisal rests with the dissatisfied party.

The presence of the appraisal clause, even though not often used, reduces the amount of litigation. Because the claimant might overestimate and the insurer underestimate the amount of loss, differences of opinion are likely. The appraisal clause helps keep differences out of court and facilitates faster loss adjustment.

SETTLEMENT OPTIONS

Insurance policies may be settled in various ways. In some kinds of insurance the insurer has the settlement option; in others, policyowners have the option. The insurer has three sets of options in settling claims—replacement, abandonment and salvage, and pair or set. Policyowners have settlement options primarily in life and health insurance.

Replacement Option

Under many insurance policies insurers may repair or replace damaged property with that of like kind and quality rather than pay the actual cash value of the loss. If insurers elect this option notice of intention is required within 30 days after receipt of proof of loss. In glass insurance insurers usually replace the broken glass. Insurers work closely with the glass companies and obtain quick service and favorable prices. Insurers seldom exercise this option in other insurance coverage because payment of cash is simpler than entering the construction business. Also, insurers would be exposed to policyowners' rejection of the repairs or replacement. The option helps insurers protect themselves against unfair loss appraisals.

Abandonment and Salvage

Except in marine insurance the insurer rather than the policyowner has the option of allowing **abandonment** and demanding **salvage** in the event of a loss.[6] The terms *abandonment* and *salvage* have been defined as follows: abandonment is relinquishing ownership of lost or damaged property to the insurer so that a total loss may be claimed; salvage is property taken over by an insurer to reduce its loss. The abandonment and salvage rights of insurers are generally found in the policy. If the policy has no abandonment clause, the courts read one into it, as expressing the parties' intention. When a total loss is paid the insurer has the salvage right. In summary, policyowners may not abandon property to insurers and claim total loss, but insurers may pay a total loss and demand salvage from policyowners.

Pair or Set

Many property insurance policies include a pair-or-set clause providing that the insurer can either: (*a*) repair or replace any part to restore the pair or set to its

[6] In some forms of marine insurance the property covered makes salvage operations by policyowners difficult. Therefore policyowners are given abandonment rights under specified conditions.

value before the loss or (*b*) pay the difference between the actual cash value of the property before and after the loss. This clause informs policyowners that a loss of one cuff link is not a total loss of the set and that the insurer will make an effort to reach an equitable settlement.

Settlement Options in Life Insurance

The proceeds or cash values of a life policy may be paid as a lump sum, as periodic payments over a limited period or for life. The policyowner or the beneficiary may select the option. The most common settlement options offered are (1) interest only, (2) installments for a fixed period, (3) installments of fixed amounts and (4) life income. These options are discussed in detail in Chapter 14.

Settlement Options in Health Insurance

The health policy might provide an elective disability income benefit for certain fractures and dislocations. If policyowners elect this benefit they are not entitled to additional disability income benefits. Under some policies election is not required; the insurer pays policyowners the higher benefit amount with the elective benefit as the minimum.

Relations with Third Parties

Some insurance contracts clarify the relationships of insurers to third parties involved in claims. A few contracts permit insurers to deal directly with third parties while others deny this right. The bailees' customers' floater provides that loss may be adjusted and paid to the policyowner or directly to the policyowner's customers at the insurer's option.

The physicians', surgeons' and dentists' liability policy, however, prohibits insurers from settling or compromising claims or suits covered by the policy without the policyowner's written consent. If insurers could settle claims out of court the effect would be to admit guilt, thus damaging the reputation of the insured doctor. A decision for the plaintiff in a malpractice case can harm the defendant more than the loss of the amount awarded to the plaintiff. The effect of this provision is to cause nearly all claims to be litigated, thus increasing expenses and in turn increasing insurance costs and the cost of medical care.

TIME LIMIT FOR BRINGING SUITS

Insurance contracts set a time limit for a policyowner's suit against the insurer. These limits may be minimums, maximums or both and supersede the general statute of limitations otherwise applicable. Time limits for bringing suits vary among contracts. If the maximum time limit in the policy is shorter than that required by state law for such policies the longer time limit governs.

INNERSCRIPT: PHYSICAL DAMAGE AND LIABILITY POLICIES

Most policies provide that no action shall be brought against the insurer unless the policyowner has complied with the policy

provisions and the action is started within a specified time after the loss occurs. The maximum time limit for bringing suits allows insurers to terminate liability within a reasonable time so that reserves for losses reported but not yet settled can be estimated more easily and so that suits are filed before the facts become blurred.

Liability policies **forbid action against the insurer until the amount of the policyowner's liability is finally determined, either by court decision or written agreement between the third-party claimants and the policyowner. No suit against the insurer is allowed while litigation between the policyowner and the third-party claimant is in process or an appeal is pending. This requirement is important because if the insurer denies liability on the grounds that the policy does not cover, the policyowner first must arrange for the case to be defended in court and wait for the judgment to be rendered before seeking to recover from the insurer. The policyowner must not allow the plaintiff to win by default and must not be indifferent to the suit or collusive with the plaintiff. Once a judgment is reached by trial the policyowner may proceed against the insurer.**

TIME LIMIT FOR PAYING CLAIMS

Insurance policies specify time limits for paying claims and these limits vary among policies. The HO provides that payment of the loss must be made within 30 days after (*a*) agreement is reached, (*b*) a final judgment is entered or (*c*) an appraisal award has been filed. The clause gives the insurer time to investigate the loss and arrange for payment. Unless a waiting period is *required* by statute insurers are expected to approve claims promptly.

SUMMARY

1. Insurance policies all have the same components:
   - *a.* Declarations—descriptive material relating to the subject, coverage and policy limits.
   - *b.* Insuring agreements—broadly define the coverage.
   - *c.* Exclusions—eliminate some of the coverages provided by the insuring agreements.
   - *d.* Conditions—obligations and rights of the policyowner and insurer.

   Many policies also have endorsements or riders which add or eliminate provisions to the basic contract.
2. Seven questions must be answered to determine if a given event is covered:
   - *a.* What perils are covered?
   - *b.* What property is covered?
   - *c.* What types of losses are covered?
   - *d.* What persons are covered?
   - *e.* What locations are covered?

f. What time periods are covered?
g. Are there hazards that exclude or suspend coverage?

In addition, in analyzing a policy four other questions must be answered following a loss:

a. What are the policyowner's duties after a loss?
b. What are the insurer's options in settling a loss?
c. What are the time limits for the policyowner to bring suit against the insurer?
d. What are the time limits for the insurer to pay a claim?

3. Policies are written on either a specified perils or all-risk basis.

4. Coverage for a peril may be limited, e.g., the homeowners policy limits coverage for the smoke peril to sudden and accidental damage from smoke.

5. The proximate cause of a loss is the efficient cause, i.e., the one responsible for the loss through an unbroken chain of events. For a loss to be covered, the covered peril must be either the proximate cause or in the chain of events that links the proximate cause with the loss.

6. Property covered may be defined comprehensively or on a specified basis.

7. Losses may be classified as direct, indirect and extra expenses. *Direct loss* is the physical loss of an object. *Indirect loss* results from (*a*) loss of net income from the inability to use the damaged property and (*b*) loss arising from direct damage to such property as a refrigerator (food spoilage) or one item in a pair or set—these losses are often referred to as *consequential losses. Extra expenses* are those incurred (*a*) in defending a liability suit, (*b*) in continuing a business following a major property loss and (*c*) in living elsewhere following a major loss to a dwelling.

8. Some policies cover only named insureds and their representatives. Others may cover additional persons.

9. Assignment transfers some or all rights held by the owner(s) to another person.

10. Insurers limit locations covered. Some policies restrict coverage to the United States and Canada while others extend coverage worldwide.

11. In defining the time of coverage, both the term of the policy and hour of inception must be considered.

12. Most insurance policies give the insurer and policyowner the right to cancel the policy upon written notice before its expiration date.

13. Provisions in some policies may exclude or suspend coverage when certain hazards are increased beyond that allowed in the rate structure. These provisions may be "while" clauses or "if" clauses.

14. Provisions dealing with the policyowner's duties after a loss are:

a. Notice of loss.
b. Protection of property.
c. Inventory.
d. Evidence.
e. Proof of loss.
f. Assistance and cooperation.
g. Appraisal.

15. The insurer has three sets of options available in settling claims with the policyowner: the replacement option, the abandonment and salvage option and the pair-or-set clause. Policyowners have settlement options primarily in life and health insurance.
16. Insurance contracts set a time limit within which a suit may be brought against the insurer by the policyowner. Usually action must be started within a specified time after the loss has occurred, and the policyowner must have complied with the policy provisions.
17. Insurance policies specify a time limit for paying claims, and these limits vary among policies.

REVIEW QUESTIONS

1. When would an insurer repair or replace damaged property rather than pay the actual cash value of the loss?
2. Why is the appraisal clause included in an insurance contract?
3. What is the purpose of each of the items required in the proof-of-loss statement described in the text?
4. A policyowner had a pair of cuff links valued at $500. One was stolen. How much will the insurer pay for the loss?
5. Is salvage important in life insurance? Why? Are you sure?
6. Explain why coverage written on a specified basis as distinguished from an all-risk basis is not limited to specified perils only.
7. Why is the hour of inception important in determining the time of coverage?
8. With reference to an increase in hazard distinguish between a "while" clause and an "if" clause.
9. Define the concept of proximate cause and explain how it is used in determining the coverage after a loss.
10. Why is the insurer required to give the policyowner advance notice before cancelling the policy?
11. Why do insurers modify insuring agreements with exclusions?
12. Explain the purpose of endorsements (or riders) in insurance policies.

CHAPTER

7 Further directions for reading a policy

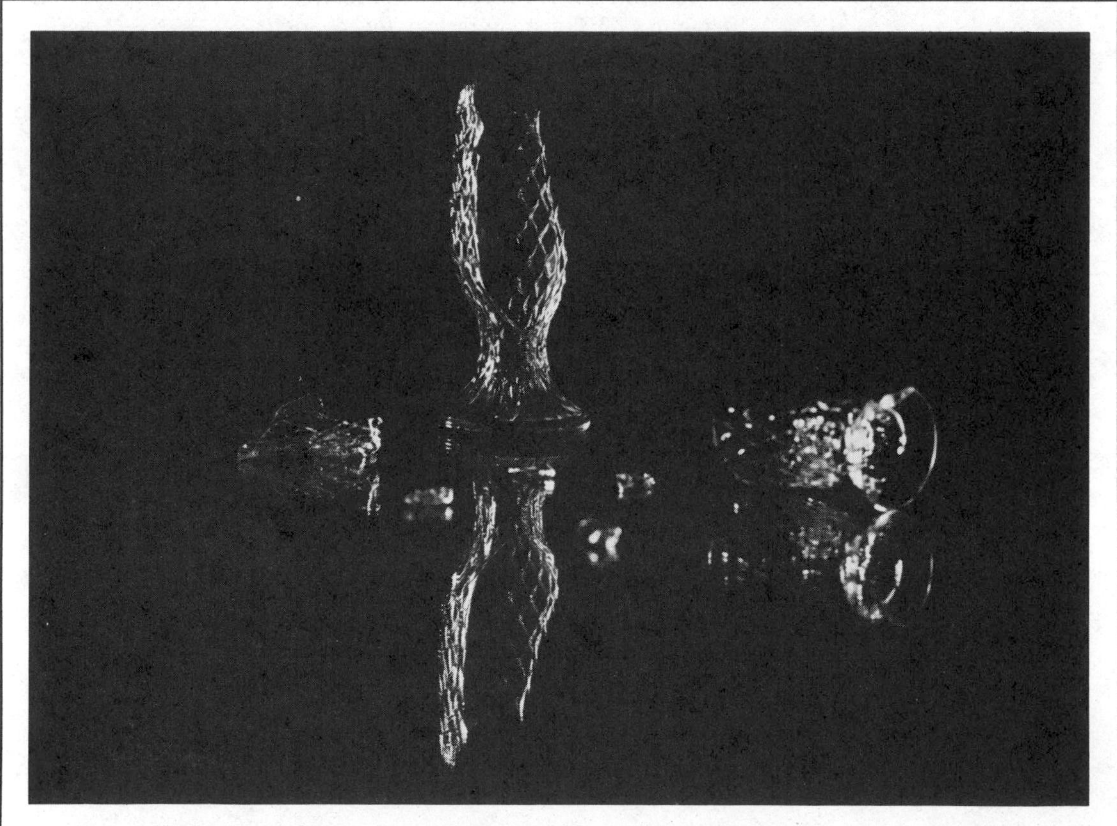

John Thoeming/Richard D. Irwin

CHAPTER OBJECTIVES

1. **To point out the factors that limit the insurer's liability in the event of a loss.**
2. **To explain the reason(s) for each of the six limitations that affect the insurer's liability.**
3. **To show how to determine the actual cash value of a loss.**
4. **To describe the various ways of stating amount limits in insurance policies.**
5. **To examine the types of and reasons for other-insurance clauses in insurance contracts.**
6. **To define coinsurance and demonstrate how it works and why it is used in some insurance policies.**
7. **To indicate the types of deductible clauses written in insurance contracts and explain the reasons for their use.**

Questions dealing with coverage and the rights and duties of policyowners and insurers are discussed in Chapter 6. In this chapter attention is directed to the question: if a covered loss occurs, how much must the insurer pay? Insurers do not issue blank checks when writing policies; they include limitations that determine their maximum liability. These limits are (1) amount of insurable interest, (2) actual cash value of the loss, (3) policy limits, (4) other insurance, (5) coinsurance clauses and (6) deductibles. Limitations with (2), (3) and (6) are the most common. The lowest of these limits is the one that governs. Any of the six may be the lowest and thus determine the amount to be paid.

AMOUNT OF INSURABLE INTEREST

Except for life insurance (see Chapter 5), to reduce or prevent moral hazard the maximum reimbursement for losses is limited to the insured's interest. In addition, reimbursement that exceeds the loss violates the indemnity principle. Suppose Joel Segall, half owner of a $10 million building, buys $10 million of fire insurance in his own name to cover the building. In the event of total loss he can collect only $5 million, the amount of his loss, although both the policy face and the value of the destroyed property are $10 million. The value of Joel's interest governs because it is the lowest.

ACTUAL CASH VALUE

Property insurance contracts usually limit the insurer's liability to the **actual cash value** (ACV) of the property at the time of the loss. What is actual cash value? The courts define it as replacement cost *new* less observed depreciation. (In a few isolated cases ACV has been equated with market value.) This rule requires that replacement cost be determined and depreciation measured, both difficult tasks.

INNERSCRIPT: REPLACEMENT COST REFINED

Replacement cost is governed by the type of property, the data available to the appraiser and whether the owner is a wholesaler, retailer or consumer. Estimated prices for labor, materials and overhead are key factors in determining replacement cost for a building and its equipment. Estimates vary among appraisers because cost figures contain subjective elements. The replacement cost of other property may be set by market values rather than cost estimates. For example, replacement cost for raw materials is based on the price quoted on commodity exchanges. The replacement cost of processed commodities depends on the policyowner's position in the trade channel. Thus the replacement cost of a commodity will be more for the retailer than the wholesaler and even more for the ultimate consumer. If an automobile burns as it rolls off the assembly line in Detroit the manufacturer's replacement cost is the cost of reproducing the automobile. If the car burned in the dealer's showroom the replacement cost for the dealer would be the wholesale price. If the car burned immediately after it was sold to the consumer the owner's replacement cost would be the retail price.

Depreciation used in determining the measure of ACV is a valuation concept reflecting total loss of value from all causes by deducting physical deterioration, obsolescence and location deterioration from replacement cost. Unlike accounting procedures, the deductions are not related directly to the age of the building but to economic and physical factors that place old property at a competitive disadvantage with new property. For example, the penalty for physical deterioration is based on the life span of each item in the building that wears out and is replaceable. If the life of a roof is estimated to be 10 years and the replacement cost is $10,000, the physical deterioration penalty would be $6,000 for a 6-year-old roof even though the building is 30 years old.

The penalty for obsolescence reflects technological and social changes. If obsolescence can be eliminated by remodeling or new equipment the penalty is their cost. If the obsolescence results from poor functional design, unattractive architecture or poor relation of the building to the site the penalty is based on the difference between the costs for an ideal building at that location and the damaged building. If the building is improperly located compared to the ideal location a penalty for location deterioration is assessed.

Measuring depreciation is a major problem in calculating ACV. Competent appraisers are relied on but disagreements between the insured and the insurer may still end in court. However, the policy has provisions (discussed in Chapter 6) designed to keep court action to a minimum.

Regardless of the method and figures used in computing the ACV of the loss, insurers limit their payment to an amount not exceeding the "cost to repair or replace the property with materials of like kind and quality within a reasonable time after such loss." Like kind and quality does not mean the *exact* kind and quality because often reproducing buildings and equipment with the same materials and construction methods is impractical. Therefore insureds and insurers use the concept of replacement rather than reproduction cost. Replacement cost is limited to the style, quality and function of the destroyed or damaged property. No allowances are made for increased costs of repair or reconstruction caused by ordinances or laws regulating construction or repair.

Actual Cash Value and Liability Insurance

In liability insurance measurement of the ACV of a loss is settled by negotiation between the claimant and the insurer, not between the insurer and the insured. If a verdict is reached in a litigated claim the verdict usually includes (1) the ACV of the economic loss including reasonable compensation for loss of use and loss of profits, (2) compensation for general damages (pain and suffering) incurred by the claimant and (3) the claimant's attorney's fees and other claim costs. In bodily injury cases the economic damages usually consists of medical expenses incurred by the claimant plus an amount the jury believes sufficient to cover future medical costs and defense costs including court costs, premiums on bonds and cost of investigation.

The question of whether insurers are liable for **punitive damages** is undecided in most states. As defined earlier, punitive damages are damages awarded in excess of normal compensation to the plaintiff to punish a defendant for a serious wrong as a means of deterring similar conduct by others. (In one respect it resembles the tale about Billy's parent who urged the teacher to smack Jimmy if Billy misbehaves because such action will so frighten Billy that he will become angelic.) For punitive damages to be awarded the defendant must be guilty of more than ordinary negligence (i.e., gross negligence or willful and wanton misconduct). Because liability policies require insurers to pay damages where the insured is legally liable, the argument is made that punitive damages should be paid by the insurer if the total amount of liability does not exceed the policy limit. But the use of insurance proceeds to pay punitive damages might eliminate any deterrent effect they might have. If punitive damages do deter antisocial behavior then public policy should preclude insurers from paying them. This dichotomy has led some courts to require liability insurers to pay punitive damages and others to prohibit insurers from paying them. Although a few states avoid the problem by denying courts the right to assess punitive damages most states leave the question to the courts.

Actual Cash Value in Life and Health Insurance

The face amount of a life insurance policy is held to be the amount of the loss and no attempt is made to place a value on the life of the deceased person. A wife collects the full face amount of her husband's policy even though two days before his death she called him a worthless bum.

Health insurance includes medical expense and disability income coverage. Medical expense limits are expressed in dollars or service. The policy might provide $150 daily for hospital room and board for a maximum period of 180 days *or* the cost of 180 days' hospital room and board in semiprivate accommodations. Major medical coverage offers a blanket amount to pay medical and hospital bills. (Many major medical policies limit the amount or type of service per day for hospital room and board.) Disability income insurance limits both the amount and the number of payments. For example, the coverage may be $1,000 a month until age 65 or $200 a week for 26 weeks.

Exceptions to the Actual Cash Value Limitation

Under several circumstances the insured may collect more than the ACV of the loss: valued policies, some duplicate coverage and replacement cost insurance.

Valued policies

A number of states have valued policy laws requiring insurers to pay the face amount of the policy *for a total loss of real property.* In these states the insurer would have to appraise all covered real property before writing the insurance to avoid the possibility of overinsurance. Because few real property losses are total, however, insurers find it less expensive to pay an occasional excessive claim than appraise all property. Valued policies violate the principle of indemnity and increase moral hazard.

Valued policies are also used to cover special types of property difficult or impossible to replace or where the value at time of loss is difficult to establish. When an item is irreplaceable (e.g., paintings, historical documents, the original manuscript of this book) ACV does not qualify as a useful indemnity measure. Valued policies are also used in life insurance. The widow can collect the $100,000 proceeds of her husband's life insurance although his death was an economic gain for her in every respect.

Duplicate coverages

A health insurance policyowner for example, may also be allowed to collect more than the ACV of the loss. Professor Neumann, who is disabled, can collect the $2,000 a month provided by a disability income policy even if the university continues to pay his $4,500 monthly salary.

For another example, even though her earnings did not exceed $3,800 a month before becoming disabled, Bertha Newhouse can collect the $1,900 a month provided by her group disability income coverage, the $2,500 monthly income from her individually owned disability income policy and the $3,000 a month **special damage** (economic) awarded her for an injury caused by a negligent golfer. In addition, she is entitled to collect any social security disability benefits for which she is eligible (see Chapter 18).

Replacement-cost insurance

Replacement-cost insurance covers the cost of repairing or replacing damaged property without deduction for depreciation. The coverage protects policyowners for the difference between the ACV and the restoration cost, thus eliminating an otherwise uncovered exposure.

POLICY FACE OR LIMITS

A property or liability insurer (unless otherwise provided) will not pay more than the **policy face amount** or its policy limits.[1] Although the face amount of the

[1] In liability insurance cost of defense, premiums on bonds, cost of investigation and so on generally are not included in the policy limits. The limits usually apply only to judgments awarded by the court. Also, indemnities under the "sue-and-labor clause" in marine policies may be in addition to the face amount of the policy. The sue-and-labor clause is discussed in Chapter 10.

policy restricts the insurer's liability, that amount is not paid unconditionally for every total loss unless the contract is a valued policy.

Types of Policy Limits

The policy face amount may be multifaceted with more than one in a policy. The simplest is found in auto physical damage coverage where no face amount is stated. Instead recovery is limited to the auto's ACV. But most policies have face amount limits and may include several internal limits applying to particular types of property, losses, locations, perils or hazards.

Divided coverage

Several types of policy limits are used, the most common being **divided coverage** where a policy has several sections with a specific face amount stated for each one. Each part of the divided coverage is independent but included in one policy for convenience and economy. Homeowners policies are examples of divided coverage: a specific amount is applied to the dwelling, another amount to personal property and so on.

Blanket coverage

When a policy with a single face amount applies to two or more locations, two or more types of property or a combination of locations and types of property the contract is called **blanket.** For example, blanket policies are written to cover goods stored at several locations. They are appropriate when total values are nearly constant but specific values fluctuate widely at individual locations.

Priority coverage

When a single policy face amount applies to all its coverages, loss settlement may be on a priority basis. For example, the boiler and machinery policy covers direct damage, expediting permanent and temporary repairs and liability for loss of or damage to property of others in the insured's care, custody or control. Bodily injury liability is covered on an optional basis with loss settlement priorities up to the face amount of the policy in the order listed, i.e., direct damage has the highest priority and bodily injury liability the lowest.

Sublimits

Sublimits are applied principally to hazardous exposures to control the cost of insurance. Coverage for amounts in excess of these limits can be bought for an additional premium or through separate policies specifically written and rated to cover the exposure. A homeowners policy with a $40,000 limit for unscheduled personal property offers an example of sublimits. Three of them are (1) $100 on money, bank notes, bullion, gold other than goldware, silver other than silverware, platinum, coins and medals; (2) $500 for loss by theft of jewelry, watches, furs, precious and semiprecious stones and (3) $500 on grave markers. Sublimits are *not* in addition to the policy's face amount.

Additional amounts

Some policy limits offer coverage in addition to the basic limits. For example, the personal auto policy provides for payment up to $10 a day, subject to a total of $300, if the car is stolen. These payments help offset expenses incurred for necessary substitute transportation and are *in addition* to the amount of insurance on the stolen car.

Limits in liability insurance

Liability insurance limits usually are stated in one of four ways. Traditionally the policy has two limits for bodily injury (one limit per person and another per accident) and one for property damage (per accident).

For example, Bill Scheel has an auto policy with limits of $10,000 per person and $20,000 per accident for bodily injury and a $5,000 limit for property damage. Suppose Bill negligently crashes into an oncoming vehicle occupied by five people. Regardless of the amounts of damages awarded by the court, Bill's insurer will not pay more than $20,000 (with a maximum of $10,000 to any one person) for bodily injury and $5,000 for aggregate property damage claims. (With courts making increasingly higher awards, buyers are unwise to purchase such low limits. Bill could have increased his limits substantially for a modest additional premium.)

Three other methods of stating policy limits in liability insurance are (1) one limit applies to bodily injury for each accident and another to property damage for each accident; (2) one limit for each accident applies to both bodily injury and property damage jointly and (3) an aggregate limit (an annual limit on claims) applies to all bodily injury and/or property damages occurring during the policy term. Of these methods (1) and (2) may be used with (3), i.e., separate limits for each accident subject to an aggregate limit for the policy term. Defense costs provided by nearly all liability policies are not part of basic policy limits and are covered without limit.

Bankruptcy and insolvency. The policyowner's ability to pay a third-party claim does not limit the insurer's liability. Liability policies contain a **bankruptcy or insolvency clause** that states: "Bankruptcy or insolvency of any insured shall not relieve us (the insurer) of any of our obligations under this policy."[2] Liability insurance policies contain this bankruptcy or insolvency clause as a matter of public policy. Society is interested in protecting injured persons for humanitarian reasons and to keep them from becoming public wards. Underwriters do not object to violating the principle of indemnity here because the clause does not create a moral hazard.

Restoration and Nonreduction of Amounts of Insurance

What happens to the insurance face amount when a loss occurs? Does it remain the same or is it reduced by the loss? The answers vary among policies.

Liability insurance

In most liability insurance contracts the payment of claims does not reduce the face amount of the insurance. The insurer promises to pay up to the limits of the policy for each loss and for all losses that occur during the policy period. The policyowner is not required to pay additional premiums after each accident to restore the amount of the policy. Aggregate limits by definition are the exception to the rule.

Property insurance

Although it is not specifically stated in the policy, courts have upheld the principle that an insurer is *not* obligated to pay more than the face amount of the policy. Thus each claim reduces the insurance by the amount of the loss paid *unless* the policy states otherwise. However, virtually every property insurance contract provides automatic restoration of the face amount of the policy after a loss. Multiple losses are included in the data used in computing the premium.

Life and health insurance

Because life is irreplaceable no questions of restoration arise in life insurance. Most health insurance does not reduce coverage after a loss although some medical expense policies have aggregate lifetime limits.

---

[2] Liabilities for the following claims are not released by a discharge in bankruptcy: willful and malicious injuries to the person or property of others; obtaining property by false pretenses or false representations; alimony due or to become due; wife or child support; seduction of an unmarried male or female or criminal conduct.

OTHER INSURANCE

The question of what happens when more than one policy covers the same loss is answered by **other-insurance clauses.** If the full amount of the loss were paid from more than one policy, the resulting gain to the policyowner would defeat the principle of indemnity, create a moral hazard and make insurance a gambling transaction, thus violating public policy.

Types of Other-Insurance Clauses

An other-insurance clause may prohibit other insurance on the same interest or provide that losses are shared with all other applicable insurance. Clauses providing claims sharing are either contributing, primary or excess.

Contributing insurance

Two methods of apportioning losses when two or more policies cover the same loss and interest are pro rata and limit of liability.

The **pro rata liability clause** operates as follows: Roger Clites has a mother-in-law and a son-in-law in the insurance business. To keep the family peace he covers his $200,000 building by purchasing $100,000 from his mother-in-law with insurer A and $100,000 from his son-in-law with insurer B. Lightning causes $60,000 damage to the building. Because each insurer writes half the insurance each pays half the loss, $30,000. If insurer A had written $40,000 and insurer B $160,000, A would pay one fifth of the loss and B would pay four fifths, or $12,000 and $48,000 respectively, computed by the following formula:

$$\textbf{Insurer A's or B's liability} = \frac{\textbf{Insurance with insurer A } \textbf{\textit{or}} \textbf{ B}}{\textbf{Insurance with insurers A } \textbf{\textit{and}} \textbf{ B}} \times \textbf{Amount of loss}$$

Some policies provide that the *limit of liability* rather than pro rata liability shall be the basis for allocating losses. Rather than apportioning the loss over the total face amounts of insurance the limit of liability apportions it over each insurer's liability as if there had been no other policy. Assume two policies cover the same interest. Policy A is written for $20,000 and policy B for $80,000. A $50,000 loss occurs. Under the **limit-of-liability rule,** insurer A will pay 20/70 or $14,286, and B will pay 50/70 or $35,714, computed by the following formula:

$$\textbf{Insurer A's or B's liability} = \frac{\textbf{Liability of insurer A } \textbf{\textit{or}} \textbf{ B, if each wrote the only policy}}{\textbf{Liability of insurers A } \textbf{\textit{and}} \textbf{ B, if each wrote the only policy}} \times \textbf{Amount of loss}$$

Excess coverage

The policy may provide that the insurer pays nothing until all other valid insurance has been exhausted in paying the loss. Group medical expense insurance covering an employee's spouse usually is written as excess insurance. Assume both spouses are covered under their respective employer's group policies and both policies include all eligible family members. If the husband incurs medical expenses the insurance provided by his employer pays all covered benefits up to the policy limits. Expenses exceeding the policy limits are covered by the insurance available under his wife's group coverage. (Among group medical expense policies this arrangement is called **coordination of benefits** and is not generally found between group and individual policies.)

For another excess coverage example, assume Carol Carillo owns an auto liability policy. While driving Ken Reeves's car she runs into a pole (or was it a Czech?). The injured party sues for damages. Both her policy and Ken's policy cover the loss. However, the coverage on the car is primary while the driver's coverage is excess. Therefore Ken's insurer pays until his policy limits are exhausted; then Carol's insurer pays the remainder of any damages up to the limits of her policy.

Primary coverage

In ocean marine insurance if more than one policy covers the same interest the policy bearing the earliest date is primary. Policies bought later are void up to the amount of the prior policy. Thus if the first policy is for $100,000 and the second for $150,000, only $50,000 of the second policy applies. The premium for the inapplicable $100,000 is refunded. However if the face amount of the second policy does not exceed the first, the second is completely inapplicable and its full premium refunded.

Apportionment clause

The apportionment clause in the extended coverage endorsement restricts the insurer's liability to the proportion of the loss that the applicable amount of *extended coverage* insurance bears to the amount of *fire insurance* on the property, whether collectible or not and whether or not the other fire insurance applies to the extended coverage perils.[3] Thus if George protects his $800,000 building with four $20,000 fire insurance policies but only one has extended coverage he can collect only one fourth of each extended coverage loss, subject to a maximum of $20,000. The purpose of the clause is to generate adequate premiums by discouraging underinsurance of extended coverage perils.

COINSURANCE

Some contracts contain **coinsurance clauses,** restricting recovery for partial losses if the policyowner does not cover the property for a given percentage of its actual cash value at the time of loss. Coinsurance is optional in some policies and required in others. The policyowner is charged a reduced rate when the policy includes a coinsurance clause. For example, a fire insurance policy on a fire-resistant building in a large central Illinois town would cost 70 percent less if written with an 80 percent coinsurance clause.

For this rate reduction the insured agrees to purchase insurance for an amount equal to at least the stated percentage of the ACV of the covered property at the time of the loss. If the percentage is not met the policyowner becomes a coinsurer. Assume a building with an ACV of $600,000 *at the time of the loss* is covered under an 80 percent coinsurance clause for $360,000. To avoid a coinsurance penalty the insured would have had to purchase $480,000 of insurance (80 percent of $600,000); so a coinsurance deficiency of $120,000 ($480,000 − $360,000) results. The insured becomes a coinsurer of this deficiency and on that basis contributes to all losses. If the building burns and damages are $64,000 the insurer pays three fourths ($360,000/$480,000) of the loss ($48,000) and the policyowner bears one fourth ($16,000). (The insurer wrote only three fourths of the required insurance and so is liable for only three fourths

[3] The standard fire policy covers the perils of fire and lightning. The extended coverage endorsement adds windstorm, hail, explosion, riot, riot attending a strike, civil commotion, damage by aircraft or by vehicle and smoke damage.

of the loss. The policyowner failed to buy one fourth of the required insurance and so must absorb one fourth of the loss.)

The following formulas show how to figure the amount payable for a partial loss where a policy is written with a coinsurance clause

1. Determine the amount of insurance required:

$$\textbf{Actual cash value of property at time of loss} \times \textbf{Coinsurance percentage} = \textbf{Amount of insurance required}$$

2. Determine the amount of recovery:

$$\frac{\textbf{Amount of insurance owned}}{\textbf{Amount of insurance required}} \times \textbf{Loss} = \textbf{Maximum amount of recovery}$$

These formulas provide the following answers in the foregoing example.

1. **\$600,000 × 80 percent = \$480,000, amount of insurance required**

2. $$\frac{\$360{,}000}{\$480{,}000} \times \$64{,}000 = 48{,}000, \text{ amount of recovery}$$

If the building's value increases and the insurance is not increased correspondingly, the coinsurance deficiency increases. Suppose that the value increases from \$600,000 to \$900,000 without a proportionate increase in the insurance. The deficiency would be \$360,000 rather than \$120,000 because \$720,000 of insurance (80 percent of \$900,000) would now be required (\$720,000 − \$360,000 = \$360,000). A \$64,000 loss under the new value would require *both* the insurer and the policyowner to bear half the loss because each is responsible for \$360,000 of insurance. The policyowner now has a 50 percent deficiency in coverage and must bear 50 percent of the loss.

Coinsurance has no effect on the insurer's liability if the loss equals or exceeds the required amount of insurance. Consequently if the loss in this example was \$760,000 rather than \$64,000 the insurer is responsible only for the policy limit of \$360,000 because it is less than half the loss. If the required amount of insurance is bought full coverage is available for losses up to the policy face amount. If a building valued at \$400,000 is covered for \$360,000 under a 90 percent coinsurance clause the insurer will pay all losses in full up to \$360,000 because the policyowner has no coinsurance deficiency.

INNERSCRIPT: THEORY BEHIND COINSURANCE

The purpose of coinsurance is to help achieve equitable and adequate rates. Fire insurance best illustrates how this purpose is accomplished. Most fire losses are partial. Less than 2 percent result in total loss and more than 80 percent produce damage amounting

(*Continued*)

to less than 10 percent of the total property value. Thus property owners can cover most losses with only 10 percent of insurance to value. However, full insurance may be necessary when the property is pledged as security for a mortgage loan. Some property owners want full insurance, recognizing that they can be among the 2 percent with total losses. But without a coinsurance rate reduction they would pay 10 times as much for protection as those insuring for only 10 percent of their property values, if the values are equal. Yet expected losses of the fully insured are not 10 times as much as those insured for the 10 percent. Thus with equal rates per $100 of insurance, persons with full coverage pay an inequitable premium.

Those realizing that most losses are partial may be willing and able to limit their insurance, e.g., to 30 percent of value. By buying only $30,000 of insurance to cover a $100,000 building they would pay an inadequate premium without a coinsurance requirement.

Equitable and adequate premiums can be developed by decreasing the rate per $100 as the insurance amount increases (called a sliding rate scale). In some types of insurance (e.g., crime), sliding rates are easy to calculate because loss estimates are simple: one truckload represents the typical burglary loss.

But not so in fire insurance where a small loss is not its absolute size but its relation to the value of the exposed property. Because parts of a building are not readily damaged by fire, total losses are uncommon. In a $2 million building $200,000 is nearly always readily destructible; in a $200,000 building, some of that value is relatively indestructible. Thus a $30,000 loss is much more likely to happen to a $2 million building than to a $200,000 building. A sliding rate scale would have to take this disparity into consideration—and that would not be easy. Coinsurance provides a much simpler solution: All policyowners are charged the same rate per $100 but are required to buy an amount of insurance equal to an agreed percentage of the value of the property to collect the full amount for partial losses. Those who fail to meet the coninsurance requirement must bear part of each loss—in effect causing them to pay a higher premium per $100 of coverage than those who purchase the required amount.

The following illustration shows the logic of coinsurance: suppose 20,000 people own identical buildings valued at $120,000 each for a total value of $2.4 billion. During the year four buildings are completely destroyed and 60 have fires causing losses averaging $12,000 each. The losses for the year are $120,000 × 4 or $480,000 in total losses and 60 × $12,000 or $720,000 in partial losses. The sum of these losses is $1.2 million and produces a loss rate of 0.05 per $100 of property exposed computed as follows:

$$\$1{,}200{,}000 \div \frac{2{,}400{,}000{,}000}{100} = \$0.05$$

The cost of fire insurance covering each building for its full value would be 5 cents per \$100 or \$60, excluding the insurer's expense addition.

Suppose the owners knowing that most losses are partial cover their buildings for only \$60,000, half their value. The losses paid for the year change as follows: \$240,000 for total losses and \$720,000 for partial losses, assuming no partial losses in excess of \$60,000. The sum of the losses paid is \$960,000 for \$1.2 million of covered property values. The loss rate per \$100 is now 0.08 computed as follows:

$$\$960{,}000 \div \frac{1{,}200{,}000{,}000}{100} = \$0.08.$$

The premium is 8 cents per \$100 or \$48 for each building not including the insurer's expenses. Thus the cost of covering the property for half its value in this particular case is 80 percent of the cost of insurance for 100 percent of its value (\$48 is 80 percent of \$60).

Given that a sliding rate scale (i.e., in this case charging \$48 for those buying \$60,000 of insurance and \$60 for those buying \$120,000 of insurance) is impractical, a logical solution is to charge both groups 5 cents per \$100 and require a 100 percent coinsurance clause.

Coinsurance clauses appear to be the simplest method to obtain a fair rate for those who insure for a high percentage of the value of their property.

DEDUCTIBLE CLAUSES

Deductible clauses have an important purpose in insurance. In some contracts they are mandatory; in others they are optional. Whether required or optional the policyowner frequently has a choice of deductible amounts.

By excluding small frequent losses deductible clauses are based on sound insurance theory. They reduce the price of insurance by eliminating small claims that are relatively expensive to handle. They also decrease moral hazard. Insureds who are forced to pay part of each loss may be encouraged to reduce their losses. Better loss experience is reflected in the rate. Some types of deductibles increase moral hazard by leading insureds to exaggerate claims to collect the full loss.

A few insurance agents oppose deductibles, believing they cause disgruntled claimants and poor public relations.[4] Agents are convinced that paying claims is their best advertising. They also suspect some insurers' rates do not fully reflect the cost savings generated by deductible clauses. Finally, lower rates mean lower commissions. Agents interested in their clients' welfare, however, understand and appreciate the value of deductibles and urge clients to buy them if (1) they can absorb the loss and (2) the rate reduction is fair.

[4] If deductible clauses lead to disgruntled claimants the problem is that agents are unable or unwilling to explain deductibles to policyowners when the contracts are written.

Types of Deductibles

Several types of deductible clauses are written to eliminate coverage for small losses.

Straight deductible

A common deductible is the **straight deductible** often found in auto physical damage and homeowners property coverages. The deductible is usually a given amount (e.g., $50, $100, $250 or more) and works as follows. Bob Witt has $100 deductible collision coverage on his car. He hits a stone wall incurring a $250 collision loss. He absorbs $100 of the loss and his insurer pays $150. The deductible means that Bob bears the first $100 of damage in *every* loss and the insurer pays the rest.

Some straight deductibles are a percentage of value rather than a fixed dollar amount. In aviation hull insurance a deductible of 2.5 to 10 percent of the insured value of the plane is common. Earthquake insurance often has a deductible of 2 percent of the actual cash value of the property.

Franchise deductibles

The **franchise,** found in ocean marine insurance, differs from the straight deductible. If the loss exceeds the franchise the insurer pays the full loss, not just the excess. Assume a shipment valued at $3,000 is covered subject to a 3 percent franchise. If a loss amounts to less than $90 the insurer is *free of liability,* but if the loss exceeds $90 the insurer is *liable for the full amount.* If this were a straight deductible rather than a franchise the insurer would be *liable only for the amount in excess of $90* (3 percent of $3,000). Marine policies are written with either franchise or straight deductibles, although the franchise is the more common. The franchise percentage varies among commodities and policies. Usually straight deductibles are found in medical expense coverage.

Waiting periods

Disability coverage deductibles are called **waiting periods.** For example, in some disability income policies no benefits are paid until after the first 14 days of illness. (Waiting periods are more common in sickness than in accident policies.) Disability riders in life insurance usually require a six-month waiting period. In some states a waiting period is required after an injury to establish eligibility for workers' compensation benefits. Often the compensation benefits become retroactive if the worker's disability continues beyond a stated period. Benefits payable retroactively after a specified period are also written in some disability income policies. This type of deductible increases moral hazard. Anyone (well, nearly anyone) can make a disability last a few more days—even weeks!

SUMMARY

1. The maximum reimbursement for losses may not exceed the policyowner's insurable interest. The amount of insurable interest does not restrict the amount payable in life insurance because life insurance policies are not contracts of indemnity.
2. In property insurance the amount payable is usually limited to the actual cash value of the property at the time of the loss. Actual cash value equals the cost of replacing the property (new) less observed depreciation.
3. Replacement cost insurance pays the policyowner the full replacement cost for a loss. To be eligible for full replacement cost coverage, a policyowner usually must cover property for at least a stated percentage of its full value.

4. Valued-policy laws require the insurer to pay the face amount of the policy for a total loss of real property.

5. Usually, property insurance contracts will not pay more than the policy face amount. In addition, most property insurance contracts contain internal limits applying to specified losses.

6. Several methods of expressing policy amount limits are:
   a. Divided coverage.
   b. Blanket coverage.
   c. Priority coverage.
   d. Sublimits.
   e. Additional amounts.

7. Liability insurance policies may be written using one or more of four methods of stating policy limits.

8. Other-insurance clauses determine how much each insurer will pay when more than one policy covers a loss. Coverage may be shared, excess, primary or prohibited.

9. Coinsurance clauses restrict the amount paid for partial losses if the damaged property is not covered for at least a stated percentage of its actual cash value at the time of the loss. The purpose of coinsurance clauses is to help achieve rate equity and adequacy.

10. Deductible clauses are included in insurance contracts to eliminate coverage for small losses and to reduce morale hazard.

REVIEW QUESTIONS

1. How does coinsurance help achieve equity and adequacy in rates?

2. Explain how a franchise deductible operates.

3. When might a policyowner use blanket coverage?

4. Giora Harpaz owns two fire insurance policies on her $600,000 office building, one with insurer A for $400,000, the other with insurer B for $200,000. If the insurers share the loss on a pro rata basis, how much will each insurer pay in case of a $240,000 fire loss?

5. If the insurers in Question 4 contribute on a limit of liability basis, how much will each pay for the $240,000 loss?

6. Explain the difference between insurable interest in property insurance and insurable interest in life insurance as a measure of the amount payable in the event of a loss.

7. Compare the different sublimits used in property insurance contracts.

8. Is the principle of indemnity violated by valued policies? By replacement-cost policies?

9. Give an example of a policy which requires the consent of the insurer prior to assignment. Why?

10. Why are some policies noncancellable while others may be cancelled by either the insurer or the policyowner?

CHAPTER

8 An analysis of the homeowners policy

John Thoeming/Richard D. Irwin

CHAPTER OBJECTIVES

1. **To identify and distinguish between the various characteristics of the seven popular forms in the homeowners "76" series.**
2. **To analyze the HO–3 policy using the techniques explained in Chapters 6 and 7.**

Homeowners policies are available to protect owners and tenants from loss or damage to their property and to provide protection against liability claims. This chapter, using the techniques developed in Chapters 6 and 7, analyzes one of the most widely sold homeowners policies, Form 3 (hereafter called HO–3).[1]

All homeowners policies have two sections: section I covers property exposures; section II covers the liability exposure. For example, section I of the HO–3 lists four coverages: coverage A, the dwelling; coverage B, other structures on the residence premises; coverage C, personal property and coverage D, loss of use. Six additional coverages are included: (1) debris removal; (2) fire department charges; (3) trees, shrubs and other plants; (4) theft of a credit card; (5) property removal and (6) reasonable repairs to protect the property after a loss.

Section II consists of coverage E, personal liability; coverage F, medical payments to others and three additional coverages: claim expenses, damage to the property of others and first-aid expenses. Sections I and II coverages are defined and explained in detail in this chapter.

THE HOMEOWNERS SERIES

Homeowners forms differ only in the coverage offered by Section I, as shown in Table 8–1.

"Readable" Forms

The current homeowners program of the Insurance Services Office (a rating bureau discussed in Chapter 20) was introduced in December 1975. The "readable" policies of this program were designed to make the policies more comprehensible to the insurance buying (and selling!) public. Readability was improved through many techniques; the number of words are reduced by 40 percent, the type size used is 25 percent larger and key words are specifically defined on the first page of the policy and always printed in boldface type when used elsewhere.

Homeowners Series Endorsements

Various endorsements are available for an additional premium to extend the coverage of the homeowners policies to satisfy policyowners' needs. The **inflation guard endorsement** increases quarterly the limits of liability of section I of HO–1, HO–2, HO–3, HO–5 and HO–8 by 1 or 1.5 percent or some other fixed amount. The endorsement allows policyowners to cover their property for increasing amounts to offset inflation. The **scheduled personal property endorsement** allows the insured to cover on an all-risk basis valuable personal property for higher amounts than provided by the basic policy. In addition, the **personal property replacement-cost endorsement** allows the insured to cover personal

[1] Note: The use of the specimen copy of the readable HO–3 policy reproduced in Appendix 3 of this text is helpful when studying this chapter. Also, see the note at the beginning of Chapter 6.

TABLE 8–1 Perils Covered Under Section I of HO Forms

POLICY FORM	*COVERAGE A*	*COVERAGE B*	*COVERAGE C*	*COVERAGE D*
HO–1	10*	10*	10*	10*
HO–2	17†	17†	17†	17†
HO–3	All risk‡	All risk‡	16§	All risk‡ or 17† (see ‖)
HO–4	No coverage#	No coverage#	17†	17†
HO–5	All risk‡	All risk‡	All risk‡	All risk‡
HO–6	Extremely limited**	No coverage**	17†	17†
HO–8	10††	10††	10*	10*

* The 10 perils are: fire and lightning, windstorm or hail, explosion, riot or civil commotion, vehicles, aircraft, smoke, vandalism or malicious mischief, breakage of glass that is part of a building, storm door or storm window and theft.

† The 17 perils are the 10 in HO–1 plus: falling objects; weight of ice, snow or sleet; collapse of buildings; damage resulting from a steam or hot water heating system; accidental discharge or overflow of water or steam; freezing of plumbing, heating and air conditioning systems and domestic appliances and accidental damage from artificially generated electrical currents.

§ The 17 perils listed in the HO–2 excluding breakage of glass coverage. Breakage of glass that is part of the building, storm door or storm window is covered under the all-risk coverage offered by coverages A and B.

‡ All perils except those specifically excluded somewhere in the policy.

‖ All risk if loss of use is caused by damage to coverage A or coverage B property and the 17 perils if loss of use is caused by damage to coverage C property.

HO–4 is also known as the "tenant's form." It applies only to the contents of the residence and is identical to the HO–2 except that coverages A and B are excluded.

** HO–6 was introduced in 1974 to satisfy the unique needs of condominium unit owners who, like apartment tenants, are exposed to losses of unscheduled personal property and losses resulting from liability exposures. HO–6 is a reproduction of HO–4 except for two changes necessary to make the policy appropriate for condominium unit owners. One change provides $1,000 of coverage for damage to additions and alterations made by the unit owners within the inside walls of the unit. The other change provides that the addition-and-alterations coverage will be excess insurance over any insurance owned by the condominium association (the owners of the building) that covers the same property.

†† The HO–8 policy is identical to the HO–1 except coverages A and B losses are settled on a ACV basis in contrast to a replacement-cost basis.

property on a replacement-cost basis rather than an ACV basis. A **watercraft endorsement** is available to extend the section II personal liability and medical payments coverage to bodily injury and property damage arising from the ownership, maintenance, use, loading or unloading of watercraft powered by outboard motors. The **theft extension endorsement** provides theft coverage for personal property left in an unlocked automobile (it deletes the requirement that the policyowner must show signs of forcible entry to recover for a theft loss).

Numerous other endorsements are available for the special needs of policyowners. These endorsements give flexibility to the homeowners forms.

Insurance for Mobile Homes

In addition to the homeowners series, insurers offer protection for mobile home owners (MP–1). Coverage A applies to the mobile home and permanent fixtures if they are located on land owned or leased by the policyowner and occupied as a private residence. Coverage B is similar to the HO personal property coverage with three additional exclusions: (1) trailers, (2) business property and (3) appliances, furniture and equipment furnished by the manufacturer or dealer as standard equipment covered under A or C. Coverage C applies to "nonpermanent" additions to the mobile home, such as awnings, carports and air conditioners. The additional living expenses coverage (coverage D) restricts benefits to $15 per day whereas the homeowners policies have no limit. The liability protection of the MP–1 is identical to that offered by the HO policy.

DEFINING THE PERILS COVERED IN THE HO–3

In the remainder of this chapter attention is focused on the HO–3 policy. The issues addressed are the covered perils, property, losses, locations, period, hazards and amounts plus the policyowner's duties after a loss. Coverages A and B in section I of the HO–3 insure against all risks of physical loss to the property described in the applicable coverage except where excluded elsewhere in the policy. Thus the policyowner must read the policy to be aware of these exclusions.

As the policy is a readable form, nothing is lost by simply reproducing the peril exclusions as they are stated in the policy. The exclusions in the HO–3 applying to coverages A (dwellings) and B (other structures) are (see also Appendix 3):

1. Losses excluded under Section I, "Exclusions":[2]
   a. *Ordinance or law,* meaning enforcement of any ordinance or law regulating the construction, repair, or demolition of a building or other structure, unless specifically provided under this policy.
   b. *Earth movement,* meaning that direct loss by fire, explosion, theft or breakage of glass or safety glazing materials resulting from earth movement is covered.
   c. *Water damage,* meaning:
      (1) Flood, surface water, waves, tidal water, overflow of a body of water or spray from any of these, whether or not driven by wind;
      (2) Water that backs up through sewers or drains or
      (3) Water below the surface of the ground, including water that exerts pressure on or seeps or leaks through a building, sidewalk, driveway, foundation, swimming pool or other structure.

      Direct loss by fire, explosion or theft resulting from water damage is covered.
   d. *Power interruption,* meaning the interruption of power or other utility service if the interruption takes place away from the residence premises. If a peril insured against ensues on the residence premises, we will pay only for loss caused by the ensuing peril.
   e. *Neglect,* meaning neglect of the insured to use all reasonable means to save and preserve property at and after the time of a loss or when property is endangered by the ensuing peril.
   f. *War,* including undeclared war, civil war, insurrection, rebellion, revolution, warlike act by a military force or military personnel, destruction or seizure or use for a military purpose and including any consequence of any of these. Discharge of a nuclear weapon shall be deemed a warlike act even if accidental.
   g. *Nuclear hazard,* to the extent set forth in the Nuclear Hazard Clause of Section I: "Conditions."
2. Freezing of a plumbing, heating, or air-conditioning system or of a household appliance or by discharge, leakage or overflow from within the system or appliance

[2] These section I exclusions apply also to coverages C (personal property) and D (loss of use).

caused by freezing, while the dwelling is vacant, unoccupied or being constructed unless you have used reasonable care to:

a. Maintain heat in the building or

b. Shut off the water supply and drain the system and appliances of water.

3. Freezing, thawing, pressure or weight of water or ice, whether driven by wind or not, to a fence, pavement, patio, swimming pool, foundation, retaining wall, bulkhead, pier, wharf or dock.
4. Theft in or to a dwelling under construction or of materials and supplies for use in the construction until the dwelling is completed and occupied.
5. Vandalism and malicious mischief or breakage of glass and safety glazing materials if the dwelling has been vacant for more than 30 consecutive days immediately before the loss. A dwelling being constructed is not considered vacant.
6. Continuous or repeated seepage or leakage of water or steam over a period of time from within a plumbing, heating or air-conditioning system or from within a household appliance.
7. Wear and tear; marring; deterioration; inherent vice;[3] latent defect; mechanical breakdown; rust; mold; wet or dry rot; contamination; smog; smoke from agricultural smudging or industrial operations; settling, cracking, shrinking, bulging or expansion of pavements, patios, foundations, walls, floors, roofs or ceilings; birds, vermin, rodents, insects or domestic animals. If any of these cause water to escape from a plumbing, heating or air-conditioning system or household appliance, we cover loss caused by the water. We also cover the cost of tearing out and replacing any part of a building necessary to repair the system or appliance. We do not cover loss to the system or appliance from which this water escaped.

Under items 2 through 7 any ensuing loss not excluded is covered.

Coverage C (personal property) in the HO–3 is written on a specified perils basis. Thus no payment will be made by the insurer unless one of the 17 specified perils is the proximate cause of the loss. These 17 perils are:

1. Fire or lightning.
2. Windstorm or hail.
3. Explosion.
4. Riot and civil commotion.
5. Aircraft.
6. Vehicles.
7. Smoke.
8. Vandalism and malicious mischief.
9. Theft.
10. Breakage of glass or safety material.
11. Falling objects.
12. Weight of ice, snow or sleet.
13. Collapse of building or any part of a building.
14. Accidental discharge or overflow of water or steam.
15. Sudden and accidental tearing asunder, cracking, burning or bulging.
16. Freezing.
17. Sudden and accidental damage from artificially generated electrical current.

This listing names the perils. The policyowner must study the policy to learn their meanings and any limitations put on them.

Section II, coverage E, of the HO–3 covers personal liability and is essentially equivalent to the comprehensive personal liability policy available as a separate contract. The comprehensive personal liability policy, in spite of its name, is a specified perils contract. The peril covered is the negligence or alleged negligence of the insured (and under certain conditions the landlord's negligence, if the

[3] Inherent vice is a latent defect in the property that may cause loss or damage to it. The insurer does not guarantee the soundness ("merchantability") of articles bought!

lease requires the insured to assume this liability). Coverage F of section II covers reasonable and necessary medical expenses of others arising from accidents.

DEFINING THE PROPERTY COVERED

The property covered under coverages A and B in the HO–3 consists of (1) the dwelling described, including structures attached to it, occupied principally as a private residence; (2) materials and supplies located on or adjacent to the residence premises for use in the construction, alteration or repair of the dwelling or other structures located on the premises and (3) other structures on the residence premises separated from the dwelling by clear space. The insuring agreements exclude structures on the premises used for business purposes and structures (except those used exclusively for a private garage) rented to or leased to persons other than a tenant of the dwelling.

Coverage is also provided for trees, shrubs, plants or lawns on the residence premises for loss caused by fire, lightning, explosion, riot, civil commotion, vandalism, malicious mischief, theft, aircraft or vehicles not owned or operated by a resident of the premises. Liability for these items is limited to 5 percent of the dwelling limit and no more than $500 per tree, shrub or plant. (Plants grown for business purposes are excluded.)

The exceptions to personal property in coverage C are:

1. Animals, birds and fish.
2. Motorized land vehicles licensed for road use and aircraft.
3. Property of tenants (broadly defined) not related to an insured.
4. Business property on and off premises.
5. Devices for transmitting, recording, receiving or reproduction of sound operated by power from a motor vehicle's electrical system.

Property separately described and covered specifically in the HO contract or any other insurance contract is excluded.

Coverage E, personal liability, does not apply to damage to property owned by the insured. Damage to property rented to, occupied or used by or in the care of the insured is also excluded from liability coverage unless the damage is caused by fire, smoke or explosion. Thus if the family rents a motel room and negligently causes a fire that destroys an upholstered chair, its liability to the motel is covered under section II of HO–3. However, if the chair is damaged by beer stains and cigarette burns during a party given by the 18-year-old offspring while the parents are out of town the policy will not cover the liability to the motel owner because the loss is not caused by a peril named in this exclusion.

DEFINING THE TYPES OF LOSSES COVERED

Although a peril may be covered by the HO–3 policy not all losses caused by that peril are covered. In coverages A and B of the HO–3 policy only direct loss or damage is covered. The policy does not provide indemnity for rebuilding expenses required by an ordinance or law regulating construction or repair. For example, some zoning laws require that a frame building more than 50 percent destroyed by fire must be replaced with a fireproof structure. Homeowners policies do not cover the additional replacement cost resulting from these codes unless the policy is endorsed to cover this loss. Nor is loss of use covered while the property is being replaced. If a building is destroyed by fire, the fire policy will cover the cost of repairing the building, but will not cover loss of business that may occur until repairs are completed. Other types of indirect losses, such as those resulting from temperature changes, also are not covered by the HO–3 unless specifically endorsed to provide the protection.

The HO–3 adds coverage for debris removal, fire department service charges (up to $250), loss of use (coverage D) and certain other indirect and extra expense losses. If, following a tornado, a house covered by an HO–3 policy must be removed from the middle of the street the removal cost will be paid under the policy. However, the insurer's limit of liability for this coverage and the coverage on the damaged property is the amount of insurance applicable to the damaged property (in this case the limit of liability applicable to section I, coverage A as stated in the declarations). If the sum of these losses exceeds that limit an additional 5 percent of that limit is available to cover debris removal expense. Coverage D, loss of use, covers the necessary increase in living expenses resulting from a property loss caused by an insured peril. The expenses covered are those incurred by the insured to continue as nearly as practicable the normal standard of living of the household for the shortest time required to repair or replace the premises, or for the household to settle permanently elsewhere. In addition, coverage is provided for the fair rental value of any part of the residence premises rented to others or held for rental that is made uninhabitable by an insured peril. This coverage is provided for the shortest time required to repair or replace the part of the premises rented or held for rent.

Under HO–3 the insurer also pays consequential loss to unscheduled personal property caused by temperature changes resulting from physical damage to the described buildings and equipment on the premises. If lightning strikes electric wires on the premises, the insured will be reimbursed for food spoilage in the freezer. If lightning knocks out a power line off the premises, the food spoilage loss is not covered by the typical HO–3. Coverage for losses stemming from off-premises interruption of power may eventually become standard because of its widespread need. As of mid-1982 only a few insurers offered coverage for this type of loss at no additional premium. The consequential loss exclusion for off-premises power failures has created confusion. Assume that lightning strikes a power line across the street from the covered dwelling, damaging its heating system, causing the plumbing to freeze. Does the HO–3 cover repair of the plumbing? Yes, because the freezing of plumbing is not an excluded peril in the HO–3; but confusion could arise because an off-premises power failure led to the loss. To eliminate confusion many territories are adopting a mandatory endorsement (HO–245) to clarify that the power failure exclusion never was intended to exclude direct damage from a specified peril. The HO–3 also provides for $250 maximum to pay fire department charges if the covered property is located outside the fire protection district that provides service to the insured.

Coverage up to $500 is included in the HO–3 for loss:

1. Arising from the legal obligation of any insured to pay because of the theft or unauthorized use of credit cards issued to or registered in any insured's name (except by a resident of the insured's household or someone who has been entrusted with the credit card).
2. To any insured caused by forgery or alteration of any check or negotiable instrument.
3. To any insured through acceptance in good faith of counterfeit United States or Canadian paper currency.

Coverage E of section II covers bodily injury and property damage claims where the coverage applies and the insured is legally liable. Under coverage F payment is made for medical expenses incurred because of bodily injury caused by a covered accident. Additional coverages in section II include expenses incurred by the insurer and charged an insured in defense of a suit: (1) premiums on bonds required in a suit defended by the insurer; (2) reasonable expenses incurred by an insured at the insurer's request, including loss of earnings (but not loss of other income) up to $50 per day for assisting the insurer in the investigation or defense of a claim or suit and (3) interest on the *full* judgment (regardless of the amount of the insurer's liability) accruing between the time the judgment is entered and when it is paid.

DEFINING THE PERSONS COVERED

In addition to providing coverage for the named insureds and their legal representatives the HO–3 provides coverage for the following residents of the household: (1) the spouse, (2) relatives and (3) any other person under the age of 21 in the care of any person named above. Section II (liability) also covers persons or organizations legally responsible for animals and watercraft owned by an insured.

The HO–3 extends coverage at the named insured's request to personal property of others while the property is on that part of the residence premises occupied by an insured.

The medical payments section of the HO–3 (coverage F) provides coverage for medical expenses incurred (or determined) within three years from the date of the accident for each person accidentally injured while on the covered location (with permission of an insured) or elsewhere (under specified circumstances). The coverage is available only if the bodily injury (1) arises from a condition on the covered location or the ways immediately adjoining; (2) is caused by activities of an insured or by a residence employee in the course of employment; (3) is caused by an animal owned by or in care of an insured or (4) is sustained by any residence employee and arises out of and in the course of employment by an insured. This coverage does not apply to the named insured or regular residents of the household, other than residence employees; nor does it apply to a residence employee if the bodily injury occurs off the covered location and does not arise from or in the course of the residence employee's employment by any insured. Persons covered under a workers' compensation law also are not insured under this section.

INNERSCRIPT: ASSIGNMENTS

The HO–3 policy requires written consent of the insurer to validate an assignment. This requirement conforms to the law that would apply in the absence of contract agreement. These policies insure the property owner, not the property, against loss. If the property is sold the insurance is still held by the former owner

(*Continued*)

unless the insurer agrees to an assignment. Insurers select their policyowners and cannot be forced by assignment to insure anyone who acquires an insurable interest in the property.

An assignment without the insurer's consent seldom voids the policy. The assignment is just not recognized. Thus if Dorothy Morey sells her home and assigns the insurance to the buyer the policy is not void. The insurer simply will not have to pay for a loss because the insured no longer has an insurable interest in the destroyed dwelling. If Dorothy repurchases the home before the policy expires the policy covers, because the insured then regains her insurable interest.

Consent of the insurer is necessary for a valid assignment of most property and liability insurance policies and may be given by the local agent of the insurer. A clause similar to the following is found in nearly all property and liability insurance contracts:

> **If, however, the insured shall die, or be adjudged bankrupt, or insolvent within the policy period, this policy, unless canceled, shall, if written notice be given to the company within sixty days after the date of such death or adjudication, cover the insured's legal representative of the insured.**

Some policies set 30 days as the time within which notice must be given. This clause is not in fire insurance policies because legal representatives of the insured are specifically covered in the insuring agreement.

DEFINING THE LOCATIONS COVERED

The HO–3 provides insurance for loss of covered property while located on the residence premises. Coverage for personal property is not restricted to the residence premises but is worldwide. Coverage for personal property *usually* situated at a residence of the insured *other* than the residence premises is restricted to 10 percent of the amount of insurance applicable to coverage C or $1,000, whichever is greater. Thus personal property of students living away from home or personal property usually situated at a summer cottage is covered subject to the 10 percent or $1,000 limitation. Insurance for direct loss *from any cause* applies for not more than 30 days to covered property while removed from the premises that are endangered by a covered peril.

The personal liability coverage of the HO–3 has no territorial exclusions. If a policy does not specifically restrict the area of coverage, then coverage is worldwide. Medical payments coverage is available to persons on the covered location with the permission of any insured or elsewhere if the bodily injury is caused by (1) an insured's activities, (2) an animal owned by or in the care of an insured, (3) a residence employee of an insured in the course of employment and (4) a condition at the covered location. The covered location is defined as:

a. The residence premises.

b. The part of any other premises, structures and grounds used as a residence and shown in the declarations or acquired during the policy period for use as a residence.

c. Any premises used in connection with the premises included in *a* or *b.*

d. Any part of a premises not owned by an insured but where an insured is temporarily residing.

e. Vacant land owned by or rented to an insured other than farmland.

f. Land owned by or rented to an insured on which a one- or two-family dwelling is being constructed as a residence for any insured.

g. Individual or family cemetery plots or burial vaults of any insured.

h. Any part of a premises occasionally rented to an insured for other than business purposes.

DEFINING THE PERIOD OF COVERAGE

The HO–3 policy begins at 12:01 A.M. standard time at the residence premises on the date of inception and continues until 12:01 A.M. standard time at the residence premises on the date of expiration. The HO–3 policy must be renewed by the policyowner annually to keep it in effect. If the insurer elects not to renew the policy, written notice must be given the policyowner at least 30 days before the expiration date of the policy.

The HO–3 policyowner may cancel the policy for any reason by notifying the insurer in writing of the cancellation date. The insurer, however, may cancel only for specific reasons stated in the policy and must give the policyowner sufficient written notice. The insurer may cancel the policy under the following conditions:

1. When the premium has not been paid, the policy may be cancelled at anytime by giving at least 10 days' notice before the date cancellation takes effect.

2. When this policy has been in effect for less than 60 days and is not a renewal it may be cancelled for any reason by giving at least 10 days' notice before the date cancellation takes effect.

3. When this policy has been in effect for 60 days or more, or at any time if it is a renewal it may be cancelled if there has been a misrepresentation of fact which if known would have caused the policy not to be issued or if the risk has changed substantially since the policy was issued. At least 30 days' notice is required in this case before the date the cancellation is effective.

4. When this policy is written for a period longer than one year, it may be cancelled for any reason at its anniversary by giving at least 30 days' notice before the date cancellation takes effect.

DEFINING THE HAZARDS THAT EXCLUDE OR SUSPEND COVERAGE

Some of the coverages provided by the HO–3 policy may be restricted if the residence premises is vacant or unoccupied. For example, loss from freezing of a plumbing, heating or air-conditioning system is excluded while the residence premises is unoccupied unless (1) reasonable care is taken to maintain the heat in the building or (2) the water system is shut off. In addition, loss from vandalism is excluded while the residence premises is vacant or unoccupied for a specified time period.

HO–3 policy also lists the following excluded hazards: "war, including undeclared war, civil war, insurrection, rebellion, revolution, warlike act by a military force or military personnel, destruction or seizure or use for a military purpose, and including any consequence of any of these. Discharge of a nuclear weapon shall be deemed a warlike act even if accidental." The nuclear hazard (any nuclear reaction, radiation or radioactive contamination, all whether controlled or uncontrolled) also is excluded from coverage. However, direct loss by fire resulting from the nuclear hazard is covered.[4]

The personal liability coverage, section II of the HO–3, excludes the business and professional liability hazard. The liability hazard from premises owned, rented or controlled by the insured (other than those premises defined as covered locations) is also excluded, except for limited coverage for property under the insured's control. Personal liability resulting from the ownership, maintenance, use, loading or unloading of an aircraft, motor vehicle or watercraft is excluded except for bodily injury to any residence employee arising from and in the course of that employee's employment by an insured. The watercraft exclusion does not apply to boats with inboard motors of less than 50 horsepower and sailing vessels under 26 feet in overall length and powered by less than 25 total horsepower. The watercraft exclusion also does not apply while the watercraft is stored or to the use of watercraft not owned or rented (e.g., borrowed) by an insured. An insured should check each policy to determine the nature of all exclusions.

LIMITATIONS ON THE AMOUNT OF RECOVERY

Six limitations on the insurer's liability for loss or damage are discussed in Chapter 7. Table 8–2 shows how these limits apply to section I of the HO–3. The limit producing the lowest amount governs the amount to be paid. The limits provided by section II are outlined in Table 8–3.

Under section II of the HO–3 only two of the six limits of recovery apply: the policy limits and other insurance. Table 8–3 outlines the applications of these limits.

Insurers specify minimum amounts of insurance that they will write under HO–3. Depending on the insurer, that amount may be as low as $8,000 or as high as $40,000 or more for coverage A. The amounts of insurance for coverages B, C and D are based on the amount of coverage A, as shown in Table 8–4. The basic limits for coverages E and F are also shown.

Since minimum limits are likely to be too low, homeowners are advised to buy an inflation-guard endorsement to maintain adequate coverage.

THE POLICYOWNER'S DUTIES AFTER A LOSS

The HO–3 policy contains the seven duties required of the policyowner, discussed in Chapter 6. Under the notice of loss requirement, the HO–3 policyowner must give immediate (not as soon as practicable) notice to the insurer. The six other duties are not discussed here as they are identical to those explained in Chapter 6.

[4] Some of these excluded hazards appear to be perils. To the extent that war and warlike acts, for example, increase the chance of loss by the perils of fire, explosion, vandalism and so on, they are hazards as defined in Chapter 2. The nuclear exposure can be a peril by causing loss by radioactive contamination, for example. To the extent that it increases the chance of loss from a tort action, the nuclear exposure can be called a hazard. As used in this paragraph the term *nuclear hazard* should be *nuclear peril*. But the insurance industry is not convinced.

TABLE 8–2
Limitations on the Amount of Recovery Applying to Section I

<table>
<tr><th>COVERAGES</th><th>ACV OR REPLACEMENT COST</th><th>POLICY LIMITS</th><th>CO-INSURANCE</th><th>OTHER INSURANCE</th><th>DEDUCTIBLES</th><th>INSURABLE INTEREST</th></tr>
<tr><td>A</td><td rowspan="2">Replacement cost*</td><td rowspan="2">Face amount listed in the declarations</td><td rowspan="2">80 percent coinsurance clause#</td><td rowspan="5">Pro rata liability</td><td rowspan="3">One deductible** (minimum $100)</td><td rowspan="5">Policyowners will not recover for an amount greater than their insurable interest at the time of loss</td></tr>
<tr><td>B</td></tr>
<tr><td>C</td><td>ACV†</td><td>Face amount listed in the declarations§‡</td><td rowspan="3">Not applicable</td></tr>
<tr><td>D</td><td>Necessary increases in living expenses for the household to maintain its normal living standard</td><td>Face amount listed in the declarations</td><td>Not applicable</td></tr>
<tr><td>Additional coverages</td><td>Any reasonable expenses and ACV‡</td><td>Sublimits and additional limits‖</td><td>The deductible applies to all but two coverages††</td></tr>
</table>

* Loss of or damage to carpeting, domestic appliances, awnings, outdoor antennas and outdoor equipment, whether or not attached to buildings, are exceptions and covered for their ACV.

† An endorsement is available to extend replacement-cost coverage to personal property otherwise available only for buildings subject to certain limits stated in the endorsement (e.g., 400 percent of the ACV).

‡ Coverages for debris removal, reasonable repairs and fire department service charge are limited to reasonable costs incurred by the policyowner. Coverage for trees, shrubs and other plants is limited to the ACV of the loss.

§ Coverage C has eight sublimits: (1) $100 for money, bank notes, bullion, gold other than goldware, silver other than silverware, platinum, coins and medals; (2) $500 for securities, accounts, deeds, evidences of debt, letters of credit, notes other than bank notes, manuscripts, passports, tickets and stamps; (3) $500 for watercraft, including their trailers, furnishings, equipment and outboard motors; (4) $500 for trailers not used with watercraft; (5) $500 for grave markers; (6) $500 for loss by theft of jewelry, watches, furs, precious and semiprecious stones; (7) $1,000 for loss by theft of silverware, silver-plated ware, goldware, gold-plated ware and pewterware and (8) $1,000 for loss by theft of guns.

‖ The applicable sublimits are: (1) under the trees, shrubs and other plants coverage, 5 percent of the insurance for coverage A but not more than $500 for any one of these items and (2) $500 for the credit card, forgery and counterfeit money coverage. The additional limits are: (1) 5 percent in addition to the face amounts for coverages A, B or C for debris removal expenses and (2) $250 in addition to all policy limits for the fire department service charge coverage.

If the policyowner purchases insurance for an amount *less* than 80 percent of the replacement cost, the greater of the following two limits applies: (1) the ACV or (2) the amount of the replacement cost less the amount assumed by the policyowner because of a coinsurance deficiency. (See Chapter 7 for a discussion of coinsurance.) Also, if the cost to repair or replace the damage is in excess of either $1,000 or 5 percent of the face amount for coverage A, the insurer will pay no more than the ACV until actual repairs or replacements are completed.

** A straight deductible applies for loss resulting from any peril.

†† Deductibles do not apply to the fire department service charge coverage or the credit card, forgery and counterfeit money coverage.

TABLE 8–3 Limitations Applying to Section II

COVERAGES	*POLICY LIMITS*	*OTHER INSURANCE*
E	One policy limit applying per occurrence	Insurance under this coverage is excess over all other valid and collectible primary insurance
F	One policy limit applying per person as a result of each accident	Other insurance does not affect the amount of recovery
Additional coverages	All additional coverages are in addition to the policy limits Two sublimits apply*	Same as coverage E†

* The two sublimits are: (1) $50 per day for reasonable expenses incurred by the policyowner in assisting the insurer and (2) $250 per occurrence for damage to property of others caused by an insured.

† The policy does not specify other insurance arrangements for additional coverages. Presumably if two or more insurers are involved they will negotiate the obligations of each. Otherwise the logical assumption is that the primary insurer under coverage E is liable for the additional coverages and an excess insurer has no liability for them.

TABLE 8–4 An Example of Coverage Limits Under the HO–3 Policy

A.	Dwelling	$20,000
B.	Other structures	10 percent coverage A
C.	Personal property	50 percent coverage A
D.	Loss of use	20 percent coverage A
E.	Personal liability	$25,000 per occurrence
F.	Medical payments	$500 per person; $25,000 per accident

SETTLEMENT OPTIONS

The HO–3 policy contains the three sets of options available to the insurer in settling losses as discussed in Chapter 6: (1) replacement option, (2) abandonment and salvage option and (3) restoration of a pair or set option.

TIME LIMITS: SUITS AND CLAIMS PAYMENT

A provision in section I of the HO–3 policy states that no action can be brought against the insurer unless such action is started within one year after the loss. In section II under coverage E, personal liability, no action can be brought against the insurer until the insured's liability to a third party has been determined by final judgment or an agreement is signed by the insurer. Under coverage F, medical payments to others, no time limit is stated and presumably the time limit is governed by the statute of limitations.[5]

Under section I the maximum time for payment of loss or damage is 30 days after an agreement is reached between the policyowner and the insurer. No time limit is specified for section II. However, under coverage E the insurer, once final judgment is entered, will be directed by the court to pay the plaintiff within a reasonable time. In the interest of reducing the probability of law suits

[5] Statutes of limitations specify the time limits in which suits can be brought following the cause of action. The time limits vary not only among states but also among types of agreements.

by the injured party the insurer is apt to expedite payment of valid claims under coverage F (medical payments to others).

SUMMARY

1. Homeowners policies are purchased to protect owners and tenants from loss or damage to their property and to provide insurance for their personal liability exposure.
2. Seven popular policies are written in the homeowners "76" series. The liability coverage (section II) is the same for all seven forms but variations are found in section I coverages primarily in the perils and property covered. (See Table 8–1.)
3. The HO–3 has two sections: section I (property coverage) includes coverage A, the dwelling; coverage B, other structures on the residence premises; coverage C, personal property and coverage D, loss of use. Section II includes coverage E, personal liability and coverage F, medical payments to others.
4. For the HO–3, perils are written on an all-risk basis for coverages A, B and D. Coverage C is written on a specified perils basis. E covers liability caused by negligence and the medical payments accident peril is covered under F.
5. As for property covered, real property is covered under A and B while personal property is covered under C. Some property not included in A, B and C is covered under additional coverage clauses. E provides protection for damage to property of others caused by an insured's negligence.
6. Direct losses of property are covered under A, B and C. C also offers limited consequential loss coverage. Both loss of use and extra expenses are covered under D.
7. HO–3 provides coverage for the named insured (and their legal representatives) plus other residents of the household broadly classified. Medical payments under F provide coverage for persons other than the named insured or regular residents of the household for accidental injuries.
8. The HO–3 provides coverage for real property and some personal property (e.g., building materials) located on the residence premises. Coverage for other personal property (coverage C) and personal liability are worldwide.
9. The HO–3 policy begins at 12:01 A.M. standard time at the residence premises on the date of inception to 12:01 A.M. standard time on the date of expiration.
10. The policyowner may cancel the policy at any time; the insurer may cancel only for specific reasons stated in the policy.
11. Under section I, hazards that can exclude or suspend coverage in the HO–3 include vacancy (under certain circumstances), war, rebellion and the nuclear hazard. Section II coverage excludes such hazards as the business and professional liability hazard.
12. Table 8–2 outlines the limitations on the insurer's liability as they apply to the HO–3 policy.

13. The HO–3 includes the usual conditions relating to the duties of the policyowner following a loss, settlement options and time limits for suits and claims payment.

14. The HO–3 contains the usual assignment clause found in property-liability insurance policies.

REVIEW QUESTIONS

1. Professor Peter Gutmann's house burns and a city ordinance requires that it be rebuilt with brick instead of wood. This change will cost him $180,000 instead of $120.000. Will Professor Gutmann's $180,000 HO–3 policy cover the full $180,000? Explain.

2. Ken Kennedy rents a cabin for a weekend fishing trip. While smoking in bed, he falls asleep. A fire ensues, causing $2,200 damage to the cabin. The cabin owner sues Ken. Will Ken's HO–3 policy cover the loss? Explain.

3. While Haig and Shultz are wrestling Haig's back is injured. Will Shultz's father's HO–3 policy cover Shultz if Haig brings suit against him?

4. Because of Betty Coleman's negligence, a fire breaks out in her basement, burns her house to the ground and spreads to the Sears's house next door. Sears sues Betty. Does Betty's HO–3 policy cover her liability? If not, how could she have been covered? Is Betty covered for the damage to her own house? If not, how could she have been covered?

5. Ali Saad's HO–3 policy provides $2 million coverage for his dwelling. A fire causes $200,000 damage to the roof and Saad must stay in a hotel suite for $1,000 a day while the house is repaired. The fair rental value of the house is $30,000 per month. How much can Saad collect under his policy?

6. If the full replacement cost of the dwelling in Question 5 is $3 million, how much can Saad recover for a covered loss if the replacement cost is $900,000 and the actual cash value is $750,000?

7. Billy, the kid next door, is 12 years old. He finds his stepfather's Saturday night special and shoots up the windows in your house while you and your family are away attending the annual National Rifle Association convention in Tombstone, Arizona. Will his family's HO–3 policy cover the loss?

8. Is replacement cost insurance available for personal property under the HO–3?

9. Roger Cannaday owns a HO–3 policy. His neighbor Soumendra De not only owns a HO–3 policy but also a German shepherd. Roger's home is well landscaped with expensive European trees and shrubs, to the dog's delight. While seeking relief on Roger's property the dog uses his favorite shrub. The shrub finally has enough and dies as a result of the constant attention. Will Roger's HO–3 policy cover the loss of the shrub?

10. A windstorm blows down two of Roger's favorite trees which land in Soumendra's backyard, killing her dog. Will Soumendra's HO–3 policy cover the cost of removing the debris (of the trees, that is)?

11. A ghoul steals the marker from your papa's grave. Does your HO–3 policy cover the loss? Explain.

12. You borrow your friend's outboard motor boat and negligently hit an experienced sailor's boat. You damage both the boat you hit and the boat you borrowed. Does your HO–3 policy provide liability coverage for both losses? Explain.

CHAPTER

9 An analysis of the personal auto policy

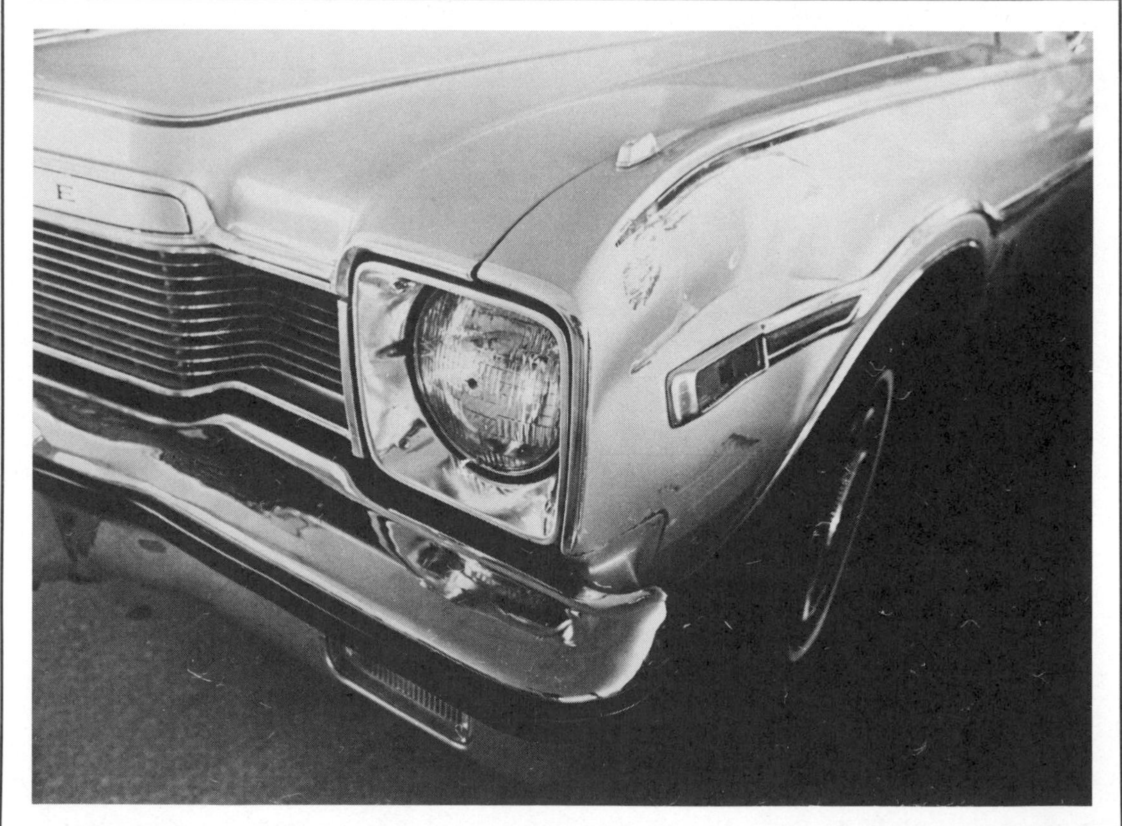

John Thoeming/Richard D. Irwin

CHAPTER OBJECTIVES

1. **To analyze the personal auto policy (PAP) using the techniques explained in Chapters 6 and 7.**
2. **To compare the three major personal auto insurance policies: the family auto policy (FAP), the special auto policy (SAP) and the personal auto policy (PAP).**

Individuals or married couples may purchase personal automobile insurance to cover private passenger autos and certain types of nonbusiness trucks they own or rent under a long-term lease. Three major personal automobile insurance policies are available: (1) the family auto policy (FAP), (2) the special auto policy (SAP) and (3) the personal auto policy (PAP).[1] The three policies offer four basic coverages: liability, medical payments to a covered person, uninsured motorists coverage and physical damage to the covered auto. However, variations among them are found both in the coverage and the eligibility requirements.

Again using the techniques developed in Chapters 6 and 7, this chapter analyzes the ISOs readable form, the PAP, which was designed to replace both the FAP and SAP. After the completion of the PAP analysis a table shows the difference between the three basic personal automobile insurance policies.

DEFINING THE PERILS COVERED

Part A (liability coverage) of the PAP covers the legal liability of an insured for bodily injury or property damage resulting from an auto accident. In part B (medical payments) the insurer agrees to pay reasonable expenses incurred for necessary medical and funeral services because of bodily injury caused by accident and sustained by a covered person. Under part C (uninsured motorists coverage) if a covered person suffers bodily injury in an accident negligently caused by either a hit-and-run or financially irresponsible driver the insurer will pay up to a specified amount as compensation for the insured's inability to collect damages from the wrongdoer. Note part C covers bodily injury only. It does not apply to damage to an insured's property negligently caused by an uninsured motorist.

Part D covers direct and accidental loss or damage to the covered auto. The perils covered under part D are divided into two classes: **collision** and **other-than-collision** (OTC). Under the PAP collision means the upset of the covered auto or its impact with another object. Perils excluded under the collision coverage are: missiles, falling objects, fire, theft or larceny, explosion, earthquake, windstorm, hail, water, flood, malicious mischief or vandalism, riot or civil commotion, contact with a bird or animal or breakage of glass. These exclusions are covered under the other-than-collision coverage even though some of them clearly are collision losses, e.g., falling objects and contact with a bird or animal. However, if breakage of glass is caused by a collision, the policyowner may elect to have it covered as a collision loss. Without this option the policyowner might have to pay two deductibles if a collision loss includes glass breakage: one for the collision loss and one for the OTC loss.

Under the other-than-collision coverage all physical damage perils are cov-

[1] Note: The use of the specimen copy of the readable PAP policy reproduced in Appendix 4 of this text is helpful in studying this chapter. Also see the note at the beginning of Chapter 6.

ered except those specifically excluded. The excluded perils are collision or upset; war losses; damage due and confined to wear and tear; road damage to tires; freezing and mechanical or electrical breakdown unless such damage is the result of other losses covered by the policy and loss caused by radioactive contamination. Many unusual losses have been paid under the OTC coverage, including damage to the finish by Halloween pranksters, damages resulting from transporting a leaking battery and loss from oil that mechanics spilled on upholstery. These losses were covered because the policy does not contain Halloween-prankster, battery-acid-spill or careless-mechanic exclusions.

When policyowners include part D in their coverage, OTC coverage is automatic, but collision coverage is included only if specified in the policy declarations. Consequently the policyowner may have OTC coverage without collision coverage. In addition, collision coverage is written with a straight deductible, most commonly $100 to $250. Traditionally OTC coverage was written without a deductible, but an effort to reduce the cost of auto insurance has encouraged insurers to offer OTC deductibles coverage, some on a mandatory and others on a voluntary basis. The amounts of the OTC and collision deductibles need not be the same; often the policyowner selects a lower deductible for OTC coverage. For collision insurance a $500 deductible costs about 40 percent less than a $200 deductible and a $250 deductible is about 10 percent less than a $200 deductible. Some insurers provide for waiver of deductibles when a car they cover collides with another auto covered by them.

Interpreting the Perils

The specific meaning of the word *collision* is hampered by the blatant rhetorical error of including the term itself in the policy's definition. An example appears necessary to clarify its meaning. Doug Cogswell had $100 deductible OTC coverage and $200 deductible collision coverage on his new sports car. A tree fell on his car during a windstorm, causing $3,500 damage. Is this loss collision or is it payable under the OTC coverage? The answer is important to Doug because if the loss is collision he must bear the first $200, but if not, then he must bear only the first $100. Obviously the tree collided with the car, but the OTC coverage states that loss caused by windstorm and falling objects shall not be deemed loss caused by collision for purposes of this coverage. Thus on two counts the loss would not be considered collision. The loss was caused both by a windstorm and by a falling object. Therefore Doug can collect the $3,400 ($3,500 less the $100 deductible) under his OTC coverage because neither windstorms nor falling objects are excluded perils for this coverage.

Assume the deductible amounts are *reversed* and Doug's car windows are smashed when hit by the rod of a smashed fisherman. If Doug is aware of the option he will elect to have the damage considered loss by collision to take advantage of the lower deductible.

The dividing line between collision and OTC is not clear. Many cases dealing with the distinction reach the courts where the decisions are often conflicting. The issues are sufficiently involved for the subject to have its own monograph. For one example, the question has been raised whether collision with a dead animal is OTC. Under the provision that contact with an animal is not considered collision, the argument is that when an animal dies it is no longer an animal but an inanimate object. Contact with it then becomes collision. But people speak of dead animals and the courts tend to apply everyday meanings rather than scientific ones when interpreting insurance contracts, although they do not always use simple everyday language in writing their opinions. So damage from contact with an animal, dead or alive, probably would be considered an OTC loss, not a collision.

The important questions in defining collision are whether an object was struck and if so, how? The problems are with the breadth of the term *object* and the many ways it can be struck. The auto can be moving, stalled, parked or waiting for a green light. It can be struck by the roadbed, a person attempting suicide or by a rising object.

Many insurance policies use the word **accident.** Under the PAP insurers pay only for *accidental* loss (part D—damage to the covered auto—also requires the loss to be direct). One judge defined accident as "an undesigned, sudden and unexpected event, usually of an afflictive or unfortunate character, and often accompanied by a manifestation of force." (Surely the judge could have simplified his definition by using everyday language.) If a burglar breaks the left front window of the car in an attempted theft the glass loss is accidental to the car owner. Even though the culprit intended both the action and the result neither was intended by the owner. On the other hand, if the owner breaks the window to recover the keys absentmindedly locked inside, the glass damage is not accidental and the OTC coverage provides no protection; both action and results were intended. A student drives the car to a beach cottage and leaves it there for several weeks. While the sun and salt water are tanning the motorist they are also tanning the powder-blue Ford. The loss, however, is *not* accidental in this case, even though the results were not intended. The term *accident* has been interpreted by the courts to mean a sudden, unexpected event, identifiable in time and place. Damage occurring gradually over time is construed as resulting from an occurrence rather than an accident. **Occurrence** is defined strictly as an accident but includes continuous or repeated exposure to conditions that result in bodily injury or property damage neither expected nor intended by the insured.

Examples indicating the necessity for a precise definition of *perils* abound. They show that it may not always be possible to depend on the everyday meaning of words and that it may be necessary to look to courts, insurance contracts or even state statutes for an interpretation. Also important is recognition that court decisions vary and that contracts and statutes undergo changes.

DEFINING THE PROPERTY COVERED

As defined in the definition section of the PAP, the covered auto means:

1. Any vehicle shown in the declarations.
2. Any of the following types of vehicles acquired during the policy period, provided a request for coverage is made within 30 days:
   a. A private passenger auto.
   b. A pickup, sedan delivery or panel truck if not used in any business or occupation.
3. Any trailer owned by the insured.
4. Any nonowned auto or trailer while used as a temporary substitute for any other vehicle described in this definition that is out of normal use because of breakdown, repair, servicing, loss or destruction.

Under part A, liability coverage is provided for: (1) the covered auto whether used by the named insured, family members or any other persons; (2) an auto owned by or furnished to or available for the regular use of *any family member* but only when used by the named insured and (3) any other auto used by the named insured or family members unless specifically excluded. Specifically excluded are autos other than the covered auto owned by or furnished to or available for the regular use of the named insured.

For the named insured and family members part A also covers damage to a residence or private garage and to nonowned private passenger autos, trailers, pickup trucks, panel trucks and vans not furnished for their regular use if these vehicles are rented by, used by or in the care of these persons. No liability coverage is provided for the ownership, maintenance or use of a motorcycle or any other self-propelled vehicle having fewer than four wheels.

Under coverage C, an uninsured motor vehicle does not include one owned by the insured or a family member, one owned by a governmental unit, one operated on rails or crawler treads, one designed mainly for use off public roads while not on public roads and one while located for use as a residence or premises.

Part D provides coverage for loss to the covered auto except loss to a temporary substitute vehicle. Liability for damage to temporary substitute automobiles is covered under part A (liability coverage) of the policy.

The PAP does not cover personal effects in a covered auto. Sound reproduction equipment *permanently installed* in the auto is covered but not loss of tapes, records or other devices for use with such equipment. Citizens' band radios, two-way mobile radios, telephones and their accessories or antennas are also excluded from coverage.

The PAP does not provide liability coverage to any person for damage to property owned or transported by that person or for damage to property other than a residence or private garage rented to, used by or in the care of that person. For example, if Ed Friedman forgets to open the door to his rented garage before backing his car out, his PAP would cover the damage to the door under part A and the damage to the car under part D. If he also ran over his bicycle while making this graceful exit his PAP would not cover that damage because the property belongs to him. But if the bicycle belonged to the owner of the garage, Ed would have liability coverage under part A of the PAP for damage to the bicycle.

DEFINING THE TYPES OF LOSSES COVERED

The physical-damage section of the PAP provides principally direct-loss coverage. Loss-of-use coverage is available only for theft. The insurer reimburses the insured under part D for expense incurred for rental of a substitute automobile, including taxicabs, not to exceed $10 a day or totaling more than $300. Reimbursement is limited to covered expense incurred during the period commencing 48 hours after the theft has been reported to the insurer and the police and terminating the day the auto is recovered *and* returned to the insured or when the insurer pays for the theft loss. The loss-of-use protection allows the insurer ample time to locate the stolen car without seriously inconveniencing the insured. The insurer pays the cost of returning the recovered automobile to the named insured or, at the insurer's option, to the address shown in the policy declarations. No rental reimbursement coverage is included for losses caused by insured perils other than theft but this coverage can be added by endorsement. The endorsement applies whenever any insured peril causes the covered automobile to be "withdrawn from normal use for a period in excess of 24 hours." The maximum reimbursement here also is $10 per day up to $300 for each disablement.

In addition to paying bodily-injury and property-damage liability claims the insurer agrees to make supplementary payments up to $250 for the cost of bail bonds required because of an accident resulting in bodily injury or property damage covered under the policy. Other supplementary payments include premiums on appeal bonds, up to $50 a day for loss of earnings because of attendance at hearings and trials at the insurer's request, other reasonable expenses incurred at the insurer's request and the usual interest payments after a judgment is entered in a suit defended by the insurer.

DEFINING THE PERSONS COVERED

Under part A covered persons are defined as:

1. The named insured or any family member (a person related by blood, marriage or adoption or a ward or foster child who is a resident of the household) for the ownership, maintenance or use of any auto or trailer.
2. Any person using a covered auto.
3. Persons or organizations exposed to liability because of acts or omissions of an insured.

As an example of (3) assume Charytyna is a United Way volunteer. She uses her car to run an errand and is involved in an accident. Her PAP covers any liability imposed on her and on the United Way arising from her acts or omissions.

The automobile liability coverage applies separately and individually to each insured. For example, if Mario has $50,000 of liability coverage on his car and lends it to Lucy to drive to Chicago both are *insureds* within the meaning of the contract. Lucy hits Neva, who is injured. Neva sues Lucy for $50,000, alleging negligence, and Mario for $50,000 for not properly preparing the car for the trip. The total liability of the insurer will be only $50,000. Although the term *the insured* includes additional persons the insurer's liability limits are not increased. The liability section of the HO–3 and most other liability coverages have a similar clause.

The PAP covers medical payments (part B) to the named insured and any family member while occupying, or as a pedestrian when struck by, a motor vehicle designed for use mainly on public roads or by a trailer of any type.

The **uninsured motorists coverage** protects:

1. The named insured or any family member.
2. Any other person occupying the covered auto.
3. Any person for damages that person is entitled to recover because of bodily injury sustained by a person described in (1) or (2) and to which coverage applies.

Coverage for collision and OTC is provided for covered autos (except temporary substitute vehicles) regardless of the person operating the vehicle at the time of the loss. However, the insurance shall not directly or indirectly benefit any carrier or other bailee. Thus if Mike White's car is damaged by a negligent mechanic while on a test drive the mechanic (a bailee) would not be allowed to benefit under Mike's PAP.

INNERSCRIPT: NO-BENEFIT-TO-BAILEE CLAUSE

The purpose of the no-benefit-to-bailee clause **is to permit the insurer to preserve its subrogation rights. Subrogation gives the insurer only those rights of action held by the insured. Suppose the mechanic working on Mike's car, aware of ways to shift the liability risk, includes a clause in the repair agreement giving him the benefit of any insurance held by Mike. The agreement, in effect, says that if Mike has insurance, the mechanic would not be liable for the loss. This agreement defeats the insurer's right of subrogation. The insurer's response is the no-benefit-to-bailee clause. Without this clause the insurer has no right of subrogation against the mechanic because the** benefit-of-any-insurance clause **in the repair agreement eliminates any rights of action against the mechanic that Mike otherwise might have had. When both these clauses are used (benefit-of-any-insurance and no-benefit-to-bailee) the insurer advances the money to Mike rather than pay the claim and then helps Mike collect his claim against the mechanic. If the mechanic pays, Mike is obligated to pay off the loan, interest free. If the mechanic does not pay the claim, Mike's debt to the insurer is cancelled. By this means, the insurer denies the benefit of the insurance to the mechanic without denying protection to Mike. The effect is the same as using subrogation: the insured is paid and the insurer seeks to collect from the responsible party.**

Like the HO–3, the PAP requires written consent for a valid assignment. The operation of the assignment clause and the reason for it are the same as for the HO–3 as discussed in Chapter 8.

DETERMINING THE LOCATIONS COVERED

The PAP restricts coverage to the United States, its territories or possessions, and Canada, or in transit between their ports. If Vic Hallman plans to drive his car to Mexico he must have his auto insurance endorsed to extend coverage to include that country. Many insurance experts recommend purchasing a liability policy from a Mexican insurer rather than adding an endorsement to an American policy because Mexican officials are more likely to accept their own policies when applying Mexican law.

DEFINING THE PERIOD OF COVERAGE

The PAP runs from 12:01 A.M. standard time on the date of inception to 12:01 A.M. standard time on the date of expiration. Standard time at the address of the named insured governs whether the coverage is in effect.

Nearly all states allow insurers freedom to cancel new insureds but only within a specified period after the inception of the policy. That period ranges from 30 to 90 days. After this period has elapsed, the insurers may cancel only for specified reasons varying significantly among states. Examples of permissible reasons for cancellation in most states include nonpayment of premium and suspension or revocation of the insured's driver's license. Other permissible reasons found in statutes of various states are:

1. Insurance obtained through fraudulent misrepresentation.
2. The named insured or other customary operator of the vehicle:
   a. Is subject to epilepsy or heart attacks without presenting a physician's statement testifying to the person's ability to operate a motor vehicle.
   b. Is convicted of driving while intoxicated or is a habitual drinker of alcohol.
   c. Has within a three-year period prior to cancellation been addicted to narcotics or other drugs.
3. The named insured or other customary operator of the vehicle who has forfeited bail or is or has been convicted within a three-year period prior to cancellation, for:
   a. Felony.
   b. Leaving the scene of an accident.
   c. Reckless driving.
   d. Theft of a motor vehicle.
   e. Conviction or forfeiture of bail for a third speeding violation during the 18 months prior to cancellation. (The 55-mile-per-hour speed limit makes this requirement a tough one, especially for those driving on interstate highways in those rare instances when the law is strictly enforced.)

Nearly all state laws specify the number of days' notice that must be given before cancelling a policy (from 10 to 60) and require that the insurer give a reason for cancellation upon the request of the insured.

In the past insurers were not required to give a reason for cancellation. To require the insurer to give one may be inhibiting, especially if the reason is suspicion of a moral hazard. Allegations of a moral hazard could induce an insured to take legal action against the insurer for slander or libel. To avoid such actions all but six state statutes requiring explanation of cancellation or nonrenewal by the insurer give the insurer immunity from any tort action that might result.

DEFINING THE HAZARDS THAT EXCLUDE OR SUSPEND COVERAGE

The PAP excludes coverage for certain hazardous exposures. Coverage for liability, medical payment, uninsured motorist and physical damage does not apply to any person or auto while the car is used to transport persons or property for a fee. The car means *any* car for the liability coverage; for the other coverages, it means *the insured's* car. This exclusion does not apply to a share-the-expense car pool. For example, if Marie Tomas takes a friend with her on vacation and shares the expenses the policy will cover. If she uses her car as a neighborhood taxi for hire, however, coverage for any resulting loss (liability or property) is excluded. Automobiles used as taxicabs, buses or rental cars are typically exposed to greater hazards than autos driven strictly for private passenger purposes. Therefore a higher premium is required for this coverage.

No coverage is provided to any person using a vehicle without reasonable belief that he or she is entitled to do so. Liability and medical payments coverages do not apply to the business use of vehicles *other than* a private passenger auto, pickup, sedan delivery panel truck or van (or trailer used with them) owned by the named insured. The PAP does not cover liability incurred by persons (*other than* a named insured, a family member or any partner, agent or employee of the named insured or family member) while employed or engaged in the business or occupation of selling, repairing, servicing, storing or parking of vehicles designed for use mainly on public highways, including road testing and delivery. The intention of this exclusion is to eliminate coverage for a garage or parking-lot attendant who may drive the car with permission of an insured. Persons

TABLE 9–1
Limitations on the Amount of Recovery Applying to the PAP

COVERAGE	*ACV OR REPLACEMENT COST*	*POLICY LIMITS*	*COIN-SURANCE*	*OTHER INSURANCE*	*DEDUCTIBLES*	*INSURABLE INTEREST*
A—Liability	Amount of award	As stated in the declarations for any one accident and some additional limits†	Not used	Pro rata subject to a major exception#	None	No amount greater than the insurable interest at the time of loss
B—Medical payments	Any reasonable and necessary expenses	As stated in the declarations per accident‡		Pro rata subject to a major exception**		
C—Uninsured motorists	Damages the covered person is legally entitled to recover*	As stated in the declarations per accident§		Pro rata subject to a major exception††		
D—Physical damage	ACV	Additional limit‖		Pro rata	Deductible for collision and OTC coverages‡‡	

* The insurer will pay damages that a covered person is legally entitled to recover from the owner or operator of an uninsured motor vehicle because of bodily injury sustained by a covered person and caused by an accident.

† The additional limits are: (1) up to $250 for bail bonds; (2) premiums on appeal bonds and bonds to release attachments in any suit defended by the insurer; (3) interest accruing for the full amount of a judgment after it is entered in any suit defended by the insurer; (4) up to $50 a day for loss of earnings, but not other income, because of attendance at hearings or trials at the insurer's request and (5) other reasonable expenses incurred at the insurer's request.

‡ Any amounts otherwise payable for expenses under this coverage shall be reduced by amounts paid or payable for the same expenses under any auto liability or uninsured motorist coverage provided by the same policy.

§ Any amounts otherwise payable for damages under this coverage shall be reduced by: (1) all sums paid because of bodily injury caused by or imputed to persons or organizations who may be legally responsible (i.e., all sums paid under part A) and (2) all sums paid or payable because of bodily injury under any workers' compensation, disability or any similar law.

‖ In addition, the insurer will pay up to $10 per day, not to exceed a maximum of $300, for substitute transportation expenses incurred because of theft of the covered auto.

Any insurance provided by the insurer with respect to a vehicle not owned by the named insured shall be excess over any other collectible insurance.

** Any insurance provided by the insurer with respect to a vehicle not owned by the named insured shall be excess over any other collectible auto insurance providing payments for medical or funeral expenses.

†† If a bodily injury liability bond or policy applies for an amount less than that required by the financial responsibility law of the state where the insured's car is garaged, the insurer providing the uninsured motorist insurance is liable for the difference.

‡‡ For OTC coverage a deductible may be optional or mandatory and may be for an amount different than that for collision. In some policies, the deductible does not apply for collision if the insurer covers all cars involved in the collision.

engaged in the automobile business are expected to buy their own automobile liability insurance. In addition, liability coverage does not apply for any intentional acts or for bodily injury to an employee of any person during the course of employment. Coverage would apply for bodily injury to a domestic employee if the employee is not eligible for workers' compensation benefits.

Medical payments and physical damage coverage exclude losses resulting from war hazards, the discharge of a nuclear weapon or nuclear radiation.

LIMITATIONS ON THE AMOUNT OF RECOVERY

Table 9–1 outlines the six limitations on the amount of recovery for loss or damage as they apply to the PAP.

THE POLICYOWNER'S DUTIES AFTER A LOSS

The PAP stipulates the usual duties required of the policyowner after a loss, such as prompt notice of loss, sufficient evidence of the loss, protection of the property from further damage and assistance and cooperation in any investigation or defense of a claim or suit. In addition, the policyowner must notify the police if a hit-and-run driver is involved or if the covered auto is stolen.

SETTLEMENT OPTIONS

Under part D the insurer has the option to pay either the ACV of the stolen or damaged property *or* the amount necessary to repair or replace the property. If the choice is to pay the ACV of the damaged or stolen property the insurer may keep all or part of the property (called the **salvage**) at an agreed upon or appraised value. However, if in the unlikely case the insured wants to retain the salvage as well as collect the ACV the salvage value must be paid to the insurer. (The customary arrangement here would be for the insurer to deduct the salvage value from the payment to the policyowner.) In the event of stolen property, if the property is returned to the policyowner the insurer will pay any damages resulting from the theft.

INNERSCRIPT: AN EMERGING DEVELOPMENT FOR TOTAL LOSSES

Because (1) auto loans are being made for longer durations and (2) people are keeping their cars longer, the amount of many outstanding loans eventually exceeds the market value of the car. Lenders prefer a better secured loan. Also for older cars the repair cost frequently exceeds their market value. Under traditional policies, a damaged auto is considered a total loss when the repair cost exceeds the car's current market value. The insurer pays the insured the current market value of the car.

Some insurers, however, explicitly recognize that the current market value of a car may not reflect its intrinsic value to the in-

(Continued)

sured. So a few insurers offer a replacement cost endorsement to cover the full expense of repairing or replacing a damaged vehicle. In 1982, one insurer (later followed by a few others) introduced coverage under which it will pay the full cost to repair a damaged car if the repairs can be made without creating an unsafe vehicle and if their cost is less than the price of a new car of the same size, class and type and containing the same equipment. If the insurer determines that the car is damaged beyond repair, it will pay the cost of replacing the damaged car with a new car of comparable quality. Under both settlement bases, these payments are made even if they exceed the car's current market value.

An example

Suppose that the insured owns a car bought five years ago for $6,000 and that its current market value is $3,000. In the event of a total loss the insured would collect $3,000 under the traditional policy even though the repair cost is $6,000 and the cost of a comparable new car is $12,000. Under the new replacement endorsement, the insured would be paid $6,000 if the car can be safely repaired or $12,000 if it cannot be repaired. That determination is made by the insurer.

The endorsement is written only on policies covering newly purchased vehicles and the policy must be continued as long as the original owner keeps the car. To control the moral hazard, fire and theft losses are excluded. The cost of the endorsement is about 10 percent of the combined collision and OTC premiums for a middle sized car.

Other plans

Replacement cost endorsements vary among insurers both as to coverage and cost. For example, another insurer writes a plan for owners of personal autos up to five years old. If the car is totally destroyed, the insurer pays the insured an amount sufficient to buy a car of the same model up to two years newer or $2,500 above the current market value of the auto whichever is less. The coverage extends to total loss by theft. The premium for the coverage is an additional 30 percent of the combined collision and OTC premiums.

TIME LIMITS: SUITS AND CLAIMS PAYMENT

The PAP states that no legal action may be brought against the insurer until full compliance has been made with all policy terms. In addition, under coverage A no legal action may be brought against the insurer until both the policyowner and insurer agree in writing that the covered person has an obligation to pay or until the amount of that obligation has been finally determined by judgment after a trial.

No time limits are specified in the policy for bringing legal action against the insurer or for the insurer to pay the loss. Presumably the maximum time limit to bring legal action is governed by the statute of limitations (see Chapter 6). However, the policyowner is expected to allow the insurer a "reasonable" period to process the claim. As in the HO–3 policy, under coverage A the insurer will be directed by the court to pay within a reasonable time. The lack of a stated time period for paying claims, however, could lead to delays and disputes, especially when interest rates are high and insurers want to retain their money.

For example, when should the policyowner expect the insurer to pay for the loss of a stolen auto? How much time should the insurer be allowed to search for the car before paying a theft loss? Does the payment of up to $10 a day, to a maximum of $300, for necessary substitute transportation relieve the insurer of any pressure for an early settlement? In many communities without rapid and convenient public transportation $10 a day is not sufficient to compensate the policyowner for a long, drawn-out search. Presumably, in this era of consumerism, in the interest of good customer relations and the desire to reduce possible law suits brought by the insured, the insurer would appear to have little choice but to pay within a "reasonable" time period.

VARIATIONS AMONG THE PAP, FAP AND SAP

The PAP was designed to replace both the FAP and the SAP as the standard form for insuring eligible vehicles. Because many insurers use nonstandard forms and the PAP has not been approved by all states, the PAP has not been universally adopted. (The ISO will discontinue the FAP when all states accept the PAP.) Many insurers continue to use the FAP and SAP (or variations thereof) to cover private passenger automobiles and certain kinds of light trucks.

A few variations among the PAP, FAP and SAP are shown in Table 9–2. These forms vary primarily as to the coverage offered and the applicable eligibility requirements.

TABLE 9–2
Variations among Three Types of Auto Policies

PAP	*FAP*	*SAP*
1. Single limit of liability per accident for bodily injury and/or property damage.	1. Split limits of liability per person and per accident for bodily injury and property damage.	1. Single limit of liability per occurrence for bodily injury and/or property damage.
2. Liability coverage provided for property damage to nonowned private passenger autos, trailers and small trucks in the custody of the insured.	2. No liability coverage for property in the care, custody or control of insured.	2. No liability coverage for property in the care, custody or control of insured.
3. Nonowned vehicles covered under liability coverage on an excess basis.	3. Nonowned vehicles covered under physical damage section of policy on an excess basis.	3. Named insured and relatives covered under physical damage coverage while using nonowned private passenger autos only if legally liable.
4. Medical expenses incurred within three years from date of accident covered under medical payments.	4. Medical expenses incurred within one year from date of accident covered under medical payments coverage.	4. Medical expenses incurred within one year from date of accident covered under medical payments coverage.

TABLE 9–2 (*Continued*)

PEP	*FAP*	*SAP*
5. Medical payments coverage made primary with respect to automobile accidents.	5. Medical payments coverage made primary with respect to automobile accidents.	5. Medical payments coverage excess over accident, disability or hospitalization insurance available to an insured.
6. First-aid coverage is not included as a supplementary payment.	6. First-aid coverage is included as a supplementary payment.	6. First-aid coverage is included as a supplementary payment.
7. Physical damage coverage provided under a single insuring agreement. However, collision coverage is optional.	7. Collision and comprehensive (OTC) coverages are written as separate insuring agreements.	7. Collision and comprehensive (OTC) coverages are written as separate insuring agreements.
8. No personal effects coverage under physical damage section.	8. Personal effects covered for loss by fire and lightning while in the owned automobile.	8. Personal effects covered for loss by fire, lightning, flood, falling objects, explosions, earthquake, theft of auto and collision.
9. No coverage for persons using a vehicle without reasonable belief that they are entitled to do so.	9. Persons (other than relatives) must have permission to use the vehicle of the named insured before coverage applies.	9. Persons (other than relatives) must have permission to use the vehicle of named insured before coverage applies.
10. Vehicles acquired during the term of the policy must be reported within 30 days for coverage.	10. Vehicles acquired during the term of the policy may be reported at any time during the policy period.	10. Vehicles acquired during the term of the policy must be reported within 30 days for coverage.

SUMMARY

1. Individuals or married couples may purchase a personal automobile policy (PAP) to cover private passenger automobiles and certain types of nonbusiness trucks which they own or lease.

2. The PAP offers four coverages: (*a*) liability, (*b*) medical payments to a covered person, (*c*) uninsured motorists coverage and (*d*) physical damage to the covered auto.

3. The PAP covers only accidental loss (sudden or unexpected). However, some insurance policies may be written on an occurrence basis (an accident, including continuous or repeated exposure to conditions).

4. Perils covered in the PAP include: (1) legal liability for bodily injury or property damage because of an auto accident (part A); (2) medical payments resulting from an auto accident (part B); (3) accidental injury to the insured by an negligent uninsured motorist (part C) and (4) direct and accidental loss or damage to the covered auto (part D). The perils covered under part D are divided into two classes: collision and other than collision. Collision is specified-peril coverage; other than collision is an all-risk coverage. Coverage may be bought for collision, other than collision or both.

5. The covered auto as defined in the policy is protected by all sections of the PAP. In addition, any auto operated by a covered person is covered under part A, B and C.

6. The physical-damage section (part D) of the PAP provides principally direct-loss coverage. Only coverage for theft includes some reimbursement for extra expenses.
7. Covered persons include the named insured, any family member, any person using the covered auto and persons or organizations with respect to their liability because of acts or omissions of an insured.
8. The PAP restricts coverage to the United States, its territories and Canada or in transit between their ports.
9. The PAP runs from 12:01 A.M. standard time (at the address of the named insured) on the date of inception to 12:01 A.M. standard time on the date of expiration. Specific reasons allowing the insurer to cancel the PAP are listed in the policy.
10. The PAP excludes coverages for certain hazardous exposures. For example, coverage is excluded for (1) liability for or physical damage to any auto used to transport persons or property for a fee, (2) any person using a vehicle without reasonable belief that the person is entitled to do so and (3) liability coverage for any person other than the named insured, any family member or any partner, agent or employee of the insured or family member while engaged in selling, repairing, servicing, storing or parking vehicles designed for public highways.
11. Table 9–1 outlines the limitations on the amount of recovery as they apply to the PAP.
12. To protect the insurer's right of subrogation, the PAP provides that this insurance shall not directly or indirectly benefit any carrier or other bailee for hire.
13. The PAP includes the usual conditions relating to the duties of a policyowner following a loss, settlement options and time limits for suits and claims payment.
14. Some insurers write replacement cost endorsements that apply in the event of a total loss.
15. Many insurers continue to use the family automobile policy (FAP) and the special automobile policy (SAP) instead of the PAP. Variations among the PAP, the FAP and the SAP are shown in Table 9–2.

REVIEW QUESTIONS

1. Sister Marie parks her car near her church. A playful student throws a missal (not a missile) to another student who misses. The volume hits and cracks Sister Marie's windshield. Does her auto collision coverage protect her for the loss? Is there any other way she might collect?
2. Under what set of circumstances would a policy written on an accident basis cover a loss that would not be covered if the policy had been written on an occurrence basis?
3. What persons are covered by the PAP for any vehicle they drive?
4. Will your PAP cover any damage to your car that occurs while a mechanic

test drives your car? Will your PAP cover the mechanic's liability if he or she negligently hits a pedestrian while test driving your car?

5. The book value of your car is $9,200. You have a collision and the lowest repair estimate is $7,900, with the salvage value of your car estimated at $2,000. How can your insurer settle in order to minimize its loss? Explain.
6. Explain the basic difference between the PAP, the FAP and the SAP in their medical payments coverage.
7. Why might a person prefer to collect under other-than-collision coverage rather than collision coverage for a covered loss? Why might a person prefer to collect under collision coverage rather than other-than-collision coverage?
8. How does the coverage for damage to a temporary substitute automobile differ under the PAP from that under the FAP?
9. Are you covered under your PAP while driving the neighborhood children to nursery school for $5 a week for each child?
10. What is the purpose of the no-benefit-to-bailee clause? How does it accomplish its purpose?
11. Why are some insurers offering a replacement cost endorsement to auto policies?
12. Give an example of how other-insurance clauses in the PAP operate.

PART FOUR PROPERTY AND LIABILITY INSURANCE COVERAGES

Attention has been directed to some economic and legal principles as they apply to risk management and insurance. Insurance was shown as generally the most efficient way to deal with the loss financing function of risk management—especially when faced with a combination of a low-loss frequency (small chance of loss) and high-loss severity (large amount of loss). The fundamental question of how to read a policy was addressed and the answer illustrated with the Homeowners–3 Special Form and the personal auto policy.

The interest now shifts to the many insurance coverages offered by private and government insurers to help families and businesses manage their loss exposures. The private insurance business is divided into two segments: property-liability and life-health. Government insurers are also composed of two segments: federal and state.

Part Four, consisting of three chapters, considers the coverages offered by property-liability insurers. Chapter 10 examines fire and marine insurance coverages, Chapter 11, liability coverages and Chapter 12, crime, surety, miscellaneous and multiple-line coverages. The purpose of these chapters is to describe the variety of property-liability forms written, point out how and why they are used and analyze a few selected policies in some depth according to the technique developed in Chapters 6 and 7. The underlying objective, however, is to serve as a self-sufficient introduction to the field of property-liability insurance and to build a solid base for those interested in pursuing further study of this specialized field at the advanced level.

CHAPTER

10 Fire and marine coverage

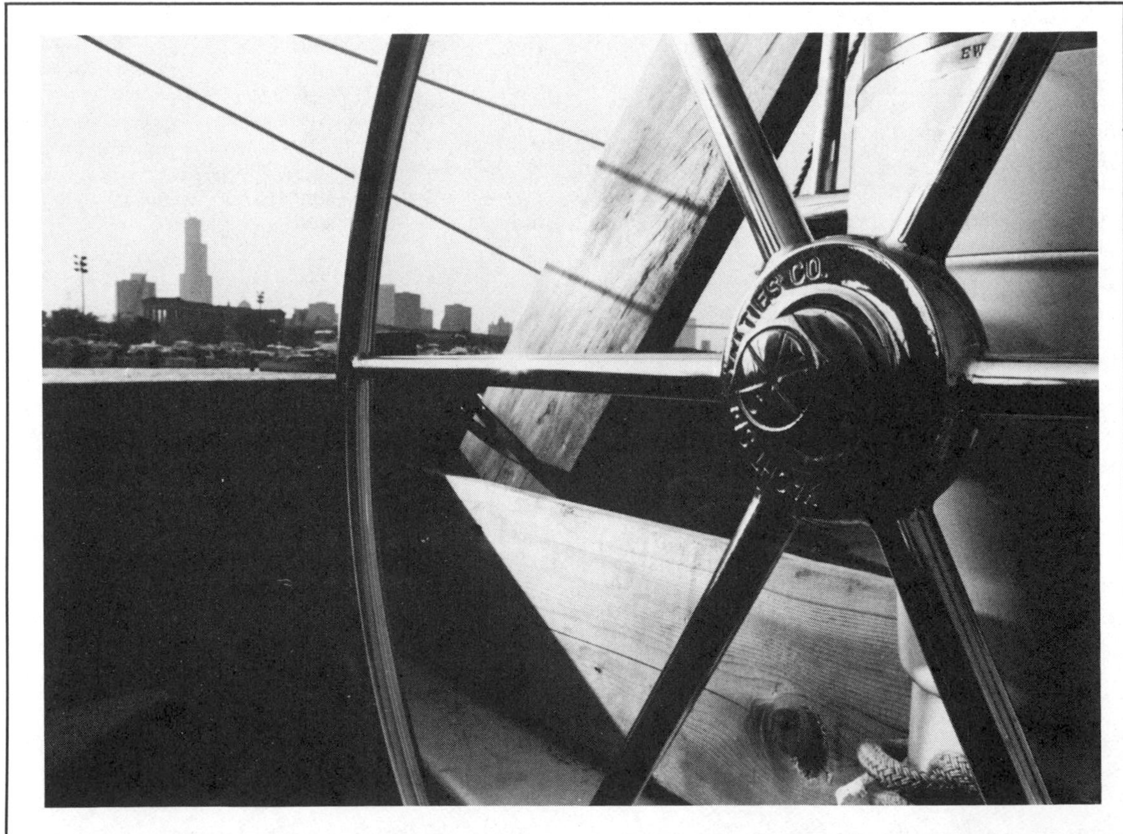

Courtesy of John Thoeming

CHAPTER OBJECTIVES

1. **To analyze the New York standard fire policy (SFP) using the techniques discussed in Chapters 6 and 7.**
2. **To describe the forms used with the SFP to provide personal and business coverages and to increase covered perils and losses.**
3. **To list the coverages classified as allied fire insurance lines.**
4. **To identify the types of interests covered, kinds of policies written and the principal clauses used in ocean marine insurance.**
5. **To classify the types of inland marine insurance coverages and distinguish between those written for individuals and families and those written for businesses.**

Many coverages are included under the classification fire and marine insurance. This chapter briefly summarizes the most important ones.

The trend in both family and business coverage is to multiple-line contracts covering many perils in one policy. These policies, called **multiple-line insurance,** are discussed in Chapter 12. Knowledge of individual coverages discussed in this and the next two chapters is essential to an understanding of multiple-line package policies.

FIRE INSURANCE COVERAGE

In 1752 the energetic Benjamin Franklin was instrumental in the formation of one of the first fire insurance companies in America. This company, the Philadelphia Contributorship for the Insurance of Houses from Loss by Fire, issued perpetual policies. Each member contributed a large sum of money that the company invested. The investment income was used to pay losses and operating costs. This firm, still in business in Philadelphia, continues to operate in this manner.

The first nonmutual (stock) company organized specifically to write fire insurance was the Insurance Company of North America (INA), organized in Philadelphia and chartered on April 18, 1792, by the State of Pennsylvania.

In 1794, after three months of study, the board of INA decided to write fire insurance on both contents and buildings, thus becoming the first insurer in America to cover contents. In 1795 INA offered fire insurance on "brick and stone houses within ten miles of the city," a departure from previous practice restricting fire coverage to areas served by volunteer fire-fighting companies. The following year INA made fire insurance available on properties anywhere in the United States.

INNERSCRIPT: BACKGROUND ON FIRE INSURERS

In the early part of the 19th century a large number of fire insurers were formed. Many small, local insurers began operation

(*continued*)

when a number of states passed discriminatory laws fostering in-state business. Massachusetts started the ball rolling in 1827 by passing a 10 percent premium tax on non-Massachusetts insurers operating in that state. Most out-of-state insurers met the challenge by raising their rates to include the premium tax but some confined their business to their home states.

In 1835 New York City was swept by a great fire that nearly destroyed the entire business district. The total loss has been estimated at about $18 million. Much of the insurance was with local insurers, because discriminatory taxes had allowed them to charge lower rates. This practice proved disastrous when all but 3 of the 26 local insurers went bankrupt. Subsequently New York reduced its premium tax on out-of-state insurers to 2 percent and the smaller insurers began to fade from the scene. Viewing the New York experience, insurers wanted to spread exposures, accumulate adequate reserves and expand sales. In 1849 a fire on the St. Louis waterfront burned 27 steamboats and engulfed the business district. Insurers had learned their lesson well. With the exception of a few western insurers the industry weathered this storm.

THE STANDARD FIRE INSURANCE POLICY

In 1873 Massachusetts prescribed the first standard fire policy, which became known as the New England standard form. In 1887 New York required the use of the first New York standard fire policy, which was modified in 1918. Today the 1943 New York standard fire policy (SFP) is used verbatim in 35 states and with minor variations in the rest. As noted in Chapter 8, the SFP is not included in the readable HO policies although many of its provisions are included. The SFP is still widely used in covering buildings and contents that do not qualify for the HO program (e.g., commercial exposures). However, readable commercial policies have been developed that include many of the provisions of the SFP but not the actual form. (The businessowners policy is an example; see Chapter 12.)

Page 1 of the 1943 New York standard policy (reproduced in Appendix 2) includes the insuring agreement, space for listing the name of the insured and mortgagee (if any), the perils covered, the amount of insurance, rate and premium for each coverage, applicable coinsurance percentages and a description and location of the property covered. Stipulations and conditions are on page 2, and because they occupy 165 lines this policy is called the **165-line form.** Included are lists of uninsurable property and property covered only if specifically named in the policy, perils not included in the coverage, conditions that suspend coverage or restrict recovery in the event of loss, provisions for policy cancellation and the procedure to be followed if a loss occurs. Page 3 is left blank for attaching one or more additional forms. Although the standard fire policy is the starting point in all fire insurance coverages the document is not complete. *At least one additional form must be attached to have a valid policy.* Some of these forms are described after completing the analysis of the SFP.

Analysis of the Standard Fire Policy

Even though the SFP is not a complete contract by itself its insuring agreement and 165 lines of stipulations and conditions can be analyzed according to the methods discussed in Chapters 6 and 7.

Perils The SFP provides coverage for the perils of fire and lightning. Coverage for property removed from premises endangered by the covered perils is also included. Removal coverage is generally considered all risk (with no exclusions) and is granted for five days following the removal. Coverage is not provided for loss by theft or loss occurring as a result of explosion or riot unless fire ensues and in that event for loss by fire only.

Property The SFP does not define the property covered. At least one additional form defining the covered property must be added to complete the contract. The SFP does list items that are not covered: accounts, bills, currency, deeds, evidences of debt and money or securities. Bullion and manuscripts are covered only if specifically named in the policy declarations.

Losses The SFP covers direct losses only. Specifically excluded are losses caused by "any increased cost of repair or reconstruction by reason of any ordinance or law regulating construction or repair and without compensation for loss resulting from interruption of business or manufacture." As shown later, forms can be added to the SFP providing coverage for these and other excluded losses.

Persons The SFP covers named insureds and their legal representatives, e.g., a guardian.

Location Property is covered only while at the location described in the declarations. Therefore an accurate description of the covered property is essential. Other forms are available to cover mobile property.

Time Coverage begins at 12:00 noon standard time at the location of the property on the inception date and ends at 12:00 noon standard time at the location of the property on the expiration date. The insurer can cancel the policy upon 5 days' written notice to the insured and 10 days' written notice to the mortgagee. The insured can cancel the policy immediately upon notice to the insurer.

Hazards The SFP does not cover losses caused directly or indirectly by: (*a*) enemy attack by armed forces, including action taken by military, naval or air forces in resisting an actual or an immediately impending enemy attack; (*b*) invasion; (*c*) insurrection; (*d*) rebellion; (*e*) revolution; (*f*) civil war; (*g*) usurped power; (*h*) order of any civil authority except acts of destruction at the time of and for the purpose of preventing the spread of fire, provided that such fire did not originate from any of the perils excluded by this policy; (*i*) neglect of the insured to use all reasonable means to save and preserve the property during and after a loss or when the property is endangered by fire in neighboring premises.

The SFP does not provide coverage for loss occurring: (*a*) while the hazard is increased by any means within the control or knowledge of the insured or (*b*) while a described building, whether intended for occupancy by owner or tenant, is vacant or unoccupied beyond a period of 60 consecutive days.

The balance of the SFP deals with the conditions of the contract. As the HO policies include many of the provisions of the SFP, the analysis of the HO–3 in Chapter 8 provides a comprehensive discussion of most of the conditions found in the SFP. The reader is referred to this chapter and chapters 6 and 7 for a discussion of contract conditions dealing with cancellation, the mortgage clause, pro rata liability, requirements in case of loss, appraisal, settlement options, abandonment, suit against the insurer and subrogation.

FORMS USED WITH THE STANDARD FIRE POLICY

Forms used to complete the coverage under the SFP are not easily classified. One simple classification divides the forms into three groups: (1) forms that describe the property and locations covered, (2) those that cover additional perils and (3) forms that cover additional losses. However, this classification creates a problem because of the extensive overlapping among the classes. For example, a form that describes the property and locations covered may automatically include forms that cover additional perils and additional losses. To remedy this problem these forms for this discussion are classified as (1) those providing personal coverages, (2) those providing commercial coverages, (3) those increasing perils covered and (4) those increasing losses covered.

Forms Providing Personal Coverages

Three forms available for use with the SFP for personal coverages are: (1) the dwelling buildings and contents, basic form, (2) the dwelling buildings and contents, broad form and (3) the dwelling buildings and contents, special form. While many homeowners prefer to buy one of the homeowners policies discussed in Chapter 8 some prefer the original method of covering their dwelling exposure: the SFP combined with one of the basic dwelling buildings and contents forms.

The dwelling buildings and contents, basic form

The dwelling buildings and contents, basic form (DB&C, basic form) can be analyzed according to the method discussed in chapters 6 and 7. In studying this section students should refer to the form used in their locale as some variation is found in the exact wording of the form among territories.[1]

Perils. The perils covered are those of the SFP plus inherent explosion. The addition of the extended coverage endorsement and the vandalism or malicious mischief endorsement (discussed later in this chapter) add other perils. Excluded in addition to those perils in the SFP are earth movement, water damage, power interruption and nuclear-related perils.

Property. Under the dwelling section the following property is covered: (1) the described dwelling; (2) if owned by the insured, building equipment and fixtures and outdoor equipment pertaining to the service of the premises; (3) materials and supplies on premises or adjacent thereto, used to make alterations, additions or repairs to the building and (4) private structures for use with the dwelling and located on the premises. Improvements, alterations or additions to the described building and to private structures appertaining to the dwelling are covered if the insured is a tenant, paid for the alterations and has an insurable interest in them. Excluded are: (1) trees, shrubs, plants and lawns; (2) structures on the premises used for mercantile, manufacturing or farming purposes and (3) structures (except those used principally for private garage purposes) rented or leased to other than a tenant of the dwelling.

Contents covered include household and personal property usual to the occupancy of a dwelling if owned by the named insured or a family member of the

[1] Sample copies of this form and others discussed in this and the following chapter, can be obtained from a local agent or sources discussed in Chapter 6.

same household. But not all property falling in this class is covered. Not only do the specific property exclusions of the SFP apply but also excluded are aircraft, motor vehicles other than motorized equipment used for maintenance of the premises, boats (other than rowboats and canoes), animals, birds and fish.

Losses. The SFP covers property only for direct loss or damage. The DB&C, basic form adds, as further coverage, protection for loss of rental value while the building is untenantable. Thus if a fire destroys the residence the insured may collect for the loss of its use until the dwelling is rebuilt. The form also covers expenses incurred in the removal of debris of property covered following loss caused by a covered peril.

Persons. The persons covered are the named insured and family members of the same household. Personal property of guests and servants while on the described premises is covered at the option of the insured.

Locations. The SFP offers coverage for *real* property only while located as described in the policy. The DB&C, basic form, however, grants limited off-premises coverage, allowing the insured to apply up to 10 percent of the contents insurance to cover personal property while anywhere in the world. This extension applies to property belonging to the insured or any family member living with the insured, but not to guests and servants. This off-premises coverage does not extend to rowboats or canoes.

Time. The time covered is for the period stated in the SFP.

Hazards. The excluded hazards of the SFP apply. No additional ones are included in the list.

Dwelling buildings and contents, broad form

The DB&C broad form differs from the DB&C, basic form primarily by including coverage for: (1) one additional loss and (2) several additional perils. The additional loss is the additional living expense coverage. The additional perils include glass breakage, burglars, falling objects, weight of ice, snow or sleet, structural collapse, rupture or bursting of steam or hot water systems, freezing or water damage from plumbing and heating systems and damage to electrical appliances or wiring (except television picture tubes) caused by manufactured electricity. Earthquake, backing up of sewers or drains and damage by flood are excluded. The coverage may be purchased for dwelling, contents or both. The protection for building structures is written on a replacement-cost basis. Ten percent of the policy's face amount may be used as rental-value insurance, additional living-expense insurance or a combination of the two. This extension is an addition to the face amount of the insurance. Five percent of the face amount may be applied to damage to trees, shrubs, plants or lawns subject to a $250 limit on each item.

Dwelling buildings and contents, special form

The dwelling buildings and contents special form covers all risks of physical loss to the dwelling and appurtenant structures subject to exclusions or limitations. The form provides for named peril coverage on contents.

The policy excludes damage to television antennas caused by wind, ice or snow, damage to plumbing by freezing if the building is vacant unless the insured has used "due diligence" to prevent such damage, insect damage, smoke from industrial operations, rust, rot, mechanical breakdown, earthquake, volcanic eruption, landslide, flood, tidal wave, backing up of sewers, theft under certain conditions, power interruptions, vandalism and malicious mischief under certain conditions, perils resulting from nuclear hazard, wear and tear and some types of water damage.

The special form covers all the losses, perils, property and so on covered by the basic and broad forms. The special form is broader because it provides all-risk coverage for buildings.

Forms Providing Commercial Coverages

Some businesses operate at a single location, others at multiple locations. Furthermore, some businesses maintain widely fluctuating inventories, others narrowly fluctuating inventories. A number of forms have been developed to meet these differing needs.

General property form

The **general property form** (GPF) is common for covering commercial buildings and contents. When attached to the SFP this form is widely used because of its versatility and can be analyzed according to the methods discussed in Chapters 6 and 7.

Perils. The perils covered are those listed in the SFP. Additional perils may be covered by buying the extended coverage and the vandalism or malicious mischief endorsements included in the form.

Property. Section I of the GPF describes the covered property; Section II describes property not covered. This form may be used to cover buildings (coverage A), personal property of the named insured (coverage B) and personal property of others (coverage C).

Coverage A includes the building, additions and extensions as well as machinery and equipment that are permanent parts of the building and used in its service. Specifically excluded are property covered by other insurance, wind and hail damage to radio or television equipment on the outside of the building, outdoor signs unless described on the first page of the policy or by endorsement and, if coinsurance is used, items like excavations, foundations and architect's fees.

Under coverage B business personal property is covered if it is owned by the named insured and not unusual to the building's occupancy. The named insured is also covered for the costs of labor and materials furnished in servicing personal property of others if that property is damaged by a covered peril while in the building or within 100 feet of it. In addition, tenants' **improvements and betterments** are included.[2] Examples of improvements and betterments include display shelves and wall-to-wall carpeting permanently installed in the building by the tenant.

Coverage C covers personal property of others for the benefit of its owners (not the named insured as in coverage B) while in or within 100 feet of the building if that property is in the named insured's care, custody or control. This coverage is subject to a limit of two percent of the amount of insurance applicable to coverage B but in *no event* more than $2,000. When a loss is covered under *both* B and C the maximum amount payable is the sum of the face amount of each coverage.

The insured must be aware of the property covered, not only to identify gaps and overlaps in the coverage but also to determine if an adequate amount of insurance is purchased to satisfy any coinsurance requirement. Table 10–1 summarizes the property covered and the amount of coverage offered for each type of property by the GPF.

---

[2] Although tenants do not own fixtures after they are attached to a rented building the tenants do retain an interest in them. This interest, called *usufruct interest,* is insurable. If the landlord has agreed to assume the responsibility for replacing fixtures in the event they are damaged the landlord is exposed to the loss and is the appropriate person to buy the insurance.

TABLE 10–1 **Summary of Property Covered and Amounts of Coverage by the GPF**

COVERAGE	*PROPERTY COVERED*	*AMOUNT OF COVERAGE OFFERED*
A	Building	Face amount as shown in the declarations
B	Business personal property Named insured's interest in the personal property of others Tenants' improvements and betterments	Face amount as shown in the declarations
C	Personal property of others for the benefit of its owners	Two percent of the insurance applicable to coverage B up to $2000

Losses. The basic fire policy with the general property form covers primarily direct loss. However, one type of extra-expense coverage is provided. At no additional charge the general property form includes debris removal coverage to pay the cost of hauling away the debris of covered property damaged by fire or any other covered peril. The total liability for both loss to property and debris removal expense shall not exceed the amount of insurance applicable to the covered property.

Persons. The GPF covers the named insured, legal representatives and the mortgagee, if any. Limited coverage is available for property of others in the insured's care, custody or control and for personal effects belonging to the named insured, officers, partners or employees. Assignment of the policy is not valid except with written consent of the insurer.

Locations. In general, coverage applies only to property within the named building or within 100 feet of the building if it is in the open or in vehicles. If the premises are threatened by any covered peril, contents are covered for five days while temporarily moved for safekeeping.

Time. The period covered by the SFP applies.

Hazards. No special conditions suspending coverage are added by the GPF, so only the SFP hazard exclusions apply. The insured is automatically granted permission to use the premises in any way required by the business even though it increases the hazard. Thus a manufacturer may try a new process that might be more hazardous without suspension of the policy. Consent is also given automatically for alterations, repairs and additions to the building. Specific authorization is needed for alterations and repairs if the building is protected by automatic sprinklers.

Amount. The SFP with the GPF is subject to the usual amount limitations: actual cash value, insurable interest, policy face, coinsurance, other insurance, special limits on particular property and the extended coverage apportionment clause. Liability for loss to books of account, drawings, card index systems and other records is limited to the cost of the blank material and the cost of copying the records. However, the insured may apply up to $500 toward the cost of research needed to reproduce, restore or replace the damaged records.

Multiple-location and reporting forms

The SFP with the GPF is used to cover specified goods in specified locations. Under this form a chain store wanting full coverage for its many retail outlets through the use of specific insurance would be forced to buy an amount of insurance for each store unit equal to the maximum value of goods expected in any one store. This approach would require a larger amount of total insurance than the average amount of exposure justifies. **Multiple-location policies** were developed for these insureds.

With the multiple-location forms came the development of **reporting forms,** a system of varying the premium collected with the amounts at risk during a given period (usually monthly). The insured submits a periodic report stating the values that have been at risk.

Provided the insured reports the values correctly and promptly and maintains a limit of insurance sufficient to cover the highest value possible at any time, the insured will be fully protected at all times and will pay a premium based on the values at risk. Because several different multiple-location and reporting forms are written, one that closely corresponds to the needs of the insured is probably available. The forms may vary according to eligible property, reporting procedures and minimum premiums.

Multiple-location reporting forms. When covered under a multiple-location reporting form the policyowner estimates the largest amount of insurance required at each specific location. The sum of these limits is the maximum liability of the insurer. The limit of insurance established at each location is the maximum the insurer will pay under the policy for losses at any one location. At the policy's inception the policyowner pays a deposit premium based on the estimated exposure. When the policy expires the deposit premium is adjusted to reflect the values actually at risk as shown by the monthly report. If the policyowner underreports the value at risk at a location and a loss occurs there the insured will be penalized through the "honesty clause" that limits payment of any loss to no more than the percentage the reported value bears to the actual value.

Multiple-location nonreporting form. A multiple-location nonreporting form is useful when values at the various locations do not fluctuate widely. Because an average rate with possible rate credits is used in calculating the premium a multiple-location nonreporting form may cost less than specific or blanket coverage. This form is used when the amount varies among locations owned by the insured but the total value is nearly constant. For example, a firm operating clothing stores in New Jersey and Florida resort areas may be able to calculate the value of the total stock in stores for the year but the values at the different locations will vary. During the summer the value will be higher in the New Jersey stores; during the winter they will be higher in Florida. The total value of the stock, however, will remain nearly constant.

Single-location reporting form. A reporting form is available for a business with one location whose stock values fluctuate considerably over the year. For example, a department store will have higher-than-average inventories before Christmas and Easter and lower-than-average inventories after these peak seasons.

Forms Increasing Perils Covered

The SFP covers only loss by fire and lightning. But forms to cover a number of other perils can be attached to the SFP.

The extended coverage endorsement

The extended coverage endorsement (EC) provides coverage against each of the following perils: windstorm, hail, explosion, riot and civil commotion, damage by aircraft or by vehicle and smoke damage. Specifically excluded are war and related hazards, the nuclear hazard and water losses. The purpose of these general exclusions is to relieve the insurers from liability unintended under EC that was thrust on them by the courts' liberal interpretation of such terms as explosion and windstorm. When EC is written on policies covering dwellings a $100 deductible is often used. In some states the deductible is mandatory; in others it is optional.

The policyowner pays a lower rate for coverage against these perils if they are included in a single form than if the protection against each is bought separately. In many rating territories the cost of the EC package is only slightly more than the cost of windstorm insurance alone because the expense of writing coverage for several perils in one policy is less than in several policies. The EC form has the advantage of removing many points where disagreement could arise following a loss. Suppose that a building is covered by fire insurance only. If an explosion occurs first, followed by fire, the difficulty lies in determining the damage caused by explosion (which is not covered) and that caused by fire (which is covered). Suppose that both fire and explosion are covered but the explosion occurs during a riot. Disagreement might arise concerning which damage was caused by riot and which by explosion. By covering these seven perils under one form, points of disagreement are minimized. So many policyowners buy EC that it is printed as part of the usual GPF and the DB&C, basic form. The protection is not extended unless a specific premium is paid. The EC is not added to the DB&C broad or special forms because coverage for these perils is included in the forms.

A reading of the EC will reveal limitations and extensions for each of the additional perils. For example, windstorm and hail coverages do not include damage by water, snow, frost or dust unless these elements enter through an opening made in the building by windstorm or hail. Under the explosion coverage damage caused by an explosion in steam pipes, turbines or flywheels is excluded if they are owned, leased or operated by the named insured.

The steam boiler exclusion is designed to reduce the cost of the explosion coverage for those who do not have a steam boiler exposure. For those who have this exposure a boiler and machinery policy may be purchased separately. Damage by aircraft must result from contact of any kind with the aircraft or by objects falling from it. Damage by vehicle is excluded if it is caused by vehicles owned or operated by the named insureds and their tenants. Smoke damage must be sudden and accidental and excludes damage occurring over a long period, e.g., by oil burners that deposit a film of smudge throughout the premises. Riot and civil commotion coverage excludes damage caused by sit-down strikers although no violence occurs. These examples illustrate only some limitations and extensions found in the EC. A study of the endorsement is necessary to complete the list.

Vandalism or malicious mischief endorsement

The vandalism or malicious mischief endorsement (VMM) provides coverage against direct loss caused by willful and malicious damage to or destruction of the covered property. Specifically excluded is damage to glass (other than glass building blocks) constituting part of a building or an outdoor sign. Coverage is suspended if the property had been vacant or unoccupied beyond a period of 30 consecutive days immediately preceding the loss. This coverage is written only with EC.

Radioactive contamination assumption endorsement

Two endorsements are available to add coverage against radioactive contamination. Form A, the limited form, covers sudden and accidental radioactive contamination resulting directly from a covered peril. Form B adds radioactive contamination as an additional covered peril. Both forms cover only contamination caused by materials used or stored on the described premises. The nuclear exclusion clause commonly attached to all fire policies does not exclude fires caused by radioactivity.

Optional perils policy

A business may obtain coverage against selected additional perils through the optional perils policy. Four optional coverages are included: (1) explosion, (2) explosion and riot and civil commotion, (3) explosion, riot and civil commotion and vandalism or malicious mischief and (4) damages by motor vehicle or aircraft. Motor vehicle damage coverage may be written separately or with any of the other coverages but riot coverage cannot be bought unless combined with explosion coverage, and vandalism coverage is not available unless both explosion and riot coverage is purchased.

The optional perils contract attracts those who want less explosion insurance than fire insurance or choose not to pay the premium for EC. By use of the optional perils policy building owners can buy as much or as little coverage against these optional perils as they choose, unrestricted by the apportionment clause discussed earlier (see Chapter 7).

Those who do not buy fire insurance may also use the optional perils policy. Some modern buildings are so constructed that their owners foolishly believe (or hope) fire insurance is unnecessary. However, they may consider explosion insurance or insurance against damage by aircraft essential.

Forms Covering Additional Losses

Under the SFP fire, lightning or another covered peril must be the proximate cause of physical damage to property for the insured to collect. An indirect loss caused by fire must be covered by a separate form attached to the SFP.

Additional living expense form

If a house is damaged by fire or other covered peril the owner may have to move the family elsewhere until the house is restored. During this period living costs probably will be much higher: the family may have to live at a motel for a few weeks, children may need transportation to school and meals in restaurants will cost more than eating at home. Additional living-expense insurance provides reimbursement for necessary additional expenses. The coverage is available as a separate policy, as a form to be attached to the DB&C, basic form and as basic coverage in a homeowners form or in the DB&C broad and special forms.

Rental-value and rent insurance

When a building is damaged by fire someone loses the use of the premises until the building is restored. Rental-value insurance is available to protect a tenant whose lease requires rent payments even during a period when the property is untenantable. In addition, rental-value insurance protects the owner from loss of use of owner-occupied property. If a lease does not require rent payments for untenantable property the landlord may buy rent insurance to protect the loss of rental income.

Leasehold interest policy

If a tenant has a long-term lease on a property and if the present rental value is greater than the rent agreed upon in the lease, the tenant has a bargain. The value of this bargain, known as a **leasehold interest,** is measured by the excess value between the market rate and the contractual rate. If the lease provides for cancellation by the landlord in the event of substantial damage by fire, not only will the tenant's property be burned but also the tenant will be deprived of the profits generated by the favorable lease. The tenant can be protected against loss of the favored position through a *leasehold interest policy.* If Terry Rose is renting a building to operate a record shop on a long-term lease at $800 a month and if the same building would rent today for $1,500 a month, Rose will lose $700 a month if the building is damaged by fire and the landlord cancels the lease. If this lease has ten years until expiration the value of the leasehold interest is equivalent to the current (present) value of the right to receive $700 a month for ten years. Leasehold interest insurance will protect Rose for this amount.

INNERSCRIPT: DEMOLITION INSURANCE

Present day construction in urban areas is regulated by local building and zoning codes. Buildings built before these codes became effective need not be torn down but the laws often provide that if a fire or other peril destroys a specified proportion of their value the entire structure must be demolished. Two forms of insurance are needed to cover the exposure fully: a Demolition form and an Increased Cost of Construction form. The Demolition form requires the insurer to reimburse the insured for the costs of tearing down the building. Under the Increased Cost of Construction form the insured will be paid the increased cost of reconstructing the building to conform with requirements of the building and zoning laws if two conditions are met: (1) the coverage is written on a replacement cost basis and (2) an adequate amount of insurance is bought. The coverage includes reimbursement for the undamaged portion of the building that must be destroyed.

Consequential loss or damage

Under consequential-loss-or-damage coverage the insurer assumes liability for losses sustained indirectly from fire or other insured perils. Losses payable under this form are of two types: (1) damage to goods by temperature changes or changes in other physical conditions and (2) damage to an integral part of a set that reduces the value of the remaining part. Protection against these losses may be provided by attaching a consequential-loss form to the SFP. In some policies consequential-damage coverage is included without an additional premium. For example, limited pair or set coverage is offered in the DB&C forms. For a small extra premium many insurers will add coverage to HO policies for food spoilage in freezers if caused by power failures.

Replacement-cost insurance

Replacement-cost insurance provides for loss settlement on the basis of the cost of replacing damaged property without deduction for depreciation. Usually to collect under replacement-cost insurance the insured must rebuild or replace the damaged property.

The homeowners forms (Chapter 8) and other multiple-line forms (Chapter 12) include replacement-cost coverage for buildings and appurtenant structures as part of the basic policy. Replacement-cost coverage initially was restricted to real property but a growing number of insurers have now extended this coverage to personal property in their HO forms. In commercial fire forms replacement-cost coverage includes specified classes of personal property, e.g., machinery, furniture, fixtures and equipment. Inventory, materials and supplies usually do not depreciate and can be replaced at their ACV. Replacement-cost coverage is unnecessary for these items.

Business-interruption insurance

Business-interruption insurance against fire and other perils covers loss of profits and those fixed charges that continue regardless of whether the business is operating. The insuring agreement states that the insurer shall be liable for the actual loss sustained for the time it would reasonably take to repair or rebuild the damaged property. While this clause limits the amount of indemnity collectible after an interruption it does not require the insured to rebuild as a condition for payment. In determining the amount payable for an interruption loss the insurer considers the experience of the business before the date of damage and the probable experience had no loss occurred.

Business-interruption forms are designed to be attached to the SFP with or without extended coverage. In addition to interruption losses caused by fire and other covered perils the forms provide limited coverage for losses arising from the interruption of business when access to the premises is prohibited by civil authority as a result of a covered peril. Thus if, as a result of a fire in the neighborhood the fire department blocks the entrance to the insured's property, the business-interruption policy will indemnify the insured for a period up to 14 days.

Two forms of business-interruption insurance are sold: the gross-earnings form and the earnings form.[3] The **gross-earnings form** covers the actual loss of business earnings. The measure of loss is the reduction of gross earnings *less* charges and expenses that do not necessarily continue during the business interruption. Heat, light and power are examples of noncontinuing expenses and may be ignored in measuring the loss. Consideration is given to the continuation of normal charges and expenses (including payroll) if such continuance is necessary for the business to resume without lowering the quality of service. A coinsurance clause ranging from 50 to 80 percent is required. As in other forms of insurance, the higher the required coinsurance percent the lower will be the rate per dollar of insurance.

Under the gross-earnings form a major decision in buying business-interruption insurance is whether to cover payroll as a continuing expense. If full payroll is covered the minimum required coinsurance percent is 50. However, if only key employees are covered (defined as officers, executives, department managers and employees under contract) 80 percent coinsurance is required.

If enough insurance is purchased to satisfy the 50 percent coinsurance requirement the insurance will provide for business shutdowns for at least six months. If a partial shutdown can be substituted for a total one the insurance proceeds can be spread over a longer period of time. Generally 50 percent coverage is sufficient for even severe business-interruption losses. Thus the success of the gross earnings form with 50 percent coinsurance is understandable. If a delay in excess of six months appears imminent the insured may eliminate some employees from the payroll, thus reducing the amount of continuing expenses and increasing the insurance available to cover loss of income beyond the six-month period.

---

[3] Because of their more complex nature gross earnings are more elaborately defined for a franchising business than for a mercantile business.

An **earnings form** of business-interruption insurance, a simplified edition of the gross-earnings form, usually is available only to mercantile and other non-manufacturing businesses. Instead of a coinsurance clause this form stipulates that no more than a stated portion of the policy's face amount can be used in any 30 consecutive calendar days. This portion is chosen by the insured and can be one third, one fourth or one sixth. A store owner with a $80,000 earnings form and a one fourth limit could collect no more than $20,000 over a 30-day period for loss of gross earnings.

Miscellaneous business-interruption forms

Contingent business-interruption insurance protects the insured if the business is interrupted by physical damage to the plant or store of another. For example, this coverage is useful for an auto dealer whose business may decline if the auto manufacturer's plant is closed from fire damage. A business making parts for the auto manufacturer might also suffer a loss of earnings if the auto plant burns.

A **tuition form** of business-interruption insurance is available. If a school building is damaged by fire the loss is not measured by the time required to restore the premises. At least a semester's tuition will be lost. The tuition form provides reimbursement for tuition loss plus board and room rents minus noncontinuing expenses. Similar forms are available for other operations like summer camps.

Profits and commissions form

Business-interruption insurance does not insure the manufacturer against damage to finished goods. For example, a fire occurs in Lou Henson's factory where he manufactures Santa Claus suits. Although a guard's quick action prevents serious damage to the building or machinery the costume stock is destroyed. Lou cannot replace the stock in time for Christmas. His SFP will provide indemnity for the cost of the suits but not for the profit lost. His business-interruption insurance will protect him for loss of production time until operations can be resumed. To protect profits on finished goods, **profits and commissions insurance** is required. A manufacturer of seasonal products has a particular need for this coverage because fire may destroy much of the year's profits even though the factory is able to continue its operation.

Fire insurance for manufacturers often includes a clause under which losses may be settled on the basis of market value instead of the usual basis of manufacturing costs. If a **market-value clause** is used the manufacturer does not need profits and commissions insurance.

Profits and commissions insurance is available to salespersons to protect them against loss if the goods they sell are destroyed and cannot be replaced in time to fill their orders. A market-value clause is of use only to salespersons who owns the goods.

Extra-expense form

To retain goodwill certain types of businesses must continue operations even though their plants are damaged by fire. A newspaper may have taken years to build circulation. If fire destroys its plant every effort will be made to continue publication, even at increased cost. To discontinue the paper with the hope of restoring circulation months later would be a dismal prospect. **Extra-expense insurance** covers the newspaper for the added cost of continuing operations following damage from a covered peril. It does not cover loss of income, profits, fixed charges or the usual expenses of a business. These exposures are covered by the business-interruption form.

Extra-expense insurance also appeals to banks, bakeries and public utilities: all of them must continue operating even at a substantial increase in cost. Because these types of concerns will operate regardless of extra expenses they have no need for business-interruption insurance unless some of their operations would be suspended during the period. A combined business-interruption-extra-expense form is written for those needing both coverages. It is priced lower than the two coverages bought separately.

ALLIED LINES

Allied lines are types of insurance provided by separate policies rather than by forms attached to the standard fire policy. Many of these coverages are of minor importance and are given only brief attention. Several of them are included in multiperil policies discussed in Chapter 12. Among the principal fire allied lines are earthquake insurance, rain insurance, sprinkler-leakage insurance, water damage insurance and crop hail insurance.

Earthquake insurance, purchased extensively in the Far West, is usually written as an endorsement to a fire contract. Elsewhere it is written as a separate earthquake and volcanic policy. (Earthquakes causing considerable property damage have been experienced in New England, New York and parts of the Midwest.)

Rain insurance is written under two standard forms: the basic form, written on an actual loss sustained basis and the optional form, written on a valued basis. Both may be written for periods of one or more days and for three or more consecutive hours each day. For example, rain insurance written for a baseball game must apply no later than three hours before the beginning of the game and terminate at the end of the fifth inning. (Unfortunately the fans of the losing team cannot buy insurance against no rain before the fifth inning.)

Sprinkler-leakage insurance provides protection for direct damage caused by discharge of fluid from (or collapse of a tank that is part of) an automatic sprinkler system. Damage to the sprinkler system itself, which may be covered by endorsement, is excluded. Other excluded perils are sprinkler-leakage losses resulting from fire, lightning, windstorm, earthquake, blasting, explosion, rupture of a steam boiler or fly wheel, riot and civil commotion and water losses from any source other than the automatic sprinkler system.

Water damage insurance covers losses arising from the accidental discharge, leakage or overflow of water or steam from such sources as plumbing, heating and refrigerating and air-conditioning systems. The insurance also covers losses from rain or snow that enters a building through open or defective doors, windows, ventilators, skylights, transoms and roofs. Damage from floods or sprinkler systems is excluded. Water damage coverage is now included in many dwelling, multiperil and homeowners forms; thus the water damage policy itself is rarely used today. (Fire insurance covers damage from water used to fight a fire.)

Crop hail insurance, covering damage for growing crops caused by hail, fire or lightning, is effective from planting until harvest or, for most crops, until some specified autumn date. The liability of the insurer usually is limited to a particular sum per acre. Some insurers write a multiperil crop-hail insurance policy that, in addition to protection against hail, covers drought, excessive heat, flood, excessive moisture, insect infestation, livestock, plant disease, wildlife, wind, tornado, sleet, hurricane, frost, freeze and snow. The Federal Crop Insurance Corporation writes an all-risk crop policy. Private insurers attempting to write all-risk crop insurance have suffered disastrous losses because of the difficulty of competing with the government in the $300 million crop insurance premium market. The government's crop insurance program is subsidized by taxpayers.

DIFFERENCES IN CONDITIONS INSURANCE

Differences in conditions insurance (DIC) usually is written to supplement existing property insurance and thus reduces the chance of an uninsured loss. DIC contracts are written on an all-risk basis with an underlying layer of basic property insurance. For losses not covered by the underlying forms a substantial deductible is charged. Although little similarity is found among available DIC policies many of them exclude fire, EC perils, vandalism, malicious mischief and sprinkler leakage.

A DIC policy offers several advantages. A firm can obtain protection against unknown perils and against perils not readily insurable separately. The contract allows the insured to reduce insurance costs by eliminating duplicate coverages. It can provide multinational firms with consistent coverages worldwide by covering the gaps that sometimes occur in contracts issued in foreign countries. Finally, the insured needing catastrophic limits for certain perils can use DIC policies to provide this protection.

TAILORED FORMS

In viewing the many specific forms available the reader might think any loss exposure can be covered by a standard printed form. Yet standard forms do not meet the needs of all insureds. Therefore risk managers of large corporations may design their own forms.

MARINE INSURANCE COVERAGE

At first glance coverages written by marine insurers seem to have no common factor. But virtually every marine policy includes an element of transportation.

Two branches of marine insurance are **ocean** and **inland marine.** Neither name accurately expresses the scope of its coverages. Ocean marine policies cover ships and cargoes on inland waters; in most inland marine coverages the use of the term *marine* does not seem justified. The two branches often are referred to as *wet* and *dry* marine respectively. These terms provide a better indication of the coverages written by each branch although they are not entirely accurate either. Ocean or wet marine concerns primarily waterborne commerce; inland or dry marine includes land transportation and other land exposures.

The first insurance policies sold in America were ocean marine contracts issued through local agents of English underwriters until 1721, when a Philadelphian advertised the opening of an Office of Publick Insurance on Vessels, Goods and Merchandizes. Soon others followed and by 1760 a substantial volume of ocean marine insurance was transacted in Philadelphia.

To meet the American challenge English underwriters cut their rates. The Philadelphia underwriters then claimed Americans had a patriotic duty to keep their money at home and argued that claims against English insurers might not be settled for months while time-consuming negotiations took place by sea mail. One advantage American underwriters could not overcome was the English groups' advantage of greater capital that permitted them to offer more insurance.

This disadvantage was eliminated in 1792 when the Insurance Company of North America was chartered with enough permanent capital and surplus to write large amounts of insurance with ease.

Inland marine insurance covers objects moving, capable of being moved or aiding in the movement of objects. These items were classified as marine insurance because they were more closely related to that branch than to fire or casualty insurance. Marine underwriters for centuries had been specialists in transportation insurance.

Aside from policies on steamboat transportation the earliest inland marine policies covered samples and personal effects of traveling salespersons. At the turn of the 20th century the tourist baggage policy was introduced. In 1912 the Postal Service began parcel-post service and inland marine policies were written for this transit exposure. By the 1920s the insurance of "instrumentalities of transportation" had been stretched to include the insurance of bridges and tunnels.

OCEAN MARINE INSURANCE

Ocean marine insurance, the oldest branch of the industry, is not substantially different from what it was many years ago. (I wish I could make the same comment about myself regarding physical condition!)

Classification of Policies

Ocean marine forms can be classified according to the nature of interest covered, valuation of interest, term of policy, treatment of insurable interest and property covered.

Nature of interest covered

Ocean navigation includes four interests: cargo, freight, hull and liability. Often these interests are held by different parties. Should the ship sink the cargo owner will suffer loss of the shipment and the shipowner will lose the value of the ship (hull). *Freight* (fare) means payment charged for transportation of goods. If the charge is not paid until the goods are delivered the vessel's owner or carrier[4] has an insurable freight interest. However, if prepaid, freight is added to the value of the cargo. Finally, the possibility of damage to others creates a liability interest.

Valuation of interest

Cargo policies are written on a valued or unvalued basis. In a valued policy the insurer agrees to pay the full face amount for a total loss. In an unvalued policy the insurer agrees to pay only the actual cash value of the loss subject to policy limits. The fluctuation of cargo values makes writing of cargo policies on a valued basis simpler. The value of the goods is expected to increase with location. Furthermore, value will fluctuate with market values. Hull coverage is written on either form. Freight policies are written on an unvalued basis. Typically, liability coverage for damaged goods is written on an unvalued basis.

Term of the policy

Ocean marine policies written for specified periods are called **time policies.** Policies covering one trip are called **voyage policies.** Policies without a terminating date are called **open contracts** and are effective until cancelled. Most cargo policies are written on open contracts, some of which have been in force for more than 50 years. Noncargo interests usually are written as time policies.

[4] The vessel may be operated by its owner or a charterer.

Treatment of insurance interest

All cargo and many freight and hull policies are written on an *interest* basis: the insured must prove insurable interest to collect and recovery is limited to the amount of the interest when the loss occurs. However, under some conditions (e.g., when freight is to be paid upon delivery) the owner or carrier has no clear insurable interest and therefore will not be indemnified under a policy written on a interest basis. Two forms, the **policy proof of interest form** (PPI) and the **full-interest admitted form** (FIA), are used to cover this intangible interest. These basically similar forms require the insurer to indemnify the insured upon submission of proof of loss without proof of interest.

Property covered

Cargo, freight and hull may be covered on the same form. Cargo policies may be written as voyage, open or time policies. A *voyage policy* covers a single shipment only. The *open-cargo policy* covers all shipments over an indefinite period. The insured reports shipments to the insurer when made and pays premiums monthly on the basis of these shipments. The policy is cancellable either by the insurer or insured. The floating or blanket form is written as a *time policy,* usually for one year. While similar to the open-cargo form it differs in the premium payment method. The value of future shipments is estimated and a premium deposit paid. The insured reports shipments when made. At the end of the period actual shipments are compared with the estimate and the premium deposit is adjusted.

Hull insurance may be written either on an individual vessel or a fleet form insuring all ships of the same owner under one policy. If a shipowner has some defective ships, insurance may be bought for them more easily and less expensively under a fleet policy covering both good and defective ships.

Special hull forms. Several special hull forms are written. *Port-risk only policies* may be written to cover ships only while docked. The insured must agree to keep the vessel in port. This coverage meets the needs of shipowners whose ships are in port for repairs.

Total-loss only forms provide protection for a total loss only and are used to cover "old" vessels or vessels that have a high value when compared with the capacity of the marine insurance market.

The builder's risk policy offers protection for a ship under construction, often until delivery is made. Nearly all physical damage perils are covered except losses resulting from strikes, riots, civil commotions and wars.

The Ocean Marine Policy

An awareness of the clauses used in ocean marine policies is helpful to the understanding of ocean marine insurance.

Insuring clause

Although many types of ocean marine insurance policies are in use, each is closely related in wording and phraseology to the policy agreed upon by Lloyd's underwriters in 1779. The archaic and delightful language of the Lloyd's insuring agreement, the basis for wording of U.S. contracts is:

> TOUCHING The adventures and perils which we the assurers are contented to bear and do take upon us in this Voyage, they are, of the Seas, Men-of-War, Fire, Enemies, Pirates, Rovers, Thieves, Jettisons, Letters of Mart and Countermart, Surprisals, Takings at Sea, Arrests, Restraints and Detainments of all Kings, Princes and People, of what Nation, Condition or Quality soever, Barratry of the Master and Mariners, and of all other like Perils, Losses and Misfortunes that have or shall come to the Hurt, Detriment or Damage of the said Goods and Merchandises and Ship, etc., or any Part thereof.

Perils of the sea include stranding, sinking, collision, lightning and tempestuous action of wind and waves. To jettison cargo is to throw it overboard to lighten the ship when it might otherwise sink. Letters of mart and countermart refer to authorizations given to people to engage in acts of war against other nations without the existence of a formal declaration of war. Surprisals are attacks without warning. Barratry is the marine equivalent of embezzlement.

Clauses modifying coverage

Clauses modifying the basic coverage (insurance agreement) of the policy are those affecting perils, hazards, property, losses or locations.

Clauses modifying perils and hazards. Two clauses cancel coverage for losses caused by perils included in most marine contracts. These clauses, called the **free-of-capture and seizure clause** (FC&S) and the **strikes, riots and civil commotion clause** (SR&CC) remove coverage for war, strikes, riots and civil commotion. Until 1982 piracy was a war risk. The 1982 revision of the Lloyd's policy, the first in more than 200 years, made it a marine risk. The 1982 revision specifically excludes strikes, lockouts, labor disturbances, riot and civil commotion in the insuring agreement.

The **running-down clause** (or *collision clause*) provides liability protection for the shipowner if the vessel collides with another. The protection is for an amount equal to the insurance covering the hull. Liability is limited to claims for loss to the other ship, including loss of use, cargo, freight and legal expenses for determining liability. However, if two ships under the same ownership collide the running-down clause offers no protection. A **sister-ship clause** protects the owners of more than one vessel if these ships collide with one another.

An **Inchmaree clause,** named for a vessel that was the subject in a court action testing basic marine policy coverage, may be attached to a policy covering hull, cargo or freight. It covers loss due to the negligence of the captain or crew.

The **free-of-particular-average clause** relieves the insurer of liability for partial cargo losses. Two forms are available: American and English conditions. Under the American form the insurer pays partial losses *caused* by the stranding, sinking, burning or collision of the vessel with another. Under the English clause the insurer pays for partial losses *if* the transporting vessel has been stranded, sunk, burned or in collision during the voyage. International competition in marine insurance often forces insurers to use the English clause.

The *explosion* clause extends coverage to include that peril unless excluded by the FC&S or the SR&CC clauses. The *fumigation clause* obligates the insurer to pay for direct loss to cargo resulting from fumigating the vessel.

Marine policies exclude *illicit or contraband* trade. The 1982 policy also excludes loss from financial insolvency or default of the vessel's owner or charterer; ordinary leakage, loss of weights or volume of cargo; insufficient packing; any weapon of war using atomic, nuclear or similar radioactive force and any terrorist action or action by a person with a political motive.

Clauses modifying property covered. Since 1748 the marine underwriters' liability for cargo has been modified by using the **memorandum clause.** It lists many goods for which the insured must bear the loss unless damage exceeds a stated percentage of its value. It also relieves the underwriters of liability for loss to specified goods. A typical memorandum clause may provide no protection for loss to musical instruments or other easily damaged items. Another group, such as special fibers (hemp, mats or matting material and tobacco stems), will not be covered unless damaged by 20 percent of value; coffee, pepper or rice must be damaged by 10 percent to be covered. This clause eliminates payments for the small losses expected in transporting these products by ship.

The *labels clause* provides that in case of damage to labels, capsules or wrappers the insurer is not liable for more than the cost of new labels, capsules or wrappers and the cost of reconditioning the goods. The *machinery clause* states that if a machine is carried as cargo the insurer is liable either for the insured value of any damaged part or, at its option, the cost (including labor and forwarding charges) of repairing or replacing the part.

Clauses affecting losses. The **protection and indemnity clause** (P&I) provides liability protection to the shipowner for damage caused by the ship to wharves, piers and other harbor installations, damage to its cargo and any injury or illness of passengers or crew. It does not cover liability to other ships.

The *delay clause* exempts the insurer from liability for delays that result in loss of sales or deterioration of property unless assumed in writing as a part of the contract.

When the ship is clearly in danger the captain is authorized to jettison cargo, incur extra expenses and take other steps to save the vessel. Under the general average doctrine costs incurred are apportioned among the interests exposed to loss (hull, cargo and freight). The **general average clause** provides that these costs and any salvage charges incurred are payable by the insurer. (A general average and salvage clause is included in the family auto policy but not in the personal auto policy.)

The **sue-and-labor clause** obligates the insured or the insured's representatives to take all reasonable and necessary steps to limit or reduce imminent losses. The insured will be indemnified by the insurer for the expenses incurred.

The **constructive total loss clause** states the conditions under which the insurer will be liable when the cost to save the damaged ship or cargo exceeds its value when restored. In claiming a constructive total loss an insured must unconditionally abandon the covered property to the insurer.

Clauses affecting locations covered. Originally, coverage was limited to cargoes only while on board. Under the **warehouse-to-warehouse clause** coverage was gradually extended until the cargo reached its destination. The *craft clause* extends coverage to include transit by craft and lighter to and from the vessel. (A lighter is a barge used in loading and unloading ships.)

INLAND MARINE INSURANCE

The definition of marine insurance adopted by most states makes three subjects eligible for coverage under inland marine forms: domestic shipments, instrumentalities of transportation and communications and movable property covered under floater policies. With the adoption of multiple-line underwriting (see Chapter 12) this latter class of property may be covered under other than inland marine forms.

Domestic Shipments

Policies covering goods in transit are the oldest sold by inland marine insurers and cover nearly every type of domestic shipment. They may be classified according to the mode of shipping. The annual transit form is used principally for shipments by truck, railroad, railway express and coastwise steamers; the parcel-post form, the registered-mail form and the first-class-mail form are for postal shipments. All forms are written as an endorsement to the **basic transportation policy.** The basic policy includes the face amount, name of the insured, nature of shipments, duration of the coverage and the general conditions. It does not contain an insuring clause stating the perils covered. The endorsements must state these perils and the exclusions.

Annual transit form

The annual transit form covers shipments of manufacturers and retailers for one year. Three benefits to the owner of a transit policy are (1) immediate indemnity for the loss even though the transit carrier eventually may be held liable, (2) indemnity for losses in excess of the carrier's liability and (3) protection against losses where the carrier is not liable (e.g., acts of God).

Perils covered by a typical annual transit policy *while the shipment is on land* are fire, lightning, windstorm, rising waters and perils of transportation such as collision, upset and derailment. Policies covering only express shipments usually include additional perils: earthquake, landslide and breakage for example. Perils covered *while the shipment is waterborne* are fire and perils of the sea. The policy may be written to include theft of an entire shipping package but pilferage (theft of part of the contents) is not covered. Excluded are strike, riot and civil commotion, unless endorsed; war, marring, scratching; dampening or becoming spotted, discolored, moldy, rusted or rotted. Leakage or breakage is not covered unless caused by one of the covered perils. Excluded properties are accounts, bills, currency, deeds, evidences of debt, money, notes and securities.

Trip transit form

The trip transit form is used when only occasional shipments are made. It is attached to the basic transportation policy to cover shipments by common carriers. The covered perils and exclusions are similar but not identical to those in the annual transit policy. The trip transit form is used mostly as personal coverage, e.g., to move household goods by public transportation.

Parcel-post form

Parcel-post policies may be used to cover merchandise against all risks from the time the post office receives it until delivered. Excluded are accounts, bills, currency, deeds, evidences of debt, manuscripts and securities; perishable merchandise except against fire, theft, pilferage or nonarrival; war; shipments made to transients at hotels; packages bearing labels describing their contents and packages not stating "return postage guaranteed." The shipper pays the insurer a deposit premium at the beginning of the policy year and reports the value of shipments monthly or quarterly for use in premium adjustments. This form usually continues until cancelled. Parcel-post policies are usually less expensive and more convenient than those the government provides as they require no waiting in line; packages may be sent with insurance after regular post-office hours and claim service is faster.

Registered-mail and express forms

Registered-mail and express forms are issued only to persons or firms acting as a fiduciary (banks, insurers, trustees, investment brokers and so on). The shipper may choose a daily or monthly reporting form or an annual premium-adjustment form. The annual value of covered registered-mail shipments determines the appropriate forms: the higher the value the more frequent the reporting.

First-class mail floater

The first-class mail floater is written for financial and fiduciary organizations to cover shipments of negotiable and nonnegotiable securities, coupons and other valuable papers. The broadest coverage is provided by form A, covering all risks to incoming and outgoing shipments. Form B covers all risks to outgoing shipments only.

Instrumentalities of Transportation and Communication

The nationwide inland marine definition states that the following transportation and communication instrumentalities may be covered under inland marine forms:

1. Bridges, tunnels and other instrumentalities of transportation and communication (excluding buildings, their furniture and furnishings, fixed contents and supplies held in storage) unless fire, tornado, sprinkler leakage, hail, explosion, earthquake, riot and/or civil commotion are the only hazards to be covered.
2. Piers, wharves, docks and slips, excluding the risks of fire, tornado, sprinkler leakage, hail, explosion, earthquake, riot and/or civil commotion.
3. Other aids to navigation and transportation, including dry docks and marine railways, against all risks.

Official interpretation of this definition has included pipelines, radio towers and airport floodlights but baseball floodlights have been held ineligible for coverage.

Dry docks and marine railways are covered for all perils. Piers, wharves and docks are covered under an inland marine form *only if* the perils commonly covered by fire insurers are excluded. Bridges and tunnels are covered by inland marine forms *if* the policy covers a peril in addition to the usual coverages written by fire insurers. So if a bridge is covered against flood damage or collapse it is eligible for inland marine coverage and may be covered against *any* peril desired. Business-interruption forms are also written to cover income loss due to physical damage to the property.

Property Floater Policies

Property floaters are written either as separate policies or as forms attached to a basic policy, most often the **scheduled property floater** (occasionally the basic transportation policy). The scheduled property floater, like the basic transportation form, contains most provisions of the policy except the insuring agreements and exclusions. These provisions are included in the property floater forms to be attached to the basic form. Property floater policies may be written to protect personal or business interests.

Floater policies for individuals and families

Forms are available to cover nearly all personal property belonging to individuals or their families.

The **personal articles floater** provides all-risk coverage for scheduled, valuable personal property. Excluded are war and nuclear hazards, wear and tear, gradual deterioration, inherent vice, insects and vermin. The *bicycle floater* provides all-risk coverage with the usual exceptions. The *wedding presents floater* provides all-risk coverage from the time the gifts are sent until 90 days after the wedding. Not covered are realty, animals, autos, motorcycles, aircraft, bicycles, boats, accounts, bills, deeds, evidences of debt, letters of credit, passports, documents, money, notes, securities, stamps and tickets. The usual perils excluded are augmented by breaking, marring or scratching of fragile articles and furniture unless caused by theft, acts of nature or conveyance upset.

The **personal effects floater** is a blanket policy covering any object usually carried by travelers. The all-risk protection is worldwide except it does not cover property at the insured's residence. The **personal property floater** is an all-risk policy covering virtually all personal property individuals have in and about their homes. This floater is deluxe and expensive coverage. Many people who formerly bought either the personal effects or the personal property floater find one of the homeowners forms (discussed in Chapter 8) sufficient.

Floater policies for business interests

Floater policies that protect business interests are classified according to property covered. The *salesperson's floater* protects against loss of samples. Two forms are available: limited and all-risk. The limited form provides insurance against specified perils: fire, lightning, windstorm, flood, perils of transportation and theft while on a common carrier or in a public checkroom. The all-risk form covers all perils with the usual exceptions. Because of prohibitions in the marine definition, coverage cannot be provided while the goods are on the insured's premises.

The *contractors' equipment floater* covers machinery and other equipment used by contractors. While this coverage may be written on a limited basis it is often written on an all-risk basis. The *mining equipment floater* and the *oil well drilling equipment floater* are two similar coverages written to meet the specific needs of operators in these fields.

The *conditional or installment sales floater* protects firms that (1) sell goods on the installment plan, (2) lend or rent merchandise or (3) send merchandise on approval. The goods are covered in transit and while in the customer's custody. The policy may be written to cover the dealer's interest only or in the case of installment sales, the customer's interest also.

The **jewelers' block policy,** a forerunner of multiple-line coverages, protects against loss of stocks of jewelry, precious stones and metals, dies and patterns and loss to customers' jewelry if damaged while in the insured's custody. Losses occurring to stock on approval with customers, on consignment from other jewelers or in possession of the insured's traveling salespersons are also covered. Merchandise shipped by sealed express or registered mail is covered. Shipments by motor carrier are covered if the shipment is by armored car, customer parcel delivery service or a passenger bus.

The *livestock floater* provides protection against named perils that cause death or destruction to cattle, sheep, hogs, mules or horses not used primarily for racing, show or delivery.

The *physicians' and surgeons' equipment floater* covers all loss to commonly used instruments. It may be extended to cover furniture and improvements or limited to portable equipment. The broader form covers building and equipment damage caused by attempted theft if the insured owns the building or is legally liable for damage.

The *radium floater,* an all-risk policy, covers radium capsules against all damage except by war and deterioration. A *radioactive contamination policy* covers damage by sudden and accidental radioactive contamination from materials used or stored on the premises. Property in transit is covered under the shippers' radioactive contamination policy. Truck operators can buy a motor truck cargo radioactive contamination policy to cover their legal liability.

Bailee Forms

Bailees—those who have possession or custody of personal property of others—are responsible *only* for their own negligence or that of employees. But a bailee who pays for damage to customers' goods only when legally liable is not likely to retain the public's goodwill or patronage. Bailees' customers' insurance providing multiperil protection for goods left for servicing is written mainly for laundries, dry cleaners, tailors, cold-storage locker operators and fur storers to reimburse the customers for loss regardless of liability.

In addition, truck lines may purchase a motor truck cargo policy to cover *liability* for damage to customers' property. A variation of the policy is available for shippers who use their own trucks to carry their goods. In these cases the policy provides *property,* not liability, insurance coverage.

Yacht and Motorboat Insurance

Yacht and motorboat coverage is divided between ocean and inland marine insurers. Insurers divide private pleasure craft into two classes: yacht insurance, written on an ocean marine form and outboard boat and motor insurance, written on an inland marine form. Coverage for outboard boats and motors is written on one of three nonstandard forms: all-risk, broad named perils or limited named perils. The all-risk form is the most popular and exclusions are similar to those generally found in inland marine contracts. In addition, this coverage does not apply when the property is used to carry passengers for hire, is rented or is engaged in an official race. Speedboats are covered like yachts. The policy excludes all loss resulting from an accident during an official race. If the policy covers two or more speedboat operators who engage in a friendly race between themselves the restriction applies only to officially scheduled contests.

SUMMARY

1. The fire insurance industry in the United States has emerged from a few insurers offering limited protection for dwellings in a small geographical area to a national (or some cases international) operation covering all types of property.

2. The standard fire policy (the SFP) is the starting point in all fire insurance coverages. The SFP covers only direct loss from fire and lightning and at least one additional form must be attached to have a valid policy.

3. Forms used to complete the coverage under the SFP are classified as to those:
   a. *Providing personal coverage*—the dwelling, building and contents forms.
   b. *Providing commercial coverages*—the general property, multiple-location and reporting forms.
   c. *Increasing the perils covered*—the extended coverage perils, vandalism or malicious mischief and the optional perils policy.
   d. *Increasing the losses covered*—additional living expenses, rental value, rental income, leasehold interests, demolition expenses, consequential loss or damages, replacement costs, business-interruption losses, profits and commission losses and extra expenses.

4. Allied lines are types of coverages written by fire insurers on separate policies rather than by forms attached to the SFP. Principal allied lines are: earthquake insurance, rain insurance, sprinkler-leakage insurance, water damage insurance and crop hail insurance.

5. Differences in conditions insurance (DIC) is written to supplement existing property insurance. It helps to protect against perils not readily insurable separately and provides multinational firms with consistent coverages worldwide.

6. Risk managers of large corporations may design their own forms to meet their own specific needs.

7. Two branches of marine insurance are ocean and inland marine. Ocean marine concerns primarily waterborne commerce; inland marine includes land transportation and other land exposures.

8. Ocean marine insurance can be classified according to the:
   a. Nature of the interest covered—cargo, freight, hull or liability.
   b. Valuation of interest—valued or unvalued.
   c. Term of the policy—voyage, time or open.
   d. Treatment of insurable interest—forms requiring proof of interest or forms where only proof of loss is required.
   e. Property covered—cargo, freight or hull.

9. Many ocean marine insurance policies are closely related in wording to those originally written at Lloyd's more than 200 years ago.

10. Clauses available to modify the basic ocean marine coverage may be classified as those affecting perils, hazards, property, losses or locations.

11. Three subjects eligible for coverage under inland marine forms are: domestic shipments, instrumentalities of transportation and communication and movable property.

12. Domestic shipment policies are available to fit the needs of a variety of insureds: annual transit, trip transit and various kinds of mail shipments. All these forms are written as an endorsement to the basic transportation policy.

13. Instrumentalities of transportation and communication cover such items as bridges, tunnels, piers, wharves, docks and other aids to navigation and transportation including dry docks and marine railways.

14. Property floater policies may be written to protect personal or business interests. These forms are written either as separate policies or as forms attached to the scheduled property floater.

15. Bailees' customers' insurance is written mainly for laundries, dry cleaners, fur storers and so on to reimburse customers for loss regardless of liability.

16. Yachts are covered under ocean marine policies while motorboats are covered by inland marine policies.

REVIEW QUESTIONS

1. What type of loss is covered by the standard fire policy? What types of losses are not covered?

2. Distinguish between the various dwelling, building and contents forms and the general property form. How do the dwelling forms differ from the homeowners forms?

3. Give an example of a business that would find a fire insurance reporting form useful. What type of reporting form would this business buy?

4. Which perils are covered under the extended coverage endorsement? When would a policyowner choose the optional perils policy rather than the extended coverage endorsement?

5. Distinguish between the gross earnings form and the earnings form of business-interruption insurance.

6. Give an example of a business that would have a need for both business-interruption insurance and extra-expense insurance.

7. How is the value of the leasehold interest measured? How can this value be protected?

8. What are allied lines? (Do they need transportation insurance?)

9. Consider the following statement: ocean marine insurance and inland marine insurance are clearly distinguishable on a logical basis. Explain why you agree or disagree.

10. Describe a situation where an ocean marine insurer will have to pay an insured for a general average loss. How is this loss computed?

11. When would a policyowner use a valued ocean marine policy rather than an unvalued one?

12. Define the three italicized words in the following term: *free*-of-*particular-average*. Why do ocean marine insurers use the English version rather than the American version of the free-of-particular-average clause?

13. What similarity do you find between fire insurance policies and inland marine insurance policies?

14. Identify three *different* types of inland marine insurance policies that *one* business firm might need. Explain.

15. Why are pleasure boats covered under inland marine insurance forms?

16. Explain why loss from nuclear or similar radioactive force was not excluded from the original Lloyd's ocean marine form.

CHAPTER

11 Liability coverages

John Thoeming/Richard D. Irwin

CHAPTER OBJECTIVES

1. **To explain the three broad areas included in the general liability insurance program: personal liability, professional liability and business liability.**
2. **To compare the three basic business liability forms: owners', landlords' and tenants', manufacturers' and contractors' and comprehensive general liability.**
3. **To identify the exposures covered by special liability policies, e.g., liquor liability and types of excess coverage.**
4. **To describe the types of auto insurance written for businesses and examine the issue of compensating victims of auto accidents.**
5. **To define the reasons for, the coverage offered and the issues involved in workers' compensation programs.**

Chapter 4 discusses liability exposures and the two types of losses that can result from them. One is the cost of defense against a law suit. The other is the obligation to pay damages on behalf of the insured. Insurance against these losses (called liability insurance) is discussed in this chapter.

LIABILITY INSURANCE POLICIES

Liability insurance is third-party coverage. (The first and second party are the insurer and the policyowner.) Nearly all liability policies require the insurer to pay the injured party directly rather than reimburse the insured. The insurer's obligations are restricted to claims under civil law and not criminal prosecution—the liability insurer will not serve the insured's jail sentence or pay the fine. In addition to covering all expenses of negotiating settlements, defending suits and paying damages the insurer agrees to pay (1) premiums on **appeal** and **release-of-attachment bonds,** (2) all reasonable expenses incurred by the insured at the insurer's request and (3) in most policies immediate medical and surgical expenses of others needed at the time of the accident.

Individuals and businesses face three types of liability exposures broadly classed as (1) general liability, (2) automobile liability and (3) employers' liability. Workers' compensation laws expose individuals and businesses to loss. This exposure is discussed along with employers' liability.

GENERAL LIABILITY PROGRAM

The general liability insurance program is similar to many fire and inland marine programs. A form must be attached to a standard policy (known as a jacket) to complete the contract. The standard policy contains the common provisions, conditions and definitions applying to all policies in the program. The forms added to the standard policy divide the general liability exposure into three broad areas:

1. Personal liability.
2. Professional liability.
3. Business liability.

Coverage for general liability exposures may be written as a separate policy rather than as a form attached to the jacket.

Personal Liability Forms

Personal liability forms provide coverage for liability losses arising from bodily injury and property damage to others. These losses must result either from the conditions of the insured's premises or the personal activities of the insured. The business activities of the insured must be covered under a business liability policy. Two types of personal liability forms are written—one for nonfarmers and the other for farmers.

The comprehensive personal liability policy

The personal liability exposure may be covered either by a separate comprehensive personal liability policy or by section II of the homeowners policy. The latter method is the more common. The basic policy limit is $25,000 but it can be increased for an additional premium. Section II of the homeowners series is discussed in Chapter 8.

The farmers' personal liability policy

The farmer needs liability protection, which is offered by the farmers' comprehensive personal liability policy. This coverage also is included in the farmowners-ranchowners program. Because these policies cover the insured while farming they include some business liability coverage. For a small additional premium the insurer will pay for the death of any cattle, horse, mule, hog, sheep or goat owned by an insured if the animal is struck while straying on a public highway. A single per-occurrence limit of $25,000 is the minimum written for the liability coverage. The accidental death benefit for covered animals is limited to $400 each. The form includes limited contractual coverage and products liability coverage. Liability for injuries to employees is excluded.

Professional Liability Forms

Professional people need liability protection against malpractice suits. The suit must result either from faulty services or failure to meet the standard of service expected under the circumstances. Coverage is needed by doctors, druggists, beauty parlor operators, architects, engineers, lawyers, employee benefit managers, corporate directors and officers, fiduciaries, insurance agents, actuaries and other professionals and has become increasingly important in this claim-conscious era.

Liability policies are written on either a **claims-made** basis or an **occurrence** basis. The descriptive names explain the difference between the two. *Claims-made* means the insurer is responsible only for *claims filed during the policy period. Occurrence* means the insurer is responsible for all claims resulting from *events occurring during the policy period* regardless of when claims are filed.

Under the occurrence basis insurers are liable for claims filed long after the policy expires, and these delays cause the insurers problems in their financial planning. The claims-made basis was introduced to remedy this problem. Because delays do not usually occur in auto liability and general liability coverages these policies are written on an occurrence basis. However, long time delays are frequent in products liability and professional liability coverages. Thus they are often written on a claims-made basis. (A new but questionable concept not restricted to products and professional liability is the *discovery* basis, i.e., the insurer is responsible for liability for injuries or damage discovered during the policy period. This basis is questionable because of the moral hazard it creates. The plaintiff can wait until the defendant increases his or her insurance before revealing a covered injury.)

Many professionals buy professional liability insurance to protect their reputations. They know that their liability insurers use some of the most competent defense lawyers available. Winning the case is important to professionals because an adverse judgment can damage their reputations.

For some professional liability claims (corporate directors and officers for example) an out-of-court settlement may be acceptable because expensive and lengthy court battles can be eliminated. For others (physicians and surgeons) out-of-court settlements usually are not acceptable. A voluntary settlement might be interpreted as an admission of guilt. Such admissions can do serious damage to the professional's practice. Thus many professional liability policies prohibit the insurer from settling out of court without the permission of the policyowner.

Basic Business Liability Forms

One of three forms may be added to the standard general liability jacket to complete a business liability policy. These forms are:

1. Owners', landlords' and tenants' (OL&T).
2. Manufacturers' and contractors' (M&C).
3. Comprehensive general liability (CGL).

Each of these forms contains coverage extensions and exclusions designed to meet special needs of the insureds. However, a common set of exclusions apply to all three forms. These latter exclusions are coverage for automobile liability, employers' liability and workers' compensation. These exposures are treated separately. (As discussed later, comprehensive auto liability coverage may be written in combination with the CGL.) In addition, no coverage is given for personal injury liability (e.g. libel, slander and defamation) and only limited coverage is included for liability assumed under contract. Personal injury liability and expanded coverage for liability assumed under contract may be added by endorsement. A reading of these forms reveals additional exclusions, e.g., the pollution hazard. A business must be aware of these exclusions to arrange adequate coverage for its liability exposures.

The CGL includes coverage for the products and completed operations liability exposure (discussed later in this chapter). Liability coverage for this exposure generally may not be written with either the OL&T or M&C forms. Therefore businesses with a products and completed operations exposure should buy the CGL form. The CGL also covers liability exposures arising from new construction, structural alterations and demolition operations. Under the M&C these exposures are excluded only if the work is performed by an independent contractor. The OL&T form excludes the exposures regardless of who performs the work. Both forms can be amended to cover these exposures.

Because the CGL policy provides the broadest coverage it is the best of the three forms to use for covering business liability exposures. While the importance of the OL&T and M&C has diminished, a description of these policies is necessary to understand the CGL.

Owners', landlords' and tenants' form

The OL&T is purchased mainly by retailers, wholesalers, service firms, owners and operators of movie and other entertainment houses, hotels, office buildings and apartments. This form provides insurance for liability claims resulting from the ownership or use of the covered premises. It covers liability for damages to those who incur bodily injury or property damage in and about the designated premises. In addition, the OL&T covers liability for damages off the premises if these damages are related to the business. An example of this off-premises liability would be an injury that occurs during the delivery of a package by the insured's employee when that package is dropped on a person's toe.

Manufacturers' and contractors' form

The OL&T form cannot be used to cover activities other than those arising from the designated premises. Liability exposures for building contractors, for example, exist at the job site as well as at the contractor's office. Thus the OL&T would not offer adequate coverage. The M&C form is available to provide liability coverage for those businesses for which the OL&T is inappropriate.

In addition to the basic premises coverage, the M&C covers liability arising from new construction, demolition operations and structural alterations changing the size and/or location of buildings, *if* such operations are performed by the insured's *own employees.* (This coverage is excluded in the OL&T form.) However, the M&C, like the OL&T, does not cover liability arising from the *use of independent contractors* in (1) demolition operations and (2) construction operations that change the size and/or location of buildings.

Comprehensive general liability form

The OL&T and M&C are not suitable for businesses that need broad all-risk coverage. Two features of the CGL qualify it as a broad all-risk form. First, the form automatically includes several liability exposures normally excluded in the OL&T and M&C. Second, the policy does not limit coverage to premises and operations existing when the policy is written. Assume a campus restaurant acquires the vacant lot next door. Part of the lot is used to provide student patrons parking facilities (the faculty can neither afford to drive nor eat out). The restaurant uses the rest of the lot to add a room to be used for the popular indoor sport of electronic games. The CGL policy will automatically cover the liability exposure from the additional premises and operations. The insured is not required to notify the insurer of these changes within a specified period. However, an additional premium will be charged at the end of the policy period. Liability exposures resulting from additional premises and operations are covered under the OL&T and M&C forms if the insurer is notified within 30 days of the acquisition.

Endorsements and Separate Policies

Table 11–1 summarizes the basic differences between the OL&T, M&C and CGL forms. Note the broad coverage offered by the CGL. An endorsement or separate policy is needed to obtain many of these coverages under the OL&T and M&C. Although the CGL offers broad coverage, endorsements may be necessary even to extend this policy to provide full coverage for the general liability exposure.

Contractual liability form

The OL&T, M&C and CGL cover only limited liability assumed under contract—liability exposures arising from **incidental contracts.** Examples of incidental contract liability exposures are those found in leases of premises, elevator maintenance agreements and **sidetrack agreements.** Thus if a lease requires the tenant to assume the owner's liability for bodily injury and property damage the tenant's OL&T, M&C and CGL forms cover this exposure.

However, special contractual liability forms are required to cover liability assumed under other-than-incidental contracts. As exposures of this type are plentiful, business owners must read every contract to identify any need for special contractual liability coverage. For example, a business that leases equipment for

TABLE 11–1
Coverage Comparison Chart: The Three Basic Business Liability Forms

	BASIC BUSINESS LIABILITY FORMS		
EXPOSURES	*OL&T*	*M&C*	*CGL*
Automobile liability	Excluded	Excluded	Excluded but may be written in combination with the CGL
Employers' liability and workers' compensation	Excluded	Excluded	Excluded
Personal injury	Excluded but may be added by endorsement	Excluded but may be added by endorsement	Excluded but may be added by endorsement
Liability assumed under contract	Limited coverage is included. Expanded coverage may be added by endorsement	Limited coverage is included. Expanded coverage may be added by endorsement	Limited coverage is included. Expanded coverage may be added by endorsement
Products and completed operations liability	Excluded	Excluded	Covered
Structural alterations that *change* the size and/or location of buildings	Excluded but the policy may be amended to include coverage	Excluded if performed by employees but the policy may be amended to include coverage for independent contractors	Covered
Structural alterations that *do not* change the size and/or locations of buildings	Covered	Covered	Covered
New construction and demolition operations	Excluded but the policy may be amended to include coverage	Excluded if performed by employees but the policy may be amended to include coverage for independent contractors	Covered
Ordinary repairs or maintenance	Covered	Covered	Covered
Additional premises and operations not present when the policy is written	Covered if reported within 30 days of acquisition	Covered if reported within 30 days of acquisition	Covered

use in its operations may find the lease requires the business (lessee) to assume the owner's (lessor) liability for bodily injury and property damage caused by the equipment.

Owners' and contractors' protective liability coverage

As mentioned earlier, the M&C form can be amended to include liability coverage for structural alterations, new construction and demolition operations performed by independent contractors. In addition, the OL&T can be amended to include liability coverage for these three activities regardless of who performs the work. Through these policy amendments the M&C and OL&T forms provide additional insurance known as owners' and contractors' protective liability coverage. This coverage protects the insured against liability claims resulting from (1) actions of independent contractors hired by the insured and (2) the insured's failure to supervise the independent contractors.

The owners' and contractors' protective coverage is automatically included in the CGL. It also may be purchased as a separate policy by an independent contractor for the benefit of a property owner or general contractor.

Products and completed-operations liability coverage

The CGL automatically includes coverage for the products and completed-operations liability exposure. This coverage may be excluded from the CGL only by endorsement. (Coverage for this exposure may not be written as an endorsement to the OL&T and M&C forms.)

The coverage for the products liability hazard is defined in the CGL form as follows:

> Products hazard includes bodily injury and property damage arising from the named insured's products or reliance upon a representation or warranty made at any time with respect thereto, but only if the bodily injury or property damage occurs away from premises owned by or rented to the named insured and after physical possession of such products has been relinquished to others. . . .

Note that this coverage provides protection against products liability claims arising *away from the premises.* The basic premises coverage under the OL&T, M&C and CGL offers *on-premises* protection for the products liability exposure.

If an insured withdraws a product from the market because of known or suspected defects, damages claimed for losses resulting from this action are not covered by products liability insurance. For example, a claim by a customer for loss-of-use of the withdrawn product is excluded. In addition, coverage can be denied for subsequent products liability claims if the insured fails to recall a product following a damage claim. A separate products recall policy is available to cover the cost of withdrawing products with known or suspected defects.

Under the coverage for the completed-operations hazard, liability insurance is provided for injury or damage caused by accidents due to operations performed by the insured at *a place away from the insured's premises.* The accident must occur after all operations have been completed or abandoned. An example is useful in distinguishing between a products liability exposure and a completed-operations hazard.

Suppose Tony Yates buys a gas stove from the Self-Cooking Stove Company. The company installs the stove. Two weeks later the stove explodes while dinner is cooking, injuring Tony and damaging his property. The cause of the explosion determines whether it results from a products liability or a completed-operations hazard. If the explosion is caused by a defect in the stove the resulting loss is a products liability loss. But if the explosion occurs because of faulty installation the resulting loss is from the completed-operations hazard.

Personal injury liability policy

Personal injury liability coverage protects against liability claims for other than physical harm and property damage allegations. It covers claims alleging such intentional torts as false arrest, detention, malicious prosecution, libel, slander, wrongful entry, eviction and invasion of privacy. This coverage, available for many years as a specialty line, is now available as an endorsement to general liability policies. Two limits of liability are used: an aggregate limit per person and a general aggregate limit. Under some policies the insured is required to participate in the defense costs; in others, insurers pay the full cost of defense.

Broad form CGL endorsement

The broad form endorsement adds coverage for a broad range of liability exposures often faced by firms but nevertheless overlooked. The 12 coverages provided by the endorsement in package form are offered at a cost lower than would be charged if each of these coverages were purchased separately. The disadvantage is that the insured may not need all 12 coverages.

INNERSCRIPT: COVERAGES IN BROAD FORM CGL ENDORSEMENT

The coverages automatically included in the broad form CGL endorsement are:

1. Blanket contractual liability—extends the meaning of incidental contract to include *any* contract unless specifically excluded.

2. Personal injury and advertising injury liability—adds coverage for these liability exposures.

3. Premises medical payments—provides coverage for medical payments for injuries sustained on the covered premises.

4. Host liquor liability—clarifies that insureds who occasionally sell or give away liquor at social events are covered for any resulting liability.

5. Fire legal liability—furnishes coverage for the named insured's *liability* for damage to rented or leased property caused by fire if the insured is found negligent.

6. Broad form property damage liability—partially supplies coverage for damage to property in the care, custody or control of the insured and damage to work performed by or on behalf of the insured. Many complicated restrictions and variations of this coverage exist. (If you need to know more about this coverage read the endorsement and see what you can make of it—better yet, see a *qualified* agent.)

7. Incidental medical malpractice liability—provides medical malpractice liability coverage for insureds not engaged in a medical, surgical or drug related business or occupation.

8. Nonowned watercraft liability—furnishes liability coverage for watercrafts under 26 feet and not owned by the insured.

9. Limited worldwide liability—extends the definition of policy territory to include, in addition to products liability, worldwide coverage for liability arising from bodily injury, property damage or advertising injury.

10. Additional persons insured (employees)—extends liability coverage to spouse(s) and employees of the named insured(s).

11. Extended bodily injury—broadens the definition of occurrence to include any intentional act by the insured resulting in bodily injury if such injury arises solely from the use of reasonable force to protect persons and property.

12. Automatic coverage, newly acquired organizations—automatically extends coverage for 90 days to include newly acquired organizations.

The storekeepers' liability policy

The storekeepers' liability form is a comprehensive liability policy tailored to meet the needs of owners and operators of eligible small shops. It is written as a form attached to the standard general liability jacket. Similar to the OL&T,

the policy covers the premises and operations hazard. It also covers the products and completed operations hazard.

Dramshop liability policy.[1] A bleary-eyed citizen charged with smashing windows in 12 shops before being arrested was hauled into police court. "Why did you get drunk in the first place?" asked the judge. "Your honor," replied the culprit, in imperfect drunkenese, "I didn't. It was the third place." Under the dramshop or liquor control laws found in a number of states and discussed in Chapter 4 the first, second and third places can be held liable for the window smashing. In addition, any individual injured by the intoxicated person has grounds under the common law of negligence to sue the bar operator who by selling liquor had caused the intoxication in whole or in part, first or last.

The general liability forms fully or partially exclude the liquor liability hazard, depending on the nature of the business owning the policy. For businesses engaged in the manufacture or distribution of alcoholic beverages, liability arising from (1) liquor control laws and (2) common-law suits is excluded. If written for owners or lessors of premises leased to businesses engaged in the manufacture or distribution of alcoholic beverages, *only* liability arising from liquor control laws is excluded. These businesses need separate liquor liability insurance to cover the excluded hazards. For businesses occasionally serving alcohol at social functions the general liability forms provide full liquor liability coverage. However, host liquor liability coverage written as a part of the broad form CGL endorsement, mentioned earlier, may be added to the general liability forms to protect the owners of non-liquor-related businesses in the event of an unusual incident that might be construed to deny coverage under the basic form.

Excess liability forms Interest has developed in three closely related forms of excess coverage: excess liability insurance, excess aggregate coverage and umbrella liability.

Excess liability insurance adds coverage above a specific amount up to a fixed limit. For instance, a student with a bad driving record might be able to obtain only minimum auto liability coverage under a basic policy. The student can seek excess coverage from another insurer specializing in writing excess liability insurance. The price of the excess coverage is higher than the cost of increasing the limits of the basic policy. The excess liability policy is needed because the primary insurer will not write the higher limits.

Excess aggregate insurance, designed for self-insurers, provides liability coverage up to an aggregate for all losses over a stated amount for the policy year. The insured must pay all liability claims until the specified amount is reached. At this point the excess aggregate insurer pays the remaining claims up to the policy limit. Through the use of excess aggregate insurance self-insurers are protected against annual losses of catastrophic proportions.

The **umbrella liability insurance** policy, in spite of its name, does not refer to claims arising from a negligent umbrella wielder at the homecoming game (covered by the comprehensive personal liability policy). It is a contract that fills the gaps in liability protection associated with basic coverages or self-insured

[1] *Dramshop* is a euphemism for bar or saloon. A commentary on the ways of legislators is the Illinois statute which forbids the use of "saloon" and "bar" in any sign or advertisement is found next to a provision forbidding the sale of unmixed whiskey, gin or rum in a container having a minimum capacity of less than one fluid ounce and requiring containers to have "at the time of sale at least one fluid ounce of the beverage being sold."

retentions. The umbrella policy is excess in three respects: (1) it provides higher limits than the other coverages owned; (2) it covers exposures not otherwise covered and (3) it provides automatic replacement for existing coverages exhausted or reduced by loss.

Typically, to be eligible for umbrella liability insurance the insured must have a minimum amount of coverage for a number of specified basic liability exposures. In addition, most insurers require the insured to retain a specified amount of the loss for uninsured or self-insured exposures. A separate umbrella policy for individuals usually is written for business executives, professional people and entertainers. The individual must first buy basic personal, auto and aviation liability policies (if applicable) before buying an umbrella contract.

Other liability forms

Several special liability policies are available to cover exclusions in OL&T, M&C and comprehensive policies, such as the hazards of nuclear energy, fire legal liability, water damage, sprinkler leakage, employer's liability, aircraft liability and automobile liability. Special forms are available to cover liability for property in the insured's care, custody or control.

AUTOMOBILE LIABILITY

Automobile liability insurance is one of the most widely held coverages purchased by both individuals and businesses and, in many states, required of all drivers. The owner or operator of an auto or other motor vehicle needs not only liability protection but in some cases also physical damage coverage. Because policies are designed to cover both these needs the discussion in this section extends beyond liability protection to include physical damage coverage.

Personal Auto Insurance

An individual driving for pleasure or to work needs protection against liability claims because of injury to persons or property of others arising from ownership, maintenance or use of the automobile. Insurance is also available to indemnify for physical damage to the car by fire, collision, theft or other perils. As discussed in Chapter 9, private passenger autos can be covered by one of three policies—the PAP, FAP or SAP. Some basic distinctions among these forms are discussed in Chapter 9. Interested readers will find it helpful to review these pages or even the chapter. The private passenger auto insurance business has become competitive; new forms and rating methods have been introduced. But according to a major study of consumer buying habits the single most important reason given for choosing a particular insurer is "reputation." And the primary reason for switching insurers is "rates."

Nonownership coverage

Individuals who own and buy insurance to cover a private passenger auto are protected to some degree by their policies (PAP, FAP, SAP) when using a nonowned auto. Not all people who drive own a car. *Named nonowner* coverage is available to protect nonowners against the *auto liability hazard.* If the insured acquires ownership of a car during the policy period the automobile is covered under the nonowner coverage for a maximum of 30 days. If the owner buys insurance on the car during this 30-day period coverage under the nonowner form no longer applies to the owned car. After graduating from college Bob Cook finds a position in Chicago, but living expenses are so high he is unable to buy a car. However, he arranges to use the Subaru owned by his friend,

Ann. Bob has learned from an insurance course in college that he will be covered under Ann's policy even if he uses the Subaru regularly. Later Ann cancels her policy. Consequently Bob buys nonownership liability coverage. Because he does not want to be exposed to a physical damage loss he also buys nonownership comprehensive and collision coverage. Three months later Bob's financial position improves and he buys both a Volkswagen and a Ford station wagon. A day later he accidentally drives the Ford into the lake; the station wagon is a total loss. Bob is indemnified by his nonownership policy because the accident occurred within 30 days of the car's acquisition. Two weeks later Bob buys a policy specifically for his VW. His nonownership policy will still apply to the Subaru and other nonowned cars but no longer to the Volkswagen.

INNERSCRIPT: AUTO RATING

In the days of few automobiles, accidents and lawsuits, automobile rating seemed almost a pleasure. Rates were applied to three categories: autos not driven by youthful drivers; autos driven by youthful drivers and autos used in business. Through the years rating has become complicated. In 1965 a rating system was introduced with 52 basic categories reflecting the age, sex and marital status of the *driver.* Classifications based on *car use* were also included: pleasure; driven fewer than 10 miles one way to work; driven more than 10 miles one way to work; cars used for business and cars used by farmers. The combination of the driver and car use categories produced 260 primary classifications. These primary classifications are modified if more than one car is covered under the same policy. The same classifications determine rates for medical payments, collision, comprehensive physical damage and liability coverage.

Often rates are further modified by the insured's accident experience. Under a safe-driving rating plan premiums are based on the insured's conviction and accident record. The more serious a conviction or accident the greater the increase in premium. Because of the apparent connection between good grades and good driving habits most insurers also offer substantial premium discounts for good student drivers ranking in the upper 20 percent of their class with a B average or better. Discounts often are given for the ownership of two or more cars by the same family when covered by the same insurer. Senior citizen discounts are also granted by some insurers.

In 1970 and again in 1976 the number of primary classifications was reduced in the majority of states—to 217 and then to 161. Further changes in auto insurance rating systems are expected due to pressure to disallow sex, age and marital status as factors in auto insurance rate making.

Related vehicles

Special policies have been developed to cover motor homes, van conversions, travel trailers, snowmobiles, golf carts, trail bikes, all-terrain vehicles, dune buggies and most other recreational vehicles. Many insurers cover this diverse collection of vehicles using a form typically called a *recreational vehicle policy*. Similar to an automobile policy, it provides liability, medical payments, uninsured motorists, comprehensive and collision coverage. Other policies have been developed to meet the needs of owners.

Auto insurance plans

The idea that all persons with valid driver's licenses should be able to purchase auto insurance is accepted by many as socially desirable. However, insurers will not write policies voluntarily to cover drivers with poor accident records. Also, very old and very young drivers are often unable to obtain coverage in the voluntary market. In response to the auto insurance availability problem most states have set up automobile insurance plans (AIPs) to provide insurance for the **residual market** (persons to whom insurers would prefer not to sell insurance). In the typical AIP each automobile insurer is assigned "extra-risk" insureds in proportion to the amount of auto premiums written by the insurer in the state. For example, if an insurer wants to write auto insurance in California it must agree to insure its proportional share of California's residual auto insurance market. A person with a record of involvement in gambling, narcotics or other illegal enterprises can be refused coverage in some states; in others, no one with a valid driver's license can be excluded from the AIP.

Although the plans provide coverage at higher-than-standard rates the increment usually does not offset the poor loss experience. Among the solutions often suggested is a further increase in AIP rates, but a strong view is that states should improve their licensing standards to prevent poor drivers from obtaining licenses.

Business Auto Insurance

Several types of autos are used in business. Various methods are available to cover the liability and physical damage exposures they present.

Private passenger coverage

Autos owned (or leased) by partnerships or corporations must be covered under the business auto policy (BAP). Automobiles owned or leased by individuals and used for business purposes qualify for the PAP. Thus Yves Roy's privately owned auto can be covered under a PAP even though he uses his car extensively for business purposes.

The BAP became effective in 1978 as a replacement for both the basic auto policy and the comprehensive auto liability policy.[2] The BAP follows the approach of the PAP and the HO series in that it is written in simplified and readable language. The mechanics of the policy allow flexibility. The BAP can be made as restrictive as the basic auto policy or as broad as the comprehensive auto liability policy (depending on the needs of the insured). Many insurers who have not yet adopted the BAP continue to write both the basic and comprehensive auto policies.

Types of coverage

The BAP provides coverage for liability and physical damage exposures. The policy can be expanded to provide coverage for medical payments, uninsured

[2] Generally the basic auto policy covers the insured's named automobiles while the comprehensive auto liability policy covers any auto used by an insured.

motorists insurance and any no-fault provisions required by law. The insured is able to create the desired scope of coverage by selecting one or more from among nine classifications of covered autos:

1. Any auto.
2. Owned autos only.
3. Owned private passenger autos only.
4. Owned autos other than private passenger autos.
5. Owned autos subject to no-fault.
6. Owned autos subject to compulsory uninsured motorist laws.
7. Specifically described autos.
8. Hired autos only.
9. Nonowned autos only.

Commercial and public vehicle coverage

Trucks are eligible for coverage under a BAP and under a truckers' policy specifically designed for long-haul truckers. Liability, physical damage and medical payments coverage is available. For rating purposes commercial vehicles are divided into classes based on "intensity of vehicle usage." Three classifications apply: (1) service use, or the transportation of personnel, supplies and equipment to job sites (least intense use); (2) retail use, or the pickup and delivery of goods to households (more intense use) and (3) commercial use, all other business purposes (most intense use).

A public auto is an auto of *any* type used as a public or livery conveyance for passengers. It can also be a private passenger car rented to others without a driver. Policies for public autos cover the named insured and any other person or organization using the auto or legally responsible for its use if permission is granted by the named insured. The rate depends on the vehicle type, its size and the territory involved. Many insurers refuse insurance on taxicabs and rental autos. The larger operators often have self-insurance plans to supplement or replace commercial coverage. Many insurers do not write insurance on public autos other than buses.

Nonownership coverage

Frequently an employee's car is used in the service of the employer. If an accident occurs the employer and employee may be sued for damages. If the court holds that the car was under the employer's direction and control the employer may be held liable. While the insurance (e.g., a PAP) on the employee-owned automobile normally covers the employer, certain actions of the employee can void the coverage. Furthermore, the liability limits of the employee's policy may not be adequate to cover fully the amount of the judgment against the employer. The nonowner form of auto liability insurance protects the employer in such cases.

Garage insurance

Garage insurance provides the appropriate coverage for those regularly engaged in auto sales, auto repair, operation of public gasoline stations, auto storage and sale and repair of self-propelled land equipment, such as tractors. Two forms may be needed: the garage liability form and the garagekeepers' legal liability form.

Garage liability insurance includes three coverages: premises and operations, products and completed operations and auto liability. The auto liability coverage may be broad or limited. If broad it applies to the ownership, maintenance or use of *any* auto. If limited, it applies to *nonowned or hired autos* *only*. In addition, the policy provides for automobile and premises medical payments and uninsured motorist coverage.

The owners of auto repair shops, storage garages or parking lots who receive customer's autos for repair or storage for a charge are legally bailees. They can be held legally liable for loss or damage caused by ordinary negligence. Because the garage liability policy excludes coverage for damage to property of others in the care, custody or control of the insured, **garagekeepers' legal liability insurance** is written to cover this exposure.

Compensating Victims of Automobile Accidents

A basic problem of auto insurance is the provision of an effective and efficient system for compensating accident victims. An *effective* system is one that guarantees that injured parties are paid amounts legally due them. An *efficient* system is one that provides **reparations** at the lowest cost consistent with social justice. The methods that states use in an attempt to provide both effective and efficient reparation of auto accident victims include financial responsibility laws, compulsory automobile insurance, unsatisfied judgment funds, uninsured motorists insurance and no-fault insurance. A brief discussion of each method follows.

Financial responsibility laws

Financial responsibility laws require drivers to furnish evidence of financial responsibility. This evidence need not be shown until after an accident (unfortunately). In general these laws provide that all drivers and owners involved in an accident causing a given amount of property damage or any bodily injury must immediately post security to guarantee payment of judgments that could arise. Proof of financial security may consist of (1) an insurer's certification that the party involved has liability limits for the minimum amount required, (2) the posting of a bond or (3) a cash deposit. In 14 states, in addition to posting security those involved in an accident must show financial responsibility for future accidents.

The diversity of required limits among the various states could create a problem for many insureds when traveling from state to state. The PAP remedies this problem by automatically providing the higher limits required by the state in which the accident occurs. The PAP also will meet the required minimum limits of the state in which an accident occurs if that state has a compulsory insurance law (see below). These provisions are either included in or can be added to other automobile liability policies.

Compulsory automobile insurance

Aside from the compulsory aspects of most no-fault laws (discussed later), less than half a dozen states have some form of compulsory auto insurance. Compulsory auto insurance requires that before a motor vehicle can be registered the owner must show financial responsibility for bodily injuries due to negligent operation of the vehicle. The responsibility may be demonstrated by depositing with the state a minimum amount in securities or cash, posting a bond or producing a liability policy with specified limits.

Unsatisfied-judgment funds

Under an unsatisfied-judgment plan, funds are available to accident victims who cannot collect judgments from negligent drivers with insufficient resources (usually because these drivers have no valid, collectible insurance). The funds are financed by a fee charged all motorists, one charged uninsured motorists or an assessment on insurers based on auto liability premiums written in the state. When a victim is compensated by this fund the negligent driver's license is revoked until that driver reimburses the fund with interest.

Uninsured motorists insurance Uninsured motorists insurance is a required coverage in several states (and strongly encouraged in others) on all auto policies. It covers the policyowner and family members if hit by a hit-and-run driver or by one who is uninsured, has insurance below limits required by financial responsibility laws or is insured by a financially irresponsible insurer. The coverage is liability insurance and not accident insurance. Payments are made only to insureds who would have been entitled to damages had there been liability insurance covering an at-fault driver. In most states the question of liability and amount of damages are determined by negotiation between the insured and insurer or by arbitration using the rules of the American Arbitration Association. The coverage is for bodily injury. Property damage is not covered.

No-fault insurance The logic of combining tort liability with insurance has been questioned and discussed from many viewpoints. The purpose of tort law is to place the accident cost on the one at fault. The purpose of insurance is to relieve the wrongdoer from the consequences of an act by paying defense costs and assessed damages. Many argue that an insurance system is in conflict with a tort system. Increasing pressures have been exerted for changes to separate insurance from tort law when applied to bodily injuries suffered by auto accident victims. One change is a no-fault system financed by compulsory insurance. The basic philosophy of no-fault plans is that one should be compensated for medical expenses and income losses by one's own insurer, regardless of fault. This idea is based on the assumption that auto accidents are similar to on-the-job accidents—they are inevitable and assessing blame serves no useful purpose.

Proponents of a no-fault system express concern for persons injured in auto accidents who receive no compensation if the injuries are not traceable to another party's carelessness. The tort system has produced claim payments in less than half the accidents in which persons have been seriously injured or killed. Many proposed no-fault plans would remove most auto cases from the courts, restrict recovery for pain and suffering and distribute limited reparations to all who experience losses. Advocates contend these changes will result in cost savings and premium reductions. Because fault will not be a factor in paying most claims a more nearly equitable disbursement would be anticipated. Proponents of a no-fault system also claim that many tortfeasors (persons at fault for accidents) escape responsibility for their wrongs because liability insurance has eroded the concept of individual responsibility and retribution.

Critics of no-fault plans contend that the basic principle of the tort-fault system is that one causing loss to another should fairly and adequately provide compensation for that loss. They state that as the true purpose is not necessarily to punish the tort-feasor, how payment is accomplished (from liability insurance or other means) is irrelevant. To say that the wrongdoer is not concerned about a possible adverse negligence judgment would be a gross misstatement. Court cases are time-consuming for the defendant and the possibility exists that the judgment will exceed the amount of insurance. Accident-prone individuals may find it difficult and expensive to buy liability limits beyond those offered under AIPs.

The principal supporters of a *pure* no-fault system (complete elimination of tort liability) are: Consumers Union, National Council of Senior Citizens, various labor unions, the Risk and Insurance Management Society, Inc. and many established stock insurers and their trade association, the American Insurance Association. Opposed to *any* type of no-fault plan are the American Bar Association and the American Trial Lawyers Association. They have been accused of opposing no-fault legislation because it would eliminate a need for lawyers in settling auto claims. About one sixth of the total income of American Bar Association members is derived from auto accident cases; a large percentage of practicing attorneys earn much of their income from these cases.

No-fault plans. No-fault plans may be classified as (1) pure no-fault plans, (2) modified no-fault plans and (3) add-on no-fault benefits. Under a **pure no-fault plan** injured parties are compensated by their insurers regardless of fault and may not initiate tort action against the wrongdoer. Under a **modified no-fault plan** if the victim's loss for medical expenses and loss of income do not exceed a specified amount the plan operates like a pure no-fault plan—the victim is compensated by his or her own insurer and may not take action against the wrongdoer under tort law. If losses exceed the limit, the injured party may sue the wrongdoer for the excess amount as well as for such noneconomic losses as pain and suffering. If the injury results in death or permanent disfigurement of the victim modified no-fault laws allow unlimited tort action against the wrongdoer. For example, under the Massachusetts modified plan the victim's own insurer provides compensation, regardless of fault, up to $2,000 for out-of-pocket expenses, including hospital bills and 75 percent of wages. The plan prohibits tort action for pain and suffering unless medical bills are more than $500 or disfigurement or death occurs.

Several states provide the addition of no-fault benefits—**add-on no-fault benefits**—to an insured's auto liability policy without impairing the right of the injured party to sue the wrongdoer. To call a plan a no-fault plan when the victim is allowed to sue the wrongdoer is a mockery. In essence, these plans grant expanded medical and disability benefit payments not found under traditional auto medical payments coverage. A system of subrogation is established in which the insurer paying no-fault benefits may recover against the negligent party. The laws usually require arbitration of disputes involving the question of liability or damages. Payments made under no-fault coverage are deducted from any damages awarded by arbitration or court action.

Modified no-fault laws are in effect in 14 states. Plans approaching *pure* no-fault are in effect in three states (Michigan, New York and Minnesota). Eight states have *add-on* no-fault laws.

Federal no-fault. A number of no-fault proposals have been considered at the federal level, the first in 1971. The bill, which failed, would have established a national compulsory no-fault system that would pay all medical and rehabilitation expenses for accident victims. Lost wages would also be reimbursed up to specified amounts. Bills introduced (but not adopted) in 1977 and 1978 would have established federal standards for state-administered no-fault automobile insurance plans. Each state could develop an independent plan if it met the minimum standards of the federal plan. As more than 1,600 insurance companies are opposed to the bills that have been introduced, passage in the near future of a federal plan seems unlikely.

WORKERS' COMPENSATION AND EMPLOYERS' LIABILITY

Every state has a system of workers' compensation requiring employers to compensate workers injured on the job or incurring job-connected diseases. Employers usually buy insurance to pay the sums for which they are liable. In six states the insurance must be bought from a state insurer called a workers' compensation fund. In 12 states the employer has a choice between state and private insurance. In the remaining states the protection may be purchased only from private insurers. In 47 states qualified employers may self-insure the exposure.

Historical Development

To understand workers' compensation legislation, the evolution of care required of employers toward workers needs to be considered.

Employers' liability

Legal liability is based on negligence law. A person has a duty to use care in dealing with others and failure to do so is negligence. To sustain a negligence action the injured person must show a direct connection between the injury and the other party's failure to use care. Traditionally the injured party must also be absolutely free of any contributory negligence. This requirement often has been modified. At one time damages were collectible only if the injured person survived, as a claim was held to die with the injured person. Negligence law is discussed in Chapter 4.

Under common law, employers must meet minimum requirements: a safe working place, proper tools and machinery for the job, suitable safety rules, reasonably competent fellow workers and warnings of dangers known to the employer but unknown to the worker. An injured worker can bring suit against an employer who fails to satisfy any of these requirements. The employer is entitled to three defenses: assumption of risk, **common employment** and contributory negligence. The *assumption-of-risk rule* is that a worker in accepting employment voluntarily accepts the risks of the job. As the employee is paid for such risks, no additional compensation should be paid for injuries. The *common employment doctrine* states that fellow workers are better judges of the competence and the fitness of fellow employees than the employer. Fellow workers discovering lapses of a fellow employee should notify the employer. The *contributory negligence defense* held that if a worker was in any way negligent in causing the accident the worker could not collect from the employer, even though the employer was grossly negligent.

Workers' compensation

The harsh doctrines of employer's liability under common law were modified beginning with the Industrial Revolution. Accidents are inherent in large-scale productions. Thus to consider job-related accidents as part of the cost of production not only is economically logical but also socially desirable. Based on this philosophy workers' compensation laws have been passed in all U.S. jurisdictions to require employers to compensate workers for income and medical expense losses regardless of fault. In return the employer, in most cases, is relieved of liability involving negligence. The modifying phrase "in most cases" is used because in a growing number of cases employers have been subject to law suits arising from on-the-job injuries. For example, employers have been held liable under common law for on-the-job injuries not considered work related. Furthermore, in some states workers' compensation laws allow spouses and dependents of injured employees to sue employers on the basis of loss of companionship.

In 1902 Maryland enacted a workers' compensation law that was soon declared unconstitutional because it restricted the employee's right to sue under common law. In the next few years Massachusetts and Illinois appointed commissions to investigate the possibility of enacting workers' compensation laws but they reached no decision. In 1908, largely through the prodding of Samuel Gompers and the American Federation of Labor, a federal bill was passed providing compensation for civilian government employees. Previously federal workers could be compensated for work-connected injuries only by a special act of Congress. New York passed a workers' compensation act in 1910 but it was immediately declared unconstitutional. In 1913 New York amended its constitution to permit a compensation act that could withstand a court test. Other states also were active and with the passage of a Mississippi workers' compensation act in 1948 compensation laws were in operation in all states.

Occupational Safety and Health Act of 1970 (OSHA)

During the 1960s employee job safety again became an issue, resulting in the passage of the Occupational Safety and Health Act by Congress in 1970. Under OSHA stringent work-safety regulations have been published and administrative machinery has been developed to enforce the rules by levying fines for violations and closing unsafe firms. Cooperation between insurers and insureds in helping businesses improve work environment and implement safe work practices can result in reduced workers' compensation claims, reduced premiums and an improved quality of life for workers.

Organization of the U.S. Workers' Compensation Program

Although each state has its own system of compensation, enough similarities exist to permit discussion of workers' compensation as a whole.

Coverage

Workers covered are specified by law. Agriculture workers usually are excluded, as are domestic servants and casual laborers in many states. The reasons for these exclusions are mainly political. The influence of farmer organizations has been a factor in excluding farm workers in spite of the appalling frequency and severity of farm accidents. All states not only provide coverage for accidental injuries arising from and in the course of employment but also include coverage for work-related diseases. In 1969 West Virginia coal miners struck for three weeks to force the inclusion of black lung disease under its workers' compensation law. The coal miners were successful and this success prompted several other states to enact similar legislation.

Compensation laws may be compulsory or elective. Compulsory laws require employers, with specific exceptions, to join the system and pay for industrial injuries as prescribed by the compensation system. Under the elective law (found in only three states) employers and employees decide whether to accept the compensation system. However, if the employer elects not to comply, the right to use the common-law defenses is denied. This restriction is a strong deterrent to employers who otherwise might elect not to participate. But a few prefer to take their chances under common law even if deprived of defenses. Some compulsory laws exempt designated employers, e.g., public employers, nonprofit organizations and employers with few employees (three to five is typical).

Benefits

Workers' compensation benefits are of three types: cash, medical and rehabilitation. Cash benefits include disability, impairment and survivor benefits. Disability benefits can be temporary or permanent and partial or total. Weekly benefits paid for permanent or temporary disability are the same: a percentage of wages, usually 66⅔ percent subject to a maximum and a minimum. The maximums and minimums are usually linked to a percentage of the statewide average weekly wage (SAWW). The maximums range from a high of 200 percent (in Alaska this percentage produces an amount close to $900 a week) to a low of 66⅔ percent. The minimums range from a high of 66⅔ percent to a low of 20 percent. Some states use specific dollar maximums and minimums rather than percentages related to the SAWW. For the maximum, the range is from about $245 to $98. The minimum range is from $159 to $15. Some states limit the number of weeks that benefits are payable and also the total dollars payable. Most states require that lifetime benefits be paid for permanent total disability.

Disability income benefits are not paid until after a specified waiting period, commonly three to seven days. If the disability continues beyond a stated period (commonly two weeks) disability benefits are paid retroactively for the waiting period. Some states require an annual cost-of-living increase for disability benefits. A few states allow social security benefits and unemployment compensation as offsets against workers' compensation benefits.

Many states require reduced benefits for temporary or permanent partial disability. Earnings of partially disabled workers are an offset against this benefit.

Special scheduled cash benefits are paid for specific physical impairments like the loss of a foot, a hand, an arm, an eye, hearing and so on. These benefits vary widely among the states. For example, the scheduled amounts paid for the loss of a leg at the hip ranges from a high of about $132,000 to a low of $6,000.

Survivorship benefits for fatal injuries are paid and include a burial allowance and a partial replacement of the deceased worker's weekly wage. These benefits are paid to the spouse until remarriage and to the children until a specified age. The payments are limited to a percentage of the deceased employee's weekly benefit and continue for a limited period. Burial benefits run from a maximum of $3,000 to a minimum of $400 with $1,000 and $1,500 the most common. The income benefits run from a maximum total for a spouse and children of $250,000 to a minimum of $44,000.

Medical benefits are usually unlimited as to both time and amount. They are not subject to the waiting period.

Rehabilitation services designed to enable injured workers to return to the labor force have received increasing attention and are assigned a high degree of importance. Rehabilitation goes beyond medical treatment and includes vocational training. Insurers are leaders in providing rehabilitation services for the industrially disabled person.

Workers' Compensation Insurance Policies

Insurers have developed a universal standard workers' compensation and employers' liability policy to protect employers under workers' compensation acts. This policy combines protection against any obligations the employer may have under the state compensation law (coverage A) and employers' liability protection (coverage B) for suits brought against them because of a negligently injured worker. The same injury can produce claims under coverage A and coverage B. Under coverage A the protection is not subject to a face-amount limit. The insurer promises to make all payments required by the state's compensation law. This section may be endorsed to cover employees injured in other states and provide workers' compensation coverage for employees excluded by the law. Coverage B covers the liability of the employer to employees for a basic limit (usually $100,000) per accident or disease. The usual provisions for supplementary payments for defense of suits, bond premiums and so on are included. Even though the state has a workers' compensation law the employer is exposed to suits arising from illegal employment of minors, losses claimed by the injured worker's spouse and, in some states, gross negligence.

Second-Injury Funds

Second-injury funds have been established to facilitate employment of physically handicapped workers. If a worker is blind in one eye when employed and later loses the other eye in a work accident the employer will be responsible for only the scale of compensation paid for loss of one eye. The additional compensation for loss of sight in both eyes (considered total disability) is paid from the second-injury fund. Usually insurers contribute to this fund on the basis of the total compensation paid during the year or on workers' compensation premiums collected. Some states support the second-injury fund through legislative appropriations.

Direction of Workers' Compensation Laws

The frequent changes made in state compensation laws are usually focused on flexible maximum weekly benefits, increases in medical benefits and improved occupational disease laws. The legislative trend continues to be one of broadening coverage and increasing benefits. An amendment to the Occupational Safety and Health Act of 1970 established a National Commission on State Workmen's Compensation Laws to examine and evaluate the state workers' compensation structure. The commission made 19 "essential recommendations" including:

1. Coverage by workers' compensation laws should be compulsory.
2. Employers should not be exempted from workers' compensation coverage because of the small number of their employees.
3. Farmworkers should be covered on the same basis as all other employees.
4. Adequate weekly cash benefits should be paid for temporary total disability, permanent total disability and to employees' survivors.
5. No statutory limits of time or dollar amount should exist for any work-related impairments.
6. Occupational diseases should be fully covered.

The findings of the commission have pressured states either to upgrade their laws or face replacement by a federal statute. States have made many changes in their workers' compensation laws following the commission's report and this impetus toward state reform is expected to continue primarily because of powerful lobbying interests that oppose any federal intervention.[3]

SUMMARY

1. The general liability insurance program operates like many fire and marine insurance programs. It covers personal, farmers', professional and business liability. Forms like the comprehensive personal liability, the OL&T and the M&C contain the insuring agreement that is inserted into a jacket contain-

[3] For an up-to-date analysis of state workers' compensation laws, including U.S. territories and Canadian provinces, see *Analysis of Workers' Compensation Laws,* the Chamber of Commerce of the United States, 1615 H St., N.W., Washington, D.C. 20062, annual. The 1982 edition includes 15 valuable detailed charts comparing specific provisions of the various workers' compensation laws. (A magnifying glass would be useful as an aid in reading its footnotes.)

ing provisions, conditions and definitions common to all contracts in the program.

2. Liability of farmers is covered by the farmers' personal liability policy and the farmowners-ranchowners program.

3. The OL&T form covers liability from the ownership, maintenance or use of premises occupied by the policyowner. The M&C form provides similar coverage for manufacturers and contractors, although altered to meet their specific needs. The CGL form, along with available endorsements, provides broad automatic coverage for all general liability exposures.

4. Products liability coverage protects the manufacturer or retailer from liability due to defective products. Insurance is also available to cover expenses of recalling defective products.

5. Professional liability policies are written for a host of professional people: doctors, lawyers, insurance agents, employee benefit managers, accountants and so on.

6. Special liability policies are available to cover exposures due to false arrests, libel, slander, invasion of privacy and liability resulting from dramshop laws. Contracts specifically designed for the needs of small storeowners are also available.

7. Excess liability insurance can be purchased to increase the amount of coverage over the basic policy. Self-insurers may purchase excess aggregate insurance to cover their catastrophic loss exposures. Umbrella liability insurance offers higher limits than the basic policy, covers exposures otherwise excluded and replaces existing insurance if the amount of coverage is reduced by losses.

8. All drivers have a liability exposure when operating a motor vehicle. They may also incur personal injury to themselves and physical damage to their cars. Auto insurance is available to protect against these loss exposures.

9. The personal auto policy (PAP) covers private passenger autos and light trucks owned by or leased to individuals or married couples. Autos owned by partnerships or corporations must be covered under the business auto policy (BAP) which offers coverage more restricted in most instances than the PAP.

10. The PAP protects an individual driving a nonowned automobile. Separate nonownership policies are available to extend nonowned coverage both for liability and physical damage. Nonownership insurance also is used to protect employers from liability resulting when employees use their own cars in their employer's service.

11. In auto rating 161 classifications group drivers according to marital status, accident record and—where allowed—age and sex. Insurers classify cars according to their primary use (pleasure, business, transportation to and from work and so on).

12. As most people believe all drivers should have access to auto insurance, states have set up automobile insurance plans (AIPs) to assign extra-hazardous insureds to insurers operating in the state. The expense and claims

experience of these plans has been poor so some states are experimenting with alternative solutions.

13. Special policies have been developed to cover all kinds of recreational vehicles.
14. Revision in auto insurance rating can be expected after a reevaluation of the factors currently used and as states eliminate sex and age as a rating factor.
15. The garage liability policy protects against liability from bodily injury and property damage.
16. Property in the garageowner's care, custody or control must be protected with garagekeepers' legal liability insurance.
17. A basic problem in auto insurance is providing an effective and efficient system for compensating accident victims. Financial responsibility laws and compulsory insurance requirements help protect the public from financial loss caused by careless and financially irresponsible motorists. In some states unsatisfied-judgment funds are available to pay victims unable to collect judgments from negligent drivers. Uninsured motorists insurance also protects the innocent victim.
18. No-fault auto insurance is the most discussed solution. The basic philosophy of no-fault plans is that persons should be compensated for medical expenses and income losses by their own insurers regardless of fault.
19. Employees once could sue employers as members of the general public. However, court decisions subsequently denied that right. Gradually laws were passed recognizing that accidents are inevitable and that employees should be compensated.
20. Workers' compensation insurance covers the benefits required by law: cash benefits, medical benefits and rehabilitation expenses for injured employees. The trend in legislation is toward broadened workers' compensation coverage and benefits.

REVIEW QUESTIONS

1. Why is liability coverage called third-party insurance?
2. In the typical liability policy what payments does the insurer promise to make on behalf of the insured?
3. How do professional liability forms differ significantly from other liability policies?
4. Under what circumstances would it be appropriate to recommend the CGL form? What liability exposures are not covered by the CGL?
5. Compare the M&C form to owners' and contractors' protective liability insurance.
6. What are dramshop laws? What is their significance with respect to liquor liability insurance?
7. Who would be interested in buying excess aggregate liability insurance?

8. How do auto financial responsibility laws differ from compulsory auto insurance laws?
9. Discuss the arguments commonly used for and against no-fault insurance.
10. What kinds of workers are typically excluded from workers' compensation? Why?
11. If a state has an elective workers' compensation law, what might encourage the employer to elect to participate in the compensation system?
12. What types of benefits are payable under workers' compensation laws? How do these benefits vary among the states?
13. Distinguish between liability policies written on an occurrence basis and a claims-made basis.
14. Distinguish between the business auto policy (BAP) and the personal auto policy (PAP).
15. Give an illustration showing how an employer may be obligated to pay workers' compensation benefits and still be subject to an employers' liability claim.

CHAPTER

12 Crime, surety, miscellaneous and multiple-line coverages

John Thoeming/Richard D. Irwin

CHAPTER OBJECTIVES

1. **To describe the crime coverages written for individuals, general businesses and banks.**
2. **To identify the categories of fidelity and surety bonds and to define the coverages offered in each category.**
3. **To explain the various miscellaneous property-liability coverages not easily classified neatly as fire, marine, liability and surety lines.**
4. **To show how multiple-line insurance programs bring together into one policy many property and liability coverages and to discuss some of these programs.**

Individuals and businesses are exposed to losses from burglary, robbery, theft, forgery, embezzlement and other dishonest acts. Losses from these acts are covered by crime insurance. In addition, businesses (and other organizations) are exposed to losses caused by the dishonesty of employees. Fidelity bonds are written to protect employers from these losses.

Crime and fidelity insurance are discussed in this chapter. In addition, attention is given to surety coverage, which offers financial guarantees that individuals or businesses will be compensated if the bonded person(s) do not accomplish certain tasks. Miscellaneous coverages discussed include glass, boiler and machinery, credit, accounts receivable, valuable papers, title, municipal bond, mutual fund and aviation insurance. The chapter concludes with a discussion of multiple-line insurance—the inclusion in one policy of most coverages discussed in this and the two previous chapters.

CRIME COVERAGES

The discussion of crime coverages is organized in this section on the basis of the customer buying the coverage.

Crime Coverages for Individuals

Most personal theft coverage is written as part of the homeowners policies, discussed in Chapter 8. Theft protection under the personal property floater is described in Chapter 10. The basic policy written specifically to protect individuals against theft is the personal theft policy.

The broad-form personal theft policy

The broad-form personal theft policy provides wide coverage against burglary, robbery, theft and mysterious disappearance of property of the insured, the immediate family, servants and guests. The typical person makes little, if any, distinction between the terms *burglary, robbery, theft* and related terms. In insurance, however, these terms have specific meanings defined in the policy. Briefly, **burglary** is forcible entry to premises; **robbery** is forcible taking from a person; **theft** or **larceny** is felonious taking of property; **embezzlement** is fraudulent appropriation of property and **forgery** is falsely making or altering a document.

In the broad form personal theft policy two basic insuring agreements (A and B) are available. To obtain coverage B, the policyowner must buy at least $1,000 of coverage A. Coverage A protects against loss from the insured's premises caused by one of the covered perils. The definition of the insured's premises is extended to include property within any bank, trust company, public warehouse or occupied dwelling not owned, occupied or rented by the insured if the insured put the property there for safekeeping. Damage to property and premises caused by theft or attempted theft, vandalism or malicious mischief also is covered. Coverage B includes the same perils away from the premises. It covers loss to personal property owned or used by the insured, a permanent member of the household or a residence employee. The policy for coverages A and B excludes animals, aircraft, automobiles, motorcycles and their equipment and articles held as samples for sale or delivery. Loss of securities is limited to $500 and loss of money to $100.

Coverage is written on three forms: specific, divided and blanket. Under the **specific form** certain articles are separately described and enumerated. Under the divided coverage jewelry and furs are covered for one amount and all other property for another amount. Under the blanket form the face amount of insurance may be used to pay losses of any type of property. The amount of insurance written for coverage B on any of the forms may not exceed the amount written under coverage A.

The limited-form personal theft policy

The limited form combining both on- and off-premises theft coverage may be written separately or endorsed to some other contract. At least $1,000 must be purchased. Theft, damage to premises caused by theft or attempted theft and malicious damage to covered property or to the interior of the premises are included. Mysterious disappearance is excluded. Property is not covered if taken from a dormitory, fraternity house or sorority house. Loss of money is limited to $100 and securities to $500.

Safe-deposit-box coverages

The bank is liable for safe-deposit-box losses only if it is negligent. Thus most losses will not be recoverable from the bank. Box owners can cover burglary and robbery losses of property in their leased boxes. Money is excluded but may be added by endorsement for an additional premium. Damage to property caused by actual or attempted burglary, robbery, vandalism or malicious mischief is also covered.

Crime Coverages for Business

A business's merchandise, furniture, fixtures, money and securities are exposed to loss by burglary, robbery, larceny, embezzlement and forgery. Several policies are available to protect against these losses. They usually contain the **general crime exclusions:** manuscripts, records or accounts; glass, letterings or ornamentation; loss due to fire and loss caused by vandalism, malicious mischief, war, nuclear hazards or dishonest acts of an associate or employee. These perils are generally excluded because they are covered by other policies the insured probably owns: fire and related coverages (see Chapter 10) and fidelity bonds and glass insurance (discussed later in this chapter). Furthermore some of these exposures (e.g., nuclear hazards) require special treatment. Most crime forms may be written as part of the special multi-peril program and other multiple-line contracts discussed later in this chapter.

Mercantile open-stock burglary policy

The mercantile open-stock burglary policy is written for businesses handling merchandise. The policy covers actual or attempted burglary, robbery of guards and damage other than fire caused by criminal action. Coverage for robbery and theft of merchandise may be added by endorsement. Although not considered burglary or robbery, loss caused by a person hiding on the premises and later breaking out is covered. Covered property includes merchandise, furniture, fixtures and equipment that the insured owns or for which the insured is legally liable. The general crime exclusions apply and premises damaged by burglars are covered if the insured is the owner or is liable.

The policy is written with a coinsurance clause. This clause is unique because it may be satisfied by meeting either an *amount* requirement or a *percentage* requirement. The **amount limit** is determined by the type of merchandise, while the **coinsurance percentage** is determined by the territory. Thus if the insurance taken at each location meets either requirement the other becomes inoperative.

Mercantile safe-burglary policy

Some businesses keep money and securities in safes while others (jewelry stores) have large quantities of merchandise in safes. The safe-burglary policy protects these firms against loss by forcible entry into safes, removal of the safe from the premises and any damage that results from actual or attempted burglary. The policy contains the usual crime form exclusions and also excludes loss resulting from lock manipulation and loss while specified protection is not maintained.

Mercantile robbery policy

Robbery is not covered by either the mercantile open-stock or mercantile safe-burglary policies. The mercantile robbery policy covers loss by actual or attempted robbery of money, securities, inventory and other property. Two coverages are available: inside (covers if the robbery is committed within the insured's premises) and outside (covers the property against the same perils but only while conveyed by a messenger outside the premises).

Money and securities broad-form policy

The safe-burglary and mercantile robbery policies may be bought separately or in combination. Broader money and securities coverage than would be obtained under the two policies combined may be purchased through the money and securities broad-form policy. It has two insuring agreements (on and off premises) and either or both may be bought. The on-premises agreement essentially provides all-risk coverage for money and securities. Coverage for loss of other property and damage to the premises is similar to that provided in the safe-burglary and mercantile robbery policies.

The off-premises agreement covers all loss of money and securities outside the premises caused by destruction, disappearance or wrongful abstraction while conveyed by a messenger or an armored car company or while within the home of any messenger. It also covers all loss to other property caused by robbery or attempted robbery outside the premises while that property is conveyed by a messenger or an armored car company and theft while the property is in the messenger's home.

Policyowners who cannot afford the broad form may still buy coverage against the destruction of money and securities by adding the money and securities destruction endorsement to the interior robbery, storekeepers' or office burglary and robbery policy.

Paymaster robbery policy

For most insureds the only need for outside coverage is payroll protection. The paymaster robbery form covers the payroll from the time it is drawn from the bank until the workers are paid. It covers loss of money and checks intended solely for the insured's payroll; the wallet, bag, satchel, safe or chest containing the payroll and all damage to the premises caused by robbery from a custodian engaged in regular payroll duties inside the premises. The policy also protects employees robbed of their pay on the premises at the time a robbery or attempted robbery of a custodian or messenger occurs.

Burglary special coverage form

A special burglary coverage form is available that includes the basic crime insurance provisions and exclusions but like the standard fire policy requires an endorsement to complete coverage. It is used to combine such coverages as mercantile safe burglary and mercantile robbery and to schedule related coverages like paymaster robbery, paymaster broad form and money and securities destruction. Coverage for many special risks (e.g., church theft, employees' or students' property burglary or theft, gravestone theft and vending machine theft) may also be included.

Package policies

The **storekeepers burglary and robbery policy,** a package policy including seven coverages often required by shopkeepers, is available to small shopowners and covers (1) inside robbery, (2) outside robbery, (3) kidnapping (using violent means to force messengers and custodians including owners and employees to open the premises from the outside), (4) safe burglary, (5) theft of money and securities from a bank night depository or from within a messenger's home, (6) mercantile open-stock burglary and robbery of a guard and (7) damage caused by actual or attempted robbery and burglary.[1]

The **office burglary and robbery policy** is intended for office building tenants who sell no merchandise. It is written only for those offices not located where the insured has property for sale, manufacture, cleaning, repairing, processing, storage or distribution. Coverages similar to those of the storekeepers policy are offered, except that the open-stock burglary protection is replaced by a theft-within-premises clause covering loss of office furniture, fixtures, equipment, instruments and supplies.

Crime coverages for banks

Crime insurance for banks is a specialized field. Bank crime coverages include bank burglary and robbery policies, safe-deposit-box policies and the bankers' blanket bond, discussed later.

The **bank burglary and robbery policy** may be written as primary coverage for smaller banks but is usually written as excess coverage for banks owning a bankers' blanket bond. Burglary, robbery or both can be bought. The burglary insuring agreement covers loss by burglary of money, securities and other property from within specified safes or vaults. Damage by vandalism and malicious mischief is also covered. The robbery insuring agreement covers loss of money and securities by robbery, vandalism and malicious mischief occurring on the premises. Damage to premises, including equipment, is covered if the insured is the owner or is liable for the damage.

The **combination safe depository policy** may be used by banks to cover their legal liability (coverage A) and to cover customers' property and the banks' equipment (coverage B). Banks are legally liable to use care in holding goods of others in safe-deposit boxes. However, even when they are not liable banks may reimburse boxholders for losses in order to retain the goodwill of their customers. Thus banks may purchase both coverages. Under coverage A the insurer pays all sums that the insured becomes *legally obligated* to pay for loss of customers' property while (1) in safe-deposit boxes in vaults on the premises,

[1] Money and securities destruction protection may be added for a small additional premium per premises.

(2) stored in vaults on the premises and (3) temporarily elsewhere on the premises in the course of deposit in or removal from such boxes or vaults. The only exclusions are contractual liability and the nuclear hazard. The circumstances under which a bank may be liable may be expanding. A California bank was held liable for customer losses caused by a safe-deposit-box burglary because the bank had advertised its boxes as "burglar proof" and "islands of absolute security." Under coverage B, the insurer pays for loss or damage to customers' property *regardless of the bank's liability.* Damage to the bank's premises and equipment is covered if caused by actual or attempted burglary, robbery, vandalism or malicious mischief.

Federal Crime Program

During the 1960s the crime rate jumped in most categories. The FBI's statistics showed that property crimes increased 151 percent and robbery 177 percent. Three fourths of all reported robberies occurred in cities of over 250,000 population, which also had a disproportionate share of auto thefts and burglaries. These developments led to dramatic rate increases and a severe reduction in the availability of crime insurance.

In 1971 the federal government launched a crime insurance program to provide coverage in those states where the Federal Insurance Agency determines it is needed. These states have the option to establish a pool arrangement or an assigned-risk plan in which all licensed property insurers operating in the state must participate. If a state does not set up a satisfactory program within the time limits the federal government can write crime insurance directly in that state. Many states are reluctant to develop programs. Why should one state incur the expenses to establish a plan when others do not? If no state plan exists the federal government writes the coverage and finances underwriting losses through reinsurance under The Department of Housing and Urban Development's riot reinsurance fund. By developing its own plan a state is denied these federal funds.

Federal crime insurance is available in 25 states and Washington, D.C. Areas designated as "high-risk" pay higher rates. Miami, New York and Trenton are in this category. Chicago, St. Louis and Atlanta are examples of cities in the "average-risk" group and have lower rates. The program provides both commercial and residential burglary and robbery insurance. The maximum coverage is $15,000 for commercial and $10,000 for residential exposures. The statute provides that "affordable rates" based on FBI statistics will be charged. All coverages have deductibles and the insured must use protective devices and other procedures to reduce loss.

BONDING

A bond is a contract binding one party financially for the performance by another in completing an obligation. A fidelity or surety contract involves three parties: a principal who promises performance; a surety who guarantees fulfillment and a third party, the obligee, to whom these promises are made. If the principal does not achieve as promised the surety must indemnify the obligee. Bonds that guarantee the principal's honesty are **fidelity bonds.** For example, your favorite movie theatre (the obligee) may purchase a fidelity bond from an insurer (the surety) to guarantee the honesty of its ticket seller (the principal). Bonds that guarantee the principal will accomplish certain tasks are **surety bonds.** For example, you hire a contractor to build a house to be completed in three months. If the house is not completed within that period you suffer a loss. Therefore you require the contractor (the principal) to furnish you (the obligee) a surety bond guaranteeing a specific daily payment (called *liquidation damage*) for each day beyond the three months that the house remains unfinished.

The Nature of Bonding

Is bonding insurance? This question has produced much heat and little light. The arguments that bonding is not insurance usually include these points:

1. Bonding always involves three parties, insurance two.
2. The bond principal is in full control while the insured ideally has no control over the event causing the loss.
3. In bonding the principal is liable to the surety for losses paid; in insurance the insured does not agree to reimburse the insurer.

In fidelity bonding, losses are anticipated and considered in the rate. But losses are not expected in surety bonding and premiums are considered to be service fees for the use of the surety's name. Therefore while most authorities agree that fidelity bonding resembles insurance they find it difficult to view surety bonding as insurance.

Fidelity Bond Coverages

Fidelity bonds are discussed under several categories: individual and schedule bonds, general blanket bonds, special blanket bonds, forgery insurance and the comprehensive dishonesty, destruction and disappearance (3D) policy.

Individual and schedule bonds

Two general types of fidelity bonds are available: individual and schedule. Individual bonds cover a particular named person. Schedule bonds may be name or position schedules.

The **name schedule bond** in effect combines several individual bonds. Covered persons must be listed along with the amount applying to each person. New employees may be added and former employees deleted at any time but all covered employees must be listed.

The **position schedule bond** lists the positions, specifying the amount for which each is bonded, so it is unnecessary to notify the bonding company of employee turnover. No change is necessary in the bond unless the number of workers in a position changes. The position schedule bond may include only positions the employer wants covered. However, all workers in a given position must be covered if any in that position is covered.

Bonds have no expiration date and are valid until cancelled. Thus if a bond has been in force since 1917, a loss occurring in 1918 but not discovered until 1983 would be covered. One can easily determine that a house has burned before the fire policy expires. A loss in the event of dishonesty, however, may not be discovered until long after the policy expires. Parks may tap the till for several years before Brody discovers it. By then the bond may have been cancelled. The time following cancellation when losses may be discovered and the bonding company held liable is the cutoff period and varies from six months to three years. However, the loss must have occurred while the bond was in effect.

If an employer terminates a schedule bond and buys a new one, continuity of coverage remains because the company selling the new bond will pay newly discovered losses that occurred under the old bond. The new bond covers losses only to the extent that they would have been covered by the old bond if discovered during its life. But if a loss under the old bond is discovered during its cutoff period the old bond must pay the loss even though the new bond is in effect.

General blanket bonds

General blanket fidelity bonds are **commercial blanket** and **blanket position.** Either is written for anyone ineligible for the bankers or brokers blanket bonds (discussed later) or any federal or other public-official bond except commission merchants, consignees, contractors and similar representatives. Because they offer broad coverage blanket bonds are the most popular method of covering employee dishonesty. No list of persons or positions appears because blanket coverage is provided uniformly to all persons in the insured's regular service. Blanket coverage means that the full bond amount (penalty) is available to pay a loss no matter how many employees are involved.

The *commercial blanket bond* guarantees employees' honesty up to the bond penalty. Loss payment cancels the coverage on the defaulting employee. However, the original amount of the coverage is automatically restored and is available for future losses and existing undiscovered losses. The penalty of the commercial blanket bond is the maximum available for any one loss regardless of the number of employees involved. If a $10,000 bond is in force and the discovery is made that one employee has stolen $60,000, the bond is cancelled instantly for this employee but the $10,000 is restored for newly discovered losses caused by other employees. The primary commercial blanket bond is issued for a minimum amount of $10,000.

The *blanket position bond* guarantees each employee's honesty up to the bond's penalty. The bond is issued with a minimum penalty of $2,500. In contrast to the commercial blanket bond the maximum liability of the bonding company for loss under the blanket position bond is the number of employees involved in the crime times the penalty of the bond. If a merchant has a $30,000 blanket position bond and three employees are involved a total of $90,000 is available to pay the loss. Payment cancels coverage on the defaulting employees but does not affect coverage on other employees.

The blanket position bond coverage sometimes leads insureds into self-deception. The merchant with the $30,000 blanket position bond may feel protected for losses larger than $30,000. However, coverage in excess of $30,000 exists only if several employees are involved in the default. One clerk operating alone for years may succeed in stealing $50,000. The bonding company, however, would pay only $30,000, leaving the merchant with a $20,000 net loss. Most blanket position bonds are written for a low penalty—not a wise decision, as most losses involve "lone wolves" and are not joint operations.[2]

Blanket bonds for financial institutions

Special blanket bonds are written for banks, brokerage houses, savings and loan associations, credit unions and other financial institutions. Many of these bonds were written before the general blanket bonds were developed. The demand for a general blanket bond arose from the interest in the bankers' blanket bond. Blanket bonds indemnify for loss of money, securities, bullion, precious metals and articles made from precious metals, jewelry, watches, necklaces, gems, pre-

[2] On the other hand, times may be changing: a loss to a large eastern manufacturer of electrical equipment involved 32 employees; a southern telephone office had a loss that involved nearly the entire staff. If these incidents reveal a trend one can expect an increase in the rates charged for blanket position bonds. If the electrical company had owned a blanket position bond with a $10,000 penalty, the bonding company could have been liable up to $320,000.

cious and semiprecious stones and specified classes of valuable documents. They are written for an indefinite period and continue until terminated. These blanket bonds are written with a single liability for each discovered loss. However, because upon discovery of a loss the face amount of the bond is fully reinstated, subsequent discovered losses remain covered under the bond for its initial limit.

The **bankers blanket bond** includes many sections. Section A, fidelity, covers loss through dishonesty of employees. Section B, premises, covers loss of covered property through robbery, burglary, larceny, theft, false pretenses, holdup, mysterious disappearance, misplacement, damage or destruction while the property is in any covered office of the insured. In addition, section B covers any loss, except by fire, to the insured's offices, furnishings, fixtures, equipment, safes and vaults from a covered peril. Property covered includes money, postage and revenue stamps, securities, precious metals, jewelry, watches and gems. Section C, in transit, insures against loss of the covered classes of property by robbery, larceny, theft, holdup, or negligence of messengers while the property is in transit. Section F covers redemption of U.S. savings bonds and section G provides counterfeit currency coverage. Check and securities forgery are optional coverages although they are printed as sections D and E. Coverage similar to bankers blanket bonds is written for savings banks, stock brokerage firms and investment banks by forms tailored to their needs.

Forgery insurance

Any business may suffer financial loss because someone forges a signature to a check. Except for the coverage sold with the bankers and other blanket bonds for financial institutions the main forgery coverage offered is the **depositors forgery bond.** Under this form the insurer indemnifies the insured and any bank in which the insured has a checking or savings account for loss by forgery or alteration of any check, draft, promissory note, bill of exchange or similar written order to pay money. The protection applies only to forgery of the insured's name (outgoing instruments). It does not apply to the insured's receipt of forged checks (incoming instruments). Protection against incoming items can be bought under a separate agreement printed on the contract.

The **family forgery bond** is intended for individual use. Any individual is exposed to loss by forgery. The chance of loss is small and so is the bond premium. Three basic coverages are included: outgoing instruments, incoming instruments and loss from acceptance in good faith of counterfeit U.S. paper currency up to $50 in one transaction or $100 in the aggregate. The bond is written for a minimum of $1,000.

The 3D policy

The **comprehensive dishonesty, disappearance and destruction (3D) policy** is a combination of fidelity and crime insurance designed to provide the widest possible protection. The basic form includes 5 standard insuring agreements plus an additional 13 under standard endorsements. The insured may select as many coverages as desired and elect the amount to be applied to each. Coverage I is an employee dishonesty bond corresponding to either the commercial blanket bond or the blanket position bond. Coverage II is money and securities coverage inside the premises. Coverage III is money and securities coverage outside the premises. These two coverages are identical to the money and securities broad form discussed earlier. Coverage IV is money order and counterfeit paper currency coverage, protecting the insured against loss from acceptance in good faith of a worthless money order or counterfeit U.S. or Canadian paper currency. Coverage V is depositors forgery coverage, corresponding to the depositors forgery bond.

INNERSCRIPT: ADDITIONAL 3D COVERAGES AND THE ADVANTAGES OF THE 3D

The 13 additional coverages available through standard endorsements are incoming check forgery; burglary of merchandise; paymaster robbery, inside and outside premises; broad-form payroll, inside and outside premises; broad-form payroll, inside premises only; burglary and theft of merchandise; forgery of warehouse receipts; securities of lessees of safe-deposit box; burglary of office equipment; theft of office equipment; paymaster robbery inside premises; credit-card forgery and extortion. Each insuring agreement is separately rated and the cost is the same as if bought individually.

The 3D policy has three major advantages. First, all coverages are with the same insurer. As the coverages are closely related, claims may occur that are not easily attributable to a specific coverage. For example, a money loss may be the result of employee embezzlement or of theft by an outsider. If the fidelity bond is with one insurer and money and securities coverage with another the loss cannot be paid until it is determined who is responsible for the loss. If both coverages are written by the same insurer the insured can be indemnified promptly while the argument continues between the insurer's bonding and crime departments as to which one should be charged with the loss. A second advantage of the 3D policy is that coverage is continuous. The lack of an expiration date eliminates the possibility of losses occurring under lapsed coverage. A final advantage is that including complete coverage against all business crimes in one package reduces the chance of ignoring important exposures.

Other comprehensive crime coverages

Two other important comprehensive contracts are the **broad-form storekeepers policy** and the **blanket crime policy.** These forms differ from the 3D as they are packaged rather than scheduled.

The *broad-form storekeepers policy* is written for single stores with no more than four employees. It has nine insuring agreements providing protection by combining the blanket fidelity bond, money and securities broad form, mercantile open-stock burglary, depositors forgery bond, money orders and counterfeit paper currency, damage to the insured's property by vandalism, malicious mischief and other specified crimes. The policy may be written for a minimum of $250 to a maximum of $1,000 *per insuring agreement.*

The *blanket crime policy* includes five coverages written *for a single limit.* The coverages are those of the commercial blanket bond, money and securities broad form, money orders and counterfeit paper currency and depositors forgery insurance. Additional agreements may be endorsed as in the 3D. The minimum coverage is $1,000. While this policy offers blanket coverage on all insured perils, premises, all messengers and so on, one drawback is that all coverages are written for the same amount. To expect the amount of fidelity exposure to be the same as the safe-burglary exposure or the off-premises money and securities exposure is illogical.

Surety Bond Coverages

Surety bonding is the assumption of responsibility by one or more persons for fulfilling another's obligations. This type of guarantee originally was given by friends. Today, except for bail bonds personal surety has nearly disappeared, replaced by corporate surety, i.e., an insurance or bonding company. Surety bonds are classified into judicial, contract, license, official and miscellaneous.

Judicial bonds

Some privileges are permitted by law only if a surety bond is furnished to protect the obligee. Judicial bonds are prescribed by law. The bonds are noncancellable and continue until the principal's obligation is discharged or until the bond is voided by the statute of limitations. Two general categories of judicial bonds are litigation and fiduciary.

Litigation bonds. Litigation bonds are required to be posted in the course of legal actions. A familiar type is the **bail bond,** used to secure the release of a person arrested on a criminal charge. The bond guarantees that the accused will appear for trial. Upon failure to appear the penalty of the bond becomes due.

A second litigation bond is the **appeal bond.**[3] If a person is dissatisfied with a court's decision and decides to appeal to a higher jurisdiction he or she must post a bond to guarantee that, if the appeal is lost, the original judgment and the costs of the appeal will be paid. As most appealed cases result in a confirmation of the lower court's decision, bonding companies stringently examine applicants for these bonds. The applicant often is required to deposit with the bonding company cash, U.S. government securities or securities guaranteed by the U.S. government in an amount equal to the sum of the original judgment and the costs of the appeal. In return for posting this collateral the bonding company will charge a lower premium. The question arises: If cash equal to the bond's full penalty must be deposited, why buy a bond? Why not deposit the cash with the court? The answer is: (1) the court may be legally forced to demand a bond; (2) often it is easier to obtain return of the collateral from the insurer than from the courts and (3) the service fee charged by courts for handling collateral may be more than the bond premium.

Fiduciary bonds. Fiduciary bonds provide indemnity if trustees, receivers, executors or administrators controlling property through court order do not faithfully and honestly perform their duties.

Contract bonds

Many business situations arise where signing a contract requires surety bonding. One example is a supply contract. A manufacturer contracting to supply semifinished articles to a finisher may be required to submit a **supply bond** guaranteeing

---

[3] A cynic defines *appeal* as "putting the dice in the cup for another throw."

that the contract terms will be fulfilled. The finisher depends on the contractor for a steady supply and if it does not arrive the finisher will incur a business loss. The bond guarantees the finisher indemnity if the goods are not delivered.

When a contractor bids on a building (offers to perform according to given specifications) often a **bid bond** must be posted guaranteeing that if the bid is accepted the contractor will sign the contract and furnish a **performance bond.** If a contract is awarded the premium on the bid bond is credited toward the premium on the performance bond. Under a performance bond the surety is responsible for completion of the building if the contractor fails. It must pay the expenses of finding and negotiating with another contractor and pay any additional construction costs incurred. The surety also must pay income losses due to delays. A contractor borrowing money for the construction will need a **completion bond** to guarantee the lender that the building will have no claims against it when transferred to the owner. Therefore if the contractor requires a loan both a performance and a completion bond are needed.

License (or permit) bonds

License (or permit) bonds are required by law in order to obtain a license or permit for a particular activity. A wide variety of license bonds is written to assure that laws and regulations pertaining to a given business will be followed. Examples are the abattoir (slaughterhouse), detective, electrician, funeral director, hack driver, housewrecker, hunter, pawnbroker, peddler, public accountant, travel agent and ticket broker bonds. Another group of license bonds guarantees payment of taxes on processed articles. The brewers' bond, for example, guarantees payment of taxes assessed against brewers. Similar bonds are sold to manufacturers of cigars, cigarettes, playing cards and other articles subject to excise taxes.

License bonds are of two types. One provides payment to the licensing authority for loss resulting from operations permitted by law or from the violation of the principal's imposed duties. The other provides funds to compensate third parties in successful actions to recover loss resulting from the principal's breach of a legal obligation. The time covered by the bond is the term of the license or permit but the right to file claims for losses sustained while the bond was in force continues for varying periods following its termination.

Official bonds

Bonds required of elected local or state officials are called **public-official bonds.** The bond may be required by statute, custom or administrative ruling. The obligee of the bond is the public body served by the bonded official. The term of a public-official bond usually corresponds with the official's term in office. The time limit for the discovery of loss may be prescribed by statute or by agreement between the surety and obligee. Sometimes these bonds are issued with no limitation as to time of loss discovery.

The **federal-official bond** is required of an official of the federal government controlling certain kinds and quantities of federal property. The bond may name as the obligee the government or the person to whom the employee is responsible.

Miscellaneous bonds

Some miscellaneous bonds are the **depository bond,** bought by banks serving as official depositories of government funds; the **lost-intrument bond,** bought by owners of stocks, bonds or similar instruments for replacement in event of loss and the **students' bond,** bought by those attending colleges that demand bonds guaranteeing payment of tuition, fees, room rent, board and other bills or to indemnify the school for damage to rooms, grounds or school property.

MISCELLANEOUS COVERAGES

A number of available coverages written by casualty insurers cannot be classified neatly as liability, auto or crime insurance, but they nevertheless are important. They are discussed here under the heading "Miscellaneous Coverages" and are written by property and liability insurers.

Comprehensive Glass Insurance

The comprehensive glass insurance policy is nearly completely comprehensive because reimbursement is made for all glass breakage except that caused by fire, war and associated perils and nuclear energy. The policy covers (1) damage to glass described in the declarations and to lettering and ornamentation separately described (the policy does not cover scratches or chemicals accidentally or maliciously applied); (2) repairs or replacement of frames encasing the glass; (3) installation of temporary plates or boarding up of openings due to unavoidable delay in repairing or replacing the damaged glass and (4) removal or replacement of obstructions other than window displays in replacing damaged glass, lettering or ornamentation. The amount limit under divisions (2), (3) and (4) is $75 per occurrence at any location. Higher limits are available for an additional premium.

For residences, glass is covered without measurement or scheduling. The residence form limits recovery on any one glass category to $50 but this limitation may be removed. Most residential glass coverage today is written on a homeowners form.

Unlike most other insurance lines glass losses usually are adjusted by replacing the damaged glass. This service is performed quickly and is often the principal reason for buying the coverage. Finding an insurer to cover glass in inner cities, however, may sometimes be difficult.

Boiler and Machinery Insurance

Most property insurance contracts exclude steam boiler and machinery losses (losses from the operation of pressure, mechanical and electrical equipment) leaving that protection to boiler and machinery policies (B&M). Insurers writing B&M are among the oldest in existence. In 1860 a group of engineers in Hartford, Connecticut formed an organization known as the Polytechnic Club which, in 1866, organized the Hartford Steam Boiler Inspection and Insurance Company to locate latent causes of explosion and provide indemnity in case an explosion or related loss occurred. This company is still in business and writes only B&M. The tradition of B&M insurance continued and today B&M insurers provide extensive safety engineering and inspection services. More of each premium dollar is spent for preventive measures than for losses.[4] The loss-preventive service is an important reason for buying B&M coverage.

Six basic coverages are offered: coverage A, damage to the insured's property; coverage B, expediting charges (reasonable cost of temporary repairs) up to $1,000; coverage C, property damage liability for loss of or damage to property of others in the insured's care, custody or control; coverage D, bodily injury liability on an optional basis; coverage E, defense costs and supplementary payments and coverage F, automatic coverage of additional covered objects acquired during the policy period. Some insurers exclude coverage D by endorsement with a premium reduction. Others add the coverage for an additional premium. The policy limit is the maximum amount payable per accident. However, the immediate medical and surgical care provided by coverage D and the legal ex-

[4] About 40 percent of the premium is used to pay for inspections.

penses and supplementary payments provided by coverage E are not subject to or deducted from this limit. The insurer pays losses first under A, then B and so on. If losses under A consume the limit then nothing is available for B, C or D.

One important exclusion is consequential damage. Boiler or machinery damage may cause property spoilage from lack of power, light, heat, steam or refrigeration. These indirect losses are not covered by the basic policy. Consequential-damage coverage may be endorsed on the basic policy or provided by separate contract. Another exclusion is loss caused by business interruption. This loss is covered by boiler and machinery use-and-occupancy insurance.

For a long time property damage and bodily injury liability coverage was standard in boiler and machinery policies. But recently the coverage was restricted, eliminated or made optional—a case of successive depletion of coverage but in this case one that does not penalize the insured. The insured's general liability insurance covers the boiler and machinery liability hazard except for property in the insured's care, custody or control. This part of the boiler and machinery liability coverage has been retained to fill the void in the general liability coverage.

Credit Insurance

Credit insurance protects eligible types of businesses from excessive credit losses due to debtor insolvency. Legal insolvency or bankruptcy of a debtor is not required for a claim. Claims may occur when a debtor absconds, a sole debtor dies, a sole debtor is adjudged insane and so on. The protection is available to manufacturers, wholesalers and service organizations but not to retailers. Protection does not extend to normal credit losses. The normal loss percentage is determined by the insured's experience or that of a similar business. If a manufacturer's line of business has a usual credit loss of 5 percent, a 5 percent credit loss is considered a normal operating cost. Credit insurance protects against only unusual credit losses.

Most policies are written under the optional collection form. At the insured's option, past-due accounts are turned over to the insurer for collection. The insurer charges a collection fee for this service. If *the insurer* fails to collect the accounts and the debtor is insolvent the insurer must pay the insured. Credit insurance usually covers all accounts of the insured although it is possible to cover only particular account classes or, in special cases, only a specific account.

Accounts Receivable Insurance

A firm may be unable to collect all outstanding accounts following the destruction of its records. Insurance is available to cover this loss plus additional expenses that may result, such as extra collection expenses, cost of reconstructing records and interest on money borrowed to offset impaired collections. The policy is written as all-risk coverage. Exclusions include dishonest acts of the insured, officers, directors or partners; loss caused by manipulation of records to conceal another dishonest act; loss due to bookkeeping, accounting or billing mistakes; loss from electrical or magnetic injury of electronic recordings, except by lightning; the nuclear and war hazards and loss where proof is entirely dependent on an audit or inventory computation.

Valuable Papers and Records Insurance

A business can cover inscribed documents and records, including books, maps, films, drawings, abstracts, deeds, mortgages, media for electronic data processing and manuscripts against all risks, either on a scheduled or blanket basis under a valuable papers and records policy. Property covered on a scheduled basis is written for an agreed amount while property on a blanket basis is written for its actual cash value. The exclusions are those found in inland marine policies, plus dishonesty of an insured, partner, officer or director. Irreplaceable property is excluded under blanket coverage but covered when scheduled. For libraries, loss by failure of borrowers to return books or other documents is excluded. Rate decreases of 10 to 40 percent are allowed if particular types of safes or vaults are used.

Title Insurance

Ownership of real property usually is transferred by warranty deed and the buyer generally hires a lawyer to verify that the title is clear. If the title proves cloudy the buyer may not have a clear right to the property. Even if the buyer can prove ownership the resulting legal battle may be long and costly. Title insurance can be bought to protect against these costs, including the loss of the property.

Specialty insurers that search the title write title insurance. If convinced that the title is clear they issue the policy. The title, however, is guaranteed during the search, and the policy when issued is effective as long as the same person owns the property. Title insurance is bought not only by prospective owners of real property but also by those who make mortgage loans on real property. The title policy issued to mortgagees is similar to that written for owners.

INNERSCRIPT: MUNICIPAL BOND INSURANCE ASSOCIATION (MBIA) AND MUTUAL FUND INSURANCE

The MBIA was formed in late 1973 to guarantee principal and interest payments for certain municipal bonds. Composed of five major insurers, the MBIA covers mostly medium-quality bond issuers. Another company (the MGIC Investment Corporation) also covers selected tax-exempt bonds. Municipalities have much to gain from the coverage, for with the guarantee many are able to boost their bond ratings to AAA, enabling them to borrow at lower interest rates. The lower rate more than offsets the insurance premiums.

The insured mutual fund redemption value program (IMF) guarantees that if, at the end of the covered period, the value of the insured's mutual fund does not equal the amount invested the insured will be reimbursed for the difference. An IMF account is subject to a minimum and maximum investment and a minimum period.

Aviation Insurance

Aviation insurance is closely related to ocean marine and automobile insurance, as the aircraft owner needs both physical damage (hull) and liability insurance.

Hull insurance

Hull insurance is available on a specified-peril or all-risk basis and may cover the plane while (1) stationary only, (2) stationary or taxiing or (3) on the ground or in flight. The policy generally contains a deductible of 5 to 10 percent of the covered value. Some policies are written on a participation form in which the insured pays a percentage (e.g., 25 percent) of each loss.

Aircraft liability insurance

The pilot needs protection against liability suits arising from operation or ownership of the plane. Basic aviation policies do not automatically cover the passenger bodily injury hazard, although that coverage can be purchased by endorsement if desired. A pilot who flies planes belonging to others may buy liability insurance to cover the exposure while flying these planes. A hangar keepers' legal liability policy is available to protect these operators from claims arising from losses that occur to planes left in their custody. This coverage is similar to the garage keepers' legal liability policy. Medical payments coverage for the pilot and passengers is available with passenger liability insurance.

MULTIPLE-LINE INSURANCE

In discussing his Ziegfield Follies comedy routines, Will Rogers said that if he needed any new jokes he would "just get the late afternoon papers and read what Congress had done, and the audience would die laughing." Today it is easier to keep up with the activities of Congress than to stay abreast of all the changes that characterize multiple-line insurance. An occasional agent may smile as he opens a bulky package of instructions and new forms but there has been no report of agents dying of laughter.

Multiple-line coverage must not be confused with other multiple-line activity that has always existed. Fire and casualty insurers for years have offered combination policies issued jointly. The auto policy provides a classic example of two former contracts that are now written in one document. The casualty insurer wrote the liability coverage and the fire insurer physical damage coverage. Either one wrote the collision coverage. Multiple-line coverage in this chapter is coverage of many perils, written by *one* insurer in one policy that previously had to be covered in several policies written by fire and casualty insurers.

The evolution of multiple-line underwriting powers is outlined in Chapter 1. Since the 1950s all nonlife insurers were granted multiple-line underwriting powers if they met required financial standards. Consequently qualified property-liability insurers could combine their coverages into one policy. To exploit this opportunity all an insurer needed for a multiple-line package was a bundle of inland marine forms, some liability policies, a few crime insurance contracts, the standard fire policy, a pair of scissors and a pot of paste. Initially, experimentation was complicated and inhibited by separate fire, marine, and casualty advisory and rating organizations. Eventually these separate organizations were combined; the major one today is the Insurance Service Office (ISO).

MULTIPLE-LINE PROGRAMS

Multiple-line insurance is widely written both for personal and business coverages. The principal personal multiple-line policies or programs are the various auto and homeowners forms discussed in Chapters 8 and 9. The major multiple-line business policies or programs consist of (1) the **special multi-peril program** (SMP), (2) the businessowners package forms and (3) the business auto policy (BAP). The BAP is discussed in Chapter 11. The SMP and the **businessowners programs** are discussed in this chapter.

Special Multi-Peril Program

Virtually any business is eligible for the SMP program. The exceptions are (1) boarding or rooming houses containing fewer than three apartment units; (2) farms or farming operations; (3) grain elevators, grain tanks and grain warehouses; (4) automobile filling or repair stations; automobile motor home, mobile home and motorcycle dealers; parking lots or garages unless incidental to an otherwise eligible class and (5) firms eligible for special rating plans, such as highly protected risks.

Four broad areas of coverage can be written under an SMP policy: section I, property; section II, liability; section III, crime and section IV, boiler and machinery. Generally an SMP policy must be written to include both property and liability insurance. In addition, the property coverage must apply to both the building and its contents if the insured has an insurable interest in them. Crime and boiler and machinery coverages are not mandatory under the program.

Under section I property coverage for buildings and contents may be written on either a named-perils or all-risk basis. (As different forms are used for buildings and for contents, any combination of named-perils and all-risk coverage may be written. For example, coverage on buildings can be all risk even though coverage on contents is named-peril.) Endorsements are available to tailor the SMP to the specific needs of the insured. The endorsements that may be added to section I of the SMP include, for example, coverage for replacement cost, sprinkler leakage, business interruption (gross earnings or the simple loss of earnings form), extra expense, accounts receivable, fine arts, glass, mercantile open-stock burglary, mercantile robbery and safe burglary, outdoor signs and valuable papers and records.

Liability coverage is provided in section II of the SMP. A basic form unique to the SMP program, its liability insurance coverage is a mandatory part of every such policy. The form provides coverage for liability arising from the ownership, maintenance or use of the covered premises and all operations necessary or incidental to the business of the named insured conducted at or from the covered premises.

The form also provides coverage for medical payments and products and completed operations. To obtain liability coverage broader than that offered under the basic form, standard general liability endorsements (as discussed in Chapter 11) can be added. Thus it is possible to achieve within the SMP format the broad coverage offered by a comprehensive general liability policy.

Under section III crime coverage can be written for the following exposures: employee dishonesty, loss inside the premises, loss outside the premises, money orders and counterfeit paper currency and depositors' forgery. The foregoing coverages are virtually identical to the coverage found in the comprehensive dishonesty, disappearance and destruction (3D) policy and the blanket crime policy.

The boiler and machinery coverage under section IV of the SMP is similar to the standard boiler and machinery policy. Endorsements provide coverage for indirect and consequential losses associated with boiler and machinery hazards.

Most commercial coverage should be written under an SMP format or some other package program. For the policyowner the SMP generally is more efficient because it provides more coverage for less money, causes fewer problems of coverage gaps and overlaps and eliminates problems in gray areas of determining which policy covers a particular loss. For the insurer the SMP reduces risk by spreading losses over many perils and lowers expenses by reducing the number of separate policies needed.

Businessowners Program

The businessowners program was introduced by ISO and became effective in March 1976. The program, written as a readable form, is designed to fill the needs of small businesses. For larger businesses or for those requiring more flexibility in designing coverages the SMP program is available.

Eligibility for the businessowners program is determined by the physical size of the premises to be covered. The businessowners policy may be used to cover buildings and buildingowners' personal property for the following eligible classes of risks: (1) apartment buildings not exceeding six stories and containing no more than 60 dwelling units; (2) office buildings not exceeding three stories or 100,000 square feet and (3) if containing no more than 7,500 square feet of mercantile space, buildings occupied principally for mercantile purposes, apartment buildings and office buildings.

Tenants' personal property can be covered under a businessowners policy if used in (1) offices not occupying more than 10,000 square feet in any one building or (2) mercantile businesses not occupying more than 7,500 square feet in any one building.

The businessowners program has two self-contained forms: the standard form and the special form. The principal difference between the standard and special forms is that the former provides named-perils property coverage while the latter has all-risks coverage. Section II of both forms provide comprehensive business liability coverage.

The property coverages of section I are written without a coinsurance clause. The amount of insurance, however, is expected to be the full replacement cost of the property. The businessowners policy includes an *automatic* increase-in-insurance clause under which the amount of insurance on the building is increased every three months by an agreed-upon percent.

Replacement cost coverage is provided for all direct property damage, including buildings, stock, contents and improvements and betterments. No reporting form is required for business personal property as an automatic 25 percent increase is provided for seasonal variations.

Loss-of-income coverage is automatically included in the businessowners policy. Coverage is provided for rental income, business interruption and extra expenses necessarily incurred to *resume normal business operations* but not exceeding 12 consecutive months.

Although one of ISO's main objectives was to clarify policy wording, in at least one instance it has succeeded in doing the opposite. In the business-interruption coverage agreement, the insurer agrees to pay for income losses "for only such length of time as would be required to resume normal business operations." The policy then defines the insured's normal business operations to be "the condition that would have existed had no loss occurred." Is this condition met when the physical facilities have been rebuilt *or* only after all customers have returned and earnings are at their level prior to the loss (as in Canada)? Or is the intended meaning somewhere in between these two extremes?

Several optional coverages are available: employee dishonesty, exterior signs, plate glass including exterior grade floor or basement glass, burglary and robbery (except that money and securities coverage is included in the special form), boiler and machinery and earthquake damage. Earthquake coverage must be added by endorsement; the other optional coverages are printed in the policy.

The liability provisions in both the named-perils and all-risk forms are identical and written as comprehensive general liability including both the completed-operations and products hazard. In each form, the insured may choose a basic per-occurrence limit of $300,000 with an option to increase the limit to $1 million. The liability coverage includes not only bodily injury and property damage but also personal injury defined as injury arising from false arrest, detention or imprisonment, malicious prosecution, libel and slander, invasion of privacy, wrongful entry or eviction and the invasion of the right of private occupancy.

Miscellaneous Multiple-Line Coverages

Several multiple-line forms designed to cover qualifying personal property are available for commercial insureds. Multiple-line forms combine fire, marine and casualty coverages into one policy. Among the casualty coverages are boiler and machinery, crime, glass and liability. Some multiple-line forms are written that combine property coverage with some casualty coverages *other than liability coverage.* The following are examples of multiple-line forms under which liability coverage must be written as a separate policy.

The **commercial property form** is used to provide broad protection for the business personal property of retailers, wholesalers and similar eligible businessowners. Coverage can be provided for a tenant's interest in improvements and betterments. The form is all risk, excluding perils such as flood, seepage and leakage, earthquake, war, mysterious disappearance, inherent vice and employee dishonesty. Limited transit coverage and limited extra-expense coverage are included in the form.

The **office personal property form** provides similar coverage for most office exposures other than a doctor's or dentist's office exposure. The form provides all-risk coverage for business personal property on or off premises. Improvements and betterments are covered at the insured's option.

The **industrial property form** is designed for manufacturing and processing businesses. The form is available only to businesses with personal property at two or more locations. The form can be written either on a specified-perils or an all-risk basis.

The **public and institutional property** (PIP) **form** provides broad coverage for churches, libraries, hospitals, government buildings, schools and other public institutions. The PIP form gives blanket coverage for real and personal property against the basic fire and extended coverage perils. Vandalism, malicious-mischief and sprinkler-leakage coverages are available by endorsement, or an all-risk endorsement may be purchased.

The **manufacturers output policy** provides all-risk coverage to manufacturers for personal property *away* from the premises. Originally designed for auto manufacturers, its availability has been extended to more than 300 types of manufacturers. Excluded perils are identical with those of the commercial property form. Flood and earthquake coverage are available by endorsement. Only direct losses are covered. The policy covers goods in the United States and goods in transit in Canada. It is written on an open basis without termination date and may be cancelled either by the insurer or insured upon 90 days' written notice. Four loss limits are established: losses per location, losses on conveyances, losses of property at conventions or fairs and losses per flood if the policy is endorsed to cover the flood peril. The annual premium (subject to a $1,000 minimum) is determined on a reporting basis. Available deductibles range up to $5,000.

SUMMARY

1. Crime coverages protect individuals and businesses against the perils of burglary, robbery, theft, forgery, embezzlement and other dishonest acts.
2. Although most personal theft coverage now is written under the homeowners policies, contracts are still available to protect individuals against crime losses, e.g., the broad-form personal theft policy. A potentially important coverage sometimes overlooked is safe-deposit-box insurance; the box owner (e.g., bank) probably will not be held liable for any losses to property within the rented box.
3. The burglary special-coverage form for business includes basic policy provisions but requires an endorsement to complete the coverage. Some endorsements often used are those that protect against mercantile robbery or burglary, mercantile safe burglary, paymaster robbery and money and securities destruction. All these coverages also can be purchased through separate policies or as a part of multi-peril packages.
4. Package policies for storekeepers and offices are available that combine coverages most often needed by these enterprises.
5. Crime insurance for banks is a specialized field. Policies have been designed specifically to cover a bank's exposure to burglary, robbery and legal liability for property in safe-deposit boxes. The bankers blanket bond protects against employee dishonesty.
6. The federal crime insurance program began operation in 1971 to provide coverage at affordable rates where needed.
7. A bond is a contract binding one party financially for the performance of an agreed-upon obligation by another. Three parties are involved: one party, the *surety,* guarantees the *principal* will fulfill an obligation for the *obligee.*
8. Bonds guaranteeing the principal's honesty are *fidelity bonds.* They may list the names or the positions of all persons covered or may offer blanket coverage for all employees of the insured. Special blanket bonds are available for banks, stockbrokers and other financial institutions.
9. Bonds guaranteeing that the principal will perform given obligations are *surety bonds.* Such bonds are often used in judicial situations (bail, appeal and fiduciary bonds), with contracts (supply, bid, performance and completion bonds), for elected governmental officials (public-official and federal-official bonds) and when licenses and permits are required by law.
10. Comprehensive glass insurance and boiler and machinery insurance are often bought because of auxiliary services offered by the insurer (speedy replacement of glass and extensive safety engineering and inspection services for boilers and machinery).
11. Coverage against unusual credit losses is available to manufacturers, wholesalers and service organizations but not for retailers.

12. Accounts receivable insurance protects against damage to account records. Other valuable papers and records also can be covered.
13. An aircraft operator has both a physical damage and a liability exposure when piloting a plane. Special contracts are available to cover aviation insurance needs.
14. The special multi-peril (SMP) program was developed in 1960. The SMP policies combine property, liability, crime and boiler and machinery coverages.
15. A special package plan for small and medium sized businesses (businessowners insurance program) was introduced in 1975 to meet the needs of eligible firms.
16. Special multiple-line policies are available to protect personal property of retail and wholesale establishments, manufacturers, offices and public and institutional organizations.

REVIEW QUESTIONS

1. Distinguish between the policies available to protect individuals and families against loss by theft.
2. Distinguish between the policies available to protect businesses against losses caused by crime.
3. Do renters of bank safety-deposit boxes need insurance to protect themselves against loss of the contents of these boxes?
4. Does the burglary special-coverage form resemble forms found in fire, marine and liability insurance? Explain.
5. Explain the justification for the general exclusions found in crime insurance policies.
6. What policies are available to cover crime exposures for banks? Explain.
7. Is bonding insurance?
8. What arguments can be made for buying a commercial blanket bond in preference to the blanket position bond?
9. How does the blanket crime policy differ from the 3D policy? Explain.
10. What types of surety bonds might be needed in the process of obtaining and executing a construction contract? Explain.
11. What are the principle arguments for the purchase of boiler and machinery insurance?
12. Under what multiple-line forms must liability coverage be written under a separate policy? Under what multiple-line form must liability insurance coverage be included in the form rather than bought under a separate policy?
13. What advantages does the SMP program provide the insured and the insurer?
14. Distinguish the standard businessowners package from the special businessowners package.
15. How does burglary differ from robbery?

PART FIVE LIFE AND HEALTH INSURANCE

The discussion of types of insurance coverages began with Part Four. It dealt with one of the two segments of the private insurance business: property and liability insurance. Part Five turns to the other segment: life and health insurance. It is composed of three chapters designed to explain life insurance, annuities and health insurance.

Chapter 13 considers the role played by life insurance in planning income for dependent survivors and for retirement. It defines the basic types of life insurance policies and considers the uses and limitations of each. Chapter 13 also explains the source of life insurance cash value.

The use of life insurance as a savings instrument is discussed along with an introduction to new types of policies that have developed in recent years to meet the competition for the savings dollar from other financial institutions. Chapter 13 also explains the annuity principle and describes the various kinds of annuities and their uses including the variable annuity.

Chapter 14 concentrates on life insurance policy provisions and their interpretations. The major emphasis is on decisions to be made by policyowners: beneficiary designations, ownership and the various options (nonforfeiture, dividend and settlement).

Chapter 15 moves to health insurance. Attention is given to the perils and losses covered and the types of policies written. The provisions of health insurance contracts are examined with attention toward points to consider in buying health insurance.

Part Five deals with individual policies. Group coverage is discussed in Part Six.

The purpose of these chapters is to provide a self-contained unit for the study of life and health insurance coverage at the introductory, though not overly simplified, level. An important objective is to rectify misconceptions about life and health insurance and to serve as a basis for further study—indeed to provide inspiration for further study—of life and health insurance.

CHAPTER

13 Life insurance and annuities

H. Armstrong Roberts

CHAPTER OBJECTIVES

1. **To explain the source of cash values included in life insurance policies.**
2. **To describe the different types of basic and special life insurance policies and to point out their uses and limitations.**
3. **To examine the issues involved in making a decision to buy term and invest the difference.**
4. **To define and classify annuities and discuss their role in financial planning.**
5. **To identify the recent trends in life insurance.**

People face four basic *contingencies* to their economic productivity: death, disability, compulsory retirement and unemployment. Life insurance is a financial instrument for (1) providing support for survivors, (2) paying estate obligations at death, (3) helping businesses offset losses caused by death of key personnel and (4) accumulating funds for retirement, emergencies and business uses. Health insurance (discussed in Chapter 15) provides the insured income while disabled and funds to help pay medical expenses. Life annuities offer insureds lifetime postretirement income. Government-provided unemployment benefits (discussed in Chapter 18) offer some financial security during temporary unemployment.

Life insurance plays an important role in personal financial planning as a supplement to employee benefit plans and government social insurance plans. In the United States at the end of 1981 about $3.2 trillion of life insurance was in force, of which 44 percent was group insurance. The amount of life insurance and annuity purchases has been spurred by the federal Employee Retirement Income Security Act of 1974 which provided tax incentives for individuals not covered by employee benefit plans to save for retirement. Further impetus to life insurance and annuity purchases was given by the federal Economic Recovery Tax Act of 1981 which liberalized these tax incentives by increasing the allowable amount of tax-sheltered contributions to individual retirement accounts and by extending the privilege to workers covered by other retirement plans. (Individual retirement accounts are discussed in Chapter 17.)

BROAD CLASSIFICATIONS OF LIFE INSURANCE POLICIES

This chapter focuses on a discussion of the host of policies and forms facing persons buying life insurance and annuities. Some explicit issues related to buying life insurance are discussed in Chapter 24.

Life insurance policies may be classified into four categories: (1) whether they are participating or nonparticipating, (2) whether they have cash values, (3) the specific type of policy written (e.g., term, endowment, whole life or some combination of the three) and (4) the kind of coverage written (i.e., ordinary, industrial or group). Each classification is discussed in order, proceeding from (1) through (4).

Policy Dividends

Life insurance is issued either as participating (par) or nonparticipating (nonpar). Par life insurance provides for **policy dividends** that reflect part of the insurer's gains when (1) investment income is higher or (2) death claims and/or operating expenses are lower than projected. Recently, higher investment income has been the major source of dividends. Inflation has either reduced or eliminated operating expenses as a dividend source. Nonpar life policies do not provide for policy dividends.

To be competitive insurers generally must charge lower guaranteed premiums for nonpar than for par policies of the same type issued at the same age. However, the net premium (premiums paid less dividends received) for par policies in force for several years is expected to be less than for nonpar policies. Nonpar advocates argue that nonpar premiums are guaranteed and point out that par policy dividends are not guaranteed. Par advocates answer with the argument that dividends, although not guaranteed, generally have been higher than those projected when the policy was sold.

Life Insurance Cash Values

Life insurance often is sold as a savings medium. Savings accumulate through life insurance from the method of paying premiums. If a policyowner purchases a series of one-year policies and pays a yearly premium just sufficient to cover his or her share of death claims and expenses for the year no cash value accumulates. If a policyowner purchases a policy with a duration of more than one year, however, and pays for it with either one initial premium or a series of level annual premiums cash values will accumulate.

An example is the simplest tool for explaining the source of savings (or cash values) for a life insurance policy. The policy used is an annual level-premium life insurance policy with lifetime coverage and premiums payable for life.

1. Assume 100,000 people aged 25 each have $1,000 of life insurance issued at the same time.
2. Each pays an annual premium of $10.25 mathematically calculated based on interest and mortality assumptions. (For simplicity the expense assumption is ignored in this illustration.) The total paid by all policyowners amounts to $1,025,000 ($10.25 × 100,000).
3. The premiums are invested for a year and earn an *assumed interest rate* of 4.5 percent. Thus the interest earned on the initial premium is $46,126 ($1,025,000 × .045). When this amount is added to the initial premium the fund increases to $1,071,125 ($1,025,000 + $46,126).
4. Based on mortality assumptions 193 of the original 100,000 die during the first year. On behalf of each person dying $1,000 is paid at the end of the year for a total of $193,000 (193 × $1,000). (Death claims are paid when incurred but for simplification the assumption is made that they are paid at the end of the year.)
5. Death claims ($193,000) are subtracted from accumulated premiums (step 3) reducing the amount to $878,125 ($1,071,125 − $193,000).
6. The $878,125 remaining is allocated to the accounts of the 99,807 (100,000 − 193) survivors. The amount for each survivor is $8.80 ($878,125 ÷ 99,807) and is the savings accumulation or cash value for the survivor's policy. The $8.80 is computed as follows:

a.	Premium paid	$10.25
b.	Plus assumed interest (4.5 percent)	.46
c.	Less contributions to death claims (193 deaths × $1,000 ÷ 100,000 persons)	1.93
d.	Plus survivorship benefit (explained below)	.02
	Total =	$ 8.80

At first glance, the **survivorship benefit** appears to be an elusive concept. But upon close examination its simplicity becomes apparent. It takes into account that the remaining fund (in this example $878,125) is composed of contributions by those who die as well as those who survive. The accumulated fund is used to pay death benefits for those who die. The remainder is used to increase the benefits for those who survive. This benefit, called a survivorship benefit, is computed as follows:

1. Divide the fund accumulated at the end of the year ($878,125) by the number in the group at the beginning of the year (100,000) to determine each policyowner's net contribution to the total fund.

   $878,125 ÷ 100,000 = $8.78

2. Multiply $8.78 by 193, the number dying, to determine the amount available to allocate to those who survive.

   $8.78 × 193 = $1,694.54

3. Divide $1,694.54 by 99,807, the number who survive, to determine the survivorship benefit.

   $1,694.54 ÷ 99,807 = $.02

Figure 13–1 summarizes both the computation of the survivorship benefit per policy and the savings per policy. For the accumulated savings at the end of the second policy year (the first year plus the second year) the computation is as follows:

1. Fund on hand at end of first year = $878,125.
2. Number living at beginning of second year = 99,807.
3. Premiums paid at beginning of second year = $1,023,021.80 ($10.25 × $99,807).
4. Total fund on hand at beginning of second year = $1,901,146.80 ($878,125 + $1,023,021.80).
5. Interest earned on total fund on hand at beginning of second year at assumed rate of interest of 4.5 percent = $46,035.98 ($1,901,146.80 × .045).
6. Total amount at end of second year before death claims = $1,947,182.80 ($1,901,146.80 + $46,035.98).
7. Number dying during the second year = 196.
8. Total death claims paid = $196,000 ($1,000 × 196).
9. Net fund accumulated at the end of the second year = $1,751,182.80 ($1,947,182.80 − $196,000).
10. Number living at the end of the second year = 99,611 (99,807 − 196).
11. Savings accumulation or cash value = $17.58 ($1,751,182.80 ÷ 99,611).

The computation starts with the fund on hand at the end of the first year ($878,125) and continues the process used for the first year. Only the figures are different.

Computation for the third and all future years follows the pattern of the second year. The result is that savings per policy continue to grow. The $10.25 premium is paid each year and the survivorship benefit and interest earnings grow larger and larger. The survivorship benefit increases year-by-year because more funds are available to release to fewer survivors. The interest earnings increase each year because more funds are available for investment.

FIGURE 13–1
Computing the Survivorship Benefit per Policy (100,000 Lives Aged 25 Each Covered for $1,000 of Insurance)

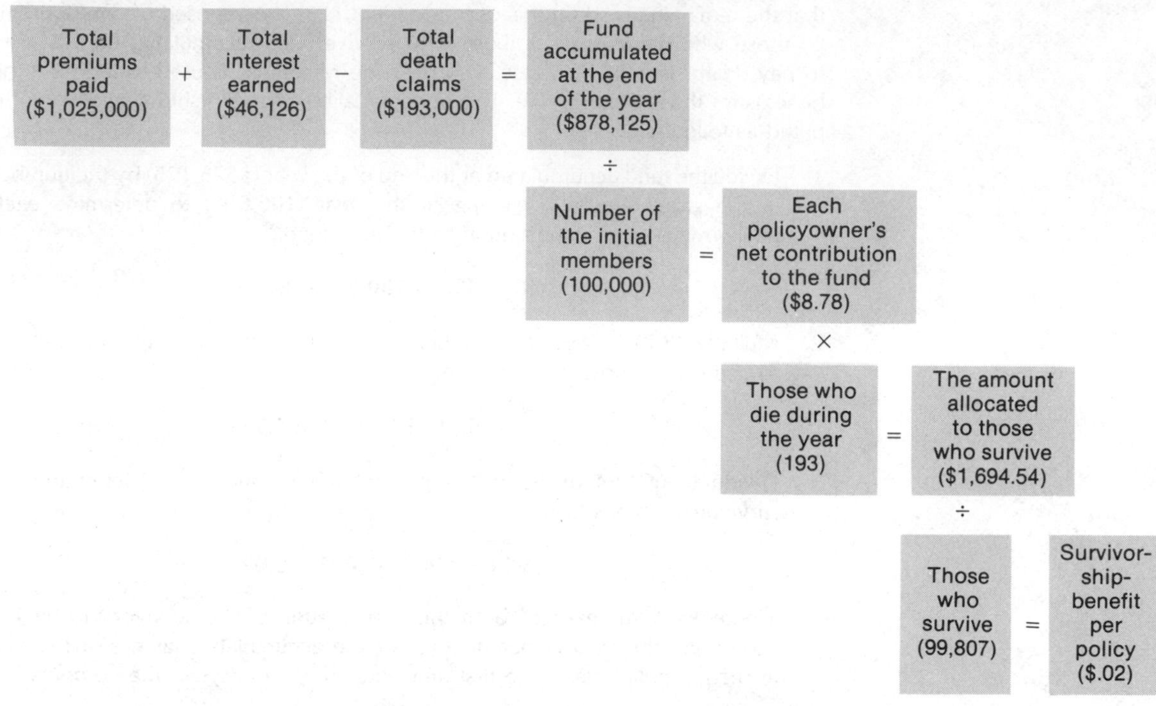

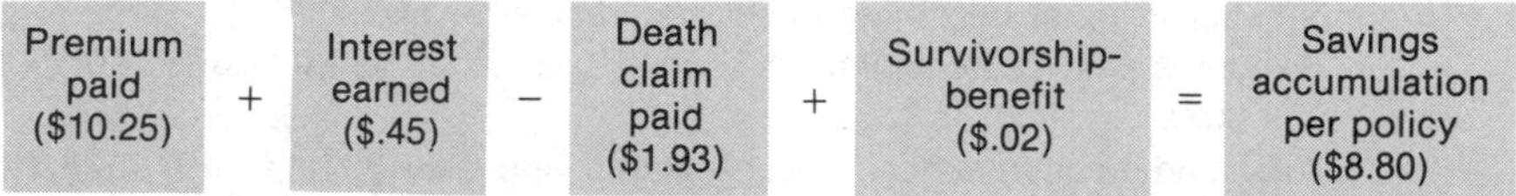

TYPES OF LIFE INSURANCE

Life insurance policies functionally are of three types: term, endowment and whole life.

Term Insurance

Term insurance obligates the insurer to pay the policy's face amount if the insured dies within a specified time. If the insured survives the period the contract expires without value. The important and distinguishing features of term insurance are that contracts are for a fixed period and have little or no cash values.

Forms

A variety of term forms are available. **Straight term insurance** is written for a year or a specified number of years and terminates at the end of the designated period. Five-, 10- or 20-year policies and term to age 65 or 70 are popular. **Renewable term** insurance allows the owner to renew the policy before its expiration date, without again proving *insurability.*[1] A 10-year renewable term

[1] As proof of insurability an insurer requires that the subject provide a statement certifying good health.

permits renewal for an additional 10 years. The renewal premium will be higher than the initial premium to reflect the higher probability of dying within the second ten years. The policy usually provides for several renewal periods or renewal up to a given age.

The purest form of term insurance is **yearly renewable term** (YRT). At the option of the owner and without evidence of continued insurability the policy may be renewed each year. The renewal privilege is limited to a specific number of years or to a specific age at which time the contract expires. Most insurers limit renewals to age 65 or 70. However, an increasing number of insurers are offering YRT to age 100 at highly attractive premiums.

Convertible term permits policies to be converted into whole life or endowment insurance (to be discussed later) within a specified period and without evidence of insurability. Some insurers remove the conversion decision from the policyowner by offering **automatically convertible term** as an option. It provides for automatic conversion at a date specified in the policy.

The renewable and convertible features may be combined into one policy called **renewable and convertible term.** For example, a 5-year renewable and convertible policy might be renewable until age 70 and convertible at any time before age 65.

The usual form of term insurance is level term, where the face amount payable remains the same throughout the period. **Increasing** and **decreasing term** insurance is available. Under decreasing term the face amount of the policy reduces periodically (e.g., monthly or yearly). This policy is useful to a parent for providing low-cost protection while the children are young. (A form of decreasing term insurance coupled with whole life insurance called **family income insurance** is discussed later.) Increasing term provides insurance that increases monthly or yearly. This policy is useful in protecting against inflation. Both increasing and decreasing term can be added as a rider[2] to whole life or endowment policies.

Premiums

Because the probability of death increases with age, premiums increase gradually as the subject grows older. However, at advanced ages premiums rise at a sharply increasing pace to reflect much higher death rates. To relieve policyowners from paying increasing premiums, term insurance is offered on a **level-premium plan** where premiums remain the same for each year throughout the life of the policy. The annual level premium for a 5-year term policy written on a nonpar basis is about $3.35 per $1,000 at age 25; $4.35 at 35 and $7.95 at 45. Premiums for convertible and renewable term policies are about 5 percent higher. Lower and higher premiums than those quoted here are found in the market. Term insurance rates are highly competitive. (Some insurers claim that their competitors are virtually giving away the insurance.)

Uses of term insurance

Term insurance is for any death protection need. A person with a 20-year mortgage loan can use decreasing term insurance wisely for additional death protection during the period of the loan. The insurance can be arranged when the loan is acquired. If the person dies before the loan is paid, the policy's proceeds can be used to complete the payments.

Term insurance is appropriate for young people who need more protection than they can afford with higher premium insurance and for those who prefer

[2] Riders are similar to endorsements in property and liability insurance.

to use other financial instruments for accumulating their savings. Term now accounts for more than 60 percent of newly issued insurance, up from 43 percent 10 years ago and from 52 percent 5 years ago.

To counteract the loss of the savings dollar life insurers are responding to the market by offering savings and investment products that attempt to compete with other financial institutions. Some insurers have purchased investment brokerage firms, various types of mutual funds and other types of savings and investment firms. They are becoming full financial service organizations rather than restricting their operations to life insurance.

Endowment Insurance

Endowment insurance obligates the insurer to pay the beneficiary a stated sum if the insured dies during the policy term (called the *endowment period*) or to the owner if the insured survives the endowment period. Thus under a $10,000, 20-year endowment insurance policy, the insurer promises to pay $10,000 to the beneficiary if the insured dies at any time within the 20-year period or to the owner if the subject is alive at the end of the period.

Premiums

Premiums for endowment policies are high. The nonpar annual premium for a $1,000 endowment at age 65 issued at age 25 is about $21; for a 20-year endowment it is about $39. Although various premium plans are available endowment policies are usually written on an annual level-premium basis.

Uses

The endowment policy can be viewed as a savings program protected by life insurance. The policyowner knows the policy's face amount will be paid no later than the end of the endowment period. The insurer must charge premiums high enough to pay this amount when due. The high premium means less death protection can be purchased with the life insurance budget.

Because endowment policies emphasize accumulated savings they can be used to fund retirement income. But as a person's most important need is usually death protection the endowment policy is inherently questionable. Young people may be sold endowment insurance when they should buy low premium insurance, e.g., term and/or, in some cases, whole life. The lure of a lump sum of money 20 years hence causes people to lose sight of the basic purpose of life insurance: to provide an efficient predeath arrangement for an effective postdeath balance between resources needed and those available.

Whole Life Insurance

Whole life (known as permanent or cash value) insurance offers lifetime coverage. It can be viewed either as endowment at age 100 or term to age 100. Some knowledge about life insurance premium calculations is necessary to understand these views. A mortality table showing the number of people expected to die at each age is one of the basic life insurance ratemaking tools. The table does not include the extreme ages on the high side and assumes all people die before their 100th birthday. Those reaching age 100 are paid the face amount of the policy because they survived the maximum period set by the actuaries. For this reason a whole life policy may be viewed as an endowment maturing at age 100. In computing the premium for a whole life policy no allowance is made for a survivor benefit at age 100 because all insureds are expected to be dead at that age. So when survivors reaching age 100 are paid the policy face amount these payments in effect are "mortality" and not "survivorship" payments. Therefore it is reasonable to view whole life as term to age 100 with "death" payments made to those who reach that age. Viewed functionally, a whole life is an endowment at age 100 because benefits are paid to those who die before age 100 and to those who survive to that age. Thus actuarially and conceptually only two basic types of policies are written: term and endowment.

Premiums

Premiums must be large enough so that when combined with accumulated investment earnings the insurer will have sufficient funds to pay expenses and honor all claims under the contract. Premiums for whole life policies may be paid under the single-premium, limited-payment or continuous-premium plan. The single-premium plan involves a large one-time initial cost. For example, the single premium for a $10,000 nonpar whole life policy issued to a male aged 25 is about $2,300.

Limited payment plans include payment periods of various durations, say, 10, 15, or 20 years or to age 65, when no further premiums are paid. (A policy that has not matured but for which no additional premiums are due is called a *paid-up* policy.) The premium-payment period is selected to meet the policyowner's need. Paid-up at age 65 has the advantage of relieving the policyowner of premium payments during retirement. For a $10,000 nonpar policy issued to a male aged 25 annual premiums range from about $175 for 20-pay life to about $120 for a policy paid up at age 65 (lower for females).

Whole life is most commonly written on a payments for life arrangement, variously known as **ordinary life, straight life** or, as in this text, **continuous-premium whole life.** Under this plan the policyowner pays a fixed annual premium for the life of the insured. The premium for a $10,000 nonpar whole life policy issued on the continuous-premium plan to a male aged 25 is about $105 annually.

Use of whole life insurance

Whole life provides resources after death regardless of when the insured dies. It is also used as a savings plan for financial emergencies or for funding a retirement income. The amount of savings accumulation depends on the premium plan selected. The continuous-premium plan offers the lowest and the single-premium form the highest cash value per $1,000 of whole life insurance.

For those seeking a level amount of insurance protection and a level premium for the whole of life the continuous-premium whole life policy is the only plan available. If one is sure of dying early, term insurance offers the best bargain. If, on the other hand, one is convinced of outliving all dependents, no insurance, except for an amount needed to pay the cost of dying is the best bargain. Under the conditions stated, a policy taken late in life but while a person is still insurable would be both appropriate and the best bargain. That policy could be either YRT to age 100 or, if level premiums are important, continuous-premium whole life. Savings through media other than life insurance cash values often appear more attractive. However, because people are not able to predict when they will die policies must be selected on a realistic basis.

Continuous-premium whole life advocates argue that it offers a compromise between term, limited-pay whole life and endowment insurance. They claim it provides a large amount of death protection per premium dollar and an effective method of accumulating savings. They allege that when continuous-premium whole life is used to cover all death protection needs cash values will provide a large part of planned retirement needs.

Term insurance is used for a temporary life insurance need to provide adequate death protection when budgets are too small for cash-value insurance and when financial instruments other than life insurance appear more efficient for accumulating savings. Endowment insurance is used to arrange for a fixed sum at a specified date upon prior death of the subject. Because continuous-premium whole life is basically term to or endowment at age 100, to some extent it combines the features of both.

The uses of **limited-pay life** are highly restricted because it overemphasizes cash values at the expense of death protection. It may be used as a gift medium—a grandparent may give a grandchild a policy to be paid up when the child reaches majority. While life paid up at age 65 or 70 offers the advantage of completing premium payments at retirement 20- or 30-pay life have no place in life insurance plans for young families. Why should a couple starting a family pay high premiums now when they cannot afford them to avoid paying premiums later when family responsibilities are reduced and income is likely to be near its highest level? It does not make sense!

Some observers claim whole life is dying and will soon be dead. They expect it to be replaced by term and by new forms of flexible cash-value policies that compete more favorably as a savings media. Other insurers vigorously deny whole life is dying or even approaching retirement. They cite their own whole life sales to support this contention. Nevertheless, increasingly competitive and attractive term policies have successfully challenged the lofty place whole life once held in the marketplace. New cash-value products (to be discussed later) have added their own embryonic challenge.

Buy term and invest the difference. Many people suggest that term insurance be purchased to provide death protection and the difference between the term premium and that for a like amount of whole life be invested elsewhere. For example, for a male aged 25 the nonpar premium for $10,000 continuous-premium whole life would be about $105 a year. The premium for $10,000 of one-year renewable term would be about $19. If one-year term is purchased instead of continuous-premium whole life the death benefit would be the same but the premium would be $86 less. This $86 could be placed in some other savings medium to build emergency or retirement values independent of life insurance. The next year, at age 26, enough term insurance could be purchased to equal $10,000 minus the amount accumulated in savings. This process would continue each year reducing the insurance so that at death the insurance plus the accumulated savings equal $10,000.

Three problems arise here. (1) Some people cannot save unless compelled to do so. Life insurance premiums are usually budgeted as a debt and a person will generally pay the premium when due. Adding to a savings deposit or the purchase of mutual funds requires a decision each month. (2) Withdrawing from a savings account not only is less troublesome but also not taken as seriously as surrendering life insurance or borrowing its cash value. (3) Most people are not investment experts. In an effort to improve investment yields some persons are tempted to invest in high-risk ventures thus exposing their principal to losses. Furthermore, some savers not accustomed to fluctuating market prices of investments might invest the "difference" in passbook savings accounts. These accounts may not offer *after-tax yields* as high as cash value life insurance.

On the other hand a possible advantage of "invest the difference" is the opportunity for savers to invest in equities—common stocks and real estate—whose values are expected by some but not all financial experts to increase *over the long run* as the dollar loses some of its value from inflation. An additional advantage is the opportunity to invest in companies in "growth industries" where some experts anticipate attractive increases in profits and dividends. However because risk not found in life insurance cash values is involved these opportunities may backfire. Still, some experts suggest that savings institutions and life insurers be required to place stickers on savings passbooks and life insurance policies containing a warning that "savings through this instrument can be dangerous to your wealth."

Universal Life Insurance

The availability in recent years of increased yields on money market funds, corporate and government bonds, various types of savings and loan accounts, bank certificates of deposit and tax-free municipal bonds has decreased the attractiveness of traditional cash-value life insurance policies. As a result consumers have been attracted to the buy-term-and-invest-the-difference program. To reverse this trend life insurers have developed policies designed to combine the advantages of cash-value life insurance (i.e., forced savings, tax-free cash buildup and income settlement options, discussed later) with the higher yields possible through the invest-the-difference plan. This class of policies when first developed was called **universal life.** Because the term *universal life* is a trade name insurers offering similar policies use various other names.[3] Regardless of the name many similarities and some differences exist among these policies.

Basically, universal life divides death protection and cash-value accumulations into separate components. This division distinguishes it from the traditional cash-value policy which is an indivisible contract with unified death protection and cash value accumulations. The distinction is not one without a difference. With universal life more competitive rates of return can be guaranteed from year to year on cash-value accumulations and greater flexibility can be achieved by adjusting the amounts of savings and protection to the needs of the policyowner.

The minimum universal life long-term interest guarantees are comparable to those of traditional cash-value life insurance—4 to 4.5 percent.[4] Besides the minimum long-term guarantees, interest guarantees for one year or less are made. These short-term guarantees are governed by money-market conditions at the time. They may be based on the insurer's appraisal of the financial markets for each period or on some interest rate index. The guarantee may be based on long-term or short-term rates or on the higher of the two. Thus during periods of high interest rates the guarantees may be 12 percent or more. During periods of low interest rates the guarantees decline but never below the minimum 4 to 4.5 percent long-term guarantee. (The short-term guarantees usually do not apply to the first $1,000 of cash value or to cash values encumbered by a policy loan.)

The flexibility universal life offers is an important advantage as the policyowner passes through the life cycle. When the children are young the more important need may be for death protection; but when the children become financially independent the more important need may be for cash-value accumulations to supplement retirement income. Unemployment may require that premium payments be skipped and that cash values be used to keep the policy in force.

[3] Three of the earlier names are the Challenger, Complete Life and the Solution. Universal life is permitted to be written in every state except New York.

[4] One form of universal life, the T-Life, has no long-term interest guarantee. It has only one guaranteed rate, the current 91-day Treasury bill rate.

Divorces, deaths of dependents, additional children, remarriages, one or more unwanted (or wanted) bastards and so on can affect the balance needed between death protection and cash-value accumulations.

An important question about universal life is its tax-sheltered status. Does it have the income tax advantages of traditional whole life insurance? In private letter rulings (which apply only to the particular parties involved and do not have the stability of a revenue ruling) the Internal Revenue Service (IRS) has said yes. The IRS has not issued a revenue ruling on the subject and until it does the tax status of universal life will continue in doubt. Cash values and interest paid in excess of the 4 to 4.5 percent long-term guarantee accumulate on a tax-sheltered basis, i.e., income taxes are paid by the policyowner *only* if these accumulations are withdrawn and if the amount withdrawn exceeds premiums paid. Then *only* the excess over premiums paid are taxable. Furthermore, the policy proceeds at death are payable to beneficiaries income-tax free. But what the IRS giveth in a private ruling it can also take away.

In 1982 the IRS ruled that interest beyond the minimum guaranteed 4 percent credited by insurers to the owners of universal life policies and annuities (discussed later) would be treated as taxable dividends thus subjecting insurers to taxation under a complex federal tax formula applied to life insurance companies.[5] This ruling does not affect earlier rulings that this interest is not taxable to the policyowners and annuitants. Its effect on them is to reduce the yield insurers can afford to pay by ½ to 1 percentage point.

SPECIAL-PURPOSE POLICIES

In addition to basic types of life insurance, insurers offer several special policy forms. Many special forms combine basic policies into packages to meet particular life insurance needs. Others reflect sales gimmicks not related to buyer needs. Often they are designed to confuse buyers seeking to compare prices and products of competing insurers. These plans add more complication to the problem of life insurance buying.

The Family Income Policy

The family income policy provides a specified monthly income from the date of the subject's death until a future date *named in the policy* (this period is called the family income period). At the end of the family income period the policy's face amount is payable to the beneficiary. If the subject lives beyond the family income period the beneficiary receives only the face amount of the policy upon the subject's death.

In structure the traditional family income policy consists of whole life insurance and monthly decreasing term insurance. Upon the insured's death, the insurer holds the proceeds of the whole life policy and pays interest until the end of the family income period. The interest provides part of the family income payments and the proceeds of the decreasing term insurance are liquidated in equal monthly installments to provide the remainder. At the end of the family income period, the proceeds of the whole life insurance held at interest are paid to the deceased insured's beneficiary. Each month the insured lives, less term insurance is needed

[5] Rev. Rule. 82–133. Because the amount to be treated as taxable dividends is the excess interest credited, the writers of the T-Life (see footnote 4) expect to be unaffected by this IRS ruling. They argue that no excess interest is possible when the amount credited is based on the one guaranteed rate.

to pay the income for the unexpired family income period, so *monthly* decreasing term is used.

The Family Maintenance Policy

The family maintenance policy provides monthly payments for a fixed period *following* the insured's death if death occurs within that period. In structure the family maintenance policy is whole life plus *level* term. The full amount of initial term insurance is needed each year to provide the family maintenance income. The use of level-term insurance for a typically decreasing term insurance need limits the legitimate uses of this policy.

Multiple-Protection Policies

Multiple-protection policies are whole life plus term. They provide a *multiple of the face amount* of the whole life if the insured dies within a specified period but only a single face amount if death occurs after the expiration of the period. The multiple-protection period expires after a specified number of years, such as 10 or 15, or when the insured reaches a given age, e.g., 60 or 65.

Mortgage Protection Policies

An important use of life insurance is to protect against loss of mortgaged property if the mortgagor dies before the debt is paid. If the breadwinner dies, mortgage protection life insurance provides the surviving spouse funds to continue mortgage payments, thus permitting the family to keep the property. Mortgage protection policies are decreasing term with the insurance amount kept approximately equal to the unpaid portion of the mortgage.

In recent years the long-term amortized mortgage loan with fixed interest rates has lost much of its popularity with lenders because of wide swings in interest rates. Several innovative alternatives have been introduced. Examples are variable rate mortgages, shared appreciation mortgages and partially amortized mortgage loans.[6] Mortgage protection policies must reflect these changes so that their face amounts automatically change to match the unpaid portion of the mortgage loan.

The Family Policy

With one policy and one premium the family policy covers the lives of the entire family—father, mother and eligible children. Insurers sell the policy in units of $5,000, written on the life of the father usually as continuous-premium whole life. Term insurance for $2,000 per unit is written on the mother's life if she is the same age as the father, more if younger less if older. Term insurance for $1,000 per unit is written on the children, usually until age 25. Children generally are excluded until they are 15 days old. The term insurance on the lives of family members usually ceases when the father reaches age 65. If the mother dies before the father the insurance on the life of the father is increased by $2,000 until age 65. If the father dies first, insurance on the other family

[6] A variable rate mortgage loan is explained by its name: the interest rate is not fixed but fluctuates with the market rate. A partially amortized mortgage loan is one where the monthly payments are made assuming a 25- or 30-year duration. However, the unpaid balance at the end of a specified period, e.g., five years, is due as a balloon note. This balloon note is then refinanced on a partially amortized basis at the interest rate in effect at that time. The shared appreciation mortgage loan is also explained by its name: the borrower agrees to share with the lender a portion of any appreciation in the value of the property over a specified period.

members becomes paid up (no further premiums are required) and remains in force until its scheduled termination date. The term insurance on the mother is convertible at the end of the term period for the full amount and for the children up to five times its amount. If the mother is the principal breadwinner, then substitute "mother" for "father" and "father" for "mother" in this and the following paragraphs.

The main advantage of the family policy is that it allows those who insist on covering dependents' lives to do so at the lowest possible cost. The right to convert the insurance on the children's lives to five times its original amount protects the "insurability" of the children at a nominal premium.

The policy has appeal, which is unfortunate because it is particularly vulnerable to misuse. A family that can afford to spend only $83.65 a year for insurance should have more than $5,000 insurance on the father; and one that can spend $167.30 should have more than $10,000 on the father. An insurance program involving less whole life and more term on the father may be more desirable.

Joint Life Policy

Joint life policies are written on more than one life. Usually the policy covers two persons with the face amount payable upon the first death only. The premium for a joint life policy is based on the ages of the insureds and costs less than two individual policies.

Preferred Risk

The "special deal" in life insurance is undoubtedly as old as the use of agents. Some agents convince customers that a "special proposition" is designed just for them. College students often are fed the story that they are in a "preferred risk" category and some swallow it. Since the turn of the century legitimate "specials" have been sold by life insurers as "preferred risk" policies. Recently, competitive interest in this type of policy has increased.

Preferred risk at one time applied *only* to contracts issued to low-hazard applicants at less than standard rates. **Standard** applies to policies written on applicants of average health, habits and occupations. The mortality experience of these average applicants is expected to reflect standard (average) mortality experience. An extra premium is charged for those who fail to meet these standards. Thus the term *preferred risk* logically should be applied only to those whose health, habits and occupations are better than standard and in most cases it is. For example, a number of insurers give special rates to nonsmokers and to persons who are physically trim. However, some insurers write preferred risk policies for other than low-hazard applicants at premiums below standard. For example, cost savings allow an insurer to offer a preferred risk policy at a lower premium per $1,000 if the policy is written for a minimum of $100,000.

Guaranteed Insurability Agreements

Under guaranteed insurability agreements the insured has an option to purchase additional insurance on his or her life at specified times without evidence of insurability. Coverage is written as a rider to whole life or endowment plans. The rider specifies the maximum amount of insurance that can be purchased during each option period. This maximum is either the face amount of the basic policy or a specified maximum (e.g., $20,000), whichever is less. The options generally are not cumulative. Failure to exercise an option results in its loss but does not affect subsequent ones.

Variable Life Insurance

A variable life policy provides a *minimum* face amount of insurance but allows the policy proceeds to increase beyond this amount if the value of the investment portfolio supporting the policy increases. Cash values also fluctuate with investment values. This policy is designed to help offset the declining purchasing power of fixed-dollar contracts in an inflationary economy but has yet to gain popularity in the United States. One disadvantage is that the stock market and the consumer price index (CPI) in recent years have not consistently moved in the same direction. The stock market has lagged considerably behind the cost of living.

The Adjustable Life Policy

An adjustable life policy provides "flexibility" to meet the policyowner's varying needs throughout life. It changes between term and whole life depending on the amount of premium a policyowner wants to pay. A policyowner can elect to adjust the policy by increasing or decreasing both its face amount and its premium level. Evidence of insurability may or may not be required when the amount of insurance is increased depending on the terms of the policy. A computer program is used to vary cash values and other benefits as well as maturity dates consistent with the premium paid as the subject passes through life and insurance needs change. A number of policies similar to adjustable life are written under other names.

Index-Linked Policies

Some insurers offer policies linking death benefits to the official consumer price index to help policyowners protect the face amount of their insurance against erosion of value caused by inflation. The policy is written as whole life. Additions based on the CPI are offered annually when the index increases, beginning on the second policy anniversary. Minimum and maximum additions are specified. Premiums are increased according to the size of the addition. The policyowner can refuse an addition but once one is declined no further additions are offered. A similar policy is also written as term insurance with its face amount tied to the CPI. The policyowner's premium is adjusted automatically to cover benefit changes.

Deposit Term

Deposit term is a term policy with a required deposit premium the first year in excess of the cost of the term insurance. At the end of the designated period (8 or 10 years), the insurer offers a cash value on the deposit premium that includes interest earned and a share of the deposit premium for policies lapsed during this term. If death occurs prior to the end of the designated term the insurer pays the deposit premium plus compound interest as an additional death benefit. Deposit term is appropriate for persons who intend to keep their policies in force and seek to avoid sharing the high lapse cost caused by discontinued policies. Most of the deposit premiums for policies lapsed during the initial 8- or 10-year term period are forfeited. Part of the amount is used to offset the high initial cost (high commissions to sales agents for example) of writing the policy. The remainder is shared by those who keep their policies in force for the full initial period thus encouraging persistency.

Other Special Policies

A detailed list of life insurance policies would include many not discussed here. Types of policies are limited only by the imagination of actuaries, creativity of insurer managements and flexibility of regulatory authorities. Some additional special policies are the *survivorship policy* where periodic payments for life (rather than a single sum) are paid to the named beneficiary (usually old) when the subject (usually young) dies; *modified life policy* where the premiums for whole life are lower than the corresponding continuous-premium policy during the first three to five years and higher thereafter and *juvenile life forms* used to write insurance on the lives of children.

CLASSES OF LIFE INSURANCE

As distinguished from *types,* several *classes* of life insurance are written. These classes are **ordinary, industrial** and **group.** They differ in type of customers, policy amounts, cash values, methods of computing and collecting premiums, underwriting standards and marketing methods. The distinction between industrial and ordinary insurance is muddled because states and insurers have their own definitions of these classes.

Ordinary Life Insurance

Ordinary life is usually issued in amounts of $1,000 or more with premiums payable annually, semiannually, quarterly or monthly. The ordinary department of most life insurers is their largest department and many insurers write only ordinary life insurance. All life insurance types previously discussed are available through the ordinary departments of life insurers. Ordinary insurance accounts for nearly 50 percent of life insurance in force in the United States and about 67 percent of the insurance currently purchased.

Industrial Life Insurance

Industrial life insurance is usually written with face amounts of less than $1,000. Premiums are generally paid weekly at the policyowner's home to an agent referred to as a **debit agent.** Although many of the same types of policies are written in industrial as in ordinary insurance, limited-payment whole life accounts for about 70 percent of the industrial life insurance in force. Presently industrial insurance equals 1 percent of the life insurance in force in the United States compared with 12 percent 30 years earlier. It represents less than 1 percent of the insurance currently purchased. Expansion of group insurance and social security, increased affluence and the exit of some large insurers from this market have contributed to the declining popularity of industrial life insurance.

Premiums charged for industrial insurance are higher than for ordinary insurance for three reasons: higher administration costs per dollar of insurance, higher mortality rates for persons covered (more liberal underwriting standards are applied in industrial than in ordinary insurance) and higher lapse rates. A 1979 Federal Trade Commission study attacked industrial insurance for its excessive costs and the sales tactics used by some agents to persuade unknowledgeable persons to purchase an excessive number of policies.

Group Life Insurance

Group life insurance is life insurance, usually issued without medical examination, on a group of persons under a *master policy,* with members of the group receiving *certificates of participation.* Group life including credit life equals about 50 percent of the life insurance in force in the United States. Group life and other group coverages are discussed in Chapter 16.

LIFE INSURANCE RIDERS

Supplemental agreements called *riders* are frequently made part of life insurance policies. Some add more life insurance, such as level, increasing or decreasing term, to a basic whole life or endowment policy. Others may add total disability benefits or accidental death benefits. Other standardized riders include waiver of premium, payor benefits and the cost of living rider.

Disability Income Rider

Disability income riders written with permanent life insurance provide that the insured will receive a stated monthly income. This amount is usually $5 or $10 per $1,000 of life insurance after a six-month waiting period if he or she becomes totally disabled. Because disability income coverage is nearly always written as health insurance, it is discussed in Chapter 15. (It is rarely written now as a rider to a life insurance policy although some life insurance policies are in force that include disability income riders.)

Accidental Death Rider

Accidental death riders (called double indemnity) provide for payment of twice the policy's face amount if the insured's death is *accidental.* Double indemnity seems like an inexpensive way to provide more death protection. But is it? The premium is high for what it buys and the need for the coverage is questionable. A reasonable approach is to have the same amount of insurance at death regardless of its cause. The funds spent for double indemnity could be better spent to add additional life insurance. (Because accidental deaths are more visible they draw an undue amount of attention. Most deaths by far are natural, not accidental.) Why is more insurance needed after an accidental death?

Waiver of Premium

Waiver of premium provides that in case of total disability of the insured the policyowner does not have to continue premium payments after a six-month waiting period. The common practice is to refund premiums paid during that time. The policy continues as if premiums were paid. The cost is low, the coverage essential and the rider nearly universally available.

Payor-Benefit Rider

The payor-benefit rider, used with juvenile insurance, provides for the premium to be waived upon the death or disability of the subject's parent. Suppose a parent buys insurance on a child's life. If the parent dies or becomes totally disabled the payor benefit permits the premiums on the child's policy to be waived until the child reaches 25 (or some other predetermined age). The annual premium for the benefit depends on the policy type and the ages of the juvenile and the payor.

Cost-of-Living Rider

Some insurers offer a rider that increases or decreases the amount of insurance to reflect cost-of-living changes measured by the consumer price index. These riders are one-year term insurance added to the basic policy. If the rider is used with a $50,000 whole life policy and the CPI advances 10 percent for the year, $5,000 of one-year term insurance is automatically added for the next year without evidence of insurability. The policyowner is billed for the additional coverage. If the CPI falls the amount of one-year term insurance is decreased proportionately. Only the amount of insurance provided by the cost-of-living rider is subject to change. The amount of the basic policy is unaffected by fluctuations in the CPI.

ANNUITIES

An annuity provides a regular periodic income for the annuitant's life or for a specified period. An annuity providing lifetime income is called a life annuity. A life annuity is true life insurance because it insures against outliving financial resources. Both the annuitant's committed resources and life are liquidated at the same time. Life annuities are important instruments in planning old age financial security.

The Annuity Principle

Often a life annuity is explained as the liquidation of capital over the annuitant's lifetime. Each payment is said to have two components: interest and principal. The interest earned declines each year as principal is gradually liquidated. As years go by more of the payment is from principal and less from interest. But what happens when all the principal is liquidated? What will be the source of the annuity payments? There appears to be no source! How can there be continued interest and principal payments when all the principal has been liquidated? Because payments do continue the traditional two-component explanation of the life annuity must be wrong.

The correct explanation is that each life annuity payment has three components: principal, interest and an insurance benefit. To illustrate, a principal sum of \$11,013 is necessary for a \$1,000 annual life income for a man age 65 (more for a woman), assuming 3 percent interest and the 1949 annuity table. (No allowance is made here for expenses.) A year later only \$10,611 would be necessary. Thus \$402 is the amount of principal (\$11,013 − \$10,611) liquidated the first year. At 3 percent interest the \$11,013 earns \$330.39, making a total of \$732.39 (\$402 + \$330.39) from interest and principal. The remaining \$267.61 needed for the \$1,000 payment is the *insurance benefit.* Those who die during the year release their principal and accrued interest to those who survive. According to the assumed mortality table enough people will die during their 65th year to release \$267.61 to pay the survivors. For the second and subsequent \$1,000 payment the insurance benefit will increase, liquidated principal will decrease and the interest earned will decrease. Under this explanation what happens when the annuitant's principal is exhausted? The answer is clear. The annuitant's principal benefits are computed on the basis of a mortality table. The assumption is that all annuitants and all principal will be exhausted at the same time.

Classification of Annuities

Annuities are classified according to (1) number of lives covered; (2) how premiums are paid; (3) when benefit payments begin; (4) use of life contingencies; (5) how long (if at all) benefit payments continue after a life annuitant's death and (6) how benefit payments are measured.

Number of lives covered

Usually the annuitant is one person, but not always. For example, the **joint-and-last-survivor annuity** covers two or more annuitants. Under this contract payments continue until the death of the last survivor. The joint-and-last-survivor annuity may be used by a husband and wife to provide an income to both of them as long as either survives. On the theory that two cannot live as cheaply as one some joint-and-last-survivorship annuities are written to reduce the monthly income to two thirds or three fourths of its initial amount upon the death of the first annuitant.

How premiums are paid

Annuities may be purchased by paying regular periodic premiums (usually monthly or annually) or by a single premium. Individuals use regular periodic premium annuities to purchase retirement income. Life insurance cash values and death proceeds frequently are converted to single-premium annuities through settlement options. In addition, both regular periodic and single premium annuities are used to fund employee retirement plans (Chapter 17).

When benefit payments begin

Annuities are classified as immediate or deferred. Benefits under an **immediate annuity** are payable immediately after purchase, usually at the end of each benefit period. If the payment is made at the beginning of the benefit period the annuity is called an **annuity due.** Benefits under a **deferred annuity** are payable after the expiration of a given period. The deferred period is usually one that lasts until retirement. An immediate annuity is usually purchased with accumulated savings or life insurance proceeds or cash values. Deferred annuities commonly are purchased on a single-premium basis in arranging employee pensions.

Single-premium deferred annuities are also bought for tax shelters. Persons buying them can shelter the interest accumulated in the annuity from current income taxes. Income taxes on the interest earnings are deferred until the annuity income is paid or the contract is surrendered for its cash value. At that time the annuitant's purchase price (called the excluded amount) is subtracted from the annuity payment to determine the taxable income. If the annuitant takes a lump sum the full excluded amount is subtracted from that lump-sum payment and the remainder is taxable income. If the annuitant takes an annuity income the excluded amount is used to compute an exclusion ratio that determines the amount of each periodic payment excluded from taxable income. The excluded ratio is the ratio of the excluded amount to the total amount expected to be received over the annuitant's expected lifetime as determined by mortality tables published by the Internal Revenue Service. For example, if a male annuitant pays $100,000 for an annuity and receives $20,000 a year for life starting at age 65, his exclusion ratio will be one third because his life expectancy according to the IRS tables is 15 years. In 15 years he will collect $300,000 or $20,000 × 15. The excluded amount ($100,000) is one third of the expected payment of $300,000. Therefore one third of the $20,000 annual payment is excluded and two thirds or $13,333.33 is taxable income. The $6,666.67 is a return of principal and therefore not taxable.

Use of life contingencies

Payments may be continued until the annuitant's death or for a given period regardless of life or death. The former is called a life annuity; the latter, an annuity certain. **Life annuities** are used in retirement plans and as a means for paying damages in serious disability cases. The **annuity certain** is used as life insurance settlement options and to pay debts on an amortized basis (i.e., where interest and principal are included in each payment).

How long (if at all) benefit payments continue after a life annuitant's death

Life annuities are straight life or guaranteed minimum annuities. Under the straight life annuity the annuitant is paid *only* until death. It offers the highest periodic income per dollar of premium. Some annuitants elect a smaller periodic payment in exchange for a guaranteed minimum return—either a full refund of the invested principal (called a **refund annuity**) or a guaranteed minimum number of payments (called a **life income period-certain annuity**).

Refund annuities are of two types: cash refund and installment refund. They guarantee that either the annuitant or beneficiary will receive payments totaling the full amount of the premium. If the annuitant dies prior to receiving an amount equal to the full premium the heirs under the cash refund receive the balance in a lump sum. Under the installment refund they continue to receive the periodic annuity payments.

Under the period-certain life annuity (e.g., 10- or 20-years certain and life thereafter) the insurer guarantees a minimum number of annuity payments whether the annuitant lives or dies. After the guaranteed payments have been made the annuity payments continue only as long as the annuitant remains alive.

How benefit payments are measured

Annuities may be conventional (fixed dollar) or variable. **Conventional annuities** guarantee the annuitant a specified minimum number of dollars for each payment period. If the annuity is written on a participating basis the amount of each payment is likely to be higher than the guaranteed minimum amount.

The variable annuity guarantees to pay a fixed number of units for each payment period. The value of the units fluctuates according to the insurer's investment portfolio supporting the annuity. Variable annuities are discussed in the next section.

Figure 13–2 should be helpful in reviewing the classification of annuities.

Special Annuity Policies

Two special annuity policies are the **variable annuity** and the **split-life** insurance policy.

The variable annuity

Under the variable annuity the dollar amount of each periodic benefit payment is based on the value of the insurer's investment portfolio purchased with variable annuity premiums. This portfolio usually consists primarily of common stocks.

FIGURE 13–2 Annuity Classifications

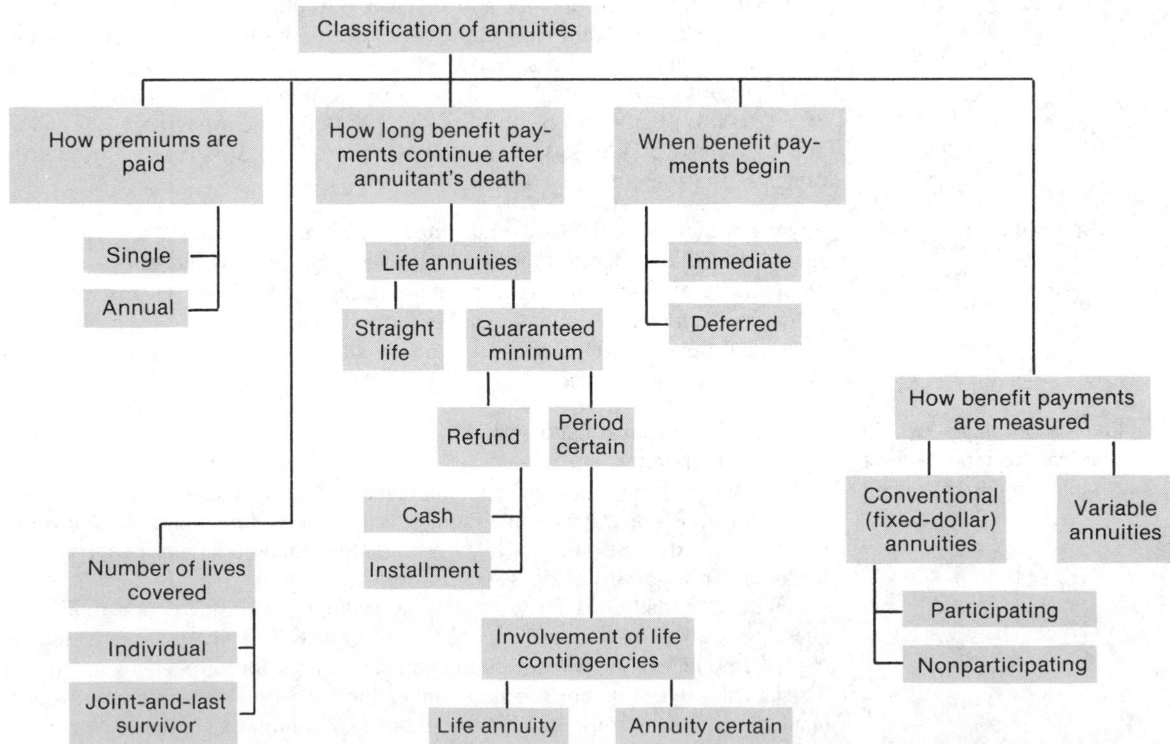

The theory behind the variable annuity is that common stock prices and the cost of living move in the same direction *over the long run,* giving annuitants fairly stable purchasing power. In the short run, changes in the market prices of common stocks and cost-of-living changes are not perfectly correlated. Frequently they move in opposite directions, as illustrated in Figure 13–3. Yet in the long run a substantial correlation between common stock averages and the cost of living had been recorded before 1969.

The long-term correlation thesis has failed the test miserably over recent years. In the 13-year period 1969–1982, the years from the end of 1969 to 1972 showed the best correlation between the CPI and the Standard and Poor 500 stock index. During this period the CPI increased steadily. The S&P 500 index decreased 18 percent from 1969 to 1970 but then rose 31 percent from 1970 to 1972. As Figure 13–3 demonstrates, the S&P 500 stock index fluctuated widely from 1969 to the present in spite of severe inflation during the latter stages of this period.

Two basic objectives of the variable annuity are (1) to give annuitants some protection against inflation and (2) to provide them an opportunity to share in the country's economic growth. Before undertaking to offer a variable annuity CREF (College Retirement Equities Fund) made impressive studies that seemed to indicate that (if the past provides any basis on which to judge the future) the variable annuity *in the long run* will provide better results than a fixed dollar annuity. Two questions now appear. How long is the long run? How long a run does a retiree have?

The following are tabulations of the results of 31 years of CREF's experience with the variable annuity. These results appear to have supported its expectation until 1973, after which the annuity value dropped nearly 39 percent in three years while consumer prices soared. The value of the CREF annuity changes yearly. Its value has been as shown in Table 13–1.

Two other objections to the variable annuity are noted. (1) Aside from the lack of a perfect positive correlation between stock prices and the cost of living, the cost of living for an individual annuitant does not fluctuate with an aggregate cost-of-living index. (2) Annuitants may be upset when their annuity decreases. This objection is both psychological and economic. Annuitants make conscious economic decisions when they buy variable annuities. They agree to take fewer dollars when stock prices fall in exchange for more dollars when stock prices rise. Yet when prices fall variable annuitants may criticize themselves for not electing fixed dollar annuity payments.

Split-life insurance

Split-life insurance is a tie-in of two contracts, an annual premium annuity and yearly renewable term insurance. The term insurance may be renewed only if the annuity premium is paid. The term insurance rate is low at every age but the annuity price is high, creating a package priced comparably to moderately priced whole life insurance.[7] The annuity and the life insurance do not have to be purchased on the same life. The term insurance can be written for several

[7] The reverse may be true for universal life discussed earlier. The charge for the death protection (term insurance) may be high leaving less of the divided premium for savings (cash values). These low cash values then accumulate at what appears to be an interest rate more competitive than it is. If a more realistic death protection charge were made then more funds would be available for savings. These higher savings amounts could accumulate at a lower interest rate and still be competitive with policies that show lower savings amounts and higher interest rates—at least for the discerning buyer.

FIGURE 13–3 **A comparison of the Consumer Price Index and Standard & Poor's index of 500 stocks, 1969 to first quarter of 1982**

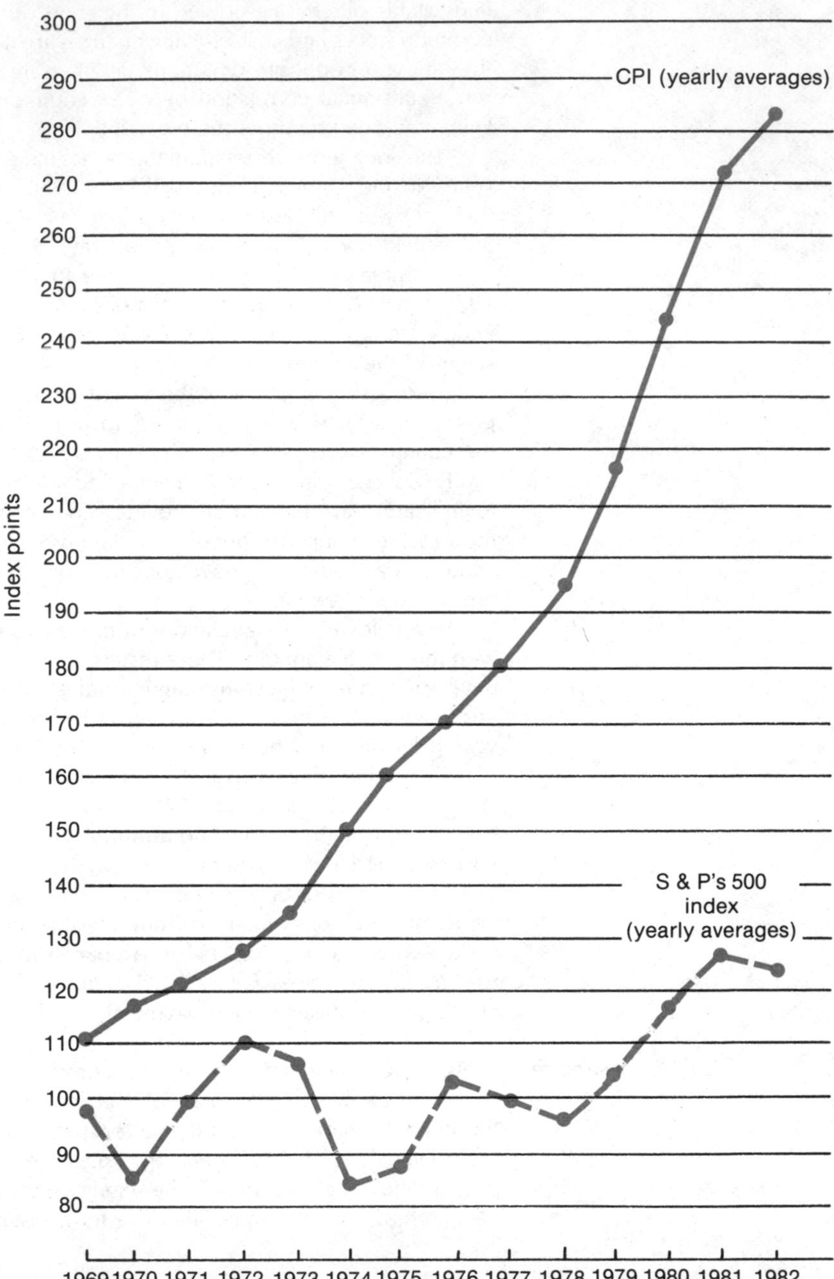

The index values are *yearly averages*. Figures were obtained from Standard & Poor's *Security Price Index Record,* 1978, p. 4, and *Current Statistics,* January 1979, p. 12, 40; *Price Indexes,* p. 76; *Survey of Current Business,* January 1981, pp. S–6 and S–18, and April 1982, pp. S–5 and S–16. The 1982 S&P average was computed by the author.

TABLE 13–1

YEAR	VALUE	YEAR	VALUE	YEAR	VALUE
1952	$10.00	1964–65	26.48	1976–77	26.24
1953–54	9.46	1965–66	28.21	1977–78	24.80
1954–55	10.74	1966–67	30.43	1978–79	23.28
1955–56	14.11	1967–68	31.92	1979–80	27.28
1956–57	18.51	1968–69	29.90	1980–81	26.27
1957–58	16.88	1969–70	32.50	1981–82	35.86
1958–59	16.71	1970–71	28.91	1982–83	30.56
1959–60	22.03	1971–72	30.64		
1960–61	22.18	1972–73	35.74		
1961–62	26.25	1973–74	31.58		
1962–63	26.13	1974–75	26.21		
1963–64	22.68	1975–76	21.83		

lives (e.g., two or more children) thus providing children with low-priced term insurance at the expense of a high-priced annuity paid for by the parent—a form of subsidy offered by parents to children. Split life is not approved in some states because of legal and tax questions and because of concern about its value to consumers.

INNERSCRIPT: RECENT TRENDS IN LIFE INSURANCE

Life insurers must remain aware of the changing needs of an increasingly knowledgeable public. As noted, insurers are experiencing a trend away from permanent (whole life) insurance toward term insurance. In their search for security individuals are seeking financial instruments that enable them to keep pace with inflation and improve their living standards. Some life insurers have introduced life insurance and annuity plans designed to help policyowners protect against inflation and provide for real financial growth. Life insurers, as noted, are beginning to expand their financial services beyond the traditional life insurance business. They have formed or acquired real estate investment firms, property and liability insurers, investment brokerage firms and other financial services organizations in order to compete with other financial institutions for the savings dollar. They are moving toward full-service financial organizations.

Americans are becoming increasingly consumer oriented. Life insurance is hardly a sacred cow. The National Association of Insurance Commissioners (NAIC) has approved a model life insurance solicitation regulation that requires insurers to supply specific life insurance price information and a life insurance buyer's guide to prospective applicants. The guide attempts to educate insurance applicants by including sections on analysis of life insurance needs and how to make cost comparisons among policies. Many states have adopted this regulation or some version of it. Its value is challenged as unnecessary and a useless burden on life insurers, lacking

(continued)

both in simplicity and in the amount of information it provides the consumer.

The Federal Trade Commission staff found the regulation helpful but inadequate. If it had its way (but it doesn't because of the insurance industry's great political power), it would give the applicant a more inclusive policy summary and buyer's guide. It would include information in the proposed policy summary showing how long the policy must be held before a policyowner could surrender it without financial loss and how policy benefits would compare to a program combining term insurance and a separate savings account. It would also require disclosure of price information before the buyer signs the application. A serious defect in the FTC staff's thinking is its misdirected emphasis on life insurance as a savings medium and on termination for its surrender value when, by the staff's own admission, life insurance should be purchased primarily for death protection. In this instance, perhaps, the industry's political power is in the public interest.

Replacement of life insurance policies is another area in which increased regulation is expected. The NAIC has adopted a model replacement bill that requires the following: the pros and cons of the proposed replacement for the buyers; a comparative information form covering a wide range of policy facts, including contract provisions and cost data; delivery of comprehensive policy summaries and an exchange of disclosure information between the replacing and replaced insurers.

Consumers will also benefit when more states pass policy readability laws. Readability laws force insurers to write and print policies a buyer will be able to read and understand. (Is this objective really possible, given the "why Johnny (or Janie) can't read syndrome"?) Some observers claim that policy readability laws are passed so that lawyers can understand the policy. Lawyers are paid to put agreements into legalese and then paid again to interpret what the contract means. So if it were not for lawyers, lawyers would not be needed.

SUMMARY

1. People face four basic contingencies to their economic productivity: death, disability, compulsory retirement and unemployment.
2. *Life insurance* provides income to dependents in the event of the insured's death. It is also used to accumulate funds to offset emergencies and to provide retirement income. *Life annuities* offer insureds lifetime postretirement income. *Health insurance* (discussed in Chapter 15) provides the insured disability income and helps pay medical expenses. *Government benefits* (discussed in Chapter 18) offer some financial security for temporary unemployment.
3. Life insurance policies may be classified according to whether they are:
   a. Participating or nonparticipating.
   b. Written with or without cash values.

   c. Term, endowment or whole life (or some combination of the three).
   d. Ordinary, industrial or group.

4. Participating life insurance provides for policy dividends.
5. Savings accumulate through life insurance from the method of paying premiums. If a policyowner purchases a policy with a duration of more than one year and pays for it with either one initial premium or a series of level annual premiums, cash values accumulate.
6. Term insurance obligates the insurer to pay the policy's face amount if the insured dies within a specified time. Term insurance may be short term, long term, renewable, convertible, level, increasing or decreasing. Term insurance may be appropriate for a temporary life insurance need. It is also appropriate for young people who need more protection than they can afford with higher premium insurance and for those needing insurance but who prefer to use other financial instruments for accumulating savings.
7. Endowment insurance obligates the insurer to pay a stated sum to the beneficiary if the insured dies during the policy term or to the owner if the insured survives the policy term. Its uses are as a gift medium, a savings medium for a particular purpose or a method of funding retirement income. It is especially subject to misuse.
8. Whole life insurance offers lifetime coverage. Viewed functionally, a whole life policy is an endowment at age 100 because benefits are paid to those who die before age 100 and to those who survive to that age. Viewed actuarially and conceptually, it is term to age 100 because the insured is assumed to be dead at that age and paid a death benefit. Whole life insurance provides for several methods of paying premiums: single premium, continuous premium or limited-payment periods such as 20 years or to age 65.
9. Some individuals advocate that term insurance be purchased to provide death protection and the difference between the term premium and the premium for a like amount of whole life be invested elsewhere. These plans may not always meet the savers' objectives because of their lack of investment knowledge and the difficulty in sticking to a well-conceived savings plan, unless compelled to do so through regular payments of life insurance premiums.
10. Universal life insurance policies have been designed by life insurers to combine the advantages of cash-value life insurance with the higher yields possible through "invest-the-difference" plans. Unlike traditional cash-value life insurance, universal life divides death protection and cash-value accumulations into separate components and adjusts the amounts of savings and protection to the needs of the policyowner.
11. Many special policy forms combine basic policies into packages to meet particular life insurance needs. Other special forms reflect sales gimmicks not related to buyer needs. Some examples of the former include: the family income policy, multiple-protection policies, mortgage protection policies, the family policy, joint life policy, variable life insurance and the adjustable life policy.
12. Life insurance policies may be classified as:
   a. Ordinary—Policies for at least $1,000 with premium payment periods at least monthly.

b. Industrial—Policies for face amounts less than $1,000 with premiums generally paid weekly.
c. Group—The group, not the individual, is underwritten.

13. Insurers frequently make riders available with life insurance policies. These riders add more insurance to the basic policy; offer waiver of premium benefits in the event of disability; provide accidental death benefits and so on.

14. An annuity provides for a regular periodic income for the annuitant's life or for a specified period.

15. Annuities are classified according to:
a. Number of lives covered—Individual or joint-and-last-survivor.
b. How premiums are paid—Single premium or periodic payments.
c. When benefit payments begin—Immediate or deferred.
d. Use of life contingencies—Life annuity or annuity certain.
e. How long (if at all) benefit payments continue after a life annuitant's death—Straight life or guaranteed minimum number of payments.
f. How benefit payments are measured—Conventional (fixed dollar) or variable.

16. Two special annuity policies are the variable annuity and the split-life insurance policy. Under the variable annuity, the dollar amount of each periodic payment is based on the value of the insurer's investment portfolio supporting the annuity. Split-life insurance is a tie-in of two contracts, an annual premium annuity and yearly renewable term insurance.

17. Life insurers can no longer be bound by traditions. They must adjust to the changing market. Many have become full-blown financial service organizations through acquisitions of or mergers with other financial service companies.

REVIEW QUESTIONS

1. This chapter provides an illustration of how to compute the savings accumulation per policy year. The second-year savings accumulation in that example is $17.58. Assuming 199 deaths in the third year, compute the savings accumulation at the end of the third year.

2. Consider the following statement: the whole life policy may be viewed as term insurance to age 100 or as endowment at age 100. Explain why you agree or disagree with this statement.

3. Distinguish between participating and nonparticipating life insurance. What arguments are advanced by those who (1) advocate participating insurance and (2) advocate nonparticipating insurance?

4. Why are so many different forms of term life insurance written?

5. What are the arguments for and against the buy-term-and-invest-the-difference plan?

6. What is universal life insurance? Why was it developed? What problems does it face?

7. Explain why buyers of mortgage protection life insurance probably want policies that now differ from the traditional mortgage protection plans.

8. Describe the family policy and explain its principal advantage(s) and disadvantage(s).
9. Identify the various types of life insurance policies or riders that have developed to help policyowners deal with the problem of inflation.
10. Each life annuity periodic payment is often said to have two components: some principal and some interest. Explain why the traditional two component explanation of the life annuity payout is wrong. What is the correct explanation?
11. Distinguish between a cash refund and an installment refund annuity. Distinguish between a refund annuity and a life income period-certain annuity.
12. Describe the variable annuity and explain the theory behind it. Do the facts support the theory?
13. Explain why so little industrial life insurance (less than 1 percent of all life insurance sold) is bought today when nearly 19 percent of the amount of life insurance sold in 1950 was industrial.
14. Give an example of a preferred-risk life insurance policy that is truly a preferred-risk policy. Give an example of a policy that is called preferred-risk that is not really a preferred-risk policy.
15. What is split-life insurance? What is deposit term insurance? Does each serve a useful purpose? Explain.

CHAPTER

14 The life insurance contract

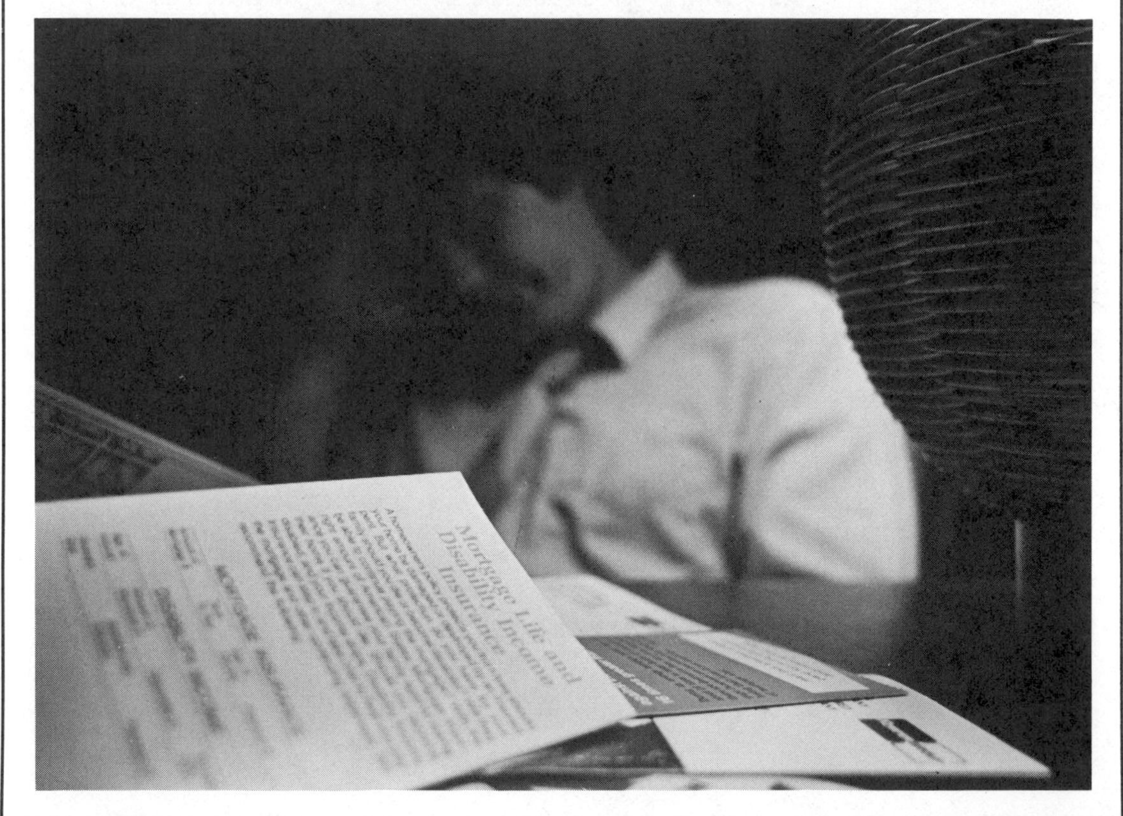

John Thoeming/Richard D. Irwin

CHAPTER OBJECTIVES

1. **To consider the contract decisions policyowners must make about their life insurance: naming the beneficiaries, determining ownership arrangements and selecting policy options.**
2. **To describe the life insurance policy provisions required by law and those permitted by law.**
3. **To point out other general provisions included in life insurance policies.**
4. **To discuss the rights of beneficiaries and creditors in life insurance policy proceeds and cash values.**

To buy, or not to buy: that is the question. True, and it is the only question if the decision is not to buy! In dealing with life insurance, if the decision is to buy, additional questions must be answered. Even after answering the fundamental questions of what kind, how much and from whom, families and businesses must face a number of questions about the policy contract itself. Yet few policyowners ever read their policies with any effort to understand them.[1] This chapter explains the contractual rights and duties of policyowners and their insurers. By understanding the contract the policyowner can make the best use of it and avoid unpleasant surprises.

Although life insurance policies are not uniformly worded they all contain basic provisions, called **general policy provisions.** They may also have three important types of options: nonforfeiture options, dividend options and settlement options. The policy's first page includes the insuring agreement between the policyowner and the insurer, the beneficiaries' names, a statement that provisions attached are part of the contract and the amount of the periodic premium payment. Next are two types of general policy provisions: *required* and *permissible.* All these provisions are discussed in this chapter.

DECISIONS BY THE POLICYOWNER

The policyowner must make decisions related to beneficiary designations, ownership and policy options. Qualified agents often help policyowners with these decisions.

Beneficiary Designations

One or more beneficiaries must be named to receive the policy proceeds upon the insured's death. Third parties may be designated as beneficiaries or the proceeds may be paid to the insured's estate. The designation may be either **revocable** or **irrevocable.** If revocable the policyowner may change the beneficiary and may also assign or surrender the policy.[2] If irrevocable, all policy rights are vested in the beneficiary and the policyowner may not assign the policy or borrow on it without the beneficiary's consent. An irrevocable beneficiary designation

---

[1] Character is itching but not scratching. Those characters itching to be among the few who have read a life insurance policy are invited to join this group by scratching deep into the specimen life insurance policy reproduced in Appendix 5.

[2] Assignment is a transfer of either some or all of the policyowner's rights in the policy. These rights include cash values, loan values, dividends and so on.

may be either *reversionary* or *absolute*. If reversionary the policy rights revert to the policyowner if the beneficiary dies first. If absolute the value of the policy is included in the beneficiary's estate for the beneficiary's heirs. These heirs may keep the policy in force or surrender it for its cash value.

The beneficiary clause, the one provision the policyowner writes, should be precise to eliminate any doubt as to who receives the policy proceeds. Contingent beneficiaries should be named in case the primary beneficiaries do not survive the insured.

Ownership

Generally the insured is also the policyowner. Life insurance policy proceeds are included in the taxable estate when the insured owns the policy. The proceeds are also included in the insured's taxable estate when *the estate* is named the *beneficiary* regardless of the policy's ownership. Thus for estate planning the subject should not be either the owner or the beneficiary. When someone other than the insured owns the policy a successor owner should be named in case the insured survives the owner. The Economic Recovery Tax Act of 1981 (ERTA) eliminated the necessity for spouses to have cross ownership of the life insurance on their lives. ERTA excludes from death taxes property transferred from the deceased spouse to the surviving spouse. However, if the value of the combined estates is high, someone other than the spouses (an adult child, for example) should own the life insurance policies to save death taxes when the surviving spouse dies.

Policy Options

Life insurance policies generally offer three sets of options: **nonforfeiture, dividend** and **settlement options.** Nonforfeiture options are found only in cash-value policies and dividend options only in participating policies.

Nonforfeiture options

If the owner discontinues paying premiums three choices are available. The policy can be (1) surrendered for its cash value, (2) converted to a paid-up policy of the same type but for a reduced face amount or (3) converted to a paid-up term policy for its full face amount for a period usually shorter than the original policy. This latter option is called extended term insurance.[3]

Assume Peter Colwell bought a $10,000 continuous-premium whole life policy when he was 20 years old, paid premiums for 10 years, then decided to discontinue payments. The value of his options are as follows: $1,030 in cash, a fully paid-up whole life policy for $2,490 or $10,000 of term insurance for 21 years and 273 days. Values vary among policies and insurers.

Most policies provide that if premium payments are discontinued the policy automatically will be changed to extended term insurance if the owner fails to elect one of the other options.

Dividend options

Dividends are paid on policies participating in the insurer's earnings. Virtually all policies mutual insurers issue are participating. Stock insurers may issue both nonpar and par policies but most stock insurers issue only nonpar policies. Dividend determination is discussed in Chapter 22.

[3] If the policy is participating the insurance under the reduced-paid-up option continues as participating insurance. The insurance under the extended term option usually becomes nonparticipating. Some insurers, however, continue the extended term as participating insurance but at higher rates; i.e., the extended term is for a shorter period than for the customary nonpar extended term.

In the absence of the owner's election dividends are *paid in cash,* but usually no money is transferred unless the policy is paid up. The insurer applies the cash dividend towards the next premium payment. Cash is the most widely used dividend option.

Dividends may be *accumulated at interest.* In this event the insurer retains the dividends and accumulates them at not less (generally more) than the interest rate specified in the policy.

Dividends may be used to buy *paid-up additions* to the policy at *net* rates. Under one continuous-premium whole life policy a $1.80 dividend would buy $6.02 of paid-up whole life insurance at age 25 and $4.35 at age 40. (The cost of insurance increases with the insured's age.) Paid-up additions offer an opportunity to acquire inexpensive insurance because these additions are purchased at net rates (i.e., without the expense allowance). A further attraction of this option is the additional insurance that can be added each year regardless of the insured's health or occupation when the dividend is paid. Paid-up additions must be of the same type as that on which the dividend is paid. This option may be selected for current dividends at any time without proof of insurability.

Another dividend option is *one-year term insurance.* Under the one-year term option the amount of insurance that can be purchased by the dividend usually is limited to the cash value of the policy. If the dividends exceed the amount required to purchase the maximum term insurance the policyowner may elect to use the excess for another option.

If the policyowner wants additional death protection either the paid-up insurance or the one-year term dividend option is a logical choice. If he or she is more interested in savings or retirement the accumulate-at-interest dividend option *might* be chosen. However, reconsideration could lead to a different choice. Interest paid on dividend accumulations is taxable income but annual increases in the cash value of paid-up additions are not subject to current income taxation. This tax incentive may encourage the owner interested in savings to elect paid-up additions.

Settlement options

The basic method of paying proceeds of a life policy is a lump sum. Two alternative methods offer periodic payments: (1) the interest-only option and (2) the annuity options. The latter include installments-for-a-fixed-period, installments-of-a-fixed-amount and an income for life.

Under the **interest-only option** the insurer retains the policy proceeds and pays interest to the beneficiary. A minimum interest rate is guaranteed with the actual interest payment determined by the amount the insurer earns. Many policies written today *promise* 3 to 4 percent but most insurers pay much higher interest rates.

Installments-for-a-fixed-period is a settlement option under which the proceeds of the policy (principal and interest) are paid in a *fixed number* of monthly, quarterly or annual installments. The amount of each payment depends on the length of the period over which payments are made. They continue until the required number of installments has been paid regardless of whether the annuitant survives. For example, a minimum monthly installment of $18.11 per $1,000 of insurance proceeds is guaranteed for a five-year period, assuming 3.5 percent interest. If the payments are guaranteed for 10 years the minimum monthly amount will be $9.83. In the likely event the insurer earns more than the assumed 3.5 percent and the settlements are participating, the monthly payments are increased.

Under **installments-of-a-fixed-amount,** insurers pay monthly benefits of a predetermined amount and continue the payments until the policy proceeds are exhausted. The duration of payments is determined by the amount of each guaranteed payment. For example, $10,000 of insurance guarantees $100 a month for a minimum of nine years and nine months (assuming interest at 3.5 percent). The difference between the fixed amount and the fixed period option is that the former guarantees the amount of each payment while the latter guarantees the period over which payments are made. Participating dividends under the fixed amount option are used to extend the payment period, not to increase each payment. To give this option flexibility, limited (or full) withdrawals are often permitted to allow an increase in the amount of each payment. The fixed amount option is usually a better choice than the fixed period option because this flexibility can be arranged. The fixed period option is inflexible. Both the fixed amount and fixed period options are called annuity-certain options because their payments do not depend upon the continued life of the annuitant.

Under the **life-income option,** insurers pay an income for the beneficiary's life, usually with guaranteed payments for a minimum number of years, e.g., 5 to 20. Although a life income seems ideal, the amount of insurance required for this option is too large to be practical especially when providing for young beneficiaries. For a 40-year-old female beneficiary, $1,000 of insurance pays a guaranteed monthly income of about $3.80 for life, 10 years certain. The interest assumption used in this example is only 3.5 percent. Thus, the insurer is likely to pay much more than the guaranteed amount. (A passbook savings and loan account currently pays about $4.58 a month income per $1,000 without liquidating principal.) Policyowners and beneficiaries should shop the financial markets before electing a settlement option.

If the insurance is inadequate to provide the beneficiary a livable lifetime income, a fixed amount option would be a better choice because it can provide an adequate income for a short period—hopefully continuing until the children are no longer dependent. Better yet, if other financial instruments provide a higher income, proceeds can be taken in cash and invested in one or more of them. Although a life income option taken when the beneficiary is age 65 or 70 offers higher periodic payments per $1,000 than at earlier ages, these higher payments could still be competitively unattractive.

Payments under the life income and installment settlement options include a return of principal. Payments under an interest only option and from investment in other financial instruments do not liquidate the principal. In comparing liquidating and nonliquidating instruments, the beneficiary must consider whether the additional income, if any, under a liquidating instrument is worth sacrificing principal. One advantage of a liquidating settlement option is that the surviving spouse receives $1,000 of tax-free interest income annually. Therefore, the after-tax return on other investments for some of the policy proceeds may be less attractive.

Under the joint-and-last survivorship option, insurers pay a minimum guaranteed periodic income during the joint lifetime of two or more persons (usually husband and wife) and for the life of the survivor. This option is used more frequently when the policy is surrendered for its cash value than as a method of settling the proceeds of a policy paid when the subject dies. Often, the payments are reduced upon the first death by about ¼ or ⅓, thus permitting higher payments than otherwise during the joint lifetimes of the parties.

OTHER POLICY PROVISIONS

In addition to beneficiary designation, ownership and settlement options (which are determined by the policyowner), life policies contain provisions required by law, provisions permitted by law and other general policy provisions.

Provisions Required by State Law

The various states require that insurers include policy provisions concerning incontestability, misstatement of age or sex, deferment, nonforfeiture, loan values, grace periods and reinstatement.

Incontestability

The incontestability clause prohibits the insurer, after a period of time, from contesting the policy on the basis of a misstatement made in the application or concealment of facts. A typical clause is: "This policy shall be incontestable after it has been in force during the lifetime of the insured for a period of two years from its date of issue except for nonpayment of premiums." The courts have interpreted the clause liberally, allowing it to become an agreement to disregard fraud. The clause is justified because of the impracticability of gathering evidence and assembling witnesses many years after the policy is issued. Furthermore, the clause is valuable to the beneficiary in preventing delayed settlements resulting from long and costly court action.

Misstatement of age and sex

The incontestability clause does not excuse the misstatement of age or sex of the subject, as they are primary life insurance rating factors. If the applicant misstates age or sex an adjustment is made in the face amount of the policy. The beneficiary is paid the amount of insurance that the premium would have purchased if the age or sex had been stated correctly. Thus if a man aged 30 states his age as 25 when buying a $10,000 whole life policy and this misstatement is discovered, the insurance proceeds will be reduced to $8,740—the amount of insurance the premiums paid would have bought at age 30. If sex is misstated the face amount of the policy also will be adjusted: decreased for a male, increased for a female. No mention is made of adjustments for surgical sex changes.

Deferment clause

In the 1930s some insurers were financially embarrassed when many policyowners wanted to borrow or withdraw the cash values of their policies at the same time. The difficulty was that to avoid suffering substantial losses the insurers were forced to sell assets at depressed prices. Since then life insurers have been required to include a clause giving them the right to defer the payment of the cash or loan value of a policy for a period not to exceed six months unless the loan is for renewal premiums. The clause does not apply to proceeds payable in cash at death, although it may apply to the lump-sum withdrawal of proceeds left with the company under the interest-only option or the prepayment of any guarantees under an installment or life income option.

Nonforfeiture

Because cash-value policies contain nonforfeiture provisions the cash-value rights in a policy are not forfeited if the policy is discontinued. The nonforfeiture provisions offer the three options previously discussed.

Loan values

If the policyowner needs money but does not want to terminate the insurance that person can arrange a loan from the insurer up to the cash value of the policy. The insurer lends the money at the guaranteed policy rate. This rate is

5 or 6 percent on older policies but on recently issued policies, in those states where allowable, the rate has been increased to 8 percent. (Some insurers offer owners of older policies the option of accepting an increase in the guaranteed loan rate in exchange for higher policy dividends.) At first glance it seems unfair that policyowners must pay interest to borrow what they consider to be their own money. However, the insurer had taken into consideration the investment income on this money in computing the premium; therefore if the policyowner withdraws the money the insurer must be compensated for the investment income lost.

The original purpose of policy loans was to provide a source of funds to the policyowner primarily for emergencies. However, sophisticated policyowners use policy loans as a source of investment funds. These policyowners borrow against their policies at guaranteed rates and invest in short-term financial paper at higher rates to earn a profit. To force life insurers to lend money at 5, 6 or even 8 percent that can be invested elsewhere at 13 percent or more puts them at a competitive disadvantage. To help solve this problem the National Association of Insurance Commissioners approved a model bill permitting a policy loan provision for new policies that allows periodic adjustments of the policy loan rate. The adjustments are based on a Moody's Investors Service index of long-term corporate bond yields. The maximum loan rate for each policy must be determined at regular intervals, at least once a year but not more frequently than once in any three-month period. The rate charged *may* be increased if the increase would be 0.5 percent or more per annum. It *must* be decreased if the decrease would amount to 0.5 percent per annum. In addition, the NAIC model bill permits a fixed policy loan interest rate of 8 percent in place of the variable rate.[4]

Grace and reinstatement

If past-due premiums are paid within a grace period of 30 or 31 days following the premium due date the policy continues in effect. If payment is not made by the end of the grace period policies without a cash value terminate. Those policies with a cash value will be placed on the appropriate nonforfeiture option. If death occurs during the grace period the premium due is deducted from the proceeds.

If the policy has not been surrendered to the insurer for cash, the terminating policyowner may reinstate the lapsed policy within a specified time upon payment of past-due premiums and upon proof of insurability. The length of the reinstatement period varies among insurers but is usually three to five years. If the policy lapsed recently the proof of insurability requirement may consist only of a simple statement by the policyowner; for longer lapses the insurer may require a medical examination.

Permissible Provisions

State laws permit insurers to include policy restrictions for suicide, aviation and war. A suicide restriction is included in nearly every ordinary life policy. An

[4] The model bill has become law in 22 states with many more states expected to adopt it. Many large insurers are reluctant to include the model policy loan provision in their policies until the model bill is enacted in a substantial majority of states. An inequity is found between borrowers and nonborrowers of cash values. Borrowers cause insurers to earn less on their investments thus reducing the amount available for policy dividends. To the extent that policy loans are not considered in dividend formulas nonborrowers are put at a disadvantage. Because large policyowners tend to be the borrowers the inequity between borrowers and nonborrowers discriminates against the small policyowner—a powerful argument for passage of the NAIC model policy loan provision.

aviation exclusion is seldom found and the war clause is contained in policies issued during war or threat of war.

Suicide If the insured commits suicide within two years (one year in some policies) from the inception of the policy the liability of the insurer is limited to a return of premiums. In the absence of this clause insurers would be subject to severe adverse selection.

Aviation As a rule insurers do not use aviation exclusion clauses. Instead they prefer to increase premiums to reflect the increased hazard. Nevertheless, four types of aviation clauses are found in some existing policies: an exclusion of all aviation deaths except those of fare-paying passengers on regularly scheduled airlines; exclusion of deaths in military aircraft only; exclusion of pilots, crew members, or student pilots and aviation death while on military maneuvers. The first and third clauses rarely are found and the second and fourth rarely are included during peacetime.

War War clauses vary widely, ranging from absolute prohibition of payment if the insured was in the armed forces at the time of death to a clause that denies payment only if the insured's death resulted from war. In any case the insurer will refund the premium or an amount equal to the policy reserve. (The policy reserve is discussed in Chapter 22.)

Other General Provisions

Several other provisions necessary for the protection of the insurer or the policyowner are included.

Deduction of indebtedness and premium refund Indebtedness to the insurer under a policy loan will be deducted from the proceeds of the policy at death or from the cash value upon surrender. Many insurers refund premiums for the unexpired period if the subject dies after paying the premium.

Change of beneficiary A beneficiary is named in the application for a life policy. The applicant usually reserves the right to change the beneficiary. Under the typical beneficiary clause the policy must be returned to the insurer's home office with a written request for a change in the beneficiary designation.

Assignment Unlike property insurance the consent of the insurer to the assignment of a life insurance contract is not needed. However, to protect the parties involved notice of assignment should be filed with the home office.

THIRD-PARTY RIGHTS IN LIFE INSURANCE

Beneficiaries and creditors have important rights in life insurance policies. The rights of a beneficiary are determined by the type of beneficiary designation and by the ownership of the policy. If the beneficiary is the owner he or she can exercise all policy rights including policy loans and assignments regardless of the type of beneficiary designation. If the beneficiary is not the owner but is revocably designated he or she has only a contingent interest in the policy—i.e., an interest contingent upon the subject dying before the beneficiary dies or is revoked. If irrevocably designated the beneficiary has a vested interest in the policy and can deny the owner permission for policy loans, assignment and any other action relating to the policy.

Creditors' rights of an insolvent insured to the cash value and proceeds of a life insurance policy have been restricted by common law, federal statutes and state statutes.

In summary determining the rights of the insured's and beneficiary's creditors in a life insurance policy's proceeds and cash value depends on (1) the beneficiary designation, (2) whether the insured is in bankruptcy proceedings, (3) state statutes (and their interpretation) governing the exemption of life insurance policy values from creditors' claims and (4) whether a spendthrift trust clause is inserted in the policy.

INNERSCRIPT: CREDITORS' RIGHTS IN LIFE INSURANCE EXAMINED

Courts have generally decided that the insured's and beneficiaries' creditors' rights to life insurance cash values and proceeds depend upon the policy's beneficiary designation. If the insured's estate is the beneficiary the policy proceeds are held to be general estate assets that can be reached to satisfy a creditor's judgment against the insured. The courts also hold that the insured's creditors can attach (take by legal authority) a life insurance policy, but the availability of its cash value to the insured's creditors depends on the policy's provisions. If delivery of the policy to the insurer for cancellation is sufficient for payment the courts will usually allow creditors to obtain the cash value. However, if as usual the right to collect is an option to be exercised by the insured, the insurer is not obligated to pay the cash value until the insured elects that option. The creditors do not have the right of election and the courts will not force election on the insured. Creditors can claim the cash value only through formal bankruptcy proceedings.

The courts rule that policy proceeds paid to a named beneficiary (third-party beneficiary) belong to that beneficiary and are not subject to the insured's creditors. They also rule that because the beneficiaries' rights take precedence over creditors' rights, the policy's cash value is also exempt from the insured's creditors' claims.

Federal statutes

Two federal statutes concern creditors' rights to life insurance: federal tax liens and bankruptcy. The federal government can collect its tax claims against the insured directly from the insurer; the amount collectible is limited to the policy's cash value. If the insured dies before the tax claim is collected the limit is the policy's cash value immediately before the insured dies.

When an insured files bankruptcy the Federal Bankruptcy Act determines how life insurance policies are treated. Section 70a of that act states that only a life insurance policy's cash value may

be distributed to creditors. Because policies payable to an irrevocable beneficiary named in good faith (i.e., without intent to defraud) give the beneficiary a vested right, the trustee has no right to these policies. However, the trustee has a right to the cash values of all policies where the insured may change the beneficiary. To offset the adverse effect of forcing insureds to surrender policies Section 70a states:

> **When any bankrupt . . . shall have any insurance policy which has a surrender value . . . he [or she] may, within 30 days after the cash surrender value has been ascertained and stated to the trustee, . . . pay or secure to the trustee the sum so ascertained and stated and continue such policy free from the claims of the creditors.**

Therefore a bankrupt insured can keep the policy in force if the trustee is paid an amount equal to its cash value. A policy loan is a source of funds available to the insured to meet this condition.

State statutes

Laws exempting life insurance from creditors' claims have been passed by nearly all states and take precedence over the Federal Bankruptcy Act. A New York court explains that these exemptions were enacted for "the humane purpose of preserving to the unfortunate or improvident debtor or . . . family the means of obtaining a livelihood and preventing them from becoming a charge upon the public."[5]

The laws vary among states. In many states the exemption extends only to policies payable to the insured's spouse and children. In others protection extends to any dependent relative; and still others provide exemption to any beneficiary other than the insured's estate. In most states the exemption includes cash values as well as policy proceeds. A few states provide protection against the claims of the beneficiary's creditors. If the statute is not applicable to the beneficiary's creditors the insured may provide this protection by including a spendthrift trust clause **in the policy settlement agreement. When this clause is used the beneficiary's creditors have no legal access to the life insurance proceeds payable to the beneficiary. To use the spendthrift trust clause the policyowner must elect an installment settlement option. Only the proceeds *held by the insurer* for the beneficiary are protected by the spendthrift trust clause. After the beneficiary receives an installment, that amount is subject to creditor's claims. (Of course the "smart" beneficiary will have spent the money before the creditors arrive.)**

SUMMARY

1. For every life insurance policy, the policyowner must make decisions about beneficiary designation, ownership and policy options. In addition, the life insurance policy contains a number of general provisions; some are required,

[5] *Crossman Co.* v. *Ranch,* 263 N.Y. 264, 188 N.E. 748.

a few are permitted and others include such necessary conditions as change of beneficiary and assignment.

2. A beneficiary designation may be either revocable or irrevocable. If revocable, the policyowner may change the beneficiary and may also assign or surrender the policy. If irrevocable, policy rights are vested in the beneficiary so the policyowner may not assign the policy or borrow on it without the beneficiary's consent.
3. The policyowner is often the subject of the insurance but can be a third party. Decisions about policy ownership can have tax and other implications.
4. Life insurance policies generally offer three sets of options: (1) nonforfeiture options (in all but term insurance), (2) dividend options (in participating policies) and (3) settlement options (in virtually all policies).
5. State laws require that insurers include policy provisions dealing with incontestability, misstatement of age or sex, deferment, nonforfeiture, loan values, grace periods and reinstatement.
6. State laws permit insurers to include policy restrictions for suicide, aviation and war.
7. Several other provisions necessary for the protection of the insurer or the policyowner are the deduction of indebtedness, change of beneficiary and assignment provisions.
8. Beneficiaries have important rights in life insurance depending on whether they are named revocable or irrevocable and if irrevocable whether reversionary or absolute.
9. The rights of the creditors of the insured and of the policyowner in the proceeds and the cash values of life insurance policies depend on (1) how the beneficiary is named, (2) whether the insured is in the process of bankruptcy, (3) state statutes and their interpretations and (4) whether a spendthrift trust clause is included in the settlement agreement.

REVIEW QUESTIONS

1. Does the Economic Tax Recovery Act of 1981 affect the policyownership decision? Explain.
2. How do the rights of an irrevocable beneficiary differ if the beneficiary designation is reversionary rather than absolute?
3. Distinguish between an installment-of-a-fixed-amount option and an installment-for-a-fixed period option with particular reference to the handling of dividends and policy loans. If a choice is to be made between the two options, which one would you recommend in virtually every case?
4. Distinguish between the interest-only option and the life-income option. What special advantage might each have?
5. Distinguish between the paid-up additions and the accumulation-at-interest dividend options. If the policyowner's principal objective is the accumulation of savings, what argument can be made for the accumulation-at-interest option? For the paid-up additions option?

6. Why does the policy loan provisions found in most life insurance policies create so much adverse financial selection? What steps are being taken to help solve this adverse selection problem?
7. Consider the following statement: "Families that fly together, die together." Does this statement suggest the inclusion of an aviation exclusion in a life insurance policy? If so, what type?
8. What types of statements made by the insured in an application for life insurance are not *fully* protected by the incontestability clause? Explain. (In your explanation, explain why the word fully is used to modify protected.)
9. How do bankruptcy proceedings affect the rights of the insured and of the insured's creditors? Would your answer be different if state statutes relating to creditors' rights apply?
10. What type of behavior would be in the best interest of the beneficiary after the insured's death if the policy included a spendthrift trust clause?
11. What considerations are important in naming the beneficiary of a life insurance policy? Explain.
12. Why should the policyowner select a nonforfeiture option when deciding to discontinue premium payments?
13. Does the deferment clause affect payment of the proceeds of a life insurance policy?
14. What would you need to know before recommending the use of a life-income option? Explain.

CHAPTER

15 Health insurance

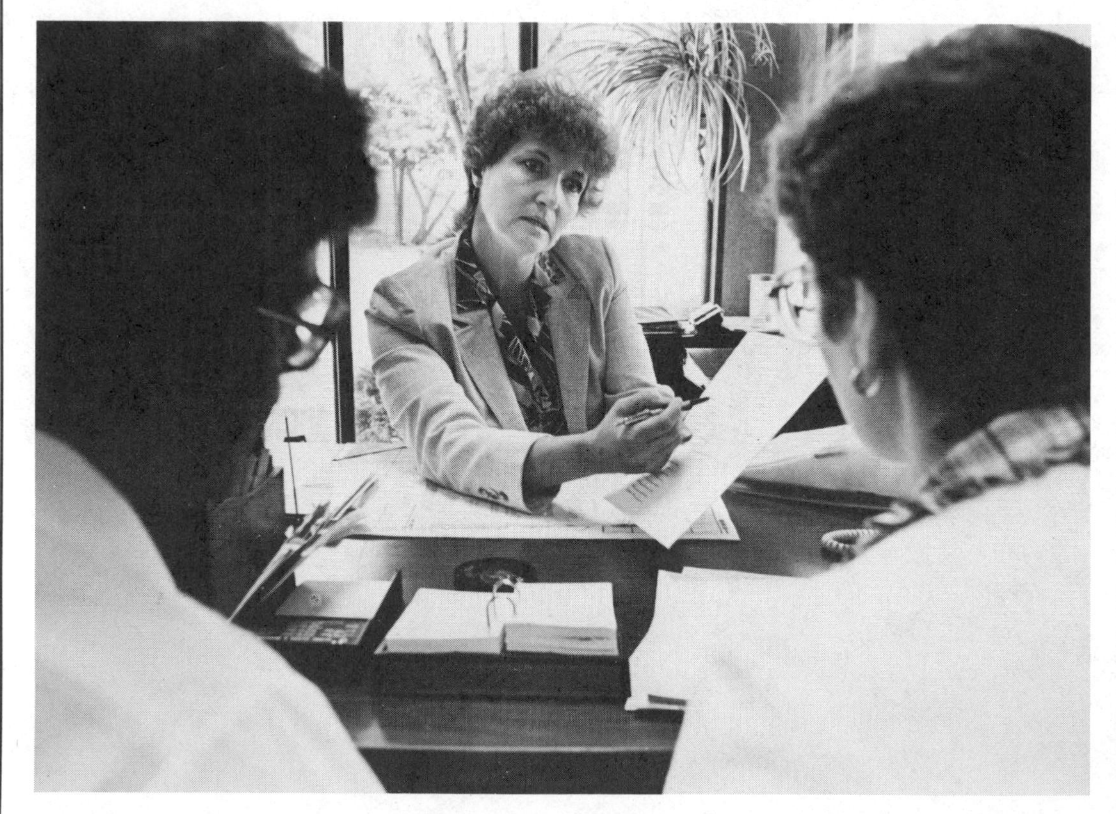

John Thoeming/Courtesy Wm. Golas Agency

CHAPTER OBJECTIVES

1. **To define the types of health insurance coverages written on the basis of perils covered and losses covered.**
2. **To classify health insurance policy according to the basis of loss payments, breadth-of-benefit provisions and underwriting standards.**
3. **To explain important terms used in health insurance contracts.**
4. **To present some guideposts for buying health insurance.**

Health insurance pays the cost of hospital and medical expenses and offsets income losses arising from accidental injury or sickness. Nearly 85 percent of all U.S. citizens are protected by private health insurance and about 35 percent of the premiums paid to life insurers is for health insurance. Yet the coverage generally is inadequate. Families able to assume the medical care and disability income risk are limited to the independently wealthy. Currently, resources for medical and hospital care and disability income are provided through public plans (Chapter 18), employee benefits plans (Chapter 16) and individual health insurance plans (discussed in this chapter).

The health insurance industry, direct consumers and employers that finance employee health benefit plans cannot ignore the increasing costs of medical care. Health care costs increased 53 percent from 1972 to 1977, decreased slightly in 1978, but resumed their upward spiral in 1979 and on into the 1980s. In 1978 an unsuccessful attempt was made to pass a federal mandatory cost containment bill. A voluntary effort by hospitals to reduce their costs has been in effect since 1977.

Many health insurers have instituted programs in an attempt to decrease health care expenditures. Examples include coverage for (1) health care facilities less expensive than hospitals (home care, nursing homes and convalescent homes); (2) care in out-patient wards, preadmission testing and well-baby preventive care and (3) discouragement of elective surgery and the encouragement of second opinions in other surgery cases. (In one study of cases where second opinions were requested nearly 18 percent of the patients were told the proposed operations were unnecessary.) Some insurers encourage use of out-patient surgical facilities to eliminate unnecessary hospital stays. Insurers are also giving increased attention to health education. An advertising campaign encourages people to accept more personal responsibility for good health, to follow better living habits and to think twice about incurring unnecessary medical expenses. Some insurers review and trim *excessive* health care charges by strict claims practices.

TYPES OF HEALTH INSURANCE COVERAGES

Health insurance coverages may be classified as to the nature of the peril, type of loss covered, basis of loss payments, breadth of benefit provisions and underwriting standards.

Nature of the Peril

Health insurance covers accident (loss by accidental bodily injury) and sickness (loss by disease). Sickness insurance may also provide benefits for expenses incurred by pregnancy, preventive and diagnostic medicine and mental illness. Accident insurance may be written separately or combined with sickness coverage. Sickness insurance is rarely sold separately except for medical care expenses covering "dread diseases," e.g., cancer.

Type of Losses Covered

Health policies classified as to losses covered are (1) disability income coverages, (2) coverage for loss of life, sight or limb and (3) medical expense coverages.

Disability income coverages

Accident and sickness policies are written to provide a stated weekly sum if the insured is disabled. Accident (and sometimes sickness) policies may be written to provide a smaller sum for partial disability, defined later. If the insured suffers specified types of fractures or dislocations many accident policies offer the option of a lump-sum settlement instead of weekly payments. Protection under disability income policies can be bought for either short-term or long-term benefit periods. The arbitrary dividing point between short- and long-term disability income protection is two years. Only one fifth of the disability income policies in force are long term. Income coverages are written on both an individual and a group basis.

Loss of life, sight or limb

Accident policies provide for a *capital sum* payment to the beneficiary if the insured dies accidentally. Most accident policies also provide payment for accidental loss of limb or sight. Accidental death and dismemberment benefits are not only the least expensive health coverage but are also the least important. As explained in Chapter 13 death benefits are best arranged using life insurance covering *both* natural and accidental deaths. Because disability income coverage protects against losses caused by a disabling dismemberment or loss of sight, separate coverage for loss of life, sight or limb appears unnecessary.

Expense coverages

Health expense coverage includes hospital, physician, surgical, nursing home and major medical expenses. Health insurance policies may range from the simple hospital expense policy providing a limited amount per day for hospital room and board to the major medical policy covering most costs of medical care. Expense coverage may be **scheduled** or **blanket.** If scheduled the maximum amounts paid for hospital room and board, miscellaneous hospital expenses and surgical procedures are listed separately as are the maximum amounts paid for nursing fees, physicians' fees and other expenses. If the coverage is blanket an aggregate maximum amount is specified for necessary and reasonable medical expenses with no specific limit for any one service.

Most health expense coverage is written independently of disability income protection. Hospital expense insurance is the most popular type of health coverage, followed by surgical expense, physicians' expense and major medical expense. The benefits paid under major medical coverage include expenses incurred for nearly all health care prescribed by a physician, subject to a deductible and a participation percentage discussed later. Expense coverages are written on an individual, family or group basis.

Basis of Loss Payments

Because health insurance need not be indemnity contracts, loss payments are not restricted to actual losses incurred. Health coverage is written on one of three bases: **valued forms, reimbursement forms** and **service forms.**

Valued forms Disability income is written to pay a specified amount per week (or month) for a designated benefit period. Specific benefit schedules are established for accidental death and dismemberment losses. Some hospital expense policies provide a flat amount per day for a maximum number of days while the insured is hospitalized. These specific benefit schedules or the flat amounts are paid regardless of incurred expenses.

Reimbursement forms More common in expense coverage is a maximum allowance, with the insurer paying the patient only the charges incurred up to the allowable limits. If the charges are more than the policy limits the insured bears the excess.

Service forms Under the *service incurred* plan payments are made directly to the hospital and doctors for services rendered and not to the patient. This payment arrangement is found in some Blue Cross (hospital) and Blue Shield (physicians and surgeons) plans as well as in some independent plans, health maintenance organization plans (HMOs) and in some insurer plans.

Breadth-of-Benefit Provisions

No health policy is free of limitations but some forms have more than others. A policy containing unusual exclusions, limitations, reductions or restrictive conditions is called a **limited policy.**

Limited health policies provide coverage only if the insured is injured in specific designated accidents or incurs specific illnesses. Some insurers pay only for accidental death. (One underwriter has characterized limited policies as paying benefits only if the insured is kicked to death by a goose in an Amtrak car.) As a sales technique newspapers have offered limited accident policies with subscriptions for a nominal charge. Coverage usually is limited to a small list of accidents with higher benefits for less frequent accidents and lower ones for the more common types. Those reading their junk mail will find circulars peddling these policies. Various types of travel accident policies are written ranging from those providing coverage for one trip by a named common carrier (the type often sold at airports) to the comprehensive travel policies marketed through associations and credit card companies.

Dread disease policies offer coverage on a blanket basis for medical expenses arising from such diseases as cancer, polio, encephalitis, spinal meningitis, tetanus, multiple sclerosis, elephantiasis and rabies. The broad coverage of major medical insurance has decreased the need for specific dread disease policies.

Most limited policies create misunderstanding. Often the large lump-sum benefits for rare accidents like those on a common carrier are emphasized in the sales pitch while the small benefits payable for more common accidents are mentioned casually if at all. Because the public is always looking for bargains many persons are motivated to buy limited policies instead of broader coverage. In recognition of the major coverage gaps in limited policies many states require these policies to include a warning overprinted on the policy face in large red letters, e.g., "THIS IS A LIMITED POLICY. READ ITS PROVISIONS CAREFULLY." This advice is good for *any* policy.

Limited accident forms available include those covering occupational accidents only, vacation accidents, accidents while participating in specified sports activity, injuries incurred while serving with a volunteer fire department, home accidents and school accidents.

Underwriting Standards

Not all prospective insureds meet the insurer's underwriting requirements for standard policies at standard rates. Policies for these persons are classified as **older age, substandard** (or **extra risk**) and **special risk.** In addition, a special policy is written for business overhead expense.

Older age policies

Older age policies are contracts issued beyond the normal insuring age of 60. A person age 65 eligible for medicare (discussed in Chapter 18) still needs private coverage. The various types of policies that can be purchased to supplement medicare are:

1. Comprehensive medicare supplement policies designed especially to provide coverage for the deductibles and the participation percentage included in medicare and to extend the days of hospital coverage beyond that provided by medicare.
2. Specified disease policies covering incurred expenses not otherwise excluded if a named disease is the cause of the expense.
3. Nursing home policies providing coverage for care in approved nursing facilities.

Many insurers write appropriate policies to fill gaps in medicare without creating overlaps. However, flagrant abuses in this type of coverage have been documented recently, causing legislative, regulatory and law enforcement agencies to focus attention on the issue. The uncovered abuses include the writing of policies with so many restrictions that the coverage is nearly worthless; the fraudulent misrepresentation resulting from private insurance agents posing as government employees; the employment of scare tactics to induce the elderly to buy and the accumulation by uninformed and fearful individuals of 20 or more overlapping and redundant policies.

Substandard policies

Substandard policies for physically impaired persons usually are written for those with an arrested serious illness, such as cancer or heart trouble. While most health policies do not cover preexisting conditions (the injury or illness must occur while the policy is in force), some substandard policies cover these conditions but for a benefit level lower than for other illnesses. Generally a higher premium is charged or a waiver of coverage for the particular medical condition(s) is required. These policies may cover both income and expense losses.

Special-risk policies

Special-risk policies cover hazards excluded in usual health policies, such as war, accidents to those involved in dangerous scientific experiments, travel to the moon and most other hazards within the realm of imagination. Many persons with incomes dependent on some special talent or personal characteristic buy high-benefit limit special-risk forms to cover their exposure. Lloyd's of London (see Chapter 19) provides underwriting facilities for many of these exposures.

Business overhead expense policies

Business overhead health insurance is a special form of disability income coverage written for a business or professional person to provide resources to pay such business expenses as rent, taxes, utilities, clerical salaries and insurance premiums that continue while the insured is disabled. The insurer reimburses the insured only for expenses incurred. Premiums paid are tax deductible and the proceeds are reportable as income. Normally premiums paid by an individual for disability income insurance are not deductible and the policy proceeds are not reportable as taxable income.

THE HEALTH INSURANCE CONTRACT

Health insurance policies are subject to the Uniform Individual Accident and Sickness Policy Provisions Act, a model law drafted by the National Association of Insurance Commissioners and passed by all but one state (Louisiana). This act contains 12 mandatory provisions that must be included in individual health insurance policies and 11 optional provisions. The 12 mandatory provisions include some familiar conditions found in other policies discussed in this text. They deal with entire contract clauses, grace periods, time limits for defenses, notice of claims, claim forms, proof of loss, reinstatement, time of payment of claims, claims payment, physical examination and autopsy, legal actions and change of beneficiary. These provisions are found in the specimen policies reproduced in Appendix 6.[1]

The 11 optional provisions include conditions relating to change of occupation, misstatement of age, other insurance with the same insurer, income insurance with other insurers, expense insurance with other insurers, relations of earnings to insurance, unpaid premiums, cancellation, conformity with state statute, illegal occupation and intoxicants and narcotics. (The most commonly used optional provisions are occupation change, age misstatement and statute conformity.) The law also specifies such additional provisions as the specific expression of the policy's consideration, the policy's effective and termination dates, the effect of false statements in the application (they may deny payment only if material to the risk and the application is a part of the policy) and the use of at least 10-point type size with no undue prominence given to any portion of the text.[2]

The uniform provisions must be followed "in substance" only, so any wording may be used if the policyowner is given the required protection. Many insurers use provisions more favorable to policyowners than the law demands.

Health insurers offer a wide variety of coverages that may be analyzed according to the procedure discussed in Chapters 6 and 7. A useful exercise for the reader at this point is to refer to the two specimen policies in Appendix 6 and analyze them according to this procedure. Please make the effort!

GUIDEPOSTS FOR BUYING HEALTH INSURANCE

A set of guideposts is useful in helping buyers make intelligent decisions in choosing among the various policies that flood the market. In the remainder of this chapter these guideposts are discussed while at the same time providing additional information about health insurance policy provisions and their interpretation.

Points to Consider When Comparing Health Insurance Policies

When comparing health insurance policies the buyer should consider (1) the insurer, (2) accident definition, (3) exclusions, (4) dimensions of disability income coverage, (5) dismemberment provisions, (6) waiver of premium, (7) renewal and cancellation, (8) change of occupation, (9) medical expense provisions and (10) cost.

The insurer

Health insurance is frequently sold by mail. Although many legitimate insurers sell by mail (called direct response selling) fly-by-night insurers thrive on mailorder business. An important rule is to buy only from home state licensed insurers.

[1] Two specimen health insurance policies are reproduced: one, a major medical policy and the other, a disability income policy.

[2] Ten-point type is one point larger than the type used in the body of this book.

Problems that can arise in transacting business with unlicensed insurers are discussed in Chapter 23. Health insurance shoppers should not overlook plans like Blue Cross, Blue Shield and health maintenance organizations (Chapter 19).

Definition of accident

Strictly worded accident policies promise payments only if the injury is caused by *accidental means.* Liberally worded policies provide payments for losses due to *accidental bodily injury.* This distinction is so widely misunderstood that courts frequently ignore it. An accidental-means clause supposedly requires the injury to result from *causes* that were accidental. Thus if the insured ruptures a blood vessel while carrying heavy textbooks (weight, not subject matter) an accidental-means policy would not cover the injury because its cause was not accidental. The cause was carrying books and that was intentional. If the insured drops the books on a foot, breaking a toe, the injury is covered by an accidental-means clause. The insured did not intend to break a toe. Carrying the books is intended; dropping them is the accidental means causing the injury. Suicide while insane has been construed to be death by accidental means.[3] For this reason most accidental policies providing death benefits exclude suicide.

Under a policy covering accidental bodily injury, payment is made if the injury was unexpected and unintended, even though the act causing the injury was not unusual, unexpected or unforeseen. Thus if the policy has an accidental-bodily-injury clause the insurer would pay any covered losses resulting from the ruptured blood vessel. For accidental bodily injury only the result, not the cause, must be unanticipated by the insured. Competition among insurers has resulted in less frequent use of accidental-means policies. However, some limited policies and life insurance double indemnity riders include accidental-means insuring agreements.

Most accident policies contain the wording "directly and independently of all other causes." This clause is designed to allow insurers to avoid claims under accident policies for a loss due to a preexisting health condition combined with a minor or imagined accident. If a student has a fainting spell, falls down the stairs and suffers a back injury, the injury has not been incurred directly and independently of all other causes and the accident insurer presumably would not be liable.

Exclusions

The fewer the exclusions the better the policy. Intentional self-inflicted injuries and war-connected disabilities are usually excluded. More restrictive policies exclude coverage while the insured is outside the United States and Canada. Some exclude disability resulting from law violations (except traffic violations).

The dimensions of disability coverage

Coverage for total and partial disability involves four dimensions: the definition of disability governing payments, the amount of the periodic payments, the maximum duration of payments and the length of the waiting period.

Definition of disability. Total disability is not uniformly defined but its definition is important in any policy covering loss of income benefits. One insurer defines total disability liberally to mean the complete inability of the insured to perform the duties of his or her regular occupation for 60 months. Then for

[3] Under Missouri law any suicide is assumed to have occurred in a moment of temporary or permanent insanity; thus in Missouri any suicidal death is deemed to be caused by accidental means. Some deep thinkers from the show-me state conclude that the law is based on the theory that those fortunate enough to live in Missouri would be crazy to kill themselves. (They use the doctrine of intuitionism in reaching this conclusion.)

the remainder of the covered disability period, total disability means the insured's complete inability to perform the duties of any occupation for which he or she is reasonably qualified by training and experience. Some insurers in defining total disability add "and does not engage in any occupation for wages or profit" after the words "regular occupation." This addition excludes benefit payments to insureds who accept positions when unable to perform their regular occupation (e.g., mentally ill professors who become deans).

Some policies contain more restricted definitions of total disability. A policy might require the insured to be under a physician's regular care. This provision has been ignored to some degree by court decisions holding that if competent medical testimony shows the disabling condition cannot be treated or improved by regular medical care the requirement is meaningless. Other policies require the insured to be house confined (continuously within doors) to be eligible for benefits beyond one or two years. Absence for brief periods to consult physicians does not violate the house confinement restriction. Policies requiring house confinement are rare and should be avoided. Patients should be allowed to follow a physician's recommendation of an ocean cruise or a visit to a health resort without losing their disability income. (Other terms like *hospital, loss of body member (leg or arm), convalescent home* and *benefit period* are defined in the policy to clarify the insurer's intentions.)

Partial disability coverage may be written as a policy provision or a separate rider. The definition of partial disability varies among policies and depends on the definition of total disability. A policy with a house-confinement total disability definition usually offers a fractional benefit (commonly one half) for a nonconfining disability. When total disability is defined as the inability to perform any occupation, the partial disability definition is usually the ability to perform some but not all the duties of any occupation. If the definition is the inability to perform the duties of one's own occupation, the partial disability definition is the inability to perform one or more of the major duties of one's own occupation.

Partial disability benefits are usually restricted to periods following total disability. Many insurers write partial disability benefits *for accidents* without requiring a period of total disability. Partial disability benefits were first written to allow insurers to shorten periods of total disability. In theory if partial disability benefits are offered, the insured may in time qualify for the lower partial disability benefits as recovery progresses rather than continue to receive the higher total disability benefits, thus reducing the cost of disability income coverage.

As a substitute for the original purpose of partial disability income, an increasing number of insurers include **residual disability benefits** in policies with a regular occupation disability definition. Residual disability coverage permits disabled insureds to work in *any* occupation if they are unable to earn as much as 75 or 80 percent of the amount earned immediately prior to becoming disabled. Both the insured and the insurer can gain from residual disability payments. Assume Bonnie owns a disability income policy paying $2,400 a month. She becomes disabled. After three months she takes a job paying $1,600 monthly. Prior to becoming disabled she earned $3,000. Her policy provides for a residual benefit. That benefit would be $3,000 *minus* $1,600 *divided by* $3,000 *multiplied by* $2,400 or $1,120. Thus she collects only $1,120 instead of $2,400 from her insurer. But this amount plus her earnings equal $2,720 so she earns $320 more by working. Her insurer saves $1,280, i.e., $2,400 less $1,120. The formula for computing the residual disability benefit is: monthly earnings prior to retirement *less* current monthly earnings *divided* by monthly earnings prior to retirement *multiplied* by original monthly disability income. Just plug in the figures as shown in the illustrative example.

The amount of periodic payments. The policy may provide for weekly or monthly payments of specified amounts for total (or partial) disability. Partial disability payments, are smaller—about 40 percent of total disability. Insurers usually limit the amount of disability income payable by writing only one half or two thirds of the insured's predisability income. A more desirable policy is one where disability income payments are flexible to offer some protection against inflation.

The maximum duration of payments. The maximum payment duration varies according to the cause and nature of the disability. The policy might provide lifetime payments for accident but only two years for sickness, five years for accident and one year for sickness or the same limits for both accident and sickness. A sickness policy might provide benefits up to one year if the insured is not confined to the house and lifetime benefits for a confining sickness. The maximum benefit period is usually less for partial than for total disability.

The ideal is a benefit period extending to age 65 or 70 for accident and sickness. Disability income benefits can then be integrated with a retirement income insurance policy protected by a waiver-of-premium rider (discussed in Chapter 13).

The length of the waiting period. Accident insurance may be written with no waiting (elimination) period but one is usually required in sickness insurance. The elimination period is generally defined as the number of days of continuous total disability (7, 14, 30, 60 and 90 days are common) when no benefits are paid. The premium decreases substantially with an increase in the elimination period. For example, the annual premiums quoted by one insurer for a $100 monthly disability income policy with benefits payable five years for sickness and lifetime for accidents are $39.50 if accident payments begin immediately and sickness payments begin after a 7-day waiting period; $34.60 (a decrease of 14.2 percent) if a 14-day elimination period is used for both; $29.60 (an additional saving of 16.9 percent) if the waiting period is 30 days and $24.80 (a further saving of 19.4 percent) for a dual elimination period of 60 days.

A waiting period as long as the insured can afford to be without earned income should be selected, subject to the consideration that premium reductions for waiting periods beyond 180 days are minor.

Provisions for dismemberment, specified fractures and dislocations

As noted, some disability income policies provide that in the event of dismemberment or other specified losses the insurer pays a lump-sum benefit instead of periodic income payments. In other policies the insured may elect either a lump-sum or periodic disability income payments. Lump-sum benefits usually are limited to the amount of disability income payable for four years. Thus the insured may make an unfortunate choice. More liberal policies make lump-sum benefits the minimum to be paid. In even more liberal policies some dismemberments are considered permanent disability. In these cases the periodic disability income payment is continued for the maximum income period. In choosing a policy the most liberal provision should be selected. The cost differentials are insignificant.

Waiver of premium

Waiver of premium in life insurance is discussed in Chapter 13. When buying *disability income* insurance the policyowner should consider a policy with a waiver-of-premium provision. The waiver of premium provides that after a period of total disability of a stated duration, usually 90 days, premiums will be waived. In some policies the insurer agrees to refund premiums paid during the waiting period. Waiver of premium is usually automatically included in noncancellable and guaranteed renewable policies (discussed next). Some insurers include this benefit in conditionally and optionally renewable policies. Retroactive waiver of premium for as long as the insured is disabled (plus three months) is the most attractive form. It gives the insured full protection against loss of disability income coverage due to the inability to pay premiums while disabled. Waiver of premium is rarely found in *medical expense coverage.*

Provisions regarding renewal and cancellation

Health insurance contracts may contain one of a variety of clauses specifying the insured's rights to retain the policy in force. The most favorable (and most expensive) is the noncancellable policy under which the insurer agrees to continue the policy in force with no change in premium until the insured reaches a specified age (typically 65). The least favorable (and least expensive) is the cancellable policy under which the insurer may terminate the insurance by giving written notice to the insured. The insured may also cancel the policy. In between these extremes, moving from the most desirable for the insured to the least desirable, are the guaranteed renewable, conditionally renewable, optionally renewable and term. The term policy has no provision for cancellation. A travel-accident policy purchased at the airport provides an example of a term policy. Figure 15–1 shows the respective rights of the insured and the insurer under the four *continuation* provisions. The figure does not include cancellable or term policies because they have no continuation provisions.

Change of occupation

Health insurance premiums vary not only with the insured's age and physical condition but also occupation. For one insurer using four occupational rating

FIGURE 15–1 An Analysis of Continuation Provisions in Health Insurance Policies

CONTINUATION PROVISION	*INSURED'S RIGHTS CONCERNING RENEWAL AND PREMIUMS*	*INSURER'S RIGHTS CONCERNING RENEWAL AND PREMIUMS*
Noncancellable	The insured is guaranteed that the policy will be renewed up to an age specified in the policy at premium rates guaranteed in the policy.	The insurer may cancel the policy only for nonpayment of premiums.
Guaranteed renewable	The insured is guaranteed renewal up to an age specified in the policy. Premium rates are not guaranteed.	The insurer may increase premiums but only for the entire class of insureds, not for an individual insured.
Conditionally renewable	The insured is guaranteed that renewal will not be denied solely on the basis of deterioration in health.	Although the insurer reserves the right to renew and adjust premiums it may deny renewal only if it declines to renew all policies of the same class.
Optionally renewable	The insured has no rights concerning renewal or premium levels.	The insurer may deny renewal, increase premiums for all or any of the classes of insureds and add restrictive policy conditions.

classes, class 1 includes salespersons and lawyers and class 3X includes laborers doing heavy manual work and motorcycle police. The age 30 rate per $100 a month for a benefit period up to five years with a 60-day elimination period is 42 percent lower for a class 1 worker than for a class 3X worker. Most health insurers specify that benefits will decrease if the insured changes to a more hazardous occupation. Thus a 30-year old salesperson who buys this policy and then becomes a motorcycle cop would, if injured, collect only 58 percent of the original stated income. More liberal policies contain no such decrease-in-benefits provision.

Medical expense provisions

Because protection against potential large losses should be bought before smaller losses are covered, major medical insurance should have priority over basic hospital, surgical and medical coverage. The most important considerations in purchasing major medical insurance are the maximum limit, the deductible and the participation percentage. The insured should determine if the maximum applies to each illness or accident, to a policy or a benefit year or to a lifetime. The aggregate lifetime maximum is the least liberal.

The amount of the deductible should be low enough to be absorbed in any one year but high enough to offer sufficient premium savings to offset the cost of increased maximum limits. A family deductible under which a yearly amount is applied and spread over all family medical expenses appears logical even though an extended illness results in the application of the deductible each year.

Under participation provisions found in major medical coverage the insured will be required to pay 20 to 25 percent of the covered charges in excess of the deductible. In addition, if the covered bills after the deductible exceed a specified amount, $10,000 for example, no participation is required on this excess amount. This liberalization of the participation feature enables many insureds to afford rapidly rising medical costs during severe illnesses. For example, an insured owns a $50,000 major medical policy with a $500 deductible and a 25 percent participation clause. The policy limits the application of the participation clause to $10,000 of the covered expenses in excess of the deductible. If the insured incurs $14,500 of covered medical expenses he or she would bear only $3,000 of this amount; $500 because of the deductible and the other $2,500 because the 25 percent participation applies only to $10,000 (25 percent of $10,000 = $2,500).

Cost

Wide variations are found among premiums for similar coverages. Therefore the wise person seeking health insurance (and other types of insurance also) realizes the importance of shopping around among reputable insurers to obtain a favorable combination of premiums and benefits. However, as both policy provisions and premiums differ greatly the comparative health insurance shopper must consider the guideposts just presented in evaluating the price of the insurance. A low premium for low-quality coverage may, in fact, be more costly than a higher premium for better coverage. Budget restrictions, however, may force the buyer to settle for less than the best coverage. Nevertheless, buyers will find bargains among policies of all quality.

Several buyers' guides to the purchase of health insurance have been published, with price the major concern. The Pennsylvania Insurance Department, a pioneer in the field of attending to consumer interests, has published one. It may be purchased from the department at a nominal cost. The guide must be studied closely where the reported comparisons do not reflect products of similar quality. Prices and quality change too, so the buyer needs to be sure the information is current, updating it where necessary.

Use of the Guideposts

These 10 guideposts to the purchase of health insurance appear logical and in some cases simple. Their apparent simplicity can be deceiving. The many variables make it difficult for the health insurance buyer to be completely certain the "best" decision has been made. The peace-of-mind solution to this problem is for the buyer to seek a "sensible" or "good" solution after considering needs, ability to pay, available products and prices, and not worry whether the best selection has been made. Who really knows what is the best selection? The best decision is one logically made, based on the facts at hand and the state of the decision maker's knowledge. A good agent may be of help if he or she knows the market and can answer questions satisfactorily based on these guideposts. The major purpose of the guideposts is to arm the buyer with questions to ask before making important decisions about health insurance purchases.

More is said on health insurance in the following chapter where group health insurance is discussed. Group is the dominant form of health coverage.

SUMMARY

1. An important issue faced by the health care industry is the spiraling cost of medical care. Efforts to control these costs are underway by the insured, industry, government, consumer of health care services and the employers who pay much of the bill..

2. Health insurance coverages may be classified as to the:

- *a.* Nature of the peril (accident and sickness).
- *b.* Type of losses covered (disability income, loss of life, sight or limb and medical expense).
- *c.* Basis of loss payments (valued forms, reimbursement forms and service forms).
- *d.* Breadth of benefit provisions, (limited policies).
- *e.* Underwriting standards (older age, substandard, special risk policies and business overhead expense policies).

3. Health insurance policies are subject to a Uniform Provisions Act. This act contains 12 mandatory provisions and 11 optional provisions for individual health insurance contracts. Furthermore, they include several other operational provisions.

4. A set of 10 useful guideposts are available to help buyers make intelligent decisions in choosing among the various policies that flood the market.

5. Points to consider when comparing health insurance policies are:

- *a.* The insurer.
- *b.* Accident definition.
- *c.* Exclusions.
- *d.* Dimensions of disability income coverage.
- *e.* Dismemberment provisions.
- *f.* Waiver of premium.

g. Renewal and cancellation.
h. Change of occupation.
i. Medical expense provisions.
j. Costs.

6. These guideposts are designed for judicious use by considering policy variations along with costs and needs.

REVIEW QUESTIONS

1. Did you analyze the two specimen health insurance policies reproduced in Appendix 6 using the procedures developed in Chapters 6 and 7? Why not?

2. Analyze one of the two specimen health insurance policies reproduced in Appendix 6 using the procedures developed in Chapters 6 and 7.

3. Explain why you agree or disagree with the following statements:

a. "Separate health insurance coverage for loss of sight or limb appears unnecessary."
b. "Death benefits are best arranged using life insurance rather than health insurance."

4. Distinguish between "accidental means" and "accidental injury." Does this question border on being an exercise in futility?

5. Explain how residual disability benefits in disability income policies may be viewed as a substitute for partial disability income benefits.

6. What factors should the insured consider in deciding the length of a waiting period when buying a disability income policy?

7. With respect to continuation provisions, which type offers the best protection? Which type offers the least protection? Should the policyowner buy a policy which includes the provision offering the best protection?

8. Identify the flagrant abuses found in the development and marketing of older age policies.

9. Explain how the business overhead expense policies differ from regular health insurance expense policies.

10. What factors should the buyer of a major medical insurance policy consider in choosing a deductible amount?

11. If a policyowner gets a second opinion about the need for surgery and that opinion differs from the first opinion, which one should influence the decision? Explain.

12. How does a change in occupation affect health insurance coverage? Explain.

PART SIX EMPLOYEE BENEFIT PLANS: PUBLIC AND PRIVATE

The type of coverage provided by property, liability, life and health insurers to meet the loss exposures of families and businesses is the core of Parts Four and Five. Emphasis is on private insurance which also plays a significant role in employee benefit plans.

Because a large part of the cost of employee benefit plans is subsidized by the federal government through favorable tax treatment, these plans can be classified as quasi-public. The stringent federal regulation governing these plans adds support to this classification.

The federal and state governments' influence in employee benefit plans is not solely indirect. They are involved directly in providing plans of their own for the labor force.

Part Six includes three chapters. Two chapters consider quasi-public plans: one deals primarily with group life and health insurance and the other with retirement plans. The third chapter is concerned with social (direct public) insurance plans. The primary thrust is on old age, survivors, disability and health insurance (OASDHI), popularly known as social security. Attention is also given to unemployment compensation, temporary disability income plans and proposed national health insurance plans, still a current issue even though it has been hotly debated for years.

Part Six is both technical and philosophical and probably requires more intense study than other parts of this book. Furthermore, it deals with more fluid subject matter. Proposed legislation that could drastically affect the important areas of income maintenance and health care is in the hopper or waiting in the bullpen. Therefore a basic knowledge of private employee benefit plans and social security is essential to the understanding of the issues that are likely to develop. Hopefully these three chapters provide that knowledge.

CHAPTER

16 Employee benefit plans: Group life, group health and other group insurance plans

H. Armstrong Roberts

CHAPTER OBJECTIVES

1. **To point out the features that distinguish group life and group health from individual life and individual health insurance.**
2. **To differentiate between group term, level premium group permanent, the unit purchase plan, group ordinary, survivor income benefit insurance, group credit and wholesale life insurance.**
3. **To describe the issues that must be resolved in establishing group life and group health insurance programs.**
4. **To outline the federal income tax treatment of premiums paid and benefits received under contributory and noncontributory group life insurance, group health insurance and qualified pension plans.**
5. **To identify and explain the issues involved in flexible compensation, group property and liability insurance and prepaid legal plans.**

Employee benefit plans may be defined as employer-sponsored plans that provide

> (1) income maintenance during periods when regular earnings are cut off because of death, accident, sickness, retirement, or unemployment and (2) benefits to meet expenses associated with illness or injury.[1]

Group insurance programs play important roles in these plans.

Employee benefit plans have been growing at a rapid rate. During the 10-year period ending January 1, 1980, employee benefit coverage for survivors, medical care, disability income, retirement income and severance pay increased from about 30 cents to 39 cents of the payroll dollar. Employee benefit plans are growing in breadth and depth. Medical care plans have expanded to include dental and eye (vision) care and prescription drugs. Also expanding are long-term disability income benefits, retirement benefits for widows or widowers of employees who die before retirement age and the continuation of earned retirement credits for disabled employees during periods of disability. Now in the early stages of development are benefits like prepaid legal aid, financial counseling and instruction programs in transcendental meditation (TM). In addition, traditional benefits are expanding for hospital care and short-term disability income.

Changes in legislation have imposed new and specific criteria and standards on employee benefit plans. The legal and tax environment is expected to undergo additional modifications to reflect changes in life styles.

This chapter concentrates primarily on group life and health insurance, group property and liability insurance and prepaid legal care.

---

[1] *Social Security Bulletin,* U.S. Department of Health and Human Services, Social Security Administration, monthly. (The employee benefits article usually is published in the April issue.) A broader definition of employee benefit plans would include paid vacations, company recreational facilities, prepaid legal services, day care centers, school tuition, and any other nonwage benefit provided by an employer.

REASONS FOR USING EMPLOYEE BENEFIT PLANS

Three reasons for private employee benefit plans are to improve employee relations, meet union demands and provide insurance benefits at low cost. Today employee benefit plans are so common that the lack of one adversely affects employee relations.

Since 1948, when the National Labor Relations Board ruled insurance and pensions subject to collective bargaining, employee benefits have been the subject of union demands and a major reason why employers have such plans. Some plans are developed because executives seek insurance at premiums lower than those charged for individual insurance. Group insurance is often written without evidence of insurability making it especially attractive to uninsurable executives. Favorable tax treatment of employer-financed employee life, health and retirement plans is another incentive for creating employee benefit plans. These tax advantages are discussed later.

GROUP INSURANCE

In group insurance the underwriting unit is the group and not the individual. Selection and rating are based on the group as a whole and the policy is issued to the group. The members are neither contracting parties nor policyowners; they are issued participation certificates and booklets describing the master policy issued to the employer.

Group insurance has experienced phenomenal growth in the United States, whether measured by face amounts of insurance in force or premium volume. For the decade ending in 1981 group life insurance in force doubled and now accounts for more than half the life insurance owned. During the same decade group health insurance premiums have quadrupled. In 1981, 80 percent of all health insurance premiums paid were for group insurance. The combined premium volume for individual annuities and group annuities increased more than five times over their 1970 levels. However, unlike group life and health, group annuities are not growing faster than individual annuities (see Table 16–1). Individual annuities increased 5.8 times while group annuities increased 5.3 times. Nevertheless, group annuities like group life and health insurance dominate the annuity business (73 percent of 1980 annuity considerations).

Distinguishing Features of Group Insurance

Several features distinguish group insurance from individual insurance.

Payment of cost

Group members do not share the full cost of insurance. Employers are generally required by statutes or insurer underwriting rules to assume part of the premium. Without employer contributions premiums charged each employee would in-

TABLE 16–1 Relative Growth of Annuity Considerations 1960–1980 ($ millions)

YEAR	*TOTAL*	*INDIVIDUAL*	*PERCENT OF TOTAL*	*GROUP*	*PERCENT OF TOTAL*
1980	$24,030	$6,504	27.1	$17,526	72.9
1970	3,721	960	25.8	2,761	74.2
1960	1,341	253	18.9	1,088	81.1

Source: *Life Insurance Fact Book* (Washington, D.C.: American Council of Life Insurance, 1981).

crease with age and become prohibitive. Charging employees an average group rate would not succeed as younger employees would have to pay more for insurance than if they bought insurance individually. When the employee bears part of the life insurance cost, contributions usually range from 30 to 60 cents monthly per $1,000 of insurance. Even so, male employees under age 35 (females under age 40) find the 30-cent rate no bargain because they can buy individually issued term insurance for less. For a 60-cent monthly contribution rate the male participant would have to be about 45 years old (female, 50) for the group coverage to be a bargain. However, to assure eligibility for group coverage at bargain rates at later ages when the coverage becomes attractive, employees are advised to participate early in the group plan.

Because health insurance premiums do not increase sharply with age, average rates can be charged without creating serious inequities between age groups. Savings in advertising and administrative expenses usually permit group premiums to be below individual premiums. Nevertheless, in most health plans employers do pay at least a part of the premiums. The trend is for employers to pay a large part of the employee's cost and to assist with dependents' coverage.

Selection of benefit levels

Employees do not choose their benefit levels. Group members receive amounts determined by benefit formulas to eliminate adverse selection that could occur if those in poor health are allowed disproportionately large amounts of insurance. Because large groups are partly self-rated[2] (the degree of self-rating depends on the group size) adverse selection could result in higher costs for the group.

Cost of insurance

Group insurance is less expensive than individual insurance. Group insurance is low-cost insurance for several reasons: (1) group insurance is written without individual underwriting, eliminating some expense; (2) commission rates are lower and decrease with premium size; (3) employers administer much of the program and (4) an income tax advantage reduces the cost of group term life insurance. Employers normally can deduct premiums they pay for employee group term life insurance.[3] Employees normally are not required to report as income the premiums paid by the employer for coverage of $50,000 or less. If the coverage exceeds that amount the employee must report as income the cost for amounts in excess of $50,000 *less* any premiums the employee pays.[4] (Disabled and retired employees are excluded from the over-$50,000 tax rule. Also excluded are policies where qualified charities are named as beneficiaries.) Premiums paid by employers for employee health plans also are deductible as a business expense. Employees are not required to report them as income.

---

[2] The experience of the group will affect the ultimate amount charged the group.

[3] Employers cannot deduct the premiums for group term life insurance covering employees whose compensation is considered excessive.

[4] The cost is determined by the Table of Uniform Premiums for $1,000 of Group Term Life Insurance Protection prescribed by the U.S. Internal Revenue Service [Reg. § 1.79–3(d)2]. The table brackets premiums into five-year bands except for (1) a broad under-age 30 class and (2) the use of the 60–64 age class for active employees 65 and over. These premiums when first developed were considered low and a break for taxpayers. Now, in many cases, they are higher than those paid by the employer for the employee. But the taxable income to employees is based on the protection received, not the premium paid. The high taxable premiums for the excess amount discourage the use of group term to provide more than $50,000 of coverage and encourage the use of employer-paid (and deductible) low-premium individual term insurance. The amount taxable to employees is then based on premiums paid rather than protection received probably resulting in a lower tax to employees.

Group Insurance Principles

Several principles apply in underwriting group insurance because (1) state statutes require them and/or (2) insurers consider them consistent with good underwriting standards. A number of insurers are willing to apply relaxed standards designed to improve their market positions. The principles are operationally important. To run a group insurance plan efficiently several plan design features must be considered.

Common purpose The group insured must have some common purpose other than obtaining insurance. Groups organized solely for insurance probably will include large numbers in poor health, engaged in hazardous occupations or with other undesirable insurance characteristics that increase cost and encourage members with desirable insurance characteristics to withdraw from the group. As a result the cost for remaining members becomes prohibitive.

Size of group The group should be large enough to reduce adverse selection and achieve savings in administrative costs. The larger the group the less likely is it to be formed for the purpose of obtaining coverage for otherwise uninsurable individuals. The minimum number of persons needed for a group has decreased over the years, indicating that less attention is given to this principle. The desire to expand group business has led insurers to seek other ways of handling the adverse effects of small groups.

Participation rates Mandatory participation rates depend on the type of plan used. Participation of all eligible employees is required for noncontributory plans (i.e., when employers pay the cost). For contributory plans (i.e., where employees pay part of the cost) 75 percent participation is usually required. These mandatory participation rates are designed to control adverse selection.

Apportioning insurance Disproportionate insurance amounts should not be allocated to a few members. Disproportionate amounts of insurance on participants interfere with group underwriting. Participants' insurance amounts should be related to amounts written for a typical employee, the size of the group and the amount written for the group. Application of this principle not only helps to control adverse selection but also is consistent with the application of the law of large numbers.

Practical application of group insurance principles. The extent to which an insurer is willing to compromise the foregoing principles poses an important question. Group insurers insist they can prevent adverse selection without requiring large groups or restricting insurance amounts by insisting on evidence of insurability from employees scheduled for large amounts of coverage. In some cases individual group members are screened before the group is accepted.

FIGURE 16–1 Differences between Group and Individual Insurance

GROUP	*INDIVIDUAL*
1. The underwriting unit is the group; selection and rating are based on the group.	1. The underwriting unit is the individual; selection and rating are based on the individual.
2. Members are not contracting parties; the policy is issued to the group and group members are given certificates of coverage. The plan design is outlined in a booklet distributed to participants.	2. Individuals are contracting parties; the policy is issued to the individuals.

Group underwriters generally are interested in whether the group can be covered—not in the individual plan's participants. They emphasize a sound group plan rather than accepting or rejecting the group. Group insurance assumes that once the group is selected individuals need not be selected. For life insurance the ideal group is *fluid,* with younger persons entering as older ones depart; otherwise the cost will become prohibitive. Figure 16–1 shows the two basic differences between group and individual insurance.

GROUP LIFE INSURANCE

A variety of group life insurance forms are available all subject to state regulation. Included is a set of mandatory policy provisions.

State Regulation

The NAIC developed the first standard definition of group life insurance and the first standard policy provisions. Soon afterward, New York and several other states established group life insurance laws. The original definition and standard provisions form the basis for group life insurance statutes.

Eligible groups

The NAIC model group life definition limits the groups eligible for life insurance. Eligible groups are employees of single employers, multiple-employer groups, labor union groups and debtors of a common creditor. Other groups may be eligible, e.g., associations, state police, army and national guard reserves, veterans, credit unions and certain cooperatives.

Group specifications

The NAIC definition specifies the minimum number of lives required for coverage, percentage rates for participating in the plan and eligible employee classifications. The definition requires the following minimums: 10 covered members for single employer and labor union groups, 25 members for multiemployer groups and at least 100 new entrants a year for creditors' groups. However, many states have no minimum number of members for single-employer groups. If the plan is noncontributory the NAIC definition requires all eligible members to be covered. If contributory, 75 percent must participate. The definition classifies employees eligible for coverage by employee groups. Corporation directors, partners and proprietors are eligible *if they are bona fide employees.*

Sharing of cost

The NAIC definition requires employers to share group insurance costs. If *employees* were required to pay the full premium, the cost of the plan for young employees would not be competitive with individual insurance. Young employees, therefore, would not join the plan. Without young employees the cost of the plan would also be unattractive to middle-aged employees so they would not join, causing a further price increase. Eventually the plan would self-destruct because the price to those remaining would probably be unaffordable. A self-destructive employee benefit plan (one that is not attractive to all age groups) would not benefit anyone. Thus compulsory employer contributions are required to make group life insurance workable.

Benefit levels

The NAIC definition prohibits employees from selecting their own benefit levels. Employees are prohibited from selecting their own benefit levels to prevent adverse selection against the group. Employers and their insurers do not want those in poor health selecting disproportionately high amounts of insurance causing the cost of insurance for the group to soar. One exception to this rule is found in cafeteria-type plans (discussed later) where employees have some limited choice in how they want their employee benefits packaged. The benefit plan needs of all employees are not alike. To the extent that employees have a choice beyond the basic package to elect additional benefits of one type or another some adverse selection can occur unless it is controlled. To accommodate cafeteria-type plans the NAIC has eliminated from its model bill the provision that prohibits employees from selecting their own benefit levels.[5]

Limits on insurance provided

The NAIC definition limits the amount of insurance that employees can be provided. The NAIC maximum limit on one life is the larger of $20,000 or 150 percent of compensation with a maximum of $40,000. This limit, known as the $20,000/$40,000, is virtually extinct. Only three states limit the amount of group life insurance that can be written on one life and these limits vary up to $100,000. Thus with 47 states without limits the insurance agent associations have lost their fight to protect their market for individual policies from group insurance. Life insurers impose their own limits. The maximum usually depends on the group's size and the average amount of insurance per member. Limits below $50,000 are rare and amounts of $100,000 or more are not uncommon. *Minimum* limits of $1,000 are predominant.

Standard Provisions for Group Life Policies

Many group life insurance policy provisions are similar to those in individual policies; others deal with the same subject matter differently while some provisions treat new subjects peculiar to group insurance. Among the standard provisions, some are required and others are optional.

Mandatory policy provisions

The model group law requires the following provisions in the master contract:

1. A grace period for late premium payments.
2. Incontestability of the validity of the master policy after it has been in force for two years from its date of issue; incontestability of the validity of the group participants' coverage (based on statements made relating to their insurability) after their coverage has been in force for two years during their lifetime. (The modifying phrase "during their lifetime" is designed to eliminate the possible advantage of a delayed filing of a death claim until after the expiration of two years even though the insured died within the two-year contestable period.)
3. The application, if any, shall be attached to the policy.
4. The participants' statements shall be representations.
5. The conditions for requiring evidence of insurability. Customarily evidence of insurability is required if the employee does not join the plan within a designated period (often 31 days) after becoming eligible.
6. A clause explaining how a misstatement of age will be handled. Participants in group life usually pay the same premium per $1,000 of coverage. Normally premiums rather than benefits are adjusted if age is misstated. Benefits are adjusted only if age is a factor in the benefit formula.
7. A facility-of-payment clause indicating that if there is no living named benefi-

[5] New York has modified its law to exclude this prohibition but has proven to be the exception. States with this prohibition in their laws seem in no hurry to remove it.

ciary at the participant's death the insurer may pay the policy proceeds to close relatives or the insured's executors.

8. A clause requiring certificates be issued to employees stating the insurance benefits, the beneficiary and the participant's rights when employment or the group contract is terminated.
9. A clause allowing withdrawing participants the right to convert the coverage to individual insurance other than term without evidence of insurability. Upon conversion the premium usually is that charged persons of the same age and sex as the converting party. The conversion time limit is 31 days. If the participant dies during the conversion period without converting, the insurer pays the full benefit provided by the group plan. This latter provision is known as the 31-day extended death benefit.
10. Conversion rights when the master policy terminates. Upon termination of the master policy every person covered for at least five years can within 31 days convert up to $2,000 of insurance without evidence of insurability. The 31-day extended death benefit also applies under this provision.
11. Master policies written for group permanent insurance must contain the appropriate nonforfeiture provisions.

Optional policy provisions

Group policies include various optional provisions in addition to statutory provisions.

1. Interruptions in employment. The typical master policy provides that group life insurance coverage continues during authentic layoffs and leaves of absence that interrupt full-time and continuous employment. Furthermore, employees are not denied coverage caused by a clerical error, e.g., failure to notify the insurer of the employee's eligibility.

2. Disability provisions for waiving premiums. Many group policies currently issued provide that if an employee is totally disabled before age 60, the insurance will continue as long as the employee is wholly prevented from engaging in any occupation for pay or profit. This provision is the waiver-of-premium clause used in many individual life insurance policies. Some group contracts provide for payment of the policy's face amount if the employee becomes totally disabled. A third type of disability clause (called an extended death benefit) provides the participant a year of coverage on terminating employment if the employee has been continuously and totally disabled since leaving employment. The extended death benefit coverage ceases at age 65. Therefore an employee with a qualifying disability starting at age 64½ will have only six months' extended benefit rather than one year.

3. Settlement options. Although most group policy proceeds are paid as a single lump-sum payment, group participants or their beneficiaries can elect an installment option. Often installment options are limited to fixed-period or fixed-amount options (see Chapter 14). Some group insurers offer either by contract or company practice a life-income (annuity) option and/or the interest-only option. Annuity payments under the life-income option depend on the rates in effect when the participant dies. Similarly, under the interest-only option the guaranteed interest rate is the current rate effective at the participant's death.

4. Limiting the employee's insurance amount. The most common methods for determining participants' insurance amounts are: (*a*) a flat fixed amount, (*b*) a fixed amount for each wage bracket, (*c*) a fixed amount for each job classification, (*d*) a variable amount based on years of service, subject to an upper limit and (*e*) some combination of these methods

5. Selecting the covered group. The employer need not cover all workers. Coverage may be limited to specific employee classes.

6. Selecting the beneficiary. The employee is usually given the right to name or change a beneficiary at any time. Statutes prohibit naming the employer as beneficiary.

7. Assigning participation certificates. Group members may or may not be allowed to transfer their rights in their participation certificates. Some master policies prohibit assignments; others allow assignments only with the employer's permission. Many master policies do not restrict the participants' assignment right. That right allows participants to exclude insurance proceeds from their taxable estates. When the estate is large enough to create a death tax problem, assignments can be made to the participant's children to reduce the taxable estate when the surviving spouse dies.

8. Records required. The employer must maintain a list of participants including the coverage date, coverage changes and coverage amount.

9. Setting premium rates and payment schedules. Premiums may be paid monthly, quarterly, semiannually or annually in advance and are determined by the participants' ages and occupations and the size of the group. The rating plan may provide for a rate adjustment based to varying degrees on the particular group's own experience. Whether the group will receive a rate adjustment depends on the *insurer's* overall claims experience for all master policies and the experience for the particular covered group. For small groups the adjustment is limited to a partial premium refund. For large groups the adjustment may be either a partial refund or an added charge.

Types of Group Life Insurance Coverage

Typically, group life is written as one-year renewable term with rates subject to change at the beginning of each policy year. The policy usually provides that from time to time coverage can be added for all new eligible employees and other eligible members. Although most group life covers the employee's life, coverage can be written to include *dependents.* Furthermore while most group life is written as term some plans are written on a *permanent* basis. Life insurance may be provided for retired employees through a retired lives reserve (discussed later) rather than through group permanent insurance. Another type of group life is *group credit insurance* (discussed later). Lending institutions and those making installment sales buy this insurance to protect themselves by covering their debtors' lives. Finally, wholesale or franchise life insurance is available for groups that are too small to meet the minimum-number-of-lives requirement.

Dependents' coverage

Group life is extended to employees' dependents to provide funds for funeral and other death expenses. Some states prohibit dependents' coverage but in those states where it is allowed, insurers will not write it for small groups. The amount written is usually small—$2,000 for the spouse with a smaller amount for children: the younger the child, the lower the amount of insurance. Premiums paid by employers for dependents' life insurance must be reported as taxable income to employees in full when the insurance exceeds $2,000. Coverage is usually written on an employee-pay-all basis. About 10 percent of master policies include dependents' coverage.

Group permanent plans

Group permanent plans include whole life insurance. These forms also may be used to provide paid-up life insurance for employees at retirement. Three principal types of group permanent plans are level premium, unit purchase and group ordinary life insurance.

The level-premium group permanent plan. Because a 1950 adverse tax ruling made premiums paid by employers for permanent life insurance taxable income to employees, level-premium group permanent is rarely used and then only to fund qualified pension plans where it receives the benefit of favorable income-tax treatment. When employment terminates, the employee may take the policy's cash value, a paid-up policy for a reduced amount, a paid-up term policy for the full amount but for a reduced period or continue the full face amount by paying the full premium.

Unit purchase plan. The unit purchase plan combines employer-financed decreasing term insurance and employee-financed paid-up units of whole life insurance. Assume a 25-year-old employee contributes $1.30 a month per $1,000 of insurance and that amount purchases $63 of paid-up life insurance. The employer buys $937 of one-year term insurance per $1,000 of coverage. The second year the employee's contribution buys $61 of paid-up insurance, increasing the total to $124. The employer will buy $876 of one-year term insurance. When the employee terminates employment the paid-up units are retained. Because the employer buys group term no tax problem arises.

The unit purchase plan funds a paid-up policy for employees at retirement while level-premium group permanent funds retirement income benefits under qualified pension plans.

Group ordinary. Group ordinary appears to be a contradiction of terms. In general group and ordinary insurance are separate classes of life insurance. Nevertheless the term *group ordinary* persists. Group ordinary, a hybrid of group term and group permanent, permits eligible participants individually to substitute a minimum amount of permanent ordinary (continuous-premium whole life, limited-payment whole life, endowment and so on) for an offsetting amount of group term. The substitution usually can be elected by a participant initially or at any subsequent premium due date. Because group permanent is substituted for group term (i.e., the group term amount is reduced by the elected group permanent amount) the total death benefit is unaffected.

INNERSCRIPT: REGULATIONS APPLICABLE TO GROUP ORDINARY

Revisions of the 1950 adverse income tax ruling applicable to employer-paid premiums for permanent life insurance has spurred a renewed but limited interest in group ordinary—often called Section 79 plans because the governing tax regulations are applicable to that section of the Internal Revenue Code (IRC). The essential features of these complicated regulations require (1) freedom of participants to elect and to cancel the permanent coverage, (2) the level group term insurance for Section 79 plans to be unaffected by the participant's decision regarding the permanent coverage, (3) a specific allocation of death benefits for each employee between that provided by group term and that attributable to group

(*continued*)

permanent insurance, (4) the *minimum* group term benefit to be that amount by which the total death benefit payable exceeds the paid-up death benefit provided by the nonforfeiture value of the permanent insurance, (5) the plan to specify that part of the premium allocable to term insurance (in making this allocation each portion of the total coverage, i.e., term and permanent, must stand on its own—not only a difficult task but one that creates confusion), (6) the employer's contribution to the plan to be limited to the premiums legally allocated to term coverage and (7) all employees covered by the plan to be eligible for the optional permanent insurance.

A formula is included in the regulations for determining the cost of the permanent insurance. Under Section 79 of the IRC, the employer pays and deducts the cost of the term insurance and the employee need not report this amount as income (except for the insurance amount in excess of $50,000). The employee pays the cost of permanent insurance with after-tax dollars.

Group survivor income benefit insurance. Group survivor income benefit insurance (SIBI) is written to supplement group term, pension plan death benefits (see Chapter 17) and social security survivor benefits (see Chapter 18). SIBI provides monthly survivorship benefits to the deceased employee's spouse and children. Typically the spouse's benefit is paid to age 62 or 65 or until prior death or remarriage. The children's benefits are paid until age 19 or prior death or marriage. The amount of benefit for the spouse is commonly from 20 to 40 percent of the employee's predeath earnings or a fixed amount—less for the children. While generally no lump-sum payment is made some plans offer an additional one-time payment upon the remarriage of the spouse.

SIBI plans vary widely. Some limit payments to 5 or 10 years while others provide spouse benefits for life. Some plans allow the insured to designate any beneficiary to receive payments for a restricted time specified in the policy.

INNERSCRIPT: RATIONALE FOR AND REACTION TO SIBI PLANS

The purpose of SIBI is to offset the "social inequalities" of typical group term life. In these plans those that need the insurance most (young people with young families and high debt) are allocated the smallest amount of insurance while those that need the insurance the least (older people with grown children and no mortgage debt) are usually given the most insurance because of higher pay and longer service. Under SIBI those that need the protection the most are likely to receive the most insurance.

Although not new SIBI is becoming increasingly important in employee benefit programs. In 1912 the first *large* (2,912 employees) group life insurance plan was written for Montgomery Ward & Co. Included was a $100 burial benefit and one year's salary up to a maximum of $3,000 payable to named beneficiaries or the estate of employees who had no dependents. For employees with dependents, the dependent spouse was given a lifetime annuity, four years certain, for an amount equal to 25 percent of the employee's salary. The payment ceased if the spouse remarried. Except for the benefits payable on behalf of employees without dependents this plan, introduced more than 70 years ago, was identical to current SIBI plans. (The prototype Montgomery Ward plan was discontinued in 1921 in favor of a less expensive traditional plan.)

Because single employees receive no benefits from SIBI and childless employees along with older employees with advanced aged spouses receive low SIBI benefits in relation to their salaries, SIBI plans are in keeping with the minority view that employee benefit plans are nonwage obligations of business. This nonwage obligation philosophy has been one of the deterrents to the further development of SIBI plans. Those who make the decisions on employee benefit programs (usually highly paid executives) find it to their interest to accept the wage concept of employee benefits rather than the theory that employee benefits are a social obligation of industry.[6] Thus they are not attuned to the philosophy of giving more insurance to new workers with low pay plus dependents with long benefit-expectancy periods than to valuable highly paid workers with a long productive service record. This attitude may be the factor that prevents SIBI from becoming the principal method of the future for providing death benefits in employee benefit plans.

Retired lives reserve

When employers use group term insurance to continue postretirement death coverage the employees' advancing age makes insurance premiums more expensive each year. Similarly, if employers elect to fund postretirement death benefits with permanent group insurance a tax problem results. Employers can deduct group permanent life insurance premiums they pay for employees but employees must report these premiums as taxable income. However, employers can avoid the tax disadvantage of group permanent life insurance and the high cost of continuing group term for retired employees by establishing a retired lives reserve.

The retired lives reserve is funded by deductible employer contributions to an irrevocable trust. Contributions are accumulated in the trust to fund postretirement death benefits or to continue group life insurance for retired employees. Trust investment earnings are exempt from federal income taxes. In addition, these contributions are not treated as taxable income to employees as long as

[6] See Robert I. Mehr, *Life Insurance: Theory and Practice,* rev. ed. (Plano, Tex.: Business Publications, 1977), p. 282.

the trust money or property is not paid to them. Unlike other irrevocable trusts the retired lives reserve tax shield is preserved as long as trust income is restricted to providing death benefits.

Group credit insurance

Group credit insurance is used by merchants making installment sales, credit unions, finance companies, banks, lenders on real estate mortgages and other creditors to cover the debtors' lives. The proceeds are used to cancel the balance of the debt when the debtor dies. The insurance protects the borrower, the family and the creditor.

Insurers and creditors negotiate the terms for the master policy. Because group credit insurance premiums are passed through the borrower to the creditor, the lender has no incentive to curb premium costs. To the contrary, creditors have an incentive to negotiate higher premiums because they receive commissions on the premiums and a share in the profits earned on the master policy. Because borrowers are preoccupied with obtaining loans they often ignore the premiums even though they are likely to be excessive. Credit insurance price regulation at state and federal levels is attempting to help borrowers obtain rates that are not higher than that reflected by loss expectancy plus expenses and a reasonable profit. Figure 16–2 summarizes the types of group life insurance.

Wholesale or franchise life insurance

Wholesale or franchise life insurance adapts some group insurance principles to cover groups ineligible for true group insurance. No master policy is issued; participants receive individual policies after applications are approved. The insurer may reject an applicant who fails to meet its standards. In a small group even one or two substandard lives, one jolly fatty, one good-hearted person with a weak heart and one with a cancerous growth (a typical company employee population group) can lead to excessive mortality costs. As in group insurance each participant's insurance amount is determined by formula. Wholesale insurance allows employers to give employees most advantages of group insurance. Generally, wholesale plans are written on a yearly renewable term basis.

FIGURE 16–2 Types of Group Life Insurance

TYPE	*PURPOSE*
Regular group term	To help provide continuing income for those surviving the deceased employee and to cover employees' funeral expenses.
Dependents' coverage	To cover funeral expenses when a dependent dies.
Group permanent	
Level premium	To fund qualified pensions with level-premium permanent life insurance.
Unit purchase plan	To provide continuing protection after retirement by combining employer financed decreasing term insurance with employee financed with units of paid-up whole life insurance.
Group ordinary	To permit eligible participants to substitute a minimum amount of permanent ordinary for an offsetting amount of group term.
Group survivor income benefit insurance:	To provide monthly survivorship benefits to the deceased employee's spouse and children.
Group credit	To cancel the balance of a debtor's indebtedness.
Wholesale life	To cover groups too small for regular group coverage.
Retired lives reserve	To accumulate funds in a trust to be used to continue group term life insurance premiums for retired employees or to pay death benefits directly to survivors of retired employees.

GROUP HEALTH INSURANCE

Group health is similar to group life insurance. Differences between the two are the perils covered and the broader definition of groups eligible for coverage. Group health insurance includes all the coverages written as individual insurance (Chapter 15). The discussion of these coverages is expanded in this chapter.

State Regulation

Group health insurance developed without special legislation. Insurers had to comply only with general statutes relating to insurance until 1937 when Illinois enacted a state group health insurance law. The model bills of the Health Insurance Association of America (HIAA) and the NAIC have influenced state group health legislation but neither has been adopted in its entirety. The laws define group health insurance and standard policy provisions.

Definition of group health insurance

The HIAA definition designates no minimum for the group. The NAIC bill requires 25 covered lives. Several states require a smaller minimum; others require no minimum leaving the decision to the insurers. The HIAA bill has no minimum participation. In contrast the NAIC bill includes a 75 percent participation requirement for contributory and 100 percent for noncontributory plans. Eligibility requirements for group health insurance are more liberal than for group life insurance. The HIAA bill provides eligibility for group health insurançe to (1) any organization eligible for group life, (2) any other substantially similar group not organized solely for the purchase of insurance that the insurance commissioner believes qualified and (3) dependents or family members of persons enrolled in an eligible group.

When group health insurance was introduced the individual market for health coverage was not developed so insurance agents had little to gain by lobbying for restrictions on group health coverage. Furthermore health insurance companies believed that group coverage was necessary to allow them to compete with organizations like Blue Cross/Blue Shield and prepayment medical groups. Thus they supported group health insurance. As a consequence adequate competition in products and rate making made further regulation unnecessary.

Standard provisions for group health insurance

The HIAA bill contains only three standard provisions: (1) oral statements cannot be used to avoid the insurance and written statements shall be interpreted as representations; (2) each group member must receive a summary statement of coverage and (3) eligible new members or dependents may be added to the group according to policy terms. A majority of states require standard provisions. Some states, for example, require a provision stating conditions under which the insurer may decline to renew the policy. As in group life insurance, the employer cannot be named the beneficiary of the insurance.

Group Health and Individual Health Contracts

Group health insurance differs from individual coverage as follows:

1. Group health covers *off-the-job* accidents only, except for long-term disabilities. Workers' compensation insurance is designed to cover on-the-job accidents. Occupational sickness is seldom covered by group health if covered by workers' compensation. Some employers integrate coverage with on-the-job accidents and occupational illnesses so that disabled employees will receive equal amounts regardless of whether the injury or illness is job related.

2. State laws require uniform provisions in individual but not group health policies.

3. Group policies omit clauses that prorate benefits when participants own other insurance. Instead, a coordination-of-benefits clause restricts the amount a covered person may collect from other group policies. In many families both spouses work and have employee group health insurance. In addition each may be covered as a dependent under the other's group plan. When the husband or wife incurs medical expenses both plans may apply in a specified order. A group participant must first exhaust the benefit of his or her employer's plan before the dependent coverage provided by the spouse's plan applies. The effect is to make the employee's coverage primary and the dependent's coverage excess. If an unemployed dependent child incurs medical expenses the coordination of benefits arrangement between spouses is not applicable. So the respective policies provide some other basis for settlement. For example, the father's plan or the plan in effect for the longest time must be primary.

Types of Coverages

Frequently written group coverages are disability income, accidental death and dismemberment, hospital expense, surgical expense, nursing home care, psychiatric expense, major medical expense, dental care, vision care and prescription drugs. Measured by number of persons covered, group insurance accounts for nearly 85 percent of major medical, 99.6 percent of dental and 100 percent of vision care coverage.

Disability income benefits have expanded to include pregnancy as a temporary disability. Insurers (and often employers who pay the bill) argued without success that pregnancy differs from illness because it occurs by voluntary means (although the results may be accidental). The courts have ruled that excluding pregnancy from disability income coverages unfairly discriminates against women in spite of its voluntarism. Guidelines designed by the Equal Employment Opportunity Commission (EEOC) require employers to offer benefits for pregnancies equal to those for other health-related conditions. An exception is nonmedical abortions. The EEOC also requires employers to cover pregnancy expenses for dependents when the plan includes dependents' coverage.

Franchise (Wholesale) Health Insurance

Franchise health insurance, like wholesale life insurance, is designed for an employee group too small to qualify for group coverage. Because the insurer underwrites individuals, not the group, and issues individual policies, not participation certificates, the franchise form at best is pseudogroup insurance. The premium is less than for individual policies but more than for group coverage. The coverage is nonoccupational. Franchise insurance is mass marketed to association members and credit card holders and the administration of franchise insurance is similar to that of group insurance.

Blanket Health Policies

Blanket insurance differs from group insurance because no insured is named and no certificates are issued. Examples of groups underwritten by blanket policies are students at a college, spectators at a sports event and members of a football squad. In general blanket group membership changes frequently and the policy covers the changing membership.

Group Credit Health Insurance

Group credit health insurance is purchased to pay a disabled debtor's payments until the debtor recovers or the debt is paid. In some plans benefits are payable

FIGURE 16–3 Types of Group Health Insurance

TYPE	*PURPOSE*
Regular group health	To cover qualified groups for medical expenses and loss of income due to accidents or illness.
Franchise	To cover groups too small to qualify for regular group health.
Blanket	To protect fluid classes of insureds who are not named in a master policy.
Group credit	To pay a lending institution the debts of disabled creditors.

retroactively to the debtor's first day of disability if the disability is continuous and lasts for a specified time. In others benefits are paid only for the time following the waiting period. Because retroactive payments lead insureds to fake the length of illness insurers tend to avoid them.

Figure 16–3 summarizes the differences between forms of group health insurance.

Administrative Service Only Group Insurance (ASO)

Since 1975 group health insurance coverage provided by ASO plans has grown from 5 percent to more than 18 percent of all group health insurance in force. ASO arrangements allow employers with predictable claims rates to self-insure health benefit plans. Employers who self-insure not only can help maintain their cash flow but also can take advantage of high interest rates by investing funds that normally are used to pay insurance premiums. However, employers must be strong enough financially to risk adverse fluctuations in claims rates if they rely solely on ASO contracts. Employers may combine ASO contracts with stop-loss insurance agreements. Under this arrangement the insurer agrees to pay aggregate claims that exceed a specified amount.

Cost of Group Health Insurance

To generalize about the cost of group health insurance is difficult as each plan is different. Competition is keen and each insurer determines its own rates. Quoted premium rates are misleading because the true insurance cost is the net cost after dividends or credits. Group premium rates vary with the age distribution, occupations covered, proportion of females in the group (women lose twice as much working time as men because of sickness) and variations in medical care costs in different localities. In major medical an additional rating factor is the earnings level of the members because high-income people demand higher-priced medical services and may be charged more for the same service than low-income persons.

INNERSCRIPT: FUNDING BENEFITS THROUGH AN INTERNAL REVENUE CODE (IRC) 501(c)9 TRUST

An IRC 501(c)9 trust is any qualified trust established by an employer to accumulate funds for self-insuring and paying em-

(*continued*)

ployee benefits. By allowing the employer to achieve the benefits of self-insurance the 501(c)9 trust offers the advantages of (1) greater control over fund contributions and disbursements, (2) the elimination of state premium taxes and (3) lower administrative costs. Qualification permits investment earnings of a 501(c)9 trust to be exempt from federal income tax.

The rules for qualifying a 501(c)9 trust are (1) the organization must be a voluntary employee association, (2) 90 percent of the membership must be employees, (3) members must hold regular meetings, (4) the purpose of the organization must be to provide life, accident, sickness and other benefits and (5) the organization must benefit members only.

Formerly under 501(c)9 trusts only life, accident and sickness benefits qualified for tax-exempt status. Now other benefits are allowed: vacation, supplemental unemployment, severance benefits and IRC 501(c)20 group legal and child-care benefits. Under collectively bargained plans scholarship and summer camp benefits are permitted for employees' dependents. Examples of benefits not allowed are auto and homeowners coverage.

The IRS has not answered the question whether payments of death benefits from a self-insured plan are tax exempt. In 1968 the U.S. Court of Appeals in *Ross* v. *Odom* held that death benefits paid by state sponsored plans are income tax exempt if actuarially determined.[7] The court did not rule on the use of 501(c)9 trusts by private corporate plans to provide employee death benefits. This uncertainty appears to make group life insurance the preferred method for providing employee death benefits in excess of $5,000. (The Internal Revenue Code permits an employer to pay a death benefit up to $5,000 to the surviving spouse or estate of a deceased employee income tax free.)

DECISIONS IN ESTABLISHING EMPLOYEE BENEFIT PLANS: GROUP LIFE AND HEALTH

Employers establishing employee benefit plans must decide (1) whether benefits will be financed by the employer alone or by contributions from employer and employees, (2) the benefits to include, (3) benefit levels, (4) eligibility rules for participants and (5) eligibility rules for benefits. Regardless of the plans considered—death benefits, health care or pension plans—the same issues must be decided for each. General issues and those applying exclusively to life and health benefits are discussed in the present chapter. Those that apply only to retirement benefits are discussed in Chapter 17.

Contributory or Noncontributory

A decision must be made as to whether the cost should be paid entirely by the employer or shared by employees.

[7] 401 F2d 464.

The noncontributory plan has the advantage of *administrative ease.* In most group arrangements, if the plan is contributory, at least 75 percent of eligible group members must elect the coverage. A noncontributory plan automatically covers everyone. Consequently employers need not exert pressure on employees to meet participation requirements. The noncontributory plan eliminates paperwork involved in withholding employee contributions and reduces clerical errors. Noncontributory plans are significantly more popular than contributory plans.

Some *cost* considerations favor contributory plans. More attractive benefits can be offered employees for each employer dollar. The additional benefits are usually better than the employee could purchase individually. However, income tax considerations favor noncontributory plans. The employer may deduct premiums paid for group life and health insurance and contributions made to qualified pension plans. Furthermore, the employee does not report the employer's group pension contributions, group health insurance premiums or life insurance premiums (unless the employer purchases more than $50,000 of life insurance for the employee). Thus in noncontributory plans the full cost of these benefits is paid with pretax dollars. In contributory plans employee contributions are not deductible. They are made with aftertax dollars.

Death benefits paid under a noncontributory plan are not reported as income to the beneficiary if these benefits are provided through life insurance. But disability and retirement income benefits under a noncontributory plan are reportable as income to the employee when received. Eligible employees may exclude disability income up to $100 a week.[8] Retired employees usually will have a double exemption (taxpayers beyond age 65 claim an extra exemption) and many will have a lower taxable income. Consequently, some retired employees will have the benefit of a lower tax rate after retirement. When disability income benefits are paid under a contributory plan that portion attributable to the employee's contribution is excluded from taxable income. When retirement income is paid under a contributory plan the employee's contribution is taken into consideration in determining taxable income.

Before the 1969 Tax Reform Act when a retiree received a single payment instead of annuity payments the funds were taxed as capital gains rather than normal income. With the Tax Reform Act of 1969 and the Employee Retirement Income Security Act of 1974 (ERISA), the treatment of lump-sum distributions in one taxable year has become complicated. In 1974 these distributions were split into pre-1974 capital gains and post-1973 ordinary income. No capital gains are accrued after 1973. Recipients of lump-sum pension distributions may be taxed in two ways. Distribution from pension contributions made before 1974 qualify for long-term capital gains treatment; those for years after 1973 are taxed

[8] Employees may exclude disability income up to $100 a week only if they are under age 65, have not reached mandatory retirement age, are permanently and totally disabled and have retired on disability. Payments are excluded up to $5,200 a year if the recipient's adjusted gross income including disability payments does not exceed $15,000. If the recipient's income is in excess of $15,000 annually the $5,200 deduction is reduced dollar for dollar. Thus if the retirement, disability-income payee has an adjusted gross income of $18,000 annually, including $5,200 of disability income, only $2,200 may be deducted by the employee. The exclusion would be phased out entirely if the adjusted gross income annually plus $5,200 of disability income is $20,200 or more. That amount equals $15,000 plus $5,200 so no disability income can be excluded. When advantageous, the recipient may elect to have qualified disability income taxed as retirement income. If a joint return is filed these rules apply to the earnings of both husband and wife. When the combined income of both spouses exceeds $20,200, disability income paid to one spouse is not excludable even if the earnings including disability income of the disabled spouse do not exceed $15,000.

as ordinary income with the option of using a special 10-year income averaging. Employees receiving lump-sum distributions after 1976 may irrevocably elect to treat them as earned after 1973 and available for 10-year income averaging. Employees who receive installment payments are taxed under the annuity rules of the Internal Revenue Service (IRS). Therefore, the payment method determines the tax consequences of a pension distribution. How benefits paid under qualified pension and deferred profit-sharing plans are taxed is discussed in depth in Chapter 17.

Specifying Coverages for Life and Health Benefit Plans

Employers must decide what benefits should be included in employee benefit plans, who should be entitled to these benefits and what the benefit level should be. Most programs include life insurance, accidental death and dismemberment benefits, hospital care, surgical expense and regular medical expense. A large majority of firms offer major medical benefits. More than half include loss-of-income protection and retirement benefits.

Because employers are unable to adjust employee benefits to inflation, **flexible compensation** (variously known as cafeteria or market-basket plans) is gaining popularity as an attractive alternative to traditional plans. For employers with sophisticated software systems geared to elaborate record-keeping, flexible compensation permits more meaningful benefits without increasing costs. The flexibility is provided by a combination of basic and optional coverages. Basic coverages include modest health and life coverages plus vacation time and pensions based on employees' length of service. Optional coverage includes full medical care, dental and vision coverage, more vacation time, increased disability income, group auto and homeowners' insurance, prepaid legal service and higher retirement pay. Employees can choose among these and other optional benefits.

Families that have two working spouses can choose their employee benefits to avoid duplicating coverages. For example, if one spouse's employer provides the family with ample medical benefits the other spouse might be satisfied with basic medical benefits and opt for more vacation time, retirement pay and so on. Most flexible compensation plans allow employees to adjust their benefit selections annually. Although employees can select any type or amount of optional coverages the total costs of flexible employee benefit plans must meet the plan's budget constraints. This budget presumably is closely related to the cost of a traditional plan. Employers have reduced basic benefit levels to free funds to finance the optional coverages. Employees are given a core of benefit credits based on such factors as age, salary and years of service. Part of these credits may be traded to obtain optional benefits.

Flexible benefit plans, introduced in the mid-1970s, are currently used by about 20 companies with another 20 giving them serious consideration. The lack of early support for these plans is attributed to (1) adverse income tax laws, (2) union opposition, (3) high initial cost of installation and (4) the normal resistance to change. Furthermore, life insurance agents oppose flexible compensation. Before the Revenue Act of 1978 the cost of benefits chosen by employees was taxable as current income. Now some benefit plan options are exempt from current income taxes. Those options not exempt can be allocated to employee contributions in a contributory plan. Organized labor fearing that workers are incapable of making intelligent choices among benefits oppose flexible compensation programs. Labor unions also believe employers will use these plans as a means of reducing the benefit cost package. Life insurance agents suspect the plan will be used as a substitute for a professionally planned life insurance program.

Flexible compensation better meets the needs of 80 percent of today's work force: only 20 percent are the breadwinners with spouse and children at home. That the modern worker views traditional plans as obsolete is attested to by the behavior of workers enrolled in flexible plans: only 10 percent elected the same benefit afforded by traditional plans.

Flexible compensation plans have advantages to employers; they (1) encourage employees to elect higher deductibles (cost control), (2) enable employers to encourage employees to contribute to the plan (cost shifting), (3) allow employers to pass cost increases to employees (cost capping) and (4) help to recruit sought-after employees. These plans are expected to be offered to hourly workers (they are now offered only to salary workers) and by small firms (they are now offered only by large firms).

The advantages of flexible compensation to employees are patent: (1) the opportunity to participate in the selection of their own benefits, (2) the elimination of duplicate coverage and (3) the feeling of sharing in an important managerial decision. The future of cafeteria or flexible benefits appears promising and is the most equitable approach to employee benefit plans in today's changing work force.

Issues in planning life and health coverage

Several issues are considered when planning an employee group life and health insurance program. To simplify the discussion of designing employee benefit plans, decisions that relate to life and health coverage are treated separately from those involving retirement benefits.

Eligibility requirements. To be eligible for coverage under group life and health plans employees usually must be regular and full time, actively at work and have served a job probationary period. A minimum number of hours worked per week is usually the test for full-time regular employees. The probationary period is customarily three months. Two special groups must be considered: employees temporarily separated from employment and retired employees. Frequently a limit is placed on the length of time coverage can be continued on an employee temporarily laid off or on leave of absence. Although the cost is high the trend is toward extending group life and medical care coverage to retired people. The employer usually pays the full cost but benefit levels are reduced to control expenses. As noted, life insurance for retired people is occasionally provided by group permanent life or a retired lives reserve. Medical care benefits for the aged under employee benefit plans are usually integrated with medicare (discussed in Chapter 18).

Benefit structure. The amount budgeted for employee benefits must be allocated among types of benefits and employees. For *group life insurance* establishing the benefit structure involves a selection of one or more of the following plans: group term, a form of group permanent, or group survivor income benefit insurance. Also of concern is whether or not to cover dependents (dependents' life) and/or retired workers (group permanent or a retired lives reserve). The issues involved in making these decisions are discussed earlier in this chapter.

The 1967 Age Discrimination in Employment Act (ADEA) permits employers to reduce benefits if age can be shown as a cost factor in covering older employees. For employee benefit plans other than retirement, age bracketing by five years is permitted. Thus group life insurance premiums spent for employees in the 55–59 year age bracket can be used to buy reduced benefits for employees in the 60–64 and 65–69 age brackets.

Decisions are more numerous for *health insurance.* Among them are disability income, accidental death and dismemberment, hospital expense, surgical expense, physicians' expense, major medical, dental care, vision care, psychiatric expense and prescription drugs. Basic coverage includes only hospital, surgical and physicians' expenses. Theoretically only disability income insurance with a waiting period and major medical insurance with a deductible should be considered because both forms exclude small losses. However, many employees fail to understand and appreciate plans that do not pay at least some small and frequent expenses. Furthermore, the advantage of having employees' medical bills paid by the employers with tax-deductible dollars often is a practical consideration. The plan must specify each coverage.

In *disability income plans* the following specifications are needed:

1. *Disabilities covered.* Should the plan cover both occupational and nonoccupational injury and illness? Most plans are nonoccupational because workers' compensation benefits are paid for on-the-job losses.

2. *Length of the waiting period.* The common pattern is a seven-day waiting period for sickness but no waiting period for accidents.

3. *Duration of the benefit period.* The usual benefit periods for short-term disability-income plans are 13 and 26 weeks although a trend toward longer durations is evident with a number of plans providing benefits for one or more years. Long-term disability income plans with benefits payable to age 65 are a major development.

Benefit levels. The various bases for determining benefit levels for life insurance are discussed earlier. The one that best fits the plan's objective must be selected and that requires management (and labor) to formulate an overall workable objective for employee benefit plans as an integrated unit. The question of a flexible compensation program could arise at this point.

The common benefit schedule for disability income is between half and two thirds of the employee's compensation. Benefits may be based on job classification, length of service, a fixed amount for all employees or some combination of these factors. Plans for professional firms (e.g., doctors, lawyers) are adding inflation-adjustment clauses that increase disability benefits 10 percent yearly until the participant reaches age 65 or 70. Inflation adjustment clauses are occasionally included in some group plans written for other than professional firms. (Many employers offer this type of protection in individual disability income policies; some small businesses buy them for other key employees.)

Accidental death and dismemberment (AD&D) benefits are frequently included in group insurance programs and usually extend to both on- and off-the-job injuries. The coverage is attractive because high dollar amounts can be purchased with low premiums and this combination lulls many employees into the belief that they are getting a bargain. The trauma of accidental death and dismemberment makes AD&D protection psychologically appealing. The basic decision here is setting the benefit level. Usually accidental death benefits are the same as the group life benefits. Dismemberment benefits are fixed by a schedule based on the accidental death benefit (e.g., 100 percent of the death benefit for loss of both hands, both eyes *or* both feet and 50 percent of the death benefit for loss of one hand, foot or eye).

In *hospital insurance* the principal decision is the benefit level. Customarily all employees receive the same benefits. Hospital room and board may be covered for a semiprivate room at its actual cost (or for a maximum amount per day). The coverage is subject to a specified number of days, most commonly 120 to

365. Miscellaneous hospital benefits are usually 15 or 20 times the daily room and board rate. Miscellaneous hospital expenses include those incurred during hospital confinement or confinement as a resident patient (i.e., laboratory or X-ray service). For miscellaneous expenses over the basic amount the trend is to allow an addition equal to the basic amount. However, the employee must participate by paying 20 percent of the costs over the base amount. Group hospital insurance in contrast to group life insurance usually includes the dependents of covered employees. When employees' coverage is written on a noncontributory basis, dependents' coverage may be written on a contributory basis.

For *surgical expense* coverage benefits may be paid according to a schedule with the policy listing the maximum benefit for each type of operation covered. However, an increasing number of plans limit benefits to the reasonable and customary charges for the covered surgical procedure.

Physicians' expense coverage provides benefits to pay fees for nonsurgical care by physicians. The coverage includes charges for home, hospital or office visits. Diagnostic X-ray and laboratory expenses may be covered up to a specified amount.

Major medical coverage requires a number of choices. Should the plan be written in addition to a basic plan, as is most common? Also what type of deductible should be used: initial, corridor or integrated? Under the **initial deductible** the insured pays the deductible amount and the insurer pays the rest, up to the policy limit and applicable participation percentage. The participation percentage (originally erroneously called coinsurance) is the percentage of *covered* expenses in excess of the deductible that the insured must bear, usually 20 percent. In many major medical plans the participation applies to expenses up to a specified amount, e.g., $5,000 or $10,000. If the deductible is $100 and a 20 percent participation applies to the first $5,000 of these expenses, the insured incurring covered medical expenses of $8,000 would be required to bear only $1,100: 20 percent of $5,000 plus $100. The insurer pays $6,900: $8,000 less $1,100. For any covered expenses within the policy limits, the maximum the insured would have to pay under this set of deductible and participation limits is $1,100. If the maximum participation limit is 20 percent of $10,000 in excess of the $100 deductible, the most the insured would have to bear for covered expenses is $2,100. The deductible frequently is offset by a basic plan including hospital, surgical and physicians' expense insurance. The **corridor deductible** does not allow the benefits of the basic plan to offset the deductible. Instead it requires the insured to pay a deductible of a specified amount after the basic benefits are exhausted and before the major medical benefits become effective. The name *corridor* is apt because the deductible is a corridor between the basic and the major medical plans.

Under the **integrated deductible** the deductible is the higher of the benefits provided by the basic plan or some fixed dollar amount. The integrated deductible is the most common. The plan's designers must decide what size deductible (flat amount or percentage of earnings) is appropriate and whether it should be per benefit period, per policy or calendar year or on a family budget basis. Most common is a flat deductible applied to a benefit period or a calendar year rather than to each disability. What should the participation level be? Usually the employee must pay 20 percent. What should the benefit limit be, and should it be per illness, per policy or calendar year, per benefit year, per lifetime or some combination of these limits? Maximum benefits for new major medical coverage written in 1980 exceeded $100,000 for 93 percent of sampled employees. In 1975 the figure was only 71 percent. Furthermore, in 1980 57 percent of the sampled employees had maximum coverage of more than $1 million. Twenty-nine percent had unlimited benefits. Benefits ranged from $10,000 to unlimited. What expenses should be excluded? Usually exclusions are expenses covered under other insurance, cosmetic surgery and workers' compensation.

Currently most health plans cover in- and out-patient treatment for nervous and mental disorders. Prescription drugs are usually covered with a calendar year deductible. Should coverage be extended to vision care? Although the coverage offers low benefits coupled with a deductible, its use in employee benefit plans is increasing. Should coverage be offered for nursing home care? Many plans offer this coverage to control hospital benefit costs.

Should dental care insurance be included? Dental care insurance usually covers 50 to 90 percent of reasonable and customary charges for diagnosis (oral examinations, X-rays), prevention, restoration, orthodontics, root canal therapy and gum disease treatment. Benefits may be limited to a specified amount, e.g., $1,000 per individual for a calendar year, and they are subject to internal limits for various procedures. Although they have no colorful symbol such as a blue cross or a blue shield, dental associations offer group dental care coverage that is frequently more liberal than commercial insurers. Nevertheless commercial insurers cover about 60 percent of those with group dental insurance.

The Age Discrimination in Employment Act (ADEA) allows medical expense coverage to be reduced at age 65 for continuing employees. Medical expense coverage may be integrated with medicare benefits. A new plan may be offered to provide coverage to fill some of the gaps in the medicare program. Employers can also reduce benefit levels and/or benefit periods for disability income payments. Changes in both medical care and disability income plans must be supported by cost data that justify the reductions. The Tax Equity and Fiscal Responsibility Act of 1982 (TEFRA) requires, beginning January 1, 1983, employers with more than 25 workers to offer employees aged 65 through 69 (and their dependents) the same health benefits available to younger workers, making medicare a secondary plan in those instances. However, the affected employees are not required to enroll in the employer's plan.

Resources for paying benefits. In group life and disability income coverage the employer may pay claims directly as they occur or use the insurer as a conduit for paying claims. The decision hinges on whether the employer can assume the risk and administer the plan more efficiently than insurers.

If death benefits are covered by insurance the employee's spouse still has an income tax advantage. Death benefits *paid by life insurers* are not subject to federal income taxes. However, payments *made directly* by an employer on behalf of a deceased employee are taxable, subject to the $5,000 exclusion mentioned earlier.

The alternatives to commercial insurance are Blue Cross and Blue Shield or similar independent plans, health maintenance organizations (HMOs) and self-insurance. In choosing between the "Blues" and commercial insurers several factors are involved. The Blues are nonprofit organizations and have tax advantages in nearly all states, thereby gaining a cost advantage. Nevertheless, commercial insurers may have an offsetting cost advantage. If the entire group package (life, disability income and medical expenses) is underwritten by an insurer, a broad base is formed giving greater weight to the group's own experience in determining its own premiums. So groups with overall good experience may be rewarded by using a commercial insurer. The Blues consider the group's own experience in setting rates but that experience is confined to medical care coverage only. In addition to cost The Blues' and the insurer's underwriting practices must be considered. The buyer has no choice unless both will write the plan. Health maintenance organizations offer employees advantages and may be used where available if employees are willing to restrict medical care service to one clinic. (Usually an HMO will refer members to other doctors if, and only if, it does not have the personnel or facilities needed.) Although not widely found the Individual Practice Association (IPA), a type of HMO, overcomes employees' objections to restricting medical service to one clinic. IPAs operate like the family physician arrangement that many people traditionally have found so comfortable.

A number of employers self-insure (or assume the risk of) their medical expense plans, particularly when plans do not cover major medical expenses. Losses covered under basic plans occur with sufficient frequency for employers to predict them accurately without having a large number of employees. Loss severity is low so the range of predictability can be wide. Most employers prefer not to self-insure; they want claims to be administered (or at least give the appearance that claims are administered) by an insurer so employee relations are not threatened when a claim is denied. Many employers that self-insure employee medical benefit plans use insurers to administer the claims under an administrative only contract (ASO).

OTHER GROUP PLANS

Several group plans other than life and health insurance and retirement (discussed in the next chapter) are offered to a limited extent to complete an employee benefit package. The two that appear to have the most promise for further development are discussed here: group property and liability insurance and prepaid legal plans. Employee benefit plans that do not include insurance are not discussed. They include supplemental unemployment benefits, formal sick leave, financial counseling, personal leave, vacations and paid holidays, recreation facilities, company cars, annual physical examinations, tuition plans, preretirement counseling, stress-control programs, company loans, annual bonuses, fat-removal plans and others that stretch the imagination.

Group Property and Liability Insurance

Both insurers and insureds are giving attention to group property-liability insurance as an employee benefit. A relatively small but growing percentage of homeowners and personal auto insurance is written on a group basis. When the major obstacles to writing group property-liability insurance are overcome the coverage will expand even more. So far these obstacles have been opposition from independent insurance agents and restrictive state regulations.

Attitudes and objectives

A management consulting firm hired by the National Association of Insurance Agents told independent agents to "accept the reality of group plans and their probable growth" and that "a negative attitude will not work toward their [the agents'] best long-term interest." The objective of group property and liability insurance is to give quality insurance at the lowest possible rates by reducing selling and administration costs. This reduction is accomplished primarily by reducing or eliminating agents' commissions and overhead. One insurer writing group-rated insurance in Michigan has reduced auto insurance cost by more than 15 percent. The National Educational Association offers group homeowners insurance to its members at a substantially lower rate than that of individual policies. Other advantages claimed for group property-liability insurance are better service to policyowners, increased potential for innovation, greater opportunity for loss-prevention activity, more convenient payroll deductions and integration with other employee benefits.

For the most part criticisms of group property and liability insurance appear to be influenced by biases. Whether one is for or against it depends on whose ox is being gored.

Limitations Some agents say that considerable structural change would be necessary to extend group principles to property-liability coverages. Similarly agents argue that writing extensive group property-liability insurance would lead to scrapping the agency system because agents' commissions would not be sufficient to pay for the services presently demanded of them. The insurer's loss-adjustment expenses would mount. To retain the group, insurers might resort to liberal claims practices eventually leading to higher premiums. Other arguments offered are that group property-liability insurance adversely affects small insurers, restricts the market for nongroup members and reduces coverage flexibility. In the early days of group life insurance those who could lose from the growth of the group marketing concepts (agents) also predicted dire results for the industry, but these predictions did not materialize. Both the life insurance industry and its agents have survived group insurance. However, the personal lines property-liability agent might not fare as well as the life insurance agent under group marketing. The market for auto and homeowners insurance, for example, is finite. The homeowners and car owners insurance need can be fulfilled with group coverage, but the need for life insurance is rarely satisfied with group insurance only. So while expansion of the group marketing concept can adversely affect the personal lines property-liability agent, nothing suggests that the industry would be severely hurt. The insurance has to be provided regardless of how it is marketed.

The legal climate Antidiscrimination laws and fictitious grouping laws have been the primary legislative blocks to group property-liability underwriting. Both kinds of laws have been administered and enforced much more stringently for group property-liability insurance than for group life and health insurance. Under the fictitious group law groups formed primarily to buy insurance are ineligible: adverse selection would result. Curiously, this law has been used to deny an employer the right to purchase group property-liability insurance for employees. The antidiscriminatory law requires insurance rates to be the same for individuals with identical rating characteristics. Because the social value of group life and health coverages has been accepted the issue of rate discrimination is ignored. The fundamental question is whether group property-liability insurance also has a social value.

The regulatory climate for mass merchandising group property-liability insurance has improved considerably in most states with repeal of the fictitious group laws and regulations. Nevertheless, statutes and administrative rulings still create a problem for writing true group property-liability insurance. *True group* means group underwriting rather than underwriting individuals within a group. Unlike true group, mass merchandising permits individual selection and rating of applicants.

Underwriting true group property-liability insurance is either illegal by statutes, not permitted by state insurance commissioners or discouraged by them. However, a number of exceptions are found.

In 1968 the Michigan Insurance Bureau broke the ice by approving a true group property-liability plan for autos. The Michigan attorney general did not challenge its legality. The group is rated and all participating employees pay the same premium for the same protection regardless of age, sex, residence or type of auto. Dividends based on experience may be returned to the group. In the approved plan both employer and employees contribute. The employer is issued a master policy and employees are given certificates of participation. However, unlike group life and health insurance employees with a bad driving record may be segregated for special treatment.

Union representatives believe property-liability insurance (auto and homeowners) is a fringe benefit to be considered but not assigned a high priority. Nevertheless, some small unions have successfully negotiated for auto coverage. If employers do not pay a part of the premium, group property-liability insurance has little appeal to some buyers. Even with true group rates premiums may be in excess of those charged by some personal-lines insurers with strict underwriting standards. If group property and liability insurance were given favorable tax treatment similar to group life and health insurance it would grow in popularity as an employee benefit.

Prepaid Legal Insurance

Prepaid legal service insurance plans provide group members coverage for legal fees up to specified maximums. Five phases of legal work are usually covered: civil, criminal, clerical, counseling and preventive law (e.g., annual legal checkup). Prepaid legal service plans first developed in the early 1900s but they have gained popularity only recently. A number of plans now in operation are offered by various groups including labor unions, consumer groups, teacher associations, credit unions, bar associations, private firms and insurers. Among other considerations (insurer efficiency, profit goals, and so on), the cost of coverage is a function of the benefits offered. However, much of the insurance activity remains in the infancy stage.

About 5 million workers and dependents are covered by prepaid legal plans providing legal service for an average cost of about $120 a year per covered worker. Prepaid legal plans have been much less popular as employee benefit plans than expected because escalating costs of health insurance plans have discouraged unions and management from bargaining for them. Also no one aggressively sells these plans. If large insurers become interested in full-blown plans and seek to market them they may increase in numbers. Several such insurers are attempting these full-scale plans in California. In the meantime a minilegal service plan called Advice and Referral is growing rapidly. These plans provide consultation and limited follow-up such as an attorney's letter. The law firm bills the employee per hour for any additional work. These limited plans cost about $20 a year.

Regulation

Regarding the question of whether prepaid legal-expense plans are insurance, the courts have expressed conflicting views about (1) the principle of indemnity, (2) the transfer of risk and (3) fortuitous events. The end result has been that some states permit insurers to write prepaid legal-expense plans but only on an individual basis; other states allow it to be written on both an individual and group basis and still others do not permit it at all. Employers' contributions to qualified legal-expense plans are deductible as a business expense, and employees do not report either the contributions or the value of legal service received as taxable income. The tax advantage applies to employer contributions for employees, their spouses and dependents. For a plan to qualify it must (1) be written separately from other employee benefit plans, (2) be initiated by an employer, (3) be for the exclusive benefit of employees, their spouses or dependents, (4) specify benefits, (5) provide for personal legal services only, (6) prepay legal fees in whole or in part by the employer and (7) be administered by a tax-exempt organization. (Any organization or trust whose exclusive function is to administer qualified legal-expense plans is treated as a tax-exempt organization.) Although the tax provisions that favor legal benefit plans are scheduled to expire December 31, 1984, recent IRS regulations suggest this favorable status will continue.

Prepaid legal expense plans are subject to federal regulation under the Employee Retirement Income Security Act. ERISA's regulations preempt state laws and set fiduciary standards and reporting requirements. State regulators would prefer to have plans file informational statements with them. Some states make ERISA-qualified plans exempt from filing, but other states ask for a duplicate copy of the plan's ERISA filing. Federal control began with a 1973 amendment to the Taft-Hartley Act of 1947, making legal services an employee benefit subject to collective bargaining with the employer sharing the cost.

However, legal benefits cannot be used to bring a legal action against an employer or labor organization or to aid labor unions in proceedings barred by the Labor-Mangement Reporting and Disclosure Act of 1959. ERISA revised the Welfare and Pension Plans Disclosure Act to include prepaid legal services as an employee benefit. This legislation further extended federal control into the legal benefits area.

Although the rationale for prepaid legal-service plans is to help middle-income persons (the poor receive free legal aid and the wealthy can afford it) the profit motive is the primary incentive. Legal insurance offers insurers another source of income and a partial solution to the exploding lawyer population.

SUMMARY

1. Employee benefit plans provide (1) income for employees and/or their dependents because of the employee's death, disability or retirement and (2) funds to pay medical expenses.
2. Three primary reasons for employee benefit plans are to improve employee relations, meet union demands and provide insurance benefits to management at low cost.
3. The cornerstone of most employee benefit plans is group insurance—life and health coverage issued to a group without medical examination under a master policy. Also included are group annuities to fund retirement plans—a subject for Chapter 17.
4. Several characteristics distinguish group insurance from individual insurance:
   a. Group members usually do not pay the full cost of insurance.
   b. Employees do not choose their benefit levels.
   c. Group insurance is less expensive than individual insurance.
   d. The covered group must have some common purpose other than obtaining insurance.

5. Several features of a group insurance plan must be considered to make it operate efficiently:
   a. The group should be large enough to reduce adverse selection and achieve savings in administrative costs.
   b. Mandatory participation (the percent of eligible employees covered) should be established to control adverse selection. Usually 75 percent is required in contributory plans and 100 percent in noncontributory plans.
   c. A disproportionate amount of insurance should not be given to a few members.
6. The original definition and standard provisions developed by the National Association of Insurance Commissioners (NAIC) form the basis for group life insurance statutes. These statutes have undergone many liberalizing changes. Among the standard provisions some are required and others are optional.
7. Typically, group life is written on a yearly renewable term basis. The protection is virtually identical with that provided by individual term insurance.
8. Group life is extended to employee dependents (called dependents' coverage) to provide funds for funeral and other death expenses.
9. Group credit life insurance is written on the lives of debtors and issued to lending institutions and those making installment sales.
10. Group life may be written on a permanent basis and includes three principal types: level premium, unit purchase plans and group ordinary life insurance. Group survivor income benefit insurance provides monthly survivorship benefits to the deceased employee's spouse and children.
11. To provide life insurance protection for retired employees when group term rather than group permanent is written, a retired lives reserve may be used.
12. Wholesale life insurance is written to provide coverage for groups too small for regular group life insurance.
13. Group health coverage usually provides benefits for accidental death and dismemberment, hospital expenses and surgical fees. Also included may be disability income, nursing home care, major medical, dental care, out-of-hospital drugs, vision care and psychiatric care. Group health insurance is less expensive than similar coverage obtained through individual policies.
14. In addition to regular group health insurance, other types of group health coverage include franchise, blanket and group credit health insurance.
15. Some employers with predictable claim rates self-insure employee medical benefit plans, shifting the responsibility of handling claims (and dissatisfied claimants) to an insurer under an administrative service only contract (ASO).
16. Several decisions must be made in designing life and health coverage for employee benefit plans: (1) benefit levels, (2) benefit structure, (3) eligibility standards and (4) financing methods.
17. Though not widespread, group property and liability insurance is written but unlike other group coverage the individual rather than the group often is the underwriting unit.

18. Prepaid legal-service insurance plans are written on a group basis to pay legal fees primarily in five legal areas: civil, criminal, clerical, counseling and preventive law.
19. Flexible compensation (benefit) plans are becoming popular to meet the needs of today's workforce.

REVIEW QUESTIONS

1. Distinguish between a narrow and a broad definition of employee benefit plans.
2. Explain why group life and health insurance costs less than individually written life and health insurance.
3. Why is on-the-job coverage usually not included under group health insurance?
4. Identify two factors that distinguish group insurance from individual coverage.
5. Explain the various types of group life insurance offered by insurers. In your explanation show why just one type would not be sufficient to meet the various needs for group life coverage.
6. What is the objective of prepaid legal insurance?
7. Why has group auto insurance been offered only to a small number of employees?
8. Distinguish between the various types of group permanent insurance.
9. What might limit the expansion of the use of SIBIs in employee benefit plans?
10. What are ASO plans? How are they used in employee benefit plans?
11. Explain a viable method for providing life insurance protection for retired employees when the employee benefit program includes group term rather than group permanent life insurance.
12. What is flexible compensation? Discuss its advantages for the employer and employees. Does organized labor have sound reasons to oppose these plans? Explain.
13. What decisions have to be made by those who are responsible for designing a life insurance plan for employees? Explain.
14. What decisions have to be made by those responsible for designing a disability income plan for employees? Discuss.
15. What decisions must be made in designing a medical care plan for employees? Discuss.

CHAPTER

17 Employee benefit plans: Retirement plans

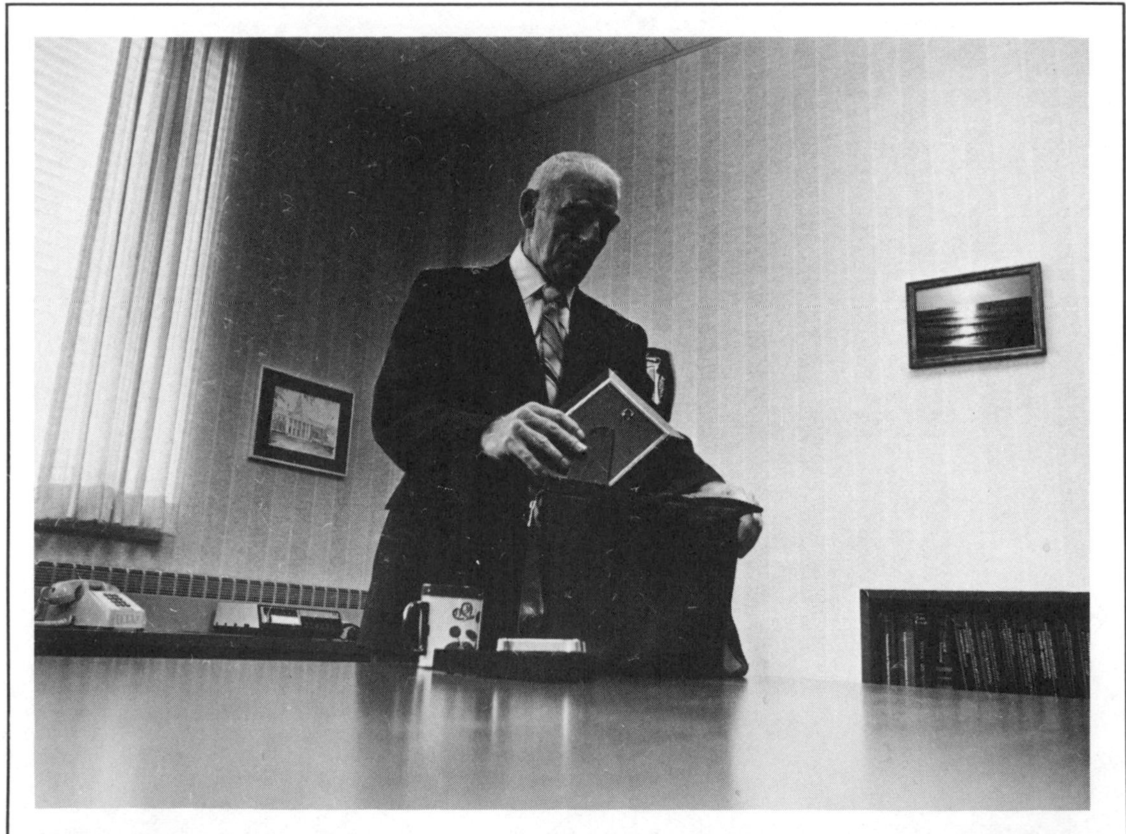

John Thoeming/Richard D. Irwin

CHAPTER OBJECTIVES

1. **To distinguish between defined benefits and defined contribution pension plans and identify the funding concerns of each type.**
2. **To define and compare the types of actuarial cost methods, pension-funding agencies and pension-funding instruments.**
3. **To discuss the basic decisions to be made when establishing private pension plans.**
4. **To describe the influence of ERISA, the IRC and the IRS on private pension plan design and administration.**
5. **To differentiate between qualified pension plans, qualified deferred profit-sharing plans, individual retirement accounts, Keogh plans, tax sheltered annuity plans, ESOPs, TRASOPs and PAYSOPs as a means of building retirement plans.**

More than 50 million wage earners and salaried employees are enrolled in nearly 600,000 private pension plans. Since 1971 private pension plans in operation have increased by 40,000. Employers and employees contribute more than $45 billion annually to these plans. Their assets equal $500 billion and have experienced an average annual *real growth* (i.e., after adjusting for inflation) of 9.2 percent since 1975. Annual retirement benefits are about $17 billion. Nearly 9 million retired workers (or their survivors) receive benefits under these plans. More than 50 percent of the recently retired couples are covered by pension plans.

The Employee Retirement Income Security Act of 1974 (ERISA) prescribes standards for funding, participation, vesting, termination insurance, disclosure, fiduciary responsibility and tax treatment of private pension plans. Prior to ERISA pension fund assets were the largest private accumulation not subject to strict federal regulation. Pension plans qualified under the Internal Revenue Code and its interpretative rulings receive favorable income tax treatment. ERISA regulations apply to all private pension plans established by businesses engaged in interstate commerce and to plans that seek favorable tax treatment.

Because of ERISA's restrictive funding standards and their effect on the incidence of pension costs and plan design, funding issues, costing methods and funding agencies are discussed first. This discussion is followed by an examination of the basic considerations in designing a retirement plan. After discussing plan termination insurance the chapter ends with an analysis of special types of retirement plans. The subject matter of retirement plans is complex and any attempt to make it simple would produce a useless chapter. The objective here is to present a difficult and technical subject as simply as possible without destroying the value of the explanation.

FUNDING ISSUES

A pension plan is funded when assets are accumulated in advance to pay benefits at retirement. These assets, administered by a trustee or an insurer, are committed irrevocably to pension benefits. A funded pension guarantees that participants will receive their full pension benefits *only if the plan is* **fully funded.**

The Concept of a Fully Funded Plan

Pension plan liabilities are divided into two parts: (1) accumulated past service and (2) current service when earned. Liability for accumulated past service includes not only liability for benefits earned before the plan is initiated (called initial past service) but also for improved benefits for past service if the plan is altered. Technically, for a plan to be fully funded a sufficient amount must be paid into the plan immediately to cover the past service liability and sufficient contributions must be made each year to cover current service benefits as they accrue.

Because the cost of discharging all past service liabilities in one payment usually is prohibitive, the technical requirements for a fully funded plan are seldom met. A less-stringent definition of a fully funded plan would allow past service liabilities to be covered by installments spread over the time until each employee retires. Even this less stringent definition of full funding may impose too large a burden on employers. Therefore federal regulations establish less burdensome minimum funding standards. These standards mandate that employer contributions include all current service costs and installment payments to cover past service liability, usually over a period of 10 years (the minimum period allowed) to 30 years (the maximum period required). Plans operating *before January 1, 1974,* have 40 years to pay past service costs. While these standards may not assure full funding by the time each employee retires, they do require employer contributions that move toward a fully funded plan.

Defined Benefit versus Defined Contribution Plans

A pension plan defines either (1) the benefits paid to employees after retirement *or* (2) the annual contributions employers must pay to buy retirement benefits for each employee. For example, under a defined benefit plan employees would receive a monthly retirement benefit of a specified percentage of final earnings. Under a defined contribution plan an employer would contribute a designated percentage of the employee's pay with the amount of the monthly retirement benefit determined by how much these contributions can buy at retirement. In either case employees may be required to contribute in order to participate in the plan. (The discussion that follows assumes no employee contributions. This assumption in no way affects the explanation of funding adequacy.) If benefit levels are fixed, the plan is called a **defined benefit plan;** if contribution levels are fixed the plan is called a **defined contribution plan.** An understanding of the funding issue requires knowledge of the fundamental difference between defined contribution plans and defined benefit plans.

Defined benefit plans

In a defined benefit plan the employer's contributions must be determined actuarially. Actuaries must make reasonable assumptions about interest rates, mortality experience, employee turnover, the ages when employees retire, salary scales and administrative expenses. The concept of reasonable actuarial assumptions is not a precise one. The term has been given various interpretations even among those whose understanding of actuarial soundness is more sophisticated than that of the typical business financial officer, accountant, lawyer or labor relations expert.

These assumptions and benefit levels determine the *estimated* cost (liabilities) of the plan. (The final cost depends on how nearly realized experience conforms to assumed experience.)

When an employee retires, the pension benefits will be paid according to the plan's schedule. The objective of adequate funding is to provide pension contributions that, when prudently invested, will accumulate sufficient funds to guarantee the payment of benefits without jeopardizing the future pensions for active employees.

In judging the actuarial soundness of a pension fund, not only its liabilities but its assets must be realistically valued. Valuation of assets requires that prudent values be placed on fund assets. Problem areas in pension asset valuations are real estate holdings, rarely traded securities (stocks and bonds), unsecured notes and other nonliquid investments.

To summarize, adequate funding for defined benefit plans requires using (1) reasonable funding standards (the minimum federal standards usually are considered sufficient), (2) realistic actuarial assumptions for measuring liabilities and (3) sound procedures for valuation of assets.

Defined contribution plans

An important distinction between defined contribution and defined benefit plans is that in the former no actuarial estimates are needed to determine employer contributions. Instead employer contributions are determined by the plan agreement, usually a percentage of employee earnings.

The lack of actuarially computed employer contributions does not cause a defined contribution plan to be actuarially unsound. As long as the employer makes the required contributions the plan is fully funded and the employee has the security promised. When an employee retires the benefit level to be paid is determined by (1) the amount accumulated in the pension account for that employee and (2) the mortality, interest and expense assumptions used to determine the pension benefit per $1,000 of accumulations.

The defined contributions are segregated and used to finance employees' retirement benefits through immediate payment either to a life insurer or a trustee, usually a bank. Funds paid to a life insurer may be used in one of two ways. First they may be used to purchase a series of single premium deferred annuities for each employee's retirement. Retiring employees will receive a pension amount equal to the sum of all these single premium annuities purchased for them during their working years. Second, the insurer may invest pension contributions until the employee retires. Then the fund is used to purchase an immediate lifetime annuity.

If pension contributions are paid to a trustee, funds may again be handled in one of two ways. First the trustee can accumulate the funds and use them to purchase an immediate lifetime annuity when the employee retires. The annuity will incorporate the insurer's actuarial assumptions. Second the trustee can accumulate pension funds, bypass the insurer and pay lifetime annuities from these funds *directly* to retired employees. The amount of the annuity depends on the interest, mortality and expense assumptions made by the trustee's consulting actuary.

Note that defined contribution plans use actuarial assumptions to determine retirement benefits rather than employer contributions thus reducing the employer's risk of failure to meet ERISA's funding standards. This lower risk has significantly affected the type of pension plan installed: 80 percent of the new plans since ERISA have been defined contribution plans. Also some shifts have been made in existing plans from defined benefit plans to defined contribution plans.

Problems of meeting minimum funding standards

Recall that the minimum funding standards for a *defined benefit plan* require (1) full funding of current service costs when incurred and (2) full funding of any supplemental liability over a designated period (normally 10 to 30 years). These requirements appear simple, but meeting them is complex. A pension plan is a long-term financial commitment and thus subject to interim changes: (1) improvements in the plan's benefits, (2) actuarial experience that deviates from original assumptions and (3) revaluations to reflect changes in the actuarial assumptions to be applied to the future. Any of these changes affect supplemental pension liabilities or alter the plan's current service costs. The poet Robert Burns put it so aptly particularly when applied to defined benefit plans when he wrote:

> The best laid schemes o' mice and men
>   Gang aft a-gley;
> An' lea'e us nought but grief and pain,
>   For promis'd joy.

The amount of a plan's supplemental liability is the present value of future benefits payable less the present value of current service costs. Present values are computed using what are considered at the time to be reasonable actuarial assumptions. The components of supplemental liability are (1) the *initial* liability for past service costs, (2) the additional liability for retroactive benefit increases for prior service, (3) an increase or decrease in liability following a revaluation to reflect changes in actuarial assumptions for the future and (4) experience losses and gains from prior actuarial assumptions that proved too liberal or conservative. Employers have 30 years (40 years for plans with an unfunded liability on January 1, 1974) to pay (1) the initial past service costs, (2) the cost of retroactive benefit increases and (3) charges or credits from changes in future actuarial assumptions. Experience losses and gains must be spread over 15 years.

To determine whether a plan meets minimum funding standards, plan administrators are required to establish a **funding standard account.** The account is *charged* each year with the plan's current service cost, the annual amount required to pay the supplemental liability, the annual amount required to offset losses from unfavorable actuarial experience (experience losses) and the annual amount required to adjust for changes in future actuarial assumptions that increase estimated cost. The account is *credited* each year with the annual contributions made to the fund, the annual allowances for gains from favorable actuarial experience (experience gains) and the annual allowances for changes in future actuarial assumptions that reduce estimated cost.

The following exhibit summarizes the various ERISA funding standards.

LIABILITY ELEMENT	*AMORTIZATION RATE*
Current service cost	Not amortized—paid each year in full
Initial past service cost	30 years maximum*
Retroactive benefit increases (plan amendments)	30 years maximum
Changes in expected actuarial experience	30 years maximum
Adjustments for experience losses and gains	15 years

* 40 years for plans in effect on 1/1/74.

An employer has met the minimum funding standard if the funding standard account has a zero balance. If the balance is positive, the employer has more than met the minimum standard ("promis'd joy"). If the balance is negative, the employer has a funding deficiency ("grief"). The funding deficiency is subject to a nontax-deductible 5 percent penalty (excise tax) if paid within 90 days;

otherwise the tax is 100 percent. Furthermore, failure to meet minimum funding standards may subject the employer to civil action ("pain").

Plans subject to ERISA funding standards must engage a qualified (enrolled) actuary to develop annual actuarial statements. The actuary certifies the plan's funding status after verifying the reasonableness of asset values and actuarial assumptions used in computing costs and liabilities. In addition, the actuary certifies the amounts required to eliminate funding deficiencies. No reports (or only simplified ones) are required for uncomplicated plans.

Funded ratio

The funded ratio is the ratio of the plan's assets to its liabilities. The ultimate goal is to achieve a funded ratio of 1.0 which means a fully funded plan. The funded ratio is not used to measure whether a plan meets regulatory standards.

INNERSCRIPT: FUNDING STANDARDS—VARIANCES AND EXCEPTIONS

A variance from minimum funding standards is provided for multiemployer plans that existed on January 1, 1974, as long as pension contributions are calculated actuarially as a fixed percentage of employees' compensation. The minimum contribution required is the sum of current service costs and interest on past service costs plus any supplemental liability created by plan amendments. Amortizations for other multiemployer and single-employer plans may be extended up to 10 years if necessary to avoid terminating the plan or reducing benefits. Furthermore, minimum funding contributions are waived in years when payments would create undue hardships for employers. The amount waived must be amortized over 15 years or less.

A plan might be based on a collective bargaining agreement (that will be in effect between one and three years) requiring a specific pension contribution (e.g., fixed contribution rates such as cents per hour). In this case any experience loss can be offset in the next labor agreement by increasing the contribution rate or reducing the benefit scale. Experience gains may be used to reduce contributions or increase benefits in the next contract.

Federal, state and local government plans and church plans are exempt from minimum funding requirements. Also plans fully funded through life insurance or annuity contracts are exempt because premiums charged by insurers are calculated to guarantee adequate funds for meeting pension obligations.

Maximum funding standards

The discussion up to this point deals only with minimum funding standards. No mention has been made of maximum funding standards (except for the 10-year minimum deductible rule) because no maximum funding standards have been established. However, the Internal Revenue Service limits annual tax deductions to that amount necessary to fully fund the plan according to the actuarial cost method used. (Actuarial cost methods are discussed in the next section.)

ACTUARIAL COST METHODS

Funding involves not only measuring pension costs based on actuarial assumptions but also spreading this cost over time. Techniques for spreading pension costs are called **actuarial cost methods.** Broadly classified, they are (1) the accrued benefit cost method and (2) the projected benefit cost method.

Pension costs usually include two elements: (1) normal costs and (2) supplemental costs. **Normal cost** is the annual cost of funding current service benefits. **Supplemental cost** is the cost of discharging the accumulated liability for service performed in the past.

The concept of normal cost needs clarifying. Assume that an employee is age 25 when entering employment but has reached age 40 when the employer installs the plan. The normal cost is computed assuming the employee is age 25. The lower entry age reduces the normal cost because of the extra 15 years over which this cost is spread. The initial past service liability is the accumulated payments assumed to have been made from age 25 to 40 and must be discharged over a period of not more than 30 years after the plan is installed. Supplemental cost (known more precisely as **supplemental liability**) includes several components. The amount required to discharge this liability within the maximum time spans allowed is the annual supplemental cost.

Under the accrued benefit cost method, normal cost and supplemental cost are calculated separately. Under the projected benefit cost method, separate amounts may be computed for normal and for supplemental costs, or one amount can be computed that includes both costs. Under both cost methods, pension costs may be computed either for individual employees separately or all plan participants in the aggregate. These distinctions are clarified as the discussion progresses.

Accrued Benefit Cost Method

The accrued benefit cost method assumes that an employee earns a precise unit of benefit for each year of credited service. The current or normal service cost for each year is the benefit earned times the cost of the benefit. If the unit benefit is $5 per month per year of credited service, the current (normal) cost for a 35-year-old employee would be the single premium for a deferred life annuity of $5 monthly purchased at age 35 and payable at age 65, assuming age 65 is the normal retirement age.

If this employee has 10 years of initial past service benefits when the plan is installed, the employer's supplemental liability is the cost of a $50 lifetime annuity payable at age 65 ($5 times 10 years of credited service). The employer can spread the estimated cost of this initial past service supplemental liability equally over a maximum period of 30 years. The number of years over which the employer chooses to spread this liability determines the annual supplemental cost. That cost must be added to the normal cost to determine the employer's annual contribution.

The accrued benefit cost method does not *necessarily* produce a *level* annual pension charge because as employees advance in age the cost of providing their service benefits increases. Note the modifying word *necessarily.* Only when employee turnover produces a constant age distribution and the supplemental liability remains constant will the employer's pension cost be a level annual charge. Both conditions are practically impossible.

Projected Benefit Cost Method

Under the accrued benefit cost method each benefit is fully funded as it accrues. When this method is used, a precisely determinable benefit must be allocated to each year of service. Most often the basis for allocation is specified in the plan's benefit formula. However, the accrued benefit cost method can be used where the plan's formula does not precisely allocate benefits to each year of service. In this event the employer makes the allocation by dividing the projected benefit by the number of years of remaining service. For example, an employee with 15 years of remaining service and a projected benefit of $1,000 a month would be allocated a benefit of $800 for each year of service ($1,000 × 12 = $12,000 ÷ 15 = $800). Because the employer's allocation patently is totally arbitrary, a better approach is to use the projected benefit cost method. This method may be used either on an attained age or an entry age normal basis.

Attained age basis Under the projected benefit cost method, the pension is funded with equal annual contributions. Normal and supplemental costs are combined. The full cost (normal and supplemental) is spread over the period elapsing from the employee's age when the plan is installed (attained age) until retirement. Contributions are level and are calculated to be sufficient to fully fund the supplemental liability by the time the employee retires. Unless the plan is fully funded by insurance or annuity contracts the attained age basis will not meet ERISA's minimum funding standards because the plan is likely to include employees with more than 30 years of remaining service thus extending the supplemental liability funding period beyond the maximum years allowed.

Entry age normal basis Usually supplemental costs and normal costs are handled separately using the entry age normal basis. In computing current service (normal) costs this basis assumes that costs accrue before the plan is installed and that the employer has funded past service benefits for each employee from the time he or she first became eligible to participate in the plan, perhaps many years ago. For a simple example, Evelyn began work at age 30 for a company that installed a pension plan 10 years later. The benefit formula granted her 10 years of service credits starting with her entry age (30). The company computes its pension costs on the assumption that it had already paid current service costs for Evelyn for these 10 years. So the plan starts off with an initial past service supplemental liability. The current service cost for Evelyn will be lower because it is computed at her lower entry age rather than her higher attained age. The initial supplemental liability offsets the lower current service cost. The employer's annual pension cost is a level contribution sufficient to cover current or normal service cost and at least the amount required to fund the initial supplemental cost in equal payments over 30 years.

Aggregate level cost basis The discussion up to this point assumes that the cost for each participant's projected benefit is calculated separately and that the employer's cost is the sum of these calculations. This method is called the individual projected benefit cost basis. An aggregate projected benefit cost basis can be used to compute the employer's annual pension cost without identifying particular individuals.

The aggregate level projected benefit cost basis requires fewer computations than the individual basis. Employees are divided into age groups (usually of five years), and the computations are made for the midpoints of each group. For example, all employees in the age 30 to 34 classification are considered to be age 32. All employment statistics needed for making pension cost computations for each age bracket are collected and tabulated. Thus the age 30 to 34 bracket may show 30 employees earning a total of $840,000, an annual average of $28,000 each. In addition, the figures show that these employees have earned an average of 9 years of past service and have 38 years of remaining future service, assuming a normal retirement age of 70. With these statistics and similar ones for other age brackets the computation of the employer's normal and supplemental pension costs is simplified.

Tables 17–1, 17–2 and 17–3 illustrate the use of the aggregate level cost basis of projected benefits. The letter *t* represents the *termination rate.* How to compute the present value of a deferred life annuity due of one and the present value of a temporary life annuity due of one payable to age 65 is explained in Chapter 21. Table 17–1 gives the employee population data; Table 17–2 gives the computations based on the unrealistic assumption of no vesting; and Table 17–3 shows the effects of different vesting methods on the projected benefit cost.

Based on the computations in Table 17–2 the employer's projected annual contribution rate to a noncontributing plan would be column 6 ($2,635,226) ÷ column 8 ($15,272,497) or 17.2547 percent of payroll. In dollars the amount is 17.2547 percent times column 2 ($1,613,000) or $278,318. For other vesting arrangements divide the appropriate column in Table 17–3 by column 8 in Table 17–2 and then multiply by column 2 in Table 17–2.

The following tabulation shows the annual projected contribution rates and the annual projected dollar cost under various vesting provisions. (Vesting provisions are explained later.)

VESTING PROVISION	*PROJECTED ANNUAL PERCENTAGE CONTRIBUTION*	*PROJECTED ANNUAL BENEFIT DOLLAR COST*
Immediate full vesting	18.4810	$298,098
100% vesting at 10 years	18.4047	296,868
Graded 5/15 vesting	18.3529	296,032
Rule of 45 vesting	18.3499	295,984

These percentages and dollar amounts are based on the unrealistic assumptions that interest and terminations are as assumed, the benefit formula and earnings are unchanged and no new employees are added. The employer, therefore, must recompute these percentages and amounts periodically.

TABLE 17–1 Employee Population Data

AGE BRACKET	*MIDPOINT IN BRACKET*	*NUMBER OF EMPLOYEES*	*TOTAL ANNUAL EARNINGS*	*AVERAGE ANNUAL EARNINGS*	*AVERAGE YEARS OF PAST SERVICE*
20–24	22	8	$ 72,000	$ 9,000	3
25–29	27	10	110,000	11,000	3
30–34	32	20	240,000	12,000	7
35–39	37	18	216,000	12,000	10
40–44	42	19	247,000	13,000	12
45–49	47	15	210,000	14,000	19
50–54	52	12	192,000	16,000	20
55–59	57	10	166,000	16,600	30
60–64	62	8	160,000	20,000	32
Totals			$1,613,000		136

TABLE 17–2
Illustration of Computation under Projected Benefit Cost Method—Aggregate Level Cost

(1) MIDPOINT AGE BRACKET	(2) TOTAL ANNUAL EARNINGS	(3) TOTAL YEARS OF COVERED SERVICE (AGE 65 − COL. 1 + COL. 9)	(4) TOTAL PROJECTED BENEFITS (1.5% OF COL. 2 × COL. 3)	(5) PRESENT VALUE OF A DEFERRED LIFE ANNUITY DUE OF ONE PAYABLE AT AGE 65 (t-3; 5%)	(6) PRESENT VALUE OF TOTAL PROJECTED BENEFITS (COL. 4 × COL. 5)	(7) PRESENT VALUE OF LIFE ANNUITY OF ONE PAYABLE TO AGE 65 (t-3; 5%)	(8) PRESENT VALUE OF FUTURE EARNINGS (COL. 2 × COL. 7)	(9) AVERAGE YEARS OF PAST SERVICE
22	$ 72,000	46	$ 49,680	0.278	$ 13,812	10.463	$ 753,336	3
27	110,000	41	67,650	0.472	31,930	10.849	1,193,390	3
32	240,000	40	144,000	0.778	112,032	11.077	2,658,480	7
37	216,000	38	123,120	1.262	155,378	11.232	2,426,112	10
42	247,000	35	129,676	1.992	258,314	11.115	2,745,405	12
47	210,000	37	116,550	3.063	356,992	10.587	2,223,270	19
52	192,000	33	95,040	4.443	422,262	9.113	1,749,696	20
57	166,000	38	94,620	6.112	578,318	6.468	1,073,688	30
62	160,000	35	84,000	8.407	706,188	2.807	449,120	32
Total ...	$1,613,000	343	$904,336		$2,635,226		$15,272,497	136

TABLE 17–3
Effect of Different Vesting Methods on Projected Benefit Cost—Aggregate Level Cost

(1) MIDPOINT AGE BRACKET	(2) PRESENT VALUE OF TOTAL PROJECTED BENEFITS NO VESTING (COL. 6, TABLE 17–2)	(3) PRESENT VALUE OF TOTAL PROJECTED BENEFITS IMMEDIATE FULL VESTING	(4) PRESENT VALUE OF TOTAL PROJECTED BENEFITS 100% VESTING AT 10 YEARS	(5) PRESENT VALUE OF TOTAL PROJECTED BENEFITS GRADED 5/15 VESTING	(6) PRESENT VALUE OF TOTAL PROJECTED BENEFITS RULE OF 45 VESTING
22	$ 13,812	$ 23,400	$ 21,462	$ 21,462	$ 20,916
27	31,930	46,950	43,432	43,432	42,416
32	112,032	154,944	148,752	147,744	145,296
37	155,378	196,992	196,992	192,682	194,160
42	258,314	299,422	299,422	296,828	298,904
47	356,992	385,198	385,198	385,198	385,198
52	422,262	430,246	430,246	430,246	430,246
57	578,318	579,170	579,170	579,170	579,170
62	706,188	706,188	706,188	706,188	706,188
Total	$2,635,226	$2,822,510	$2,810,862	$2,802,950	$2,802,494

ADVANTAGES OF FUNDING

Besides protecting employees against losing their pensions if the funding is inadequate, funding provides income tax advantages to plans approved by the IRS. The tax advantages result in reduced pension costs. For example, investment income earned on funds deposited with the insurer or trustee accrues income-tax free until distributed (taxation of pension distributions is discussed later). Funding also allows employers tax deductions for current service benefits in the year incurred and past service costs in the years funded. Under some actuarial cost methods, the employers' annual tax deduction for contributions is limited to the amount required to pay current service costs and an amount necessary to amortize any supplemental liability over 10 years.

Funding also offers the advantage of increasing pension benefits without increasing employers' cost by requiring employees to share in the financing. Furthermore, funding gives the employer flexibility in financing the plan. When cash flow falls, payments to a fund can be reduced or postponed. However, a reduction or postponement must not violate ERISA's funding standards.

FUNDING AGENCIES

When a bank or individual trustee is the funding agency, the plan is called a **trust fund plan.** When a life insurer is the funding agency, the plan is called an **insured plan.** When both agencies are used, the plan is unimaginatively called a **split-funded plan.**

Trust Fund Plans

In trust fund plans employers turn the contributions over to trustees who invest them and pay the benefits according to the plan's specifications. The plan is suitable for employers with sufficient employees to predict mortality within an acceptable range and who are financially able to absorb the losses when mortality experience exceeds the expected range. The trust fund plan is popular with multiemployer and union pension plans.

Insured Plans

In an insured plan employers transmit the contributions to an insurer who invests them and pays the scheduled benefits. Guarantees made by the insurer depend on the insurance contract selected (technically known as a **funding instrument**).

When insurers serve as pension funding agencies, two types of funding instruments are used: (1) those where cash-value life insurance or deferred annuities are immediately purchased for each participating employee and (2) those where the funds accumulate (as in trust fund plans) and are used later to purchase immediate annuities for employees at retirement and pay any contractual benefits due terminating employees. The first type of contract (technically called **allocated funding instruments**) has three forms: individual life or annuity contracts, group permanent life and group deferred annuities. The second type of contract (technically known as **unallocated funding instruments**) includes group deposit administration contracts, immediate participation guarantee plans and guaranteed investment accounts. Unallocated funding instruments grew from efforts of insurers to improve their competitive position with banks as pension funding agencies.

Individual policy plans

Some retirement plans that include fewer than 10 covered employees are funded by individual insurance policies even though some insurers are willing to write group annuities for very small groups. When individual policies are purchased and held by a trustee, the arrangement is called an **individual policy pension trust.** Employers frequently designate one of their executives as trustee to receive contributions and apply for, retain and pay premiums for the individual policies. The insurer pays benefits directly to those eligible for them.

In individual policy pension plans interest, mortality and expense rates are fixed. Thus the employer's maximum cost for each employee's pension is guaranteed when the policy is purchased. The maximum cost of additional coverage for present and new employees depends on the insurer's premium rates when the additional policies are bought.

Group permanent life insurance

Group permanent life can be used to fund pensions. Premiums are paid to the insurer who pays the benefits to employees upon retirement. Guarantees are similar to those in individual policy plans with the added guarantee that initial rates are applicable to purchases of additional units during the first several years (usually five) of the master contract. Rather than using group permanent life insurance to combine death protection with the funding of qualified pension plans, the simpler approach is to use group term life insurance to provide life insurance benefits and to fund pension benefits through group annuity contracts.

Group deferred annuities

Some insurers write group deferred annuities for 10 or even fewer employees. Insurers establish minimum total premiums or minimum premiums per employee as an eligibility standard to achieve adequate size for administrative efficiency. These underwriting rules are established to provide adequate funds for plan administration rather than to prevent adverse selection. A separate charge is made for a small group or for relaxed underwriting standards.

Typical group deferred annuity plans provide for buying specified amounts of fully paid deferred annuity units each year for eligible employees. The units are single-premium deferred annuities. If a fully paid deferred annuity of $30 a month is purchased each year, an employee with 35 years of service at retirement will have a guaranteed retirement income of $1,050 a month ($30 × 35). Group annuity contracts usually provide that paid-up units can be purchased at the initial rates for the first five years. Under some plans, employees have immediate ownership of the paid-up annuity units. However, annuity pay-outs are deferred until the employee is eligible to retire. Under other plans employee ownership is deferred until after a designated period of service.

Deposit administration plans

Under the deposit administration plan (DA), annuity units are not bought immediately with each contribution. Instead, insurers accumulate the deposits to buy annuities for employees at retirement. Before retirement the plan is similar to a trust fund plan. After retirement the plan is similar to a group deferred annuity because funds are "transferred" within the insurer from the DA account to "purchase" a single-premium retirement annuity. For the conventional DA plan, interest and annuity purchase rates are guaranteed for all funds deposited within the first five years.

The contract describes the basis for crediting interest earned. At one time the interest credited was often related to the *average net rate earned* by the insurer's total investment portfolio, but the average rate is no longer competitive. The use of new money rates is discussed in the next section.

The immediate participation guarantee plan. Under the immediate participation guarantee (IPG) DA plan the fund is credited annually with the net rate of interest earned by the insurer, charged annually with administration expenses and credited or charged with mortality gains or losses. At retirement the employee's pension is paid directly from the fund. By this method the employer participates immediately and fully in the plan's favorable or unfavorable investment and mortality experience. However, because of currently high interest rates, the present method, called the **investment year** or **new-money approach,** is generally used to allow insurers to compete with other pension funding agencies. This method relates the guarantees to current market rates available for deposited funds.

Separate or segregated accounts. Another variation of DA plans, separate accounts, is designed for employers electing to invest a part of their deposits in equities without subjecting their funds to the restrictive regulations applicable to the insurer's general assets. Separate accounts are maintained by the insurer who selects the investments. Generally the accounts are pooled for all employers, although some insurers offer individual accounts for plans large enough for a diversified investment portfolio. Insurers may maintain pooled accounts for common stocks, real estate mortgages and corporate bonds, and employers can split contributions among these accounts.

In contributory plans, only employer contributions can be placed in segregated accounts. The Securities and Exchange Commission requires that employee contributions be included in the insurer's general investment funds and accumulated at a guaranteed minimum rate of interest. No investment guarantees are made for separate accounts. However, annuity purchase rates are guaranteed just as in other DA plans.

Guaranteed investment contracts (GICs). Many insurers offer special single-sum investment contracts designed to attract pension funds. These popular contracts offer guaranteed rates competitive with current market rates. The guarantees are for a number of years. The length of the guarantee to a large extent depends on the duration of the insurer's particular investment(s) in which these funds are committed.

Unallocated funding instruments are the most popular ones used in insured plans. Individual policy pension trusts, group permanent and other allocated plans account for less than 10 percent of insured plans.

TERMINATION OF PLANS

Upon termination of plans, the funds are allocated to employees according to their equitable interest. The termination provisions must not discriminate in favor of officers, stockholders and highly paid employees. ERISA provides the following priorities for allocating employees' retirement benefits:

1. Voluntary employee contributions.
2. Mandatory employee contributions.
3. Benefits for the employees who have been retired at least three years or who were eligible to retire at least three years before the plan's termination date. (The provisions of the plan in effect five years prior to the plan's termination date are used to determine the amount of these benefits).
4. All other benefits guaranteed by the Pension Benefit Guaranty Corporation (PBGC). PBGC is discussed later.
5. All other vested benefits.
6. All other benefits accrued under the plan.

If gains result from actuarial assumptions that proved to be conservative, the funds remaining after meeting these priorities may be returned to the employer.

BASIC DECISIONS IN ESTABLISHING RETIREMENT PLANS

Retirement plans are more complex than group life and health plans. In addition to tax constraints, questions of finance as well as employee relations must be considered. ERISA, the Internal Revenue Code and the Internal Revenue Service rulings set broad requirements for a qualified pension plan. Basic decisions that must be made are eligibility qualifications, conditions for paying benefits, benefit levels and types of benefits. Requirements for qualifying pensions do not specify the precise funding policy but they do establish minimum funding standards. Cost, competitive conditions in the labor market and the desire for an effective personnel and employee relations policy are important considerations in designing retirement benefit plans.

A qualified retirement plan must be (1) established by the employer; (2) for the exclusive benefit of employees and their beneficiaries; (3) written; (4) permanent; (5) communicated to the employees; (6) financed by contributions from the employer, the employee or both; (7) nondiscriminatory with respect to coverage and benefits; (8) based on a defined contribution or defined benefit formula and (9) protected so that no part of the fund assets or income may be recaptured by the employer until all employee liabilities under the plan are satisfied.

Eligibility of Coverage

Under the IRC provisions a qualified plan must benefit employees (and their beneficiaries) in general, not special designated employees. The plan must meet one of the following tests: (1) at least 70 percent of all employees must be covered (or 80 percent of all eligible employees in a contributory plan, provided that 70 percent or more are eligible) or (2) if only specific classes of employees are covered, the classification must not discriminate in favor of officers, stockholders, supervisors or high-salaried employees. Plans meeting the percentage test (test 1) automatically satisfy the IRC coverage requirement. Plans that fail the percentage test can qualify by meeting the classification test (test 2). In this event the plan is subject to the discretionary power of the IRS. For the classification test nearly any classification is acceptable if it does not violate the nondiscriminatory requirement. One classification not permitted is union employees or nonunion employees.

ERISA requires that 25-year-old employees with one year of service be covered. However, three years of service can be required if employer contributions are immediately 100 percent vested (vesting is discussed later). Employees within five years of normal retirement age may be excluded in defined benefit plans (discussed later).

One of the common eligibility standards in pension plans is that employees be actively employed on a full-time basis. However, ERISA has eliminated many requirements and improved the status of part-time, seasonal and reemployed participants. Some plans require no probation period for eligibility.

Eligibility for Benefits

Pension plans may specify the normal retirement age when an employee is eligible for full benefits and a compulsory retirement age. Using social security as a guideline most plans initially set age 65 for normal retirement. Because federal legislation prohibits compulsory retirement before age 70 that age has now become the compulsory retirement age. In some industries or occupations for which age 65 seems inappropriate, the normal retirement age may be lower. Some flexibility may be permitted in the normal retirement age by allowing early or late retirement. If early retirement is at the employer's request, benefits are not reduced. For delayed retirements, employees may be entitled to an increased pension but pension credits do not necessarily accumulate beyond the normal retirement age. The Age Discrimination in Employment Act (ADEA) prohibits compulsory retirement before age 70. However, for a defined contribution plan employers are allowed to discontinue contributions on behalf of employees after they reach normal retirement age. Employers are not required to cover new employees hired beyond the normal retirement age.

Benefit Levels

As noted, pension benefits depend either on the contributions to the fund (defined contribution plans) or on the plan's benefit formula (defined benefit plans). Benefits under a defined contribution plan are usually conventional fixed dollar payments. However, some defined contribution plans incorporate the variable annuity principle where each payment is a function of the pension fund's investment performance. So, for a defined benefit plan, the employee's retirement benefit depends on the accumulated amount of the employer's and employee's contributions, the annuity rate used and whether the plan is a fixed-dollar or variable annuity plan.

Under a defined benefit plan pension benefits are determined by formula. The formula may be one of several types: flat amount, flat percentage, flat amount unit benefit or percentage unit benefit. The **flat amount formula** provides all participants the same benefit regardless of earnings, age and to some extent years of service. For example, participants with the minimum service (e.g., 25 years) receive a $300 monthly retirement benefit. Those with less than the minimum service (e.g., 20 years) receive proportionately less, e.g., $240 monthly. The flat amount formula is used in a number of negotiated plans. The **flat percentage formula** relates benefits to earnings. Under this formula a pension equal to a percentage (e.g., 40 percent) of an employee's average annual wage is paid to all employees completing a minimum number of years of service. This percentage may be applied to the average annual earnings for all years of service with the employer (*career average*) or limited to the average annual earnings during the three or four consecutive years of highest earnings (*final average*). Inflation has made career-average benefits inadequate. Consequently, the final average earnings formula is more popular because it increases retirement benefits.

The formula provides no increase in benefits for time worked that exceeds the minimum length of service. However, employees who fail to meet the minimum service required are given a proportionately reduced pension. The exact percentage used and the average compensation to which the percentage applies vary widely among plans.

The **flat amount unit benefit formula** relates pension benefits to years of service but not to earnings. Under this plan the employee accumulates one unit of benefit for each year of credited service. An employee with 30 years of service receives 30 benefit units. If each unit is worth $10 a month the employee's monthly pension is $300 (30 × $10). The flat amount unit benefit formula also is used in negotiated plans. The **percentage unit benefit formula** may be used to relate benefits to both years of service and earnings. Under this formula the employee is given percentage points for each year of service, e.g., 2 percent.

An employee with 30 years of service receives a monthly pension benefit equal to 60 percent of earnings (30 × 2). The earnings to which the percentage applies may be either the career average or the final average. When a pension plan is installed an established company will have employees with many years of service. These years are usually rewarded at a lower rate than service after the plan becomes effective. The difference is justified by the higher cost of funding past service benefits. Interest and employee terminations play a significant role in pension finance. No interest will have been earned on unfunded past service benefits and no gains from terminations will have accrued. Furthermore, in contributory plans past service benefits must be financed entirely by the employer.

The discrimination against past service may be insignificant if the benefit is based on earnings in the year the unit is applied. The percentage used to determine the past service benefit is applied to the employee's current earnings at the time the plan is installed rather than to the amount earned when the service was rendered. Because earnings normally increase over time the higher base might compensate for the lower rate. Past service credits can be limited by ignoring some past service, counting only those earned beyond a specific age or a specific employment period. Some plans grant no past service credit, setting a minimum benefit instead.

In some unit benefit formulas, a higher percentage is applied to annual earnings that exceed the social security tax base. Pension formulas that consider social security payments are called integrated plans. Under IRS regulations two types of integrated plans are approved: the offset and the excess plan.

The **offset** plan provides that at retirement the benefits otherwise provided employees by the benefit formula are reduced by a percentage of the employee's social security benefit. The effect is to reduce partially the payment required from the employer, thus denying the employee the full social security increase. The offset plan is seldom used because employees do not like it and for good reason, of course.

An **excess** plan covers employees only if their annual earnings exceed a given amount, usually the social security tax base. The excess plan is the popular method of integrating private pension plans with social security. Special IRS rules must be followed to establish benefit formulas for qualified integrated plans.

Under defined benefit plans the employer's cost is not known until the final pension check is paid. The employer knows only the actuarial cost projections.

The employer's costs will fluctuate as experience varies from actuarial assumptions. Because some business firms are averse to pension costs that fluctuate and cannot be precisely determined, they are willing to give employees a pension only if the costs can be budgeted in advance and related to payroll cost. Thus these firms use defined contribution plans. While the absence of a definite benefit formula is admittedly unattractive to employees, the definite cost associated with the defined contribution plan appeals to the employer.

Some employers prefer to relate contributions for retirement benefits to profits rather than to payroll, especially if profits fluctuate widely. These plans are called **deferred profit-sharing plans.** Under some plans the employer determines on a year-to-year basis the amount of profit to be allocated to the deferred profit-sharing plan. Other companies use a formula: a percentage of gross profits, net profits, profits available after the payment of a minimum dividend on common stock, net profits available after deducting a fixed percentage of invested capital or a graded percentage of net profits. These plans must meet IRC and ERISA guidelines for participation, vesting, benefits, lump-sum distributions, fiduciaries and reporting standards, and employers must make frequent and recurring contributions. In some deferred profit-sharing plans employees are required to contribute in order to participate.

Profits to be shared may be allocated among employees on the basis of earnings, years of service or both. The IRS prohibits allocation on the basis of age. To illustrate, assume that the Uptight Corporation distributes $100,000 of this year's profits to its 100 employees using both years of service and earnings as the bases. Points are given as follows:

YEARS OF SERVICE	*POINTS*	*EARNINGS*	*POINTS*
0–5	0	Less than $10,000	1
5–10	1	$10,000–$19,999	2
10–15	2	$20,000–$29,999	3
15–20	3	$30,000–$49,999	4
20–25	4	over $50,000	5
Over 25	5		

Assume that the 100 employees have a total of 500 points. Thus each point is worth $200 of shared profits. In this example an employee with 16 years of service who earns $25,000 a year will be allocated 6 points or $1,200. Another employee with 28 years of service who earns $71,000 a year will be allocated 10 points or $2,000.

Regardless of whether the retirement plan is a defined benefit, defined contribution or deferred profit sharing, pension experts agree that retirement income should be at least 70 to 75 percent of preretirement income including social security for long-service employees. Nevertheless, if the benefit is fixed throughout retirement, the retired employee is exposed to purchasing power loss. Furthermore, retirees are unable to share improved standards of living that develop in a growing economy. Variable pensions with cost-of-living adjustments are growing in popularity because labor and management believe the national economy has built-in inflation.

Achieving adequate benefit levels is important to low and middle income workers. However, ERISA imposes limits on benefits for high income workers. Annual retirement benefits funded by *employer* contributions in a defined benefit plan are limited by ERISA to the *smaller* of (1) 100 percent of the participant's average compensation for the highest three consecutive years or (2) $75,000 adjusted for inflation ($136,425 as of January 1, 1982). For defined contribution plans, including profit sharing, the annual addition to a participant's account is limited to the smaller of (1) 25 percent of the participant's annual compensation or (2) $25,000, adjusted for inflation ($45,475 as of January 1, 1982). (How these limits and other aspects of pension plans are affected by the Tax Equity and Fiscal Responsibility Act of 1982 are discussed later.)

Types of Benefits

Although a qualified pension plan must be primarily for retirement benefits, other benefits may be included.

Vesting

A decision must be made on vesting provisions. If the plan is fully vested a terminating employee retains equity in both employer and employee contributions. ERISA requires that a participant's rights to accumulated benefits from employee contributions be nonforfeitable. This requirement makes it necessary in a contributory plan to determine benefits attributable to employee contributions. The employee's account balance measures the benefits attributable to employee contributions in defined contribution plans. In defined benefit plans these benefits are computed by applying a conversion factor to the employee's accumulated contributions. ERISA states how the applicable interest rates and conversion factors are determined. Once the amount attributable to employees' contributions is determined the remainder is the amount attributed to the employer's contributions.

Terminating employees covered under a contributory pension plan have two options regarding *their own* contributions: (1) a paid-up pension payable at normal retirement age for an amount based on their contributions or (2) a lump-sum cash payment of their own contributions. If option (2) is selected the employer may include or withhold interest. Most commonly, employers pay interest at a nominal rate.

Regarding employer contributions ERISA has 3 minimum vesting standards: the **10-year rule,** the **graded 5–15 rule** and the **rule of 45.** The 10-year rule grants employees full vesting after 10 years of service. The graded 5–15-year vesting standard requires 25 percent vesting after 5 years of service; then 5 percent a year, reaching 50 percent after 10 years of service; then 10 percent a year, arriving at 100 percent after 15 years of service. The rule of 45 requires that the benefits for an employee with at least 5 years of service must be 50 percent vested whenever the employee's age and service years add up to 45. The percentage of vesting required increases 10 percent each following year until 100 percent vesting is attained. If the employee has 10 years of service 50 percent vesting must be granted immediately regardless of the age-plus-service figure and increased by 10 percent for each additional year thereafter.

The IRS has added a fourth vesting standard—the **4–40 rule,** under which a plan must be 40 percent vested for a participant after 4 years of service, 45 percent after 5 years, 50 percent after 6 years and then 10 percent additional for each of the next 5 years. Its purpose is to prevent "actual or potential discrimination" in favor of "highly compensated participants" against the "rank and file" participants. The IRS requires 4–40 vesting for qualification of plans that cannot pass the discrimination tests. Multiemployers can be exempt from the discrimination tests if these tests are "unduly burdensome." The IRS may require more rapid vesting to cure a pattern of employer abuse or to prevent discrimination in favor of officers or stockholders.

In all but the 10-year rule, partial vesting of employer contributions occurs before full vesting. For example, under the graded 5–15 year vesting standard, if an employee terminates employment with 5 years of covered service, the employer's contributions are 25 percent vested. If the plan is noncontributory, the vested amount is 25 percent of the accumulated benefit at the time of termination. If the plan is contributory, the employee's contributions when added to the employer's contributions increase the pension benefits to an amount exceeding 25 percent of the accrued benefit at the time of termination.

The principal advantages of restricted vesting for employer contributions are (1) lower costs because employers retain their contributions when employment terminates prior to vesting and (2) lower employee turnover. The employer must weigh these advantages against the social benefits of liberal vesting.

An employee's vested benefits from employer contributions may be forfeited (1) if the employee dies (unless a joint-and-survivor option is in effect) or (2) if the employee withdraws his or her contributions from a contributory plan that is less than 50 percent vested. However, the employee may "buy back" and restore forfeited benefits by repaying the withdrawn contributions at 5 percent interest. If the plan is at least 50 percent vested the employee may withdraw his or her contributions in a lump sum and still retain the vested benefits from the employer's contribution.

Death benefits Under contributory plans the employee's accumulated contributions are paid to the employee's beneficiary if the employee dies before retirement. Occasionally a *true death benefit* is provided in both contributory and noncontributory plans, but death benefits more commonly are arranged through group life insurance plans. When the pension is funded through individual life insurance policies death payments are a fundamental part of the plan. According to ERISA requirements pension plans must make available to participants who have been married at least one year at the time of death a joint and 50 percent survivorship annuity for the spouse. This annuity is optional for the participant who has attained the earliest retirement age under the plan. Unless the employee elects a different plan a joint and 50 percent survivorship annuity is automatic for employees attaining normal retirement age. The participant generally pays the cost of this benefit by accepting a reduced pension.

Disability benefits Although long-term disability income benefits may be included in pension plans, many planners are reluctant to incorporate them because they increase pension costs and are difficult to administer. When disability benefits are included, safeguards are used to protect against adverse selection and faked claims. These safeguards include a long service eligibility period, a precise disability definition, low benefits and periodic checkups following disability.

Medical expenses Some pension plans incorporate provisions for accumulating funds for medical benefits for retired employees, their spouses and dependents. The accumulated funds are used to pay medical expenses directly or to pay premiums for group health insurance or supplementary medicare insurance. Payment of these expenses from qualified pension funds is not treated as taxable income to the participant, an added tax advantage of qualified plans.

Funding the Benefits

Management must decide whether the funding agency is to be a trust company (e.g., bank) or an insurance company. If insurance is used a variety of funding instruments are available, each having its special use.

The decision factors for choosing between trust fund plans and the several types of insured plans are the (1) degree of freedom sought in investment decisions, (2) plan administration cost, (3) value of the insurer's services in administering benefits to retired employees, (4) importance of investment guarantees, (5) emphasis given to mortality guarantees, (6) flexibility desired in actuarial assumptions and funding methods, (7) concern about fiduciary liability under ERISA and (8) freedom desired in benefit design.

The extent to which insured plans meet the eight decision factors varies widely among available funding instruments. As noted, these instruments vary from the conventional annuity (with the most pension guarantees and least investment and design freedom) to the least restricted segregated account (with the least guarantees and most investment and design freedoms).

The employer may balance pension guarantees against investment and design freedoms (implicit in the eight decision factors) by using a split-funding approach. Split-funding distributes pension contributions between an insurer and a trustee.

INNERSCRIPT: INCOME TAXATION OF BENEFITS—QUALIFIED PENSION AND PROFIT-SHARING PLANS

Benefits under qualified pension and deferred profit-sharing plans sometimes are paid as a lump-sum distribution but more often as a lifetime annuity. How the benefits are paid determines how they are taxed. The Internal Revenue Code (IRC) defines a lump-sum pension distribution as a payment to an employee who has died, terminated employment, reached age 59½ or was disabled within the tax year. An employee's cost basis is subtracted from the lump-sum distribution to find the total taxable amount (TTA). If employer securities are part of the distribution, unrealized appreciation in them is also subtracted to compute the TTA. The minimum distribution allowance (MDA) is 50 percent of the first $20,000 of TTA reduced by 20 percent of the TTA amount over $20,000. The MDA is designed to reduce taxes for relatively small distributions. For distributions over $70,000 the MDA works out to be zero: 50 percent of $20,000 = $10,000; 20 percent of $50,000 = $10,000; $10,000 − $10,000 = 0.

The special 10-year income averaging device, known as the initial separate tax (IST), treats the post-1973 portion of the lump-sum distribution as ordinary income received over 10 years. The IST is computed by subtracting the minimum distribution allowance (MDA) from the total taxable amount (TTA) and multiplying the tax on the sum of $2,300 plus 1/10 of the remainder by 10. The tax rate used is that for a single person. The $2,300 used here is the zero bracket amount for that person in 1982. (Do not memorize these figures because the zero bracket amount and the tax rate for single people will change with changes in the income tax law.) An employee must be a participant in the pension plan for at least five years to qualify for IST treatment.

The next step to determine the taxes payable on a lump-sum distribution is to find the percentage of the TTA that is ordinary

(continued)

income and the portion that is a long-term capital gain. The ordinary income portion is the number of participation years after 1973 divided by the total years of participation in the plan multiplied by the TTA. The balance of the TTA is a long-term capital gain. If this discussion is confusing (and it probably is), do not worry because a clarifying illustration appears later just when needed.

When employees elect to receive retirement benefits by installments, the taxes payable depend on whether the employees have a cost basis in the distributions. Without a cost basis the employee must report the distributions as income in the year received. If the employee has a cost basis, pension benefits are taxed under either of two IRS rules: (1) the three-year cost recovery rule or (2) the annuity exclusion ratio. *The three-year cost recovery rule* provides that if the installment payments received during the first three years equal or exceed the employee's basis, all the pension payments are excluded from gross income until the employee has recovered the cost basis. Afterwards 100 percent of each distribution is included in gross income. *The annuity exclusion rule* allows the employee to recover the cost basis by excluding only part of each pension payment. Two factors are necessary to compute the exclusion ratio: the employee's cost basis and the expected return from the annuity. The exclusion ratio is used to calculate the percentage of benefits received each year that are a recovery of the employee's cost and therefore not subject to tax. The amount an employee can exclude from income is determined by life expectancy tables published by the IRS. The amount excluded each year is the employee's cost basis divided by the remaining life expectancy as shown in the IRS tables.

Tax calculation for a lump-sum pension distribution—an example

On December 31, 1982, Hun Park, age 65, received a $100,000 lump-sum pension distribution that included his employer's stock worth $35,000. The cost basis of the stock was $10,000. Hun had participated in the plan since January 1, 1951, with 32 years of service and had contributed $25,000 towards his retirement plan. The tax on the ordinary income portion of the pension distribution is calculated as follows:

Step 1. Determine the TTA (total taxable amount)

Total distribution		$100,000
Less:		
Employee contributions	$25,000	
Unrealized appreciation in employer's stock ($35,000 fair market value − $10,000 basis)	25,000	
	$50,000	−50,000
Net distribution (TTA)		$ 50,000

Step 2. Determine the MDA (minimum distribution allowance)

50 percent of the first $20,000 of the distribution	$ 10,000
Less 20% of the net distribution over $20,000: 20% ($50,000 − $20,000)	− 6,000
MDA	$ 4,000

Step 3. Determine the TTA − MDA

TTA	$ 50,000
Less MDA	− 4,000
TTA − MDA	$ 46,000

Step 4. Determine the percentage of the distribution taxed at ordinary income rates

Percentage of distribution taxed at ordinary income rates:

$$1 - \frac{\text{Number of years of plan participation before 1974}}{\text{total number of years of plan participation}} = 1 - \frac{24}{32} = 25\%$$

Step 5. Perform income averaging

Amount taxable	
Zero bracket amount for single taxpayers (using no credits)	$2,300
1/10 of TTA − MDA (0.1 × $46,000)	4,600
Averaged annual income	$6,900

Step 6. Determine the taxes on averaged annual income

Taxes on $6,900 = $608 plus 17 percent of amounts in excess of $6500 = $676

Step 7. Multiply the taxes in Step 6 by 10

10 × $676 = $6760

Step 8. Determine the ordinary income tax due

Percentage of distribution taxed at ordinary income rates—25 percent (see Step 4) times tax on 10 times averaged annual income:

25% × $6760 = $1,690, the taxes on ordinary income portion

Step 9. Determine the percentage taxed at capital gain rates

Percentage of distribution taxed at capital gain rates:

1 − Percentage taxed at ordinary income rates (See Step 4)
= 1 − 25% = 75% taxed as capital gain

Step 10. Determine the amount of capital gain

Amount of capital gain 75% of TTA (See Step 1)
= 0.75 × $50,000 = $37,500 long-term capital gain

(continued)

Step 11. Determine the capital gain exclusion

60% of capital gain excluded = 0.60 × $37,500
= $22,500 capital gain exclusion

Step 12. Determine the amount of capital gain included in gross income

Total capital gain (See Step 10)	$37,500
Less: Amount excluded	−22,500
Capital gain subject to tax	$15,000

Step 13. Determine total taxes payable
Total taxes payable include the $1,690 of taxes payable on ordinary income and any tax that might be attributable to the $15,000 capital gain. (Note: Hun might have other capital gains or offsetting capital losses.)

Suppose Hun had elected to receive his pension by installments of $10,000 per year for life rather than a lump sum. In this event his tax liability is determined by the three-year cost recovery rule or the annuity exclusion ratio rule whichever is applicable.

Example 1. The three-year cost recovery rule. If Hun receives a pension distribution equal to his cost basis within three years, he will be taxed by the three-year cost recovery rule. Because Hun's cost basis is $25,000 (his contribution) his taxes will be as follows:

PENSION YEAR	*DISTRIBUTION*	*AMOUNT TAXABLE*
1983	$10,000	None
1984	10,000	None
1985	10,000	$5,000 ($30,000 received to date less $25,000 cost basis)

Example 2. The annuity exclusion ratio rule. If Mr. Park had elected to receive his pension in installments which amounted to $8,000 a year for his remaining life, the amount taxable would depend on his life expectancy. The three-year cost recovery rule does not apply because Park will not recover his cost basis within three years ($8,000 per year times three years = $24,000). The amount of each distribution that is taxable depends on (1) the cost basis in the contract and (2) the expected return from the contract. Assuming the cost basis is $25,000 as before, the expected return is determined as follows:

Life expectancy taken from IRS annuity tables for a 65-year-old man	15 years
Annual distribution	$8,000 per year
Amount of distribution excluded each year:	
Cost basis	$25,000
Life expectancy	15 years

Annual exclusion

$$\frac{\$25{,}000}{15 \text{ years}} = \$1{,}667 \text{ excluded per year}$$

Therefore, the amount of Hun's taxable pension is

Annual distribution	$8,000	
Less: Amount excluded each year	−1,667	
Taxable pension	$6,333	Taxed for each full year Hun lives

PLAN TERMINATION INSURANCE

Earlier, defined contribution plans were distinguished from defined benefit plans. Under defined contribution plans no specific benefit is promised. The employer promises only to make annual contributions to the plan. Thus employees are not exposed to the problem of inadequate funding.

Under a defined benefit plan employees are promised a specified level of benefits and the employer's annual contribution to the plan depends on the amount eventually needed to pay them. Although this amount is computed actuarially, accumulations may be inadequate to fully fund retirement benefits. Therefore employees are exposed to the risk of losing all or part of their earned benefits. This risk is handled by **plan termination insurance** (PTI). PTI guarantees *qualified defined benefit pensions* up to a specific amount, despite inadequate funding. (Note that PTI does not apply to defined contribution plans or nonqualified plans.)

The Pension Benefit Guaranty Corporation (PBGC), operating within the U.S. Department of Labor, administers PTI, collects the premiums from employers and guarantees payment of nonforfeitable benefits. When a pension plan is forced to terminate operations after five years all the benefits are guaranteed. If the plan has operated for *less* than five years, each participant is guaranteed a benefit equal to the number of years the plan has been in effect multiplied by the higher of $20 or 20 percent of the monthly benefit. Monthly limits on guaranteed benefits, assuming benefits begin at age 65, are the lesser of (1) the participant's average monthly income during the five consecutive years of highest income or (2) $750 adjusted for increases in the social security taxable wage base. The first-year premium per participant in a single-employer plan once was $1 and later increased to $2.60 but could climb much higher. The employer is held liable for 100 percent of the underfunding up to 30 percent of its net worth.

FIDUCIARY RESPONSIBILITIES

Under ERISA a plan must designate a fiduciary to administer its operation. Persons exercising managerial control over the plan or its assets are fiduciaries, regardless of their formal titles. Fiduciaries are responsible for compliance with the laws and must use the "care, skill, prudence, and diligence . . . [of] a prudent . . . [person]." Furthermore, fiduciaries have the responsibility to diversify assets and refrain from "prohibited transactions" where conflict-of-interests could arise and are held personally liable if regulations are violated.

DISCLOSURE

Annual reporting to the IRS also is required. Furthermore, the plan administrators must file an annual report with the secretary of labor and furnish participants with a description of the initial plan agreement and changes in the plan at least every five years. In addition, the plan administrators must provide descriptions of plan amendments, plans for termination, participants' rights and the annual financial report. The annual report must include a statement from the enrolled actuary that reasonable actuarial assumptions and methods have been used. A formal valuation must be made in support of the actuary's certification at least every three years.

SPECIAL RETIREMENT PLANS

IRSs, Keoghs, TSAs, ESOPs, TRASOPs and PAYSOPs provide additional methods with special income tax advantages to allow eligible persons to build retirement and other funds.

Individual Retirement Account

An individual employee may set up a retirement savings program known as an Individual Retirement Account (IRA) in addition to participating in a qualified employee pension plan. The funds may be invested in a trusteed account, custodial account (banks, S&Ls or mutual funds) or annuity contract. A participant may take an income tax exemption up to $2,000 for contributions to IRAs. This limit does not affect the amount that can be contributed—only the amount that can be deducted. If IRAs for both employees and their nonworking spouses, called spousal IRAs, are bought, the maximum deduction is increased to $2,250. A terminating employee may be allowed to transfer vested amounts held in a company pension plan into an IRA. These funds are transferred free of income tax if the transfer is completed within 60 days after the funds are available. They are called **tax-free rollovers.** In addition, employers can contribute and deduct annually as a business expense the lesser of $15,000 or 15 percent of an employee's compensation to an employee's IRA. Employees do not report these contributions as income until they receive the funds at retirement. This type of plan is called a **simplified employee pension (SEP).**

Self-Employment (Keogh) Retirement Plan

Prior to 1963 owners of sole proprietorships and partnerships could not be included in the qualified pension and deferred profit-sharing plans that covered their employees, even if the sole proprietor or partner was actively engaged in the business. However, if their businesses were incorporated they could be covered. To remedy this inequity Congress passed the Keogh Act to allow employees of unincorporated businesses and other self-employed persons to be covered under qualified retirement plans. The maximum annual deduction for an approved Keogh (HR–10) plan is the lesser of $15,000 or 15 percent of earned income. When an owner-employee (a sole proprietor or a partner who owns more than 10 percent of either the capital interest or the profit interest in a partnership) with employees establishes a Keogh plan, all employees who meet the minimum eligibility requirements must be included. To assure that plans do not favor owners employers are required to contribute at least the same percentage of earnings for employees as for themselves. (This rule does not apply to defined benefit Keogh plans.) In applying this limitation employers can deduct only contributions made on the first $200,000 of earned income. Although 15 percent of $200,000 is twice the maximum $15,000 annual deduction allowed, the $200,000 limitation is needed to encourage reasonable contributions on behalf of employees. To illustrate, for employers earning $200,000 or more to take advantage of the maximum deductible contribution, the contribution rate would have to be 7.5 percent: 7.5 percent of $200,000 is $15,000. Thus employers would have to contribute at least 7.5 percent on behalf of all employees. The minimum deductible contribution to a Keogh plan is the lesser of 100 percent of earned income, or $750. In these cases the 15 percent limitation does not apply.

Keogh plans normally are written as defined contribution plans. However, they may be written as defined benefit plans. In this event a special table developed by the IRS is substituted for the 15 percent and $15,000 limits to determine deductible contributions. The table includes the starting ages of participants and the applicable percentages. The amount obtained by applying the appropriate percentage to the employee's salary is the deferred pension the employee can earn for each service year until retirement. The maximum earnings to which the percentage applies is $100,000. The sum of these deferred benefits is the employee's final pension. The employer may deduct the level annual contribution necessary each year to fund the total benefit.

As in other pension plans benefits under a Keogh plan can be coordinated with social security if not more than one third of the total contributions are made on behalf of owner-employees. However, a unique social security integration formula is used. Rather than employees' earnings, the formula is based on social security taxes paid by the employer for employees. Only defined contribution plans may be integrated with social security benefits.

Tax-Sheltered Annuity (TSA)

Nonqualified annuity plans for 501(c)3 organizations and public school systems meeting specified standards receive special tax treatment. Section 501(c)3 organizations include nonprofit corporations operated exclusively for religious, charitable, scientific, public safety testing, literary or educational purposes or for the prevention of cruelty to children or animals. (Not included are organizations for prevention of cruelty to students and their professors.) The employer must purchase a nontransferable annuity contract or mutual fund shares for participating employees. The participant's rights are nonforfeitable. However, unlike other nonqualified plans TSA participants incur no federal income tax liability until the funds are withdrawn. TSA plans have the same advantage as qualified pension plans but avoid ERISA's nondiscriminatory regulations.

ERISA considers TSA plans defined contribution plans. Consequently annual contributions are limited to the lesser of $25,000 adjusted for inflation ($45,475 in 1982) or 25 percent of the participant's annual compensation. However, these limitations apply only if they produce less than the following: 20 percent of the employee's salary multiplied by the number of service years less the total contributions in previous years and employer contributions to qualified plans made currently or previously. Employees of educational institutions, hospitals and home health care plan agencies are allowed to make larger contributions to TSA plans.

Employee Stock Ownership Plans (ESOP and PAYSOP)

An ESOP is similar to a profit-sharing plan except ESOP contributions do not depend on profits, and benefits are distributed in employer's securities (e.g., common stock). Thus employees acquire an interest in the ownership and growth of the employer's business through ESOPs, making them similar to stock bonus plans. ESOP plans are administered by trusts and are subject to the same ERISA rules as profit sharing plans with respect to contributions, participation, benefit limits and vesting. ESOPs resemble defined contribution plans because the value of the stock contributed during the employees' working years may increase or decrease but benefits are always fully funded.

Employers' contributions made to qualified ESOPs are tax deductible in the year made. Investment earnings accumulate in the trust tax free and are used to purchase additional shares for employees. Employees do not pay income taxes until the trustee distributes the stock. The amount subject to tax is the original cost of the securities and does not include increases in market value.

The ERISA fiduciary regulations for ESOPs are different from those that apply to other qualified retirement plans. ESOPs are not required to diversify their investment portfolios. Some or all trust assets can be invested in employers' securities. Fiduciaries must still follow the prudent man standard for investing trust assets and must always act for the exclusive benefit of employees. Qualified businesses are allowed a normal investment tax credit of 10 percent. The Tax Reform Act of 1976 allows up to an additional 1.5 percent investment tax credit *provided that* an equal amount is contributed to a qualified ESOP. These more liberal stock ownership plans are called Tax Reform Act Stock Ownership Plans (TRASOP). An even greater tax incentive for investment will occur between 1983 and 1985 when the 1.5 percent additional investment tax credit will be replaced by a tax credit based on 0.75 percent of payroll creating another SOP, the Pay-Related Stock Ownership Plan (PAYSOP). This change is designed to encourage investment by labor-intensive companies that are not making significant levels of qualified investments. The provision is currently scheduled to expire in 1987.

Estate tax advantages of qualified pension and profit-sharing plans, TSAs, Keogh plans, IRAs, ESOPs, TRASOPS and PAYSOPs.

Death benefits from qualified pension or profit sharing plans are excluded from the decedent's gross estate under specified conditions: they must be paid from employer contributions to a named beneficiary in other than a lump sum unless the lump-sum income-tax advantages explained earlier are forfeited. Benefits attributable to employee contributions are included in the decedent's gross estate unless these contributions are income-tax deductible (e.g., voluntary contributions up to $2,000 annually as an alternative to an IRA).[1]

Keogh plan death benefits are excluded from the deceased's estate if contributions to the plan were income-tax deductible and the beneficiary elects not to claim capital gains or 10-year income averaging if benefits are taken as a lump-sum distribution.[2] IRA death benefits are excluded from the decedent's estate if

[1] If employees' contributions and interest earnings are precisely known that amount is included in the decedent's taxable estate. Otherwise, the amount included in the taxable estate is a percentage of total benefits (the employee's contributions divided by the employer's contributions). The estate tax exclusion may be preserved if the survivors' benefits are paid to a living trust and proceeds are not used to discharge the estate's debts.

[2] Death benefits are excluded from the gross estate if the employee died before reaching retirement age. If the employee had started to receive retirement benefits, the value of these death benefits can be excluded from the employee's estate *only* if the employee could not have elected to receive a lump-sum distribution. The estate tax exemption is lost if (1) a lump-sum distribution option is available, (2) an interest only option is available (where an employee is considered to have *constructively received* the pension at retirement) or (3) the employee receives a lump-sum distribution and then dies (the distributed proceeds have become personal property and mingled with the rest of the estate). Ten-year income averaging and capital gains treatment for income taxes are available for beneficiaries of employees who die after five years of participation in a Keogh plan. However, beneficiaries cannot exclude benefits from estate taxes if they elect income averaging and capital gains treatment. Thus a trade-off is offered between a possible estate tax and some income tax liability. Armed with the necessary input an intelligent decision can be made.

payable to the beneficiary as an annuity, defined as an arrangement providing substantially equal periodic lifetime payments or for a period of at least 36 months.[3] If an IRA owner dies before the full amount of the IRA is distributed, the remainder must be paid under one of three options to be selected within five years: (1) in cash, (2) an immediate-life annuity for the beneficiary or (3) an annuity certain for a period not to exceed the beneficiary's life expectancy. When the decedent's remaining interest is distributed in one installment to a rollover IRA, the distribution is excluded from the decedent's estate as long as the rollover IRA will distribute benefits as an annuity.

The estate-tax status of death benefits from TSA plans depends on whether the employer is a **favored institution.** Favored institutions are IRC Section 501(c)(3) organizations defined earlier. Nonfavored organizations are public school systems. Death benefits paid to a named beneficiary of a deceased employee of a favored institution are not included in the decedent's estate if these benefits are from employer contributions that were excluded from the employee's gross income.[4] Lump-sum distributions are not given favorable treatment because TSAs are not qualified plans. Death benefits paid to a named beneficiary or the estate of a deceased employee of a *nonfavored* organization are included in the employee's estate.

Employer contributions to ESOPs, TRASOPs and PAYSOPs are exempt from estate taxes when distributed to the participant's beneficiaries. However, if the participant withdraws the stock and still owns it at death, that stock is included in the participant's estate.

TEFRA AND RETIREMENT PLANS

The Tax Equity and Fiscal Responsibility Act of 1982 (TEFRA) includes several provisions that affect retirement plans. The principal changes are: (1) A reduction of the limit on contributions to a defined contribution plan from $45,475 to $30,000 per participant. (2) A decline in the limits on annual benefits from a defined benefit plan from $136,425 to $90,000. (3) A three-year freeze on cost-of-living adjustments of these limits from 1983 until 1986 when they are scheduled to be increased to reflect post-1984 inflation. (4) A lowering of the limit on the amount an individual can receive from both a defined benefit and a defined contribution plan to the lesser of 125 percent (formerly 140 percent) of their combined dollar limits or 140 percent of the law's existing percentage test. (5) A requirement that dollar limits be actuarially reduced if benefits are paid before age 62 rather than age 55, but no less than $75,000 at ages 55 to 61. (6) Permission is granted for benefits starting after age 65 to be actuarially increased. (7) Loans over $10,000 from qualified plans are considered as distributions and thus taxable, with the exception of loans up to $50,000 that will be repaid within five years or will be used to buy a house. (8) An increase in the dollar limits on Keogh and simplified employee pension plans to $30,000 over a four-year period to make them comparable to the limits on other defined contribution plans. (9)

---

[3] Death benefits are excluded from the decedent's estate if the beneficiary receives them as an annuity paid over at least 36 months—or *paid over the survivor's remaining life expectancy,* if less.

[4] For a deceased employee of a favored institution when a part of employer contributions were not excluded from the employee's gross income, the amount exempt from estate taxes is

$$\frac{\text{Excluded employer contributions}}{\text{Total employer contributions}} \times \text{Amount in TSA account}$$

Requires faster vesting on "top-heavy" plans, defined as those in which 60 percent or more of the nonforfeitable benefits are for key employees. (10) A requirement that employees receive a minimum level of benefits when the plan is integrated with social security. (11) A requirement that employers, insurers and trustees withhold tax from retirees' periodic pension payments that exceed $5,400 unless the retiree elects otherwise. (12) A requirement that taxes on lump-sum distributions be withheld according to tables that reflect 10-year forward averaging and capital-gains treatment, unless the recipient elects otherwise. These provisions are called the "dirty dozen" and they must be dealt with by pension designers and administrators until changed—the latter not entirely unlikely.

Withholding of taxes is scheduled effective January 1, 1983. This provision is an expensive one for plan administration. It involves not only enormous costs of notifying retirees and record keeping, but also counseling retired employees. The law requires that the retirees be notified each year of their option. Why a one-time notice is insufficient is difficult to comprehend. It seems to be an example of an expensive convenience. The changes in maximum benefits and contributions become effective January 1, 1983. The loan provision became effective in August of 1982. The faster vesting provisions exceed the "4–40." The pension must be fully vested after three years, or a six-year graded plan can be used in which the pension is 20 percent vested after two years and vested at the rate of 20 percent a year until fully vested in six years. This provision affects a large number of smaller plans.

The Keogh and simplified pension plan increases are scheduled to begin in 1984. The full increase to the maximum is programmed to take effect in four years.

INNERSCRIPT: TAXATION OF JOINT AND SURVIVORSHIP ANNUITIES

The amount of income tax payable by a surviving spouse is not found by using the usual annuity exclusion ratio formula discussed earlier. For annuities that decrease after the death of a spouse-participant, the short-cut annuity exclusion rule is replaced by a special formula that calculates the expected return for a joint and survivorship annuity as follows:

1. **Find the joint and survivor life expectancy at the annuity's starting date (in IRS Table 2) and adjust it for frequency of payment.**
2. **Repeat step 1 using IRS Table 2A.**
3. **Compute the difference between step 1 and step 2 and multiply it by the payment to the survivor.**
4. **Multiply the factor in step 2 by the larger annuity when both spouses are alive.**
5. **Add the results of steps 3 and 4 to find the *expected total return.***

The exempt portion of each annuity is the sum of the employee's contributions divided by the expected total return. This percentage

is applied to the surviving spouse's annuity to determine the amount excluded from income tax.

Under a joint and survivorship option, the estate tax status depends on whether the plan was contributory or noncontributory. The same rules discussed earlier apply. Because under a joint and last survivorship annuity the annuitants are usually husband and wife, no estate taxes are involved because as of 1982 any transfers at death between spouses are excluded from federal estate taxes (the Economic Recovery Tax Act of 1981—ERTA).

SUMMARY

1. Pension plans are funded if the employer sets funds aside in advance to pay retirement benefits. Fully funded pension plans have no unpaid liabilities for past service or current service.
2. Pension plans define the annual contributions employers must make to the plan (defined contribution plans) or the amount of benefits employees will receive after retirement (defined benefit plans).
3. Defined benefit plans make actuarial assumptions about interest rate, mortality experience, employee turnover and so on.
4. Adequate funding for a defined benefit plan depends on reasonable funding standards (time schedules for eliminating the pension's supplemental liability), realistic actuarial assumptions for measuring liabilities and sound valuation procedures for assets.
5. For defined contribution plans no actuarial estimates are used to determine employer contributions. The plan specifies the annual contribution.
6. Defined contributions are segregated by employee accounts and accumulated to buy an immediate annuity for the employee at retirement or are used to buy the employee a series of single-premium deferred annuities payable at the scheduled retirement date. (In the unlikely event the contributions are level an annual premium deferred annuity can be purchased.)
7. Defined contribution plans use actuarial assumptions rather than the employer's contributions to the pension fund to determine retirement benefits.
8. A pension liability can increase when the plan is improved, when actuarial experience deviates from original actuarial assumptions or when the plan is revalued to account for new actuarial assumptions about the future.
9. *Supplemental liability* is the present value of future pension benefits payable less the present value of current service costs.
10. A *funding standard account* shows plan administrators whether minimum funding standards are being met.
11. *Variances* from minimum funding standards help employers comply by extending the periods to amortize pension liabilities and changing contribution schedules.

12. Actuarial cost methods are computational techniques for determining the pension costs over time. The two types of actuarial cost methods are: the *accrued benefit cost method* and the *projected benefit cost method.*

13. The accrued benefit cost method calculates normal costs and supplemental costs separately. The projected benefit cost method calculates normal costs and supplemental costs together *or* separately.

14. The accrued benefit cost method assumes an employee earns a precise unit of benefit for each year of credited service. The cost of providing the benefit increases with the employee's age.

15. The projected benefit cost method assumes each unit of benefit is fully funded as it accrues and a precisely determinable unit of benefit is allocated to each year of service.

16. Under the attained age basis method, the pension cost is funded with equal annual contributions, and pension costs are spread over the time when the plan is installed (the employee's attained age when participation begins) until retirement. The attained age basis also makes level contributions sufficient to fully fund the supplemental liability by the time the employee retires.

17. Under the *entry age normal basis* supplemental and normal costs are handled separately. The employer has an initial supplemental liability because the method assumes the employer has been funding past service costs since the employee was first eligible to participate in the plan. Annual contributions are level charges sufficient to cover current service costs and the minimum supplemental liability.

18. The *aggregate level cost basis* is used to compute employers' annual pension costs without identifying particular employees. Employees are divided into age groups, and pension computations are made for the midpoints of each group.

19. Funding agencies include insured plans (when a life insurer is the funding agency), trusteed plans (when a bank or other trustee is the funding agency) and split-funded plans (when a trustee and an insurer are used).

20. Insured plans can use allocated funding instruments (individual life or annuity contracts, group permanent life contracts or group deferred annuities).

21. Insured plans also can use unallocated funding instruments (group deposit administration plans or immediate participation guarantee plans).

22. Normally the plan should be designed to qualify for favorable tax treatment under the IRC. For this purpose the plan must (1) be established by the employer, (2) benefit employees only, (3) be written, permanent and communicated, (4) be financed by employer and/or employee contributions, (5) be nondiscriminatory and (6) be based on a defined contribution or defined benefit formula.

23. Benefit formulas for defined contribution plans can be a flat amount formula, a flat percentage formula or, a flat amount unit benefit. An offset or excess plan formula (to integrate the benefits with social security) can be used.

24. Vesting standards approved by ERISA are the 10-year rule, the graded 5–15 and the rule of 45. ERISA requires that a joint and 50 percent survivorship annuity be provided automatically.

25. To determine the proper funding agency (bank or insurer) the employer must consider the degree of freedom in investment decisions, administrative costs, investment guarantees, selecting funding methods, choosing actuarial assumptions and designing benefits.

26. Plan termination insurance benefits are available to plans that operate for more than five years. Monthly benefits are limited to the employee's average monthly income or $750 (adjusted for inflation). Nevertheless, employers are liable for underfunding up to 30 percent of corporate assets.

27. IRAs allow participants to exclude up to $2,000 from annual income. Spousal IRAs allow husbands and wives to exclude $2,250 per year (when filing joint tax returns). IRAs can be invested in a trusteed account, annuity contract or custodial accounts.

28. Keogh plans allow employees of unincorporated businesses and self-employed people to be covered under qualified retirement plans. The maximum annual deduction for a Keogh plan is $15,000 or 15 percent of earned income. Employers are required to contribute the same percentage for employees as for themselves.

29. IRS section 501(c)3 organizations and public schools that establish a tax sheltered annuity plan allow employees to contribute up to $25,000 (adjusted for inflation) or 25 percent of the employee's salary each until contributions are 20 percent of the employee's salary multiplied by the number of service years *LESS* the total contributions made in previous years and contributions made to qualified plans. Employees of educational institutions and hospitals and home health care agencies are allowed larger contributions to their TSAs.

30. An ESOP is similar to a profit-sharing plan, but contributions are employer's stock and do not depend on profits. ESOPs are administered by trusts and are subject to ERISA's rules for profit-sharing plans.

31. The effects of ERISA on pension plans has been to promote defined contribution plans and insured plans because employers' worries about adequate funding and investment performance are kept at a minimum by these plans.

32. The Tax Equity and Fiscal Responsibility Act of 1982 affects 12 aspects of retirement plans.

REVIEW QUESTIONS

1. What is a funded pension plan?
2. When is a pension plan fully funded?
3. Explain the difference between a defined contribution and defined benefit pension plan.
4. Are actuarial estimates ever important to participants in defined contribution plans?
5. What does adequate funding depend upon for defined benefit pension plans?
6. What problems are encountered in meeting funding standards?
7. How does the funding standard account show plan administrators whether minimum funding standards are met?

8. Explain the difference between the two types of actuarial cost methods: accrued benefit cost method and projected benefit cost method.
9. Explain the advantages of funding a pension plan.
10. What kinds of funding instruments are available for insured pension plans (allocated and unallocated)?
11. List the basic requirements for a pension plan to be "qualified" under ERISA.
12. Explain the following vesting standards permitted by ERISA: 10-year rule, graded 5–15, rule of 45.
13. Does the funding agency affect the employer's investment decisions, administrative costs, earnings guarantees and actuarial assumptions? Should an employer choose a bank or an insurer to be trustee?
14. Does an employee have investment freedom if he/she participates in an IRA? Can employers contribute?
15. What is a 501(c)3 organization? How do 501(c)3 organizations benefit from ERISA?
16. Explain the difference between ESOP, TRASOP and PAYSOP plans. How do ERISA fiduciary regulations for these "SOP" plans differ from those that are applied to other qualified retirement plans?
17. Explain how retirement plans are affected by the Tax Equity and Fiscal Responsibility Act of 1982.

CHAPTER

18 Social insurance

John Thoeming/Richard D. Irwin

CHAPTER OBJECTIVES

1. **To define social insurance and explain the need for it.**
2. **To analyze the insurance coverage under social security using the techniques developed in Chapters 6 and 7.**
3. **To point out the financial problems facing the social security system and identify some possible solutions.**
4. **To outline the major aspects of unemployment compensation plans and state temporary disability income plans.**
5. **To identify and discuss the major issues in the controversy over proposed national health insurance plans.**

The government insures more persons than do private insurers. Broad governmental schemes to provide income for old age, unemployment, death and disability and to pay the cost of medical care are called **social insurance.**

THE NATURE OF A SOCIAL INSURANCE SYSTEM

Broadly conceived, social insurance covers social risks, which are whatever a particular society considers them to be at a given time. Whether the burden of medical care is a social risk has been debated for years. Now medical care for the aged and long-term disability at any age are treated as social risks. The risks of loss of income from unemployment, old age and death of a working spouse (or parent) became social risks in the middle and late 1930s. Even earlier (during the 1920s) loss of income and medical expenses of workers were considered social risks. Replacement of some liability exposures with *pure* no-fault laws (see Chapter 11) could expand the number of social risks covered. Thus social risks change over time.

Definition of Social Insurance

The Committee on Social Insurance of the Commission on Insurance Terminology of the American Risk and Insurance Association has defined social insurance *as a device for pooling risks by transfer to a governmental service organization.* According to the committee the characteristics of social insurance are:

1. Coverage is compulsory by law in nearly all cases.
2. Benefit eligibility arises from contributions made to the program by or for the claimant; the individual is not required to demonstrate inadequate financial resources although a dependency may have to be established.
3. The method to determine the benefits is prescribed by law.
4. Benefits are not usually related directly to contributions but generally redistribute income to groups with low wages or large numbers of dependents.
5. The benefit financing plan must be designed for long-range adequacy.
6. The cost is borne primarily by contributions from covered persons, their employers or both.
7. The plan is administered or supervised by the government.

The social security system violates the foregoing conditions in several respects, as will become apparent. But because of inevitable compromises what can be expected of a definition or any other output from a committee?

Kinds of Social Insurance in the United States

Social insurance in the United States includes the federal social security system with its old-age, survivors, disability and health care coverages; and state unemployment compensation, workers' compensation and temporary disability plans. (Workers' compensation is discussed in Chapter 13.) Other forms of insurance are available under government auspices. These include crop, war damage (including aircraft), flood, auto accident (Puerto Rico), life (Wisconsin) and crime insurance. Various government reinsurance plans are also written, but they are not considered social insurance.

INNERSCRIPT: THE NEED FOR SOCIAL INSURANCE

Why are social insurance programs regarded as a government obligation? Demographic, economic and social changes explain the reasons. In earlier cultures society saw no need for social insurance. Most people were self-employed. Individuals hunted or gathered food for themselves and their families. Among many primitive peoples the economic problem of old age presented no difficulties. The perils of the jungle, as well as those of disease, resulted in a low rate of longevity. In the earliest cultures the individual would starve to death upon reaching an age beyond self-sufficiency unless some charitable friend or relative was willing to assume the burden of care. Some tribes are reputed to have solved the problem by killing the aged. However, with the factory system, the Industrial Revolution and the end of the family as the principal economic unit, the problem of unemployment became serious. The family no longer produced sufficient goods for self-maintenance. Workers traded money wages for goods and services to meet their families' economic needs. This economic development made workers "wage slaves" and victims of the business cycle.

Along with the end of the family as a self-supporting economic unit has come the additional problem of increased numbers of persons reaching old age. At one time the United States had a young population but by 1980 the proportion of people over 65 reached 11 percent. Much of the increase is due to a long-term declining birthrate. The number of births per thousand of population at the turn of the century was about 55. Currently that figure is about 15. Economic pressures requiring two-career families, women's desires for careers and over-population problems continue to depress the birthrate. Scientific advances in medicine have increased the number of old people. Although the maximum life span has not lengthened significantly more people are living to become old. Actuaries expect these trends to continue.

With the increase in the number of the elderly, changes have occurred that make old-age problems more acute. The social unity

of the family has changed. Aged parents who could participate in the economic life of the family used to be a welcome adjunct. Today, however, the aged have few ways to contribute economically to the family and have become unwelcome burdens. As a young man in George Ade's *Fables in Slang* muses about his father: "Here is an Ancient Party without any Assets, who lives with me Week in and Week out and doesn't pay any board. He is getting too Old and Wobbly to do Odd Jobs around the Place, and it looks to me like an awful Imposition." Even the performance of domestic tasks by an older person no longer is as welcome as in the past. The changes in modern living require less from the homemaker than before. At one time a grandparent would be welcome in the home to help with laundry, cooking, housecleaning and child care. These tasks have been so reduced by modern appliances, frozen dinners, attractive easy-to-care-for modern living quarters and day-care centers provided by the government or employers that grandparents have become technically obsolete, at least for these purposes.

In former days two people reaching 65 might have a family of 4 to 10 children who could pool resources to provide a comfortable old age for their parents without undue hardship falling on one child. However, today's parents are likely to have only two children to help them. Even a *willing* only child would find it difficult financially to provide adequate support both for parents and a young family.

A final and important reason for social insurance is to provide protection against losses from perils that are uninsurable privately. As noted in Chapter 2, unemployment is an example. One large New York life insurance company once developed rate tables for unemployment insurance and sought permission from that state to write the coverage. Nothing more has been heard from that abortive effort.

Social insurance operates where compulsory coverage seems to be an effective way to protect large population segments. Experience has shown that without legal compulsion some people will not, or cannot, provide income and medical expense protection for themselves and their families. This observation has become apparent now as people tend to view old-age support, medical payments, unemployment compensation, and disability payments as a governmental responsibility or at least their endorsement as a political necessity for reelection. The result has been the expansion of governmental programs to the point where many observers question whether benefits justify costs.

This chapter discusses old-age, survivors, disability and health insurance; unemployment compensation; temporary disability income benefit plans and national health insurance.

OLD-AGE, SURVIVORS, DISABILITY AND HEALTH INSURANCE (OASDHI)

Under the Social Security Act benefits may be classified as either public assistance or social insurance. Public-assistance benefits are disbursed on the basis of need; insurance payments are made to those entitled to them regardless of need. *Entitled to them* means having a right or grounds for laying claim to benefits based on the provisions of the Social Security Act applicable at the time. Unlike private insurance the Social Security Act does not provide contractual benefits. The law can and will change thus changing the **entitlements.**

INNERSCRIPT: PUBLIC-ASSISTANCE PROGRAMS

The Social Security Act of 1935 encouraged a system of state plans for old-age assistance (OAA). The states were permitted freedom to form plans within limits of specified broad principles. These principles required that the program be statewide and that the state consider an elderly person's other income. States were required to participate in the program but the act did not specify the exact amount of participation.

Under the 1935 act the federal government agreed to pay qualified states a subsidy equal to one half the amount given to each needy person over 65. Congress has increased maximum dollar amounts of federal participation several times. The initial assistance programs included aid to the aged, to families with dependent children (AFDC) and to the blind (AB). In 1950 aid to the permanently and totally disabled (APTD) was added. In 1960 amendments to the Social Security Act provided federal matching funds for states to improve medical care programs for the aged unable to pay for medical care.

The 1972 amendments to the Social Security Act established the supplemental security income program (SSI) to replace federal grants to states for care of the aged, blind, and disabled. The program is administered by the Social Security Administration and financed by general revenues of the U.S. Treasury. States are allowed to supplement federal payments. The SSI program established basic benefit standards for the eligible aged, blind and disabled. The eligibility of applicants is based on need rather than contributions. Benefit levels differ widely among the states. States may save money by shifting the administration of benefits to the federal government. The theory behind SSI is to provide a benefit program with uniform eligibility standards and benefit levels to remedy the wide variations in the previously existing state programs of OAA, AB and APTD.

In 1965 Title XIX of the Social Security Act created a separate medical assistance program called medicaid. In 1970 Title XIX replaced all medical assistance programs. Payments are made directly to the vendors of the service (hospitals, physicians, and druggists, for example). Under this program states must cover at least inpatient

and outpatient hospital care, skilled nursing home care, laboratory and X-ray services and physicians' services. However, most states go beyond minimum requirements and cover dental care, prescription drugs, eyeglasses, and prosthetic devices.

The Insurance Coverage

In contrast to the assistance program the federal old-age, survivors, disability, and health insurance program (OASDHI) is a system of social insurance administered by the federal government. Benefits are determined on the basis of earnings and are financed by a tax on wages levied on each insured worker and employer. For 1982 the first $32,400 of each individual's annual wage was subject to the tax. The maximum annual taxable wage is subject to automatic increases based on legislation and economic indicators. The life expectancy of social security tax schedules is extremely short. The tax rate in 1982 was 6.7 percent each from the employer and employee. For the self-employed the rate was 9.35 percent. Rates are to be raised gradually until 1990, when they are scheduled to be 7.65 percent for employees and employers and 10.75 percent for the self-employed. These contribution rates were set by the 1977 act. Who knows what they will be in years to come or even before this text is released? Up-to-date information on social security might be found by telephoning the local social security office, assuming a knowledgeable person answers the phone, the question is clearly presented and has a clear-cut answer. The system is nationwide and virtually compulsory in private employment. Although defined by law rather than contract the coverage can be analyzed by using the techniques developed in Chapters 6 and 7. This analysis of OASDHI is based on the law in effect in 1982.

Perils The perils covered are death, injury, sickness and old-age.

Persons covered Coverage is provided for insured workers and their dependents. Nearly every worker including the self-employed (more than 90 percent of all employed persons) in the United States is covered. The exceptions are some governmental employees; college students working for sororities, fraternities, the college or a college club; some members of religious orders who have taken vows of poverty; student nurses; inmates of penal institutions; employees of special types of charitable and other nonprofit organizations (unless they elect coverage); railroad workers; newspaper carriers under age 18; individuals employed by their spouses and children under age 21 employed by their parents. Clergymen, Christian Science practitioners and members of religious orders who have not taken vows of poverty are covered but may claim exemption on the grounds of religious principle or conscientious objection. Excluded as self-employed are limited (silent) partners if no personal services are performed. (Other individuals are covered as self-employed even though they perform no personal service, e.g., absentee businessowners.) Farm operators are covered on an elective basis. Federal employees and railroad workers are generally covered by their own retirement programs.

State and local government employees may be covered by agreement with the secretary of health and human services (HHS). Members of the armed forces have been covered since 1957.

The social security system provides two types of insured status: fully insured and currently insured. The workers' *insured status* determines the *types of benefits* for which they qualify as shown in Table 18–1. These benefits are discussed later.

To be **fully insured** workers must have: (1) a minimum of 6 quarters' coverage with one quarter of coverage for each calendar year *commencing* one year *after* 1950 (or the quarter when they reached age 21 if later) and *ending* one year *before* they die, become disabled or reach age 62 whichever is the earliest *or* (2) at least 40 quarters of coverage. For the years before 1978, employees earned a quarter of coverage when they were

1. Agricultural workers (after 1954) credited with $100 or more cash wages in a calendar quarter.
2. Paid $50 or more in wages for covered employment in a calendar quarter.
3. Credited with $100 or more of self-employment income in a calendar quarter and had at least $400 in net earnings from self-employment in that calendar year. (Self-employed workers are given four quarters of coverage if they earn more than the maximum social security earnings base for that year even if they worked only one quarter.)

TABLE 18–1 Types of Cash Benefits

RETIREMENT	
Monthly payments to:	*If worker is:*
Worker and spouse and/or child*	Fully insured
SURVIVORS	
Monthly payments to:	*If at death worker is:*
Widow or widower 60 or over or disabled widow or widower 50–59*	Fully insured
Mothers or fathers (regardless of age) if caring for a child under 16 who is entitled to benefits or over 15 and disabled if the disability began before age 22*	Either fully or currently insured
Dependent child	Either fully or currently insured
Dependent parent at 62	Fully insured
Lump-sum death payment	Either fully or currently insured
DISABILITY	
Monthly payments to:	*If worker is:*
Worker and the worker's dependents if worker is disabled	Fully insured and worker has at least 20 quarters of coverage in the 40-quarter period ending with the current quarter†

* Under certain conditions payments can also be made to the worker's divorced spouse or surviving divorced spouse.

† If disabled before age 31, worker qualifies with (1) a minimum of 6 quarters of coverage and (2) coverage for one half of the quarters elapsing after age 21 until disabled (or, for those disabled before age 24, 6 quarters of coverage in the last 12 quarters). A blind person needs only fully insured status to qualify for disability benefits.

For 1982 all workers including the self-employed received one quarter of coverage for each $340 of annual earnings. (Self-employed workers still needed a minimum of $400 in annual earnings from self-employment to qualify for any quarters of coverage for the year.) For the years following 1977 the earnings required for a quarter of coverage increase annually with increases in the national average annual earnings. These amounts for 1978, 1979, 1980 and 1981 were $250, $260, $290 and $310 respectively. In no event will a worker be credited with more than four quarters in one year.

To be *currently insured* the worker must have at least six quarters of coverage out of the last 13 quarters ending with the quarter of death or eligibility for retirement or disability income.

Conditions suspending benefits

Persons receiving old-age benefits, their eligible dependents and eligible survivors of insured workers may lose some benefits if they receive wages or self-employed income over a specified amount. Payees under age 65 may earn up to $4,400 (1982) a year as wages or self-employment income in any employment without a reduction in benefits. For payees age 65 through 71 the maximum earnings allowed without a reduction in benefits is $6,000 (1982). For earnings over these amounts the individual loses benefits equal to half the excess. Earnings for the month the insured becomes 72 are excluded from the computation. Investment income is not considered earned income. Upon attaining age 72 the payee receives full benefits regardless of earnings. In these cases a loss is presumed—a strange presumption but it does recognize belatedly that social security benefits are not based on need but are earned. The maximum level of exempt earnings automatically increases each year. The amount is indexed to national average annual earnings.

For the year the worker applies for benefits, a monthly earnings limit is applied. For any month the worker earns less than $500 in that year and does not perform substantial service in self-employment the worker is entitled to benefits for that month. For the ensuing years only the annual earnings test applies: if the full annual maximum is earned in one month the employee loses all benefits for that year.

The age at which full benefits can be paid regardless of earnings is scheduled to drop to 70 in 1983. But who can be sure of any currently scheduled changes today.

Amounts

Six steps are required to determine the amounts payable for each of the social security benefits payable to eligible recipients: (1) index the covered earnings, (2) compute the average index monthly earnings (AIME), (3) apply the primary insurance amount (PIA) formula to AIME, (4) allocate the percentage of the PIA payable to each beneficiary, (5) redistribute benefits to amend for excesses if total allocated benefits exceed the family maximum limit and (6) adjust for cost-of-living increases.

Index the covered earnings. Column 1 of Table 18–2 shows the maximum covered earnings from 1951 through 1982. If the worker earned the full amount (or more) of covered earnings the *maximum amount of covered earnings* are indexed. If the worker earned less, only the amount of covered earnings are indexed. For example, if the worker earned $10,000 in 1972, only $9,000, the maximum covered earnings, are indexed. If the worker earned $8,000 in 1972 that amount is indexed because it is less than the $9,000 maximum covered earnings for that year.

TABLE 18–2 Maximum Covered Earnings under the OASDI Program Indexed at 1977 Levels

	(1) MAXIMUM COVERED EARNINGS	(2) NATIONAL AVERAGE ANNUAL EARNINGS*	(3) MAXIMUM POSSIBLE INDEXED EARNINGS TO 1977 EARNINGS LEVEL
1951	$ 3,600	$ 2,799.16	$12,577
1952	3,600	2,973.32	11,841
1953	3,600	3,139.44	11,214
1954	3,600	3,155.64	11,157
1955	4,200	3,301.44	12,441
1956	4,200	3,532.36	11,628
1957	4,200	3,641.72	11,279
1958	4,200	3,673.80	11,180
1959	4,800	3,855.80	12,174
1960	4,800	4,007.12	11,714
1961	4,800	4,086.76	11,486
1962	4,800	4,291.40	10,938
1963	4,800	4,396.64	10,677
1964	4,800	4,576.32	10,257
1965	4,800	4,658.72	10,076
1966	6,600	4,938.36	13,070
1967	6,600	5,213.44	12,380
1968	7,800	5,571.76	13,690
1969	7,800	5,893.76	12,942
1970	7,800	6,186.24	12,331
1971	7,800	6,497.08	11,741
1972	9,000	7,133.80	12,338
1973	10,800	7,580.16	13,933
1974	13,200	8,030.76	16,074
1975	14,100	8,630.92	15,976
1976	15,300	9,226.48	16,217
1977	16,500	9,779.44	16,500‡
1978	17,700	10,556.03	17,700§
1979	22,900	11,479.46	22,900
1980	25,900	12,513.46	25,900
1981	29,700	†	29,700
1982	32,400	†	32,400

* National average annual earnings for the next indexing year are published in the *Federal Register* each year on or before November 1 by the Department of Health and Human Services.

† The national average annual earnings for 1981 were published by November 1982—too late to be included in this table. (This book went to press before HHS published that figure.) The 1982 figure will have been published by November 1983.

‡ The $16,500 is indexed because according to the index adjustment formula the numerator and denominator for the indexing year are the same, yielding an index adjustment factor of 1.0.

§ No index adjustment applies to years after the indexing year—in this case 1977. Thus the figures in columns 1 and 3 for the years 1978 through 1982 are the same.

The formula for indexing each year's covered earnings is

$$\text{Actual covered earnings for the year indexed} \times \frac{\text{National average annual earnings for the indexing year}}{\text{National average annual earnings for the year indexed}}$$

Column 2 of Table 18–2 gives the national average annual earnings from 1951 through 1980. The **indexing year** is the second year before the worker reaches age 62, dies or is disabled, whichever is first. Assume the worker dies in 1982. The indexing year will be 1980, two years before the worker dies. If this worker earned $10,000 in 1972, the $9,000 of covered earnings for that year would be indexed as follows: $9,000 × $12,513.46/7,133.80 or $15,787. If the earnings in 1972 were $8,000 they would be indexed to $8,000 × $12,513.46/7,133.80 or $14,033. The worker's earnings would be indexed for each year using the same formula. For the years beyond the indexing year (in this case 1981 and 1982) the covered earnings up to the maximum are used in computing AIME. Column 1 of Table 18–2 shows these maximums to be $29,700 and $32,400 respectively.

Computing the average index monthly earnings (AIME). The **average indexed monthly earnings** (AIME) formula averages the indexed earnings over the years to be included. It uses the worker's annual wages up *to the maximum social security wage base* to calculate the **primary insurance amount** (PIA), discussed later. The AIME formula uses two time periods: (1) the benefit computation years and (2) the computation base years. The **benefit computation years** are those over which the worker's indexed earnings are averaged. The **computation base years** are those selected to calculate the worker's average indexed earnings. Don't worry! These concepts become clearer as the discussion progresses.

To find the number of *benefit computation years* begin by calculating the number of elapsed years. Elapsed years begin in 1951 (or the year the participant becomes 22, if later) and end in the year *before* the participant dies, reaches age 62 or is disabled. When computing AIME for retirement or death benefits the number of benefit computation years is the elapsed years minus five. An additional reduction in the benefit computation years can be made if the worker established a disability period (discussed later). Any part of the calendar year in which the worker has a qualified disability counts as a full year. So if a worker is disabled in December 1978 and that disability continues through January 1980, three years of disability can be excluded. This exclusion is called a disability freeze. If a worker earns a substantial income in part of a year in which the disability occurred that year can be counted if it increases the worker's AIME. When computing AIME for disability benefits, the number subtracted from the elapsed years is the number of elapsed years divided by five. Fractions of a year are disregarded. The number of subtracted years may not exceed five. In no case can the number of computation base years be less than two.

The next step is to determine the number of computation base years. Computation base years usually extend beyond the benefit computation years because they (1) nearly always begin in 1951 regardless of when workers become age 22,[1] (2) end later for those who claim death and retirement benefits and (3) are not reduced by five years as are the benefit computation years.[2] For workers who die, computation base years extend from 1951 *through* the year the worker

[1] A special alternative benefit computation method is available if earnings before 1951 are used in the computation base years. One quarter of coverage can be credited for years before 1951 in which $400 of wages were earned if the worker will achieve fully insured status by including these quarters plus any acquired after 1950 *and* the worker's elapsed years are more than six.

[2] The number of *benefit computation* years is more than the elapsed years minus five for persons who become disabled before age 47. The number of dropout years allowed in computing disability benefits is four from age 42–46, three from 37–41, two from 32–36, one from 27–31 and zero under 27. It is five at age 47 and over. Up to three years can be subtracted from the elapsed years if the disabled person had no earnings in those years and had a child under three years of age living with him or her.

FIGURE 18–1 **Relevant Time Periods to Calculate AIME**

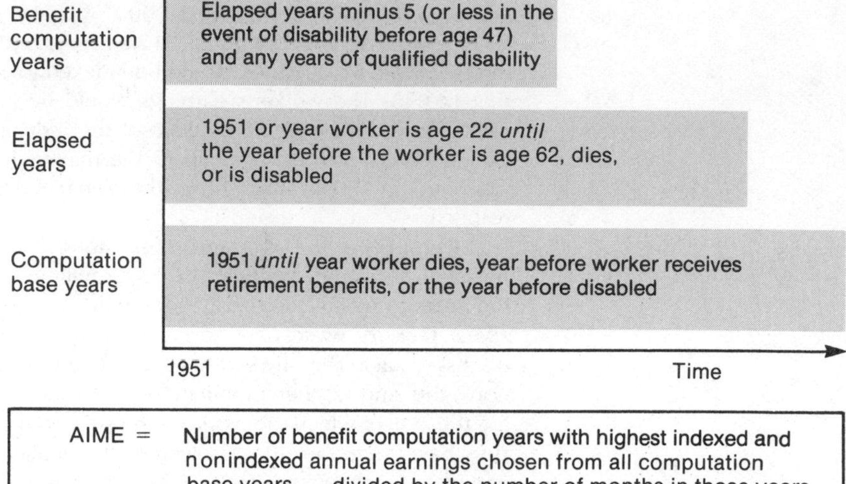

AIME = Number of benefit computation years with highest indexed and nonindexed annual earnings chosen from all computation base years . . . divided by the number of months in those years.

dies. For workers who retire, the computation base years extend from 1951 to the year *before* they receive retirement benefits (without regard to the year when the workers reach age 62). For disabled workers computation base years extend from 1951 to the year *before* they become disabled.[3]

After the number of computation base years is determined, the annual credited earnings (i.e., the worker's earnings up to the social security wage base) for each year are indexed by applying the prescribed formula.

Benefit computation years are chosen from the computation base years with the highest indexed and nonindexed annual earnings.[4] Average indexed monthly earnings (AIME) is the total of indexed and nonindexed annual earnings for the selected years divided by the number of months in those years dropping cents. See Figure 18–1 for a graphic display of relevant time periods for calculating AIME.

Apply the primary insurance amount formula. The primary insurance amount (PIA) is the basis for all social security income benefits. It is determined by applying a formula to the average indexed monthly earnings. That formula for those becoming *eligible* in 1982 is

90 percent of the first $230 plus
32 percent of the next $1,158 plus
15 percent of the remainder of the AIME.

Becoming eligible for benefits does not mean becoming *entitled* to benefits. Entitlement is established in the year an eligible person applies for benefits. A covered worker becomes eligible for retirement benefits at age 62 but usually

[3] Although the year in which a person applies for retirement or disability benefits is not included in the computation base years, the AIME will be recomputed with earnings for that year substituted for the lowest earnings year if it increases the AIME.

[4] The nonindexed earnings will be the covered earnings following the indexing year, i.e., those following the second year before the worker reaches age 62, dies or is disabled.

will not apply for them until age 65 or later. Regardless of when that worker applies for benefits, as long as eligibility is established in 1982, the 1982 PIA formula will apply upon entitlement. The percentage figures are the same for the PIA formula each year, but the dollar amounts (called the bend points) to which they apply are adjusted annually according to the national average annual earnings. These bend points are published by the Social Security Administration in the *Federal Register* on or before November 1 each year for use the following year.

For a person entitled to benefits in 1982 who first became eligible in 1981 the formula and bend points are

90 percent of the first $211 plus

32 percent of the next $1,063 plus

15 percent of the remainder of the AIME.

Note the amounts are lower but the percentages are the same (these lower amounts are offset by the automatic cost-of-living increases explained later). For 1980 the bend points are $194 and the next $977; for 1979 they are $180 and the next $905. The final 15 percent always applies to the excess. These excess bend points are $1,389, $1,275, $1,172 and $1,086 for 1982, 1981, 1980 and 1979 respectively.

Allocate the percentage of the PIA to each beneficiary. Beneficiaries entitled to social security are paid a percentage of the PIA. For *retirement* benefits the worker receives 100 percent of the PIA if entitlement is at age 65. If benefits begin between age 62 and 64 they will be reduced by five ninths of 1 percent of the PIA for each month between the month the benefits start and age 65. Thus if they begin at age 62 the benefits are 80 percent of the PIA. The percentages for 63 and 64 are 86⅔ and 93⅓ respectively. If the benefits begin four months before age 65 they will be 96⅔ percent. The initial percentage of the PIA remains the same throughout the recipient's life. Thus if a worker starts receiving benefits at age 62, the initial 80 percent will continue, i.e., it is not increased each month by five ninths of 1 percent until age 65. If the worker postpones retirement, benefits are increased by one quarter of one percent for each month of delayed retirement between ages 65 and 72. Thus a worker retiring and entitled to benefits at age 70 receives 115 percent of the PIA. The worker's *disability* benefits are 100 percent of the PIA.

Table 18–3 shows the percentages of the PIA payable to other eligible recipients for the type of benefit for which they are entitled. The table gives the PIA percentages only. The benefits are discussed in some depth under the rubric losses.

Redistribute benefits if their total exceeds the maximum family benefit. The maximum family benefit for those who become eligible in 1982 are

150 percent of the first $294 plus

272 percent of the next $131 plus

134 percent of the next $129 plus

175 percent of the remainder (in excess of $554) of the *PIA*

eliminating any cents. For 1979 the formula is 150 percent of $230 plus 272 percent of $102, plus 134 percent of $101 plus 175 percent of the remainder (in excess of $433) of the PIA. These amounts (not the percentages) are adjusted each year based on the national average annual earnings. For 1981 the amounts

TABLE 18–3 Percentage of PIA Payable to Other Beneficiaries

BENEFICIARY (TYPE OF BENEFIT)	*PERCENTAGE OF WORKER'S PIA**
Husband and wife (of retired or disabled worker) caring for the deceased worker's child (under 16 or disabled)	50
Benefits beginning at age 65	50
Benefits beginning at age 62 through 64	50, reduced (see text)
Child	
Of retired or disabled worker	50
Of deceased worker	75
Mother or father (widow or widower) caring for the deceased worker's child under 16 or disabled	75
Widow or widower (not caring for a child)	
Benefits beginning at age 65	100
Benefits beginning at age 60 through 64	100, reduced (see text)
Disabled widow or widower	
Benefits beginning at age 50 through 60	50 to 71½
Parents (dependent parent of deceased worker)	
One	82½
Two	75 each

* The amounts produced by these percentages are reduced to the lower dollar, i.e., the cents are dropped.

are $270, $120, $118 and the excess over $508; for 1980 they are $248, $110, $109 and the excess over $467.

For a *disabled* worker, family benefits are limited to 85 percent of the worker's AIME or 150 percent of the amount paid to the worker whichever is lower. The amount, of course, cannot be less than that paid to the worker.

If the amount of benefits allocated to family members exceeds the maximum based on the formula, the benefits must be adjusted. Only the living worker's benefit (disability or retirement) is untouchable. To redistribute benefits, deduct the living worker's benefit from the family maximum and apportion the remainder pro rata among the others entitled to benefits. If the worker is deceased, the survivors are paid a proportionate share of the applicable limits in accordance with their full shares. Assume a worker died in 1982 and is survived by her 55-year-old husband and their 14-year-old child. Her PIA is $703.80. Her surviving husband is entitled to 75 percent of $703.80 or $527; her child is also entitled to $527. These benefits total $1,054 which is below the 1982 maximum family monthly benefit of $1,232. But suppose she is also survived by her dependent father. He would be entitled to 82.5 percent of $703.80 or $580 bringing the total to $1,634, $402 in excess of the maximum, so the benefits must be reduced pro rata. The maximum is 75.4 percent of the total ($1,232 ÷ $1,634) so each recipient receives 75.4 percent of their scheduled benefits, dropping the cents. Her surviving husband and child each receive $397 a month and her dependent father receives $437 a month, making a total of $1,231. Rounding to the lower dollar gained an extra dollar for a social security system that needs every dollar that it can find. When the 14-year-old child reaches age 16, the full benefits are restored because the husband's benefit ceases until he reaches age 60. By that time the child will have reached 18 and will no longer be entitled to benefits.

Benefits paid to a divorced wife are not included in the family maximum.

Adjust for cost-of-living increases. An automatic cost-of-living adjustment is granted whenever the Department of Labor's consumer price index increases by at least 3 percent from the first quarter (called the base quarter) of one year to the first quarter of the next year unless Congress enacts a general benefit increase. The CPI for a quarter is the arithmetic mean of the index for the three months of the quarter. The cost-of-living increase equals the percentage increase in the consumer price index for the year rounded to the nearest 0.1 percent. These increases were 9.9 percent for 1979, 14.5 percent for 1980, 11.2 percent for 1981 and 7.4 percent for 1982. They become effective in June and are included in the July 1 check. These prior increases are important to know. For example, the PIA of a worker who first becomes eligible for benefits in 1979 is computed for that year, but the cost-of-living adjustments from 1979 onward are added to the PIA when the worker becomes entitled to benefits.

The base quarter is the cost-of-living computation quarter. If Congress enacts a general benefits increase, the base quarter is the calendar quarter in which the increase becomes effective. If a general benefit increase is granted in the prior year, no cost-of-living computation quarter can be declared for the current year.

The secretary of health and human services must notify the House Ways and Means Committee and the Senate Finance Committee of the proposed increase within 30 days after the close of the cost-of-living computation quarter and publish an announcement of the increase in the *Federal Register* within 45 days after the close of the quarter.

INNERSCRIPT: A SUMMARY ILLUSTRATION OF A PIA COMPUTATION

The discussion of amounts payable may be brought together and clarified by a summary example of the method of calculating the PIA. (See the appendix for this chapter for the average monthly wage (AMW) method that can be used until 1984.)

Consider the case of Professor Kingsfield, who becomes 65 years old in January 1982. He has earned at least the maximum covered earnings in each year since 1950 and decides to retire at age 65. The benefit computation years start with 1951 and continue through 1978, the year before Kingsfield reached age 62. Thus the number of elapsed years is 28. This number is reduced by 5. It would be reduced further if the professor had any qualified disability. But Kingsfield was always healthy and never missed a day in the library. So the number of his benefit computation years is 28 minus 5, or 23.

To compute the AIME for Kingsfield, use the 23 years of highest indexed and nonindexed earnings from 1951 through the year before Kingsfield retires. The national average wages and the maximum covered earnings indexed at 1977 levels are shown in Table 18–2. The computation base years are 1951 through 1981. A 1977

(*continued*)

amendment to the Social Security Act requires covered wages to be indexed for every year except the last two immediately before the worker reaches age 62, dies or is disabled, whichever is first. The purpose is to adjust prior earnings upward to reflect changes in wage levels over the years so that workers are not given a double adjustment for inflation. The combined effect of inflation-induced increases in the taxable wage base and in wages was to project retirement benefits for some workers in excess of their preretirement income—not the purpose of the system nor one it can afford. The AIME method is designed to confine cost-of-living increases to workers and their beneficiaries to the time following the period when they become eligible for benefits. The assumption is that wage increases during working years will provide the necessary inflation protection. The process is called decoupling.

Professor Kingsfield's indexed earnings are calculated by multiplying the covered earnings by the ratio of the national average annual wages in 1977 (the second year prior to the one in which Kingsfield reaches 62) to the national average annual wages in the year indexed. The average annual wages for the years 1951 through 1977 are listed in column 2 of Table 18–2. The maximum possible indexed earnings for Professor Kingsfield are shown in column 3. Note that his indexed earnings for 1951 are $12,577 computed by dividing the 1977 figure in column 2 by the 1951 figure in that column and multiplying the result by the figure in column 1 for 1951: ($9,779.44 ÷ $2,799.66) × $3,600 = $12,577. Earnings for those years following the indexing year (1978 through 1981) are not indexed but are the earnings shown in column 1.

The 23 years of highest earnings in this example are 1951, 1952, 1955, 1956, 1959 to 1961 and 1966 through 1981. The total covered indexed earnings are $347,253. The average indexed monthly earnings are

$$\frac{\$347{,}253}{23 \times 12} = \$1{,}258$$

The PIA is determined by the formula (using 1979 values as is appropriate)

90 percent of the first $180 =	$162.00 plus
32 percent of the next $905 =	289.60 plus
15 percent of the next $173 =	25.94
Total PIA =	$477.55 which is rounded down to $477.50

In this example the PIA is $477.50 plus the 9.9 percent benefit increase that was made in June 1979 and the automatic adjustments of 14.5 percent, 11.2 percent and 9.4 percent in June 1980, June 1981 and June 1982 increasing the PIA for 1982 to $717.30. This figure compares to $839.30 using the average monthly wage formula

(see Appendix). Because the average monthly wage (AMW) formula produces the higher PIA, the AMW formula is used to compute Professor Kingsfield's benefits.

Again, because social security benefit formulas and amount levels are subject to rapid change, an individual should check with the local social security office for up-to-date information.

Losses

Covered losses include retirement income, disability income, dependents' loss of support, lump-sum death payments and medical expenses for those reaching age 65 or receiving disability benefits for at least 24 consecutive months.

Retirement and disability benefits. Covered workers are entitled to retirement and disability benefits. Their spouses and dependent children are also entitled to benefits on the retired or disabled worker's account.

A *fully insured* worker retiring at age 65 is entitled to a monthly benefit equal to the PIA. An eligible worker may elect to retire as early as age 62 with benefits reduced by 5⁄9 of 1 percent for each month of retirement before age 65. Thus a worker retiring at age 62 receives 80 percent (1 − 5⁄9 × .01 × 36) of the PIA. The reduction is not restored at age 65; it is for life. However, a recomputation of benefits is made at age 65 for an adjustment upward of 1/180 for each month that the worker loses benefits. Benefits are lost primarily because of excess earnings. (The adjustment is not made unless it amounts to at least $1.) If the worker delays retirement beyond age 65 an increase of one quarter of 1 percent of the PIA is paid for each month retirement is delayed until age 72.

Two principal disability provisions affect fully insured workers: (1) a disability freeze (discussed earlier) preserves the worker's insured status and benefit level during the disability period and (2) monthly disability benefits are paid eligible workers after a five-month waiting period during disability periods before age 65. Disability is defined as the inability to engage in substantial gainful activity by reason of medically determinable physical or mental impairment that can be expected to result in death or that has continued or can be expected to continue for at least 12 months.

After the five-month waiting period the applicant receives the PIA calculated when the application was filed. If a worker becomes disabled a second time within five years, no additional waiting period is required if the new disability is expected to continue for at least 12 months or result in death. If a disabled worker under age 65 is paid workers' compensation benefits or other public disability benefits provided by federal, state or local programs, social security payments to the worker and family are reduced to keep the sum of the two below 80 percent of average current earnings as defined in the law.

Disability under social security is *strictly* defined. An individual is considered disabled only if the physical or mental impairment is so severe that the person is not only unable to do his or her previous work but based on age, education and experience cannot perform any other substantially gainful work regardless of whether (1) that work is available in the immediate area, (2) a specific job is available and (3) he or she would be hired for that job. A special definition applies for a blind person age 55 or over. That definition is the inability "by reason of such blindness to engage in substantial gainful activity requiring skills or abilities comparable to those of any gainful activity in which he [or she] has previously engaged with some regularity and over a substantial period of time."

Payments to the blind are suspended during months of substantial gainful work and are resumed when no such work is performed. Other disabled persons suffering from severe medical disability who meet other eligibility requirements are permitted to work up to 9 months without loss of eligibility. If the gainful activity continues beyond this 9-month trial work period, benefits are payable 3 more months. Continued eligibility for disability payments (called technical eligibility) lasts 15 months. The final 12 months are without benefits. But if the worker discontinues employment during this 15-month period, disability benefits are again paid without the worker reapplying for them.

Benefits are forfeited if a disabled worker refuses to accept rehabilitation services without an acceptable reason. Loss of benefits to the worker also means loss of benefits to the spouse and children.

Wives' and husbands' benefits. The 65-year-old spouse of a fully insured worker receiving retirement or disability benefits is entitled to a monthly payment of one half the worker's PIA. A spouse age 62 through 64 may elect to receive benefits reduced permanently by 25/36 of 1 percent per month for each month that benefit payments are started before age 65. If the spouse of a fully insured worker is also fully insured the payment will be the larger of one half the PIA or the spouse's own monthly benefit. A spouse of any age receives a benefit equal to 50 percent of the primary worker's PIA if he or she cares for the worker's disabled child or an eligible child under age 16.

Starting in 1983 the spouse's monthly benefit is reduced by any amount received as federal, state or local government retirement benefits based on earnings in noncovered employment. Also the loss of benefits because of excess earnings applies if the worker or the spouse earns in excess of the designated amount.

A divorced wife (for some unknown reason, not husband) is entitled to benefits if married to the worker at least 10 years, has not remarried, or, if so, that marriage ends in a divorce or death.

Children's benefits. If a fully insured worker retires at 62 or later or becomes disabled, any unmarried children under 18 receive a monthly payment equal to half the parent's PIA. Stepchildren, adopted children and illegitimate children are covered provided they achieved that status at least one year before the benefits begin. Unmarried full-time college students at least 18 years old who received a child's benefit in August 1981 are entitled to a decreasing benefit until they reach age 22 if they began college before May 1982. These benefits are paid from September through April and are not eligible for the cost-of-living adjustment. The benefit decreases 25 percent a year beginning September 1982 and phases out April 1985. A child entitled to payments under two workers' social security accounts (e.g., a disabled mother and a retired father) receives the higher of the two benefit amounts. The loss of benefits because of excess earnings also applies to children's benefits.

Survivor benefits. Benefits are available to widows, widowers, mothers and fathers of dependent children, children and dependent parents of a deceased covered worker. Widows', widowers' and parents' benefits are payable only if they survive a fully insured worker. The mothers' or fathers' benefit; children's benefit and the lump-sum death benefit are payable if the deceased was either fully or currently insured.

Widows and widowers. A widow or widower who is at least age 60 (50 if disabled) is entitled to a benefit. The benefit is equal to the spouse's PIA if taken at age 65. If taken at ages 60 through 64 the benefit is reduced 19/40 of 1 percent for each month under 65 when the benefits begin. The reduction is for life. Thus a surviving spouse receives 71.5 percent of the PIA for life if the benefits start at age 60 $(1 - 19/40 \times .01 \times 60)$. If the deceased worker deferred retirement benefits between ages 65 and 72 the surviving spouse receives an additional one fourth of 1 percent for each deferred month.

The benefit for a disabled widow or widower at age 50 is reduced by 19/40 of 1 percent for each of the 60 months between age 60 to 65 and by 43/240 of 1 percent for each of the 120 months between age 50 and 60. Thus if benefits start at age 50 they are 50 percent of the PIA. A waiting period of five months is required for disability benefits. A strict definition of disability is used.

If the widow or widower remarries at age 60 or later the benefit is not affected. If the new spouse is collecting an old-age benefit, the benefit based on the deceased spouse's PIA continues, i.e., a widow's or widower's benefit rather than a wife's or husband's benefit is paid. Effective in 1983, benefits are reduced by the amount of government pensions received based upon earnings in noncovered employment. Also the excess earnings test applies to the widow's and widower's benefit.

The benefit for a surviving divorced wife is the same as that for a widow.

Mothers and fathers. Surviving spouses are entitled to a mother's or father's benefit of 75 percent of the PIA at any age when caring for their natural or adopted child under age 16 (beyond 16 if a child is disabled) if the child is eligible for benefits based on the deceased worker's account. This entitlement is conditioned upon the surviving spouse remaining single, not being eligible for a widow's or widower's benefit or a retirement benefit based on his or her own social security account. (The mother's benefit will not cease if she marries a person receiving old age, disability, widower's, parent's or disabled child's benefits.) The previously discussed reduction provisions for excess earnings and for government pensions based on earnings in noncovered employment apply to these benefits. The benefit extends to divorced mothers and fathers.

Children. Unmarried children under age 18 are entitled to a benefit equal to 75 percent of the deceased parent's PIA. If disability occurs before age 22, benefits continue until two months after the child's disability terminates. The excess earnings test applies to reduce the child's benefits but only to the child's earnings. The parent's earnings do not affect the child's benefits, and the child's earnings do not affect the parent's benefits. Much of the earlier discussion of the benefits for a child of a retired or disabled parent applies to a child of a deceased worker.

Parents. A parent age 62 receiving at least half support from a fully insured worker is paid a benefit of 82½ percent of the deceased worker's PIA. The parent must be the natural parent, a stepparent before the worker became 16 or a person who adopted the worker before his or her 16th birthday. If both parents are alive and dependent, each receives 75 percent of the worker's PIA. Benefits are paid until the parent dies or, if single, remarries. Marriage to a person receiving one of the types of social security benefits mentioned earlier does not disqualify him or her for the parent's benefit. The excess earnings test applies to this benefit.

Social security retirement benefits are payable to a worker and his or her spouse only in months in which all conditions of eligibility are met for the *full* month. So only persons born on the first day of the month are eligible for benefits for that month. This provision does not apply to survivorship benefits. Social security benefits are exempt from federal income taxes and are not subject to attachment by creditors except for delinquent federal taxes and failure to pay alimony and child support. If a person is eligible for more than one type of social security benefit, he or she is paid the highest one. To receive benefits, the insured worker must file an application and submit proof of age. Benefits available to widows, widowers, parents or children are also available upon formal application.

Lump-sum death benefit. A lump-sum death benefit of $255 is paid if an eligible spouse survives the worker or if a child is entitled to benefits based on the deceased's account.

Medicare benefits. Medicare has two parts: Part A, hospital insurance and Part B, medical insurance. Part A is financed by a hospital insurance tax which is a part of the social security tax. For 1982 that tax was 1.3 percent of wages up to $32,400 paid by the employer and the employee. It is a part of the 6.70 percent social security payroll tax. The tax is the same for the self-employed (actually less because it is not matched by an employer) and is a part of the 9.35 percent social security tax. Under the Tax Equity and Fiscal Responsibility Act of 1982 (TEFRA), federal civilian employees are required to pay the hospital portion of the social security tax. Part B is voluntary and is paid for partly by the insured and partly by the government. In 1982 the cost to the insured was $12.20 effective July 1. (The cost to the government is more than twice the cost to the insured.)

Basic hospital insurance. Basic hospital insurance automatically covers those who became 65 before 1968. Those reaching 65 in 1968 must have had either fully insured status (on their own or their spouse's earnings record) or at least three quarters of coverage for each calendar year after 1965. For persons reaching 65 in 1974 or later, fully insured status is required for coverage. The coverage extends to all persons age 65 or over who are eligible for monthly social security benefits and to railroad workers. (Railroad workers must pay only the hospital insurance tax because they are not covered for social security income benefits.) Persons under 65 who have been entitled to disability benefits for 24 consecutive months also are covered: disabled workers at any age, disabled widows and widowers at age 50 or older, persons age 18 or more receiving disability benefits beginning before age 22 and qualified railroad retirement annuitants. Persons with permanent kidney failure who require dialysis or a transplant are eligible for medicare protection. Disabled persons are automatically eligible for medicare without the 24-month waiting period if they qualified as disabled not more than five years earlier (seven years for disabled widows, widowers and children). Medicare coverage continues for disabled persons 36 months after disability benefits terminate because of a return to work.

Persons covered by medicare may continue to work, and their earnings are not subject to limitations. If 65 or over, a dependent or survivor of a worker entitled to medicare is also eligible for basic hospital insurance under medicare. Persons ineligible for automatic coverage under the basic plan usually can purchase it by paying its full cost ($113 a month effective July 1, 1982, up from $89 one year earlier).

The basic hospital services program provides the following benefits:

1. A maximum of 60 days in a participating hospital, subject to a $260 (1982) deductible per illness and then all but $65 (1982) a day for an additional

30 days. This benefit is paid for each *spell of illness,* that is, the period beginning with hospital admission and ending after 60 consecutive days following the patient's discharge from the hospital or a nursing home. An additional 60-day lifetime reserve is available at a $130 (1982) daily cost to the patient. Benefits for psychiatric hospital services are subject to a lifetime limit of 190 days.

2. Full cost up to 20 days in a skilled nursing home and all but $32.50 (1982) per day for an additional period of 80 days for each spell of illness. Nursing home benefits become effective after a stay of at least 3 days in the hospital and generally within 30 days of discharge. Benefits cover only continued treatment of the medical condition involved in the hospital stay.

3. Unlimited home health visits by nurses, interns or other health workers from qualified home health agencies (excluding doctors) if the patient is house-confined, needs the medical service (nursing, physical therapy or speech therapy) and a doctor arranges the plan with a participating home health agency.

4. When a person becomes entitled to medicare because of permanent kidney failure, the coverage begins the fourth month after a course of maintenance dialysis treatment begins. However, coverage can begin the first month if the patient participates in a self-dialysis training program in a medicare-approved training facility. To qualify, the training must start before the third month of dialysis and the patient must be expected to complete the training and then self-dialyze. Medicare begins the month the patient is admitted to an approved hospital for a kidney transplant or a procedure pertaining to a transplant if it takes place within 3 months. Medicare ends 12 months after the patient no longer requires maintenance dialysis treatments or 36 months after the kidney transplant.

The benefit payments for hospital or nursing home service covers semiprivate accommodations unless a private room is medically indicated, plus the cost of the usual auxiliary services, such as drugs, regular nursing service, special diets, cost of special care (e.g., intensive care units), lab tests, X-rays, medical supplies, use of appliances, use of operating and recovery rooms and rehabilitation services such as physical, occupational and speech therapy. The patient pays for the first three pints of blood unless they are replaced.

The medicare law includes a waiver of beneficiary liability law that frees the patient of responsibility for the cost of care if he or she could not reasonably be expected to know that the care is not covered. This provision applies primarily to custodial care (care primarily for the purpose of meeting personal needs such as help in walking, eating, bathing and so on—help that can be provided by a nonmedical professional) and for diagnosis or treatment not reasonable or necessary.

Deductibles and participation rates increase with medical costs. The secretary of health and human services is required by law to make annual reviews of medicare costs and adjust the basic plan deductibles. The increases of $180 to $204 and from $204 to $260 in 1981 and 1982 were about 14 and 27.5 percent respectively. The law requires that when the hospital deductible changes, comparable changes should be made in the amount medicare patients pay toward hospital stays of more than 60 days, in charges for remaining in a skilled nursing home for more than 20 days and in the amount the patient will pay for each of the *lifetime reserve* days used. Consequently these costs also increased about 27.5 percent in 1982.

Medical insurance. The supplementary medical insurance is voluntary and costs the participant a monthly premium. The secretary of health and human services may increase the rate if it proves inadequate. The original cost in 1966 was $3 a month and deductibles were low. The cost jumped to $9.60 by 1980, $11 by 1981 and $12.20 by 1982. Further increases to $13.70 and $25.30 beginning July 1983 and July 1984 respectively were scheduled by TEFRA. The supplementary medical insurance plan is administered by private insurers under contract with the federal government.

Nearly everyone at least age 65 is eligible to buy social security supplementary medical insurance. Nonsocial security and railroad retirement beneficiaries may enroll if they are U.S. citizens or legal aliens living in the United States continuously for five years. The effective date of coverage is the month in which the participant becomes age 65 assuming enrollment is before that month. A person who does not enroll in the initial enrollment period (the seven-month period from three months before until three months after the month of the 65th birthday) may enroll during the general enrollment period (January 1 through March 31) but must pay an additional premium equal to 10 percent for each full 12-month period that enrollment is delayed.

The supplementary medical insurance program provides the following benefits:

1. Physicians' and surgeons' fees at home, at the office or in the hospital on an in- or out-patient basis, in a skilled nursing facility or any other location in the United States. (The medical insurance also pays for doctors' services on an in-patient basis in Canada or Mexico under specified conditions.) The insurance pays for a second opinion regarding the need for surgery. (What happens if the second opinion contradicts the first? Whom should the patient believe?) Patients reluctant to ask their own doctors to refer them to another doctor can use medicare's second-opinion referral center. (Routine physical examinations, eye examinations for corrective glasses, examinations for hearing aids, immunizations and cosmetic surgery are not covered.)

2. Limited coverage for optometrists (examination services related to aphakia), podiatrists (removal of plantar warts or routine care for a medical condition such as diabetes affecting the lower limbs), dental care (only if surgery of the jaw or related structure is required), psychiatric care (up to $250 a year as an out-patient) and chiropractic care (only manual manipulation of the spine to correct a subluxation). Regular foot care, eye care and dental care are not covered.

3. Radiology and pathology services by doctors for 100 percent of approved charges while an in-patient in a qualified hospital.

4. Full cost of unlimited home health care under an approved home health plan without prior hospitalization as medically necessary.

5. Full approved charges for diagnostic service received in a hospital's out-patient department or a doctor's office within seven days prior to admission.

6. Other medical and health services like prescription and nonprescription drugs and biologicals that cannot be self-administered, prescription maintenance drugs, anesthesia, medical supplies, physical therapy and speech pathology services, X-ray treatment, surgical dressings, rental of medical equipment and services of the doctor's office nurse (whatever that may be!).

7. Necessary ambulance transportation except to the doctor's office.

8. Prosthetic devices such as lenses after a cataract operation (dental plates are not covered).

9. Blood transfusions as an out-patient for 80 percent of the charge after the first three pints unless they are replaced.

10. Laboratory tests.

11. Service in an emergency room or out-patient clinic.

12. For people with permanent kidney failure 100 percent of the recognized cost of home dialysis equipment if an approved facility or hospital provides the equipment for exclusive use of medicare patients on home dialysis; nearly all supplies necessary to perform home dialysis; periodic support services furnished by an approved facility necessary to assist the patient to remain on home dialysis; the surgeon's services for performing a kidney transplant operation including pre-operative and follow-up care and the doctor's services provided to the kidney donor during his or her hospital stay.

Nearly all benefits are subject to an annual cumulative deductible of $78 (1982) and a 20 percent patient's participation. Payment is based on the reasonable cost of the service (the prevailing charge in the area) and the amount the doctor charges whichever is less.

THE SOCIAL SECURITY LEVIATHAN

The social security system is an instructive case study for analyzing the democratic political process. Problems involve conflicting aims of governmental social programs and fiscal responsibility, uncertainties of economic and demographic forecasting and the apparent unwillingness of the various news outlets to keep the public adequately and objectively informed about important and complicated social issues.

Social Security and Politics—Siamese Twins

Politicians' desire to gain popularity in election years is illustrated by preelection increases in social security benefits, or by its nearly untouchable status when trying to move toward a balanced budget. The need for fiscal responsibility is often met by postelection increases in contributions. Numerous forecasts by actuaries and economists about inflation rates for wages, prices, birthrates and early retirement have proved to be overly optimistic. The social security issue is as complicated as any issue facing elected officials. Any changes in the program will directly affect all workers paying social security taxes and all beneficiaries, making its impact nearly universal.

A great irony concerning social security often debated is that civilian government workers, including the legislators who determine benefit and contribution levels and the employees of the Social Security Administration, are not covered by social security. Federal workers are covered by their own separate retirement program that is even more generous than that available to workers covered by OASDHI and private pension plans. It is argued that the long-run financial future of the social security system would not be so uncertain if legislators and administrators were participants in the program and had to rely on the system for their own retirement benefits.

Brief History of the Social Security System

The social security system developed in 1935 was established to provide supplementary retirement assistance to some of the working population recovering from the Great Depression. The 1935 act provided retirement coverage for workers in industry and commerce. The initial benefit formula would have provided eligible retired workers a monthly benefit of $10 to $85, depending upon their cumulative wage credits. The employer and employee were each taxed 1 percent of the first $3,000 of their annual earnings in 1937–39 for a maximum total annual contribution of $60. Since then at least 15 amendments to the Social Security

Act have been enacted to (1) provide benefits for more recipients, (2) increase the benefit levels and (3) increase the contribution level.

The major increases in the types of recipients covered came in 1939 when dependents and survivors were included and in 1956 when the disabled were added. Monthly benefit levels as measured by the PIA have increased from the initial $10 to $85 levels to the $820 to $1,103 levels of 1982. Further increases are scheduled to adjust benefits automatically for the inflation rate. The period of greatest benefit escalation was 1970–1972, when benefit levels were increased 51.8 percent. Many of the financing problems described later developed because benefit increases were excessive.

The maximum contributions level has grown at a rate even faster than the benefits level. Table 18–4 lists the maximum contributions for employees, the combined contributions of employees and employers and the maximum contributions by the self-employed for each year since the social security program began. The maximum tax is paid by any worker earning the maximum covered earnings listed in Table 18–2. Earnings lower than the maximum would be subject to a proportionately lower tax. The maximum contribution level for an employee has increased from $30 to $2,170.80 in 1982, an increase of 7,136 percent. With increases of this magnitude the taxpayers' concern about social security financing should not be surprising; many families pay more in social security taxes than in federal income taxes.

TABLE 18–4 Maximum Annual Taxes Payable under OASDI and HI

YEAR	*MAXIMUM FOR EMPLOYEES*	*COMBINED MAXIMUM FOR EMPLOYERS AND EMPLOYEES*	*MAXIMUM FOR SELF-EMPLOYED*
1937–49	$ 30.00	$ 60.00	No coverage
1950	45.00	90.00	No coverage
1951–53	54.00	108.00	$ 81.00
1954	72.00	144.00	108.00
1955–56	84.00	168.00	126.00
1957–58	94.50	189.00	141.75
1959	120.00	240.00	180.00
1960–61	144.00	288.00	216.00
1962	150.00	300.00	225.60
1963–65	174.00	348.00	259.20
1966	277.20	554.40	405.90
1967	290.40	580.80	422.40
1968	343.20	686.40	499.20
1969–70	374.40	748.80	538.20
1971	405.60	811.20	585.00
1972	468.00	936.00	675.00
1973	631.80	1273.60	864.00
1974	772.20	1544.40	1042.80
1975	824.85	1649.70	1113.90
1976	895.05	1790.10	1208.70
1977	965.25	1930.50	1303.50
1978	1070.85	2141.70	1433.70
1979	1403.77	2807.54	1854.90
1980	1587.67	3175.34	2097.90
1981	1975.05	3950.10	2762.10
1982	2170.80	4341.60	3029.40

Current Financial Status of the Social Security System

The current social security system is widely recognized as financially unsound. Although receipts are expected to exceed expenditures over the short range the projection for the future indicates deficits will occur unless legislative changes are enacted. The 1977 amendments made major improvements in the short-range financial outlook but did not eliminate the long-term difficulties. This short-range financial strengthening arose from a series of increases in the tax rate and wage base. Some experts considered these changes unfair to low-income workers and a possible cause of an economic recession. However, social security's financial position will deteriorate if either the wage base or tax rates, or both, are not increased.

Reasons for Problems

An important question is why a social security financing problem exists. A major reason lies in the baby boom of the post–World War II era. During the 1970s and 1980s baby boomers entered the labor force providing additional tax revenue to finance current benefits. However, as this population reaches retirement age, providing baby boomers their benefits will become increasingly difficult. In 1950 8.1 percent of the U.S. population was over 65 and potentially eligible for retirement benefits. In 1982 this percentage had increased to 23.1. Social security operates on a pay-as-you-go basis, i.e., collecting money from current taxpayers to pay current beneficiaries. (Owe-as-you-go is a more appropriate name for this basis because the system incurs liabilities for future benefits without accumulating sufficient funds to pay them.) Thus contribution levels will be forced to rise with the increase in beneficiaries. Otherwise benefit levels will have to drop or the minimum retirement age will have to be raised.

Contributing to the problems of financing the social security system is the difficulty of developing accurate economic forecasts. In the past 75 years annual inflation has varied from a negative 10.7 percent to a positive 17.5 percent. Unemployment has ranged from 1.2 percent to 24.9 percent and life expectancy has increased from 49 to 74 years. Developing an accurate long-range forecast of these factors would be a matter of luck rather than economic or actuarial expertise.

Another factor that has led to growth in the labor force and helped finance more generous benefit levels for current beneficiaries is the increased participation of women in the work force. This change has created additional problems by focusing attention on inequities in the benefit structure. The benefit structure was developed by people envisioning a typical one-worker family unit. Upon retirement at age 65 the worker would receive a monthly benefit equal to the PIA. If the worker had a nonworking spouse of the same age the spouse would receive one half the PIA. If both husband and wife had worked in covered employment, the family would receive the *higher* of two separately calculated PIAs *or* one and one half times the higher PIA. Although the lower-paid spouse contributes a full share into the social security system, the most that he or she can receive is the amount by which his or her PIA exceeds one half of the spouse's PIA. The increased number of two-career families has made this inequity widespread and brought about calls for reform.

What can be done

The solution to social security financing problems requires adopting one or more of the following changes: raising tax levels, reducing benefit levels, eliminating some benefits, financing benefits from general revenues, including benefits as taxable income, tightening benefit eligibility requirements (e.g., raising minimum retirement age to 68) and indexing social security payments to wage increases rather than to the CPI. As of this writing some changes have been made in benefits. The workers' death benefit has been modified; the college students' educational benefit is being phased out; the mother's and father's benefit period has been reduced and the workers' minimum social security benefit has been eliminated. Furthermore the current tax rates are scheduled to increase 25 percent from 1980 to 1990. The maximum covered earnings will probably double during the period but even more increases are necessary unless benefits are reduced and/or alternative financing methods are adopted.

The Committee for Economic Development (CED), a private research organization, has gathered social security financing recommendations from leaders in education and business. The consensus among these leaders is that social security must be viewed as a three-tiered system of retirement benefits. The CED recommends that the two other tiers, private pension plans and employees' personal savings, should play more prominent roles in retirement benefit planning. They should not only supplement but also partially replace social security benefits. How successfully personal savings and private pension plans can accomplish the goals set for them by the CED depends on additional tax incentives for: (1) personal savings and (2) employee contributions to company pension plans. The Economic Recovery Act of 1981 made some efforts in this direction by liberalizing IRA and Keogh plans, for example. But the Tax Equity and Fiscal Responsibility Act of 1982 partially counteracts these developments by reducing the contributions and benefits allowed under qualified pension plans.

UNEMPLOYMENT COMPENSATION

In contrast to OASDHI, unemployment compensation is not financed or administered by the federal government. The states administer the program with some federal participation. The Federal Unemployment Tax Act provides for a 3.4 percent levy against covered employers on the first $6,000 earned by each employee. (The tax rate is 3.4 percent if the state has no outstanding loans from the U.S. Treasury.) Employers may credit the federal tax with any state taxes paid if the state plan is federally approved. Because state plans are experience rated (discussed later), employers may receive an additional credit against the state tax. The total credit from these two sources may not exceed 2.7 percent of currently taxable wages. The remainder of the tax is collected by the federal government to offset federal and state administrative expenses and to strengthen reserves of state programs. The federal government's portion of the tax will reduce to the normal level of 0.7 percent when the trust fund has repaid loans from the U.S. Treasury that were used to finance a special extension of benefits enacted during the 1975–77 period of high unemployment (expired in 1977). The maximum number of weeks of benefits during the period was increased from 26 to 52. The Federal Unemployment Tax Act covers industrial and commercial employers, certain state employers and nonprofit groups who employ at least one worker for 20 or more weeks or who pay wages of $1,500 or more quarterly or $6,000 or more in a calendar year. In 1981, 19 states had an unemployment insurance wage base higher than $6,000. The state-collected unemployment insurance taxes are held by the U.S. Treasury in a reserve fund where separate state accounts are maintained. TEFRA provided for an increase retroactive to January 1, 1982 of about $1.20 a month per worker in employer-paid taxes for unemployment compensation.

Coverage Provisions

Except for a few federal administrative regulations states can design their own unemployment insurance programs, including coverage, benefits, eligibility and financing provisions. Most states include only those types of employment covered by the federal law. As a result domestic servants, some farm workers, some government workers and casual laborers are not covered. More than 60 percent of all workers are covered by the current program. Railroad employees have their own unemployment compensation system.

Variations are found among state systems. Hawaii covers agricultural workers. Domestic servants are covered in three states: Alabama, Hawaii and New York. In most states a minimum employment period is required before an employee is covered. Some states require a minimum payroll for an employee to be covered in addition to a minimum employment period.

Benefits

Unemployment compensation is designed to pay the unemployed worker a weekly benefit equal to roughly half the worker's wage but limited to no more than half the average weekly wage in the state. Many government officials, however, have been urging an unemployment benefit up to two thirds of the state's average wage. A comparison of current state unemployment compensation laws with those in effect during 1939 shows that increases in benefits have not kept pace with earnings levels. Weekly benefits vary among states. In the majority of states they are determined by applying a given percentage to the highest quarter of earnings in the base period. The base period is defined in terms of some previous employment period. This method is called the high-quarter basis. Some states use a schedule weighted to give proportionately higher benefits to low-income workers. The typical benefit period is 26 weeks.

Eligibility for Benefits

The federal act requires that no worker can be denied benefits for refusal to accept a job if wages are substantially lower than wages for similar work in the same area, the worker refuses a job offer for unsuitable work (as defined by the state's unemployment insurance law), a strike is in progress or acceptance of the job would mean joining a company union or signing a "yellow-dog" contract, i.e., a contract prohibiting the worker from joining a union.[5] Neither can a worker be denied eligibility while attending vocational training courses approved by the head of the employment security agency.

State unemployment compensation laws contain both *positive* and *negative* eligibility tests. Positive tests include the following: the worker must (1) have been employed for a designated number of weeks by a covered employer, (2) be registered for work, (3) file a claim for benefits, (4) be able to work, (5) be available for work and (6) meet any waiting-period requirement. In all but 10 states waiting periods are required to reduce moral hazard and to prevent insureds from filing claims for small affordable losses. In many states applicants are subject only to one waiting period in a benefit year.

[5] "Yellow-dog" contracts are outlawed under other federal statutes.

To receive benefits workers must have worked in employment covered by the act. The states provide that the workers must prove they earned a given amount of wages in some prior period, usually referred to as the "base period." This amount usually is 20 to 30 times the weekly benefit. The purpose of the earnings requirement is to restrict coverage to members of the labor force. This system generally excludes part-time and low-income workers whose average weekly wage is less than the state's minimum benefit.

Certain conditions provide a basis for denying benefits. The following are principal types of negative tests: the claimant (1) is receiving severance pay from a former employer, (2) is receiving workers' compensation benefits, (3) is receiving federal old-age insurance benefits greater than the unemployment compensation benefit, (4) voluntarily quits the job without just cause, (5) was discharged for just cause, (6) refuses "suitable" work or (7) fails to comply with the rules and regulations prescribed by law. Until recently, under most state laws women who left their jobs for marital reasons or pregnancy were denied unemployment compensation. As of early 1980 less than half the state laws still contained such provisions, compared to more than three fourths in 1972.

Financing

Except in Alabama, Alaska and New Jersey, where employee contributions are required, unemployment insurance is financed entirely by taxes levied on the employer. Alabama provides for the elimination of the employee tax whenever the state's unemployment compensation fund rises above a specified amount.

Although a tax of 3.4 percent of covered payroll is provided under federal law to pay benefits most employers pay much less because the federal law allows experience rating. Employers who maintain stable employment (low employee turnover) are given tax credits for their role in reducing unemployment benefits. The purpose of the credits is not only to lower payroll taxes for these employers but also to motivate other employers to maintain stable employment. Experience rating, however, has had little influence on employment policy. Its effect is primarily to reduce contributions during economic prosperity. The merits of experience rating in unemployment compensation insurance are vigorously debated but the system seems to be in little danger of abandonment.

Frequent changes are made in the state unemployment insurance laws. These changes cover nearly all important areas, including benefit amounts, financing, eligibility requirements and coverage. Up-to-date information on unemployment insurance in a particular state is available from the local office of that state's division of unemployment compensation.

TEMPORARY DISABILITY INCOME BENEFIT PLANS

Temporary disability benefit plans provide partial replacement of lost wages during a limited period of sickness or injury unrelated to employment. These plans have been adopted in Rhode Island, California, New Jersey, New York, Puerto Rico and Hawaii.

Rhode Island provides that the coverage must be purchased from a state fund. In four states private insurers are allowed to compete with state funds. Hawaii has a special fund to pay workers of bankrupt firms and workers who become disabled while unemployed.

Altogether nearly 25 percent of all wage and salaried workers in private industry are covered by a state temporary disability income benefit plan.

Finance

Employees contribute to the cost of the plans in all six jurisdictions. In California and Rhode Island, *only* employees contribute. The rate and the rate base vary from a combined low of 0.5 percent of the first $3,120 of wages in New York to a combined high of 1.5 percent of the first $9,000 of annual wages in Rhode Island, a state with a monopolistic state fund. In New Jersey the worker and the employer pay the same amount if the insurer is the state fund. If a private insurer is used the employer pays the balance of the cost of benefits, if any. In New York if the contribution of the worker is not sufficient the employer pays the balance. These state-sponsored plans provide for a compulsory non-occupational health insurance system. If contributions are made to a state fund rather than a private insurer they are considered state income taxes and deductible for federal income taxes (when the deductions are itemized).

Eligibility

Generally employers who must participate in state unemployment compensation systems must also participate in the temporary disability income system. Those excluded are workers in agriculture (covered in Hawaii and Puerto Rico), domestic service (covered in New York), government service and railroad workers.

Benefits

A seven-day waiting period is imposed in each of the six jurisdictions. In California and Puerto Rico the waiting period is waived if the insured is confined to a hospital. In all but Rhode Island the waiting period is for each disability; in Rhode Island it is for each benefit year. In New Jersey the participant is not paid for the waiting period (seven days) until after receiving benefits for three consecutive weeks. Benefit durations are 26 weeks in all states except California where it is 39 weeks or until the worker collects 50 percent of the base year wages, if sooner. The plans of three states (California, New Jersey and Rhode Island) have submaximums that apply to low-income workers or to other situations. For example, the California plan has a minimum of six weeks for low-income workers, and the New Jersey plan applies an eight-week minimum to pregnancies (four weeks before and four weeks after childbirth). Disability from normal pregnancies is covered only by the plans of Hawaii, New Jersey and Rhode Island. (The Rhode Island plan allows a maximum of $250.) Sickness from abnormal pregnancies is covered by all plans. Benefit amounts are generally based on the formulas used for unemployment compensation except the amounts are usually higher—55 rather than 50 percent of the average weekly wage. The Rhode Island plan allows a supplement of $4 a week for each child up to a maximum of $16 (four dependent children). Maximum benefits run from a high in Hawaii (66.55 percent of the state average wage which exceeds the next highest of $146 in California) to a low of $91 in Rhode Island for a family with no dependent children. The New York maximum of $95 would be lower than the Rhode Island plan for a family with more than one dependent child. Minimum benefits run from a high of $30 in California to a low of $7 in Puerto Rico. (Under the Puerto Rico plan a $3,000 death benefit is paid.) The average weekly wage applies if it is less than the minimum.

The Future of Temporary Disability Laws

Although nonoccupational temporary disability benefit plans have been discussed in many legislatures over the past 30 years, only Puerto Rico and Hawaii have enacted plans since 1949. Reasons advanced to explain the slow growth of state plans include the reluctance of lawmakers to burden employees and employers with more taxes and the success of unions through collective bargaining in gaining temporary disability income benefits for their members. Approximately two thirds of the work force now has some form of nonoccupational temporary disability income coverage—compulsory, union bargained or unilaterally installed by employers. However, some persons believe that more employees should be covered and advocate that OASDHI be expanded to provide for nonoccupational temporary disability income benefits—an unlikely development given the present problems of the social security system.

NATIONAL HEALTH INSURANCE (NHI)

The philosophy behind national health insurance (NHI) proposals is that every American should have access to quality health care regardless of income, age or residence. Advocates of NHI maintain that the present U.S. health care system does not accomplish this objective. Many Americans cannot obtain satisfactory health care because they cannot afford it. Nearly 20 percent of Americans have no health insurance. Furthermore, the 80 percent of Americans with health insurance have inadequate coverage.

Because of rising health care costs a serious illness could bankrupt many American families. The result is an outcry of NHI advocates for the replacement of a woefully inadequate health care system that produces such inhumane effects.

Those who oppose NHI argue that it would destroy the doctor-patient relationship, interfere with the free choice of doctors, lower the standard of medical care, increase the cost of medical care, add an unreasonably high tax burden to an already over-taxed society and subvert the free enterprise system. Many of these arguments lack substance and are put forth by physicians' lobbyists who have not succeeded in destroying what appears to be overwhelming pressue for some type of NHI. The question seems to be what form of NHI would best mold all attitudes into an acceptable compromise.

Basic Principles for a NHI Plan

Basic principles for a NHI plan include (1) every American should have adequate health care; (2) the quality of care should not be based on a person's income; (3) the government should not interfere in the private insurance system; (4) financing should not burden the lower- and middle-income classes and (5) the plan design must control overutilization of medical facilities.

Three Basic NHI Proposals

Although NHI legislation was expected to be passed in the early 1970s little progress had been made until 1978 and 1979 when several NHI proposals were introduced in Congress. The economic downturn and the changed political climate since then have made NHI a low priority item. If a NHI program eventually passes, the form it takes will be a compromise among three basic proposals that can be classified as liberal, moderate and conservative.

The liberal proposal would provide comprehensive benefits for every resident of the United States through mandated health insurance plans with federal financing for the poor, the unemployed and the aged. The public would obtain health insurance coverage through Blue Cross and Blue Shield facilities, private health insurers and health maintenance organizations. The NHI plan would be administered by a public authority to assure equal coverage for all Americans. Individual insurance companies and Blue Cross and Blue Shield plans would be certified and regulated by this authority.

The liberal plan would be financed through a combination of employer and employee contributions with federal support for the poor, aged and unemployed. The employer's contributions would be based on payroll and paid to an insurer. All employees would pay the same rate. The total premium would cover the full costs of benefits.

The liberal plan includes built-in cost controls for hospital and physician costs. The NHI authority would budget hospital and physician expenditures; hospitals and doctors would be paid prenegotiated amounts. The total cost of health care would be less because of the cost controls applied.

The American Medical Association believes that the liberal program would bring total federal domination over health care. Another criticism is that the absence of deductibles and coinsurance might lead to overuse of facilities and services.

Unlike the liberal proposal the moderate NHI plan would divide the responsibility for providing health insurance between the federal government and the private insurance industry. Under both plans employers and employees would pay the cost of insurance. Like the liberal plan the moderate plan would not involve the government in catastrophic medical coverage for employees. The major difference between liberal and moderate NHI plans lies in their provisions. The liberal plan would provide public comprehensive health care for all citizens regardless of economic condition. The insurance/health care industry (i.e., HMOs, Blue Cross and Blue Shield and private insurers) would be completely regulated. The moderate proposal, on the other hand, would provide comprehensive coverage (catastrophic and basic medical care) for the poor, aged and welfare recipients but the employed worker would have an option to buy private catastrophic medical coverage.

The conservative plan differs from the moderate and liberal plans by relying much more on the private insurance industry. The employee would not have a choice between a public or a private plan. Public insurance would be available only to the aged, poor and needy. Uninsurable employed workers would be guaranteed the right to buy private insurance at "reasonable" rates. The federal government would require employers to guarantee a core level of health protection to full-time employees and their families. The principal feature of the conservative program is that employees must share health care costs with insurers up to a specified maximum, such as $2,500 a year. No cost-sharing features are required for the aged and poor.

Solutions

Solutions to the problem of rising costs and inadequate treatment have been suggested by many different sources. In addition to NHI some have suggested wider use of such group practice plans as HMOs. The largest of these is the Kaiser Foundation Program with 2 million members, originally designed as a method to provide medical care for Kaiser Corporation employees, many of whom lived and worked in remote locations. The foundation now owns a network of hospitals and outpatient clinics in Oregon, California and Hawaii. The members pay a monthly fee and are entitled to a wide range of medical services. Contrary to private health insurance, the theory of group practice plans places primary emphasis on preventive medicine.

Overall, the plans appear to provide high-quality service at costs that average

15 to 20 percent lower than the average for the areas where they operate. Length of hospital confinements has also been below average, partially because the emphasis on preventive medicine reduces the number of serious illnesses incurred.

In summary, what is needed in the health care delivery system is action to improve the supply and efficiency of the health labor force, develop ambulatory health care services, improve comprehensive health planning, establish national health care goals and priorities, create controls on health care and quality and grant comprehensive health insurance for all.

APPENDIX: AVERAGE MONTHLY WAGE CALCULATION FOR THE SOCIAL SECURITY PRIMARY INSURANCE AMOUNT

Before 1979 the average monthly wage (AMW) method was used exclusively to calculate the worker's primary insurance amount (PIA). The 1977 amendments to the Social Security Act adjusted benefits so that they would offer protection against inflation only after benefits begin. The process, called decoupling, made it necessary for the worker's PIA to be calculated by the average indexed monthly earnings method (AIME) rather than the AMW method. However, the amendment provided a transition period between 1979 and 1983. A worker who retires or dies after reaching 62 during this period is given assurance that the method (AMW or AIME) which yields the higher benefit will be used. The assurance only applies to workers with credited income for one year prior to 1979 and who were not disabled before 1979. The transition period does not apply to disability benefit computations. The result of this amendment is that benefits during this period must be computed by both the AMW and the AIME method.

The steps involved in computing the PIA under the AMW system are as follows, using Professor Kingsfield as an example:

1. Calculate the number of years elapsing after 1950 until the year before Professor Kingsfield becomes age 62. That will be in 1978, so the number of years is 28.

2. Subtract five years and the number of calendar years that Kingsfield was disabled. If a person is disabled for at least five months, a full calendar year is deducted from the elapsed years even though the disability lasts only a fraction of that calendar year. For example, if Kingsfield was disabled from December 1970 through January 1973 four years of disability (1970, 1971, 1972 and 1973) are subtracted from the elapsed years. However, Kingsfield was not disabled, so 23 years (28 minus 5) are used in computing his AMW.

3. Calculate the number of years from 1951 until the year before Kingsfield becomes *entitled* to retirement benefits—in this case 1981 for a total of 30 years.

4. Select the 23 years of highest covered earnings for these 30 years. They are from 1959 through 1981 during which Kingsfield had total covered earnings of $253,100.

5. Divide this amount ($253,100) by the 276 months in the 23 years to compute the average monthly wage. That amounts to $917.

6. Check the appropriate social security table for the PIA. The table shows that the PIA for an average monthly wage of $917 is $781.50 with a maximum family benefit of $1,366.70.

7. These amounts are increased by the 7.4 percent cost-of-living adjustment effective June 1982 bringing the PIA to $839.30. The $839.30 PIA computed using the AMW compares to a PIA of $717.30 using the AIME.

So, the AMW method would have been used in computing Professor Kingsfield's PIA.

SUMMARY

1. Social insurance covers social risks, i.e., whatever a particular society considers to be a social risk.
2. Earlier cultures felt no need for social insurance because unemployment and old age were not problems. The few unemployed were allowed to starve and few persons survived to old age. Economic development and social change have created unemployment and old age problems. Attitudes have changed so that government now assumes responsibility for these problems.
3. The social security system provides public assistance payments based on need (SSI) and social insurance payments to persons entitled to them, regardless of need (OASDHI).
4. Supplemental security income makes payments to needy persons, including the blind, aged, disabled and dependent children. The medicaid program pays specified medical expenses for the needy.
5. Old-age, survivors, disability and health insurance benefits include payments to covered workers and their dependents for death, disability and retirement. Furthermore, OASDHI benefits help pay medical care costs to persons over 65 and to the long-term disabled.
6. The social security system is currently widely recognized as financially unsound. Even though payroll taxes to support the system have increased dramatically, expenditures will soon exceed receipts unless additional changes are made either in the benefit structure, the tax system or both.
7. Proposed solutions to the financing problems of social security include raising tax levels, reducing benefits or reducing beneficiaries by restricting coverage.
8. Unemployment insurance is financed primarily by state taxes on covered employers to provide compensation to the covered unemployed for periods usually up to 26 weeks. States have wide authority to design their own systems. So state plans vary.
9. Five states and Puerto Rico have temporary disability income laws requiring payments to workers nonoccupationally disabled. Other states have not enacted such laws primarily because unions have been successful in persuading employers to provide this protection without state compulsion.
10. Numerous national health insurance proposals have been introduced in Congress over the years. The principle behind these proposals is that every American has the right to adequate health care regardless of age or income or increasing health care cost. The future of national health insurance is uncertain both as to the type of plan and when it will be passed. Some form of national health insurance protection seems likely, probably starting with a modest plan and later expanding to become more nearly comprehensive.

REVIEW QUESTIONS

1. Is all insurance written by government (state or federal) social insurance?
2. Review the definition of social insurance in this chapter and the programs discussed. Do they adhere to this definition?
3. What makes a person eligible for public assistance payments? For social insurance payments?

4. What benefits are paid under OASDHI? Who are eligible for those benefits?
5. How do the administration and financing of unemployment compensation differ from OASDHI?
6. What determines whether a person is fully insured, currently insured or uninsured under OASDHI? What difference does it make?
7. The current social security system is widely recognized as financially unsound. How would you propose to put the social security system on a financially sound basis?
8. Why have so few states passed temporary disability benefit laws?
9. What reasons are given in support of NHI? What reasons are given by opponents of NHI? Distinguish between the basic characteristics of liberal, moderate and conservative proposals for NHI.
10. What factors have influenced the expansion of social insurance systems during the 20th century?
11. Explain why Professor Kingsfield's PIA is higher using the AMW rather than the AIME method.
12. Explain the importance of the PIA in computing OASDI benefits. What other considerations are important in determining benefit levels?
13. Explain the difference between the two parts of the medicare program.
14. Explain how a person might be qualified for medicare benefits but not for retirement benefits under OASDHI.

PART SEVEN ORGANIZATION AND ADMINISTRATION OF INSURERS

Emphasis now shifts from risk management and the insurance product to insurers and their operations. Part 7 consists of four chapters, 19 through 22. Chapter 19 classifies types of insurers all the way from the fascinating operations of the underwriters at Lloyd's of London to the small county assessment mutuals that write only fire insurance. Chapter 20 outlines the management organization of insurers that if charted would look like the defensive lineup of the Chicago Bears or the offensive lineup of the Fighting Illini. (Are there other football teams?)

A smoothly functioning insurance organization encompasses several operations. The insurance product must be marketed, claims must be handled promptly and efficiently and an effort must be made to encourage loss prevention and control. These functions are discussed in Chapter 20.

Chapter 21 zeros in on the two functions that most directly affect buyers and sellers, the A.A. Not *the* A.A. even though some insurance executives and risk managers *are* driven to drink by the hectic insurance market in which they operate but the A.A. that stands for availability and affordability which are governed by the underwriting and pricing function. Insureds must be selected and premiums must be computed. Underwriting and pricing are interrelated and this interrelationship is demonstrated in Chapter 21.

The finance function is discussed in Chapter 22. Insurers must operate within the legal environment peculiar to insurance, using intelligent and modern financial principles although they are forced to use unconventional financial reporting principles.

The four chapters of Part 7 describing the organization and administration of insurance companies are not designed solely for those readers who will make insurance a career. Buyers of insurance and those interested in business in general will find this group of chapters not only informative but also useful as practical background information about one of the nation's largest and most powerful industries. These chapters are important to anyone claiming to know something about insurance.

CHAPTER

19 Types of insurers

Subscription room at "Lloyd's"/The Bettman Archive

CHAPTER OBJECTIVES

1. **To distinguish between proprietary and cooperative insurers.**
2. **To differentiate and explain the principal types of unincorporated insurers: Lloyd's of London and reciprocal exchanges.**
3. **To define and classify the principal types of incorporated insurers: capital stock companies and mutual insurance companies.**
4. **To identify and describe the various types of producers' and consumers' cooperatives engaged in insurance activity.**
5. **To point out the types of insurance written by federal and state agencies.**

An industry is composed of many business units and their ownership is organized under several legal forms. The insurance industry is no exception.

A PREVIEW

Insurers are owned privately or are parts of governmental units. Broadly conceived, privately owned insurers are either proprietary, organized to earn profits for their investors, or cooperatives, nonprofit-making enterprises organized to benefit policyowners. Government insurers are operated by state or federal governments. The dominant type of proprietary insurer is the capital-stock company; the dominant type of cooperative insurer is the mutual insurance company. The principal state insurer is the workers' compensation fund; the principal federal insurer is the old-age, survivors, disability and health insurance program.

Motives for Formation

Several motives can lead to forming a private insurer: (1) to earn profits for its owners, (2) to enrich its promoters, (3) to earn management fees for operating cooperative insurers, (4) to lower insurance costs for its owners, (5) to provide its owners with a type of insurance protection not otherwise available to them and (6) to sell services (medical, legal or administrative) on a prepaid basis.

The difference between a proprietary and a cooperative insurer is that proprietary insurers operate for profit and cooperative insurers operate to furnish insurance at cost to members. While this distinction between proprietary and cooperative insurers is often used, it oversimplifies the real world of insurance. Proprietary insurers are formed and operated by other businesses to obtain their insurance at cost. (These insurers are called *captives.*) Cooperative insurers are formed and operated for the profit of separate insurance management companies.

Similarities and Differences

Whether the insurer is proprietary or cooperative is usually unimportant to the buyer. More important are the differences among the various *types* of proprietary insurers and the various *types* of cooperative insurers. The similarities between proprietary insurers and cooperative insurers are many. An increasing number of life insurers, for example, use independent agents and brokers along with exclusive agents to reduce marketing costs and to increase market exposure. Cooperative insurers use a similar marketing arrangements in property and liability insurance. The dominant marketing method used by proprietary property and liability insurers is an agency system where the agent usually represents more than one insurer.

Proprietary and cooperative insurers may have the same pricing policy: a fixed premium with no partial return of premium ("dividend") and no additional charge ("assessment.") However, some cooperative insurers operate on an assessment basis and some proprietary and cooperative insurers pay regular dividends to policyowners. Insurance contracts under which dividends are paid regularly are participating policies, described earlier. In life insurance all cooperative insurers and many proprietary insurers (especially the older ones) write participating policies. In property and liability insurance proprietary insurers rarely write them and only some cooperative insurers issue dividend-paying contracts.

A principal difference between proprietary and cooperative insurers is that policyowners of cooperatives must own the insurer or be insurers themselves. They cannot enter a simple buyer-seller relationship as customers purchasing insurance from proprietary insurers. As the discussion progresses it becomes apparent that this distinction often is unimportant. Currently, cooperative insurers have the dominant position in life insurance and proprietary insurers dominate property and liability insurance.

UNINCORPORATED PROPRIETARY INSURERS

Proprietary insurers may be unincorporated or incorporated. The underwriters at Lloyd's of London and to a far lesser extent members of the New York and Chicago insurance exchanges are the principal unincorporated proprietary insurers operating in the United States. A few Lloyd's-type American organizations also write insurance in this country.

Lloyd's of London

In 17th-century England the coffeehouse was the center of the insurance world. Shipowners seeking insurance for a voyage would write a proposal stating the name of the ship, its ownership, captain, cargo, destination, the amount of insurance desired and so on. The would-be insured would place the proposal on a sideboard in the coffeehouse then go about his coffee drinking and wait for would-be insurers to act. Merchants wanting to "take a flyer" in the insurance business as well as established underwriters would study the proposal. An underwriter might note that a proposal asked for £100,000 of insurance. Available resources would permit assumption of only one tenth of that amount. So the underwriter would accept £10,000, indicate the rate (for example, 5 percent), then sign the proposal. The insurer's custom of signing under the proposal is the origin of the word *underwriter.* Eventually the entire £100,000 would be written. It was no coincidence that England became the largest exporter of marine insurance and also the greatest trading nation the world had ever seen. The adequately insured merchant would undertake ventures undreamed of without insurance.

Most successful among the coffeehouse proprietors was Edward Lloyd. Lloyd perceived that information about the condition of ships, tides, size and types of cargoes, weather conditions and anything remotely connected with seagoing commerce interested the coffeehouse patrons. These men would wander from coffeehouse to coffeehouse picking up the latest gossip. Lloyd reasoned that if he could gather the news and relay it to those in his coffeehouse his patrons would stay in his shop instead of roaming among competitors in their quest for news.

Edward Lloyd's coffeehouse soon became known as the place to hear all the news first and his business prospered. In 1696 he began publishing *Lloyd's News,* a flyer appearing three times a week. By this time Lloyd's was in undisputed first place as an insurance center and underwriters who frequented Lloyd's coffeehouse became the most prominent in the business. Eventually Lloyd's stopped serving coffee and moved to London's financial district. The underwriters at Lloyd's constitute one of the richest, most powerful and important insurance groups in the world.

Nature of Lloyd's

Contrary to the belief of the lay public Lloyd's is not an insurer and does not issue policies. It is an association of individuals who write insurance for their own account. The New York Stock Exchange that began as an open-air mart under a buttonwood tree at Broad and Wall streets bears the same relationship to stock purchases and sales "on the exchange" as Lloyd's bears to insurance purchases from its members. The New York Stock Exchange, like Lloyd's, provides a hall and procedures for transacting business. Neither organization engages in any trade. The direct facilities of Lloyd's are open to three groups: members, subscribers and associates.

Lloyd's has two *membership* classes: underwriting and nonunderwriting. Underwriting members, or "names" as they are often called, are entitled to accept risks on their own account. Currently about 10,000 underwriting members conduct business through underwriting agents accepting (or rejecting) proposals presented by Lloyd's brokers. Nonunderwriting members have all the facilities of Lloyd's except the privilege of acting as insurers. They can act as brokers, placing business with underwriting members.

In 1968 a major change was made: foreigners were admitted as members primarily for additional capital (16 of the 240 new members elected that year were non-British). In 1969 new ground was broken again when 46 women were elected to membership. Soon afterward Lloyd's membership included more than 700 foreigners and 1,300 women.

Annual *subscribers* are more than 200 firms who have the privilege of operating as Lloyd's brokers. *Associates* are technicians: lawyers, claim adjusters and actuaries who perform services for members and subscribers. Members, subscribers and associates (nearly 19,000 in all) must be approved by the governing body—called the Committee of Lloyd's—an elected group of members who serve four-year terms.

Functions of Lloyd's

Lloyd's obtains worldwide underwriting information on marine and aviation risks, maintains a complete record of losses, aids in loss settlements and supervises salvage and repairs throughout the world. Lloyd's provides underwriting quarters for its members and a place for the member underwriters to conduct business. It establishes regulations for business transactions, arbitrates disputes, develops policy forms and processes policies underwritten by members. Members of Lloyd's resist rules and regulations they believe are unnecessary to protect the public. While freedom is highly valued, members recognize that independence does not excuse them from observing a number of unwritten rules. The Committee of Lloyd's does not have the authority to establish underwriting rules, make rates or prescribe policy conditions. An underwriter is free to write any kind of insurance and to set the premium. Committee regulations are designed chiefly to assure the solvency of underwriting members.

But changes are taking place even at institutions like Lloyd's of London. When a reputation for impeccable integrity earned over so many years appears to be threatened, steps have to be taken quickly to counteract the threat. The reactionaries must react. So in 1982 Lloyd's of London adopted a set of new membership regulations to prevent threatened regulation by the British Parliament.[1] The need for additional regulation became clear following a string of underwriting losses that brought Lloyd's reputation into question—a development that raised the eyebrows of many Lloyd's advocates. These losses were the result of arson, particularly affecting large buildings in the U.S. central-city areas, ships reported sunk under questionable circumstances (scuttled supertankers) and the widespread cancellations of leases of computers that became obsolete with the introduction of silicon chips. The arson losses caused one syndicate to go broke owing $37 million. Lloyd's was sued for malfeasance and settled out of court for $28 million to protect its name. The arrival of the silicon chips cost Lloyd's syndicates $185,000,000.

Lloyd's new regulations provide that:

1. A new 25-member supervisory committee with authority to fire, suspend or expel members without fear of retaliatory prosecution must be created.
2. Lloyd's brokers are prevented from engaging in underwriting activities to protect against conflicts of interest. They are given five years to sell their Lloyd's underwriting agencies.[2]
3. Members (names) of underwriting syndicates must delegate all underwriting authority to the syndicate's managing agent.
4. New members must have net worth of at least $185,000—excluding the value of their residences.[3]

These new regulations are the most significant changes in the 300-year history of Lloyd's. They update and tighten self-regulatory powers exercised under bylaws set out in five acts passed since 1871.

Operations of Lloyd's

Authorized brokers place proposals for insurance before Lloyd's underwriting members or their agents. The broker prepares the policy, submits it to the policy signing office and if it conforms to agreed-upon rules a stamp is placed upon it. The policy then is submitted to underwriters and those who participate in the policy will affix their signatures. Today the underwriting is usually by one or more of 431 syndicates, each managed by an agent. The syndicate members

[1] One member of Parliament said he believes "the leadership of Lloyd's in disciplinary matters has shown itself to be judicially, intellectually and morally inferior to any other regulated body in Britain." A person speaking on behalf of Lloyd's acknowledged that "we have found the old bylaws to have rubber teeth" and that "we need very much tighter self-regulatory powers under today's conditions."

[2] About 115 agencies will have to be sold for about $175 million.

[3] Mini-name memberships are available for persons with a net worth of $92,500. Mini-names are allowed to write up to $185,000 in insurance premiums. The collateral value of a residence can be used if the residence is pledged to a bank in exchange for the bank's guarantee of that amount of the member's net worth. The advantage of joining Lloyd's as an underwriting member is the opportunity to earn a double return on capital. The net worth required for membership can be invested elsewhere while sharing syndicate underwriting profits. The disadvantage is that losses as well as profits are possible. The worry about being wiped out financially by a jumbo jet crash, earthquake or a volcanic eruption may not be worth it all except to a born gambler. Syndicates are obliged to present a seven-year record of performance to those interested in joining. The record must show how the syndicate protects itself against a disaster. The best syndicates in 1981 paid their members between $1,850 and $7,400 for each $18,500 pledged—not bad! The worst syndicates had a loss—not good!

furnish the capital. The syndicate stamp lists the participating members showing the proportion of the total risk each member assumes. The agent in charge attests the stamp. Any number of members may be in a syndicate and any number of syndicates may be involved in one policy.

Underwriters who specialize in given lines of insurance are known as *leaders* for those lines. A broker seeking to place a risk will try to get a leader to be the first to accept a share of the risk. If the broker is successful other underwriters are willing to follow suit.

Members of a syndicate are responsible only for their own share of the risk. Enforcement of the contract in court can be obtained only by proceeding against each underwriter separately. However, all underwriters generally pay their share if one of them is judged liable.

The underwriters at Lloyd's never have written much life insurance and what is written is limited to short-term policies. But the Committee of Lloyd's sponsors Lloyd's Life Assurance Ltd. to write long-term life insurance. Stock ownership in the life insurance company is limited to Lloyd's members.

Financial strength of Lloyd's

The strength of Lloyd's lies in its resources and in the integrity of its underwriters. Lloyd's will admit only underwriters with substantial financial assets who place no limit on their liability.

Efforts are made to assure continuing financial responsibility of underwriting members. Their accounts are examined periodically. The association oversees the fulfillment of insurance contracts. Solvent underwriting members have assumed the liability of defaulting members. As a further safeguard members of Lloyd's reinsure with one another in order to reduce their individual exposure. (See Chapter 21 for an explanation of reinsurance.)

Specific guarantees of financial security to Lloyd's policyowners are:

1. *Underwriting deposits.* Deposits with the Committee of Lloyd's must be made by underwriting members. The amount required depends on the type and volume of business the underwriter intends to handle.

2. *Premium trust fund.* Each underwriter must pay into a trust fund all premiums received for insurance business transacted. Withdrawals are allowed only for payment of underwriting expenses and claims. Each member must maintain a minimum deposit in the premium trust fund. As long as this deposit remains intact underwriting profits are distributed to the members when earned. Premiums collected in dollars from Americans are deposited in a voluntary American trust fund which is used to pay claims on American policies. The fund helps assure prompt payment of legitimate claims, even catastrophic ones.

3. *Central guarantee fund.* The committee holds a fund of several million pounds obtained from an annual levy on premium income of all underwriting members to pay obligations of insolvent members.

4. *Reserves held by underwriting agents.* Underwriting agents generally do not distribute the full net profits members earn. Instead they hold funds in trust to pay future claims. These funds are protected from claims of general creditors.

Kinds of policies written by Lloyd's

Although the chief business of the underwriting members of Lloyd's is to provide property and liability covers for the usual everyday exposures all members do not confine themselves to these risks. It is virtually folklore that members of Lloyd's will underwrite any type of risk. Lloyd's accepts no bets. It is true that some underwriters at Lloyd's often will issue "insurance" against the election of a particular candidate; but the person seeking the insurance must have an insurable interest; that is, the person must stand to lose by the event insured against before the risk will be underwritten.

INNERSCRIPT: LLOYD'S OF LONDON: DEFENSE INSURANCE AGAINST A TAKEOVER BATTLE

In 1980 a Lloyd's syndicate began writing insurance for corporations to protect them against the cost of *successfully* fighting a hostile takeover attempt by another corporation. Note the word *successfully!* The insured must win to collect, a reasonable condition because the expenses will be paid indirectly by the corporation that succeeds in its takeover bid. The big worry by corporate executives and their risk managers is that the company might be sued by stockholders who object to the corporation's spending many thousands of dollars for insurance to save the jobs of the company's top executives from unwanted suitors especially when the takeover could well be in the stockholders' interest.

The coverage is written with a $50,000 deductible and the insurer pays 80 percent of the loss in excess of the deductible up to the policy's face amount. Originally the maximum amount written was $1 million at a cost to the insured of as little as $35,000 for a small company to more than $100,000 for a company vulnerable to a takeover. The policy excludes payment of the cost of seeking "white knights" that would not give control to the suitor. The rate or cost of the insurance is based on the company's size, financial condition, stock price, stock ownership distribution and whether the bylaws include an antitakeover amendment. An unlimited number of takeover tenders are covered during the policy period. The coverage is marketed through large brokerage firms in the United States through a Chicago Lloyd's broker.

In America the underwriters at Lloyd's of London are licensed insurers only in Illinois and Kentucky. In this capacity they can do business only with an agent or broker who has a "surplus lines" license (see Chapter 20). American insurance buyers can purchase insurance directly from underwriters at Lloyd's (without the services of a licensed surplus line agent or broker) by contacting an Illinois or Kentucky broker.

An important service Lloyd's performs is to provide coverages unavailable elsewhere. American insurers may be unable to write all the insurance demanded and Lloyd's has been particularly helpful in providing underwriting capacity. The underwriters at Lloyd's contribute by developing new covers (e.g., rain insurance and comprehensive coverage for banks) and encouraging other insurers to follow their lead.

American Lloyds

The success of Lloyd's of London has led to forming private underwriters' associations in the United States that call themselves *Lloyds Associations.* These organizations have no connection with Lloyd's of London. They have neither the same name (note the lack of an apostrophe) nor the same reputation. American Lloyds organizations are unincorporated associations of individuals who assume liability for a part of each policy issued. For example, Lloyds, New York, the oldest American Lloyds (1892), currently has 11 individual underwriters who have agreed to assume between 2 and 21 percent of the liability for each policy. These associations of individual underwriters operate through an attorney-in-fact who, using a staff of technical specialists, selects risks, develops rates and adjusts losses. Individual underwriting members bear the financial risk. Each underwriter is liable for only his or her share of the loss.

American Lloyds operate under a variety of different plans. In some associations underwriters make deposits with the attorney-in-fact to guarantee payment of their policy obligations with no further liability assumed. In other associations, in addition to the deposit the underwriter assumes liability for further payments if needed to pay claims. This additional liability is unlimited in some organizations but limited in others. An American Lloyds association may operate under a plan that permits an underwriter to withdraw from accepting new business and eventually from the association. Withdrawal from the association may create a problem because some states require minimum deposits from underwriters before new business can be written. If these deposits fall below the required minimum because underwriters withdraw from the association, the association is immediately liquidated even if it is solvent.

Best's Insurance Reports lists only 25 active American Lloyds organizations, 22 in Texas plus one each in New York, Indiana and New Mexico. Rating laws in Texas do not apply to American Lloyds, which explains the large number there.

Legislation has been passed in New York, Illinois and Florida to allow the establishment of an insurance exchange modeled after Lloyd's of London. The New York Insurance Exchange (NYIE) began operating in 1981 with 16 underwriting syndicates and 43 brokers. By mid-1982 the NYIE had 31 underwriter syndicates and 59 brokers. This exchange provides additional insurance capacity to write a large share of the business now written by Lloyd's of London. Its principal operations are expected to concentrate on reinsurance and exposures located outside the United States.

The Illinois Insurance Exchange (IIE) began writing policies in Chicago in November 1981. Because members operate similarly to Lloyd's of London they jokingly refer to themselves as "Lloyd's of LaSalle Street." The IIE requires a minimum premium of $50,000 for an exposure to be eligible for coverage. Like Lloyd's of London the IIE will underwrite exposures unacceptable to other insurers. The underwriters on the IIE engage in both direct writing and reinsurance. As of mid-1982 six syndicates and 25 brokers were operating on the IIE. IIE officials do not expect to offer a serious challenge to the underwriters at Lloyd's of London. (However, with the establishment of the NYIE and the IIE, brokers in the United Kingdom are beginning to think of the United States as the insurance market of the future.) The IIE has two main functions: reinsurance routing and adding capacity to excess and surplus coverage lines.

Several American insurers have the word *exchange* in their names. They are entirely different from the NYIE and the IIE. They are reciprocal exchanges and are discussed later in this chapter.

INCORPORATED PROPRIETARY INSURERS

The typical capital-stock insurer is like any business corporation: its objective is to earn a profit for its owners. Stockholders provide its capital and paid-in surplus. Shareholders do not directly underwrite the risk like underwriters in a Lloyds association. Both underwriting and investment gains and losses are reflected in the insurer's surplus position. Unlike members of Lloyds associations, stockholders cannot withdraw their funds directly from the organization but they can dispose of their interest by selling their shares of stock. Capital stock insurers usually acquire their business through independent agents and brokers although the second largest "direct writer" (nonagency company) is a capital-stock company. However, that company (Allstate) is experimenting with the use of independent agents through a subsidiary insurer.

CONSUMER-TYPE COOPERATIVE INSURERS

Cooperative business organizations in the United States consist of two types: consumers and producers. Consumers' cooperatives usually are formed by those wanting lower prices. Sometimes the purpose is to control the quality of goods or services offered members. Those who wish to provide members with efficient marketing facilities form producers' cooperatives. An example of a consumers' cooperative is a campus bookstore organized to furnish student members textbooks at cost. An example of a producers' cooperative is the organization of citrus fruit growers in California that sells the members' crops.

Both types of cooperatives operate in the insurance industry. Consumers' cooperatives—more prevalent than producers' cooperatives—include reciprocal insurance exchanges and mutual insurers. Producers' cooperatives include Blue Cross/Blue Shield organizations sponsored by hospitals and doctors and cooperative underwriting organizations. Unincorporated cooperative insurers are called **reciprocal insurance exchanges;** incorporated ones are called **mutual companies.**

Reciprocal Insurance Exchanges

The reciprocal insurance exchange originated in 1881 in New York when a group of cost-conscious dry-goods merchants reacted to inadequate fire insurance rate-making. Broad rate classifications were used that charged hazardous and non-hazardous exposures the same rate. These merchants thought these broad classifications gave them the short end of the bolt causing them to pay more than their share of the losses. So they decided to insure one another by exchanging insurance contracts.

A reciprocal exchange in its basic form operates as follows. A thousand dwellers in suburbia who own houses worth $80,000 each form an interinsurance exchange. Each subscribes for $80,000 of insurance coverage and in turn accepts (underwrites) $80,000 of risk on the 1,000 houses. If a subscriber's house is totally destroyed by fire the interinsurance exchange will reimburse the loss by $80 contributions from the 1,000 subscribers. The effect of the reciprocal arrangement is that subscribers have an $80,000 loss exposure spread among 1,000 properties instead of having an $80,000 loss exposure on their own property. With this large number of exposure units, losses become predictable. The subscriber's share of the predicted losses and expenses is the premium charged.

A separate account is held for each subscriber. To this account are credited premiums paid plus interest earned. The account is debited with the subscriber's share of losses and expenses. A credit balance may be retained or refunded to the subscriber and a subscriber who terminates participation may withdraw any credit balance. A subscriber is held liable only for the agreed-upon share of losses and expenses and the maximum amount of this liability may be a multiple of the annual premium.

A reciprocal exchange usually operates under a trade name and is managed by an individual or organization known as an attorney-in-fact. The insurance operation is nonprofit because members pay only their share of losses and expenses. The attorney-in-fact may be a profit rather than a not-for-profit organization. Some reciprocals use agents to acquire business; others write business directly or through a trade association. In one respect reciprocals are like Lloyd's of London because the exchange issues no policies, merely furnishing a mechanism for members to insure one another. An important difference is that membership in the exchange is required for insurance. No one can buy insurance without offering insurance in return. Members of Lloyd's, however, insure outsiders and do not insure one another. This feature makes reciprocals cooperative insurers and Lloyd's underwriters proprietary insurers. The reciprocal is not a corporation or a partnership. Corporations or partnerships may be members of a reciprocal and the attorney-in-fact usually incorporates; but still the organization is individual. The foregoing describes a reciprocal exchange in its pristine form. Operational and legislative changes have modified the form to some extent, as will soon become apparent.

Operation of a reciprocal

The operation of a reciprocal exchange usually follows a general pattern. The attorney-in-fact's authority comes from an agreement (called the *subscriber's agreement*) inserted in each application blank and signed by the subscriber. The attorney-in-fact, the principal administrative officer, must be qualified to direct the managerial functions of underwriting and rating risks, sales promotion, claims administration and handling finances. An advisory committee often controls the attorney-in-fact.

The attorney-in-fact may be paid a salary but usually receives a percentage of the premiums collected. What happens when the entire premium revenue is not needed for claims and expenses or when it is inadequate to cover these expenses? At this point reciprocals change from their original form. In the simplest form surpluses are divided among individual members and no group surplus is retained. If the funds are insufficient the subscribers are assessed for their separate liability up to an agreed-upon amount. Reciprocals generally retain some surplus because surplus funds are necessary to absorb investment losses, smooth the effects of irregular claims experience, and finance expansion. This surplus cannot be depleted by dividend payments and all assets must be available to meet claims.

Some exchanges, particularly those writing only auto insurance, do not maintain surplus accounts for each subscriber. Instead all surplus funds are held undivided as property of the exchange. Terminating subscribers receive nothing. These exchanges function virtually as mutual insurers and the subscriber's relationship to the exchange is similar to a mutual policyholder's relationship to the insurer. Reciprocals writing fire insurance, however, usually maintain individual accounts and return surplus to subscribers when they withdraw.

Reciprocals can issue nonassessable policies when their unallocated surplus (called *free surplus*) equals the minimum capital and surplus required for stock insurers writing similar business. Under the basic reciprocal form subscribers participate in savings and assume limited liability for assessments needed to pay their share of unpaid claims. However, some auto reciprocals charge fixed premiums, return no savings and include no assessment provision; or they include an assessment provision but return no savings.

Mutual Companies

A mutual insurer is a cooperative corporation organized and owned by its insureds. An accounting student reviewing a mutual insurer's balance sheet will be surprised to find that the net-worth account includes no capital stock but only surplus. Policyowners of mutual insurers in many ways occupy a position similar to stockholders of stock insurers. Voting control is in their hands. Profits earned by a mutual company can be used (1) to pay policy dividends to policyowners and (2) to strengthen the insurer by building its surplus. Policyowners absorb losses through lower dividends, assessments (if permitted by policy provisions) or by reducing surplus. In a mutual company the concept of surplus as an ownership interest is cloudy. A policyowner is not entitled to a pro rata interest in the surplus at withdrawal. The surplus, therefore, represents the ownership interest only of those who remain policyowners.

A distinction between principle and practice is necessary. The stockholders of a stock insurer technically control the company through their votes for the board of directors. In practice, however, stockholders are so widely scattered that control rests with those who hold an amount of stock sufficient to provide the majority of votes ordinarily cast at stockholders' meetings. The active management of the corporation often holds working control.

Theoretically in a mutual company the policyowners who elect the board of directors hold control. In practice control is generally in the hands of a few officers and directors who have proxies, i.e., authority to vote on behalf of policyowners. Just as few stockholders ever attend a stockholders' meeting few policyowners attend policyowners' meetings. Therefore the organization usually is controlled by its existing management.

Mutual insurers may be arrayed according to pricing arrangements. At one extreme is the **pure assessment mutual;** at the other is the **perpetual mutual.** In between are varying arrangements of premium prepayment plans.

Pure assessment mutuals

Pure assessment mutuals primarily write fire insurance on farm property. Hundreds of such mutuals are in operation (Illinois alone has about 200) but their premium volume is small. Assessment mutual insurers are also found in life insurance but usually write only burial insurance. Assessment mutuals are the purest form of cooperative activity for handling risk. Their organization is simple; usually no more than one or two officers receive a salary. Some farm mutuals are too small to have full-time paid officers. One of several plans of operation may be used:

1. The insurer may issue the policy charging a small fee and assess each member for expenses and claims.

2. The insurer may issue the policy charging a premium large enough to pay expenses and small losses. To provide for large losses members sign premium notes payable if losses and expenses exceed the advance premiums. Their liability is limited to the amount of these notes.

3. The insurer may issue the policy charging a cash premium sufficient to pay expenses and small losses. If additional funds are necessary for claims and expenses the assessments are unlimited. Most assessment insurers operate on this principle.

Considerations for insurance buyers. Would-be insureds usually cannot buy from pure assessment mutuals. Their insureds are members of a local community banded together to furnish mutual aid. That operation works for a group of neighbors but it would prove difficult to administer if extended over wide areas and different groups. Buying from a pure assessment mutual may not be advisable even for those who have the opportunity. The caliber of management varies widely. Particularly important are the insurers' reinsurance facilities. Insurers writing coverage on properties in only one community are subject to catastrophic loss. Furthermore, even well-managed pure assessment mutuals might levy large assessments in high claim years, a factor that could deter purchasing insurance from them. Well-managed assessment mutuals are plentiful though, and insurance buyers who do not object to the assessment principle will find them attractive.

Advance-premium mutuals

Full advance-premium mutuals charge annual premiums large enough to provide funds to pay claims and expenses and strengthen surplus. Many of the larger mutuals charge an advance premium comparable to that of stock insurers and anticipate returning a refund. A few advance-premium mutuals charge premiums equal to those of stock insurers without returning dividends to policyowners. However, many charge an initial premium lower than dividend-paying mutuals. When claims exceed those assumed in the premiums some advance-premium mutuals assess policyowners. However, the large advance-premium mutuals have accumulated sufficient surpluses to write nonassessable policies.

Some advance-premium mutuals conduct their business on the same basis as stock insurers. They use independent agents, write a variety of coverages and operate over a wide geographical area. Others write business on a national scale through salaried representatives or through exclusive agents. Distribution systems are discussed in Chapter 20. Some limit their coverages to a specialty line—auto insurance, for example. The largest mutual insurers are advance-premium mutuals issuing only nonassessable policies.

Perpetual mutuals.

The name *perpetual* describes the coverage period. Perpetual policies are written without a termination date and the policyowner pays a large initial premium. The premium is calculated to provide a fund to yield enough investment income to cover expenses and claims and contribute to surplus. After the policy has been in force for a number of years the insured is paid an annual dividend. The policy may be cancelled either by the insurer or the insured. If cancelled the initial single-premium deposit is returned.

The issuance of perpetual policies is not restricted to mutual insurers. For example, in 1949 the Green Tree Mutual formed the Stock Insurance Company of the Green Tree to provide perpetual policies for its policyowners for perils in addition to fire.

Perpetual policies are not available for most insurance buyers. The geographical area covered is small and the eligible insureds are restricted. Types and amounts of coverage written are also limited. For those who qualify a perpetual policy can be an attractive investment offering income-tax savings as well as high dividends on deposit-premiums. The cost of the insurance is paid from investment income earned on the policyowner's single-premium deposit. The investment earnings that the company uses to pay losses and expenses are not treated as taxable income to the policyowner. The insured, therefore, pays for insurance with tax-free dollars.

Factory mutuals

In 1822 in North Providence, Rhode Island, Zachariah Allen built a textile mill. Allen, whose hobby was fire prevention, vowed to build a factory with near-zero probability of fire although at substantially high cost. Allen believed reduced fire insurance premiums would offset construction costs. Imagine his shock when told that he would pay the same as the owner of the ramshackle factory across the millpond. The fire underwriters advised Allen that they were in the business of paying losses, not of preventing them. After making a thorough study of insurance Allen became one of the moving forces in organizing the Manufacturers Mutual Fire Insurance Company of Rhode Island.

Four factory mutual fire insurance companies now operate. Although they are separate companies they share each risk through The Associated Factory Mutual Fire Insurance Companies that provide underwriting and rating services. Because the basic philosophy of factory mutuals is loss control, applicants for insurance are inspected before policies are approved. Periodic inspections also are made after policies are issued. Only sprinklered premises are acceptable and because inspection cost is so high only large insureds can qualify financially. The factory mutuals own and operate a stock insurance company (the Affiliated FM Insurance Company) that issues participating policies to cover properties that fail to meet factory mutual standards.

To compete with factory mutuals 12 large stock fire insurers formed the Factory Insurance Association (FIA) in 1890. Today 45 of the leading stock fire insurers are members. In December 1975 the FIA merged with the Oil Insurance Association to form the Industrial Risk Insurers (IRI) to improve its financial ability to write more insurance. The IRI, like the factory mutuals, writes insurance on large, high-grade, sprinklered buildings and emphasizes loss prevention. Inspection, underwriting and loss adjusting are performed through regional and field offices. Covered properties are inspected quarterly.

Factory mutuals charge an advance premium many times larger than the amount needed for claims and expenses. At the end of the policy period a large dividend is returned as an offset against the premium for the next policy period. This pricing method results in added safety to the insurers, increased underwriting capacity and a substantial permanent investment account for the insurers. The same premium is charged for one-year as for three-year contracts. Typically the dividends amount to about 81 percent on one-year contracts and from 40 to 45 percent on three-year policies.

The factory mutuals, though small in number, are an important factor in the insurance market. Insurance by factory mutuals is unavailable to the typical buyer. For those who qualify factory mutuals provide an attractive source for insurance protection because of low costs and excellent service facilities.

Fraternal insurance

A **fraternal** is an insurer organized under the section of a state's insurance code related to social organizations that provide insurance benefits for members. To qualify as a fraternal the insurer must have some type of social organization—usually a lodge system. Fraternals sell only life and health insurance and usually operate on an advance-premium basis although a few operate as assessment insurers. In some instances the fraternal's insurance activity has become more important than the lodge, and some insurers seeking to take advantage of lenient insurance regulations for fraternals have a lodge system in name only.

Savings bank life insurance

In 1907 Massachusetts passed legislation necessary to permit mutual savings banks to establish insurance departments. The law required that insurance department funds be separate from banking funds. The insurance funds are not liable for obligations of the banking department nor are the banking funds liable for obligations of the insurance department. Originally policies were limited to $500 each. The amount was raised gradually to the present $15,000 limit. The insured may hold $15,000 policies in several banks but total coverage cannot exceed $53,000. All the insurance may be purchased through one bank acting as agent for the others. These limits do not apply to group insurance.

In order to offer low-cost insurance, sales agents are forbidden but banks do advertise extensively. Applications for life insurance are taken by banks, employers, credit unions and others. Any of these organizations except employers may retain a small collection fee. Insurance may be written for residents only or those regularly employed in Massachusetts.

Rate computation, medical examination and underwriting are performed by the Division of Savings Bank Life Insurance, a department of the state government. The banks pay for the services. The General Insurance Guaranty Fund, a special fund to which each bank with a life insurance department must contribute, is used to apportion death claims among the banks.

In 1938 savings bank life insurance was authorized in New York and in 1941 in Connecticut. In New York all insurance must be purchased from one bank and the limit is $30,000 a person. In Connecticut the maximum amount of life insurance that can be purchased from an individual bank or from all savings banks is $15,000 ($10,000 for group life). Savings bank life insurance in other states has been proposed from time to time but none has passed the necessary legislation.

PRODUCERS' COOPERATIVES

Several types of producers' cooperatives are found in the insurance business. Illustrative of one are the dozens of organizations operating under the trade names Blue Cross/Blue Shield. Hospitals and doctors in these organizations provide the insurance and in that sense are producers. Health maintenance organizations (HMOs) composed of physicians who provide medical care to the public are another type of medical-care-producers' cooperative although they also may be organized as consumers' cooperatives.

Medical and Hospital Service Plans

Many nonprofit hospital and medical-care plans have been organized under special state statutes. These organizations are an interesting hybrid of mutual and proprietary forms. The best known hospital plans are those members of the American Hospital Association calling themselves Blue Cross. The most familiar medical-care plans are those sponsored by physicians' groups that are members of the Blue Shield Medical-Care Plans Association. These two associations are now merged into one with the same governing board with no name change. Blue Shield and Blue Cross plans are coordinated to offer a medical and hospital care package under the name Blue Cross/Blue Shield. Boards of directors or trustees that include representation from hospitals, the medical profession and the public govern these plans. In most plans the directors are appointed by hospitals and the medical profession. In others the plan's subscribers elect governing boards and these tend to become self-perpetuating because the people nominated by the board are usually elected. The plans are not mutual insurance corporations because the controlling "members" are the hospitals and physicians who furnish the protection rather than the persons who "subscribed" to the insurance. The controlling members bear the financial risks (and determine the allocation of surpluses). Most jurisdictions consider Blue Cross/Blue Shield organizations charitable and benevolent institutions. As such they are entitled to tax exemptions. Also, a growing number of dental societies offer dental care on a prepaid basis, usually under group plans.

These hospital, dental and medical-care plans differ from insurance because they sell services (medical and hospital care) not insurance. The cost and coverage associated with medical and hospital service plans are so varied the prospective buyer must study each plan before making the decision to join one.

Health Maintenance Organizations

HMOs are formal organizations of physicians who provide medical service to subscribers and divide earnings. Each subscriber to a group practice plan pays a premium in exchange for the right to medical care when desired. HMO plans may be organized tightly (prepaid group practice) or loosely (medical foundation or individual practice). Furthermore, prepaid group practice plans may be civic sponsored and operated as consumers' cooperatives where physicians are under salary contracts or they may be sponsored and owned by doctors and operated as profit-making producers' cooperatives.

HMOs emphasize prevention. Their benefits are broader than group insurance or Blue Cross/Blue Shield plans. They are not limited to treatment resulting from accident and illnesses but extend to preventive medicine. Because the physicians receive the same total compensation regardless of the amount of service rendered they have an incentive to keep members well in order to reduce required services.

The HMO Act of 1973 stipulated that employers with more than 25 employees must offer enrollment in a HMO as an option to their health insurance plan if a qualified HMO is located near the employer's business. However, the employer is not required to pay more for HMO services than under the existing employee health-care benefit plan.

GOVERNMENTAL INSURERS

Government insurance, for the purpose of this discussion, includes insurers established, maintained and administered by a branch of the government—federal or state—and organized primarily to insure other than government employees or government property.

Federal Insurers

The federal government offers insurance of several types: (1) *The Federal Crop Insurance Corporation* (FCIC) offers insurance against crop failures resulting from perils of nature; (2) *the Veterans Administration* (VA) offers life insurance to members (and veterans) of the armed forces; (3) *the Department of Health and Human Services* offers coverage for death, disability, medical care and old age through the old-age, survivors, disability and health insurance program operated by the Social Security Administration (similar coverages are provided for federal civil service employees and railroad employees through other federal organizations); (4) *the Federal Deposit Insurance Corporation* (FDIC) provides bank deposit insurance; (5) *the Federal Savings and Loan Insurance Corporation* (FSLIC) protects savings accounts in federal savings and loan associations and in state-chartered thrift and home-financing institutions; (6) *mortgage and prop-*

erty improvement loan insurance programs provide mortgage insurance to aid home buyers and mortgage lenders, both urban and rural; (7) *the Securities Investor Protection Corporation* (SIPC) protects customers' securities held by registered broker-dealers up to $100,000 and (8) *the National Credit Union Administration* insures credit union accounts.

Other federal agencies participate in the insuring of properties against crime, flood, riot and risks abroad. For instance the *Overseas Investment Group,* composed of a group of private insurers and the U.S. government's *Overseas Private Investment Corporation* (OPIC), provides coverage for private American investments against foreign political risks of expropriation and currency inconvertibility.

State Insurers

State insurers offer hail insurance, life insurance, workers' compensation, unemployment, nonoccupational temporary disability income insurance, title insurance, medical malpractice insurance and auto insurance. Not every state has all these funds. Only Wisconsin has a life insurance fund and Maryland an auto fund. Just a few states have hail insurance, title insurance or disability income funds.

Special Contributions of Governmental Insurers

Government insurers' principal contribution is to provide coverages that other insurers are unwilling or unable to offer. They can offer insurance without operating under the rigid actuarial principles that private insurers must follow. A frequent argument is that unless actuarial principles are adhered to, the protection is not insurance and the government agencies offering it are not insurers. The beneficiaries under these programs, however, are not concerned with semantics when they collect their social insurance benefits (and, for that matter, neither are the tax collectors when they gather in the social insurance taxes) nor are the legislators when they cast their votes for social insurance programs just prior to an election.

SUMMARY

1. Insurers are either privately owned or operated by a government agency. Private insurers are organized as proprietorships or cooperatives. The dominant type of proprietary insurer is the capital stock company, the principal cooperative insurer is a mutual company.
2. Lloyd's of London is not an insurer; it is an association of individuals who write insurance for their own account. Lloyd's provides a building and procedures for transacting business. It obtains worldwide underwriting information on marine and aviation risks, maintains a complete record of losses, aids in loss settlements and supervises salvage and repairs throughout the world. The Committee of Lloyd's also governs and disciplines the members as the operation is self-regulated.
3. Lloyd's policyowners have financial security guarantees from its underwriters who must make security deposits to the Committee of Lloyd's and to the premium trust fund. Withdrawals are allowed from the trust fund only to pay underwriting claims and expenses. Premiums collected in dollars from Americans are deposited in a voluntary American trust fund to pay claims on American policies. The purpose of the premium trust fund is to help assure prompt payment of losses, even catastrophic ones. Several million pounds from an annual levy on premium income is available to pay the

obligations of insolvent underwriters. Full net profits are not distributed to members: some are retained to pay future claims.

4. Nearly 300 years later insurance exchanges were formed in New York and Illinois. Both began operating in 1981. Their principle operations are expected to be reinsurance and foreign insurance business. The Illinois exchange is given wider powers and is expected to write business difficult to place elsewhere.

5. Lloyd's success led to formation of American Lloyds associations where an attorney-in-fact selects risks, develops rates and adjusts losses. Risks are borne by individual underwriting members. American Lloyds do not have the reputation accorded Lloyd's of London. Most of them operate in Texas where they are exempt from that state's rating laws.

6. Consumers' cooperatives include reciprocal insurance exchanges and mutual insurers. Producers' cooperatives include Blue Cross/Blue Shield organizations sponsored by hospitals and doctors. Unincorporated cooperative insurers are the reciprocal insurance exchanges; incorporated cooperatives are mutual companies. HMOs can be organized as producers' or consumers' cooperatives.

7. Reciprocal exchanges operate by giving each member a separate account that is credited for premiums paid plus interest earned. The account is debited for the member's share of losses and expenses.

8. Reciprocal exchanges operated by an attorney-in-fact provide a mechanism for members to exchange insurance on a nonprofit basis. The attorney-in-fact may be an individual or a corporation and may operate for profit.

9. Mutual companies are organized by pricing arrangements. Pure assessment mutuals write fire insurance on farm property. Assessment mutuals have only one or two officers who receive salaries. Policyowners may be assessed (1) for expenses and claims only, (2) for notes payable or (3) for unlimited amounts to cover large losses as they occur.

10. Advance premium mutuals charge annual premiums large enough to provide funds for claims and to strengthen surplus.

11. Perpetual mutuals write policies without a termination date. The large initial premium is calculated to provide a fund to yield investment income to cover expenses and claims and contribute to surplus.

12. Factory mutuals charge a premium many times larger than the amount needed for claims and expenses. A dividend is returned by deducting from the premium for the following policy period. High standards for loss control must be met to obtain coverage.

13. Fraternal insurers must have some type of social organization. Fraternals operate on an advance premium basis and sell only life and health insurance.

14. Savings bank life insurance is available in three states through banks. Sales agents are not used. Rate computation, medical examination and underwriting are performed by the states' Division of Savings Bank Life Insurance.

15. Producers' cooperatives like HMOs and Blue Cross/Blue Shield are not mutuals because the policyowners are not owners of the business. They

do not underwrite the risk. Hospital, dental and medical care plans are not insurers because they sell services, not insurance.

16. The HMO Act of 1973 provided that an employer with more than 25 employees working near an HMO must offer the HMO alternative to the existing benefit plan. HMOs provide wider benefits for medical coverage than the Blues because they emphasize prevention not just cure.
17. Federal government insurers offer crop insurance, social security, bank deposit insurance and so on. State insurers offer hail insurance, life insurance, workers' compensation, unemployment and disability income insurance.

REVIEW QUESTIONS

1. What is the difference between a proprietary and a cooperative insurer?
2. Is Lloyd's of London considered an insurer by the general public?
3. How does Lloyd's of London guarantee its solvency? Why have recent changes been made in the governance of Lloyd's?
4. Describe how a reciprocal exchange operates. How does Lloyd's of London differ from a reciprocal exchange? How is a reciprocal like Lloyd's of London? Do fire insurance reciprocals operate differently from automobile insurance reciprocals? Explain.
5. Explain what distinguishes a mutual insurer from (1) a reciprocal insurer and (2) a Blue Cross/Blue Shield plan.
6. How might assessment mutuals bill their insureds?
7. Explain the tax advantage for insureds who belong to perpetual mutuals.
8. Do members of perpetual mutuals ever receive dividends?
9. Explain the origin of factory mutual insurers.
10. Are HMOs producers' cooperatives or consumers' cooperatives? What difference does it make?
11. Does the HMO Act of 1973 benefit employees? What are the advantages of an HMO plan?
12. Select one insurance plan offered by a state agency and one offered by a federal agency. Why are these plans offered? Do you think they should be offered?
13. What is the distinguishing characteristic of the factory mutuals?
14. Why does the law require mutual savings banks to limit the amount of life insurance written on one life?
15. What are fraternal insurers? What kinds of insurance do they write? Are their insurance policies different from competing insurers?

CHAPTER

20 Management organization and functions: Marketing, claims and loss control

John Thoeming/Courtesy Wm. Golas Agency

CHAPTER OBJECTIVES

1. **To define the functional departments of an insurer.**
2. **To identify and describe the types of insurance marketing systems.**
3. **To explain the process of claims administration.**
4. **To discuss the role of insurers in loss control.**
5. **To examine the areas of cooperation among insurers.**

A study of insurance management organization and function reveals the many types of job opportunities available in the insurance industry. Insurers, like other businesses, are organized by function into divisions, departments and sections. No standard organization chart is adaptable to all insurers but a few basic departments are common to most.

MANAGEMENT ORGANIZATION

The primary source of authority is the stockholders in a stock company and the policyowners in a mutual company. Theoretically they have the final say on company administration but this authority is generally delegated to the board of directors. The board is organized into committees to formulate company policy. Responsibility for daily company operations is delegated to the chief executive officer, usually the president. The president delegates some authority to other executive officers. The levels of authority depend on the size and scope of the operations.

DEPARTMENTALIZATION

Insurers organize departments on the basis of the functions performed, products sold, territories, customers and executive interests. A small insurer may have employees performing in several departments. Departments organized by functions are underwriting, legal, investment, agency, claims, loss control (engineering) and so on. Life insurers' departments organized by products are ordinary, weekly premium, group and health insurance. For property-liability insurers departments organized by products are fire, inland and ocean marine, liability, auto, health and crime.

Territorial departments are determined by the territory they control. A large insurer may have an eastern department, a western department and others. Customer departmentalization establishes departments by the class of customers dealt with by an insurer and this classification is often difficult to distinguish from product departmentalization. Customer departments might consist of a reinsurance department managing sales to other insurers, a special-risks department controlling large self-rated accounts and a group department selling to employee and association groups. Finally, departments may be organized according to *executives' interests* even though those interests may be diverse. Only the functional departments are discussed here.

The agency department's function is to recruit, train, supervise and direct special agents, general agents, branch managers and local agents. The agency department of an insurer is its sales department.

The underwriting department sets selection standards and chooses among insurance applicants. Underwriters review not only new business but also business already accepted. Underwriters check policy rates and forms for all business submitted and also help develop new forms. (See Chapter 21.) The underwriting department is responsible for line limits and reinsurance.

The legal department defends the insurer against complaints from insurance commissioners and litigates the case whenever the insurer is the plaintiff. It assists the investment department by reviewing real estate titles, bond indentures and corporate charters and helps in foreclosure proceedings. It aids the underwriting department in preparing policies. The claims department uses the help of the legal department in investigation and defense of claims, as does the agency department in preparing agency contracts. Finally, the legal department advises the executives on conformity with federal law and state insurance codes and helps with lobbying activities in state and federal legislatures, insurance departments and government committees. Some insurers decentralize legal work, with various departments having their own legal staffs.

The investment department selects and services the insurer's investment portfolio. Insurers' investments are subject to the regulatory constraints discussed in Chapter 23.

Property and liability insurance claims usually are settled in branch offices or by independent adjusters. Home-office claims departments are responsible for claims administration. They operate as a personnel and records office responsible for selection and supervision of adjusters and for maintenance of adequate claims records. By reporting the causes of each loss claims departments help underwriting and loss control departments develop loss prevention measures. Claims departments work with police forces, detective agencies, special investigators, lawyers and physicians to recover losses or reduce their severity.

Life and disability insurance claims usually are handled in the home office. Life insurance claims are easy to handle as contract exclusions and conditions are few. Double indemnity, sickness, accident and medical claims present problems, and claims departments must be staffed with technicians especially trained to cope with them.

The actuarial department is responsible for the calculation of insurance rates, dividends, loss and loss adjustment expense reserves, unearned premium reserves, commission scales, preparation of annual reports and development of operating forecasts. Actuaries establish settlement options, develop formulas for nonforfeiture values and perform other functions concerned primarily with mathematics. Property and liability insurers in the past have used statisticians rather than actuaries, primarily as a result of a scarcity of casualty actuaries. With the increasing emphasis placed on scientific rating methods and regulations requiring certification of annual statements by qualified actuaries, however, the statistician is giving way to the professional casualty actuary.

Another active insurer department (excluding life insurance) is the loss-control department. In some insurance coverages the insured is as interested (if not more so) in loss-control services as in indemnification of loss. Boiler and machinery insurance is an example. To improve loss ratios insurers inspect property and operations to develop recommendations to reduce loss. They also engage in safety research and loss-prevention education. Loss-control departments cooperate with underwriting departments and also help with rating problems. In fact, fire insurance engineers, as distinguished from other property and liability loss-control experts, are principally engaged in ratemaking and only indirectly in loss prevention.

Where a variable such as payroll is used as the rate base an insurer needs a staff of traveling auditors to determine the correct payroll to use in calculating the final premium. The auditor's job is not only that of checking the total payroll but also of classifying the payroll into the applicable rate classifications.

Several departments are self-explanatory and not peculiar to insurers. They include the accounting, stenographic, filing, purchasing, supply, mail, research, personnel, publication, communication, electronic data processing and education departments. They may operate separately or as subdivisions of other departments.

MARKETING INSURANCE COMPANY PRODUCTS

Marketing is an important insurer function. Unless an insurer's products are easily obtainable by a large number of prospective buyers an insurer cannot accomplish its objective of writing a sufficient amount of business to make its losses predictable and its operation profitable. Marketing consists of offering desirable insurance products to qualified buyers and developing new products to meet the changing needs of these buyers.

Sales Organizations

The insurance principle cannot operate effectively without a large number of exposure units. If the volume of business is too small, loss experience might be unstable. In order to build a large volume of business, insurers develop strong sales organizations. Most businesses have production departments and sales departments. The sales department's function is to sell products manufactured by the production department. An insurer's sales department must not only sell the product, but produce it as well. Selling a $100,000 life insurance policy automatically produces an additional $100,000 of insurance in force. Thus an insurance sales department is also an insurance production department: no insurance exists until it is sold.

Agency systems

The majority of insurance is written through agents and brokers. Agents operate under one of two systems: the **American agency system** or the **exclusive agency system.**

The American agency system. Most capital-stock and many mutual property and liability insurers operate under the American agency system. Agents are independent, usually representing several insurers. They issue policies, collect premiums and retain exclusive rights to solicit renewals from customers. Insurers operating under this system are called **independent agency companies.** Some independent agency insurers administer details usually handled by agents like policy writing and billing. In return for performing these operations insurers pay reduced commissions to agents which enables these insurers to be more price competitive with exclusive agency insurers.

The exclusive agency system. Some property and liability insurers use the exclusive agency system where agents represent only one insurer or group of related insurers. The insurer reserves the rights to ownership, use and control of policy records.

Exclusive agency insurers have made substantial inroads on independent agency business. Five exclusive agency insurers write more than one third of the private passenger auto insurance premiums. Exclusive agency insurers write auto insurance at premiums below those of many other insurers. Some premium reduction results from lower selling costs and the rest from stricter underwriting. Independent agency insurers occasionally, although these days rarely, relax underwriting standards to accommodate their most productive agents. Because exclusive agents represent only one insurer the incentive to meet insurer's production goals and training requirements is much greater than for agents representing many insurers. This factor encourages improved sales performance of exclusive agents.

The principal distinguishing feature of the independent agency system is that the agents own the renewal rights on the insurance they sell. Property-liability agents usually are paid the first-year commission each time the policy is renewed. Because the operational pattern of life insurers does not include renewal rights to insurance sold, the independent agency system normally is not used in life insurance marketing. Life insurers generally use the exclusive agency system. Life insurance agents are usually paid a high commission the first year, a much smaller one for several years and then a token commission for the policy's remaining life.

Agency forces

Insurer agency forces may be organized under one or more of three systems: **general agency, branch office** and **direct reporting.** Some insurers use at least two systems in their production operations.

The general agency system. A contract with the insurer authorizes the general agent to represent it in a given area. The territory may be a group of states, a state or several counties. Among the general agent's functions are appointing sub-agents, hiring salaried sales representatives, soliciting business and developing brokerage accounts. General agents must produce business or they will lose their contracts. They earn commissions on all business sold through their offices. These commissions pay operating costs, salaries and commissions to sales agents. Sometimes general agents share in profits earned on business submitted by their offices or receive a bonus for attaining a given sales goal. Some general agents, especially in life insurance, are given service fees, expense allowances, and a small salary in addition to commission income.

A general agent's specific duties vary among agencies. In life insurance the principal task is to develop and service business and involves recruiting, selecting, training, supervising and motivating agents. In property and liability insurance the agent may have duties beyond that of a sales manager, e.g., underwriting and claims administration. Large general agencies employ their own special agents, loss-control experts, adjusters and auditors. Although large property and liability general agencies commonly represent more than one insurer, life insurance general agents represent only one. The general agency is the oldest form of field organization and is still used in life insurance, although to a rapidly decreasing extent. It is not widely used in property and liability insurance.

The branch office system. A later development in field organization is the branch office system where the insurer establishes its own office in a territory. The branch office performs the functions of general agencies. The manager is paid a salary and usually an incentive bonus. The insurer pays all office expenses. Unlike the general agent, the branch manager is not independent but is supervised by the insurer. The manager's employees are employees of the insurer. The branch office is increasingly popular because the insurer gains more direct control over product marketing and servicing.

Direct-reporting system. Under the direct-reporting or home-office system the agent deals directly with the home office rather than a branch office or general agency. The home office maintains many contacts with the field and provides numerous services. Local agents receive exclusive rights to their territories. They obtain brokerage business for the insurer as well as originate business themselves and also may employ solicitors. In life insurance, except for the smallest insurers, the direct-reporting system is rare but it is used frequently by property and liability insurers.

Direct-selling systems

Many insurers write business directly, eliminating agents from the transaction. They solicit business through vending machines, direct mail (now called direct response) campaigns, newspaper advertisements and salaried sales representatives. Insurers using the direct-selling system are known as direct writers to distinguish them from agency insurers. The exclusive agency system insurers often are incorrectly called direct writers. The latter term is reserved for insurers using salaried sales personnel or direct mail. Direct-selling insurers often operate through well-placed branch offices staffed with salespersons who solicit and service business in its territory. Insurers do not always adhere to one marketing system. They may sell directly in some areas and use independent agents elsewhere.

Mass merchandising

The concept of mass merchandising in insurance is not new. Life insurance group policies have been written on a mass-merchandising basis for more than 70 years. However, mass merchandising in property and liability insurance is a relatively new concept. It consists of selling and underwriting insurance on a group basis. Mass merchandising is expected to increase faster in commercial lines than in personal lines because it allows both insurers and insureds to reduce costs. Members of trade and business associations or franchises can purchase insurance as a group, enabling the insurer to eliminate many underwriting and processing costs because individual selection is eliminated. In addition commissions can be lower because less agent solicitation is required. These cost reductions allow the insurer to charge a lower premium. During an economic recession businesses are especially cost conscious thus increasing the demand for low-cost group insurance.

Many agents fear that mass merchandising will reduce the need for their services. Others view it as a useful sales tool to increase their production rather than eliminate the need for agents.

Is the insurer a seller or a buyer?

Insurers generally sell insurance to buyers. However, the reverse often seems true. Applicants for insurance try to sell their risks to insurers. Consider a 21-year-old male driver with a history of two accidents and three traffic citations. He may experience difficulty in obtaining insurance. Few agents except those representing high risk insurers will attempt to sell him insurance. Businesses may also need hard-to-place insurance, e.g., products liability. These individuals and businesses must try to sell their risks to insurers. They often use insurance brokers to make the sale.

Producers

Those who market insurance are called insurance producers. The insurance market contains many kinds of producers: **general agents, local agents, brokers, surplus** or **excess-line brokers or agents** and **solicitors.**

The general agent

Because true or supervising general agents assume many responsibilities and have many expenses they are paid the highest commissions. In property and liability insurance many sales agents with general agents' contracts do not function as general agents but are important enough to their insurers to receive general agents' commissions. General agency contracts sometimes are used as a competitive device to obtain (or retain) a particularly outstanding agent.

Local agents The local agent represents an insurer in one city or town. Except in life insurance the local agent ordinarily will represent more than one insurer. The commission paid is less than general agents receive. The local agent usually does not perform technical insurance services; the true general agent or branch or home offices offer these services. The local agent is principally a salesperson who acquires business and counsels clients.

Brokers Not all insurance producers are tied to insurers by agency contracts or by employer-employee relationships. Some are free-lance operators called *brokers* who seek the best coverage possible for clients. Theoretically brokers are agents of insurance buyers and not of insurers. Nevertheless they are paid commissions by insurers, not fees by buyers. Premiums charged buyers include the cost of commissions, of course, so the client indirectly pays the commissions of both agents and brokers. The broker usually is paid a lower commission than the agent, allowing the agent to accept business from a broker and still retain a profit margin. However, brokers occasionally place business directly with the insurer rather than through an agent.

Some brokers operate solely as salespersons, providing no technical insurance service. They depend on the insurers to provide the service. Other brokers maintain a loss-control staff to help clients obtain the best rate possible. The engineers check clients' exposures and rating procedures of insurers and advise on loss-prevention activities. They also have underwriters who prepare policy forms to fit the needs of clients.

Brokers are more prominent in metropolitan areas, operating extensively among businesses with large exposures. In a sense they operate as insurance and risk managers for some corporations. While most brokers are local some are national and international. Many brokerage firms offer their clients innovative suggestions for risk management. Brokers are not yet as active in life insurance as in property and liability insurance sales; they play their most significant role in ocean marine insurance.

Surplus or excess-line brokers or agents Sometimes an insured will seek a highly specialized coverage not written by an insurer licensed in the home state. The market is limited for many coverages. A partial list includes auto plan excess liability, auto racing liability, strike insurance, oil-pollution liability, dramshop liability, nonappearance insurance for paid lecturers or their sponsors and tuition refund insurance for colleges returning fees to withdrawing or dismissed students. To handle business with nonadmitted insurers, states license surplus or excess-line agents and brokers (see Chapter 23).

Solicitors A final type of producer is the solicitor who usually cannot bind the insurer or issue policies. The solicitor seeks insurance prospects and then handles the business through a local agent, broker, company branch or service office.

Special agents Salaried representatives known as **special agents** maintain contact between property and liability insurers and their agents. The special agent is responsible for the insurer's business in an assigned territory and may work directly for an insurer or general agency. The special agent's duties involve appointing agents, assisting them in approaching prospects when requested, helping them plan a sales program, keeping agents informed of new coverages and forms, helping them with technical problems involving coverages and procedures and in general maintaining the agents' goodwill and confidence. Some local agents regard the special agent simply as the nice fellow who picks up the luncheon check on each visit, but the special agent's job is also to monitor the quality of business written to assure the development of profitable business. If an agent persists in placing poor business the special agent must investigate the cause. If the condition continues the special agent must terminate the agent and appoint a new one.

Insurance buyers and consultants

Large industrial concerns with complex insurance problems often employ full-time insurance or risk managers who study their companies' loss exposures. They may deal with agents, brokers or direct-writing home offices. Some large firms own their own insurance agencies and trade directly with agency insurers as well as with direct writers, thus saving the agent's commission. Other large firms organize their own insurers (called *captive insurers*) and buy reinsurance rather than direct insurance.

The insurance or risk manager's job includes keeping up with developments in the insurance business. Aside from buying insurance, corporate insurance managers must study loss-prevention techniques and attempt to minimize losses. Some insurance managers have broadened their operations to become full scale risk managers (see Chapters 2 and 3). Insurance buyers sometimes rely on insurance consulting firms acting as advisers and charging a fee. The consultants study the coverages owned by the client, survey exposures and, where necessary, recommend changes. The consultant's advice also may be sought here. (In some cases the consultant will write the insurance and apply the commission against the fees.)

CLAIMS ADMINISTRATION

The purpose of insurance is to provide a mechanism for reducing risks and sharing losses. For insurance to serve its function properly claims must be paid promptly and fairly. Valid claims must not be underpaid. Claims chiseling will result in an unfavorable reputation and an insurer that continually underpays legitimate claims soon will be without customers. Equally dangerous is consistently overpaying claims because it eventually leads to financial difficulty.

The Mechanics of Loss Adjustment

The loss-adjustment process begins upon prompt notification of loss to the insurer or agent. If reported to the agent, notice will be forwarded to the insurer unless the agent has authority to adjust losses. In addition to agents four types of loss adjusters are used: company adjusters, adjustment bureaus, independent adjusters and public adjusters. Independent adjusters and public adjusters differ in that the former represent insurers and the latter represent insureds. Regardless of the adjuster used, the procedure is the same and involves checking the coverage, investigating the claim and filing necessary reports. If the claimant and adjuster do not agree on the amount of settlement arbitration is required. The greater amount of time and energy the insurer expends in loss adjustment the greater the chance of a fair settlement. However, insurers must seek an optimum tradeoff between loss-adjustment expense and equitable claims settlement. Payment of a few invalid or exaggerated claims may be more economical than spending large sums for claims investigation.

Checking the coverage

Once notice of loss is received the insurer makes a preliminary inspection to learn if the adjustment process needs to be continued. Several questions arise that must be answered positively if the loss adjustment is to proceed.

1. Has a policy been issued and is it *still in force?*
2. Is the loss the result of a covered peril?
3. Is the property covered by the policy?
4. Is the loss covered?
5. Is the claimant entitled to the payment?
6. Did the loss occur in a place covered by the contract?

The foregoing questions are answered on the basis of facts submitted by the claimant. If the insurer determines that a basis for a claim exists the claimant will be sent proof-of-loss forms. If the insurer finds the claim fails to meet any of the requisites settlement proceedings will not continue.

Investigation of the claim

Sending proof-of-loss blanks to a claimant does not mean that the insurer admits liability but only that after studying the facts the insurer has found nothing that disqualifies the claimant. A more complete investigation is necessary before the insurer can determine its liability. Claims investigation involves ascertaining if a loss occurred, determining whether actions by the insured have invalidated the claim and establishing the amount of loss. The investigation includes validating facts submitted in the proof-of-loss statement.

If a loss has occurred usually it is simple to verify, but occasionally the investigator finds no evidence of a loss. Persons with substantial amounts of life insurance have disappeared only to reappear later in remote places.

The second object of claims investigation is to determine whether the insured has fulfilled the obligations under the insurance contract. Has the insured with a homeowners policy "protected the property from further damage, separated the damaged and the undamaged personal property and put it in the best possible order?" Has the insured done everything reasonably possible to prevent the spread of the fire? Did the insured report the loss promptly? The investigation may disclose factors that nullify evidence contained in the notice of loss.

The third function of investigation is to determine the amount of loss. When the amount of loss is reported the adjuster examines the claim and estimates the amount owed the insured. If the adjuster's estimate is not in agreement with the insured's most often they can work out a satisfactory solution. If not the policy specifies the steps that must be taken to arbitrate the dispute.

Preparation of proof of loss

Once the investigation is complete and coverage established final papers are prepared. The papers, called the proof of loss, are usually prepared for the insured by the adjuster and filed with the insurer. The adjuster usually files a separate report summarizing conditions found and recommendations concerning loss settlement. When the insured signs the proof of loss or cashes the check further rights to pursue the claim are waived.

Salvage, subrogation and arbitration

The adjustment process may require the adjuster to determine if the insurer can recover some of the money paid in claims. Salvage occurs when damaged property can be sold by the insurer's representative for the insured or the insurer. Sometimes the insurer settles the claim as a total loss then seeks to salvage damaged goods to obtain funds. More often, however, the adjuster helps the insured protect the damaged property and realize its best possible disposition.

When the insurer pays a claim, that payment becomes subrogated to the insured's claim against wrongdoers responsible for the loss. Thus if a neighbor carelessly sets fire to dry grass and the fire spreads to the insured's house the insured is entitled to damages from the neighbor. The fire insurer acquires right of action against the neighbor for the amount of the loss paid. The adjuster of any loss, with the exception of life and most health insurance claims, must be aware of subrogation rights. Sometimes these rights produce enough funds to reimburse the insurer completely for a claim payment.

Arbitration

Although in nearly all cases the adjuster and the insured can reach an agreement concerning settlement every policy provides terms for settling claims when disagreement about the amount of loss occurs. Arbitration is provided in such cases. Typically the insured and the adjuster each appoint a disinterested party to act as arbitrator. The two arbitrators select a third disinterested party. An agreement meeting the approval of any two will be binding on both the insured and the insurer. In liability lines the court replaces the arbitrator and the policy has no arbitration clause.

Difficulties Encountered by the Adjuster

Because the adjuster must often satisfy the claimant without making unreasonable concessions, the attitudes of many insureds make the adjuster's work difficult. These problem claimants are either mistaken, misled or dishonest although many troubles of claims adjusters come from honest mistakes of insureds in overestimating the loss. When the damaged and undamaged goods have been separated and the latter put in the best possible condition the insured often finds that the damage is not as severe as originally estimated. Another source of conflict is that many insureds place a higher-than-market value on their property. For example an auto often is worth more to the insured than in the market.

The adjuster faces more problems from misled insureds than mistaken claimants. Most people refuse to take the time to read their policies and possess only a general grasp of the provisions. Nevertheless they have definite ideas concerning their coverage. The adjuster has studied the policy in detail and usually knows if coverage applies. If the claimant is mistaken about coverage the adjuster must deny payment but attempt to do so in a way that will keep the claimant as a client.

Claimants are also misled by lack of knowledge about adjustment procedures. In the early days these procedures were not standardized. Some insurers advised adjusters to delay settlement so that claimants would tire of pressing their claims. Policies often were constructed to be misleading. This experience has built a feeling among policyowners that they must engage in a war of wits with adjusters. They believe they must file excessive claims to be in a better bargaining position. Furthermore, some claimants, noting that insurers have impressive home-office buildings and extensive investments, consider them fair game. Jurors' hearts seldom bleed for an insurer.

Far different from the misled claimant who pads a claim report for strategic reasons is the claimant who seeks to defraud the insurer with faked claims or self-inflicted losses. To these claimants the adjuster should be merciless. No selling powers are needed because the insurer has no interest in keeping such claimants as clients. Insurers would like to have these persons off their books and preferably in jail.

Examples of Loss-Adjustment Problems

Although basic principles of loss adjustment are similar in all fields of insurance each branch has its own problems.

One of the most complex problems of fire loss adjusting occurs when two or more policies are issued on the property and the policies are not written alike; that is, they are not concurrent. Many basic fire insurance policy forms have a warning printed in boldface: if the property is covered by more than one policy, insuring agreements should be worded identically. Despite this warning many policies are not concurrent. In simple cases the claimant may have one policy covering the property generally, e.g., stock and machinery, and another specifically covering stock. The question is how to apportion the payment between the two insurers when a loss occurs. Resolving this question could cause confusion, payment delay and in some cases recovery for less than the full amount of the loss. The advice printed on the policy is excellent. Be sure that all policies are worded identically. Also, where possible all policies on the same property should be bought from the same insurer. Then if a question arises about which policy covers it will not concern the insured. The insured is paid without delay.

In marine insurance the basic problem is determining the amount of indemnity. Settlement is complicated because what remains of the ship or shipment may be at the bottom of the sea. The ship manifest is a document giving a "complete" cargo inventory. Occasionally insurers doubt all goods listed were on board when a ship sinks (if the ship did indeed sink and was not spirited away). Fortunately, attempts at deception are rare. The chief problem is determining the values lost. In *valued policies,* values will be no problem because insurers pay the agreed amount without question if the loss is total.

A second problem in ocean marine insurance is adjusting general average losses. A loss voluntarily undertaken to save (and succeeds in saving) the venture is borne by all interests and not solely by the owner of the destroyed goods. If cotton is thrown overboard during a storm to lighten the load to save the ship it would be unfair for the entire loss to fall on the cotton owner. Under the rule of general average all other cargo owners, the ship's owner and persons who profit from the freight charge for hauling the cargo must share proportionately in the loss. Because each interest must be valued this rule introduces many complications into ocean marine loss adjustment.

In settling liability claims *speed* is essential. Nearly every fire could have been extinguished by a glass of water if it had been thrown on the fire soon enough. Many liability claims could be settled quickly with a few kind words and immediate assurance that medical expenses will be paid. After the injured person has thought it over, it may be too late for an amicable settlement. Second is the problem of *obtaining relevant facts.* Each witness may have a different version of the accident. A third problem is *preservation of facts.* Obtaining facts is not enough. Adjusters must preserve the facts by signed depositions, photographs, medical reports and so on.

A fourth problem is the *cash settlement,* if any, to be offered. The facts pieced together from statements of witnesses must be analyzed from the point of view of a judge and jury. From this study the decision can be made to offer a settlement or fight the claim in court. When the decision is to go to court another problem arises. Assume the insured has a policy with $100,000 limits and the claimant offers to settle for $100,000 but the insurer refuses. Suppose the court awards the claimant more than $100,000. Numerous court decisions hold the insurer liable for the full amount awarded. The grounds are the insurer acted negligently or in bad faith by refusing to settle for an amount within the policy limits.

Insurers, particularly those writing auto insurance, have experienced much criticism from the consumer movement. One complaint is the method and delay of claims adjustment. The traditional method has been to tender settlement for an absolute release. Today the loss adjuster may make partial payments without a release.

One of the insuring agreements under a liability policy is the promise to defend any suit against the insured for claims covered by the policy even if the suit is groundless, false or fraudulent. Under this agreement the insurer must defend suits against the insured if the insurer would be liable for the claim in a successful suit. Thus in a suit against an insured restaurant owner for bodily injury alleging assault and battery what should the adjuster do? In many business liability insurance policies coverage applies only for an occurrence "that is neither expected nor intended by the insured." Assault and battery would be neither unexpected nor unintended by the insured. If the court rules the restaurant owner guilty the insurer is not liable for the defense or the damages awarded. But if the insured wins the case (it proves to be self-defense not assault and battery), the insurer is liable for the cost of defense. The adjuster must investigate the facts before denying defense on grounds of a contract exclusion.

Life insurance

Adjustment of life insurance policy claims is the simplest of all. If the policy matures during the life of the subject, as in an endowment policy, the insurer need only check its records before paying the claim. When policies mature by the subject's death that death must be verified along with the beneficiary's claim to receive the proceeds. Problems of loss valuation do not occur because partial losses are not possible.

The beneficiary is usually found by consulting the insurer's records. If doubt arises about the proper beneficiary (as it might if a person names "my spouse" and then marries three times) the insurer has an efficient procedure. The insurer pays the proceeds to a court and designates the court to pay the proper claim. One widow entangled in legal proceedings was quoted as saying, "This settlement is so much trouble I almost wish my husband hadn't died." Two difficulties causing problems in a life insurance settlement are: the insured has given misinformation when applying for the policy or fraud has been perpetrated against the insurer. Because the incontestable clause found in every life policy gives the insurer only two years to uncover deception these problems seldom appear. One clause, double indemnity, often attached to life policies may cause headaches. In borderline cases the claims adjuster investigates the facts to determine whether the beneficiary is entitled to double payment.

LOSS CONTROL

Loss control is as important as prompt settlement. Historically insurers were not concerned with loss control and considered their business one of paying losses not preventing them. Rates were based on loss experience and insurers were content to let the law of averages produce their usual profits without worrying about loss prevention.

Cooperative Efforts of Insurers in Loss Control

Insurance executives today have a different attitude. Insurers of all types are concerned with loss control. Just after the Civil War fire insurers formed the National Board of Fire Underwriters. This organization, through the use of engineers, research, investigation and education, was instrumental in reducing life and property loss from fires, windstorms, explosions and other perils. In the mid-1960s the board merged into the American Insurance Association, which continued the work for several years. In 1970 the American Insurance Association discontinued the Fraud and Arson Service that began with the National Board of Fire Underwriters more than 100 years before. The arson and inland marine theft portions of their surveillance have been discontinued and their casualty investigation and statistical work merged into the Casualty Insurance Fraud Association.

In 1970, 12 major insurers formed the Casualty Insurance Fraud Association (CIFA). This organization, now known as The Insurance Crime Prevention Institute (ICPI), was formed to conduct investigations into losses in an effort to break up organized rings. The ICPI places special emphasis on rooting out dishonest lawyers, police officers and doctors who damage the nation's bar, law enforcement agencies and medical profession. Other fire insurance organizations engaged in loss prevention are the Associated Factory Mutual Fire Insurance Companies and the Industrial Risk Insurers.

Marine insurance offers another example of early interest in loss prevention. The information center operated by Lloyd's had as one of its chief purposes supervising ship construction to attain greater safety. Marine insurers are active in the Yacht Safety Bureau, the American Bureau of Shipping, National Cargo Bureau, the Power Squadron and the American Hull Insurance Syndicate, all of which are active in loss prevention. In 1971 the major insurers writing motorcycle coverage formed the Association of Motorcycle Insurers to advance motorcycling safety and theft prevention through education. (Those of us on college campuses who have to dodge motorcyclists are thankful for this mission but wonder about its success.)

The American Insurance Association has an accident-prevention department that concentrates on industrial safety codes and standards, traffic safety and safety education. The National Association of Mutual Insurance Companies engages in accident prevention and rehabilitation. The National Council on Compensation Insurance cooperates in loss-control activity. Property and liability insurers support the National Safety Council. This organization provides leadership in safety of all kinds. Auto insurers support the Insurance Institute for Highway Safety, an industrywide traffic safety organization.

The Alliance of American Insurers, the American Insurance Association, the National Association of Independent Insurers and the National Association of Mutual Insurance Companies all support mandatory installation of air bags (real ones, not politicians) in automobiles. These associations believe that air bags will reduce serious injuries and deaths and result in lower auto insurance premiums.

Life insurers were among the last to recognize the importance of loss control. Who can blame them for failing to discover methods to prolong life? Several large insurers, however, notably the Metropolitan Life Insurance Company, inaugurated a health information service many years ago. In 1945 nearly 150 of the nation's leading life insurers formed the Life Insurance Medical Research Fund. The organization's purpose is to provide research funds for the discovery of treatments and cures for various illnesses and diseases.

Individual Efforts of Insurers in Loss Control

The Hartford Steam Boiler Inspection and Insurance Company, organized in 1866, has boiler accident prevention as its major purpose. It employs a large staff of engineers and other experts to aid in loss control. With the coming of workers' compensation laws in the 20th century insurers have conducted extensive research programs in the prevention and control of industrial accidents. Loss-prevention and control services also are offered to insureds for general liability exposures, elevator hazards, crime exposures, glass breakage and fire exposures.

In addition to direct services, insurers contribute indirectly to the insured's loss-control program by distributing general loss-control information and encouraging the insured to practice loss control by using a merit-rating system (Chapter 22). Some observers believe that insurers are not doing nearly enough in the loss-control field—that many losses occur that could be prevented through more research by insurers on unsafe physical conditions and practices. Insurance and loss control complement each other. Both the insured and the insurer must be aware of loss-control economics. Preventing loss is as important to risk management as insurance against losses. To obtain insurance prospective insureds frequently must institute loss-control programs. Loss control and loss financing are the major functions of risk management.

Loss Control and the Firm

Modern-day businesses are becoming increasingly aware of the importance of methods for loss control. For many years businesses installing loss-control devices have been entitled to lower fire insurance rates. Businesses are currently investigating other possible measures of loss control, especially in the workers' compensation area, prompted by the Federal Occupational Safety and Health Act of 1970 (OSHA) and in the product safety field, motivated by the Federal Consumers Products Safety Act of 1972.

However, loss-control techniques cannot be instituted indiscriminately. If the cost of installing loss-control equipment or procedures exceeds the expected saving in losses the measure should not be implemented. The question of whether the benefits of a particular loss-control method exceed the costs is usually a difficult one. Many variables must be considered, including the cost of implementation, expected reduction in losses, duration of the loss reductions, social welfare considerations, productivity reductions caused by losses and many other factors. The firm may also have to choose between alternative loss-control techniques.

Once all these factors are considered the risk manager must decide on the proposal's profitability. Even if the risk manager believes the proposal will reduce losses the difficult job remains of convincing top executives and production line managers about the utility and profitability of loss-control measures and getting cooperation in enforcing them.

COOPERATIVE ORGANIZATIONS

Sometimes it is said that insurers "compete in a great spirit of cooperation." The existence of many different types of associations in the insurance business is partly responsible for this statement. A complete directory of cooperative insurance organizations would include associations for company executives, technicians, loss control, insurance agents, intercompany claims settlement, educational groups, public relations, buyers' groups and so many others the reader would be drowned in a complete list.

Why Cooperate?

Traditionally in America, competition in insurance has been controlled either by governmental regulation or cooperative action among insurers. Many insurers prefer the latter method. Therefore they make efforts to discourage destructive competition despite strong opposition from two groups: those believing in state control and those believing in free competition.

The more difficult obstacles to cooperative action involving trade practices come from within the industry. Some insurers refuse to cooperate—among them the rugged individualist, the new insurer seeking growth and the insurer that does not believe that either the public interest or its own interest is best served by cooperative action among insurers. These insurers tend to believe that government regulation best protects the public from "undesirable" competition *and* from "restrictive" trade practices.

Competition in insurance may be classified into four categories: prices (rates), products (policy terms), service and representation in sales outlets (agencies).

Controlling competition is not the only reason for cooperative organizations. Most industries maintain one or more trade associations for activities handled best on an industrywide rather than individual company basis. These associations lobby for or against legislation, engage in cooperative advertising to improve public relations, establish codes of ethics for the business, gather industrywide statistics, sponsor periodic meetings to discuss industry problems and engage in cooperative educational and research activities. Cooperative organizations also aid in loss-adjustment activities and in providing underwriting facilities.

Ratemaking Organizations

Many insurers find that cooperative ratemaking is essential. Cooperation is maintained openly through ratemaking organizations or secretly when such organizations have been ruled illegal. The ratemaking organizations may be independent bodies offering advisory rates to insurers at a contract price or organizations owned, financed and managed by member insurers. Where membership in rating bureaus and adherence to the rates and rules they promulgate are required these organizations are closely regulated to assure fair and nondiscriminatory practices. Even if membership is not mandatory many insurers find it desirable to join a rating bureau to eliminate the expense of independent rate filings in various states. In addition, combining loss statistics from many insurers increases the reliability of the calculated rates. Nevertheless, some insurers prefer to remain outside the rating bureau and file rates independently. These are called nonbureau insurers and by using rate-cutting practices they become an irritant to bureau insurers. The Insurance Services Office (ISO) was formed in 1971 through consolidation of six national insurance rating or service organizations. Since its beginning the ISO expanded its scope of operations to include product development and research. The American Association of Insurance Services is another rating, statistical, and advisory organization composed principally of small to medium sized insurers. They provide forms for both personal and business lines.

Rating bureaus collect statistics to develop rates and rate schedules for approved policy forms. (They are not allowed to supply gross rates in Illinois, only loss statistics.) They often standardize insurance policies because rate development and administration are difficult if contracts are not standardized. The bureaus also aid insurers in preparing merit rates for individual exposures. Rating bureaus usually administer rates by auditing each policy for the proper rate assignments, forms and endorsements. Sometimes the audit bureau is independent of the rating bureau. Life insurance rating bureaus do not exist because rates are not set cooperatively.

INNERSCRIPT: OTHER ASSOCIATION FUNCTIONS, UNDERWRITING ASSOCIATIONS AND PUBLIC RELATIONS

Cooperative organizations are formed to engage in numerous other functions. National, state and local insurance agents' associations are organized to promote agent welfare. These associations engage in lobbying activities, promote educational programs for members and in general protect the agents' relations with insurers.

The Insurance Federation on state and national levels is another lobbying organization designed to protect private insurers from undesired governmental interference and competition. The American Insurance Association provides a forum for the capital-stock insurers to study their common problems. The industry also has such social organizations as the Order of the Blue Goose, a fire insurance society. College teachers of insurance have organized the American Risk and Insurance Association.

Underwriting Associations

Associations are also formed to provide underwriting facilities for a particular industry or for a special class of property. Through these organizations greater insurance capacity for large or perilous exposures is available than individual insurers could offer. The associations—sometimes called pools, associates, syndicates, or federations—perform rating, loss-adjustment and engineering services more economically than each insurer could by operating alone. Profits and losses are shared by member insurers. Underwriting associations established by state and federal authority make insurance available in central-city areas against riot, theft and fire and provide flood insurance in selected areas. The insurance business is probably the most organized of all industries. Just name the type of organization and the insurance business probably has it.

Public Relations

All branches of insurance have formed organizations to improve public relations through efforts to educate the public. The oldest major public relations organization is the Alliance of American Insurers, sponsored and supported by the mutual property and liability insurers of America. Capital-stock property and liability insurers founded the Insurance Information Institute to coordinate public relations work carried on by several regional organizations. It publishes *Insurance Facts,* statistics about property and liability insurance. The American Council of Life Insurance is the public's prime source of life insurance information. It conducts invaluable studies on public opinion and collects massive statistics. Its *Life Insurance Fact Book* is an important information source. The Health Insurance Institute performs similar services and publishes the *Source Book of Health Insurance Data,* a valuable source of health insurance statistics.

Company Fleets

Insurers often operate in interrelated groups. A few examples are the Aetna group, the State Farm group, the Hartford group, the Kemper group, the Sentry group and the Nationwide group. A group or **fleet** is composed of more than one insurer owned or managed by the same interests. Many groups include a life insurer.

Insurance executives form groups for several reasons. One is to develop size to take advantage of economies of scale. Another is to be able to write many insurance coverages. Before multiple-line underwriting powers were granted, fire insurers could write marine but not casualty lines and casualty insurers could not write fire or marine lines. However, several insurers could be grouped to give one management organization underwriting outlets in all coverages. A third reason that insurers form fleets is to provide a means for companies within the group to specialize in different markets. For example, fleets might consist of three companies with one catering to preferred-risk drivers, another handling standard-risk drivers and the third accepting high-risk drivers. Once an important reason for forming groups was to increase the number of agents representing an insurer group. If there were six insurers in a group there could be six agents in a territory with "exclusive rights" for one of the group's insurers. Just as multiple-line underwriting powers reduced the need for two or more insurers the declining use of sole-representation agency contracts has reduced the need for several insurers of the same kind. As a result consolidations have taken place. Property and liability insurers acquire or form life insurers and life insurers acquire or form property and liability insurers to offer all-lines insurance.

SUMMARY

1. Insurers include a number of specialized functional departments that offer a variety of career opportunities in the insurance business.
2. Agents operate under one of two systems: the American agency system or the exclusive agency system. The American agency system has independent agents that represent several insurers. Agents collect premiums and retain exclusive rights to solicit policy renewals. Insurers who operate under the American agency system are known as independent agency companies. Independent agencies own renewal rights to policies and administer details like policy writing and billing. Some insurers perform these functions for the agents and pay lower commissions to make policies more competitive with prices charged by exclusive agency insurers.
3. The insurers who use the exclusive agency system have agents that represent only one insurer or group of insurers. The insurer retains the rights to ownership, use and control of policy records.
4. Insurers' agency forces are organized by three systems: The general agency system is based on a contract with the insurer that authorizes the general agent to represent the insurer in a given region. The general agent appoints agents, hires sales representatives, solicits business and develops brokerage accounts. General agents earn commissions on all business sold through their offices. Operating costs, salaries and commissions to sales agents are paid by the general agent. Property and liability general agents' responsibilities may extend to underwriting and claims administration. Large general agencies employ special agents, loss control experts, adjusters and auditors. Life insurance general agents represent only one insurer.

5. Under the branch office system the insurer establishes its own office in a territory. Branch offices perform all the functions administered by a general agency. Managers are paid a salary, and the insurer pays all office expenses. Unlike the general agent the branch manager is supervised by the insurer.
6. Under the direct reporting or home office system the agent is appointed by and deals directly with the home office rather than a branch or general agency. Local agents have exclusive rights to their territories.
7. Direct selling systems use vending machines, direct mail campaigns, newspaper ads and salaried sales representatives to solicit business.
8. Mass merchandising is selling and underwriting for groups thus allowing reduced costs and lower prices. Commissions are lower because less solicitation is required.
9. The sales activity in insurance is often reversed: the insured sells the risk to the insurer in those cases where the insured has undesirable characteristics.
10. Local agents are salespeople who acquire business and counsel clients. In property and liability insurance, local agents represent more than one insurer.
11. Independent brokers are not agents or salaried salespeople. Theoretically, brokers seek the best coverage for clients and are agents for the client. Premiums paid for insurance acquired through a broker include a commission to the broker and to the agent. Large brokerage firms have loss-control staffs, risk management advisers and underwriters. Surplus line or excess line brokers provide highly specialized coverage not written by an insurer licensed in the client's home state, e.g., strike insurance and liquor liability insurance.
12. Solicitors seek insurance prospects and cannot bind the insurer. Solicitors work with local agents, brokers or company branch or service offices.
13. Special agents monitor the quality of business written to assure a profitable line of business.
14. When the claims adjuster and the insured cannot reach agreement on loss settlement, arbitration is used. The insured and the adjuster each appoint a disinterested party to arbitrate and the arbitrators select a third party. The court settles liability cases.
15. If the ship is saved by jettisoned cargo, the rule of general average says that all cargo owners, the ship's owner and people who profit from the freight charge for hauling the cargo must share in the cargo loss.
16. The Insurance Crime Prevention Institute was formed to investigate losses and break up organized crime rings. Insurers contribute to loss control by distributing loss-control information and contributing to loss-control research.
17. Insurers use independent ratemaking organizations that provide advisory rates at a contractual price. Although costs of independent rate filing are less, some insurers prefer to make and file their own rates.
18. Underwriting associations provide facilities for a particular industry or special class of property. Underwriting syndicates can provide rating, loss adjustment and engineering services more economically than individual insurers.

REVIEW QUESTIONS

1. Describe the American agency system and the exclusive agency system.
2. How are agency forces organized?
3. Explain the term direct writer.
4. What are the advantages and disadvantages of mass merchandising?
5. Do insureds ever sell risks to insurers? Explain.
6. Are independent brokers salaried salespeople? Who pays the broker's commission?
7. When does an insurance buyer need a surplus line broker?
8. How do special agents support the sales staff?
9. If a claimant does not agree with the settlement offered by an adjuster, what is the usual arbitration process for a property loss?
10. Define a general average loss. Explain the logic of the method by which they are absorbed.
11. How are insurers involved in loss control?
12. Discuss the benefits of membership in a rate making bureau. Are there any disadvantages to this membership? Explain.
13. Insurers support air bag legislation. Do they support the air bags that favor such legislation?
14. What are risk management consultants? How are they compensated?
15. Classify insurance claimants according to the attitude they have toward claim adjusters.

CHAPTER

21 Underwriting and pricing insurance

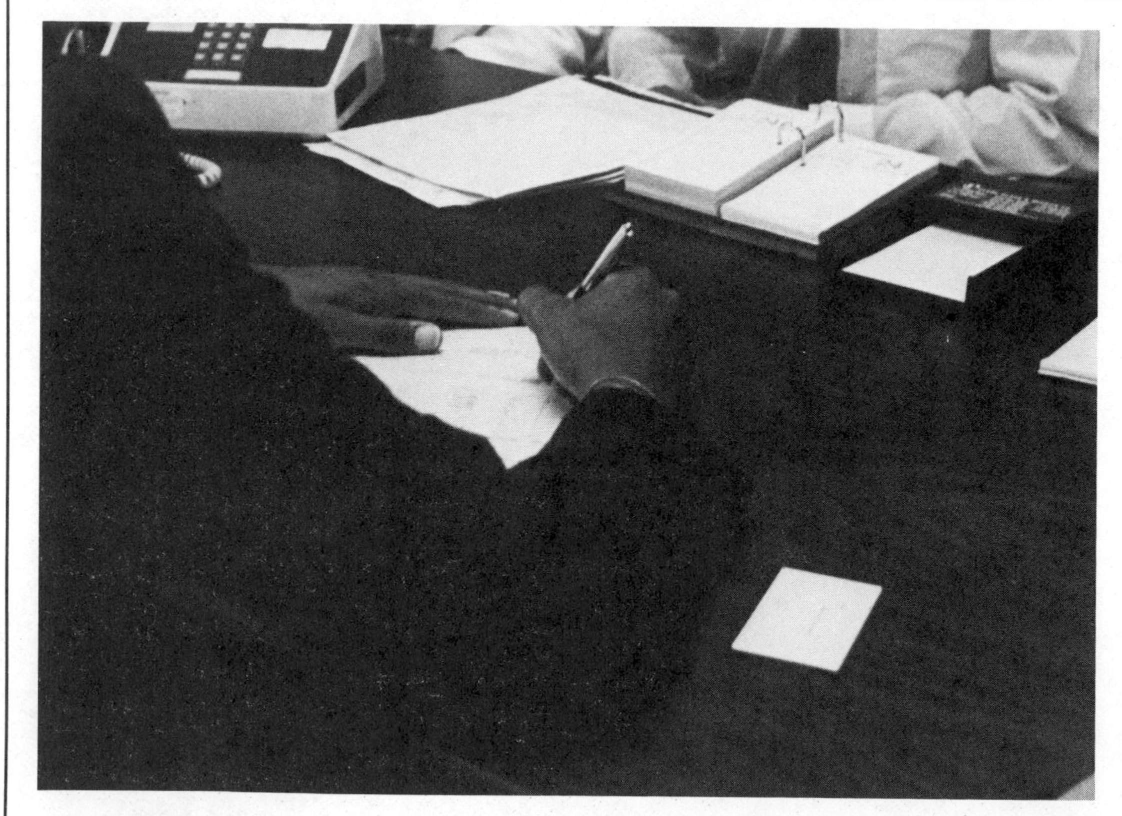

John Thoeming/Richard D. Irwin

CHAPTER OBJECTIVES

1. **To describe the underwriting function in insurance.**
2. **To explain and classify reinsurance.**
3. **To identify the characteristics of a sound insurance rate.**
4. **To contrast the various types of insurance ratemaking systems.**
5. **To show the interrelationships between underwriting and ratemaking in insurance using fire and life insurance as examples.**

Any exposure can be underwritten if the price is sufficient. Thus the underwriting and pricing of insurance are interrelated—one function can not be discussed without the other. The interrelation between underwriting and pricing becomes apparent as the discussion progresses.

This subject is of interest to both insureds and insurers. The insured's interest is in finding answers to such questions as what makes an applicant eligible for insurance, what determines the premium charged and what can the buyer do to become an acceptable risk and to lower the premium rate applicable. The insurer's interest is in knowing whom to accept as insureds and what price to charge to be both profitable and competitive in the long run.

UNDERWRITING INSURANCE

Underwriting is the process of accepting or rejecting applications for insurance. If the application is accepted underwriting is further concerned with the terms under which the insurance is written. The underwriting profession was well established in 16th-century coffeehouses in London where persons willing to acccept risks signed their names under marine insurance proposals, indicating how much they would accept (Chapter 19).

A student considering the theory of insurance might comment: "Because insurance is based on the law of averages why not accept all applicants and trust the laws of probability?" This comment is simplistic. To rely on the law of averages would be inefficient and unprofitable. In a competitive market, selection always occurs in insurance either by insurers or insureds.

Select or Be Selected Against

All insurance applicants do not have the same loss expectancies. Classification systems are established with different rates for each class; an example is age classification in life insurance. However, even within classes variation in loss expectancies are common. If insurers can determine a method of eliminating insureds with higher-than-average loss expectancy within each class, they will earn higher underwriting profits on their business than those that accept all insureds indiscriminately. Selective insurers can then lower rates, attract more business and increase overall profits. Meanwhile, nonselective insurers will lose the better (more profitable) insureds to the selective ones. Because nonselective insurers attract a greater proportion of poor insureds their rates must be increased, thus widening the gap between premiums charged by selective and nonselective insurers. This wider gap encourages even more preferred insureds to move to selective insurers, placing the nonselective ones in a vicious cycle. This illustration explains why all insurers must be selective.

Some government officials and consumer advocates claim that insurers are overly selective in underwriting and give too much attention to statistical analysis of insurance data, neglecting social equity. The term *actuarial equity* often is used to describe the condition where each risk is charged a premium in accordance with its chance of loss. Given (1) the necessity of insurance for many activities (e.g., obtaining a mortgage loan on a house and driving a car) and (2) the inability of some individuals to afford insurance at actuarially fair rates, consumer advocates often pressure insurers to provide subsidies to high-risk insureds by charging premiums below actuarially fair rates. These people argue that losses should be spread over larger numbers of people: insureds in suburbia should subsidize those in central cities and those outside the insurance system should subsidize the system through tax dollars as in social insurance plans.

If an insurer without government help were forced to insure any prospective buyer, rates eventually would move so high that self-insurance and risk assumption would be widespread. Among those with less hazardous exposures only the most security minded or those required by creditors to do so would buy insurance. Others would wait until a loss was imminent before insuring. If an insurer accepts all applicants selection occurs, but by insureds, especially if competing insurers practice selective underwriting. Selection by buyers is called *adverse selection* because the insurer is left with the short end of the stick.

Profitable Distribution of Exposures

The primary purpose of underwriting by an insurer is to obtain a profitable distribution of policyowners. The goal of a profitable distribution of exposures does not mean that insurers try to avoid claims. They expect claims. Without them the insurance business could not exist. But an insurer does not want an excess of claims over those provided for in the rate. Sometimes houses burn the same day they are covered but insurers probably would refuse to insure a person whose houses consistently burn immediately after the insurance becomes effective. The story is told of a client who, upon buying a fire policy one morning, asked the agent: "Now that I've bought this policy, what would I get if my house burned this afternoon?" The agent, a born underwriter, replied, "About 10 years!"

WHO IS THE UNDERWRITER?

Although the agent selling the policy should make a preliminary appraisal of the exposure the bulk of underwriting is done by full-time underwriters in home and branch offices. Groups outside the insurer, such as engineering, auditing and credit rating firms, furnish information and recommendations to aid in the underwriting decision.

The Agent as Underwriter

Many insurance agents refer to themselves and their colleagues as "underwriters." Agents, however, are not underwriters according to the true meaning of the word, i.e., they do not personally underwrite losses.

In property and liability insurance and to a much lesser extent in life insurance, however, the agent can perform an important function in the underwriting process. If an agent knows an insurance applicant will not be a good insured the applicant should be rejected. Agents who sell persistently to persons with high loss expectancies may find their agency contracts terminated. Insurers keep records of the loss experience of their agents. They cannot afford to retain agents who fail to make even a rudimentary selection.

Insurer Underwriting Departments

No matter how good agents are in selecting suitable insureds the ultimate responsibility of efficient underwriting falls on the insurers' underwriting departments. These departments are divided into two sections, staff and line, according to their function. Staff underwriters are concerned only with the insurer's overall underwriting policy. They make recommendations pertaining to underwriting policy, product development and rate structures. Another function is to analyze operating statistics to determine if desirable results are achieved. Because of the supervisory nature of staff underwriters they usually operate from the home office.

Line underwriters are responsible for the acceptance and rejection of individual applications. They may work either at the home office or in branch offices and are closely involved with producers (sellers) of insurance. Line underwriters are properly referred to as "underwriters" because their responsibility is to make specific underwriting decisions and establish a profitable business foundation. Expert line underwriters are invaluable to an insurer as they are the backbone of a profitable operation.

THE UNDERWRITING PROCESS

Underwriting includes both preselection and postselection of insureds. Preselection involves gathering relevant information concerning the exposure and arriving at a decision whether to accept or reject the applicant. Once the exposure is accepted the insurer must practice postselection, the process of reviewing persons already insured and terminating those no longer desirable.

Preselection

Rules governing selection of new insureds begin with the instructions to agents to refuse certain types of applicants. For example, agents of life insurers may be told to refuse steeplejacks, stunt flyers or professional football players (other than those sponsored by universities seeking powerhouses). Property-insurance agents may be told to refuse burglary insurance to persons living alone who are employed outside the house.

Obtaining information

The underwriter must have adequate information for making equitable and profitable underwriting decisions. The amount and type of information needed depends on the kind of insurance offered and the applicant involved. The most important types of information are (1) the applicant's past loss experience, (2) the financial qualifications of the applicant, (3) the applicant's living habits, (4) the physical condition of the applicant or property and (5) the character of the person requesting insurance.

Many sources of information are available to the underwriter. The sources chosen are a function of the particular risk, practicality and cost.

Agents provide underwriters with valuable information, beginning with the application that contains basic information regarding the risk. Agents also usually submit a report with the application answering questions regarding the risk and giving their recommendation as to its acceptability. In a number of cases the underwriter accepts or rejects a risk solely on the basis of the agent's report.

Another important source of information is the inspection company. These organizations provide insurers with a nationwide investigating service, submitting reports concerning a prospective insured. They can tell a life insurer how much liquor the neighbors (and other informers) think the applicant drinks or they can tell a liability insurer whether a prospective insured is considered a careful driver or has had serious accidents. A typical insurance applicant would be amazed at the amount of information (and sometimes misinformation) these investigating organizations can uncover.

Underwriters' Laboratories, Inc., of Chicago is one of the most important agencies performing useful underwriting services. This company began as a cooperative organization of western fire insurers at the time of the Columbian Exposition of 1893. Insurers who were asked to cover the flimsy, combustible buildings of the exposition organized a group to investigate the best ways to wire buildings to prevent fire. The Chicago fire of 1873 (20 years earlier) allegedly caused by the Cow O'Leary still burned in their memories. The organization tested methods of wiring and the electrical equipment. Insurers, perceiving the value of such work, expanded the lab so that now more than 90 years later Underwriters' Laboratories, Inc. has become a mammoth testing organization. Virtually no fabricated device or material is used that has not been tested—everything from corn poppers to locomotives. Items meeting its high standards are permitted to bear the UL label. Others are returned to manufacturers for changes if they want their product to have that valuable label. The use of items approved by Underwriters' Laboratories is often required by insurer underwriting rules and by building codes. The UL label has become the hallmark of safety.

Many other sources of underwriting information are available. Insurers often consult loss-control engineers who provide safety information to help identify liability hazards and examine motor vehicle records on prospective insureds on file in state departments of motor vehicles. Although many other sources are available, the value of additional information may not be worth the cost and problems involved in obtaining it.

Making the decision

After gathering the relevant facts underwriters must analyze the information. The reliability of the information and whether it is subjective or objective are important factors affecting the underwriting decision. Underwriters rely on their experience and knowledge in deciding whether to accept the application, offer modified coverage or reject the application.

If the underwriter decides the particular risk is **standard** the applicant is accepted. The applicant will be issued the standard coverage for the standard premium. In some cases the information may establish that the applicant has a lower-than-average loss experience, which along with other factors allows the applicant to be classified as a **preferred risk.** Preferred risks usually receive standard coverage at a lower premium. However, in most nonstandard cases information may indicate the applicant has a higher-than-average loss expectancy. Underwriters recognize that some of these risks can be made profitable. So in selected cases they may offer alternatives to rejection. In this event, the applicant is classified **substandard** and when accepted is offered modified coverage for the standard premium, which usually is more restrictive than standard coverage and/or may include a larger deductible. Instead of modified coverage, standard coverage might be offered at a higher premium.

Some risks are ineligible. Insurers do not believe that these applicants can be profitable at any *feasible* premium or at any reasonable coverage modification and therefore reject them.

Postselection

Underwriters review renewal applications using techniques similar to those employed in considering whether to renew or decline the coverage for new applicants. They also review claims to determine whether to cancel a policy before it expires. However, one claim does not necessarily mean refusal to renew or even policy cancellation unless the claim investigation reveals some fact not discovered during the original underwriting. Postselection, however, has several unique aspects. Allowing for public criticism by those insisting that insurers have a social obligation to provide insurance to anyone at "affordable" prices, underwriters may easily refuse to renew an application. A refusal, however, creates difficulties for the agent who lives in the community with the rejected applicant. More difficult is the problem of dealing with a current insured now considered undesirable. The insurer has several choices.

One choice is for the insurer to refrain from cancellation until the policy expires, then notify the agent that the contract will not be renewed. The agent may place the client's business with another insurer who follows less strict underwriting rules.

Circumstances may require the insurer to terminate the policy as soon as possible. If, for example, a follow-up inspection of the insured premises reveals undesirable physical conditions or unsound practices the underwriter will recommend immediate cancellation. In one case in which a policy inadvertently was written on property belonging to a convicted arsonist, the insurer maintained a 24-hour-a-day vigil near the premises to notify the fire department should fire occur before the cancellation notice became effective.

Postselection is available only if the policy is cancellable or not guaranteed renewable. The life insurance policy, for example, is noncancellable. The insurer must gather and weigh all underwriting data before issuing the policy. Once the contract is delivered to the insured, the insurer has only a two-year period in which to discover and act upon misrepresentations and concealments in the application. Upon discovery of certain types of misrepresentations and concealments the insurer can rescind the contract. (See Chapter 5.)

In health insurance many noncancellable and guaranteed renewable policies are issued. Many auto insurers write liability contracts that give the insurer only limited cancellation rights. In most instances, however, the policies are not guaranteed renewable. If renewal is denied the insurer in most states must (1) give the insured a written explanation for nonrenewal or (2) notify the insured that on written request such information will be provided.

RETENTION

After the underwriters have accepted an application, decided on the type of policy to be issued and determined the rate to be charged, the question of the amount of insurance the insurer wants to retain must be answered. Underwriters make this decision. If they do not want to retain the full amount they may offer a portion of it to other insurers. This process is called reinsurance and is discussed later in this chapter.

Even if underwriters are able to select the best applicants limitations are established on the amounts of insurance that one insurer can sell. Underwriters seek a safe distribution of exposure units. The financial condition and size of the insurer are important determinants of how much it can underwrite safely. A basic question is: What is the largest single amount the insurer can afford to lose on one exposure? This question must be answered by the insurer's financial officers and approved by the board. Its answer helps to establish **line limits**—the maximum amount of insurance an insurer will write on one exposure. The line limits for particular exposures are compiled into a line book that serves as a guide to underwriters.

Line Limits in Life Insurance

Determining the line limit is simple in life insurance. The board of directors decides the maximum amount of insurance the insurer will write on one life and the maximum amount of coverage under a policy the insurer will retain without seeking reinsurance. The largest insurers write several million dollars on a life and retain the entire amount. Many smaller insurers write only limited amounts, e.g., $300,000 or $400,000, but will reinsure all but some such amount as the first $50,000 to $100,000. A new insurer might reinsure nearly all its business during its first several years of operation.

Line Limits in Property and Liability Insurance

Establishing line limits in property insurance is more complicated. These lines vary among coverages, insureds, geographical areas and other factors. For example, assume the line book shows that brick buildings in Champaign, Illinois are subject to a $200,000 limit. However, these line limits do not represent the amount of insurance the insurer can write on these buildings but rather the largest amount it is willing to lose on one of them. Assume the owner of a $400,000 brick building in Champaign applies for fire insurance. The underwriters, on the basis of an engineering report, note that if the building burns its probable maximum loss would be half the value of the building ($200,000). Thus since the insurer is "willing" to accept a loss of $200,000 on a brick building the underwriters can approve a $400,000 policy for this building. If the owner wants more than $400,000 of insurance the insurer can write higher limits if reinsurance is available.

REINSURANCE

Reinsurance is the insurance of insurance. When an insurer receives an application for insurance exceeding its retention limit the excess amount may be reinsured. Furthermore, if business submitted by all agents exceeds the amount supportable by the insurer's financial position part of that business can be reinsured. Reinsurance prevents the strain that might result on insurer-agency relations if the insurer had to return the application to the agent with a notation that the business could not be accepted because line limits or the insurer's financial capacity had been exceeded. The amount of business placed with the reinsurer is called the **ceded** amount. The placing of business with a reinsurer is called **cession.** Reinsurers frequently reinsure part of their exposure. This process is called **retrocession.**

The reader may wonder why an insurer does not accept contracts of questionable soundness and pass most of the exposure to a reinsurer. The answer is: a ceding insurer that continually cedes poor business to reinsurers would eventually lose its reinsurance facilities. Reinsurance markets are carefully guarded, thus preventing the passing of questionable exposures to reinsurers.

Types of Reinsurance

Reinsurance may be classified broadly as treaty, facultative or a combination of the two. It may be written as proportional or nonproportional.

Facultative and treaty reinsurance

Under **treaty** (sometimes called automatic) **reinsurance** the insurer must cede the amount of insurance required under the contract agreement and the reinsurer must accept the amount offered. Treaties may cover a range of perils and they avoid the time-consuming negotiations necessary when reinsurance has to be arranged for each contract. When an insurer writes a policy covered by the treaty the reinsurance is activated and applies to that policy. Under **facultative reinsurance** the insurer determines for each case whether reinsurance is desired and if so the reinsurer retains the right to accept or reject each proposal on its merits. A new contract must be negotiated for each case. Two hybrids (see Figure 21–1) have been developed: (1) the insurer has the option to cede but the reinsurer must accept all reinsurance offered, subject to the treaty and (2) the insurer has the option to cede or retain and the reinsurer has the option to accept or decline each submission. The method for handling reinsurance, however, is determined by contract.

INNERSCRIPT: PROPORTIONAL AND NONPROPORTIONAL REINSURANCE

Under proportional (**or** pro rata) reinsurance **an insurer shares with a reinsurer on a proportional basis both premiums and losses. The originating (ceding) insurer writes the full amount of the policy for an insured but has an agreement with the reinsurer to share in the premiums and losses. The reinsurer might receive 30 percent of the premiums less a commission in exchange for an agreement to pay 30 percent of all losses. The commission reimburses the ceding insurer for initial expenses. Pro rata reinsurance is used, for example, by new insurers that lack underwriting talent.**

Two types of proportional or pro rata reinsurance are quota share **and** surplus share. **For quota share reinsurance the same proportion of every policy, large or small, is shared with the reinsurer. For surplus-share reinsurance the percentage of reinsurance participation is calculated separately for each policy. Nonproportional reinsurance can be classified into two major categories:** excess loss **and** stop loss. **Under excess-loss reinsurance the reinsurer is required to bear only those losses in excess of the ceding insurer's retention limit, leaving the ceding insurer to bear losses in full up to the retention amount. For example, an insurer has a $500,000 retention limit but writes a $750,000 policy. Under excess-loss reinsurance the insurer cedes $250,000 of the insurance to the reinsurer. Excess loss reinsurance may be written as individual** per risk **reinsurance or** catastrophe risks **reinsurance. Under per risk reinsurance the reinsurer agrees to pay losses on a single risk in excess of the ceding insurer's net retention limit. Under catastrophic risks reinsurance, the reinsurer agrees to reimburse the reinsured, up to a stated maximum, for catastrophe losses in excess of a given retention amount per disaster.**

(continued)

Stop-loss reinsurance is used by a ceding insurer to control its loss ratio, i.e., the ratio of incurred losses to earned premiums. Under this plan, a stop-loss limit is used. *That limit* is the higher of a given percentage of the ceding insurer's net earned premium or a specified dollar amount. The reinsurer is liable only for the insurer's aggregate losses *exceeding* the applicable stop-loss limit up to a specified maximum. *This maximum* is either a predetermined percentage of the insurer's net earned premium or a fixed dollar amount, whichever is less. For example, assume an insurer negotiated a stop-loss reinsurance agreement. The stop-loss limit is established at 70 percent of the ceding insurer's net earned premium or $300,000, whichever is greater. The reinsurer's maximum liability is set in this agreement at 50 percent of the ceding insurer's net earned premium or $300,000, whichever is less. Thus a ceding insurer with a net earned premium of $500,000 must incur losses of $350,000 (70 percent of $500,000) before the reinsurer incurs any obligations. The reinsurer's maximum liability in this example is $250,000 (50 percent of $500,000) because it is less than $300,000. Thus the ceding insurer is protected against a loss-ratio greater than 70 percent if incurred losses do not exceed $600,000 ($350,000 is retained and $250,000 is reinsured.)

Figure 21–1 illustrates the types of reinsurance used in property and liability insurance. An insurer can have any combination of types moving from the top to the bottom of the figure.

Arrangements unique to life insurance

Life insurance reinsurance is of two types: the **yearly renewable term** (YRT) **plan** and the **coinsurance plan.** Under the YRT plan (sometimes called **risk premium reinsurance**) the insurer reinsures only the difference between the *net amount at risk* and the net retention of the insurer. The net amount at risk is the policy face amount less its terminal reserve. As the terminal reserve increases throughout the life of the policy the amount of the policy reinsured continually decreases. For example, assume the Lowe Life Insurance Company has a net retention limit of $10,000. It writes a $25,000 policy on Donna Jessee. The insurer reinsures $15,000 at the time the policy is issued. Years later, however, the terminal reserve is $13,000 so the net amount at risk is only $12,000. That year the amount of reinsurance will be down to only $2,000 ($12,000 − $10,000 = $2,000). The YRT plan is preferred by most small life insurers as it permits them to retain more risk on each reinsured contract and thus retain more premium receipts for investment.

The coinsurance plan provides for reinsuring the amount by which the original face amount exceeds the net retention limit. This amount continues throughout the life of the contract. In the previous example, $15,000 of Donna's policy would be reinsured for its duration.

FIGURE 21–1 Types of Reinsurance*

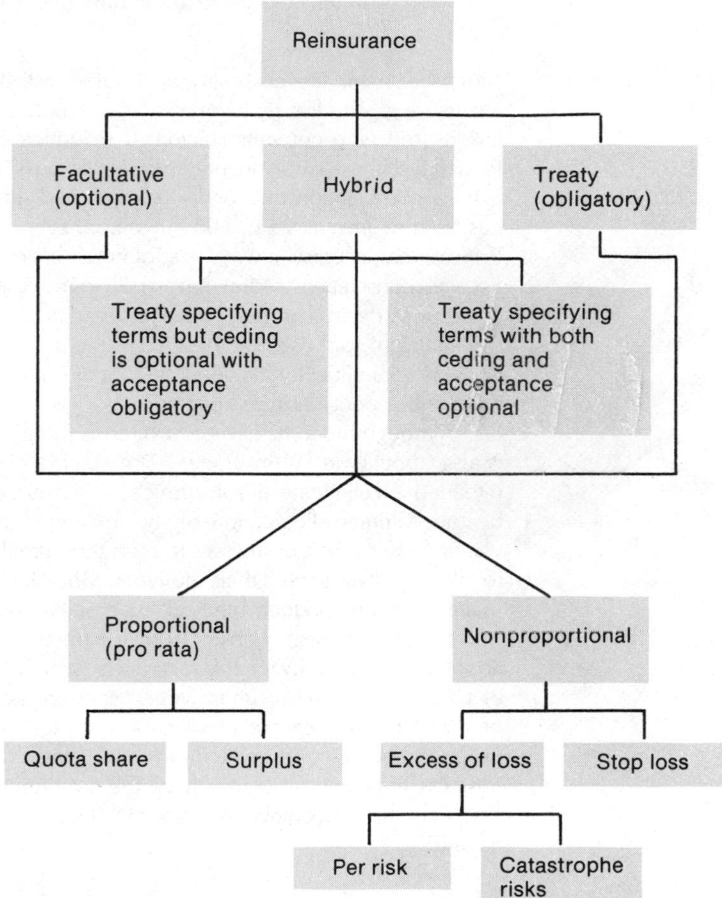

*A modification of a diagram developed by Stan E. Whitfield, C. T. Bowring and Co., (Insurance) Ltd., London, England.

Reasons for Reinsurance

Reinsurance is purchased for several reasons. Most important, by eliminating the possibility of excessive losses in one occurrence, operating results of ceding insurers are stabilized. Additionally, insurers can accept more business than their underwriting capacity otherwise would support. Finally, reinsurers can provide underwriting advice to new insurers or insurers expanding into new territories and coverages. Because of its vested interest in the success of the ceding insurer the reinsurer offers its clients assistance on many technical matters and helps in the operation of the ceding insurer.

SPECIAL PROBLEMS OF UNDERWRITING

Besides the aspects of underwriting outlined in the preceding section underwriters are faced with special problems concerning applicants, agents, and public pressures. These problems are those of moral hazard, conflicts between production and underwriting departments and governmental pressures to insure applicants who would be rejected under traditional underwriting rules.

Moral Hazard

Moral hazard is the possibility an insured will deliberately cause a loss insured against; e.g., the fire policyowner who sets fire to the covered property or the life insured who commits suicide. If evidence shows that an applicant intends to defraud the insurer no underwriting is possible. Moral hazard usually arises from a combination of moral weakness and financial difficulty. Fire by friction has been defined as a $100,000 inventory rubbing against a $200,000 fire policy. Professional arsonists always are looking for new clients with a large policy and a small conscience. Moral hazard is found not only if the applicant has the intention to destroy property but also when factors are present that may encourage the applicant to do so. Factors suggesting moral hazard besides moral weakness and financial difficulty include a history of questionable acts, evasion of responsibility and a poor business reputation.

Although moral hazard most often is found in property and health insurance it also appears in life insurance. The suicide clause in life insurance policies is intended to eliminate life insurance as a source of funds for liquidating debts by the voluntary liquidation of the insured. However, the number of persons willing to burn their businesses to feed their families greatly exceeds those willing to take their lives to feed their survivors. Moral hazard in health insurance produces malingering and padded medical expenses as well.

Moral hazard also arises from indifference concerning loss, often brought about by the security of the insurance, which leads to carelessness. This form of hazard is difficult to underwrite. Many insureds are guilty in varying degrees of moral hazard. People leave cars unlocked with the keys in the ignition, an unsound practice and unlawful in many states. An insured with an unprofitable business may not set a match to the structure but may do little to prevent a fire. Poor housekeeping becomes the rule; trash accumulates and causes a fire hazard.

Conflict between Underwriting and Production

Conflict between underwriting and production is inevitable. Each group sometimes believes the business would be much better, or at least more pleasant, without the other. The production department's function is to sell as much insurance as possible. The underwriting department must obtain a safe and profitable distribution of exposure units. To the production department underwriters often appear overly conservative. Agents want borderline applicants accepted but underwriters may have a different perception. To minimize ill will and improve relations with agents underwriters should explain the reasoning behind decisions adverse to agents.

INNERSCRIPT: CONFLICT BETWEEN UNDERWRITER AND AGENT—A SING ALONG

The following poem (sung to the tune *Oh, My Darling Clementine*) **depicts the gist of a lot of correspondence in the files of the medical departments of many life insurance companies.**

"My Dear Agent," wrote the Doctor,
"Application of Jim Brown
Is declined for valid reasons;
Sorry, but we've turned him down."
"My Dear Doctor," wrote the Agent,
"Your form letter just received,
And the information given
Makes me just a little peeved.
In the first place, my dear Doctor
I have known this man a year,
And I've never seen him drinking
Much of anything but beer.
He don't chew nor smoke tobacco;
He don't toddle to the jazz;
I can't detail all the virtues
That this super-standard has."
"My Dear Agent," wrote the Doctor,
"You are certainly some kidder.
Case-of-Jim-Brown still is turned down;
Sorry; cannot reconsider."
"My Dear Doctor," wrote the Agent,
"Your decision makes me sigh—
Brown's entitled to a contract;
If he isn't—*tell me why*."
"My Dear Agent," wrote the Doctor,
"Brown's case shows much albumin,
Mitral murmur, high blood pressure,
And the fat man's prize he'd win."
"My Dear Doctor," wrote the Agent,
"Brown has trivial ills, that's true,
But they're family characteristics;
So it's safe to pass him through.
Why, his father had a murmur
You could hear a block or more;
His old grand-dad had albumin,
And he lived to ninety-four.
Note the weight's good distribution;
Pressure shows the heart is strong.
He has never had a hemorrhage;
So please rush the contract on."
"My Dear Agent," wrote the Doctor,
"Application of Jim Brown
Is declined for valid reasons;
Sorry, but we've turned him down."
When the Agent got this letter
He just settled back and sighed,
For he couldn't argue further,
'Cause his "prospect" had just died.

Governmental Pressures on Underwriting

Underwriters are subject to pressure from various governmental units, particularly to write auto and property insurance in inner-city areas and to write various types of liability coverages. The strong consumer movement has led to public examination of nearly every aspect of auto insurance. Allegations are made that people living in the inner cities pay inordinately high insurance rates. During the 1970s the government exerted pressure upon liability insurers to provide products liability and medical malpractice insurance protection even if unprofitable. Underwriters defend their practices by insisting that insurers are not meant to be charitable institutions and that the levels of loss experience in these lines support higher rates and in some cases prohibit coverage.

Various measures have been undertaken by the industry and government to make insurance available to nearly everyone at reasonable rates. Often these programs require governmental subsidies.

PRICING INSURANCE

The price paid for insurance, called the **premium,** is the *rate per unit of coverage* multiplied by the *number of units of insurance purchased.* Units of insurance are measured differently according to the type of coverage. For example, a unit can be a specific amount of insurance ($100 for fire insurance and $1,000 for life insurance); a vehicle for auto insurance; 100 square feet of area in a building for some types of liability insurance or $100 of payroll for workers' compensation insurance.

Rates once were made individually. Underwriters judged separately each insurance application. As business volume increased new ratemaking methods became necessary. Insurers found it too expensive to inspect all individual properties. Cooperative ratemaking bureaus were formed in most insurance lines to develop equitable rates. They published rates that were used by most insurers. Subscribers sometimes deviate from bureau-published rates but they are a basing point for these deviations. (Life, health and ocean marine insurers set their own rates and some "nonbureau" insurers writing other types of insurance develop premiums independently.) Today's trend is strongly toward independent ratemaking for all types of insurance.

Principles of Ratemaking

Modern ratemaking involves adherence to fundamental principles. Rates should be adequate, not unfairly discriminatory and not excessive. Also they should be economically feasible and encourage loss prevention. State laws require the first three principles. The others represent more an ideal than a requirement.

Adequacy

Rates must be sufficient to pay losses and reasonable expenses of the insurer's operation. State laws require rate adequacy, as inadequate rates could result in the insolvency of an insurer and losses to policyowners.

Equity

Rates must be equitable, which means that all insureds pay their fair share of projected claims and expenses. But in practice equity is impossible. Its achievement would require each insured to be placed in an individual class, as no two insureds have the same loss probability, risk or expenses. If each insured were placed in a separate class of its own, the principle of insurance—prediction of total loss values through large numbers of homogeneous units—would be unworkable. Thus complete equity in insurance is a contradiction.

Pooling similar exposure units into classes produces a practical degree of equity even though the degree of similarity among units in a class may vary widely. In homeowners insurance the same rate is charged for most one-family residences of frame construction with fire-resistant roofs in a given town. Although some houses are more likely to burn than others, further classification is too expensive. More classifications also might produce classes with so few members that the basic principle of risk pooling would be violated. The number of exposure units would be too small to allow loss prediction.

Not excessive

Rates can be excessive. State regulatory authorities and insurers sometimes do not see eye to eye on specific rate levels. Insurance commissioners in observing loss statistics may question whether or not insurers are making excessive profits from a particular type of insurance. So they ask insurers to justify their rates or reduce them. Regulatory authorities, however, are supposed to be just as concerned with inadequate rates as with excessive ones but for political reasons they seek more vigorously to correct rates that they judge to be too high.

Economic feasibility

Adequate, equitable and not excessive rates are sufficient to meet state regulatory requirements but insurers also must consider other ratemaking principles. An economically feasible rate is one that makes insurance attractive. For the rate to be attractive the loss insured against must have a low frequency and high severity rate. For example, full coverage for auto collision damage would require a premium so high that few insureds could afford it. However, deductible clauses make collision insurance economically feasible for the typical auto owner by reducing claims frequency.

Inducement of loss-control activities

Ideally rates should be constructed to encourage loss control. Discounts can be allowed for protective devices and safe practices. Because economic gains from loss control accrue to both insurers and insureds loss control discounts when properly used are a good insurance rate making practice. But rate discounts are abused. Insurers use these discounts as competitive weapons to discriminate unfairly on behalf of their more favored customers. Insurance commissioners who seek to eliminate unfair discrimination in rate practices do not easily detect such actions.

Types of Ratemaking

Ratemaking may be divided into three broad categories: **judgment rating, manual rating** and **merit rating.** These classes are not mutually exclusive: a rate may combine all three types.

Judgment rating

Judgment rating reflects complete individuality in rating. Each exposure is rated on its own merits independent of any established class, schedule or formula. Although it is the least scientific rating method judgment rating is still used in some coverages, especially in marine insurance, when credible statistics are unavailable. Judgment rating is not wholly unscientific as ratemakers often use some crude statistics in judging each exposure. In fact no rating system can be developed and applied without some judgment (good or bad) entering into the final rate.

Manual rating

Manual rating, defined as **class** or **blanket** rating, combines large groups of similar exposures into classes. All exposures in the classification are charged the same rate. The ability to establish similar classes and identify factors governing class boundaries is assumed. Manual rates reflect the average loss experience of the group and are the most widely used in ratemaking. Class rates in homeowners insurance, for example, apply to most residential property. In a specific town, all one- or two-family frame dwellings with standard roofs are assigned the same rate per $100 of insurance; all one- or two-family brick dwellings in the same community are given another rate. The important consideration in determining each class is that the units are alike in structure, exposed to similar hazards and thus likely to have comparable loss experience over time.

Merit rating

Merit rating or **modification rating** varies the rate charged insureds in the same classification based on the insured's past experience and/or anticipated experience for the policy term. The purpose is to help achieve equity by providing a rating system that reduces premiums charged large insureds whose experience is consistently better-than-average and increases premiums charged large insureds with poorer-than-average experience. The three types of merit rating are schedule rating, experience rating and retrospective rating.

Schedule rating requires a physical evaluation of the applicant's exposure. Based on this evaluation the manual classification rate is adjusted upward or downward. Because of the significance of physical factors in schedule rating it is important only in fire insurance on commercial properties. It is used to a limited extent in liability, burglary and glass insurance.

Under an **experience rating** system a modification is made in the manual rate to reflect the insured's experience. The premium for the period covered will not be affected by the experience for the current year but is later averaged with the experience of past years. Because experience modifies future rates this rating plan is known as *prospective experience rating* to distinguish it from *retro-*

FIGURE 21–2 Three Types of Merit Rating

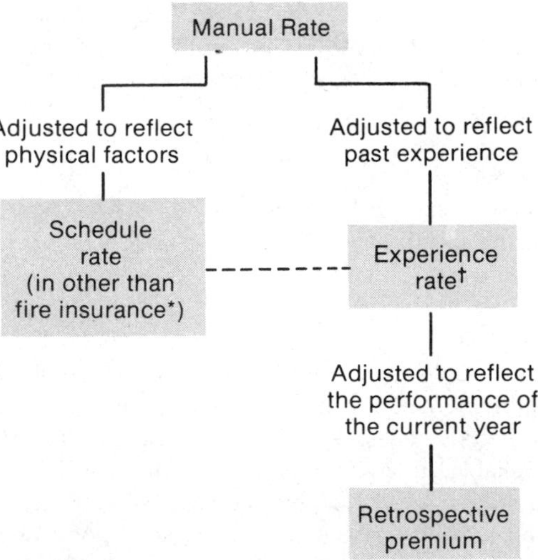

* For fire insurance, the building to be rated is compared to a standard building and adjustments are made to reflect differences.

† The experience rate for workers' compensation insurance may be modified in some instances by a schedule.

spective experience rating. The degree to which the manual rate is modified depends on the credibility (believability) of the data available to reflect the insured's experience and that in turn depends on the amount of data generated.

Retrospective rating further modifies the experience premium (called the *standard premium*) to reflect performance in the current year. The insured is charged a *basic premium,* which is a percentage of the *standard premium.* The basic premium includes an amount sufficient to pay expenses and a risk charge to cover losses in excess of a fixed maximum. Losses including loss adjustment expenses incurred during the period and the state premium tax are added to the basic premium. The total is the retrospective premium, subject to a maximum and a minimum. Several plans of retrospective rating are available. They vary according to the maximum and minimum premiums. The least risky plan for the insured is the one with the highest minimum and lowest maximum premium. The most risky plan is the one with the lowest minimum and highest maximum. Figure 21–2 illustrates three types of merit rating.

Class rates are also modified to reflect lower costs per unit of insurance as the number of units purchased increases. In life and workers' compensation insurance the quantity discount is based solely on reduced expenses per unit; in liability and crime coverages the discount is based both on reduced expenses and reduced loss costs per unit. For example, the second $25,000 of liability insurance does not produce as much loss as the first $25,000.

EXAMPLES OF UNDERWRITING AND PRICING OF INSURANCE

Factors that affect insurance underwriting often affect insurance pricing. Two examples illustrate this interrelationship: one from fire insurance the other from life insurance.

Underwriting and Rating of Fire Insurance

The methods used by underwriting departments of fire insurers are typical of those followed in underwriting most property and liability coverages. For this reason fire insurance is used to illustrate the underwriting of property and liability coverage.

Underwriting procedures

Applications are submitted by agents who usually have already issued the policies. (The local agent generally can issue a fire policy knowing it will be approved by the underwriting department of the insurer at the manual rate quoted to the customer.)

Factors that affect the building underwriting and rating decision include the type of roof, number of dwelling units, the building's age, neighborhood, value, size, construction, occupancy, exposure and degree of protection. Of these factors the last four are the most important. Underwriters weigh these and other factors to arrive at a decision. The decision is obvious when a moral hazard is found: reject the application. (No *reasonable* price is available for this type of hazard.)

Construction. Construction means building materials used. For fire insurance buildings are classified as frame, brick or fire-resistant. All three types of construction are insurable. But construction of the building when considered in its geographical location or with its occupancy may have an important bearing on the underwriter's decision whether to accept the application and, if so, at what price.

Occupancy. The occupancy of a building is defined as its use. To the underwriter a frame structure may be acceptable for office work but unacceptable as a dry-cleaning plant. The effects of occupancy may be divided into three parts: ignitability, combustibility and damageability.

Ignitability is a measure of the chance of the occurrence of fire from a given occupancy. The ignitability of a dry-cleaning plant will be high and that of a church will be low except during a hell-fire-and-brimstone sermon. (The devil does a nice business for such a lousy location.) *Combustibility* measures the burning capability of a given occupancy once a fire has started. A lumberyard would have high combustibility. Lumber is unlikely to cause ignition, as anyone who has tried to produce flame by rubbing two pieces of wood together will testify. However, once a fire has started lumber burns quickly. *Damageability* measures the susceptibility of contents to severe loss. Damageability is closely related to values. A characteristic of damageability also is susceptibility to water or heat damage in addition to combustion.

Exposure. Exposure is the likelihood of damage occurring to an object caused by an outside source. A building's location next to a powder plant may be sufficient to warrant rejection for insurance although the premium supposedly reflects the adverse exposure.

Protection. Protection may be private, like fire alarm systems, fire doors, fire blocks, automatic sprinkler systems and so on. Protection also includes public protection furnished by fire departments.

Pricing procedures

All this fire insurance underwriting information is necessary to develop a fire insurance rate. Fire insurance rating offers examples of both manual (class) and schedule rating. Dwellings are class rated. In one small midwestern town, for example, all frame dwellings (without an unusual exposure) built for one-family occupancy may be charged $0.18 per $100. As no fire insurance quantity discount is offered the rate for each $100 is constant. The rate is not the same in every town because the chance of loss by fire differs among localities. In 1916 a "Standard Schedule for Grading Cities and Towns with Reference to Their Fire Defenses and Physical Conditions" was adopted and is the starting point of fire insurance rating. Each town is rated according to factors affecting the frequency and severity of fire losses. A system of deficiency points is used in grading the towns. After an inspection they are assigned a classification ranging from 1 to 10, according to the number of deficiency points assessed. The importance of the different factors is shown by the relative weights given the 5,000 deficiency points that can be assessed against a town:

FACTOR	*DEFICIENCY POINTS*
Water supply	1,700
Fire department	1,500
Fire alarm	550
Police protection	50
Building laws	300
General hazards	300
Structural conditions that might lead to a general conflagration	700
Total	5,000 points

A town with 500 or fewer deficiency points assessed against it would be in class 1 but there is no such town.[1] Class 2 runs from 501 to 1,000 deficiency

[1] It is rumored that one once existed—but it burned.

points and so on down to class 10, with more than 4,500 points. The grades along with recommended improvements are explained to town authorities.

Commercial properties are individually rated according to a comprehensive rating schedule. Two widely used rating schedules are the **universal mercantile system** and the **Dean's analytic system.** (It is difficult to conceive of a dean being analytical much less having a system.)

INNERSCRIPT: THE UNIVERSAL MERCANTILE SYSTEM ILLUSTRATED

Fire schedule rating is illustrated using the universal mercantile system. Under this system, the guide applied to measure chance of loss is a standard building in a standard town. The assumed building is so high grade that few structures can meet it. The city assumed also is high grade. The basis rate **for this standard building in the standard city is the schedule's starting point. Next, the** key rate, **i.e., the rate assigned to the standard building in the actual city in which the structure is located, is determined. The city is compared with the standard city as to the building code, fire department adequacy, water supply and the efficiency of the police department. Credits are given for items where the city is better than the standard city and deductions are made for items where the city is poorer than standard. Once the key rate is determined the actual building is compared with the standard building. Additions are made to the key rate for building features (including occupancy, neighbors and construction) poorer than the standard. Deductions are made for features that exceed the standard.**

For example, a five-story frame mercantile building in a medium-sized eastern town might be rated as follows under one of several schedules available under the universal mercantile system. The basis rate would be 25 cents per \$100 of valuation. Using the grading system for cities and towns a charge of 50 cents per \$100 is added to produce a \$0.75 key rate. Then additional charges are made for various characteristics of the building. These charges are as follows: 50 cents if the structure is frame rather than brick; 5 cents if the total floor area is 10,000 square feet as compared with the standard 5,000; 15 cents if the building has 5 stories rather four and 5 cents if the occupancy is by 3 tenants instead of 2. The final rate increases to \$1.50 per \$100 of coverage (\$0.25 + 0.50 + 0.50 + 0.05 + 0.15 + 0.05 = \$1.50). Other factors for which charges often are made include stairways, heating systems, lighting systems, roof construction, elevators, interior finish, electrical defects and exposure. Because the schedule requires a nearly perfect building as its starting point, few credits are given. The structure could have received small percentage credits for guards, fire extinguishers and other "exceptionally good features."

(*continued*)

After weighing the basic underwriting data against the rate, the underwriter decides whether the insurer wants to underwrite the applicant. As mentioned, a large part of the underwriter's judgment may be subjective. The business will be accepted if the underwriter perceives it to be potentially profitable.

Underwriting and Pricing of Life Insurance

The underwriting procedure in life insurance is similar in many respects to that in fire insurance. A major difference is that an applicant for life insurance submits a formal written application for a policy through the agent to the insurer. The underwriting department's approval is required before the policy is issued. In contrast, many fire policies are issued before the underwriting department sees and approves the application. This dichotomy is reasonable in that fire policies are cancellable while life insurance policies are not.

Underwriting procedures

Underwriting information for life insurers is developed from many sources: the application, the agent's certificate, the inspection report and the medical information bureau. Factors affecting underwriting primarily are the insured's age, occupation and physical condition.

The application. The life insurance application is a detailed document in two parts. Part 1 consists of data supplied by the applicant including birth date, address, former addresses, occupation, negotiations pending for other policies, membership in the armed forces or in organized military reserves, contemplated changes in occupation or residence, type of policy applied for, the premium to be paid, when premiums are payable, special riders or benefits to be included, disposition of dividends (if the policy is participating), the beneficiary designation and so on. Part 2 contains the report of the medical examiner. It reports the physician's answers to questions and records the applicant's answers to the physician's questions which concern medical treatment received, physical examinations taken in recent years and diseases suffered by the applicant. A series of questions is asked about the applicant's family: age of parents, brothers and sisters; if any are dead, how old were they when they died and the cause of death. In addition, part 2 includes the physician's report of the medical examination, if required.

Many policies are written without requiring a physical examination. The maximum amount that can be written without medical examination usually varies with the applicant's age—the young applicant can buy more "nonmedical" insurance than can an older applicant. The maximum also varies with the kind of policy. The maximum age limit is usually 40 and the maximum amount is usually $25,000. In these nonmedical cases the underwriter makes a decision based on answers the applicant has given to questions in a special nonmedical section of the application. The underwriter can request a medical examination if answers to the nonmedical section are unsatisfactory.

The agent's certificate. The agent's certificate (included in part 1 of the application) contains information about how the agent met the applicant; how long and how well the agent knew the applicant and the agent's knowledge of factors concerning the applicant's employment, marital status, financial standing and so on. The agent is asked whether or not the applicant is recommended for insurance. This document is a minor detail in underwriting life insurance because agents are not likely to forward applications for clients they are not willing to endorse.

The inspection report. The insurer may obtain an inspection report of personal matters concerning applicants. From this report the underwriters learn if there is any reason to doubt information contained in the application. The inspection report supplies information about the applicant's finances, occupation, participation in hazardous sports, health, habits, character, appearance and home environment.

Medical information bureau. The underwriters check the files prepared by the Medical Information Bureau (MIB). This cooperative organization of life insurers was formed to centralize information of special interest to members about the physical condition of previous applicants for life insurance in a member company. MIB's file cards, however, do not record the action taken by the insurer on the application. The information is made available to member companies for use in making their own underwriting decision. Underwriting philosophy and practices differ among insurers so an applicant refused insurance by one insurer does not necessarily mean refusal by another.

Factors affecting underwriting. In many respects life insurance underwriting is much simpler than property and liability underwriting. The basic underwriting factors are age, occupation and physical condition. In addition, residence, financial status and family and personal history are considered.

Age. All insurers have maximum age limits and a few have minimum limits for accepting applicants. The maximum age limits are 65 with some insurers and 70 with others. Few insurers will write policies on those over 70 years old. At this age the premium may be prohibitive and the probability of having sufficient applicants for the law of large numbers to operate is low. Where minimum age limits are set they usually are one day, one week, one month or one year. Age is important in consideration with other underwriting factors. For example, excessive weight for those under 25 is not so serious but it is given more importance beyond that age.

Occupation. The occupation of the insured is considered because some jobs present greater-than-average hazards. Those in some occupations are not eligibile for life insurance under any circumstances. With most insurers these include steeplejacks, motorcycle racers and deep-sea divers.

Physical condition. Physical condition is of major importance in life insurance underwriting. If the applicant's health is impaired a policy may be offered at a higher premium or under one of the other plans discussed later, unless the application is flatly rejected.

Minor factors. Residence, financial status and family and personal history are secondary in importance. The residence of the applicant is of no interest to the underwriter if the applicant lives in the United States. A person may live or travel anywhere in the United States including New York City without having to pay a higher premium.

The financial status of the applicant interests underwriters for two reasons. If a person seeks an unusually high amount of life insurance the indication may be either a moral hazard or a hidden physical hazard soon to end in a death claim. Even if the overindulgent applicant is healthy the insurer still will want to limit the life insurance to a reasonable amount. To issue an insurance policy is costly. An oversold buyer is apt to lapse the policy within a short time making it impossible to recoup the funds spent in selling it. Underwriters often refuse to insure those who have records of nonpayment of bills and who appear to be buying more insurance than they can afford.

A favorable family and personal history is of little effect if the underwriters have found unfavorable information among the other factors. On the other hand an unfavorable family and personal history may be cause for rejection. Underwriters weigh all factors in arriving at a composite judgment.

Treatment of extra-hazard applicants. Applicants for life insurance fall into one of two broad classes: insurable and uninsurable. The insurable group may be divided further into those insurable at standard premiums and those who must be charged premiums higher than standard. Those in the latter category do not meet the insurer's underwriting standards but are sufficiently better than the uninsurables to warrant policies under some conditions. Usually the extra-hazard applicant is issued a policy at a higher-than-standard premium with a flat additional amount charged for each $1,000 of insurance or, more often, with the standard premium increased by a given percentage to reflect the expected percentage mortality increase.

Another often-used method of handling the extra-hazard applicant is to issue a policy other than the one for which the application is made. A policy requiring a higher premium (such as limited-payment or endowment) will be issued instead of term or continuous-premium whole life. These higher-premium policies build higher reserves; hence the amount the insurer has at risk is smaller than in either the continuous-premium whole life or term policy. In some instances the insurer might issue the policy that the extra-hazard applicant applied for but for a smaller amount. In other cases an insurer will write life insurance at standard rates but refuse to write double indemnity or disability insurance. For example, one company insures professional football players at standard rates for life insurance but they must pay twice the standard rate for double indemnity and disability-income insurance riders.

Pricing procedure

Life insurance premiums are computed by using assumed mortality rates, interest and expenses. Mortality rates are assumed death rates at each age, usually expressed on per 1,000 basis. The *Commissioners 1958 Standard Ordinary Mortality Table* (1950–54), commonly known as the 1958 CSO Mortality Table, relates the probable number dying and living at each age from 0 to 100 assuming 10 million at the initial age. The basic data underlying the table are drawn from the combined mortality experience of 15 large U.S. insurers between 1950 and 1954. A section of the table is reproduced as Table 21–1 and is used here for illustrative purposes. The table considers only male lives but can be used for women by making an age adjustment of four to six years. Thus the mortality rate for women aged 40 is approximated by that listed in the table for men aged 35. Although a person's sex does affect mortality rates so do such other factors as race, place of residence, work habits, travel and health.

Insurers may use the mortality table of their choice or develop their own for computing life insurance premiums. But they are subject to minimum-reserve liabilities based on the 1958 CSO Mortality Table at interest from 4 to 4.5 percent on newly issued policies depending on the insurers home state (Chapter 22). The 1980 amendments to the National Association of Insurance Commissioners' standard valuation law (adopted in most states) require the use of the 1980 CSO mortality table by 1989 and interest rates based on monthly averages of a Moody's corporate bond index. These interest rates are variable not only by the year of policy issue but also by the duration of the interest guarantee. In 1981 they

TABLE 21–1 Commissioners 1958 Standard Ordinary Mortality Table

(1) AGE	(2) NUMBER LIVING	(3) NUMBER DYING	(4) DEATHS PER 1,000	(5) EXPECTATION OF LIFE-YEARS
0	10,000,000	70,800	7.08	68.30
1	9,929,200	17,475	1.76	67.78
2	0,911,725	15,066	1.52	66.90
3	9,896,659	14,449	1.46	66.00
4	9,882,210	13,835	1.40	65.10
5	9,868,375	13,322	1.35	64.19
6	9,855,053	12,812	1.30	63.27
7	9,842,241	12,401	1.26	62.35
8	9,829,840	12,091	1.23	61.43
9	9,817,749	11,879	1.21	60.51
10	9,805,870	11,865	1.21	59.58
11	9,794,005	12,047	1.23	58.65
12	9,781,958	12,325	1.26	57.72
13	9,769,633	12,896	1.32	56.80
14	9,756,737	13,562	1.39	55.87
15	9,743,175	14,225	1.46	54.95
16	9,728,950	14,983	1.54	54.03
17	9,713,967	15,737	1.62	53.11
18	9,698,230	16,390	1.69	52.19
19	9,681,840	16,846	1.74	51.28
20	9,664,994	17,300	1.79	50.37
21	9,647,694	17,655	1.83	49.46
22	9,630,039	17,912	1.86	48.55
23	9,612,127	18,167	1.89	47.64
24	9,593,960	18,324	1.91	46.73
35	9,373,807	23,528	2.51	36.69
36	9,350,279	24,685	2.64	35.78
37	9,325,594	26,112	2.80	34.88
38	9,299,482	27,991	3.01	33.97
39	9,271,491	30,132	3.25	33.07
95	97,165	34,128	351.24	1.80
96	63,037	25,250	400.56	1.51
97	37,787	18,456	488.42	1.18
98	19,331	12,916	668.15	.83
99	6,415	6,415	1,000.00	.50

ranged from 6 percent for durations of 10 years or less to 5 percent for durations of more than 20 years. In 1982 the comparable range was from 6.75 percent to 5.50 percent. (See Chapter 22 for some further discussion.)

The reproduced table presents mortality rates as a function of age only. Mortality rates are also a function of occupation and physical condition. Most jobs do not require special attention in ratemaking but a few hazardous ones sufficiently influence the death rate to justify an extra premium. For example, bartenders and jockeys (other than the disc variety) are charged higher premiums. Most insurers will underwrite applicants in some extra-hazardous occupations and a few write insurance for nearly any occupation if the applicant pays a premium high enough to reflect the expected loss. In addition, some applicants

TABLE 21–2 Present Value of 1 at Compound Interest

YEAR	*4%*	*YEAR*	*4%*	*YEAR*	*4%*
1	.9615	13	.6006	25	.3751
2	.9246	14	.5775	26	.3607
3	.8890	15	.5553	27	.3468
4	.8548	16	.5339	28	.3335
5	.8219	17	.5134	29	.3207
6	.7903	18	.4936	30	.3083
7	.7599	19	.4746		
8	.7307	20	.4564		
9	.7026	21	.4388	35	.2534
10	.6756	22	.4220		
11	.6496	23	.4057		
12	.6246	24	.3901	40	.2083

are charged extra because of an adverse physical condition. Insurer practices differ regarding whether the applicant will be insured and, if so, whether the premium will be standard, an amount in excess of standard or an amount below standard. Some insurers offer preferred-risk policies to applicants with higher-than-average probabilities for a longer life. These applicants are given discounts from 3 to 5 percent if they are slim and do not smoke. A person who gives up smoking and controls eating habits probably will be concerned about health and therefore acts accordingly. Discounts are also given to physical fitness freaks.

Each insurer computes its own premiums. The actuary, a life insurance mathematician, assumes an interest rate in premium calculations. As the policy is a long-term contract, the assumed interest rate has an important effect on the premium. Today most insurers use rates from 2.5 to more than 4 percent. The following example assumes 4 percent. Table 21–2 lists the present value of 1 at 4 percent compounded for 1 through 40 years. This table shows how much must be invested *now* at 4 percent to accumulate to 1 at the specified time. The present value of 1 (dollars, apples or units of any kind) due at the end of 40 years is 0.2083. Thus if $0.2083 were invested today at 4 percent compounded annually it would amount to $1 in 40 years.

Table 21–3 shows the calculation of the net single premium for a $1,000 whole life policy for a man age 98. Of course no one buys a whole life policy at 98 but a late age is best to use for a simple illustration. According to the mortality figures in Table 21–1, 12,916 of the 19,331 people alive on their 98th birthdays will die within that year; of the 6,415 who reach 99 none will reach age 100. Of course a few may reach 100 but this accomplishment(?) does not matter to oblivious actuaries. The policy's face amount is paid to those reaching

TABLE 21–3 Net Single Premium, $1,000 of Life Insurance at Age 98*

AGE	*NUMBER DYING*	*AMOUNT OF INSURANCE*	*TOTAL CLAIMS*	*PRESENT VALUE OF 1 AT 4%*	*PRESENT VALUE OF CLAIMS*
98	12,916	$1,000	$12,916,000	0.9615	$12,418,734
99	6,415	1,000	6,415,000	0.9246	5,931,309
					$18,350,043

* Note number living at age 98 = 19,331. $18,350,043 ÷ 19,331 = $950, the net single premium.

age 100 as though they had cooperated with the actuaries by dying in accordance with the mortality rate of 1.00 (1,000 deaths out of 1,000 alive) shown for age 99 (Table 21–1).

If 12,916 people will die at age 98 the insurer must have on hand $12,-916,000 to pay each beneficiary $1,000 by the end of the year. The insurer does not wait until the end of the year to pay claims; they are paid when incurred. (Many insurers pay interest on the proceeds from time of death until the settlement is made.) The assumption that claims are paid at the end of the year is to simplify the calculation.

Because premiums are paid at the beginning of the year the insurer has the funds for the full year. If these funds are invested at the assumed 4 percent, a deposit of about $0.9615 is required to equal $1 in one year. Thus $12,916,000 multiplied by the present-value factor of 0.9615 (Table 21–2) is needed to provide $12,916,000 at the end of the year. This product of $12,418,734 is the amount necessary to assure enough funds to meet estimated claims for the year. At this point the assumed interest rate makes a significant difference in computing premiums. If the rate were 10 percent only $0.9091 would be needed at the beginning of the next year to equal $1 at the end of the year, and only $11,741,936 would be needed by the insurer to pay its claims for that year.

For the second year $6,451,000 will be paid in claims. Again the insurer has the funds, in this case for two years. About $0.9246 at 4 percent interest for two years will accumulate to $1. Therefore only $5,931,309 ($6,415,000 × .9246) will be needed now to pay claims of $6,415,000 two years hence.

The total present value of future claims is the amount the insurer must have on hand today to guarantee $1,000 to the beneficiaries of each of the 19,331 people now aged 98, assumed to buy $1,000 whole life policies. As these payments are undertaken on behalf of 19,331 insured persons the cost is divided among them. By dividing the total cost of $18,350,043 ($12,418,734 + $5,931,309) by 19,331, the net single premium to be charged each insured is computed to be about $950. (If the interest assumption is 10 percent the net single premium will be $882. At younger ages the difference in premiums will be far greater, much lower at 10 percent than at 4 percent.)

The premium is very close to the policy face amount because in this example each insured is very close to death. This premium is the amount that will be sufficient to pay the face amount upon death without allowing for the insurer's expenses. Expenses are provided by adding a loading charge to the net premium. Various loading methods are used for different types of policies.

Thus far the assumption has been that a single-premium policy is written. But most premiums are paid on an installment basis, usually annually for the life of the insured. Thus rather than pay $950 for $1,000 of insurance, the 98-year-old would prefer to pay two annual installments. Each installment would exceed $950 divided by two, i.e., it would be more than $475 a year. Therefore the single premium must be divided by a factor less than two. How is this factor determined? The premium is paid at the beginning of each year if the insured is alive. This type of arrangement resembles a life annuity due paid by the *policyowner to the insurer* rather than by the insurer to the annuitant. The annual premium is determined by dividing the single premium by the present value of a life annuity due of one per year (yes *one,* not $1 or one pizza). Two steps are necessary: (1) compute the present value of an annuity due of one per annum based on the insured's age and applicable interest and mortality rates and (2) divide the net single premium by this figure.

Table 21–4 shows how the present value of a life annuity due of one per annum is computed at age 98, using the 1958 CSO Mortality Table and 4 percent interest. Because the first payments of 19,331 are made immediately their present value is their full amount, i.e., not discounted. The 6,415 payments are discounted for one year because they are made at the beginning of the second year. They amount to 6,168. The total present value is 25,499, or 19,331 plus 6,168. By dividing this figure by the number living at the beginning of the period—19,331—the present value of an annuity due of one is found to be about 1.32. Thus the level annual premium is about $720, or $950 ÷ 1.32. (If 10 percent interest is assumed the present value of the life annuity due would be 1.27 and the net level annual premium would be the net single premium ($882) divided by 1.27 or about $694.)

TABLE 21–4 Present Value of a Life Annuity Due of One Per Year Using 1958 CSO at 4 Percent*

AGE	*NUMBER LIVING*	*PROMISED PAYMENTS OF ONE PER YEAR*	*PRESENT VALUE OF ONE AT 4%*	*PRESENT VALUE OF PROMISED PAYMENTS OF ONE PER YEAR*
98	19,331	19,331	1.0000	19,331
99	6,415	6,415	.9615	6,168
				25,499*

* 25,499 ÷ 19,331 = 1.32

The annual level premium is greater than the net single premium divided by the maximum number of years over which the premiums are to be paid (two in this over-simplified example) because (1) most insureds die before reaching 99 and can no longer pay the premium and (2) the insurer earns less interest because the full premium is not collected in advance.

The policy size is a factor in rating life insurance. The rate per $1,000 generally is lower for large amounts than small amounts. In calculating life insurance rates electronic computers are used with the necessary assumptions plugged in to perform the computations in the program.

SUMMARY

1. Underwriting is the process of accepting or rejecting applications for insurance. If the application is accepted underwriting is further concerned with the terms under which the insurance is written.
2. Underwriting in insurance is patent. The issue is whether the insurer or the applicant will do the selecting. If the insurer does not select it will be selected against. Therefore, the insurer must select to avoid adverse selection.
3. The primary purpose of underwriting by an insurer is to obtain a profitable distribution of policyowners.
4. The bulk of underwriting decisions is made by full-time underwriters in home and branch offices. Professional people other than insurance technicians aid in the underwriting process. They include doctors, engineers, auditors, lawyers and so on. Also useful are investigating firms in evaluating moral hazard. Furthermore, agents, especially in property and liability insurance, perform important functions in the underwriting process.

5. Underwriting includes both preselection and postselection of insureds. Preselection involves gathering relevant information concerning the exposure and arriving at a decision whether to select the applicant at superior, standard or substandard rates or to reject the applicant entirely. Postselection (not available in life insurance) involves monitoring the exposure to determine whether to continue the policy in force at the renewal date or in serious situations whether to cancel the policy.
6. The maximum amount of insurance an insurer will write on one exposure is called a line limit. Line limits are simple in life insurance because all losses are total (so we are told). Most losses in property insurance are partial, complicating the determination of line limits.
7. When insurers accept applications for insurance beyond their line limits they can shift the excess exposures to other insurers through a process called reinsurance.
8. Reinsurance may be classified as treaty, facultative or a combination of the two.
9. Reinsurance may be further subdivided into proportional (quota share or surplus share) or nonproportional (excess loss or stop loss).
10. Reinsurance in life insurance may be written either on a yearly renewable term or a coinsurance plan.
11. Underwriters are faced with special problems: moral hazard, conflicts between the underwriting and production departments and governmental pressures on underwriting.
12. The price paid for insurance, called the premium, is the rate *per unit of coverage* multiplied by the *number of units of insurance* bought.
13. Rates are required by law to be adequate, not unfairly discriminatory and not excessive. They should also be economically feasible and encourage loss control.
14. Ratemaking may be divided into three broad categories: judgment rating, manual rating and merit rating. Merit rating is further classified into schedule rating, experience rating and retrospective rating.
15. Commercial properties are individually rated according to a comprehensive rating schedule. Two widely used rating schedules are the universal mercantile system and the "Dean's analytical" system.
16. For fire insurance the factors that affect the underwriting and rating decision for a building include the type of roof, number of dwelling units, the building's age, neighborhood, value, size, construction, occupancy, exposure and degree of protection.
17. Fire insurance rating offers examples of both manual and schedule rating.
18. Life insurance underwriting information is gathered from many sources: the application, the agent's certificate, the inspection report and the medical information bureau. Factors affecting life insurance underwriting primarily are the insured's age, occupation and physical condition.
19. Life insurance rates are computed using interest and mortality assumptions and then adding an allowance for expenses. The mortality and interest as-

sumptions are conservative (mortality is overstated and interest is understated) in order to meet unrealistic reserve requirements imposed by state law (discussed in Chapters 22 and 23).

REVIEW QUESTIONS

1. Distinguish between preselection and postselection.
2. Explain why life insurers do not engage in postselection. Are there any other types of insurance in which postselection is not found? Explain.
3. Name two types of noninsurance professionals who aid in the underwriting process. Explain their functions.
4. What is adverse about adverse selection? Could adverse selection be an advantage to the insured?
5. Explain the statement, "Reinsurance is the insurance of insurance." In your answer point out why insurance might have to be insured.
6. Two types of excess loss reinsurance are per risk reinsurance and catastrophic risks reinsurance. Distinguish between the two.
7. Distinguish between the yearly renewable term and coinsurance plans used in life reinsurance contracts. What factors would encourage a life insurance company to seek (*a*) a yearly renewable term plan or (*b*) a coinsurance plan?
8. Does the term line limits have anything to do with fishing? If so, can an analogy be made between fishing line limits and insurance line limits? Explain. If not, then what is an insurance line limit?
9. The underwriting department of an insurance company is frequently faced with conflicts. Identify and explain two of these areas of conflict and sing a song about one.
10. Explain the following statement, "Although judgment rating is one of three major ratemaking systems, no rating system can be developed and applied without the use of some judgment."
11. With the development of machines, manual rating has become less important. Do you agree or disagree with this statement?
12. Assuming 4 percent interest and the mortality figures reproduced in the text: (*a*) compute the net level annual premium for a five-year term policy issued at age 35 and (*b*) compute the net level annual premium for a five-year endowment policy issued at age 35. Will these be the premiums charged by the insurer? Explain.
13. Identify and explain a set of common factors that affect both underwriting and rating in fire insurance. In life insurance.
14. Suppose the applicant for fire insurance is a well-known arsonist. What premium would you charge to insure her against a loss of her $100,000 house by fire? Are you sure?
15. Consider merit rating. Could a *one single merit rate* (or premium) be prospective, retrospective *and* also involve schedule rating? Explain.

CHAPTER

22 Financial structure

John Thoeming/Richard D. Irwin

CHAPTER OBJECTIVES

1. **To distinguish insurance accounting from general business accounting practices.**
2. **To explain the types of reserve liabilities of property and liability insurers and their importance.**
3. **To examine the nature of the life insurance legal reserve.**
4. **To identify the sources of surplus for property-liability insurers and for life insurers.**
5. **To define the sources of dividends for life insurance participating policies and point out how funds available for dividends are apportional among policyowners.**

Knowledge of insurer finances is particularly important to large insureds because it helps them appraise the insurer's potential ability to pay claims promptly and fairly, to maintain a long-lasting stable relationship in the market and to negotiate equitable arrangements for experience-rating plans. This latter reason for knowing insurance finance applies to insureds large enough to qualify for these plans. How insurers establish values for their loss reserves is of special interest to these insureds because it helps them determine whether their own losses and thus their retrospective premiums are excessive. During periods of high interest rates and cash flow problems insureds want their experience-rate credits as soon as they are earned. Thus insureds find it convenient in dealing with insurers to have a basic working knowledge of their financial structure. The subject is not simple but careful study of it should be rewarding not only to insurance buyers but also to those who invest in insurance company stocks.

This discussion can be simplified by first looking at skeleton balance sheets of a property-liability insurer and a life insurer. A balance sheet is a statement of assets, liabilities and net worth. Assets are what the company owns; liabilities are what it owes and net worth is the difference between the two. Figures 22–1 and 22–2 show that an insurer's principal liabilities are its reserves. For property and liability insurers reserves represent obligations to policyowners for premiums received but not yet earned and for losses incurred but not yet paid. For life insurers the reserve is an actuarial, though not accurate, measure of the insurer's net obligation to its policyowners. When assets or liabilities are understated or overstated the effect is to understate or overstate net worth. The methods used by insurers for valuing assets and liabilities (discussed later) cause their reported net worth to differ from their true net worth.

ASSETS OF INSURERS

Insurers' assets are either admitted or nonadmitted. **Admitted assets** include most financial investments, the company-owned office buildings and electronic data processing equipment. **Nonadmitted assets** include such items as company supplies, furniture, office equipment, autos, advances to agents, unsecured loans and prepaid expenses. Only admitted assets are considered when measuring insurer solvency because nonadmitted assets are not easily converted into cash without a loss.

FIGURE 22–1

The Fisherman's Multiline Insurance Company
Balance Sheet
December 31, 1983

Assets	
Bonds	$29,920,000
Common stocks	13,735,000
Preferred stocks	1,880,000
Real estate	460,000
Cash	570,000
Premium balances receivable	4,270,000
Investment income accrued	110,000
Other assets	3,980,000
Total assets	$54,925,000
Liabilities	
Unearned premium reserve	$10,740,000
Loss and loss expense reserve	24,150,000
Reserve for taxes and expenses	1,280,000
Reserve for all other liabilities	3,915,000
Total liabilities	$40,085,000
Net Worth	
Capital	$ 1,265,000
Surplus (including retained earnings)	13,575,000
Total net worth	14,840,000
Total liabilities and net worth	$54,925,000

FIGURE 22–2

The Same Old Line Life Insurance Company
Balance Sheet
December 31, 1983

Assets	
Cash	$ 225,000
Bonds	58,965,000
Stocks	7,125,000
Real estate	3,280,000
Mortgage loans	70,860,000
Policy loans	11,095,000
Premiums receivable	3,795,000
Investment income accrued	1,015,000
Other assets	221,000
Total assets	$156,581,000
Liabilities	
Net policy reserves	$118,980,000
Policy claims	1,005,000
Dividend accumulations	10,987,000
Reserve for dividends	2,190,000
Reserve for taxes and expenses	795,000
Securities valuation reserve	1,345,000
Premium deposit funds	1,160,000
Other liabilities	964,000
Total liabilities	$137,426,000
Net Worth	
Capital	2,000,000
Surplus (including paid-in surplus and unassigned surplus)	17,155,000
Total net worth	19,155,000
Total liabilities and net worth	$156,581,000

Valuation of Assets

Some admitted assets are more easily valued than others. *Cash and bank deposits* are valued at face amount. *Real estate* may be valued at book value (cost less depreciation) or market value (estimated value based on a fair appraisal). *Mortgage loans* are valued at the amount of the outstanding debt. If not properly secured these loans must be valued at less than the loan amount. Bonds amply secured by earning power and not in default are valued at amortized value. Bonds in default or inadequately secured according to standards of the National Association of Insurance Commissioners are valued at market. Stocks are valued at their market prices. Where no market prices are available the NAIC uses estimated values, which insurance commissioners generally accept.

Regulation of Insurers' Investments

When trouble besets life insurers it is usually a result of investment problems. Property-liability insurers are in financial trouble more often from underwriting than from investment problems. To protect policyowners, discourage concentration of economic power and encourage the commitment of funds for socially desirable purposes, state laws regulate the investment of insurer assets. Laws vary widely among states although the NAIC seeks to reduce the variations. The laws are concerned with both qualitative and quantitative restrictions and deal with types of investment media, portfolio distribution among approved media, amount of security required for authorized media to qualify, percentage of a firm's outstanding common stock that may be held, percentage of admitted assets that may be invested in a single corporation, percentage of admitted assets in a single investment issue of a corporation and the source of investment funds.

Property-liability insurers

Some states require property-liability insurers to invest assets equal to their minimum required capital and surplus in the investments available to life insurers (discussed later). They may invest assets exceeding their required capital and surplus in stocks of solvent corporations. Other states are more realistic and apply the stricter standards to assets equal to the amount of the required unearned premium and loss reserves rather than the minimum required capital and surplus. The following regulations illustrate the restrictions placed on property-liability insurers:

1. Assets representing the required minimum net worth are limited to U.S. and state bonds, mortgage loans and, in some cases, railroad and public-utility bonds.
2. Assets representing required reserves are limited to the foregoing investments plus bonds and preferred stocks of corporations that satisfy requirements for solvency and earning power.
3. Assets that exceed the amount representing the required minimum capital and surplus can be invested in common stocks. The exact restrictions vary among states. Various other limitations may be prescribed as to the quality of securities and percentage of assets that may be invested in foreign government bonds, real estate and the securities of a single private corporation. While insurance commissioners have no power to dictate the investments an insurer must make they can disapprove investments they consider not in the best interests of insureds.

Life insurers

Because they generally deal primarily in long-term, fixed dollar contracts with premiums and reserves computed on the basis of specific interest rates, life insurers are largely restricted to investing in high-grade bonds and mortgage loans. The laws of many states limit the amount that can be invested in preferred stocks, common stocks and real estate. Life insurers can establish separate accounts subject to less stringent limitations than those for general funds. These accounts allow life insurers to compete with other financial institutions for equity-funded retirement plans. Some states authorize the investment of life insurance assets in multiple-housing projects and commercial rental properties under strict limitations as to proportion of total assets so invested. Life insurers' real estate holdings include apartment complexes, multipurpose skyscrapers, neighborhood shopping centers and downtown centers. Life insurers purchase commercial properties and lease them back to their former owners or developers. These transactions provide the insurer a profitable outlet for large volumes of funds. They also relieve the original owners of the necessity of tying up capital in fixed assets, releasing more funds for working capital.

Life insurers may invest in real estate to the extent necessary for transacting business—primarily home-office and regional office buildings. Real estate acquired by foreclosure must be disposed of within a limited time, usually five years. The commissioner can extend this period if the insurer would suffer from a forced sale. Mortgage loan investments usually are limited to first mortgages and restricted to a stated percentage of the property's appraised value. A liberalizing provision in many state laws permits life insurers to commit a small percentage of admitted assets to unregulated investments.

RESERVES OF PROPERTY AND LIABILITY INSURERS

Property and liability insurers maintain three types of reserves: unearned premium, loss and voluntary reserves.

Unearned Premium Reserve

When an insurer prepares its financial statements it is required to show the amount of unearned premiums on all policies outstanding. This amount is called the unearned premium reserve (UPR). For example, assume a one-year fire insurance policy is written on the first day of the month for an annual premium of $120,000. The premium earned on this policy is $10,000 a month. The unearned premium would be $110,000 at the end of the first month, $60,000 after six months and zero at the end of the year.

If an insurer's monthly premium is stable, its UPR will remain constant. A property insurer writing exactly $1 million of premiums each month ($12 million per year) will always have an UPR of $6 million. The reason is that only one half the annual premiums written will be earned at any one time. If the premium volume is declining, the reserve will be reduced; if it is expanding, the reserve will be increased. This latter point is important because it has an effect on the insurer's ability to continue to expand its premium volume. Therefore it is closely related to the subject of insurer capacity—mentioned again later.

Overconservatism in the reserve

The UPR is based on the gross premium, which is the amount needed to cover losses and expenses and to provide a profit. Expenses for writing a policy are agents' commissions and home-office expenses. Most of the expenses are paid shortly after the policy is issued. However, the rules for computing the reserve assume that expenses are spread evenly over the policy term. Including paid expenses in the UPR causes the reserve to be overstated and thus overly conservative. Overstating the UPR liability causes an understated surplus.

Why then is overconservatism required in the UPR? The answer is that for some reason state regulatory authorities require insurers to show a liability for all amounts they might be called upon to pay. When an insurer cancels a policy it must refund the unearned gross premium to the policyholder. Thus state authorities reason that insurers must use the gross premium to report the reserve liability. Given this explanation the overconservatism in the UPR is neither necessary nor desirable. It is not necessary for two reasons.

First, if the insurer should withdraw from the business the cost of reinsuring (placing its business with another insurer) should be less than the amount charged its policyowners. Suppose an insurer with a $1 million UPR terminates its business. How much must it pay another insurer to assume its policy obligations? If the other insurer acquired $1 million in gross premiums through its own agents it would have to pay commissions and other expenses associated with writing policies. So the withdrawing insurer would have to pay less than $1 million, thus retaining a portion of its UPR. *Second,* even if an insurer should have to refund policyowners their pro rata share of premiums the amount needed would be less than the full unearned premium reserve. When a refund is made, the agent refunds the commission. Thus the UPR is higher than required to meet all policyowners' refund claims. Because an insurer's ability to write insurance depends on its surplus an understated surplus can contribute to a capacity problem. A capacity problem exists when insurers are unable or unwilling to write the amount of insurance the public needs. Overconservatism in the UPR is undesirable because of its negative effect on insurer surplus.

Loss Reserves

The loss reserve is the insurer's estimated liability for unpaid claims and settlement expenses. This liability includes (1) claims reported and adjusted but not yet paid, (2) claims reported but not yet adjusted and (3) claims incurred but not yet reported.

The size of the loss reserve relative to total liabilities varies among coverages. Some coverages under which periodic payments are made (workers' compensation, disability income and medical care) require the use of discount factors to reflect the time value of money and mortality factors to reflect the probability that the claimant will not live to collect maximum benefits. Estimates of claims from pending litigation often are needed for developing loss reserves for liability and workers' compensation insurance. Furthermore, some types of insurance (health, workers' compensation, liability, and crime) use estimates of claims incurred during the policy period but not reported until after the policy expires. Fire losses are less complicated. They include (1) those few losses incurred too recently for the claim report to be received and (2) claims in process of settlement.

Calculating the loss reserve

A variety of methods are available to calculate the loss reserves. In general these methods rely on the individual insurer's loss experience.

If many claims approximately the same size are outstanding, the **average value method** can be used. Under this method the loss reserve is approximated by multiplying the number of claims outstanding by their average value.

Another method is the **individual case approach** where the claims department estimates each loss. Total estimated claims are then multiplied by a correction factor to adjust for unreported claims and to correct any biases discovered in past reserving practices. The advantages of the average value over the individual case method are greater efficiency (especially when many claims are involved) and less dependence on individual judgment. State laws require insurers to use a formula called the **loss ratio method** to determine their minimum loss reserve for auto and other liability insurance, medical malpractice insurance and workers' compensation. Under this method the minimum loss reserve for each of the three most recent accident years is based on the expected loss ratio: 60 percent for auto and other liability and medical malpractice and 65 percent for workers' compensation. (Remember the loss ratio is the ratio of incurred losses to earned premiums.) However, if more than two of the five years before the current three-year period have a premium volume of at least $1 million the expected loss ratio is the lowest ratio reported in this five-year period. In no case can the expected loss ratio be less than 60 percent (65 percent for workers' compensation) and no more than 75 percent. In computing the minimum loss reserve the insurer subtracts losses and loss adjustment expenses paid from the figure produced by applying the loss ratio formula. Insurers may use a loss reserve rate higher than that required. However, the minimum loss reserve rates apply whenever the insurer's loss reserve is below the loss and loss adjustment expenses allowed by the insurer.

Still another method is the **payment development method.** Under this method the amount of the loss reserve is based on historical rates of loss payments. This method considers the value of losses paid to date in light of historical loss payment rates. Then necessary adjustments are made to reflect current experience.

Sufficiency of the loss reserve

The loss reserve, unlike the UPR, is not automatically overly conservative. However, an insurer may establish an overly conservative loss reserve. Insurers cannot set loss reserves so low that they arouse state insurance regulators concerned with insurers' solvency. On the other hand insurers cannot set loss reserves so high that the IRS will consider them excessive. Excessive loss reserves reduce the insurer's reported profits and thus reduce its tax liability. Furthermore, the excessive loss reserves and the lower profits that accompany them help to provide the insurer with convincing documentation when it seeks a rate increase in those states requiring the commissioner's expressed or tacit approval. A disadvantage of excessive reserves for stock insurers is that understated profits from overstated reserves disappoints shareholders and depresses the insurer's stock price. *In summary,* setting the loss reserve calls for balancing many interests and objectives.

Voluntary Reserves

The unearned premium and the loss reserve are required by law. Insurers also set up many reserves commonly found in other businesses, such as reserves for taxes and dividends. Like property insurers, life insurers also have mandatory and voluntary reserves. Unlike property insurers, life insurers are required to maintain only one type of mandatory reserve liability: the policy reserve.

Reserves of Life Insurers: The Policy Reserve

The life insurance policy reserve measures the amount that together with future **net valuation premiums** and assumed interest will produce the exact amount needed to pay policy obligations as they become due if the mortality rate is as assumed. The net valuation premium and the gross premium are not the same for the following reasons: (1) the net valuation premium does not include the expense allowance, (2) the mortality and interest assumptions for computing the policy reserves are governed by law and may not be the same used for premium rates and (3) reserve standards are permitted to be modified by law and thus allow the valuation premium to reflect the modifications as explained later.

The Nature of the Policy Reserve

Although the policy reserve is an aggregate figure it is helpful to think of it as divided among blocks of business and apportioned to each policy in the block. A **block of business** is defined as a number of identical policies (i.e., same face amount, type of policy, year of issue, subject's age at issue and subject's risk classification). The total reserve is the sum of policy reserves for each block of business. The policy reserve arises because most life insurance policies require annual premiums that exceed the amount needed to pay claims during all but the later policy years. Consider the following example.

Based on the 1958 CSO Mortality Table and a 3.5 percent interest assumption, the net level annual premium for a $1,000 continuous-premium whole life policy issued at age 35 is $15.03. However, the projected mortality cost for the first year is only $2.51. The projected mortality cost rises each year but remains below the net level premium ($15.03) until after age 56. At age 57 the projected mortality cost reaches $15.54 and continues to increase, reaching $1,000 at age 99. The net annual premiums collected each year plus accumulated interest at the assumed rate (3.5 percent) build the fund from which death benefits are paid. The amount of this fund is shown as a liability to policyowners and is called the policy reserve. The size of this reserve increases each year until the mortality cost for the block of business exceeds the sum of the premium and investment income allocated to the block. At that point the fund will decrease, reaching zero when final projected claims are paid.

For another example assume that the number insured is equal to the 9,373,807 living at age 35 shown on the CSO Mortality Table (reproduced in Chapter 21). If these people each pay $15.03 for a $1,000 continuous-premium whole life policy the insurer will collect $140,888,319. Invested at the assumed 3.5 percent the fund grows in one year to $145,819,410. According to the mortality table 23,528 insureds will die before reaching age 36. Each death costs the insurer $1,000 making a total of $23,528,000 for all deaths. Upon paying these claims the fund is reduced to $122,291,410. The insurer must show this amount as a liability to its 9,350,279 policyowners. Rounded to even cents the reserve is $13.08 for each $1,000 of coverage. Note the two reserve figures: $122,291,410 and $13.08. The first is the reserve for the block of business; the second is the reserve for each policyowner in the block.

Over the life of a policy these reserves behave differently. The reserve for the block of business increases each year as long as the amount by which the net level annual premiums collected plus the assumed interest earned exceed the projected amount needed to pay claims. In this particular case that point is between the 30th and 40th policy year. The reserve for the block increases to $634,515,846 at the end of the fifth policy year, to $1,309,495,065 at the end of the 10th policy year and $2,273,575,920 at the end of the 30th policy year. At the end of the 40th policy year it is $2,520,927,953 having passed its peak a few years earlier. It drops to $865,533,152 at the end of the 50th policy year and to $5,997,778 at the end of the 63rd policy year. While the insurer's reserve shown on the balance sheet is the combined figure for all blocks of business, as it should be, many people view the reserve as allocated to each policy. When the block reserve starts to decline the reserve allocated to an individual policy continues to increase. The reason is that the policy reserve is divided each year among the number of surviving insureds. Because the yearly decline in the number of insureds is larger than the decline in the block reserve, the reserve per policy (block reserve divided by the number of insureds) increases. For example, the individual reserve at the end of the fifth policy year is $68.90. At the end of the 10th policy year it is $145.49. It continues to increase, reaching $497.16 at the end of the 30th year, $658.74 at the end of the 40th policy year, $786.82 at the end of the 50th policy year and $934.96 at the end of the 63rd year, two years before the policy matures.

Reserve computation

To compute the policy reserve the unrealistic assumption is made that premiums are paid at the beginning of the policy year and death claims are paid at the end of the policy year. Also, the insurer's actuary makes mortality and interest assumptions. The reserve may be calculated retrospectively or prospectively. Figured under the **retrospective method,** the reserve is based on what is assumed to have happened since the policy was issued even though the insurer knows the amounts of claims incurred and interest earned. Deviations of realized experience from assumed experience either increase or decrease the surplus account. The **prospective method** looks at the present value of claims assumed to be paid over the life of the policy subtracted from the present value of the net valuation premiums assumed to be collected. The difference is the policy reserve.

The retrospective method for computing the policy reserve accumulates the assumed net valuation premiums for the year at the assumed interest rate and then subtracts the assumed mortality claims for the year. The remainder is the reserve for the first year. For the second year the net valuation premium is added to the first year reserve and that sum is accumulated for the year at the assumed rate of interest. The assumed claims for that year are subtracted to compute the second year reserve. This process is continued each year to compute the reserve retrospectively for the ensuing year. Because the assumptions are the same the reserve will be the same under both methods. It makes no difference whether the reserve is computed looking backward or forward. The following illustrations should clarify the difference between the two methods.

Assume that an insurer issues $1,000 continuous-premium whole life policies to 9,373,807 people aged 35. What is the third year policy reserve? The calculation of the reserve computed retrospectively is illustrated in Table 22–1.

TABLE 22–1
Third-Year Reserve, Retrospectively Calculated, for a $1,000 Continuous Premium Whole Life Policy Issued at Age 35 to 9,373,807 Insureds (1958 CSO, 3.5 Percent, Full Reserve); Net Valuation Premium $15.034902*

(1) YEAR	(2) NUMBER LIVING	(3) NET VALUATION PREMIUM	(4) TOTAL FUND	(5) TOTAL FUND ACCUMULATED AT 3.5 PERCENT FOR ONE YEAR	(6) DEATH CLAIMS ASSUMED TO HAVE BEEN PAID FOR THE YEAR	(7) TOTAL RESERVE FOR YEAR	(8) RESERVE PER POLICY
1....	9,373,807	$15.034902	$140,934,270	$145,866,969	$23,528,000	$122,338,969	$13.05
2....	9,350,279	15.034902	262,919,497	272,121,680	24,685,000	247,436,680	26.46
3....	9,325,594	15.034902	387,646,072	401,213,684	26,112,000	375,101,684	40.22

* Differences in this table and Table 22–2 are a result of rounding the figures. For example, column 7 in this table should be the same as column 4 in Table 22–2.

TABLE 22–2 Third-Year Reserve, Prospectively Calculated, for a $1,000 Continuous Premium Whole Life Policy Issued at Age 35 to 9,373,807 Insureds (1958 CSO, 3.5 Percent, Full Reserve); Net Valuation Premium $15.034902

(1) NUMBER SURVIVING THIRD YEAR	(2) PRESENT VALUE OF FUTURE CLAIMS	(3) PRESENT VALUE OF FUTURE NET VALUATION PREMIUMS	(4) TOTAL RESERVE (col. 2 − col. 3)	(5) RESERVE PER POLICY
9,325,594	$3,121,745,504	$2,746,643,457	$375,102,047	$40.22

Table 22–2 illustrates the same reserve calculated prospectively. The net valuation premium based on the 1958 CSO mortality table with 3.5 percent interest is $15.034902. The reserve for the third year is $375,101,684 for the block of business and $40.22 per $1,000 as shown in columns 7 and 8 in Table 22–1. The total fund (column 4) is the reserve at the end of the previous year (column 7) plus the product of the net valuation premium ($15.034902) times the number living at the beginning of the year (column 2). The fund is accumulated at 3.5 percent (column 5) and assumed death claims (column 6) are subtracted to arrive at the total reserve (column 7). The reserve per policy (column 8) is the total reserve divided by the number surviving the year (column 7 ÷ column 2).

The reserve calculated for the block of policies in Table 22–2 is $375,102,047 (column 4), the present value of future claims (column 2) less the present value of future net valuation premiums (column 3). The $40.22 reserve per $1,000 (column 5) is the total reserve (column 4) divided by the number surviving the year (column 1).

The prospective method is the most common and the one described in state statutes regulating reserve liabilities. However, when benefits are expressed in terms of the market value of an investment portfolio (variable annuities, for example) the present value of future claims is unknown. In these cases the retrospective method is appropriate.

Modified reserve standards

Reserve methods to provide relief for insurers whose surpluses are insufficient to cover the full first year reserve are available. Life insurers incur most of their expenses during the initial policy year. Once expenses are paid the remaining first year's premium will not be enough to cover the policy reserve. Because the first-year liability for a policy exceeds assets retained from the first-year premium, surplus is decreased. Younger and small insurers using a full (normal net valuation premium) reserve system will soon find themselves sold out of business if they grow rapidly.

One method, the **full preliminary term reserve plan,** requires no policy reserve for the first policy year. For every year thereafter the reserve is the full reserve for a policy issued one year later for a premium payment period one year shorter. For example, a continuous-premium whole life policy issued at age 35 is treated as a one-year term policy issued at age 35 plus a continuous-premium whole life policy issued at age 36. Because the reserve is zero at the expiration of a term contract no first-year reserve liability is required for this policy. At the end of the second year, the reserve is the full (normal) reserve for a one-year-old continuous-premium whole life contract issued at age 36.

This method allows the insurer to use the full first-year premium for initial expenses and first-year claims without depleting its surplus account.

Other but more complicated minimum reserve standards are required for high premium-types of policies (e.g., 20-payment life and endowment insurance) because for these policies insurers are given too much relief from first-year reserve requirements.

The **Commissioners Reserve Valuation Method (CRVM)** is the minimum legal reserve standard permitted. CRVM is a variation of the full preliminary term reserve method. Under the CRVM, policies are divided into two classes. Class 1 policies are those where the level valuation premium is equal to or less than that charged for a 20-pay life policy issued at the same age for a like amount. The reserve on all class 1 policies may be valued on a preliminary term basis. Thus no first-year policy reserve is necessary. The effect is to release additional funds that can be used for expenses.

Class 2 policies are those where the level valuation premium exceeds that for a 20-pay whole life policy issued at the same age for the same amount. For class 2 policies the full preliminary term method would defer more reserves then necessary to cover first-year expenses. Therefore the CRVM requires a modification of the preliminary reserve method for class 2 policies. The CRVM involves an understanding of two premium concepts: the initial premium and the renewal premium. An illustration is helpful to define these premium concepts. For example, for a 20-pay whole life policy issued at age 25 the initial premium is the valuation premium for a one-year term policy issued at age 25. The renewal premium is the valuation premium for a 19-pay policy issued at age 26. The modification requires that the difference between the initial and renewal premiums for class 2 policies equal the difference between the initial and renewal premiums for a 20-pay life policy issued to a person of the same age for the same face amount.

To compute the renewal premium (1) take the difference between the renewal premium and the initial premium for a 20-pay life policy, (2) divide this difference by the present value of a life annuity due of 1 for the class 2 policy paying period and (3) add its level valuation premium. To compute the class 2 initial premium (1) take the difference between the renewal premium and the initial premium for a 20-pay life policy and (2) subtract it from the renewal premium for the class 2 policy. The following example of a first-year reserve computation for class 2 policies helps clarify this elusive concept. In this example, the various premiums, present values and accumulation factors are given without complicating the discussion by showing their actuarial calculations. However, how these figures are used to determine the first-year reserve is shown.

Example. Based on the 1958 CSO at 3.5 percent interest the first-year reserve for a $10,000 15-pay whole life policy issued to a person age 25 using the CRVM involves several steps:

1. Calculate the initial and renewal premiums on a $10,000 20-pay whole life policy issued to a person age 25. (These values are $18.65 and $70.58 for the initial and renewal premiums, respectively.)
2. Determine the net level premium for the 15-pay whole life policy. (This premium is $196.42.)
3. Compute the present value of a 15-year annuity due of 1 for a person age 25. (This value is 11.760868.)

The renewal premium for the 15-pay whole life policy based on the CRVM is $200.84 computed as follows: [($70.58 − $18.65 ÷ 11.760868) + $196.42]. The initial premium for the 15-pay whole life policy based on the CRVM is

$148.91 computed as follows: [$200.84 − ($70.58 − $18.65)]. The CRVM first year reserve can be calculated by the prospective method. The present value (net single premium) of a $10,000 whole life policy issued to a person age 26 is $2376.17. The present value of a 14-year annuity due of 1 to a person age 26 is 11.159033. Thus the CRVM first-year reserve is $135.08 computed as follows: [$2376.17 − ($200.84 × 11.159033)]. Using the retrospective method the cost of a $10,000 one-year term policy at age 25 and the future value of 1 compounded for interest and mortality for one year are $18.65 and 1.037 respectively. Thus the CRVM first-year reserve is $135.08 computed as follows: [1.037 ($148.92 − $18.65)].

Overconservatism in Computing Policy Reserves

The life insurance policy reserve, like the property-liability unearned premium reserve, is considerably overvalued. Recall that the use of gross premiums to compute the unearned premium reserve for property-liability insurers overstates the reserve. However, using a premium *less than* the gross premium for computing the life insurance policy reserve overstates this reserve. If the present value of the gross premium (rather than the lower valuation premium) were subtracted from the present value of future claims the reserve would be lower. Because the net valuation premium is usually less than the gross premium minus expenses the reserve is overstated. Furthermore, the reserve is overconservative because of two additional factors: overly conservative mortality assumptions and overly conservative interest assumptions. Nearly all states require the reserve to be no less than that produced using the 1958 CSO Mortality Table that has built-in safety margins and a low 4 to 4.5 percent interest assumption (3 to 3.5 percent for older blocks of policies). But as mentioned in Chapter 21, these overconservative assumptions are now undergoing long overdue major changes for newly issued policies.

INNERSCRIPT: A WELCOME INNOVATION—FLEXIBLE STANDARD VALUATION AND NONFORFEITURE LAWS

An effort to update and create flexibility in reserve requirements was made by the National Association of Insurance Commissioners' 1980 amendment to its model standard valuation law. Based on its adoption rate as of mid-1982 presumably this amendment will be the law in all states by the middle of the decade and many life insurers will comply with it before the January 1989 mandatory date. The law includes mechanisms for future changes thus making it dynamic. Maximum interest rate assumptions will change automatically and other changes can be made by regulators instead of legislators—a less time-consuming process. The commissioners can issue new rules to allow the development of new products and will do so if they are in the public interest. The amendment requires the use of the 1980 CSO mortality table with its two unique characteristics: (1) mortality rates for men and women are separated and (2) both a select-ultimate table (one including recently selected lives, thus showing lower mortality rates for the first five years)

(continued)

and the traditional ultimate table (one excluding recently selected lives, thus continuing to show a higher mortality rate for the select years) are included. Insurers are allowed to use either one, for example, the select-ultimate for term insurance and various preferred risk policies and the ultimate table for the traditional whole life policies. The amendment gives insurance commissioners the authority to update the mortality tables based on ongoing mortality studies such as those by the Society of Actuaries.

The system for updating interest assumptions is based on monthly averages of a Moody's corporate bond index with the weights given to current market rates varying with the kinds of insurance and annuity contracts. For life insurance the rates are governed by the lower of the 12-month and 36-month running averages ending June 30 of the previous year. Higher valuation interest rates are permitted for policies of shorter guarantee periods—a new feature that should encourage variable guaranteed rate policies. One problem is that the valuation interest rate will not be known until the third quarter of the previous year making it important for insurers to review interest rate trends. (By early 1982 life insurers were convinced that 1983 valuation of interest rates would not be below those of 1982.) The law does not permit an increase in valuation rates unless that increase is at least half of 1 percent in each category. Under the amendment valuation interest rate assumptions for life insurance ran from 5.5 percent for guarantees of more than 20 years and 6.75 percent for those of 10 years or less. Between 10 and 20 years the guarantee was 6.25 percent. Annuity valuation rates in 1981 ran from a high of 12 percent to a low of 5.5 percent. The 12 percent valuation rate was for a five-year guarantee and either restrictive withdrawal rights or withdrawals that adjust the principal for changes in interest rates. The 5.5 percent valuation rate was for annuities with guarantees of more than 20 years and the most liberal withdrawal privileges. (Annuity rate guarantees are delayed one year so 1982 rates are not available until mid-1982. The 1982 rates for life insurance are available in mid-1981.)

The 1980 amendment also affects nonforfeiture values. The interest rates for these values in 1982 ran from 8.5 percent for guarantees of 10 years or less to 7 percent for guarantees of more than 20 years. The change allows for more attractive nonforfeiture values. (The change in the valuation law allows for more innovative products.)

Other Reserve Accounts

Other reserve accounts of life insurers have secondary importance. The reserve for policy claims includes claims reported but not yet paid plus those incurred but not yet reported. Life insurance claims are reported and settled promptly so this reserve is usually small. Life insurers provide settlement options and annuities that require payments over long periods. Liability for these items appears in the reserve for annuities and the reserve for supplementary contracts. They are a part of the net policy reserves shown in Figure 22–2. Also shown is a liability for policy dividends left with the insurer to accumulate at interest, for dividends declared but not yet paid, for funds deposited with the insurer in advance to pay premiums when due and for taxes, commissions and other expenses incurred but not yet paid.

EARNED SURPLUS OF PROPERTY-LIABILITY INSURERS

An insurer's capital and surplus represent the excess of assets over liabilities. Stock insurers' net worth consists of the capital stock plus surplus accounts. Mutual insurers have no capital-stock account; net worth is represented by surplus accounts only. Total net worth is always referred to as the policyowners' surplus because the excess of assets over liabilities is available to pay policyowner claims. Property and liability insurers have two sources of earned surplus: underwriting profit and investment profit.

Underwriting Profit

Underwriting profit arises from insurance operations. Because of a peculiarity in accounting for income in relation to expenses, reported and actual profits differ. When income is deferred the normal accounting practice in other businesses is to defer directly associated expenses but property and liability insurers are not allowed to defer expenses. To illustrate insurance accounting procedures, Table 22–3 shows the monthly accounting activity for a one-year auto insurance policy written on January 1, 1983.

Column 1 indicates that the entire *written premium* is credited in January. Column 2 shows that *earned premium* is credited evenly throughout the 12-month policy period. Only one twelfth of the total premium is earned in the first month. Column 3 illustrates the expected pattern of incurred losses and

TABLE 22–3
Illustration of Statutory Accounting Procedures Applicable to an Individual Auto Insurance Policy

	(1) WRITTEN PREMIUM	(2) EARNED PREMIUM	(3) INCURRED LOSSES AND LOSS ADJUSTMENT EXPENSES	(4) OPERATING EXPENSES*	(5) MONTHLY UNDERWRITING GAIN	(6) CUMULATIVE UNDERWRITING GAIN
January	$120	$ 10	$ 7	$30	$−27	$−27
February	0	10	7	0	3	−24
March	0	10	7	0	3	−21
April	0	10	7	0	3	−18
May	0	10	7	0	3	−15
June	0	10	7	0	3	−12
July	0	10	7	0	3	− 9
August	0	10	7	0	3	− 6
September	0	10	7	0	3	− 3
October	0	10	7	0	3	0
November	0	10	7	0	3	3
December	0	10	7	0	3	6
Total	120	120	84	30	6	(not applicable)

* Not amortized for financial reporting—expensed immediately.

loss adjustment expenses for each month. Although each individual policy will not produce losses every month, the ratio of incurred losses and loss adjustment expenses to earned premium tends to be nearly constant for the insurer. The figures in column 3 represent the average incurred losses and loss adjustment expenses related to the policy's earned premium.

Column 4 reflects the distribution of the insurer's expenses for this policy. Although some expenses are incurred throughout the policy term a substantial proportion of them occurs within the first month. For simplicity, the example in Table 22–3 assumes that all expenses are incurred in the first month.

Column 5 illustrates the statutory underwriting gain for each month. Underwriting gain is calculated by subtracting the incurred losses, loss adjustment expenses and the operating expenses from the *earned* premium. In January a $27 underwriting loss is reported because the expenses incurred in the initial month of the policy exceed the earned premium. Each subsequent month yields an underwriting gain of $3 because the incurred losses and loss adjustment expenses are less than the earned premium. Column 6 shows the cumulative underwriting gain. Throughout the first nine months of the policy the insurer is in an underwriting-loss position. Not until the policy term has expired does the cumulative underwriting gain reflect the true profitability of this policy.

Because an insurer has thousands of policies with different effective and expiration dates it is not practical for management to wait until all policies have expired to determine the profitability of the company. The method used to measure profitability involves calculating the combined ratio, which is the sum of two ratios: the **loss ratio** and the **expense ratio.** The loss ratio is the ratio of incurred losses and loss adjustment expenses to **earned premiums.** The expense ratio is the ratio of expenses to **written premiums.** Although these two ratios have different bases they are added to determine the **combined ratio.**

In the example shown in Table 22–3 the incurred loss and loss adjustment expense ratio for January is 70 percent, column 3 divided by column 2. The operating expense ratio is 25 percent, column 4 divided by column 1. The combined ratio is 95 percent, the sum of these two ratios. The combined ratio indicates that the insurer is paying out 95 percent of the premium for losses and expenses. Therefore the underwriting profit is 5 percent of the premium (100 − 95). The insurer in Table 22–3 earned an underwriting gain of $6 on $120 of premium, or 5 percent. Therefore the combined ratio provides a procedure to determine underwriting profits without waiting for each policy to expire.[1]

Because operating expenses are not amortized, financial statements understate underwriting profit in the first accounting period and overstate it in later periods. Financial analysts adjust the reported figures. A percentage of the increase (or decrease) in the total **unearned premium reserve** for the period is added to (or subtracted from) the reported statutory underwriting results to introduce

---

[1] The formula for the adjusted underwriting result is:

$$\textbf{Earned premiums}\left[1-\left(\frac{\textbf{Incurred losses}+\textbf{Loss adjustment expenses}}{\textbf{Earned premiums}}+\frac{\textbf{Operating expenses}}{\textbf{Net premiums written}}\right)\right]=\textbf{Adjusted underwriting profit or loss}$$

In the foregoing example, the adjusted underwriting profit is $6:

$$120\left[1-\left(\frac{84}{120}+\frac{30}{120}\right)\right]=\$6,\ \textbf{the adjusted underwriting result.}$$

some realism into financial reporting. Although the percentages vary among analysts 35 percent is an intermediate figure. For example, in 1983 an insurer reported a statutory underwriting loss of $1,030,000 but 35 percent of the *increase* in the unearned premium reserve for the year was $2,456,000. The adjustment (−$1,030,000 + $2,456,000) converted the $1,030,000 statutory loss into a trade-underwriting gain of $1,426,000 before taxes.

Underwriting results are affected by the precision used in determining loss reserves. Unlike the unearned premium reserve no neat formulas are available to adjust the loss reserve. Underwriting losses are determined by subtracting the beginning loss reserve from the sum of losses paid during the year and the loss reserve at the end of the year. The incurred losses for the period will be overstated if the beginning loss reserve is understated or the ending reserve is overstated. In these events the underwriting profit will be understated. Because the loss reserve must be estimated, underwriting profits may be understated in some years and overstated in others.

Investment Profit

The components of an insurer's investment profits are: (1) investment income, (2) realized capital gains and (3) unrealized capital gains. These investment profits often offset adjusted underwriting losses. Therefore during periods of high interest rates insurers knowingly underprice their insurance to obtain investable funds. Returns on their investment operations are expected to exceed losses on their insurance operations. For example, insurers experienced underwriting losses of $5.6 billion in 1981. However, these record underwriting losses were more than offset by a record investment profit of $13.0 billion. Many experts advise insurers against relying too heavily on expected investment returns to offset heavy underwriting losses.

Property and Liability Insurer Profitability

The rates charged by property and liability insurers have provoked much attention. Consumers believe premiums are too high and profits excessive. Industry analysts argue that premiums are too low and profits are inadequate. If profits are too low resources will leave the industry. If profits are too high market forces will operate to diminish prices or consumers will seek other alternatives.

Because earnings of property-liability insurers include unrealized capital gains and losses their variability far exceeds that of other industries. A study by Citibank of New York shows that profits (as a percentage of net worth) for stock property and liability insurance companies were 11.6 percent in 1971 and 15.4 percent in 1980. During the intervening years these percentages fluctuated from a high of 21 percent in 1977 to a low of 4 percent in 1975. The average for the 10-year period 1971–1980 was 13.1 percent. (These figures compare to 4.2 percent for the decade 1961–1970 and 5.5 percent for the decade 1951–1960.) Earnings were more stable for other industries, as shown in Table 22–4.

Table 22–4 shows that stock property-liability insurers' earnings were slightly more than the average of all industries for 1971–80. The extraordinarily high earnings in 1977 and 1978 increased the 10-year average significantly. Table 22–4 also shows that stock property-liability insurers earn much less than the average for any industry during the decades of the 1950s and 1960s.

Property-liability insurers seem more concerned with profit cycles than with long-term profit levels. Not only are underwriting results cyclical but so are investment results. Problems of adequate pricing in relation to losses (losses are rarely

TABLE 22–4
Selected Annual Rates of Return on Net Income after Taxes as a Percent of Net Worth*

SELECTED YEARS	*PROPERTY LIABILITY INSURANCE†*	*PUBLIC UTILITIES*	*COMMERCIAL BANKS*	*SERVICE INDUSTRIES*	*MANUFACTURING*	*ALL INDUSTRY AVERAGES*
1971	11.6	10.3	10.6	11.1	10.8	10.2
1980	15.4	12.8	15.1	20.4	16.6	15.2
Interim high	21.1	13.0	16.0	21.2	18.4	16.7
year	(1977)	(1979)	(1979)	(1978)	(1979)	(1979)
Interim low	4.0	10.3	10.3	11.1	10.8	10.2
year	(1975)	(1971–2)	(1975)	(1971)	(1971)	(1971)
1971–1980 average	13.1	11.4	12.6	16.3	14.6	13.0
1961–1970 average	4.2	10.6	9.3	13.0	12.1	9.9
1951–1960 average	5.5	9.5	8.4	11.0	12.5	10.4

* Net worth at the beginning of the year

† Capital stock companies only

as predictable as some theorists lead their followers to believe) in a dynamic market cause underwriting cycles. Widely fluctuating and unpredictable interest rates plus the erratic behavior of the stock market produce cycles in investment results. All is well only when the cycles offset one another.

PROFITABILITY OF LIFE INSURERS

Life insurers do not face the same profitability problems as property-liability insurers. They have stability in underwriting results. Because investment earnings are explicitly tied to life insurance pricing life insurers have only limited problems there—they use conservative interest assumptions which prepares them for wide swings in investment results. However, changing financial markets (high interest rates) are causing life insurers problems particularly with policy loans (discussed in Chapter 14) and policy replacements (surrendering policies for their cash value and purchasing new policies elsewhere that offer an opportunity for lower costs and higher investment returns) but they have taken steps to correct these problems.

Earned Surplus of Life Insurers

Life insurers use conservative mortality, investment and expense assumptions to set premiums. Surplus is increased when investment earnings (including net realized and unrealized capital gains) are more than anticipated and claims and expenses are less than anticipated. Two financial statements show the degree and direction of the change in surplus: the summary of operations and the surplus account.

Summary of operations

The summary of operations shows the source of gain (or loss) from the insurer's operations. Table 22–5 shows the source of gains flowing from operations of a

TABLE 22–5 Summary of Operations ($000)

COLUMN 1		*COLUMN 2*	
Gross premiums accrued (including all considerations received for life and health insurance, annuities and policy proceeds left with the insurer under settlement options, but excluding reinsurance premiums paid to other insurers) . .	$290,433	Claims paid (including death, endowment, annuity, health, surrender, settlement options, divided accumulations, and interest on policy funds)	$191,055
Net investment income (including interest, dividends, and rents less investment expenses such as investment management expenses, investment taxes, depreciation, and depletion)	57,365	General insurance expenses (including administrative expenses, taxes other than federal income taxes, licenses, and fees)	55,952
Sundry receipts and adjustments (including fees for handling deposit administration pension plans, reserve adjustments with reinsurers, uncashed checks cancelled after a reasonable period, and so on) . .	635	Increase in reserves (including those for life, health, and annuity insurance contracts and for settlement options and dividend accumulations) . . .	63,417
Total	$348,433	Total	$310,424
Gains from operations before dividends to policyowners and federal income taxes			$ 38,009
Dividends to policyowners	$ 17,019		
Federal income taxes incurred	6,150		−23,169
Net gain from operations			$ 14,840

large stock life insurer. The item *increase* in reserves could be a *decrease* if, for example, reserves released from terminating policies exceed the increase generated from the advancing duration of old policies and writing of new ones. Because policy reserves are conservative, profit is understated when reserves increase and loss is overstated when reserves decrease.

Surplus account

Surplus at year end is reconciled with that at the beginning of the year through the surplus account. An example is shown in Table 22–6. The increase in surplus for the year is $8,062, the ending surplus of $121,332 less the beginning surplus of $113,270.

Several items need explanation. The mandatory securities valuation reserve (MSVR) is designed to reduce the impact of rising and falling securities markets. The annual addition to the MSVR is determined by a complex formula. Percentages from 0.1 to 1.0 are applied to the statement values of special stocks. The maximum value of the MSVR is also subject to a complex formula. Percentages vary from zero to 33.33 of the statement values for particular securities. Net realized and unrealized capital losses are allowed as a deduction against the MSVR, again

TABLE 22–6 Surplus Account ($000)

Beginning surplus	$113,270	Dividends to stockholders	$ 5,239
Net operating gain	14,840	Net capital loss (realized and unrealized)	12,248
Decrease in mandatory securities valuation reserve	10,745	Net loss from nonadmitted assets	34
		Increase in liability for unauthorized reinsurance	2
		Ending surplus	121,332
Total	$138,855	Total	$138,855

subject to a complex formula. Note the insurer reported a net capital loss of $12,248; $10,745 was absorbed by a decrease in the MSVR rather than by a decline in surplus. (After the devastating stock market experience in the mid-1970s, some authorities urged a MSVR for property-liability insurers.) The net loss from nonadmitted assets is the net amount of admitted assets converted into nonadmitted assets during the year. Reinsurance due from insurers not authorized to operate in the state must be shown as a liability.

Policy Dividends

Life insurance surplus management is closely related to policy dividend practices. Two decisions are how much surplus should be allocated for dividends and how the allocated funds should be apportioned among policyowners.

How much?

To be competitive insurers try to maintain a liberal dividend policy while building surplus as a cushion against poor investment and mortality experience. How much of the annual operating gain should be retained rather than paid in policy dividends is a matter of judgment, particularly considering that conservative actuarial assumptions and valuation methods overstate reserves and understate surplus. But the surplus that can be accumulated by an insurer writing participating policies is limited in some states to 10 percent of the policy reserve. As reserves increase insurers try to increase surplus. Thus dividends paid will usually be less than gains from operation. Insurers want to maintain stable dividend payments. Therefore, no fixed relationship exists between operating gains and dividends. However, any clear and lasting trend in gains must be reflected in dividends paid.

Apportionment

States require that policy dividends be apportioned and paid annually. Most insurers use the contribution plan of dividend apportionment. This system apportions dividends to blocks of policies based on the amount that each block contributes to surplus. Contributions to surplus arise from three sources: (1) excess interest earnings, (2) mortality savings and (3) expense savings. Thus the contribution plan is called the three-factor system. For any block of policies the amount contributed to surplus is found by crediting the block of policies with

1. The aggregate reserve at the beginning of the year.
2. The excess of aggregate expense loadings over incurred expenses (expense savings).
3. Interest earned for the year on items 1 and 2 (interest earnings).

and debiting the block of policies with

1. The aggregate reserve at the end of the year.
2. The aggregate mortality cost experience.

The result is the amount that the block of business contributed to surplus. It gives the insurer a basis for prorating the total dividends to be paid among the blocks and the policies within them.

Insurers' investments. Table 22–7 shows the assets held in 1980 by property-liability and life insurers as a percentage of total assets. Financial requirements and legal restrictions account for the differences. Property and liability claims are not as predictable as life insurance claims and are more subject to catastrophic losses. Therefore financial requirements dictate that property and liability insurers, more than life insurers, maintain investment portfolios readily convertible into cash.

TABLE 22–7 Assets Held by Property-Liability Insurers and Life Insurers as a Percentage of Total Assets (1980)

	PERCENTAGE OF TOTAL ASSETS HELD BY	
TYPE OF INVESTMENT	*PROPERTY-LIABILITY INSURERS*	*LIFE INSURERS*
Corporate bonds	13.3	35.0
Stocks*	25.1	9.6
Mortgages	0.6	27.3
Real estate	0.5	3.4
Policy loans	NA	8.9
Government securities†	60.4	6.8
Miscellaneous	0.1	9.0
Total	100.0	100.0

* Includes both preferred and common stocks.

† Special revenue bonds and foreign bonds are included with government securities.

FINANCIAL REPORTING

Concern has been shown over insurer accounting practices. Earnings are reported on a statutory basis and are appropriate for revealing insolvencies. However, for the investor this method fails to reveal the insurer's earning capacity. Under statutory reporting an expanding insurer may report little or no profits while a stagnating one may show large profits. The cause of under or overstated profits, as explained earlier, is the statutory requirement that expenses be reported and charged when incurred rather than spread over the policy term. The result is clearly a distortion of earnings.

To correct this condition in property and liability insurance the NAIC has developed a standard form for measuring insurance company profits and several insurance regulators urge that insurers be required to use it. They see a need for a standard reporting technique to evaluate insurers' profits. Without a standard accounting method the result is not only public confusion but also public mistrust. Even so, the industry opposes what it calls an imposition of "artificial formulas" to control profitability. Insurers maintain that insurers' profits cannot be determined by one standard formula method because differences in the risks assumed require differences in rates of return. These differences in risks result from

1. The mix of insurance written. (Some lines of insurance are riskier than others and require higher returns.)
2. The different investment strategies. (Insurers with an aggressive investment strategy should earn a higher rate of return.)
3. Differences in rate regulatory systems in various states and in how the systems are administered. (Some state rate regulatory climates create more risk than others for insurers.)

The American Institute of Certified Public Accountants has issued accounting guidelines to adjust life insurers' statutory earnings to make them more meaningful to security analysts and investors. Life insurers would still report their conservative statutory earnings to regulatory agencies but would compute earnings under these new guidelines. Under them the costs of acquiring new business would not be expensed immediately as under statutory reporting but would be spread over the expected premium-paying period. The method of reporting the policy reserve also would be more realistic. Although the concept of two different financial reports (one to investors and one to regulators) does not appeal to some insurance experts, many believe it is a step forward. The ideal would be to have one set of financial reports to serve both purposes. Hopefully the time will come when that will be the case. The 1980 changes in the NAIC's 1980 amendment to its standard valuation law should be helpful in reaching this ideal.

SUMMARY

1. Insurer's assets are either admitted or nonadmitted. Only admitted assets are considered when measuring insurer solvency.

2. Some admitted assets are more easily valued than others. The law prescribes the method of valuation of insurer's assets.

3. Because of the nature of the business, life insurers are more restricted by law in investing their funds.

4. Property and liability insurers are required to maintain unearned premium reserves and loss reserves.

5. The unearned premium reserve is the unearned portion of the gross premiums written for policies outstanding at the time of valuation. The loss reserve estimates claims and settlement expenses as of the valuation date.

6. The law regulating the unearned premium reserve causes that reserve to be excessive but the law does not require overstatement of the loss reserve. The loss reserve by practice may be either overstated or inadequate.

7. Life insurers are required to maintain policy reserves. The policy reserve measures the amount that together with future net valuation premiums and interest will produce the exact amount needed to pay policy obligations as they become due if the mortality and interest rates experienced are identical to those assumed.

8. The law specifies several valuation methods that can be used in computing policy reserves.

9. The life insurance policy reserve, like the property and liability unearned premium reserve, is considerably overvalued primarily because of unrealistic low interest and unrealistic high mortality assumptions used. More realistic interest and mortality assumptions for reserve valuation are included in the NAIC's 1980 amendments to its standard valuation law.

10. Property and liability insurers have two sources of earned surplus: underwriting profit and investment profit.
11. True underwriting profits differ from those reported in statutory financial statements because property and liability insurers cannot defer expenses.
12. Investment profits sometimes offset underwriting losses.
13. A life insurer's surplus increases when (1) mortality is lower, (2) interest earned is higher and (3) expenses are lower than assumed in calculating premiums.
14. Life insurers writing participating policies use part of their earned surplus to pay dividends to policyowners.

REVIEW QUESTIONS

1. For valuation of the assets of insurers, how are common stock investments valued? How are bond investments valued?
2. What types of reserves of insurers are overstated by statutes?
3. How can insurers overstate or understate underwriting profits through their loss reserve? Why would they want to overstate or understate their profits?
4. Explain how the net valuation premium in life insurance differs from the gross premium.
5. How is the full preliminary term reserve computed?
6. Given the following information about a fire policy:

Net written premium	=	$2,400
Earned premium	=	200
Loss + loss adjustment expenses	=	120
Allocated overhead	=	20
Commissions	=	600
Premium taxes	=	100
Underwriting expenses	=	240

   Calculate the statutory underwriting result produced by this policy. Also compute the adjusted underwriting result. Why do these two figures differ?
7. Why are policyowners interested in how their insurers value their loss reserves?
8. What affect do investment profits have on the price of property and liability insurance?
9. Explain the source of surplus for property and liability insurers. Explain the source of surplus for life insurers.
10. Explain how the overstatement of unearned premium reserves can affect the capacity of a property and liability insurer to expand its business.
11. Explain how the NAIC's 1980 amendment to its standard valuation law can help improve the financial reporting of life insurers.
12. What accounts for the variability of profits in the property-liability insurance industry?

PART EIGHT THE PUBLIC AND INSURANCE: REGULATORS AND CONSUMERS

Insurers are not permitted to perform their functions without some control. That control is exercised by regulators and the marketplace. Part Eight contains two chapters, one covering insurance regulation and the other insurance buying.

Chapter 23 considers the nature and purpose of public control over the insurance business. The principle objective of insurance regulation is to protect the consumer against unfair trade practices, financially inept insurers and a lack of insurance facilities. The chapter on regulation is near the end of the book because those who discuss the regulation of any business should know something about that business first—not always the case even among some principal regulators. A former governor of Illinois appointed an insurance commissioner a few years ago whose only knowledge of insurance was that he owned a life insurance policy—probably a group life insurance certificate!

Part Eight and the book end with a chapter on how to buy insurance. The reason should be patent. Knowledge of the subject is a prerequisite to insurance buying, and that knowledge is at its peak upon completion of the previously assigned chapters.

Insurance buyers face the problems of deciding what insurance to buy, how much, from whom and at what price. The job is not an easy one. It involves careful planning and the application of well-defined principles. Chapter 24 presents some principles of insurance buying and discusses their application. The chapter serves as a summary of much of the text, and the reader is advised to think beyond the printed page and apply the knowledge accumulated from other parts of the text.

CHAPTER

23 Regulation of the insurance business

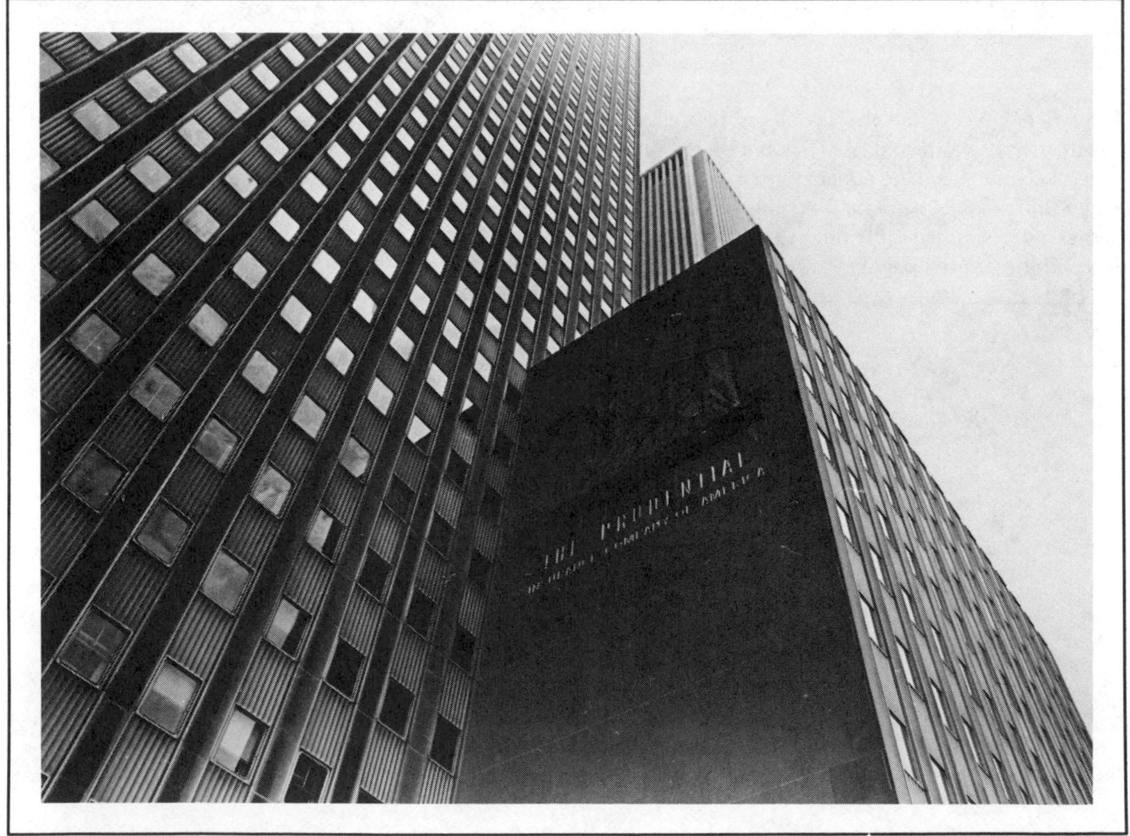

John Thoeming/Richard D. Irwin

CHAPTER OBJECTIVES

1. **To identify the objectives of government regulation of the insurance business.**
2. **To trace the evolution of government insurance regulation.**
3. **To explain and evaluate the roles of the state and the federal governments in insurance regulation.**
4. **To define the aspects of insurance company operations that are regulated.**
5. **To outline the types of taxes and fees applied exclusively to insurers.**

The insurance business performs many functions. Public regulation affects nearly all of them.

OBJECTIVES OF REGULATION

Insurance requires public confidence. Incompetency and dishonesty caused many insurer failures in early American history. Failures reached a peak during the period of expansion following the Civil War when policyowners lost money and the entire industry became suspect.

Why is there public concern over the continued solvency of insurers but not over most industrial and mercantile companies? The reason is that insurance buyers rely on the insurer's promise to pay if a covered loss occurs. If an insurer is unable to honor its promises its customers lose not only the purchase price but also resources relied on to replace damaged property, meet liability claims, provide income during periods of disability, pay medical expenses or support surviving dependents. Furthermore, persons winning judgments against insureds may be unable to collect damages, creating a social injustice.

A Business Affected with a Public Interest

Insurance long has been a regulated business but not until 1914 was it held by the U.S. Supreme Court to be a business "affected with a public interest." The court ruled that insurance was affected with a public interest because it plays an important role in other businesses. Therefore the public interest is served by regulating insurance.

INNERSCRIPT: THE CHANGING CONCEPT OF PUBLIC INTEREST

The concept of a business affected with a public interest originated in 1676 with the British jurist Lord Chief Justice Matthew Hale. However, not until 200 years later did the U.S. Supreme Court establish *first* that a business was affected with the public interest and *then* apply due process. In this case the Court affirmed the

(*continued*)

state's right to regulate "properties . . . with a public interest." The Court reasoned that when people devote their property to a use where the public has an interest they grant the public an interest in that use and must submit to control by the public for the common good. Such control was held to be a legislative question and not a judicial one involving due process. Thus the courts cannot substitute their judgment for the legislature on a regulatory policy under the guise of due process.

What determines whether a business is affected with a public interest? The Court said that property has a public interest when used to affect the community at large. The concept of a public interest is not a fixed one. It varies with court opinions, social and economic conditions and shifts in public opinion. At one time the Court held a narrow concept, that of protecting public utility consumers from excessive charges and inadequate service. Public regulation was deemed to be more effective than competition to regulate public utilities because utilities could operate more efficiently as monopolies. The public interest concept was enlarged to include other situations where participants had unequal bargaining power. States protect the weaker party to a contract as a matter of public policy. The Court held that the concept "affected with a public interest" is not limited to public utilities but extends to any industry that should be controlled for the public good. The Court said if public policy demands regulation for the public welfare no constitutional principle bars the state from regulation by legislation.

Regulation and Competition

Two studies by the New York legislature in the early 1900s dealt with the effect of regulation and competition in the insurance industry. The Armstrong investigation of 1905, a study of the life insurance industry, disclosed serious financial reporting abuses. The Merritt Committee investigation of nonlife insurers in 1910 concluded that price competition led to insurance rate wars and insolvencies. The basis of this report was that marginal insurers attempted to gain fire insurance business by lowering rates. The better managed insurers would be forced to match these rate reductions. This action and reaction would lead to inadequate rates and result in insurer insolvencies. The effect of the report was to support cooperative insurance pricing. The committee did not accept the economic argument that competition could lead to a more efficient industry.

Most current studies of the insurance industry refute the Merritt Committee. Effectively regulated price competition should increase the availability of quality insurance and reduce insolvencies by discouraging marginal insurers. Regulation and competition should reinforce each other in the interest of the consumer. Price competition should be the prime factor for allocating resources in the industry and regulation should be the main factor for assuring fair competition.

In summary, the prevailing regulatory sentiment is that competition in insurance should be fostered if it is healthy. A wide range of opinion is found regarding what constitutes healthy competition and how to promote it. The various state rating laws and their administration reflect these differences of opinion. However, there appears to be little opposition to the regulatory objectives that premiums be adequate, not excessive and not unfairly discriminatory. The fundamental question is how to achieve these objectives. How freely should insurers be allowed to price their product? The answer is unclear. Variation exists in state laws, in the administration of similar laws and in the regulations applicable to different types of insurance. The various attitudes toward rate regulation and the role of competition can be summarized in the following diverse hypotheses:

1. Open competition is the most effective means of assuring insurance availability at adequate rates.
2. Fair rates can be assured only by requiring the insurance commissioner to review and pass judgment on every rate change.
3. State made rates are the optimal form of rate making.

These hypotheses illustrate the conflicting viewpoints toward insurance regulation and how to achieve efficient insurance pricing.

Other Reasons for Regulation

Another reason for government regulation of insurers is its *fiduciary nature*. Public control is appropriate both to prevent insolvencies and to protect the public if one should occur. The U.S. Senate Commerce Committee proposed a federal insurance guaranty agency to provide a nationwide plan for indemnifying victims of insolvent property-liability insurers. As of early 1982 insolvency laws have been enacted in 48 states, the District of Columbia and Puerto Rico, most of them after the federal bill was introduced in 1970. These laws assess solvent insurers to satisfy claims against insolvent ones.

Regulatory authorities are concerned with the *availability of insurance* to applicants who should have coverage. Insurers in general are free to accept or reject any applicant. Underwriting standards presently are not subject to public regulation. However, insurers writing automobile liability insurance (in some states automobile physical damage insurance also) and workers' compensation insurance are required to accept their pro rata share of rejected business. A government-industry program known as FAIR (Fair Access to Insurance Requirements) was introduced in 1968 to make fire and extended coverage insurance available to persons unable to obtain this insurance in the traditional market, particularly persons with property in central-city areas. Some plans include homeowners insurance; however, these plans generally exclude manufacturing operations. **FAIR plan** facilities are established in some but not all states.

While insurers generally are free to establish their own underwriting rules they cannot engage in racial or sexual discrimination. In many states insurers are subject to anticancellation laws—particularly for automobile liability insurance—prohibiting indiscriminate cancellation of policies.

Equity is another purpose of regulation. One former commissioner asserts that the objective of maintaining equity "accounts for more than half the work done by insurance departments."[1] He divides his concept of equity into reasonableness, impartiality and fairness, defining these subdivisions as follows:

> Reasonableness means equity to policyholders as a group, impartiality implies equity between one policyholder and another, and fairness refers to the treatment

[1] Allen L. Mayerson, "An Inside Look at Insurance Regulation," *The Journal of Risk and Insurance*, vol. 32, no. 1 (March 1965), p. 52.

of the individual insured. Under reasonableness, for example, comes regulation designed to assure holders of participating life insurance policies a fair share of the companies earnings. Under impartiality comes regulation requiring that these earnings be distributed equitably among the participating policyholders. And under fairness, for example, comes the effort of regulatory authorities to hear policyholders' complaints (usually regarding claim payments) and to take whatever action deemed necessary to correct any abuses.[2]

Regulatory Goals

The purpose of insurance regulation can be reduced to two objectives: (1) to assure that the industry is sufficiently solid financially to meet the expanding demand for coverage and (2) to assure that the industry operates with a sense of fairness, equity and reasonableness in the market.

In summary, the objectives of insurance regulation are to assure fair competition, monitor the solvency of insurers, help make insurance available to those who need and are entitled to coverage and to assure equitable treatment of the insuring public. Regulation also protects innocent parties outside the insurance transactions, such as injured parties in liability claims and life insurance beneficiaries. Public regulation is welcomed by many people in the business because they believe it is necessary to control the brigands. Those in the business favor controls that provide the best regulatory climate in which to operate. Of course no universal agreement is found regarding any specific piece of regulation. In the final analysis one's attitude toward a given regulatory act boils down to the question of whose ox is being gored.

METHODS OF REGULATION

The American form of government operates through three divisions: legislative, judicial and executive. All are involved in the regulation of insurance. Self-regulation is a fourth regulatory system.

Legislative Control

To govern the operations of insurers all 50 states, the District of Columbia and Puerto Rico have their own insurance laws and rules. They legislate on many matters: insurance rates, availability, solvency, licensing, policy types and provisions and business methods. The police power gives the states the right to legislate in the interest of the safety, health and welfare of its citizens. This power is one not delegated by the states to Congress but reserved for themselves. States are free to legislate as long as such legislation is not in conflict with federal law although such regulation may incidentally affect interstate commerce.

Drafting legislation in the various states has not been left solely to legislators. Individuals and groups (generally associations of insurers, agents or consumers) submit model bills to be sponsored. Sometimes insurers sponsor legislation that agents oppose, e.g., more lenient rules for writing group insurance. Agents may sponsor legislation that insurers oppose, like stricter licensing requirements for agents. State legislatures rely on the insurance department to sponsor legislation and to appraise proposed bills; and the state's attorney general assists in drafting proposed laws. The National Association of Insurance Commissioners drafts model legislation. Also, the New York insurance code has influenced the codes of other states.

---

[2] Ibid.

Judicial Control

Insurance is also regulated through judicial procedure. The courts interpret legislation when its meaning is challenged and settle disputes among contracting parties. A court ruling on the constitutionality of insurance legislation or actions of the insurance commissioner becomes part of the body of insurance regulation.

Administrative Control

Because insurance requires specialized knowledge its regulation cannot be left to untrained lawmakers. State insurance departments are responsible for administering insurance regulation. The state official in charge is known as the commissioner, superintendent or director. Regardless of the official title the person occupying the position generally is referred to as the commissioner.

Insurance departments operate under legislative authority and make and enforce rules within that authority. Decisions and rulings of the commissioners are subject to judicial review if any affected parties wish to challenge them. In making decisions the commissioners create rules known as *administrative law*. Administrative law grew from the necessity for both flexibility and technical understanding impossible in the normal legislative or judicial processes.

Qualifications of the insurance commissioner

Insurance regulation could profit by having better informed insurance commissioners and staffs. Regulators too often fail to (1) examine their objectives in depth, (2) look for new approaches to solve problems and (3) measure the total effects of their actions. In addition, the financial and mental resources available to state insurance departments limit the quantity and quality of insurance regulation.

After extensive hearings and study the Senate Judiciary Antitrust Subcommittee concluded that many departments operated with inadequate budgets and were lax in dealing with monopoly, restraint of trade, unfair trade practices, mergers, insurer examinations and licensing foreign insurers. (A foreign insurer is one domiciled in another state; an alien insurer is one domiciled in another country.) The quality of insurance departments varies among states with the strong tending to upgrade the weak.

The National Association of Insurance Commissioners

The National Association of Insurance Commissioners, a voluntary organization, was formed to achieve some uniformity in state insurance laws. Over the years the NAIC has grown into a constructive force by studying legislation, encouraging industry representatives to state their positions and preparing model bills that commissioners can present to their respective legislatures. The NAIC has a number of task forces consisting of members from industry and the public. These study a broad range of insurance regulatory issues with the objective of preparing model bills. Issues studied include early detection of possible insurer insolvencies, certification of loss reserves by qualified professionals, the role of investment income in ratemaking, life insurance price comparisons, life insurance policy loan requirements, acceptable classifications for automobile insurance rating and comprehensive health insurance.

Duties of the insurance commissioner

To regulate *the financial solvency* of insurers the commissioner in general has the power to (1) license insurers that meet the state's financial requirements, (2) revoke licenses of insurers that no longer meet these financial requirements, (3) examine insurers periodically and make spot examinations, (4) check adequacy of assets and reserve valuations, (5) approve classes of investments, (6) require adequate rates, (7) require insurers to file standardized annual statements, (8) limit insurer expenditures, (9) act as a depository of securities in those states with depository laws and (10) liquidate insolvent insurers.

To regulate *trade practices* the commissioner usually has the power to (1) approve policy forms, (2) require that rates not be unfairly discriminatory, inadequate or excessive, (3) investigate complaints from policyowners and others and (4) act as an agent for unlicensed foreign insurers by accepting notices of suits from resident insureds.

To regulate *insurance marketing* the commissioner has the power to license insurance agents, brokers, adjusters and in some cases counselors.

Statutory regulations affecting insurer solvency, trade practices and marketing are discussed later.

Self-Regulation

In Chapter 20 several cooperative organizations of insurers and agents are discussed. These associations exert some control over the business through codes of ethics and various cooperative agreements. For example, standards for policy forms, advertising, education and so on have been adopted to protect the public. The fear of more public regulation has instilled a "conscience" into some individual insurers, forcing them to act in the public interest. Self-regulation was the first type of regulation in the United States.

THE HISTORY OF REGULATION IN THE UNITED STATES

Although insurance regulation can be traced to a time long before the discovery of America the concern here is with its development in the United States. The objective is to focus on state versus federal insurance control.

Regulation by Charter

The first type of public control over insurance was by charters issued to insurers. These charters contained regulatory measures now in insurance codes: investment restrictions, reserve requirements and limitations on insurance offerings. A few chartered insurers operate today.

State Insurance Departments

Direct control of insurance by legislatures proved inadequate. Therefore legislatures appointed state regulatory officials to assume the authority of public control over insurers but to these officials regulating insurers was a sideline. Administrative departments headed by commissioners then were created solely for insurance regulation so that it could receive more attention. Insurance commissioners are generally appointed by the governor but they are elected in a few states. The insurance commissioners wield substantial control over the industry.

Paul v. *Virginia*

No one questioned the constitutionality of state insurance regulation until Samuel Paul of Virginia became an agent for a group of New York insurers. Virginia law provided that nonresident insurers and their agents be licensed before doing business in the state. A security deposit was required to obtain the license. Paul was unwilling to make the deposit so the license was denied.

Paul continued to sell fire insurance, was arrested, convicted and fined $50. He sued the state of Virginia and the case reached the U.S. Supreme Court. Paul's defense was based on two grounds: (1) the Virginia license law violated that portion of the Constitution granting citizens of each state all the privileges and immunities of citizens in the other states and (2) insurance written by nonresident insurers was interstate commerce and the Virginia license law was illegal interference by a state in interstate commerce. The Court decided that (1) corporations are not considered citizens within the meaning of the equal-rights clause and (2) insurance is not commerce within the meaning of the interstate commerce clause. With respect to the latter argument the Court said:

> Issuing a policy of insurance is not a transaction of commerce. The policies are simple contracts of indemnity against loss by fire, entered into between the corporations and the insured, for a consideration paid by the latter. These contracts . . . are not commodities to be shipped or forwarded from one State to another and then put up for sale. They are like other personal contracts. . . . Such contracts are not interstate transactions, though the parties may be domiciled in different States. . . . They are, then, local transactions, and are governed by the local law.[3]

This position was upheld for 75 years in many cases that involved insurers' efforts to obtain a ruling that insurance was commerce and therefore not subject to state regulation.

The South-Eastern Underwriters Association Case

The South-Eastern Underwriters Association (SEUA) controlled 90 percent of the fire insurance and related lines in its area. The U.S. attorney general accused it of violating the Sherman Antitrust Act and the association was indicted in 1942 for (1) restraining interstate commerce by fixing noncompetitive premium rates on fire and related lines and (2) monopolizing the insurance business. The SEUA was also charged with fixing agent's commissions, using boycotts and compelling prospective insureds to buy only from SEUA members. Nonmembers of the SEUA were refused reinsurance opportunities and the SEUA disparaged their services and facilities. Agents who represented nonmember insurers were denied the right to represent members, and customers who purchased insurance from nonmember insurers were threatened with boycotts and withdrawal of patronage. In the ensuing court case the SEUA relied on the defense that the Sherman Antitrust Act does not apply because insurance is not commerce. The federal district court upheld this view and dismissed the case, citing *Paul* v. *Virginia.* The attorney general appealed to the Supreme Court, contending that insurance was commerce and subject to the federal antitrust laws. The Court reached a decision in 1944 that insurance is commerce and when it traverses state lines it is interstate commerce. The majority opinion stated:

> . . . the power to govern . . . [commerce between] . . . the states . . . is vested in the Congress. . . . No commercial enterprise . . . which conducts its activities across state lines has been held to be wholly beyond the regulatory power of Congress under the Commerce Clause. We cannot make an exception of the business of insurance.[4]

Even the dissenting justices disavowed *Paul* v. *Virginia.* They conceded that Congress had the power to regulate insurance but had not exercised that power. The SEUA decision led to confusion about its meaning. Some concerned parties believed that the decision placed insurers in an uncomfortable position. Insurers could not obey two conflicting laws. For example, some states had laws requiring

---

[3] 8 Wall 183 (1869).

[4] *United States* v. *South-Eastern Underwriters Association et al.,* 322 U.S. 533 (1944), p. 552.

ratemaking organizations. However, the federal law (Sherman Antitrust Act) considered cooperative ratemaking a restraint of trade and thus illegal. Therefore if the insurer obeyed one law it would violate the other. However, the matter was not that serious. State laws contrary to federal legislation were nullified. States retained the power to regulate insurance as long as state laws were not contrary to federal legislation. If the Supreme Court had upheld the states' right to regulate insurance in *Paul* v. *Virginia* on the grounds that states may regulate interstate affairs as long as Congress is silent it could have been spared the embarrassment of reversing an awkward decision that had held for 75 years.

Public Law 15

To avoid confusion Congress passed Public Law 15 (the McCarran-Ferguson Act) in 1945. Public Law 15 stated that continued regulation and taxation of insurance by the states is in the public interest and that congressional silence is not to be construed as a barrier to state regulation. The law exempted insurers from the Sherman, Clayton and Federal Trade Commission Acts until 1948. At that time the federal fair trade and antitrust acts were to apply to insurance in states having no such laws. The 3-year moratorium allowed states time to enact their own fair trade and antitrust laws and avoid federal regulation of insurance. However, under section 3(b) of Public Law 15 the Sherman Antitrust Act still applied to boycotts, coercions and intimidations.

Some interested parties interpreted Public Law 15 to mean that only *voluntary* action in concert is to be sanctioned and then only when regulated by states. However, the court ruled that North Carolina's law requiring all insurers writing automobile liability insurance in the state to be members of the North Carolina Automobile Rating Office with no rate deviations permitted is not in conflict with Public Law 15 or the Sherman Act. The Court said that states are authorized to regulate the insurance business completely if they desire. Thus the state can also limit methods of competition.

Developments after Public Law 15

If it becomes apparent that state regulation is deficient in serving the public Congress is apt to assume the primary regulatory role. It is expected periodically to review state insurance regulation. Following the passage of Public Law 15, states passed laws to strengthen insurance regulation.

Model rating laws

The NAIC formed an all-industry committee to study the effects of federal antitrust acts on insurance. NAIC committees developed model fire and casualty insurance rating bills. An area of disagreement among committees was whether filing rates with the commissioner for review was necessary where rates were not made in concert.

Another disagreement focused on when rates were to be effective. Should rates have the commissioner's prior approval before they could be used or should they be effective immediately after filing? The compromise provided that filed rates could be used after a specified time unless specifically disapproved by the commissioner. However, the commissioner would retain the power to disapprove rates at any time even though they had been tacitly approved by failure to act during the initial period. A few states with model rating laws have adopted the file-and-use provision rather than the compromise recommendation.

Most rate laws followed the NAIC's all-industry commissioners bills that neither require nor prohibit membership in rating organizations. Under these laws if an insurer has its rates filed by a rating organization it must use those rates unless it has the commissioner's permission to deviate. The rating organization may oppose the deviation at a commissioner's hearing. Any aggrieved insurer or rating organization can demand a hearing on any commissioner's order and following the hearing it has the right to a judicial review.

Other rating laws

Model laws are not in force in every state. Other types of laws are classified broadly as mandatory and permissive.

Mandatory laws require either membership in a specified rating bureau or that ratemaking responsibility be placed in a state agency. Mandatory rating bureaus are required in some states for workers' compensation or for fire or fire and casualty insurance. In some states, rates are state-made for workers' compensation, automobile liability, fire and general casualty insurance.

Under the permissive laws if filing is required insurers must file rates for information only. Rating bureaus are authorized but their use cannot be required. Members are free to use whatever bureau's rates and policy forms they wish. An agreement among members and subscribers or with the bureau to charge uniform rates is illegal. Insurers are free to charge bureau rates with the limitation that these rates not be excessive, inadequate or unfairly discriminatory.

In several states with the *permissive-type laws* the terms *excessive* and *inadequate* are defined. A rate is excessive only if unreasonably high *and* no reasonable degree of competition prevails. A rate is inadequate only if unreasonably low *and* its continued use would either endanger the insurer's solvency or create a monopoly. The concepts of unreasonably and reasonable are not defined.

Permissive-type laws (known as no-filing and open-rating laws) have been enacted in more than half the rating jurisdictions. One state with model rating laws applies them only to those insurance lines where the commissioner determines that competition is lacking. Another state has no insurance rate regulatory law except for workers' compensation. An argument against open rating is that competition fails to prevent unfair price discrimination. Open rating has led to a variety of policies and rating systems that can produce unfair price discrimination. Insurance departments must be aware of possible abuses and attempt to prevent them.

Fair trade laws

The NAIC approved a model unfair trade practices bill and all states have enacted it or a similar one. The bill defines unfair methods of competition or unfair or deceptive acts. In general the unfair trade practices model bill grants the commissioner broad power to regulate unfair competition and unfair trade practices.

Federal Regulatory Issues and Public Law 15

The general belief prevailed that the passage of state regulatory laws similar to the Sherman, Clayton and Federal Trade Commission Acts would free insurers from federal regulation. That was not the case. The Federal Trade Commission (FTC) sought jurisdiction over interstate insurance advertising in spite of state laws covering the subject. The Supreme Court denied the commission this jurisdiction. The FTC also sought jurisdiction over mailorder insurers. The courts finally ruled that the FTC has jurisdiction to prevent unfair trade practices by mail order insurers through its power to initiate cease and desist orders or investigative actions.

The U.S. Justice Department questioned various mergers involving insurance companies. A U.S. district court upheld the Justice Department in a case involving the merger of two insurers domiciled in different states. Another merger case involving a large insurer and a large conglomerate resulted in out-of-court settlement. Later the Justice Department regretted not having a Supreme Court ruling on the applicability of existing antitrust laws to big mergers involving insurers. As noted, Public Law 15 continued the applicability of the Sherman Act regarding boycotts, coercions and intimidations. Before the SEUA decision many insurance practices would have been in violation of the Sherman Act had this act applied to insurance. After that decision the Justice Department had to force discontinuation of these practices.

When life insurers began writing variable annuities the Securities and Exchange Commission (SEC) claimed jurisdiction. Because Public Law 15 is limited to insurance an important issue was the meaning of "insurance." The question was whether variable annuities are insurance and entitled to exemption from the Securities Act of 1933 and the Investment Company Act of 1940. The Supreme Court held that variable annuities are not insurance because the issuing insurer assumes no risk in the insurance sense. Thus, the SEC's position was upheld and variable annuities became subject to jurisdiction of the SEC, the Securities Act of 1933 and the Investment Company Act of 1940.

State versus Federal Regulation

The issue of state versus federal regulation of the insurance industry is not new. The controversy intensified during the *Paul* v. *Virginia* case and the SEUA case, and is again increasing. In the late 1970s the president appointed a National Commission for the Review of Antitrust Laws and Procedures. One area of concern was the antitrust immunity that Public Law 15 provides. The commission produced the following recommendations:

1. The current antitrust immunity should be repealed and replaced with legislation allowing cooperative activities only for limited endeavors.
2. Competition should be relied upon as the most effective regulatory method.
3. The federal government should undertake additional analysis of insurance regulation.

Preferred regulation: state or federal?

A question frequently discussed is whether federal or state insurance regulation is preferable.

Arguments claimed for federal regulation. Until Franklin D. Roosevelt's New Deal many insurers favored federal regulation. Starting with *Paul* v. *Virginia* and continuing until the SEUA case they presented brief after brief against state regulation, insisting that insurance was commerce. They favored federal supervision because they believed it less burdensome and for many years the states were more active than the federal government in controlling business. In recent years many insurers have shown increased interest in federal regulation. They and others have advanced the following arguments in favor of federal control:

1. The lack of uniformity in state codes and rulings complicate the problem of insurers operating in more than one state.

2. State regulation is expensive. Insurers are required to file reports in each state where they operate. Maintenance of 51 regulatory bodies also is required.

3. Federal control would be more competent. Under a system of state regulation insurers must guard against "bad" legislation in 51 jurisdictions while under federal control lobbying activities could be limited to Washington. Because they are full-time representatives members of Congress should be better legislators

than state lawmakers. They have more time to study legislation and are less subject to local pressures. Federal regulation advocates argue that a federal insurance commissioner appointed on merit would be better qualified than many state commissioners.

4. Exclusive rather than partial federal control of insurance would eliminate confusion created by conflicting and overlapping regulation.

5. The national scope of insurance supports the logic for federal control. States find it difficult if not impossible to deal with some foreign and alien insurers.

Many of these arguments are illusory. First, a federal regulatory system probably would have regional offices issuing inconsistent rulings among regions. Second, other federal regulatory agencies are likely to increase their involvement in insurance regulation resulting in confusion, conflict, feuds and overlapping jurisdiction.

Arguments claimed for state regulation. Several arguments in favor of state control have been advanced.

1. State regulation helps assure equity by considering local conditions that Washington authorities may not understand.

2. Federal regulation might be arbitrary and bound in red tape. Insurers can communicate more effectively with state lawmakers and regulators.

3. The NAIC tends to eliminate some disadvantages of state regulation (e.g., nonuniformity, multiple examination of insurers and poor legislation).

4. An error made in regulation is restricted to one jurisdiction. Experiments in regulation are possible in limited areas without adversely affecting the entire country if the experiment fails.

5. Federal control could become a leveling factor weakening regulation in those states where both the code and its administration are strong.

6. Decentralized political power is desirable. Problems that can be handled effectively by states should not be shifted to the federal government.

7. State regulation is a known entity. To cure the ills and build on the strengths of the present system is better than creating a new one.

Which is better? The strength of the foregoing arguments depends on one's biases and perception. At the present time political considerations suggest that states' rights are to be protected but not at all costs. If the public interest can be served efficiently by state regulation, then states should be encouraged to meet the challenge. Federal control should be exercised only to fill a void in state laws. Those who fear federal regulation are aware that state regulation is now on probation. The question of regulation of insurers is in a state of flux. Most parties do not want to abandon state regulation without giving it a chance to survive. At this writing it is too early to predict the outcome of the controversy.

WHAT IS REGULATED?

Insurance regulation focuses on insurers' finances, products and business methods.

Financial Regulation

To control insurer solvency the law regulates many aspects of the business such as rates, expenses, reserves, valuation of assets, investments, surplus, policyowners' dividends, organization and licensing of insurers, annual reports and liquidation of insurers.

Rate regulation

Because rate regulation for property and liability insurance is so different from life and health insurance the two are discussed separately.

Property and liability insurance rate regulation. Insurance rate regulation is discussed earlier in this chapter in connection with the SEUA decision and Public Law 15. In summary, property and liability rates in most states are regulated in accordance with the model rating laws. These laws provide that rates reflect past and prospective loss and expense experience, catastrophe hazards, reasonable margins for underwriting profits and contingencies. In these states insurers must file premium rates, rating plans, coverage and rules for the commissioner's approval. Supporting data consisting principally of statistics on losses and expenses are required. An insurer may satisfy this obligation through a licensed rating organization that files for members and subscribers.

Rating organizations must be licensed by the commissioner. Every rating organization must permit any qualified nonmember insurer to subscribe to its services. Furthermore, each rating organization must furnish its services to members and subscribers without discrimination. Rating bureaus are subject to supervision and examination by the commissioner. Members and subscribers of rating bureaus are required to adhere to bureaus' rates unless the commissioner approves an application for a deviation. The commissioner will not approve a rate modification that produces inadequate, excessive or unfairly discriminatory premiums. These standards are general so the commissioner needs guidelines to determine if a rate qualifies. To help commissioners with rate supervision, rating laws include technical requirements concerning methods of recording and reporting loss and expense experience, exchange of rating plan data and consultation with other states. The commissioner may designate one or more rating or other organizations as statistical agencies to assist in collecting and compiling the required data.

Many states have withdrawn their support of direct regulation of property-liability insurance rates. This retreat is based on two contentions. First, the property-liability insurance industry has enough sophistication in statistical analysis of data to determine profitable rates and insurance is sufficiently competitive to eliminate excessive rates. Second, even if some insurers are overly optimistic in measuring loss potential and unknowingly charge inadequate rates, a growing number of commissioners are confident of their ability and facilities to detect insurers bordering on insolvency before the public is hurt. The thought is that supervision of various financial accounts is sufficient to protect the public without specific attention to the price at which insurance is sold. The foregoing beliefs have resulted in proposals for the removal of insurance regulators from the pricing decision. Under a no-file law statistical support for a rate change does not have to be filed and rate changes can be initiated without notifying the commissioner. However, most no-file laws require that the commissioner be notified of rate changes within a specified period.

While the nonprior-approval laws remove the state insurance departments from the initial pricing decision the laws still require that rates be adequate, not excessive and not unfairly discriminatory. Even under no-file laws commissioners may (and usually do) make periodic examinations of rates to determine if these criteria are met.

Ratings laws generally do not apply to ocean marine insurance in order to give American insurers flexibility to compete in world markets. Furthermore, because buyers are generally represented by knowledgeable brokers, bargaining power between parties in ocean marine insurance transactions seems to be equal.

Life and health insurance rate regulation. Life insurance rates are regulated indirectly by rules applying to the valuation of the insurer's reserve liability. The legal reserve requirements for life insurers are not directly related to the premium charged. If the insurer's premium structure is inadequate, its assets will be insufficient to offset the required reserve. In life insurance as in property-liability insurance unfair price discrimination among buyers of the same policy from the same insurer is prohibited. However, unit prices may vary inversely with the policy size and the applicant's insurability. The theory has been that competition would assure nonexcessive rates. However, the effectiveness of competition as a regulator of life insurance prices is questionable. The typical buyer has neither the technical competence nor the data needed to analyze the prices of cash-value life insurance. The life insurance industry has offered formulas for preparing indexes for price comparisons. These price indexes are widely published and available to concerned insureds. Life insurance price comparisons are discussed in Chapter 24.

In many cases credit life and health insurance rates are negotiated between the insurer and the lending agency and tend to be set at levels that will provide the highest profit in commissions and policy dividends to the lender. This practice is known as reverse competition. To avoid abuses, rates for these coverages are subject to control in nearly all states. In group life insurance the initial premiums are regulated in some states. The renewal premiums are free to reflect the group's experience.

Many states require that rates and occupational classifications for health policies be filed with the commissioner. In many jurisdictions the commissioner may disapprove health insurance forms if benefits are unreasonable in relation to premiums. A few states require estimates of expected loss ratios with health insurance rate filings. All states require the filing of annual statements of loss ratios in health insurance by policy types. Although public interest requires supervision of health insurance rates they often escape regulation because of the conviction that they cannot be regulated effectively. So many widely different health policies are issued that understaffed insurance departments are unable to check rates against benefits. Blue Cross and Blue Shield rates, however, are controlled.

Expenses

Insurer expenses must be controlled for effective financial regulation. Expenses are not specifically regulated in property and liability insurance; their regulation is tied directly to rate regulation. An important expense is the cost of acquiring business. Since the SEUA decision the activity of organizations that once controlled commission rates became illegal. If commission wars jeopardize public interest commissioners generally have the power to restore order.

Only two states limit the amount of expenses life insurers can incur. Because one of them is New York these limitations have widespread applications. A New York insurance code provision known as the Appleton Rule requires all insurers licensed in New York to "substantially comply" with New York laws in all states where they operate. New York law limits total expenses and acquisition costs. It restricts commission and fees on individual policies, and prizes or bonuses based on the volume of business written are controlled. It sets complicated aggregate limits on first-year expenses. Renewal commissions and policy service fees are also limited. In addition to compensation allowances the insurer may pay training allowances for new agents subject to a set of statutory limitations.

Reserves

Property and liability insurers are required to maintain unearned premium reserves and loss reserves. The principal reserve for life insurers is the policy reserve. These reserves are discussed in detail in Chapter 22. A primary concern of regulators is that insurers do not undervalue loss reserves because understated liabilities lead to insolvencies. On the other hand, to allow insurers to overreserve can result in excessive rates. Insurance departments usually do not have the qualified personnel necessary to determine adequacy of loss reserves on a company-by-company basis. Thus on occasion insurers have been able to conceal financial weaknesses that have led to insolvencies. Experts who have studied the problem of regulating loss reserves insist that the regulatory approach needs reform. Life insurers frequently value their policy reserves in excess of the statutory minimum. The result is an understated surplus and an altered statutory profit pattern. Reported profits are usually understated in periods of high growth and are overstated when growth declines.

Capital stock and surplus accounts

An insurer's surplus consists of a paid-in surplus and earned surplus. A capital-stock insurer will also have paid-in capital.

Capital-stock accounts. An insurer's capital-stock account represents the dollar value nominally assigned to stockholders' shares. Most states require that stock initially be issued at a premium (i.e., the value assigned to the stock must be less than the money paid in by stockholders) thus creating a paid-in surplus. For example, New York stock life insurers must have a minimum paid-in fund of $3 million—$1 million is assigned to the capital account and $2 million to paid-in surplus.

Paid-in surplus account. A minimum paid-in fund is required for mutual insurers. But because mutuals have no capital stock this fund is assigned entirely to paid-in surplus. The minimum paid-in fund is $150,000 for a New York domestic mutual life insurer and $500,000 for a domestic multiple-line insurer. These initial funds are usually supplied by lenders but are not treated as liabilities. Interest may be paid on these funds and the principal may be repaid from earnings.

Dividends to policyowners

Policyowner dividends are usually associated with participating life insurance policies. (Some mutual property-liability insurers pay dividends to policyowners but these dividends generally are not subject to government regulation.) The amount of the annual gain from operations that should properly be paid to life insurance policyowners as dividends is a matter of judgment. Some states regulate dividends by limiting the surplus that an insurer writing participating policies may accumulate. Limits are imposed to prevent building a large surplus at the expense of current dividends to protect equity among policyowners and to help prevent extravagance among insurers in the use of their assets.

Requirements for organizing and licensing insurers

Insurance codes prescribe conditions for forming new insurance companies. They deal with the insurer's name, notice of incorporation, organization, organizers and promotion. Some states are trying to reduce the birth rate among life insurers by increasing minimum capital and initial paid-in surplus requirements for insurers. The law attempts to exclude those promoters whose interest is not in providing insurance but in profiting from the sale of stock. The organizational laws for insurers vary among states, types of insurers, types of coverage to be written and over time.

States also have authority for licensing insurers and control the insurance business chiefly through this power. A license is a document stating that the insurer has complied with the state laws and is authorized to engage in the insurance business. Insurers, however, may operate without a license in a state by conducting their business through the mail.

A license to write insurance may be issued to a domestic, foreign or alien insurer. The state can establish stricter licensing requirements for alien and foreign insurers than for domestic ones. This practice is justified because domestic insurers' assets are generally in the state and more easily subject to the commissioner's control through court procedure.

Licenses are usually permanent for domestic insurers. However, foreign and alien insurers are licensed only for one year, subject to renewal. The commissioner may revoke a license, forcing the insurer to discontinue business in the state. The insurer may seek a court reversal of the commissioner's decision; the burden of proof is on the insurer to show that its license should not have been revoked. Licensing power is an effective control because it is nearly impossible to succeed in reversing the commissioner's action. The commissioner will license qualified insurers if no director has a record of fraud or dishonesty and if the licensing does not jeopardize the public interest.

Unauthorized insurers. The regulation of unlicensed insurers (called nonadmitted or unauthorized insurers) creates special problems. *Doing business* in a state is broadly defined to include soliciting, writing, rating, administering and servicing an insurance contract by mail or otherwise. Excluded from the definition are reinsurers, insurance owned by residents before moving into the state and insurance bought outside the state without using a licensed agent in the state. The law makes unauthorized insurers subject to state jurisdiction in actions brought by the state to enforce its laws (and in suits brought by resident policyowners against the insurer). Unauthorized insurers are subject to fines and state premium taxes.

Two uniform acts deal with unauthorized insurers: (1) the Unauthorized Insurers Service of Process Act (UISPA) and (2) the Uniform Reciprocal Licensing Act (URLA). The UISPA gives commissioners authority to accept summonses for court suits against unlicensed foreign insurers, as mentioned earlier. The URLA gives commissioners the authority to revoke licenses for domestic insurers who operate without a license in other URLA states. States control unauthorized insurers by limiting them to business placed by licensed surplus-lines agents or brokers. Insurance may be purchased from unauthorized insurers only under specified conditions discussed later.

Annual reports

Insurers must file annual reports with the states where they do business. Reports are filed according to standards developed by the NAIC and contain details about premium income, expenses, investments, reserves and other financial information. State insurance departments verify the information by direct examination not more than once every three years. Financial regulation also requires standards for valuation of insurers' assets and restrictions on insurers' investments. These controls are discussed in Chapter 22.

Liquidation of insurers

When an insurer is found to be technically insolvent the commissioner takes over the insurer's business. Grounds for liquidation are usually outlined in the insurance code and include insolvency, failure to cooperate fully with examiners, impaired capital, refusal to remove a dishonest officer or director or willful violation of state laws. The insurer is entitled to a court hearing but the insurer's assets are controlled by the commissioner when the liquidation order is entered. If the takeover proves to be unsupportable the insurer's assets must be returned to management. The Uniform Insurers Liquidation Act is designed to obtain uniformity in handling claims and distributing assets for insurers doing business in more than one state. The act allows creditors in each state to share losses equitably. Creditors in the insurer's home state receive no preferential treatment.

Product Regulation

The inability of policyowners to interpret a policy presents insurers an opportunity to take advantage of their insureds. Insurers may unintentionally use clauses and policy forms that are misleading. Some states encourage insurers to simplify policy language. As a result a rate advisory bureau filed a new readable homeowners policy in 30 states, reducing the number of words by about 40 percent and increasing type size by 25 percent. Readable policies have been developed for personal and business insurance as well as life and health insurance.

Approval of policy forms

To protect the public and reputable insurers insurance departments are empowered to disapprove policies that are ambiguous, deceptive or misleading. In some states special "gimmick" life and health insurance policies are outlawed. In some coverages (e.g., fire and workers' compensation) standard policy forms are required. In others (e.g., life and health) certain provisions must be included and others are prohibited. Generally the commissioner may disapprove a policy if it contains provisions that are inequitable or encourage misrepresentation. Unfortunately, most insurance departments do not have sufficient funds to give policy forms a thorough examination. In states where model rate laws are in effect supervision of policy forms and rates is interrelated. When an insurer or bureau files a rate it must include a description of the coverage offered. A policy issued subject to that rate must contain the coverage contemplated when the rate was filed.

Regulation of Business Methods

Insurance regulation seeks to protect the public from incompetent and dishonest agents and to maintain fair competition. The states regulate methods insurers use to acquire new policyowners.

Licensing of agents and brokers

Agents and brokers must be licensed by states where they do business. Qualifications for a license vary. More and more often applicants for an agent's license must pass a written examination. A few states require formal courses in insurance, sometimes particular courses, before the examination. In some states where no written examinations are required the law assumes the insurer will select its agents with care. The NAIC is studying state licensing laws with the goal of proposing a model uniform agents' and brokers' licensing bill.

Agents' licenses usually are issued for one year and renewed automatically. The commissioner may refuse or revoke licenses. Dishonesty usually is grounds for rejecting a license application or revoking an existing one. Misrepresentation, rebating, unfair discrimination or other violation usually is sufficient cause for revocation. A few states regard incompetence or ignorance as grounds for revocation. In some states licenses are issued only to residents. A few states license counselors. If licensing of agents is to be more than a source of state revenue, increased attention must be given to professional qualifications.

Surplus-line agent or broker

In all but one state an agent or broker who wishes to place business with a nonadmitted insurer must have a surplus-line license. The surplus-line laws vary among states but they generally include the same types of restrictions: (1) the insurance must be unavailable in the admitted market; (2) the surplus-line agent or broker must pay the premium tax; (3) only those nonadmitted insurers meeting specific requirements are acceptable (requirements include filing a financial statement, appointing the commissioner as attorney for service of process, obtaining a certificate of compliance from the state or country of the insurer's domicile and maintaining a trust fund in the United States by alien nonadmitted insurers) and (4) the surplus-line agent or broker must pay a special license fee, post a bond and be a resident of the state. Surplus-line laws have been attacked for restricting competition. If coverage is available in the admitted market buyers are not allowed to place insurance with an unauthorized insurer even if it is financially stronger, offers lower prices and will write a better contract than that found in the admitted market.

Misrepresentation and twisting

State statutes usually prohibit a misrepresentation of facts about a policy and its coverage or the relationship between the insured and the insurer. **Twisting** refers to misrepresentation by an agent in order to induce a policyowner to substitute one contract for another. The definition of twisting must include failure to disclose all facts. An agent's recommendation to an insured to replace one policy with another is not necessarily twisting. Unfortunately, fear of accusation of twisting discourages some agents from making sound recommendations involving dropping one policy in favor of another. Furthermore, misrepresentation and twisting are not easy to prove and often go undetected or unpunished.

Twisting, found principally in life insurance, is referred to as the **replacement problem.** The NAIC has developed a model replacement bill requiring that complete and accurate written information on a proposed replacement, including a comparison between the existing and proposed policies, be supplied to policyowners. The bill requires that each insurer with a policy in force likely to be affected by a replacement be given the opportunity to evaluate and comment on the comparative information given the policyowner.

Rebating

Agents who refund part of the commission to the applicant are violating antirebating laws which are designed to maintain fair competition among agents and to protect career agents from part-time agents. A rebate may be not only a return of part of the premium paid but also an inducement not specified in the policy. Few rebating cases reach court because they are difficult to prove. Both the buyer and seller are guilty and will not want to testify against each other. Insurance departments are challenging the advisability of rebating laws. The belief is that knowledgeable insurance buyers should not be prevented from driving a bargain any more than purchasers of other goods and services. For certain coverages, in fact, it is not uncommon for the agent's commission to be subject to lawful negotiation.

Unfair discrimination

Discrimination that gives one insured a lower premium rate than others with the same underwriting characteristics is prohibited by state insurance codes. A growing number of social reformers support the concept that private insurance is a method of spreading losses without adequate regard for actuarial cost. As a result "unfair" discrimination is sanctioned in the private insurance system. For example, insurers yielded to heavy political pressure when they agreed to organize automobile insurance plans (formerly called assigned-risk plans) at the expense of sound underwriting principles. Assessing solvent insurers to pay claims on behalf of insolvent insurers is another example of actuarially inequitable loss spreading. Loss spreading by private insurers without full attention to actuarial costs represents a shift from actuarial equity to social equity. However, if the private sector is to provide the public with the insurance it needs at "affordable rates" the shift may be necessary.

INNERSCRIPT: TAXATION OF INSURANCE COMPANIES

Insurers must pay a host of taxes and fees. Except for federal income taxes all are paid to state governments and local communities.

Insurers pay federal income taxes according to complicated Internal Revenue Code formulas. Several states impose an income tax on insurers. In some states a tax is levied on the net investment income of domestic insurers. License fees include those for licensing insurers and agents. Filing fees are charged for filing the annual statement and supporting documents. The examined insurer pays the cost of examination. To examine the Prudential Insurance Company of America or some other giant insurers requires three years. Real and personal property is taxed on the same basis as that of any taxpaying owner. Some states impose a franchise tax on insurers. Many states tax the underwriting profits from ocean marine insurance instead of taxing ocean marine insurance premiums. Most states levy a special tax on fire insurance premiums to support the state fire marshal's office or local fire departments. A special tax is levied on insurers writing workers' compensation insurance to pay costs of administering the system, build security funds and finance second-injury funds. (Second-injury funds are used to pay additional workers' compensation benefits that might be required if a handicapped worker is injured. The purpose of the fund is to relieve the employer of this obligation, thus eliminating an obstacle to employing handicapped workers.)

The premium tax

The most debatable of all insurer taxes is the premium tax. These taxes were originally imposed to offset the costs of regulation but state insurance departments now receive only a small part of the revenue from the premium tax. The remainder is used to finance other state services. Many insurance departments are understaffed and are unable to perform their required functions effectively. These departments believe premium taxes should be used for their original purpose rather than for general revenue.

The argument for premium taxes is that the revenue from them is easy to collect and policyowners who indirectly pay these taxes have shown no resistance to them. One advantage of premium taxes to insurers is their simplicity. For example, although a number of states now have an income tax in addition to or instead of the premium tax they recognize the problem of measuring an insurer's

true income. States vary widely in how they measure income. However, insurers object to premium taxes because they are not uniform. Rates for premium taxes vary from 1.7 to 4 percent with 2 percent the most common. Most states levy a retaliatory premium tax on out-of-state insurers. Retaliatory taxes eliminate the effects of different premium-tax rates on domestic insurers. To illustrate: if a domestic insurer in state A must pay a 3 percent premium tax in state B, then state B's domestic insurers must pay 3 percent in state A even though A's premium-tax rate is 2 percent. The extra 1 percent is a retaliatory tax. Its purpose is to control tax increases on out-of-state insurers. The NAIC is seeking to eliminate retaliatory taxes. The lack of uniformity of premium taxes among states is burdensome to insurers. Furthermore, inequities are created when policyowners in low premium-tax states must pay the same rate charged policyowners in high premium-tax states, as is usual for individual life and health policies.

SUMMARY

1. Because insurance is a business "affected with a public interest," it is subject to regulation.
2. The purpose of insurance regulation is to assure that the industry is (1) financially sound and (2) competes fairly.
3. Insurers are regulated by legislative, judical and executive authority. To some extent insurance also regulates itself.
4. The U.S. Supreme Court in the 1944 SEUA decision ruled that insurance is commerce, reversing the 75-year-old *Paul* v. *Virginia* decision. Nevertheless, regulation is predominately exercised by the states.
5. In 1945 Congress passed Public Law 15 (the McCarran-Ferguson Act) stating that continued regulation and taxation of insurance by the states is in the public interest. However, the debate continues as to whether state regulation should be replaced by federal regulation. Insurers are subject to federal regulation of some of their practices.
6. Insurance regulation focuses on insurers' finances, products and business methods.
7. Financial regulation is designed to control solvency and is concerned with rates, expenses, reserves, valuation of assets, investments, surplus, dividends, organization and licensing of insurers, annual reports and liquidation of insurers.
8. Product regulation includes approval of policy forms to eliminate those that are ambiguous, deceptive or misleading.
9. Business methods are regulated by licensing of agents and brokers and by prohibiting misrepresentation, twisting, rebating and unfair discrimination.

10. Insurers like other businesses must pay taxes and some special fees. The most debatable tax of all insurer taxes is the premium tax.

REVIEW QUESTIONS

1. Define the concept of a "business affected with a public interest."
2. How do the goals of insurance regulation conflict with each other?
3. Why did Congress pass Public Law 15?
4. Regarding the debate of state versus federal regulation:
   a. What are the arguments claimed for federal regulation?
   b. What are the arguments claimed for state regulation?
5. Distinguish between mandatory and permissive rating laws.
6. What is the justification for state regulation of dividend payments to policyowners?
7. What is a "readable" policy? Are these policies readable?
8. On what grounds have surplus-line laws been attacked in the interest of the insurance buyer?
9. Why have rebating laws been subject to challenge by some insurance departments?
10. Why is the premium tax debatable?
11. Give three examples of federal regulation of insurers.
12. What is the replacement problem in life insurance? Why is it a problem? How do insurance regulators deal with the problem?

CHAPTER

24 How to buy insurance

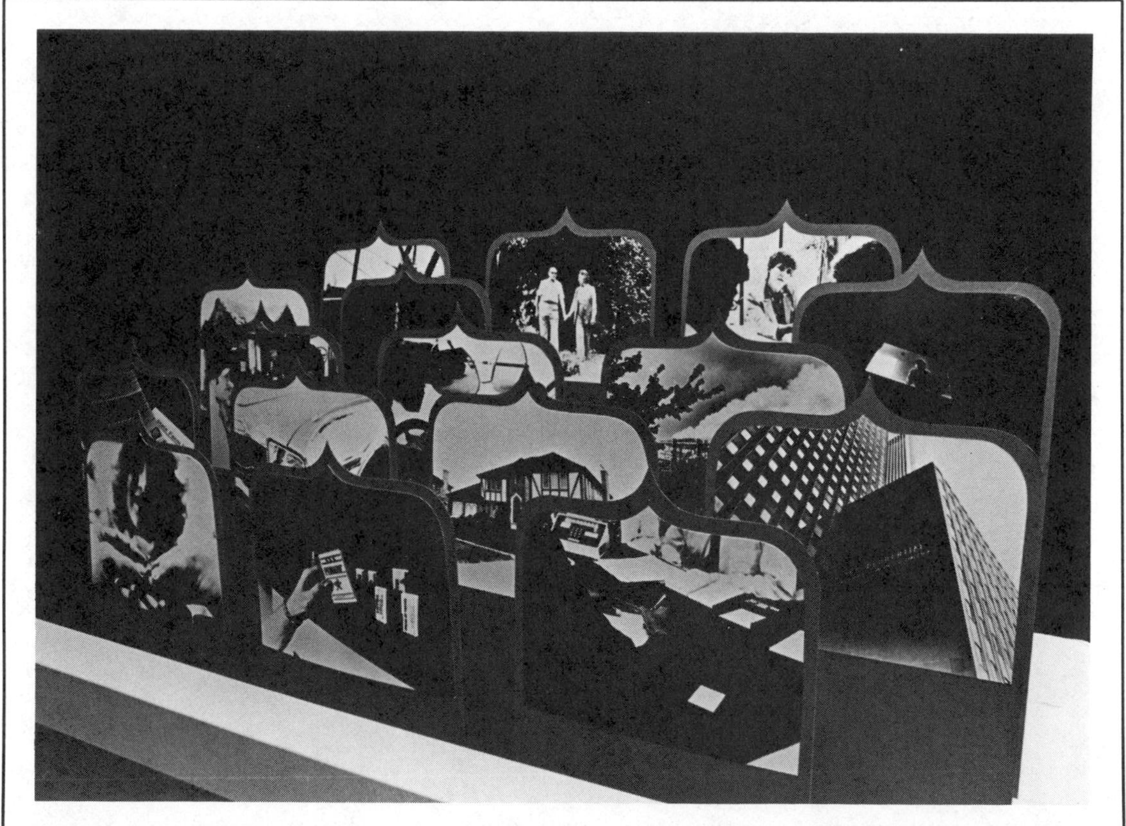

John Thoeming/Richard D. Irwin

CHAPTER OBJECTIVES

1. **To define the essential conditions for self-insurance.**
2. **To identify and explain the application of basic principles of insurance buying.**
3. **To describe a process for personal and business insurance planning.**
4. **To consider the issues involved in selecting an insurance agent and an insurer.**
5. **To point out and discuss the uses of several prominent methods of comparing the prices of cash value life insurance policies.**

Individuals, families, businesses and public institutions are exposed to losses from many perils. As a result a basic problem facing everyone is how to deal with all these possible losses. In this chapter only one of the methods available for handling loss exposures is discussed: insurance. Other methods are discussed in Chapter 2.

Insurance may be classified into self-insurance and commercial insurance. Self-insurance is discussed first but the principal focus here is on the purchase of commercial insurance, i.e., what kind, how much and from whom.

SELF-INSURANCE

For most insurance buyers the question of whether to self-insure will never arise. Self-insurance requires a large number of noncatastrophic and similar exposure units so that losses can be reasonably predicted. Exposures that meet these requirements may be self-insured if the insured has the financial strength to fund the plan and to absorb unpredicted losses. Sufficient understanding of insurance to administer the plan is also needed.

When a self-insurance plan is used a regular deposit is put into a self-insurance fund. In low-loss years the fund will grow; in high-loss years it will be depleted. Because losses can occur early, before adequate funds are accumulated, self-insurance should be installed gradually. Thus a decreasing amount of commercial insurance can be purchased each year that the self-insurance fund increases. In this way the self-insurer is protected until the fund matures. When using self-insurance, coverage with commercial insurers is usually desirable to cover losses exceeding some basic figure.

Self-insurers must provide efficient loss-inspection and loss-prevention activities that for some coverages are as important as indemnity. If a firm is not in a position to provide these services it may purchase them from an insurer. Those few firms that can qualify might find self-insurance more economical than commercial insurance because selling costs and premium taxes are eliminated and administrative costs might be lower. Lower administrative costs may not materialize, however, if the self-insured is not equipped to perform the engineering and claims functions as efficiently as commercial insurers.

One disadvantage of self-insurance is the lack of an impersonal claims service, particularly in workers' compensation and group health insurance. An adverse relationship is created between employer and employee when a self-insured employer denies a claim; if commercially insured the employer can blame the insurer.

In addition, self-insurance may create an unnecessary income tax burden. Contributions to a self-insurance fund are not deductible expenses; only losses incurred are deductible. Premiums paid to commercial insurers are deductible in the year paid. Therefore the annual tax deduction for commercially insured losses is spread over high and low profit years. However, the result under self-insurance is that several high profit years might pass with small tax deductions while high deductions may be realized in low-profit years.

PRINCIPLES OF COMMERCIAL INSURANCE BUYING

Insurance should be bought according to sound theory. As with all theories, though, several principles must be considered.

The Large-Loss Principle

The basic insurance principle is the substitution of a *small* certain cost for a *large* uncertain one. Many insurance buyers seem to avoid this principle and substitute small certain costs for *small* uncertain ones: As one agent remarked, "People are not smart insurance buyers. Sure, they *ought* to buy insurance protection against the large losses rather than small ones; but many times the only way to get them to buy protection against catastrophic losses is by tying it in with protection against the small losses, too."

Curious buying behavior is often found in auto insurance. Some people buy low deductible collision coverage at the expense of more essential protection. If a person loses an auto by fire, theft or collision the most that can be lost is the value of the car. But if someone is injured by the car all the driver's property, as well as future income, can be lost in a lawsuit. Yet some people who cannot afford both physical damage and liability insurance buy physical damage and leave liability uninsured.[1]

Why do so many intelligent people suddenly seem so ignorant when buying insurance? Perhaps the more frequent the losses the more aware they are of the perils producing them and therefore the more likely they are to insure against them. Insurance of small losses is uneconomical. The cost of writing the coverage, when added to the loss cost, makes the insurance too expensive. Moreover, when losses are frequent they can be considered expenses. Insuring them becomes unnecessary unless valuable special-service features are associated with the coverage (for example, speedy replacement of broken glass under glass coverage) or the coverage is required by law or contract (minor claims under workers' compensation laws or for auto physical damage under mortgage loan contracts).

In purchasing insurance too much weight may be given to the *probable chance of loss* and *the cause of loss* and not enough to the *possible size of loss.* If a $40,000 loss would ruin a family why does it matter if the loss has only a 0.01 percent chance of occurring or if it is caused by fire, windstorm, illness, death or an adverse legal judgment?

Gradation of Insurance Coverages

After analyzing loss exposures as discussed in Chapters 3 and 4, risk managers realize they cannot afford all the insurance desired. So they classify exposures and budget for those they consider the most essential.

[1] Finance companies frequently require physical damage insurance on financed autos. They do not require liability insurance. Many car owners believe they have all the insurance needed when satisfying finance companies' requirements.

INNERSCRIPT: THE LOSS THAT COULD NEVER HAPPEN!

Consider the following story concerning the experience of one harried insurance agency manager:

I remember a case called The Loss That Could Never Happen. A number of years ago we were asked to insure a collection of fine Egyptian statuary and John Rogers, who's our partner in charge of Fine Arts and Special Risks, sent young Ad Taylor out to survey the place. Taylor came back and said "Mr. Rogers if I ever saw a perfect risk this is it. The statues are six feet high and weigh a ton or more each. Frankly I don't see how they ever got them in there and it would take a railway car to get them out. They're housed in a separate fireproof building and anyway, they're stone and they can't burn. And they have a watchman and dogs around the place. There hasn't been an earthquake in Jersey for as long as I can remember and meteorites don't scare me. What could possibly happen to them?"

We underwrote that risk and practically no sooner had we done so than we had to write out a check for close to $500,000 for a total loss. It seems the statues were waxed to keep them at a high finish and one day a little fire broke out in a bundle of old rags they kept around for that purpose. The fire got going on the wax and the next thing you know the statues are red hot. Then the firemen came and sprayed the darn things. Inside of two minutes those statues had split into pieces you could pick up in your hand.

Essential coverage

An important principle of insurance buying is to buy protection first against all losses potentially so large as to be financially disastrous. Insurance against these losses is essential. The size of a possible loss, not its frequency, should be the determining factor. Insurance *might* be considered even if the chance of loss is negligible.

The decision to insure may not rest with the insured. Some insurance is essential because it is required by contract; other types are required by law. When property is mortgaged, the mortgagee usually requires fire insurance. Some labor contracts require the employer to buy group life and health insurance and annuities. Workers' compensation insurance usually is required by law. Some jurisdictions require auto liability insurance. When required, insurance coverage becomes essential regardless of the large-loss principle.

Desirable coverage

Some losses are not large enough to cause bankruptcy for a family or business. However, they may be sufficient to impair accumulated savings seriously or create a burdensome debt. Physical damage to the family car might be an example of this type of loss. While insurance against such losses is not essential, it is desirable if the budget is sufficient to cover more than just the essential coverages.

Aside from essential and desirable coverages, a number of coverages are available that should be ignored by all buyers except those who are (1) psychologically unable to handle losses of any size *and* (2) willing to pay for the luxury of buying insurance simply because it is available.

Boundaries between the classes

The boundaries between essential and desirable coverages are highly variable. They depend on the insured's property, income, financial status, responsibilities, desires and attitude toward loss retention. Coverage that was essential last year may be only desirable coverage this year.

Liability protection is always essential coverage because large claims may arise at any time from various sources. Bodily injury damage claims resulting in awards in excess of $100,000 are common and accidents involving several persons can produce claims for millions of dollars. Liability claims could exceed total business assets and except for certain exemptions, a person's entire property can be attached to pay a liability judgment. The future also can be "mortgaged"—wages earned and property acquired in the future may be attached to satisfy unpaid judgments.

To some families a $2,000 hospital bill might be enough to make hospital insurance essential while other families would find such insurance only desirable. A few families might be able to absorb the expense without any financial difficulty, thus requiring no insurance for that amount. Coverage that may be only desirable for well financed businesses or families becomes essential for the marginally financed ones creating a dilemma in insurance planning: those who need certain coverages cannot afford them and those who can afford them do not need them.

The loss-unit concept

In determining whether insurance is essential or desirable the **loss-unit concept** is helpful. A loss unit is defined as the aggregate losses resulting from a single event. A peril can cause a loss that develops into catastrophic proportions. For example, a steam boiler explosion can cause an *aggregate* loss that would cripple a business even though several of the individual losses composing the aggregate might be handled without stress.

The loss-unit concept requires that prospective insurance buyers consider all losses from a single happening rather than focus on individual losses only. Thus in the event of a steam boiler explosion such losses as damage to the boiler, direct damage to the building and contents and profit losses from business interruption must be considered. Furthermore, compensation paid to injured employees, judgments at law for bodily injuries and property damage, loss of service of key persons injured or killed in the explosion and benefits payable under employee benefit plans to employees and their survivors must be considered. These fragmented losses all add up to *one* loss when deciding whether a large loss exposure exists.

Of course the explosion is unlikely to occur and any loss sustained is unlikely to be the estimated maximum potential. The probability that a large loss will *not* occur should not be a controlling factor in insurance buying, however. In deciding what losses *not* to insure the buyer must consider the loss-unit concept and the reality that the same free assets that may be used to offset *uninsured* losses also must be used to offset *uninsurable* losses. Because these assets may be needed to cover business or family financial reverses they may be unavailable to meet losses that could have been insured.

Integrated Insurance Planning

Insurance buying is a budgeting problem. The insurance budget should be overall, not separate for each coverage. Insurance planning involves integrating all coverages: life, health, property and liability; otherwise premium dollars will not be used efficiently. The danger inherent in nonintegrated planning is that a policy is bought because it fills a particular need without consideration of priorities.

Some family finance authorities, however, do not advocate a separate insurance budget. They suggest that auto insurance be included in the transportation budget, homeowners insurance in the housing budget and life insurance in the savings budget. This view can be defended but it does not force the buyer to think in terms of buying insurance on a "first-needs-first" basis. Integrated insurance planning for a business is different. The use of profit centers may force efficiency-conscious managers to consider alternatives to insurance as a risk management device. Top management also may consider pure risk more carefully in planning new ventures.

CHOOSING AMONG COVERAGES: PERSONAL INSURANCE NEEDS

Ideally the prospective insurance buyer determines the applicable loss exposures and then instructs the insurer to "cover this property, income and expense against whatever perils might cause loss." But the present state of the art does not permit such perfection in obtaining coverage.

The Life and Health Insurance Programming Process

Programming life and health insurance is a complex process. For this text an introduction and treatment of each need separately is sufficient, leaving to specialized life insurance textbooks the development of an illustrative program.[2] The separate treatment of each need must not be interpreted to mean that a separate policy is bought for each need; i.e., that the same policy does not also cover other needs. One policy can cover multifaceted needs by using the global approach and the discounting technique to determine the amount and types of policies to buy. After determining the purposes for which postloss funds are needed, five basic steps should be considered in the programming process.

Determine the amount of postloss resources needed to satisfy each purpose

In the absence of constraints the postloss resources normally sought are those required to provide the exact amount needed. However, because of constraints, primarily involving limited preloss resources, the decision normally includes tradeoffs between spending one's resources or committing them to provide financial security following disability, death or retirement. The tradeoff varies among individuals and is a function of such factors as living styles, income levels, asset accumulation, attitudes toward risk and sense of family responsibility.

Even if one is willing and financially able to purchase sufficient disability or death benefits another constraint may be faced: insurers' underwriting standards. The applicant must be insurable and the insurer must be willing to write the amount necessary for the required postloss resources. For example, it is difficult to obtain sufficient coverage to provide the required amount of disability income in those cases where this amount exceeds the "normal" underwriting limits available in the market. But don't give up! A knowledgeable agent can be helpful.

Determine the current resources available to meet the needs

Available resources generally include social security benefits, payments under employee benefit plans, individual insurance policy benefits, annuities, real and personal property (including savings and investments), assets to be inherited, credit lines available to survivors and the survivors' earning power.

---

[2] See Robert I. Mehr, *Life Insurance: Theory and Practice,* rev. ed. (Plano, Tex.: Business Publications, 1977), Chap. 19.

Determine the amount of additional resources required Resources that will be available must be subtracted from resources needed to determine the additional amount required. This amount can be accumulated through savings and investments or by the purchase of insurance. The problem with the accumulation method for nonretirement loss exposures is that the loss may occur before necessary resources are accumulated. So in most circumstances the safest method of providing postloss resources is through appropriate insurance policies.

Coordinate the postloss resources into a plan As noted, determining resources needed usually requires a decision on the minimum income level at which a family can operate effectively and involves tradeoffs. When considering tradeoffs among coverages for different needs two action rules are helpful.

1. *Keep first needs first.* Some policies have greater appeal than others and "unthinking" insurance buyers often purchase the wrong policy. One coverage with high appeal is the college endowment education policy. High sales commissions on this policy may compound the problem if some agents selfishly push high-premium plans. What has a child gained if a parent inappropriately purchases a $10,000 endowment on the child's life at age 18 rather than $30,000 of continuous-premium whole life insurance on the parent's own life and then dies before that child completes elementary school? Instead of $30,000 of life insurance proceeds the surviving family has a policy on the child requiring an annual premium of about $450. Insurance buyers should realize that using high-premium-high-cash-value policies reduces the insurance available for the premium spent. Additional life insurance is needed in nearly every program.

2. *Look to the future.* A sound financial program must provide flexibility for the future. Young unmarried persons usually should not contract for high-premium retirement income policies. Even though their current status may permit payments for high-premium policies their future status as parents may rule out high-premium commitments if they want sufficient life and health insurance to protect their families. To change from high- to low-premium policies they must once again prove their insurability.

Insurance programming also must consider the forces likely to change the balance between needed and available postloss resources. Changes in income, financial responsibilities, investment values, price levels and social security benefits can affect that balance. A way to maintain the desired balance is to purchase policies that offer the flexibility needed such as some form of adjustable life (discussed in Chapter 13).

Arrange safeguards to protect the plan When the final program is formulated the insurance must be arranged to pay the proceeds to the appropriate persons and to assure that these funds are held until needed to satisfy their planned objectives. Dividend and settlement options also must be chosen properly. (See Chapter 14.)

Executor Fund

The need for an executor fund to pay final expenses is continuous. Therefore the appropriate policy is whole life or YRT to age 100. Whether a limited- or continuous-premium whole life policy or YRT to age 100 should be bought depends on the money available for premiums and on alternative financial opportunities for this money.

Technically the cost of last illness is included in the final expenses the executor will pay. But the same medical insurance that covers nonterminal illnesses also covers last illness expenses. Still, many life insurance planners include this expense as part of the executor fund—needlessly arranging for life insurance to cover a health insurance need. This action is an unfortunate waste of premium dollars because no special fund is needed to pay last illness expenses if adequate health insurance is bought.

Because medical expenses are unpredictable they are best provided for by major medical insurance offering virtually blanket coverage for medical, hospital, nursing, surgical and similar expenses. Major medical is discussed in Chapter 15. Various deductibles and maximums are available. Because all expenses are not covered by the major medical policy other resources must be provided to pay specified expenses excluded from coverage, the deductible, the insured's participation and amounts in excess of the policy limits. Medicare provides coverage of major hospitalization expenses for those over 65. Some excess coverage complementing medicare is desirable. Medical expense insurance should cover both dependents and the breadwinners.

Mortgage or Rent Fund

The appropriate disability and life insurance policies depend on the provisions of the mortgage loan agreement. They should provide the amount of monthly income required until the debt is retired. With the introduction of variable interest rate mortgage loans and other innovations in mortgage lending the policyowner has the additional responsibility of matching the insurance with the obligations under the mortgage loan agreement. Lump-sum life proceeds should not be used to repay an old loan that has a low interest rate.

Special mortgage loan protection plans provide nothing for taxes and upkeep when the mortgage loan expires. Therefore additional disability income and life insurance should be added to cover these expenses. If the family does not own a home it must arrange sufficient disability income and life insurance to provide funds to pay rent. The possibility of rent increases must be considered in determining the amount of insurance purchased.

Adjustment Income

Because of the probability of a sudden decrease in standard of living following loss of the breadwinner's income, insurance should be purchased to provide an adjustment income. This income allows the family to decrease its living standard gradually over several years without severe emotional stress. An appropriate disability income policy, if affordable, is a noncancellable or guaranteed renewable contract; otherwise an optionally renewable form may have to be purchased. These forms are discussed in Chapter 15. For life insurance the policy may be either term (if renewable to retirement age or convertible) or continuous-premium whole life. With either of these forms the insurance does not expire before the need for adjustment income.

Family Period Income

The family income policy provides a stated monthly income from the time of the insured's death until a given date. The period should be selected to provide the required income until the youngest child is expected to become self-supporting. Family income is available in three types of plans.

1. Decreasing monthly term insurance for an initial amount necessary to pay the guaranteed income to the end of the income period.

2. Family income rider usually attached to an endowment or whole life policy.
3. The traditional family income policy.

The premium for the decreasing term form is the lowest because no cash value is involved, but death protection for a growing family is usually considered a more basic need than the accumulation of cash values. Building a retirement income through cash values can be deferred until the children are financially independent. In many families 15 to 20 years will remain in which to build a retirement fund after the children have grown.

If the insured wishes to use premium money to accumulate cash values either a permanent policy with the family income rider or the traditional family income form would be appropriate. In families with no budget problem and an attraction to life insurance as a savings medium the family income need can be met solely through the purchase of traditional forms of cash-value policies.

No standard policy is available for the family period disability income need. The ideal policy would decrease the benefit period by a month for each month the insured remains healthy. The period finally reduces to zero if the insured reaches the end of the family period while still able to work. Disability income insurance programming specialists have urged development of such a policy and the buyer should ask his or her agent to search the market for a policy to meet this need.

Lifetime Income for the Spouse

A lifetime income guarantee requires large amounts of life insurance, as indicated in Table 24–1. Thus the lifetime income need must be filled with the least expensive insurance. Even then a compromise usually will have to be made between the income a person would like to guarantee the spouse and what can be afforded. Term insurance requires the lowest premium. As shown in Table 24–1 each year the insured lives, less face amount of insurance is required to provide a given dollar income to the surviving spouse. If the insured assumes this given dollar income will be sufficient, a form of decreasing term may be purchased. However, unless the rate of inflation declines significantly the dollar income needed will increase substantially over the years, thus reducing the attractiveness of decreasing term for this need. Therefore either renewal or convertible term insurance or the lowest premium form of permanent insurance (continuous-premium whole life) appears to offer the best coverage for this need. The amount

TABLE 24–1 **Amount of Life Insurance Needed to Guarantee a Woman a Minimum Lifetime Monthly Income of $500 from the Starting Ages Shown Based on 3 Percent Interest***

AGE INCOME STARTS	*FACE AMOUNT NEEDED†*
45	$140,000
50	131,000
55	121,000
60	100,000
65	87,500

* Less for a male.

† The insurer is likely to pay more than this guaranteed minimum. Thus the face amount needed to pay a *nonguaranteed* $500 monthly is likely to be *much* less at today's rates. But insurers are conservative and offer low long-term guarantees. The policy proceeds can be converted into an annuity probably paying and guaranteeing much higher interest rates.

of insurance purchased should be based on less conservative interest assumptions than those used by insurers.

Education Insurance

Insuring an income for the college period in case of the breadwinner's disability is awkward because no policy is available for that purpose. A delayed-benefit policy is needed that pays only during the college years; no benefits are paid until the child is 18 if the parent is totally disabled before that time. The best current arrangement is to buy enough disability income protection to support the family so that the child can borrow funds and supplement them with employment income while attending college. In case the breadwinner dies the cash values of life insurance arranged for education can be used. If a premium waiver is included with the policy the contract remains in force during the insured's total disability without requiring premium payments. When the child enrolls in college the cash value can be borrowed and the funds used to help pay college expenses.

An ideal arrangement for a college income is the juvenile endowment at age 18 with a waiver-of-premium rider in event of the parent's death or disability. Such policies commonly are too expensive for the typical family. So the best education insurance plan for most families is a policy on the parent's life that provides a sufficient income to the children during their college years if the parent dies. The assumption is that a living parent will contribute toward the child's college expenses from current income. If term insurance is bought the education fund provided by insurance would mature only upon the parent's death. But if cash-value life insurance is bought and the parent survives, the policy's cash value may supplement other available resources to finance the child's college education. Funds maturing from college education policies should be left with the insurer at interest subject to withdrawal so they can be used, if necessary, to guarantee a gradeschool or highschool education or to offset inflation or a family financial setback.[3]

Emergency Fund

An emergency fund can be established by setting aside a few thousand dollars of life insurance proceeds to be held by the insurer at interest, subject to withdrawal in whole or in part. This fund covers emergency needs of a surviving spouse only. For the family of the disabled breadwinner the best way to meet the need is to include disability waiver-of-premium coverage for all life insurance policies so that cash values continue to grow while the insured is disabled. The cash values can serve as emergency funds.

Retirement Insurance Needs

Neil Doherty has programmed the income needs of his family. He has adequately provided for them upon his death with cash-value life insurance. In contemplating his retirement Neil expects that much of his income need will be arranged automatically. When he retires he can convert his cash-value policies into retirement income for life. Insurers offer many types of annuities to liquidate cash values

[3] Some persons insist that the withdrawal privilege could be abused and money intended for college used for unnecessary purposes. However, if the beneficiary is that irresponsible a trust rather than policy options should be used. The discussion in Chapter 14 of selecting options should be reviewed at this point.

systematically. Furthermore, single-premium life annuities may be purchased to liquidate capital accumulated independently of life insurance, e.g., savings accounts, stock and bond portfolios and so on. Individual retirement accounts (IRAs) and other retirement programs discussed in Chapter 17 are available through life insurers and other financial intermediaries for building retirement income on a tax-sheltered basis. These instruments should not be overlooked in planning retirement. An important consideration in arranging life annuities for retirement is that some of the income be continued to the surviving spouse. This objective may be met through the use of a joint-and-last survivor annuity discussed in Chapter 14. But if sufficient capital is available to provide an attractive income without liquidating cash values or other investments, the annuity may not be an efficient financial instrument unless one is willing to sacrifice capital for additional income benefits. Illness often is more frequent and severe after retirement. Retirees should continue medical coverage because retirement income and social security medical benefits often are inadequate to pay medical expenses. Private plans that integrate with medicare are written to cover the gaps and eliminate the overlaps. Restrictive medicare supplement policies often sold by unscrupulous agents and insurers should be avoided.

Family Insurance Needs

Income insurance planning tends to stress insurance needs of the breadwinner while overlooking the needs for other family members. These needs include an estate clearance fund and insurance written on the lives of spouse and children.

Estate clearance fund

The death of any family member costs money. Therefore a fund for final expenses for each member should be considered. Death taxes can substantially reduce an estate. The Economic Recovery Tax Act of 1981 eliminated federal death taxes on an estate if it is transferred to the surviving spouse but the estate of the surviving spouse may be subject to a heavy death tax burden. A life insurance policy written on the lives of the spouses and payable upon the second death can be used to provide funds to pay this tax without forcing the sale of estate assets. The beneficiary, however, should be someone other than the spouse's estate. Furthermore, medical coverage should be included to pay the cost of illness.

Insurance on the life of the spouse

The death of a parent of young children may cause financial loss. First, the surviving parent may have to pay someone to care for the children. This cost is deductible in part from taxable income but the deduction is only a small part of the cost. Second, in many families both spouses work and contribute to the family's living standard, so income insurance should be arranged to offset the loss arising from a spouse's death. Third, upon the death of a non-wage-earning spouse the family will be subject to higher income tax rates. Disability income insurance covering the spouse should be bought to offset these losses if he or she is disabled. Adequate medical expense insurance also should be purchased to cover the spouse's expenses in excess of the family's budgeted amount.

Insurance on the lives of the children

Life insurance on children has several legitimate uses. However, because these uses have high sentimental appeal they often attract buyers who ignore more basic insurance needs. Children are better protected by insurance on their parents' lives than on their own lives. Insurance on children should not be bought until higher priority needs have been filled. Although the expenses involved in a child's death can adversely affect family finances the family would face a greater hardship if a parent died without adequate insurance.

The family plan

A policy often appropriate for family life insurance needs is the family plan discussed in Chapter 13. The children's insurability is guaranteed as each $1,000 of term on the children may be converted into a maximum of $5,000 of whole life when the term expires. Adequate insurance is provided for most children but more insurance often will be needed for the spouse. In that case a separate policy must be purchased.

Caution: Inflation Ahead?

Inflation imposes a serious threat to long-term financial planning for income security. Therefore the life insurance buyer with the help of competent insurance agents and financial planning advisers must keep abreast of new life insurance policies and other financial instruments designed to help offset the eroding effects of inflation on these plans. These new life insurance policies are discussed in Chapter 13.

Property and Liability Insurance Planning

In addition to life and health insurance, families must plan for their property and liability insurance needs. Important coverages are those for dwellings, general personal property, automobiles and personal liability.

Dwelling coverage

In selecting dwelling coverage the buyer must decide if the benefits of the broader forms with additional covered perils are worth the cost. Several of the added perils cover losses that would not have a disastrous economic effect. Glass is an example. The broader forms tend to exclude perils that can cause major losses, e.g., earthquake and flood. In favor of the broader forms are their coverages against landslide, building collapse, water damage and vandalism.

In addition to coverage against loss to the dwelling a family should protect itself against loss of use while a destroyed house is rebuilt. This loss may be covered by rental value insurance—a limited amount of this coverage is included in fire dwelling forms. Often after a loss or damage to a dwelling additional living expenses are incurred until the dwelling is restored. Additional living expense insurance reimburses the insured for this extra financial burden. Rental value insurance is usually insufficient to cover these expenses, so additional living expense insurance is the solution to this problem. The broader dwelling forms often include broad "loss-of-use" and additional living-expense coverage as part of the physical damage form. Under some of the broader forms insurers pay full replacement cost for losses without deduction for depreciation, a form of extra-expense protection—the expense incurred because "old" must be replaced with "new."

Another coverage related to the dwelling is liability insurance. Property ownership obligates its owner to maintain the property in good repair so that it causes no one bodily injury or property damage. Residence liability covers the homeowner's liability for damages traceable to the maintenance and use of the residence. The comprehensive personal liability policy covers not only residence liability but also additional liability hazards. Broad liability coverage is included in homeowners forms and usually offers the appropriate coverage for nearly all families.

Nonautomobile personal property coverage

For most insureds, personal property will be covered by one of the homeowners forms. The extent of coverage available ranges from coverage for ten specified perils to all-risk protection. For articles of high value a personal property floater providing worldwide all-risk protection is recommended. The insured must be aware of the special amount and other limits applying to personal property and modify the basic coverage if warranted. For example, an insured who has property located in a safe deposit box should consider the purchase of safe deposit box coverage to offset losses of securities and other property held in the box—unless the bank is negligent, it is not liable for the loss.

Property excluded from homeowners coverage must be covered under other policies if such coverage is deemed necessary. For one example, if a person owns a recreational vehicle, coverage for that vehicle should be considered. A reading of the exclusions and inclusions in homeowners and auto policies will reveal other areas where additional coverages might be needed.

Personal activities

A negligent act causing bodily injury or property damage to others can be costly, depleting accumulated wealth and tying up future earnings. Persons engaged in sports are exposed to liability hazards. The exact destination of a golf ball the typical player hits is not known. An injured party may claim the golfer failed to give adequate warning and is thus guilty of negligence and liable for damages. The defendant needs liability insurance to pay the defense costs and any awarded damages. The liability exposure is not restricted to the sports lover: everyone is exposed to liability claims resulting from his or her actions. For example, entering a building through a revolving door could cost thousands of dollars if the entering party pushed the door at such speed as to injure an exiting person.

The family's best liability coverage is comprehensive personal liability protection. Special business and personal activity endorsements generally are available. High limits are recommended. Homeowners policies incorporate a comprehensive personal liability section. The standard amounts are $25,000 for each occurrence, $500 per person for medical payments and $250 for physical damage to property of others when there is no liability. Because one of the homeowners forms discussed in Chapter 8 will probably meet the need for dwelling coverage, personal property other than auto coverage and personal liability coverage, the reader might find it useful at this point to review these pages. These forms are available for homeowners, condominium owners and renters. A special farmowners form is also available.

Motor Vehicle Coverage

An auto owner is exposed to two basic losses: loss of or damage to the auto and loss from liability for bodily injury and property damage to others resulting from ownership, operation or use of an auto. These exposures, the available insurance policies and their proper uses are discussed in Chapter 9. No further elaboration is needed here.

CHOOSING AMONG COVERAGES: BUSINESS INSURANCE NEEDS

Business loss exposures are analyzed in Chapters 3 and 4. Property and liability insurance needs vary with the industry and the individual firm. A firm's life and health exposures can also be handled by insurance.

Property and Liability Insurance

Most property and liability exposures can be discovered using the process outlined in Chapters 3 and 4. Although insurance can be purchased to cover most of these loss exposures, in some cases the use of other risk management tools may be more efficient. Each firm must determine the amount of funds it can have accessible to offset losses. Funds from within the firm and credit sources should be considered in this determination. If gaps remain between needed and available funds, insurance can be purchased to fill them. Applicable policies and their uses are discussed in Chapters 10 through 12. A quick perusal of these chapters should be helpful in identifying these coverages.

Business Life and Health Insurance

Businesses have many uses for life and health insurance. One use discussed in Chapter 16 and 17, is for employee benefit plans. Other uses include plans to attract and retain key employees and to finance buy-and-sell agreements in the event of the disability or death of an owner. Business life and health insurance is a highly technical subject. These technicalities center on ownership of the insurance and tax implications and are best discussed in a specialized text on life and health insurance. Only the simplest plans are discussed here to provide a background for understanding the role of life insurance as a basic solution to some business financial problems.

Key-employee life and health insurance

Key personnel are employees whose loss might materially affect the firm's profit. Key-employee insurance is a simple coverage. Usually life and disability income policies are bought and *owned by the employer.* When a key employee is lost through disability or death the proceeds are paid to the firm. The premiums are not tax deductible nor are the policy proceeds taxable.

Individual life and health insurance may also be purchased to attract and retain employees. This type of insurance commonly is written on and *payable to or on behalf of the employee.* The employer pays the premium. Under a documented medical care and disability income plan the employer can deduct the premium without the employee reporting it as taxable income if the benefits are reasonable in relation to the employee's salary for services rendered.

The income-tax consequences of a life insurance plan for the benefit of the employee are more complex. They depend on how the plan is set up. Under some arrangements the premium is deductible by the employer but reportable as taxable income to the employee. In others the premium is not deductible by the employer and is not taxable to the employee. The taxability of the proceeds also depends on the type of plan. The advice of a competent life insurance agent *and attorney* should be obtained before the plan is established. These qualified specialists can offer a wide range of suggestions for the use of individual life insurance for the benefit of the key employee. The regulations against practicing law without a license require life insurance agents to restrict their advice to life insurance plans; legal and tax advice must be left to the attorneys.

Sole proprietorship insurance

The loss exposures peculiar to the sole proprietorship are examined in Chapter 3. Life and health insurance can be used in dealing with some of these exposures.

A sole proprietor may need life insurance to provide funds to protect the personal estate against business debts. If the sole proprietor has no suitable heirs for the business the sole proprietor may want to find a buyer to purchase the business at a fair price upon the owner's death. In this instance a buy-out agreement with a key employee may offer a solution, with the key employee buying life and disability income insurance on the sole proprietor to help purchase the business. The employee would own and purchase the insurance. The premiums would not be tax deductible nor would the proceeds be taxable. The sole proprietor could make some arrangement to help the employee pay premiums.

To offset the loss of an owner who is also a key person, adequate insurance should be purchased to preserve the value of the business following loss of the owner's services. If the proprietor becomes *temporarily* disabled disability income insurance can help pay for needed extra help and offset an anticipated earnings drop resulting from the owner's absence. The policy can be written with a waiting period for the number of days the business can function during the proprietor's absence without serious loss. Again, premiums are not tax deductible nor are insurance benefits reportable as taxable income.

Partnership insurance

Disability income and life insurance also are important for partnerships. If a partner's disability is long term the partnership may want to buy the interest of the disabled partner. Similarly, if a partner dies the surviving partners may want to buy the interest of the deceased partner. A mandatory buy-and-sell agreement offers a solution to the problem especially when funded by life and disability income insurance. Either a **cross-purchase plan** under which each partner buys and owns the insurance on the other partners or the **entity plan** under which the partnership itself owns the policies on each partner may be used. The entity plan is simpler when the number of partners is large, because fewer policies are required.

Close corporation insurance

If an employee stockholder becomes disabled the disability will create the same problems as that of a disabled partner. The recommended disability insurance and its arrangement are identical in most respects with those used for a partnership. As the corporation's existence is not affected by a shareholder's death the heirs may legally sell their shares to anyone unless the corporation's bylaws provide otherwise, as in closely held corporations (often called close or closed corporations). Often the surviving shareholders or the corporation may want to buy the shares of an active stockholder who dies or becomes totally disabled. Life and disability income insurance can help provide the money for this purchase.

Credit and collateral uses

Business life and health insurance can strengthen company credit, provide collateral for loans and bolster the confidence of customers, suppliers and employees. Adequate insurance to absorb the shock of the loss of a key employee or to guarantee business continuation following an owner's disability or death often affects the firm's credit rating. If creditors know that death or disability of an owner or other key employee will not disrupt the firm, credit may be granted more readily.

INNERSCRIPT: POLICY STANDARDIZATION

In the early days the insurer and the policyowner had complete freedom in designing the policy. As insurance became highly technical this freedom was a disadvantage to policyowners and insurers. A policyowner with several insurance policies often discovered

overlapping and conflicting coverage. The policyowner might own two policies with each policy containing a provision that denies coverage if other insurance was maintained on the property. More often than not these distressing facts became known only after a loss had occurred. The need for some standardization was evident. The HO–3 and the PAP (discussed in Chapter 8 and 9 respectively) are examples of standardized policies.

Methods of standardization

Policies are standardized by custom, statute and intercompany agreement. Not all policies are standardized, and even when they are, risk managers for large businesses do not have to purchase the standard form. Instead they might develop forms of their own to meet particular needs and then seek insurers to write the tailored coverage. A *standard policy* may be defined as one that is substantially like that written by the majority of insurers.

Custom

As early as 1764 the underwriters at Lloyd's coffeehouse realized that it was to their advantage and that of their policyowners to adopt a standard policy. In 1779 they agreed to use a standard marine form developed by fellow underwriters, known as "Lloyd's standard policy." Through the years a body of insurance law developed from many court decisions concerning the policy. Nearly every word of the Lloyd's policy has been subject to court interpretation so that, in spite of its archaic wording, any insurer writing the policy is confident of the meaning. By custom marine insurance policies written in the United States stem from the Lloyd's policy even though some variations are found among the policies as a result of competition.

Standardization by state law

Standardization by state statute is accomplished either by prescribing a particular contract or minimum standard provisions.

The only example of a standard policy where the exact wording of the contract is prescribed by law is the fire insurance policy.

Rather than require a standard policy for some coverages the states prescribe minimum standard provisions. Some are mandatory; others are optional. The use of specified additional provisions is expressly forbidden. Life and health policies are standardized through standard provisions. Although life insurance forms are not identical they must contain prescribed provisions concerning grace periods for premium payments, nonforfeiture options, reinstatement and incontestability. Life insurers cannot exclude or restrict coverage except for war, suicide, aviation and hazardous occupations (see Chapter 14). Health policies achieve a measure of stan-

continued

dardization through required "uniform provisions." These provisions are discussed in Chapter 15. The uniform provisions do not deal with benefit clauses so benefits vary widely among policies, also noted in Chapter 15.

Standardization by intercompany agreement

Recognizing the advantages of standard policies insurers often develop uniform contracts through intercompany agreement. Standard policies eliminate undesirable "fine-print" competition among insurers and simplify interpretation of policies. Standardization by intercompany agreement also eliminates the need for standard policy laws. Insurers prefer voluntary intercompany action to legislative compulsion.

Automobile insurance provides the best known example of standardization through intercompany agreement. The original 1936 standard automobile policy (called the basic policy)**, covered liability only. Through many revisions coverage has been extended to include physical damage and to some extent personal accidents. Automobile insurance is not the only field where policies are voluntarily standardized. Such policies as the comprehensive personal liability, comprehensive general liability, glass and many crime coverages are also standardized.**

Many insurers do not use standard forms. Indeed, for competitive reasons the current trend appears to be away from them. Policies, therefore, are likely to vary widely among insurers and over time. Insurance buyers should compare policies rather than rely on some standard form or some previously owned policy.

CHOOSING THE AGENT

Too many writers on the subject of how to buy insurance give selecting the insurer primary emphasis. Frequently they have little or nothing to say about choosing the agent. (The word *agent* is used in its broadest, nontechnical sense to include anyone involved in the marketing of insurance: agents, brokers, direct salespersons and so on.) What are the characteristics of a good agent? In addition to an interest in their clients' welfare well qualified agents must be able to provide: knowledge of the insurance business; time and facilities for providing necessary services; good contacts with the insurance market; knowledge of insurers to use for special situations; an effective claims follow-up service and, finally, the respect and cooperation of clients, competitors, insurers and claim adjusters.

What readily visible earmarks enable the buyer to select agents wisely? The answer is: none. Two sources of information not readily visible are available: other insurance buyers and insurance agents. The opinions of other insurance buyers vary with the extent of their insurance knowledge and their experience with insurance representatives. Although insurance problems of one's neighbor may be the same as one's own, the neighbor's judgment may be inexperienced and faulty. For these reasons one must build a composite opinion from several sources.

In general an agent's competitors are a valuable source of information, but here an important point must be noted: certain agents' comments will reveal more about these agents than about their competitors. Good business practice requires caution in making critical remarks about competitors. Thus a freely critical person may be telling the listener his or her own weakness. Still, the ethical agent usually cannot condone clearly unethical practices and so in such cases will make specific comments but refrain from drawing general conclusions.

The buyer needs the answers to pertinent questions. What is an agent's experience in years and breadth of practice? Is the agent a specialist in any coverage? Does the agent deal mostly with personal lines, small or large firms or across-the-board? What is the reputation of the insurer or insurers the agent represents? Are the agent and the staff regular attendants at schools, forums and professional educational conferences? The answers offer some measure of the quality of an agency if the source is informed and honest.

The agents themselves are the ultimate source of information. They must be persons with whom the buyer is willing to discuss business and family financial details. What should the buyer expect of the agent in addition to knowledge? How should the agent show a sense of responsibility for clients' welfare? How should agents use their time and facilities for providing service? To what end should they organize their market contacts? The agent has the responsibility (in addition to acquiring and keeping up with product and market knowledge) to become fully acquainted with the client's problems. He or she should help the buyer identify loss exposures as described in Chapters 3 and 4.

By applying knowledge of insurance and risk management to the client's loss exposures, professional agents will help their clients reach intelligent risk management decisions. However, wise agents seldom make decisions for their clients. Regarding the potential insurance portion of the program professional agents will keep up to date on their clients' loss exposures and will inform them of relevant changes in insurance rules, forms and rates. They will seek to provide insurance at the lowest cost consistent with quality. These tasks require regular contact and cooperation between the agent and the insured.

Finally, agents may play a role in claims settlements although they have little or no official position in loss adjustments for other than small losses. In large agencies and sometimes in moderate-sized ones claims may be handled by the agency, but this arrangement is uncommon. When agents have no official standing regarding claims settlement their services may consist mainly of interpreting the positions of the insurer and the insured and in seeking a rapid and smooth settlement. The wise agent tends to be more active on behalf of the insured than the insurer. The insured, however, should not expect an agent's support in other than a valid position. Some agents have not followed this rule and those who persist on such a course sooner or later find themselves without reputable insurers to represent.

Agents' services cost money—money from premiums paid by insureds. Differences in premium levels are often explained by differences in agency services. As students of marketing put it, distribution costs are reduced by shifting part of the service to the customers. How much service insureds wish to buy and how much they wish to supply themselves are personal determinations. However, the importance of the services of a *good* agent should not be underestimated.

INNERSCRIPT: THE STORY OF POOR HERMAN AND HIS BEVY OF AGENTS

The story of Poor Herman emphasizes the importance of *buying insurance* rather than *collecting policies.*

Once upon a time, in the rich land of America, in the village of Sunnyside, there dwelt a citizen known as Herman. He was a righteous and respected businessman who, since early manhood, had applied himself diligently to his trade. And not without success. Somewhat abundant was his store of worldly goods and bright indeed his prospects. Now Herman was not alike unto all of his fellowmen for he was a believer in insurance. And he let this be known since his belief was founded upon the conviction that only insurance can remove the risk of loss. And the people to whom he spoke, spoke of it among themselves and the word spread and the agents of insurance did one after another seek him out. To each of these did he renew his faith saying: "Yea, I am a believer in insurance and I feel it is a good thing. For has not insurance the power to lift the crown of care from the brows of the worried?"

And to him they displayed their policies and from them did he take insurance. Even the property floater which is personal and the personal liability which is comprehensive. From one he sought security against loss by automobile and to yet another did he entrust the fire insurance on his dwelling. And thus at last was his mind at rest and to himself he said: "Secure must I be against misfortune for have I not of policies a full bushel and of agents a round half dozen? Surely ease and prosperity shall follow me all the days of my life."

But it came to pass that on a day when Herman and his family visited in a neighboring village a sudden and accidental rupture of the steamheating boiler did rend asunder the house of Herman. . . . Yea from gable to foundation. And Herman upon his return did summon unto himself all of his agents of insurance and they together examined his bushel of policies. And then at last as the truth broke upon them did they all fall back aghast; for of all the policies of Herman none there was which would make good the destruction and all of his good intentions availed him naught. Then truly did Herman tear his hair, beat his breast and cry out: "Oh Lord, what is the use?"

SELECTING THE INSURER

Few insurance buyers begin by choosing a type of insurer—a stock or mutual company for example. They are following sound insurance buying instinct in this regard. Considerations in choosing an insurer are broadly summarized in a paraphrase of Pope's "Essay on Man:"

> For forms of companies let fools contest
> Whate'er is best administer'd is best. . . .

General Considerations

The management's quality and philosophy are the most important criteria in selecting an insurer. Unfortunately these criteria are intangibles that statistical or financial reports do not reveal. Published figures can be used to determine the insurer's financial condition but they tell little about its claims policy or service. Then where is this information found?

If one can depend on the agent to put the client's interests first and not be tied too closely to particular insurers that agent probably is the best source of information about insurers as well as about contracts. The agent must keep the interest of the clients above any close ties to particular insurers. Thus the presumption is that the agent uses a particular insurer or insurers because of the belief that they are good for clients. If unusual policies that suit the client's need are unavailable from the agent's insurers the good agent helps the client obtain that special protection from other insurers. Financial condition, underwriting philosophy, claims policy, service and price are more important in selecting an insurer than whether it is a reciprocal, stock or mutual. The quality of insurers differs and discriminating among them is not easy for the layman.

Alfred M. Best, Inc. publishes two insurance yearbooks, one for property and liability and the other for life and health insurance. *Best's Insurance Reports* includes details on company history, personnel, investments, operating results, underwriting results and other financial data. This information is reported for all types of insurers. Ratings assigned to insurers usually are based on an analysis of their financial statements. Best examines five criteria to arrive at its "general policyholders' rating," intended to measure the financial stability and general reliability of the insurer from the buyer viewpoint. The assigned ratings range downward: excellent (A+ or A), very good (B+), good (B), fairly good (C+) and fair (C). If Best's does not have adequate information (either because the insurer does not cooperate or does not have a 5-year operating history) the rating is omitted.

For property and liability insurers Best also supplies a financial rating intended to evaluate these insurers' net safety factor. These ratings begin with class I, representing a net safety factor of less than $250,000 to class XV representing a net safety factor in excess of $100 million. Some observers consider these "canned" ratings of value only in excluding low-rated insurers from consideration. However, many corporate insurance buyers give serious attention to them. (For further discussion of the ratings in *Best's Insurance Reports* see the latest editions.)

Once people have decided to buy an item they become interested in how much (quantity and quality) they can get, what it will cost and how quickly they can get it. The insurance buyer's "how much" is determined by the amount of protection and auxiliary services. A quality product in insurance demands a financially sound insurer. Insurance protection and services are sold in the present for indefinite future delivery. Whether buyers want protection or service they will receive neither unless the insurer is financially able to deliver. In choosing insurers an estimation of future liquidity and solvency should be a principal factor.

Factors in Insurers' Finances

Most insureds are poor judges of insurance finance. The reliable insurer is both solvent and liquid. **Solvency** means owning more than one owes: total assets exceed total liabilities. **Liquidity** means the ability to pay off liabilities as they become due: current assets exceed current liabilities. Insureds want their insurers to be liquid and solvent at the time of loss. But because that time is in the indefinite future wise buyers must consider the factors that affect an insurer's continued ability to pay losses when they occur. Factors like the insurer's loss and expense ratios, net income earned on investments, the size and growth of surplus and quality of assets are discussed in Chapter 22.

Services to the Policyowner

One question regarding an insurer's service can be settled quickly: does the insurer offer buyers the policy they want? Many special coverages are available only from some insurers. Furthermore, valid differences in underwriting philosophy allow one insurer but not another to underwrite a particular exposure. Thus some insurers are automatically eliminated from consideration. Most life insurers, for example, do not write disability income riders. Insurance protection for lumberyards is a specialty line for some property insurers while others cater to flour mills or coal mines. Insurers lacking necessary specialized facilities or experience often will accept neither of these exposures.

Many times underwriters will ''take the bitter only with the sweet,'' meaning that undesirable (unprofitable) coverages are written only if the profitable ones are also purchased. Workers' compensation might be considered an undesirable line and will be offered only along with the generally more profitable property lines (or, for some underwriters, vice versa!).

The speed and fairness of an insurer's claims service are a consideration. Finding this information is difficult because prejudiced and limited observation obscures many observers' opinions. Human nature being what it is, not all claimants receive what they think is due. Considering how few policyowners read, let alone understand, their policies and the room for honest differences of opinion about values of lost property, it is surprising that more problems do not arise. To hear that an insurer has had a dissatisfied claimant is to learn no more than that the insurer is in the insurance business.

Yet if the buyer is to form a judgment of the speed and fairness of an insurer's claims service the buyer has at best only two sources other than trustworthy agents: the insurer's customers and competitors. Both must be used cautiously with considerable weight given the experience, knowledge and character of each informant. As for the claims policy, extremes are undesirable. No insured wants coverage with an insurer that regularly pinches claims pennies. On the other hand, overly liberal payments can damage an insurer's financial structure.

In some insurance lines an additional service is important: loss control. The quality of this service varies among insurers. A qualified corps of inspectors might tip the balance in favor of an insurer for boiler and machinery coverage; an imaginative loss control department might be the deciding factor in selecting a workers' compensation insurer.

Costs of the Insurance

When buyers have decided on the best coverage for their needs their buying problem still is not solved. Costs vary widely among insurers for essentially similar coverage.

Property-liability insurance costs comparisons

If the policy, the quality of services provided (claims, loss control and so on) and the financial soundness of the insurers are identical the cost of the insurance should be the same in a perfectly competitive market. However, the market is not perfect. Therefore the buyer must compare the prices of several insurers to find the one with the lowest cost.

Families in their market search will find homeowners policies and auto policies with widely differing premiums. In some cases these differences are justified by the quality of the product and services. In other cases the differences may not be justified. One service that should be considered in cost comparisons is the quality of the agent. Another consideration is the importance of maintaining a stable relationship with an insurer. Insurance markets undergo cycles. In some periods underwriting is lax and premiums are low. In others the reverse is true. Policyowners who frequently shift from company to company to obtain the lowest premiums may find it difficult to buy insurance at a reasonable price when insurers become more restrictive in their underwriting.

Business insurance buyers often develop their own specifications for coverage and services. They practice competitive bidding based on these specifications to find the most economically attractive insurers. Only insurers that meet the financial ratings desired are invited to bid.

The foregoing discussion of property-liability cost comparisons also applies to health insurance and short-term life insurance.

Life insurance cost comparisons

Because life insurance policies often include cash values and provide for dividend payments, cost comparisons among them are difficult. Over the past two decades attempts have been made to develop methods for making life insurance cost comparisons. These attempts have not been easy because of the desire to develop methods that are both accurate and simple—apparently conflicting goals. A few of these methods are discussed here.

The traditional net cost method. The traditional method of comparing life insurance costs per $1,000 of insurance has been to take the sum of all the premiums for a specified period (usually 10 or 20 years) *less* (1) the cash value at the end of the period, (2) the sum of the policy dividends, if any, for that period and (3) the current applicable terminal dividend, if any. This sum, either positive or negative, is divided by the number of years in the illustrated period to compute the net cost per $1,000 per year. For example, assume that a prospective insured compares the costs of a $1,000 continuous premium whole life policy with a similar policy issued by a competing insurer. Assume further that the sum of all premiums for the initial 20 policy years is $264 ($13.20 a year); total dividends based on the current scale are $60; the cash value at the end of 20 years is $229 and the terminal dividend is $6. The net cost per $1,000 per year would equal

$$\frac{\$264-(\$60+\$229+\$6)}{20}=\frac{-31}{20}=-\$1.55 \text{ per } \$1{,}000 \text{ per year}$$

Thus the prospective buyer would use the figure −$1.55 per $1,000 of insurance per year in comparing the cost of that policy with another similar policy. A cost comparison technique that shows life insurance to have a negative price has to be suspect. The use of this method was a prime cause for the development of other techniques.

The surrender cost method. The surrender cost method resembles the traditional cost concept but by using interest assumptions some of the major deficiencies of the traditional cost method are overcome. The surrender cost method differs from the traditional method in three respects: (1) the premiums are accumulated at interest, (2) dividends also are accumulated at interest and (3) instead of dividing the total by 20 (for a 20-year comparison) the new sum is divided by the amount to which one per annum payable in advance will accumulate in 20 years at the assumed interest rate. That amount at 5 percent interest is 34.719.

This formula produces a higher but more nearly accurate cost estimate. Using the previous example and 5 percent interest with the surrender cost method, accumulated premiums equal \$458 (i.e., \$13.20 × 34.719) and accumulated dividends equal \$82. The other figures in the numerator remain the same. The figures in the denominator change from 20 to 34.719 to reflect the assumed interest. The cost per year per \$1,000 equals

$$\frac{\$458-(\$82+\$229+\$6)}{34.719}=\frac{\$141}{34.719}=\$4.06 \text{ per } \$1{,}000 \text{ per year}$$

This figure compares to a −\$1.55 cost under the traditional cost method.

The net payment cost method. The net payment cost method is calculated in the same manner as the surrender cost method except that the cash value at the end of the specified period and the terminal dividend are not subtracted from the accumulated premiums. This cost method does not assume that the prospective buyer will surrender the policy after the specified period; rather the net payment cost method shows how much a policyowner will have to pay to keep the policy in force for the specified period. Using this method for the previous example the cost of the policy per \$1,000 equals

$$\frac{\$458-\$82}{34.719}=\frac{\$376}{34.719}=\$10.83 \text{ per } \$1{,}000 \text{ per year}$$

However, the surrender cost and net payment cost methods are still subject to criticism. The assumption is that the current dividends remain unchanged although future dividends are unknown.

Average annual rate of return. Some persons advocate using the rate of return method as a basis for policy cost comparisons: a policy showing a high rate of return is regarded as a low priced policy and vice versa. The average annual rate of return on a cash value life insurance policy can be determined by using a method developed by M. Albert Linton. This method is based on the "buy term and invest the difference" concept discussed in Chapter 13. It determines the rate of interest compounded annually that must be earned on the separate investment fund so that the fund will equal the guaranteed cash value of the life insurance policy at the end of a specified period. Calculating this rate of return requires trial and error. Various rates of return are tried until the rate is found that creates equivalence between the assumed accumulated fund and the guaranteed policy cash value at the end of the period selected. The average annual rate of return provides information to buyers seeking to purchase life insurance as an investment. A buyer interested in life insurance as an investment can use this method to compare the rates of return of two different life insurance policies.

Use of the cost-comparison methods. After studying different cost comparison methods one might be concerned as to which methods, if any, are worthwhile. All of them, with the exception of the traditional net cost method, could be useful to a prospective purchaser. (The traditional net cost method is probably more misleading than helpful to a consumer.) The purchaser should use the method that satisfies his or her needs. For example, a buyer who plans to keep the policy in force should use the net payment cost index instead of the surrender cost index. The purchaser also must realize that the cost of the policy is not the only aspect to consider when buying life insurance. The quality of services offered by insurers, their financial standings and policy provisions must be compared.

CONCLUDING REMARKS

Before offering a summary of this chapter and questions for review, several closing observations are in order.

Risk management is the name of the game. Its components are loss control and loss financing. Insurance is the most common and in many cases the most effective method of loss financing. Therefore the budding risk manager, and that includes nearly everyone, does well to learn about insurance first. What is it? What makes it tick? What kinds of insurance are available? How are insurance contracts written and interpreted? What types of organizations write insurance and how is it sold? What are the legal and regulatory problems involved? What problems are faced by those who buy and sell insurance? These and an array of other theoretical and institutional aspects of insurance have been discussed in these pages. Some of them have not been assigned reading. But that is all right! Classtime is always limited and the unassigned material will be there when needed. As time passes and educational growth continues those sections and chapters not assigned (and many of those assigned) will become more meaningful and understandable.

The story of insurance, or at least a good part of it, has been told (hopefully nonfictionally). It includes a number of characters: insurers, insureds, agents, brokers, mail carriers, physicians, claimants, lawyers, regulators, consumer advocates, risk managers, a host of technical insurance company personnel, students and professors.

AND THEY ALL LIVED HAPPILY EVER AFTER
THE END

Meanwhile, back to the chapter's summary and review questions:

SUMMARY

1. Self-insurance requires a large number of noncatastrophic and similar exposure units so that losses can be reasonably predicted. Exposures that meet these requirements may be self-insured if the insured has the financial strength and knowledge to fund and administer the plan.
2. When buying insurance, several principles should be considered:
   a. The large-loss principle in which a *small* certain cost (the premium) should be substituted for a *large* uncertain one.
   b. The gradation of coverage is used to provide a basis for trade-offs between limited premium dollars and the loss exposure to be covered. Essential coverages should be purchased first, then desirable coverage. Available coverages should be purchased only by worrywarts or people whose best friend is in the insurance business.
3. In determining whether insurance is essential or desirable, the loss-unit concept is helpful. The loss-unit concept requires that prospective insurance buyers consider all losses from a single happening rather than focus on individual losses only.
4. After determining the purposes for which postloss resources are needed, five basic steps should be considered in the process of buying life and health insurance:
   a. Determine the amount of postloss resources needed to satisfy each purpose.
   b. Determine the current resources available to meet the needs.

c. Determine the amount of additional resources required.
d. Coordinate the postloss resources into a plan.
e. Arrange safeguards to protect the plan.

5. To meet personal life and health insurance needs, the life insurance planner should consider a number of possible needs: an executor fund, a mortgage or rent fund, adjustment income, family period income, lifetime income for the surviving spouse, an education fund, an emergency fund, retirement income coverage and coverage on individual family members.

6. Families must also plan for their property and liability insurance needs. Important are physical damage insurance and liability insurance covering losses arising from the ownership and/or use of dwellings and contents, automobiles and other personal property. Personal activity also creates a liability exposure that must be protected by insurance.

7. Businesses own assets, rent property, engage in activity and have a work force—all of which are sources of losses. Insurance can be purchased to cover most of these loss exposures. However in some cases the use of other risk management tools may be more efficient.

8. Business life and health insurance is used for employee benefit plans as well as to attract and retain key employees, to finance buy-and-sell agreements for sole proprietorships, partnerships and close corporations and to strengthen company credit.

9. Policies are standardized by custom, statute and intercompany agreement, thus simplifying some of the buyer's problems but complicating others.

10. Good insurance buyers carefully select their agents. A good agent has the following characteristics: responsibility for the client's welfare; knowledge of the insurance business; time and facilities for providing necessary services; good contacts with the insurance market and the respect and cooperation of clients, competitors, insurers and claims adjusters.

11. The management's quality and philosophy are the most important criteria in selecting an insurer. Published figures can be used principally to determine the insurer's financial condition (solvency and liquidity), but they tell little about its claims policy or service.

12. Property and liability insurance cost should not be viewed in a vacuum. The quality of the agent, the product offered and the need for a stable relationship with an insurer should be considered along with the cost.

13. Life insurance cost comparisons are complicated because of cash values and dividend payments. Attempts have been made to develop methods for making meaningful as well as simple life insurance cost comparisons without much success. The modern cost comparison methods are interest-adjusted and include the surrender cost index and the net payment cost index. Also gaining support is the average annual rate of return method.

14. The prospective policyowners should consider only the life insurance cost methods that best meet their needs.

REVIEW QUESTIONS

1. Name the characters involved in the saga of insurance and explain why they all lived happily ever after.

2. Consider the advantages and disadvantages of self-insurance. Develop a situation in which the advantages would outweigh the disadvantages. Develop a situation in which the disadvantages would outweigh the advantages.
3. Point out some curious principles that often are applied in the purchase of insurance. Explain why you consider these principles to be curious.
4. Boundaries exist between essential and desirable coverages. Are these boundaries fixed or variable? Explain.
5. Define the loss-unit concept and explain its importance to the insurance buyer.
6. Identify and explain the five basic steps in the life and health insurance programming process.
7. Evaluate the postloss needs for personal life and health insurance in terms of their relative importance.
8. A family is planning its property and liability insurance program. What are the typical loss exposures of a family and what types of policies best cover them?
9. Explain how life insurance can be used by business to attract and retain key employees.
10. Distinguish between a cross-purchase plan and an entity plan in financing partnership buy-and-sell agreements.
11. What procedures would you recommend in selecting an insurance agent? Do you follow these procedures? Why not?
12. Do you think you are better equipped to buy insurance now that you have taken this course?
13. Distinguish between solvency and liquidity. Is it more important to you for your insurer to be solvent or liquid? Choose one or the other.
14. Describe the surrender cost index and the net payment cost index. Which index is the most useful? Explain.
15. What are some resources available to a firm after a loss other than insurance?

Glossary

Abandonment: Relinquishing ownership of lost or damaged property to the insurer when permitted under the contract.

Absolute liability: Liability for injury to others imposed, in the absence of negligence or intent, on those best able to control the occurrence.

Accident: A fortuitous event, unexpected and unintended, occurring suddenly and causing measureable loss.

Actual cash value: Replacement cost of property new, minus that sum equal to accrued financial depreciation, technological obsolescence and location deterioration.

Actuarial cost methods: Technique for distributing the incidence of pension costs, both current and supplemental, over time.

Add-on no fault benefits: Provision adding no fault benefits to automobile liability coverages without restricting the right of the victim to sue the wrongdoer.

Adhesion: Contract prepared and made available by an insurer to an applicant who must accept or reject it in the form offered.

Admitted assets: Assets, including most legal portfolio investments, whose values are permitted by state law to be included in the insurer's annual statement as a measure of solvency.

Affirmative: Form of warranty stating a fact is true now but promising nothing about the future.

Agency by ratification: Creation of an agency relationship, in the absence of a formal agreement, by the principal sanctioning the actions of another party after a transaction has been completed.

Aleatory: A contract in which the dollar amount to be exchanged will be unequal; e.g., if a loss is suffered, the payment will be far greater than the premium and if there is no loss, there is no payment.

All-risk: An insurance policy covering real or personal property against any loss except those specifically excluded.

Allocated funding instrument: The deposits made by an employer to an employee retirement plan are segregated and identifiable for each participant.

American agency system: Independent agents represent one or more insurers, own all policy records and are compensated by commissions.

Amount limit (coinsurance): The amount of insurance specified in an open stock burglary policy beyond which the coinsurance percentage limit does not apply.

Annual policy: A policy issued for a 12-month period.

Annuity certain: Benefits paid for a given period regardless of the life or death of the annuitant.

Annuity due: Payment is made to the annuitant at the beginning of the first income period.

Compiled by Irving L. Finston, M.A., CPCU, CLU.

Apparent authority: Authority which the agent has exercised and in which the insurer, with full knowledge, remained silent.

Appeal bond: Bond guaranteeing payment of original judgment and cost of appeal should the appeal to a court of higher jurisdiction be unsuccessful.

Assault: An unsuccessful attempt at violence or a physical or verbal threat of violence to another.

Assignment: Partial or total transfer of policyowner rights to another party.

Assumption of risk doctrine: A defense arguing that the plaintiff consented, expressly or by implication, to relieve the defendant of the duty to protect and accepted the chance of injury from the particular risk causing the injury.

Attractive nuisance: Any novel device particularly enticing to children and potentially dangerous to them, creating a significant liability hazard for the owner.

Automatically convertible term: Term life insurance policies programmed to convert to permanent insurance at a predetermined date without an express direction by the insured at that time.

Average indexed monthly earnings: Workers average covered monthly wage, after adjusting for the rising national average annual earnings, used in determining the primary insurance amount for social security benefits.

Average value method: A method for determining the claim reserve by taking the average value of claims of various types, adjusting it to trend projections and then multiplying by the number of unsettled claims.

Bail bond: A guaranty that an accused, if released, will voluntarily appear for trial.

Bank burglary and robbery policy: A combination of burglary, robbery, vandalism and malicious mischief as primary coverage for the smaller bank and as excess coverage for larger banks.

Bankers blanket bond: A hybrid form covering employee dishonesty under one section and crime and miscellaneous coverages, other than fire, under another section.

Bankruptcy or insolvency clause: Affirms the responsibility of an insurer despite bankruptcy or insolvency of the insured.

Basic policy (automobile): Liability and physical damage insurance provided with options available to expand scope of coverage.

Basic rate (schedule rating): The rate assigned to a well-built structure with high-grade fire protection used as a starting point in the Universal Mercantile System of fire schedule rating.

Basic transportation policy: The basic policy for domestic shipments, applicable to most transportation exposures and completed by endorsement specifying perils covered and pertinent exclusions.

Battery: The intentional, unpermitted and unprivileged contact with the person of others.

Beneficiary: That person, named in the policy, entitled to the proceeds of the policy upon the death of the subject.

Benefit computation years: The year 1951 or year a worker is age 22 until the year before the worker is age 62, dies or is disabled, minus five and minus any years of qualified disability.

Benefit of any insurance clause: A clause frequently found in a bill of lading transferring the benefit of any insurance to the carrier or bailee.

Bid bond: A guarantee that should a bid be accepted, the successful bidder will sign the contract and furnish a performance bond.

Bilateral: A contractual agreement to exchange one promise for another promise.

Blanket (health coverage): An aggregate amount is specified for necessary and reasonable medical expenses.

Blanket coverage: A single face amount of the policy applies to all the various coverages contained therein at one or more locations.

Blanket crime policy: Provides a single limit of insurance for fidelity and crime coverages with minimum coverage of $1,000.

Blanket health: A contract protecting all members of a given group against insured perils without naming individuals or issuing individual certificates.

Blanket position bond: Each employee's honesty is guaranteed up to the bond penalty with maximum liability equal to the bond penalty limit multiplied by the number of employees.

Blanket rating: Refer to **Manual rating.**

Block of business: Life insurance of the same type and face amount, issued in the same year to a homogeneous group of the same age.

Bottomry: Early form of marine insurance to secure a loan for a maritime venture by pledging the ship as collateral.

Branch office: Regional or local office of an insurer providing all company services in a given geographical territory.

Broad form storekeepers policy: Designed for the single retail store with four or fewer employees, providing fidelity and crime coverages with limits of insurance from $250 to $1,000 per insuring agreement.

Broker: An agent of the insured, paid a commission by the insurance company and authorized to deliver contracts and collect premiums only on behalf of the insurer.

Burglary: Unlawful abstraction of property from within the premises by someone using force or violence on the structure to effect entry or exit.

Businessowner's program: Provides limited or broad form physical damage insurance on smaller apartment, office or mercantile structures, covering building and contents for full replacement cost, plus liability insurance.

Catastrophe risks reinsurance: Reinsurer agrees to reimburse the ceding insurer up to a stated maximum for catastrophic losses in excess of a given retention amount per disaster.

Ceded: The amount of insurance placed with a reinsurer.

Cession: The process of placing business with a reinsurer; or the unit of insurance transferred by the ceding company to a reinsurer.

Chance of loss: The long-run relative frequency of loss, best expressed as a fraction or percentage.

Civil law: That part of the law, based on the common law and statuatory acts, which is employed by the injured party to redress private wrongs.

Claimants: Parties or party making formal demand for payment for a loss construed to be covered under the terms of an insurance policy.

Claims-made basis: Insurer has responsibility only for claims filed during the policy period.

Claims-occurrence basis: Insurer has responsibility for all claims resulting from events occurring during the policy period whenever the claim is filed.

Class rating: Refer to **Manual rating.**

Coinsurance amount limit: Requirement under burglary insurance policy that a minimum amount of insurance be maintained, determined by the nature of the merchandise.

Coinsurance clause: Determines the amount of recovery for partial loss if the property is not insured for a specified percentage of its cash value at the time of loss.

Coinsurance percentage: Provision in the mercantile open stock burglary policy, determined by geographical location, indicating the amount of insurance required to avoid penalty in the event of loss.

Coinsurance plan (life reinsurance): Reinsurance of the difference between the face amount of a life insurance policy and the ceding insurer's net retention limit.

Collision: Sudden and unintended damage to a vehicle caused by upset or contact with another object.

Combination safe depository policy: Covers bank's legal liability and customers' property and bank's equipment against loss by crime.

Combined ratio: An approximation of fire and casualty company underwriting profitability obtained by adding the operating expense ratio to the incurred loss and loss adjustment expense ratio.

Commercial blanket bond: Covers employee dishonesty involving one or more employees up to a fixed, maximum penalty.

Commercial property form: Covers business personal property of retailers, wholesalers and some other businessowners against physical loss on an all-risk basis.

Commissioners reserve valuation method: A method that, in essence, limits initial expenses to that amount available by treating a 20 payment life policy for establishing reserves without depleting surplus as a one-year term policy plus a 19 payment life policy issued to a person one year older.

Common employment: A defense against recovery by an injured employee, alleging fellow employees are better qualified than the employer to judge another worker's ability to prevent injuries to other workers.

Common law: A body of law, subordinate to constitutional law and statutory law, comprised of appellate court decisions and that part of post-renaissance English law reflecting local public policy.

Commutative: A contract in which each party relinquishes goods or services deemed to be of equal value.

Comparative negligence: Doctrine designed to permit recovery in a negligence action despite the plaintiff having contributed to the accident, with both parties sharing the financial burden according to their respective degrees of negligence.

Completion bond: A guarantee provided by a contractor through a bonding company to a lender that a building will be free of claim when turned over to the owner.

Comprehensive dishonesty, disappearance and destruction policy (3D): A combination policy providing elective coverage for fidelity and crime coverages.

Computation base years: Those years, starting in 1951 and ending with the year the worker dies, the year before the worker begins to receive retirement benefits or disability benefits.

Concealment: Intentionally withholding known adverse facts when obligated to reveal them.

Conditional: Contract of insurance requiring the insured to meet specified conditions to obtain payment for insured losses.

Consequential losses: Losses arising indirectly from an insured peril, e.g., fire damaging refrigeration equipment resulting in food spoilage.

Constructive total loss: Partial loss where the cost of repairs would exceed the value of the restored property.

Contingent business-interruption insurance: Provides monetary benefits to the insured if his earnings are diminished because of an insured peril damaging another business on which his business is dependent.

Continuous premium whole life: Refer to **Straight life.**

Contracts: In insurance, an agreement in which an insured pays a sum of money to obtain stipulated benefits from an insurer should specified events occur.

Contributory negligence: A defense arguing that if the plaintiff's conduct or performance failed to meet the standard required for protection and that this failure contributed in causing the injury or damage, the plaintiff shall be denied recovery.

Conventional annuities: Annuitant is guaranteed a specified minimum dollar amount for each payment period, subject to increase if the annuity was issued on a participating basis.

Conversion: Wrongful disposition or detention of the personal property of others by one who has lawful possession of the property.

Convertible deductible: The initial premium charged is less than the manual premium and, following a loss, the balance of premium is due to qualify for payment.

Convertible term: Term life insurance which can be converted to any permanent or endowment form without evidence of insurability subject to time limitations.

Coordination of benefits: Provision of group medical expense policies to prevent profiting where more than one group policy is involved.

Corridor deductible: That amount the insured must pay for medical charges between the amount payable under a basic policy and that payable under a major medical plan.

Criminal law: That part of law, based on statute and enforced by government, which deals with actions harmful to the public.

Cross purchase plan: Each partner or stockholder in a closely held corporation is the applicant and owner of the life insurance policies on the other partners or stockholders.

Cumulative and participating deductible: Insured pays half the premium, assumes all losses until they equal the balance of the premium and then the insurer pays all future losses during the policy period.

Dean's Analytic System: A system of fire insurance rating under which cities are divided into 10 categories and buildings into 3 categories, each respectively indicating a different degree of fire protection and fire resistance quality.

Debit agent: An insurance company representative empowered to collect weekly or monthly payments from the insured.

Decreasing term: Insurance benefits reduce monthly or yearly with the premium remaining constant and payable for a period slightly shorter than the term of the policy.

Defamation: Actions which injure another's reputation, intentionally or negligently communicated to someone other than the defamed party.

Deferred annuity: Benefits begin after a given number of years or at optional ages specified in a contract purchased with a single premium or annual premiums.

Deferred profit-sharing plans: Employer funded programs with no predetermined or targeted benefits and with employer contributions related to profits rather than to payroll.

Defined benefit plan: A retirement benefit plan under which benefits are specified using a predetermined formula.

Defined contribution plan: A retirement plan under which contribution levels are established with future benefits determined at the time of retirement.

Depositors forgery bond: Indemnifies insured and any depository for loss by alteration or forgery of an order to pay money, e.g., check, draft or promissory note.

Depository bond: Bond provided by a bank serving as an official depository for government funds.

Differences in conditions insurance: Contracts written on an all-risk basis to supplement an existing, underlying layer of basic property insurance.

Direct reporting (agent): Agent deals directly with his or her home office rather than with a general agent or branch office, a system of operation found most frequently in the property and liability business.

Disappearing deductible: Losses below a specific dollar amount are excluded; those above a second dollar amount are paid in full; and those in between are paid a multiple of the loss, usually 111 percent or 125 percent.

Divided coverage: Specific amount of coverage is allocated to each section of the policy.

Dividend options: Alternative ways in which dividends paid under participating life insurance policies can be used by policyowners.

Earned premiums: The proportional share of each policy's written premium applicable to the expired part of the policy.

Earnings form: Business interruption insurance which pays a stipulated amount to the insured when loss is caused by an insured peril.

Embezzlement: Fraudulent use of money or property held or controlled by an individual to whom it has been entrusted.

Endorsement: A written form modifying a fire and casualty policy to meet special conditions, to change policies in effect or to complete a policy.

Entire-contract statute: Holds that the policy and the application made part of its constitutes the entire contract between the parties precluding unwritten misrepresentations as a defense by the insurer against claim payment.

Entitlement: The benefits payable to a social security recipient starting with the year the participant elects to take these benefits.

Entity plan: Under a compulsory partnership or closely held corporation, the entity owns the life insurance policies on each partner or stockholder and upon the death of any such party uses the proceeds of the policy to purchase the share of the decedent.

Equitable remedies: Procedures in civil law when adequate legal remedy is unavailable, including reformation or rescission of contracts.

Estoppel: If one party to a contract had led the other party to believe certain contractual provisions would be ignored, resulting behavior relying on this action cannot be used to allege nonperformance.

Excess aggregate insurance: Coverage designed to meet the needs of self-insurers who wish to limit maximum potential loss in a designated time period.

Excess plan: A pension formula integrated with social security that provides benefits to the retiree only to the extent that his or her pension exceeds the amount of social security benefits at time of retirement.

Excess liability insurance: Coverage against loss in excess of coverage provided under another insurance contract.

Excess loss reinsurance: The reinsurer bears losses in excess of the ceding insurer's retention limit.

Exclusive agency system: Agents represent one insurer or a group of related insurers and retain no ownership interest in the policy records.

Experience rating system: Establishes premiums for various forms of insurance by modifying the manual rate to reflect, to varying degrees, the insured's past experience.

Expressed authority: Refer to **Stipulated authority.**

Extra-expense insurance: Provides for payment of extraordinary charges incurred in maintaining business operations following a loss caused by an insured peril.

Extra risk: An insurance applicant who does not fall into a standard premium range and can be accepted by increasing the premium cost, decreasing the scope of coverage or both.

Facultative reinsurance: Insurer determines for each case whether reinsurance is desired, requiring negotiation of a specific contract subject to acceptance or rejection by the reinsurer.

False imprisonment: The intentional restraint of another's freedom of movement by physical action or the threat of force.

Family forgery bond: Covers all family members for nonbusiness financial transactions against loss through (1) forgery of outgoing instruments, (2) accepting forged documents or (3) accepting counterfeit U.S. currency, subject to policy limits.

Family income insurance: Life insurance policy under which the beneficiary receives a fixed monthly income upon the insured's death, until the end of a specified period beginning when the policy was issued.

Favored institution: Nonprofit organizations classed by the IRS under Sec. 501(c)(3) of the Internal Revenue Code, including but not limited to private educational institutions, religious organizations and charitable institutions.

Federal-official bond: Bond required of any official of the federal government controlling certain kinds and quantities of federal property.

Fidelity bond: Guaranty of the principal's honesty, usually issued to protect an employer against loss by the dishonest acts of an employee.

Fire: Unintended rapid combustion, evidenced by a flame or glow, occurring outside its intended confines, e.g., fire escaping from a furnace.

Fitness for a particular purpose: Warranty affirming fitness for use when the seller is aware of the intended use and sanctions this use to the buyer.

Flat amount formula: The amount of the pension benefit is uniform for all retirees.

Flat amount unit benefit formula: The amount of pension benefits is determined only by the years of service completed.

Flat percentage formula: All eligible retirees receive the same percentage of annual wage as a retirement income.

Flexible compensation: Employer-provided fringe benefits, including but not limited to health and life insurance and vacation benefits, subject to partial selection by the employee.

Forgery: Falsely making or altering a document in writing.

4–40 rule: An incremental vesting formula requiring 40 percent vesting after 4 years with full vesting after the 10th year.

Franchise deductible: Should loss exceed a stipulated percentage of the value of the property, the loss is paid in full and no payment is made if the loss falls below this percentage.

Fraternal: An insurer related to a social organization to provide insurance benefits for members.

Free-of-capture and seizure clause (FC&S): Excludes coverage for piracy, war and capture under ocean marine insurance.

Free-of-particular average clause: Relieves a marine insurer of obligation for partial cargo losses.

Full-interest admitted form: Ocean marine form which requires payment of claim upon submission of proof of loss without proof of interest (basically similar to policy proof-of-interest form).

Full preliminary term reserve plan: Foregoes any reserve liability for the first year and requires a reserve account beginning the second year, assuming a policy issued at an age one year greater for a policy term one year shorter.

Fully funded: Retirement plan that provides for payment of funds sufficient for the liquidation of past service liabilities together with current payments to cover cost of benefits as they accrue.

Fully insured: A worker who has (1) a minimum of 6 quarters' coverage with 1 quarter of coverage for each calendar year commencing one year after 1950 (or the quarter when the worker reaches age 21 if later) and ending one year before the worker dies, becomes disabled or reaches age 62 whichever is the earliest or (2) at least 40 quarters of coverage.

Funding instrument: A trust agreement or an insurance contract stating the conditions under which the funding agency performs, specifying the terms under which the funding agency will accumulate, administer and disburse plan assets.

Funding standard account: A statistical tool to determine if the funding for a specific plan meets minimum funding standards for current service costs, initial past service costs, retroactive benefit increases, changes in expected actuarial experience and adjustments for experience losses and gains.

Garage liability insurance: Designed for automobile-related business firms, providing coverage for the premises; for the operations, products, completed operations; and for automobile liability.

Garagekeepers legal liability: Covers customers' vehicles, either on a primary basis or as excess over the customers' insurance, without regard to legal liability, against specific perils.

General agency: Agency represents a company, as an independent contractor, in a given territory, performing all operating functions for the company, including claims adjusting, collections and underwriting.

General agents: Refer to **General agency.**

General average clause: Basic provision of the ocean marine policy, in accordance with marine law, guaranteeing a shared assumption of costs to reimburse parties whose goods are sacrificed to save a vessel, if the effort succeeds.

General crime exclusions: Perils excluded because they are usually covered under other policies or because they require special treatment.

General policy provisions (life): Statutory constraints, identifying provisions which are prohibited, permitted or required in life insurance policies.

General property form: A standard form for insuring commercial buildings and contents used widely because of its versatility.

Good-faith contracts: Mutual reliance by the parties at interest on the truthfulness of the representations made and the legality of purpose in a contract.

Graded 5–15 rule: Provides for incremental vesting reaching 50 percent at the end of 10 years and 100 percent at the end of 15 years for participants in a funded pension plan.

Gross earnings form: Business interruption coverage which replaces actual loss of business earnings, i.e., gross earnings minus terminable expenses.

Group life insurance: Life insurance issued to an employer or association under a master policy for the benefit of employees or members.

Hazard: A condition that may create or increase the chance of loss arising from a given peril.

Hedging: Making commitments on both sides of a transaction so the risks offset each other.

Hold-harmless agreements: Contractual agreement in which one party agrees to release another party from all legal liability resulting from the occurrence of specific events.

Immediate annuity: Benefits are purchased with a single premium and begin at the end of the first income period.

Immediate notice: In the event of actual or presumed loss, notice must be provided the insurer or its representative as soon as is reasonably possible.

Implied authority: Power which the public may reasonably expect an agent to possess.

Improvements and betterments: The use interest in fixtures, alterations, installations or additions made to a part of a building occupied but not owned by the named insured.

Imputed negligence: One person becomes responsible for the negligent acts of another.

Inchmaree clause: Affirms coverage in an ocean marine policy even if due to negligence of master or crew or if due to defective machinery.

Incidental contracts: Contractual liability covered under most liability policies, limited to lease of premises, elevator maintenance agreements and railroad sidetrack agreements.

Incorporation: Forming an entity, under statute, legally distinct from the owners and which can be held legally liable for the acts of its employees.

Increasing term: Provides life insurance benefits which increase monthly or yearly.

Indemnity: Legal doctrine limiting recovery under an insurance policy to the lesser of the sum which will restore the insured to his or her financial position prior to the loss or to the actual cash value of the loss.

Independent agency companies: Those companies which market insurance through independent agents who are compensated by commissions and who own all policy records.

Indexing year: The second year before the worker reaches age 62, dies, or is disabled, used in determining social security benefits.

Individual case approach to loss reserving: A subjective approach, based on experience, of estimating the costs of discharging unsettled claims.

Individual policy pension trust: Individual policies of life insurance are purchased under qualified plans and held by the trustee to fund employee pension plans.

Industrial life insurance: Policies of $1,000 or less face value, paid weekly or monthly to a company employee, the "debit agent," who is assigned to service a limited geographic area.

Industrial property form: Specific peril or all-risk form available to manufacturing or processing businesses with two or more locations.

Inflation guard endorsement: Provision included in the homeowners policy automatically increasing the amount of coverage by a predetermined amount each quarter.

Initial deductible: A flat amount deducted by the insurer prior to insurer assumption of its proportion of the balance of covered charges.

Inland marine insurance: Covers domestic shipments, movable property and instrumentalities of transportation and communication.

Installments-of-a-fixed-amount option: Insurer pays a monthly benefit to the recipient of a predetermined amount until the policy proceeds are exhausted.

Installments-for-a-fixed period option: Proceeds of the policy, principal and interest are paid to the recipient in a fixed number of periodic payments.

Insurable interest: Created by exposure to financial loss in the event of damage or destruction to property or in the event of death or injury to an individual.

Insurance policies: Loss-sharing arrangements executed between individuals and members of a selected group who are exposed to similar losses.

Insured: That party to an insurance contract to whom or on behalf of whom the insurer has specific contractual obligations.

Insured plan: A pension plan administered by an insurance company.

Insurers: Organizations which administer insurance plans by pooling the payments of many contributors to offset the losses of the few.

Integrated deductible: Under major medical coverage, the higher of the benefits provided under the basic plan or fixed dollar amount is deducted from benefits payable to the insured.

Interest-only option: Insurer retains life insurance policy proceeds and pays the interest to the beneficiary.

Investment year: Refer to **New money approach.**

Irrevocable beneficiary: The beneficiary has been named under a life insurance policy with no reservation of the right to change beneficiary designations.

Jewelers block policy: Inland marine policy developed specifically for the jewelry trade covering most property losses to which they are exposed.

Joint-and-last-survivor annuity: Income is payable throughout the joint lifetimes of two or more annuitants, continuing until the last survivor's death.

Joint-and-last-survivorship option: Insurers pay the cash value or proceeds of a life insurance policy as an income payable until the death of the last survivor of two persons.

Judgment rating: Each exposure is rated on its own merits without recourse to schedule, formula or refined statistical data.

Judicial risk: The risk that a judicial interpretation may disturb accepted rules and may create, rather than follow, precedents.

Juridicial risk: The possibility that judicial interpretation may alter the assumed intent of a contract.

Key rate: Under the Universal Mercantile System for fire insurance rating, it is that rate assigned to a standard building in an actual city.

Larceny: Refer to **Theft.**

Last clear chance: Argument in a negligence action which holds that the defendant with the last clear chance to avoid the accident is guilty of contributory negligence by failure to use that last clear chance.

Leasehold interest: Reflects the advantage to a tenant under an existing lease compared to higher rental costs currently demanded for comparable property.

Legal remedies: Procedures in law, including waiver and estoppel, to settle disputes among parties to a contract regarding rights and obligations.

Level premium plan: Premiums remain the same, disregarding any dividend payment, for each year throughout the life of the policy.

Liability without fault: Imposed as a matter of public policy even though an injury may be unintentional and inflicted without negligence.

Life annuities: Benefits are paid annually or more frequently until the death of the annuitant.

Life income option: Policy proceeds are retained by the insurer and paid periodically for as long as the payee lives or for a specified minimum number of years, whichever is longer.

Life income period—certain annuity: Annuitant is promised a life income with a minimum number of guaranteed payments.

Limit of liability rule: When there is more than one policy covering a loss, each pays according to a predetermined formula which assumes no other insurance was in force.

Limited-pay life: Premiums are payable in level installments for a stated period or until the insured reaches a certain age.

Limited policy (health insurance): Health insurance policy with unusual exclusions, limitations, restrictions or reductions in coverage.

Line limits: Maximum amount of insurance any one insurer will issue on any one exposure.

Liquidity: Financial condition of a firm reflecting it can pay liabilities as they are due and that its current assets exceed current liabilities.

Local agent: An insurance agent representing several insurers in a restricted geographical area, performing sales functions primarily.

Loss frequency: Frequency of loss by a specific peril to a given body of homogeneous properties during a particular time period.

Loss ratio method: A technique of claims reserving in which the minimum loss reserve for each of the three most recent accident years is based on expected loss ratio.

Loss severity: The average claim cost, statistically determined by dividing dollars of losses by the number of claims.

Loss unit concept: The aggregate of diverse losses resulting from a single event.

Lost-instrument bond: Bond issued to a firm guaranteeing that the owner of a lost financial instrument will hold the firm harmless against loss if it will issue a duplicate instrument.

Malicious prosecution: Instituting criminal proceedings against another person without justification.

Manual rating: Exposures sharing common characteristics and grouped into classes with each class charged specific rates and each insured in the class charged the same rate.

Manufacturers' output policy: Covers direct loss to property situated off premises but owned by a manufacturer.

Market-value clause: Clause which permits settling losses on the basis of market value rather than on actual cash value.

Memorandum clause: Ocean marine cargo policy provision which relieves insurer of small losses to be expected in ocean transportation.

Merchantability: Implied warranty held to be extended by the seller relating to fitness, proper packaging and truthful representations.

Merit rating: The rate charged members of a specific class is modified by past experience or anticipated experience or both.

Mistakes: A valid justification, under limited conditions, for an intentional tort.

Modification rating: Refer to **Merit rating.**

Modified no-fault plan: Maintains the right to initiate action against the wrongdoer dependent upon the monetary loss incurred and if death or permanent disfigurement results from the event.

Multiple-line insurance: Insurance contract providing coverage against many perils, usually combining liability and physical damage coverages.

Multiple-location forms: Insurance on property owned or controlled by one entity and situated in more than one location.

Mutual companies: Incorporated cooperative insurers with no stockholders.

Named nonowner: Policy available to protect nonowners who may drive an uninsured or underinsured vehicle.

Name schedule bond: Fidelity bond listing the person or persons covered.

Negligence: An act of commission or omission demonstrating failure to exercise a degree of care expected of an ordinary person of reasonable prudence in a specific circumstance.

Net valuation premium: Gross premium for a life insurance policy less an adjusted expense allowance.

New money approach: Relates interest guarantees for some life insurance policies and annuity contracts to current market rates at the time of issue, rather than to overall portfolio return.

No-benefit-to-bailee clause: Preserves insurer's rights of subrogation against a third party who is responsible for the loss.

Nonadmitted assets: Insurance company assets that are excluded under state law in measuring solvency and includes such assets as supplies, office furniture, unsecured loans, prepaid expense and advances to agents.

Nonforfeiture options: Options available to a life insurance policy owner on discontinuing premium payments, including cash value, paid up insurance and extended term insurance.

Normal cost: The annual cost of funding current service benefits under a pension plan.

Notice as soon as practicable: Notice to the insurer as soon as practical relative to all the facts.

Notice of accident: Written notice to the insurer or its representative as soon as practicable with all pertinent available information.

Notice of claim or suit: Policy provision which requires the insured to forward immediately to the insurer every notice, demand, summons or other process received by the insured or his or her representative.

Ocean marine: That form of insurance which covers ships and cargoes involved in waterborne commerce against physical damage, liability exposure and loss of revenues.

Occurrence: A sudden event causing loss as well as continuous or repeated exposure to conditions that result in unintended bodily injury or property damage.

Office burglary and robbery policy: Policy covering office building tenants who have no stock for sale.

Office personal property form: Provides all-risk coverage for all office occupancies, except for medical or dental offices, against physical damage only.

Offset plan: A pension plan integrated with social security under which an employee's benefits are reduced by a predetermined percentage of the social security payment based on an approved formula.

Older-age policies: Health insurance policies issued beyond the normal insuring age of 60, with benefits usually coordinated with and supplemental to medicare benefits.

165-line form: The fire insurance policy form approved in New York in 1943 and still used as a model in most states.

Open contract: Ocean marine policy with no expiration date specified.

Ordinary life insurance: Refer to **Straight life.**

Other-insurance clause: Specifies procedure to follow when another contract of protection embraces the same interest and loss.

Other than collision coverage: Loss or damage to a vehicle caused by a peril other than collision, upset or other enumerated perils.

Owner: That person specifically named in a life insurance policy who has the authority to exercise all rights in the policy.

Parol evidence rule: Excludes any statements made prior to the creation of a formal contract, disallowing any evidence that the terms of the policy are other than those included in the contract.

Payment development method: The amount of the loss reserve is based on historical rates of loss payments.

Per-risk reinsurance: Reinsurer agrees to pay losses in excess of ceding insurer's net retention limit on every policy.

Percentage unit benefit formula: Retirement benefits are determined by a formula involving years of service and earnings.

Performance bond: A guarantee by the bonding company that it will assume responsibility for completion of the contract should the contractor default.

Perpetual mutual: Insurer requires a very large initial payment and provides coverage with no termination date, assuming the dividend income will be adequate to cover all expenses incurred.

Personal articles floater: A policy, or an endorsement to a homeowners policy, which provides all-risk coverage for scheduled valuable personal property, subject to a minimum number of exclusions.

Personal effects floater: A blanket policy covering personal effects carried by travelers.

Personal property floater: An all-risk policy covering virtually all individually owned personal property situated in and about the home and worldwide.

Personal property replacement cost endorsement: Amends coverage under the homeowners policy from an actual cash value basis to a replacement cost basis on personal property, subject to a limitation of 400 percent of actual cash value.

Plan termination insurance: A compulsory program of the U.S. Department of Labor guaranteeing limited benefits under qualified defined benefit pension plans.

Policy dividends: The return to a policyholder of a part of premium paid for a policy issued on a participating basis.

Policy face amount: The maximum amount payable under a contract, usually stated on the face of a policy.

Policy limits: The amount of coverage provided for each area of coverage when the policy has several such identified areas of coverage.

Policy proof-of-interest forms: Ocean marine forms which require the insurer to indemnify the insured upon submission of proof of loss without proof of interest.

Policyowner: Holder of ownership rights in an insurance policy and who may be the insured and/or the policyholder.

Position schedule bond: Fidelity bond on which positions are listed along with amounts for which each is bonded so that no notification of employee turnover is required.

Preferred risk: That insurance applicant possessing lower than average loss expectancy.

Premium: Rate per unit of coverage multiplied by the number of units of insurance purchased.

Presumed negligence: Doctrine which, in the absence of proof of negligence, assumes the party allegedly responsible could have intervened at some point in the sequence of events to prevent the occurrence of the injury and, further, that the injured party lacked such ability.

Presumptive agency: Created when an insurer's behavior causes a reasonable person to believe that a particular person is an agent of the company.

Primary insurance amount: The amount of monthly payment to which a worker is entitled upon retirement or disability under the federal social security system and is the basis for all other benefits.

Privity of contract: Doctrine which held manufacturers immune and retailers vulnerable to negligence actions instituted by consumers.

Pro rata liability clause: Formula whereby various insurance companies covering one property share equitably in any loss.

Profits and commissions insurance: Reimburses insured for loss of prospective profits on finished goods damaged by an insured peril.

Promissory: Warranty which states a fact is true at present and will continue to be true.

Property insurance contract: A personal contract insuring the individual property owner, assuming utmost good faith on the part of all contracting parties.

Proportional (pro rata) reinsurance: Insurer shares premiums and losses with a reinsurer on a proportional basis.

Prospective method (life insurance reserves): The present value of assumed claims minus the present value of assumed net valuation premiums.

Protection and indemnity clause (P&I): Covers the liability of a shipowner for damage done to wharves, piers, harbor installations, damage to cargo and injury or illness of passengers or crew but excludes liability for damage to other ships.

Proximate cause: A breach of duty initiating an unbroken sequence of events resulting in an injury to a person or damage to property.

Public and institutional property form: Provides limited or broad form physical damage coverage on real and personal property owned by churches, libraries, hospitals and other public institutions.

Public official bond: Bond required of a public official payable to the public body served by the official, guaranteeing faithful performance of duty.

Punitive damages: A monetary award to a plaintiff in a tort action in excess of the cash value of the economic loss as a punishment to the wrongdoer and as a deterrent to similar conduct by others.

Pure assessment mutual: A cooperative insurer with few employees, levying a small initial premium, subject to additional payment for policyowners to cover losses incurred.

Pure no-fault plan: Injured parties are compensated by their insurers regardless of fault and forego all rights of action against the wrongdoer.

Quota share reinsurance: The same proportion of every policy is shared with the reinsurer.

Reciprocal insurance exchanges: Unincorporated cooperative insurers operated by attorneys-in-fact empowered to act in behalf of the subscribers who exchange insurance with one another to reduce their risk.

Reformation: Process of changing policy terms to meet the original intentions of the insurer and of the insured.

Refund annuity: Guarantees the annuitant or the beneficiary will receive payments equal to no less than the total consideration paid.

Reimbursement form: Hospitalization coverage in which the insurer reimburses the insured up to allowable limits with insured bearing the cost if charges exceed policy limits.

Release-of-attachment bonds: Given by defendant to plaintiff to defeat any action to attach property in question previous to court decision, guaranteeing the safety of the property and that the appraised value of the property attached will be surrendered if legally required.

Renewable and convertible term: Term life insurance that may be renewed for another period of time or converted to a permanent life or endowment policy within a given period before the term contract expires.

Renewable term: Term life insurance policies which may be renewed at the rate for the attained age without evidence of insurability.

Reparations: Compensation paid by a wrongdoer to an injured individual or to the owner of damaged property.

Replacement problem: The unjustified replacement of one life insurance policy by another where such exchange results in no increase in the policyholder's expected wealth or in no demonstrable enhancement of his or her insurance objectives.

Reporting forms: Commercial property insurance which requires periodic reports of inventory value to the insurer, usually submitted monthly or quarterly, so that requisite amounts of insurance will be in effect and the insured would pay premiums on the average amount at risk.

Representations: Statements by the applicant to the insurer in the process of obtaining a policy, accepted as being true to the best of knowledge and belief of the applicant, but not part of the contract.

***Res ipsa loquitor* (the thing speaks for itself):** A legal doctrine eliminating the need for the plaintiff to prove negligence because (1) the defendant has superior knowledge of the cause of the accident, (2) the instrument causing the injury would not ordinarily do so without negligence or (3) the injuring instrument is solely controlled by the alleged wrongdoer.

Rescission: Having the contract declared void from the onset because of fraud or misrepresentation in the inducement.

Residence theft: Provides theft coverage from insured's residence with options to extend coverage off premises and to include mysterious disappearance.

Residual disability benefits: Reimbursement to a partially disabled policyowner equal to the monthly benefit payable adjusted by the ratio of (1) earnings after resuming work to (2) predisability earnings.

Residual market: That group of insurance buyers most companies would prefer not accepting as policyholders.

Respondentia bond: An early form of marine insurance, attributed to Ancient Greece, in which the ship's cargo was pledged as security for a loan to finance the venture.

Retrocession: The sequential reinsurance of some part of assumed obligations by reinsurers.

Retrospective method: A system of reserving used by life insurance companies basing the reserve on what is assumed to have happened since the policy was issued, disregarding information relative to actual claims incurred and interest earned.

Retrospective rating: The final premium for an insured relies heavily on the loss experience incurred during the policy term.

Revocable beneficiary: Policyholder retains the right to change the beneficiary and to assign or surrender the policy.

Rider: A written attachment to a life or health policy that changes the original policy to meet special conditions.

Riot: An act, lawful or unlawful, committed with force or violence by no fewer than two persons against the property or person of another.

Risk: Uncertainty concerning loss.

Risk premium insurance (reinsurance): Refer to **Yearly renewable term plan.**

Robbery: Forcible and unlawful taking of another person's property by violence or the threat of violence.

Rule of 45: Any employee with five years of completed service must be 50 percent vested when employee's age and service total 45

Running down clause: Provides liability protection to the shipowner equal to the value of insurance on the hull of his ship, should his vessel collide with another vessel.

Salvage: The property transferred to an insurer to reduce its loss.

Schedule rating: The manual classification rate adjusted by a physical evaluation of the exposure.

Scheduled personal property endorsement: Provides all-risk insurance to highly valued property for higher dollar limits than are provided in the basic policy.

Scheduled coverage (hospitalization insurance): Maximum amounts payable for room and board, surgical procedures and miscellaneous hospital expenses are stated in the contract.

Scheduled property floater: Inland marine insurance coverage on business or personal property completed by endorsement specifying perils covered and applicable exclusions.

Service form (hospitalization insurance): Payments for services rendered are made directly to the doctors and hospitals.

Settlement options: Alternative modes of taking the proceeds of a life insurance policy available to the payee in lieu of a lump sum.

Short rate: Policies written for a period of less than 12 months.

Short term: Refer to **Short rate.**

Sidetrack agreement: Contractual agreement obligating a railroad to construct and maintain a switch track on a business premises in exchange for which the business releases the railroad, partially or totally, from liability.

Simplified employee pension: Employer-funded plan for Individual Retirement Accounts with contributions limited to the lesser of 15 percent of earnings or $15,000.

Sine qua non: A rule invoked in determining liability, defined as an indispensable thing or condition without which the event would not have occurred.

Sister-ship clause: Ocean marine policy provision guaranteeing payment under the collision or running down clause irrespective of ownership.

Sliding rate scale: The rate per $100 of insurance diminishes as the amount of insurance increases.

Smoke: A mixture of gasses and partially oxidized carbon particles suddenly and accidentally discharged affecting covered property, excluding smoke generated by industrial operations or agricultural smudging.

Social insurance: Government programs designed to provide benefits to consumers not currently served by commercial insurers, usually compulsory.

Solicitors: Individuals appointed by an agent and authorized to solicit and receive applications as a representative of the agent with no authority to obligate an insurer in any way.

Solvency: Financial status in which assets exceed liabilities.

Special agents: Company employees who maintain contact with agents, introduce new products and procedures and act as an intermediary in resolving problems.

Special damages: Reflects economic loss in wages, additional living expenses and transportation expenses.

Special multiperil program: Package policies adaptable to the needs of most commercial and industrial businesses in which physical damage and liability insurance coverages are combined in a single contract.

Special risk (health insurance): Individually underwritten policy offering the benefits of orthodox health policies with higher than ordinary benefits to meet unusual conditions.

Specific coverage (residence theft): Coverage is limited to articles specifically described and enumerated.

Specified perils contract: Insurance coverage on real and/or personal property in which those perils insured against are specifically listed and described.

Spendthrift trust clause: Provisions, valid in some states, shielding policy proceeds paid under a settlement option from creditors of a beneficiary.

Split-funded plan: A retirement plan combining individual policies of whole life insurance and a separate equity investment fund, administered solely by an insurer or, alternatively, by an insurer and a trustee.

Split-life policy: Combination of a life annuity deferred until age 65 and a yearly renewable term policy.

Standard (risk): Insurance applicants displaying potential average loss experience.

Statutory law: Written law, enacted by a legislative body and incorporated into a formal document.

Stipulated authority: Bestowed by the terms of the contract between the agent and the insurer specifying the types of insureds, types of coverage and amounts of insurance which may be written.

Stock company: An insurer organized and owned by stockholders to earn a profit.

Stop-loss reinsurance: An agreement between a primary insurer and a reinsurer in which the reinsurer intervenes and assumes loss responsibility when losses exceed a plateau, either a given percentage of the ceding insurer's net earned premium or a fixed dollar amount up to a specified maximum.

Storekeepers burglary and robbery policy: A package crime insurance policy covering seven areas of potential loss.

Straight deductible: A constant amount or percentage of value which the insured bears on every loss.

Straight life (ordinary life, continuous premium whole life): Coverage for which the policyowner pays a fixed annual premium for the life of the insured.

Straight term life insurance: Life insurance policy written for a specific number of years and which then terminates.

Strict liability: A legal doctrine holding manufacturers and merchandisers of goods liable for injuries caused by defective products sold by them, irrespective of fault or negligence, so long as the claimant can prove the product defective and that the defect made the product unreasonably dangerous.

Strike, riot and civil commotion clause (SR&CC): Marine insurance policy provision excluding coverage for war, strikes, riots and civil commotion.

Students' bond: Assurance from a student to a school guaranteeing payment of costs for tuition, lodging or for damage to property.

Subcontracting: Transferring an obligation, in its entirety or in part, to another.

Subject: In life insurance, the person whose death triggers payment of the policy proceeds.

Subject-owner-beneficiary rule: Either the owner or the beneficiary must have an insurable interest in or be the subject of the insurance.

Subrogation: The right of an insurer to substitute for the victim in recovering the amount of the loss paid from a third party responsible for the loss.

Substandard risk: An applicant for insurance displaying characteristics forecasting higher than average loss expectancy.

Substandard risk (or policies) (health insurance): Policies designed specifically to cover physically impaired persons, usually issued at higher premiums or with reduced benefits.

Sue-and-labor clause: Insured's obligation, under a marine policy, to take all reasonable and necessary steps to limit or reduce imminent loss and to protect the salvage.

Supplemental cost: The cost of funding the accumulated retirement benefit for services performed in the past, spread over a time period not in excess of 30 years nor less than 10 years.

Supplemental liability: The sum that measures the total pension liability for past services performed by all eligible employees.

Supply bond: Guaranty provided by a supplier to a finisher affirming compliance with a delivery contract.

Surety bond: Guarantees the principal will accomplish certain tasks subject to payment of monetary damages in the event of default.

Surety bonding: A three-party agreement in which the bonding company (surety) and the principal promise a third party (obligee) that a job will be completed according to contract.

Surplus or excess line brokers or agents: Insurance procurement specialists who obtain unusual or marginally profitable coverages from insurers not licensed to operate in the state of location.

Surplus share reinsurance: The percentage of participation in each policy is separately calculated.

Survivorship benefit: That part of a life insurance premium payment made by a deceased policyholder allocated to the account of surviving policyholders.

Tax-free rollovers: A transfer of funds from a company pension plan, IRA or other tax-sheltered plans into an IRA, completed within 60 days after funds are available.

Ten (10) year rule: The pension plan must be fully vested at the end of 10 years with no vesting prior to that time.

Term insurance: Form of life insurance issued for a number of years specified in the contract or to subject's age 65 or 70.

Term policies: Policies issued for a period in excess of 12 months.

Theft: The felonious taking of money or property.

Theft extension endorsement: Extends theft coverage to property taken from an unlocked automobile and waives the requirement of signs of forcible entry.

Third-party coverage: Insurance to pay damages on behalf of the policyowner for negligent acts covered under the policy.

Time policies: Ocean marine policies written for specified periods.

Tort: A wrongful act, other than breach of contract, committed by one person against another creating a possible legal liability.

Treaty reinsurance: The insurer must cede the amount of insurance required under a contractual agreement and the reinsurer must accept the amount offered.

Trespass: Wrongful entry on to the land of another, failure to remove property from another's land; intentional interference with the possession or physical condition of personal property.

Trust fund plan: A pension or profit-sharing plan administered by a bank or individual trustee.

Tuition form: Business interruption insurance which provides reimbursement for tuition loss plus board and room rents minus noncontinuing expenses when due to the occurrence of an insured peril.

Twisting: Misrepresentation by an agent to induce a policyholder to substitute one life insurance policy or annuity contract for another.

Umbrella liability: An excess liability policy, providing higher limits than other policies owned, covering an additional spectrum of exposures and providing automatic replacement of existing coverages reduced by low.

Unallocated funding instrument: Employer contributions to retirement plans are commingled and not identifiable as to each employee.

Underwriting decision: Decision made by an insurer to offer or withhold insurance predicated on the pooled information supplied by employee technicians in an attempt to maximize profits.

Unearned premium reserve: The amount equal to the unconsumed portion of the gross premium of all outstanding policies at the time of valuation.

Unilateral: Contractual agreement in which it is agreed to exchange an act for a promise.

Uninsured motorist coverage: Insurance to pay damages to an insured for which another motorist is liable but which is uncollectible.

Universal life: An interest sensitive form of life insurance, indexed to money market yields, offering variable cash values and mobility between permanent and term life insurance plans.

Universal Mercantile System: A system for establishing a base fire classification for a specific community from which fire rates are derived, assuming a high standard of fire protection.

Valued form: Under hospital indemnity or income disability insurance, a specific dollar amount is paid to the insured when disabled or hospitalized irrespective of expenses incurred.

Variable annuity: Payment is predicated on the accumulation of a fixed number of annuity units with the value of each unit determined by the investment portfolio supporting the annuity.

Vested: The incremental increase in ownership rights to the dollar value of a life insurance policy or pension plan accumulation contributed by an employer.

Voyage policy: Ocean marine policy covering one trip.

Waiting period: A form of deductible most frequently found in income replacement policies excluding payment until the disability has persisted beyond a stipulated time period.

Waiver: A voluntary abandonment by one party of some right or advantage under a contract.

Warehouse-to-warehouse clause: An extension of marine coverage insuring cargo until it reaches its destination.

Warranty: Stipulation in an insurance policy that some statement about the subject of the insurance is true.

Watercraft endorsement: Extension of the liability portion of the homeowners policy to cover losses due to the ownership or operation of certain types of watercraft.

Written premiums: The entire amount of insurance premium collected on contracts issued by the insurer during a 12-month period.

Yearly renewable term: Term policies written for one-year periods and renewable each year without evidence of insurability.

Yearly renewable term plan: Reinsurer insures the difference between the net amount at risk, i.e., the policy face amount less its terminal reserve and the net retention.

APPENDIXES

1. Policy declarations page
2. Standard fire policy
3. Homeowners 3 policy
4. Personal auto policy
5. Whole life insurance policy
6. Major medical and disability (recovery) income policies
7. A mathematical note

Appendix 1 Policy Declarations Page

NAME OF COMPANY

HOMEOWNERS POLICY
DECLARATIONS

RENEWAL OF NUMBER

No. H

Named Insured and Mailing Address (No., Street, Apt., Town or City, County, State, Zip Code)

Policy Period: Years From: To: ☐ 12:01 A.M. ☐ 12:00 Noon, Standard Time at the **residence premises**

The **residence premises** covered by this policy is located at the above address unless otherwise stated: (No., Street, Apt., Town or City, County, State, Zip Code)

Coverage is provided where a premium or limit of liability is shown for the coverage.

Coverages and Limit of Liability	Section I Coverages				Section II Coverages	
	A. Dwelling	B. Other Structures	C. Personal Property	D. Loss of Use	E. Personal Liability Each occurrence	F. Medical Payments to Others Each person
	$	$	$	$	$	$

Premium	Basic Policy Premium	Additional Premiums				Total Prepaid Premium	Premium if paid in installments	Payable: At Inception (and)	At each subsequent anniversary
	$	$	$	$	$	$	$	$	$
		Premium for Scheduled Personal Property				$	$	$	$
Form and Endorsements made part of this Policy at time of issue:		Combined Premium				$	$	$	$

Form HO- Endorsement(s) HO-

Insert Number(s) and Edition Date(s)

DEDUCTIBLE	SECTION I	OTHER	
	$	$	In case of a loss under Section I, we cover only that part of the loss over the deductible stated.

Section II	Other **insured locations:** (No., Street, Apt., Town or City, County, State, Zip Code)

Mortgagee (Name and address)		Special State Provisions S. Car. Valuation Clause (Cov. A) $

Countersigned:

By________________________
Authorized Representative

RATING INFORMATION

NUMBER OF FAMILIES — Not Town/rowhouse— Number of Families: 1 Code (1) ☐; 2 (3) ☐; 3 (6) ☐; 4 (8) ☐ | Town/rowhouse— Family units in Fire Div.: 3-4 (2) ☐; 5-8 (4) ☐; 9 over (9) ☐ | HO-4 HO-6 Self-Rating: Code No Yes (9) ☐ ☐ | If YES Number of Families— HO-4 and HO-6 Not rented to others: 1-4 (1) ☐; 5-10 (2) ☐; 11-40 (3) ☐; over 40 (4) ☐ | HO-6 Rented to others: 1-4 (5) ☐; 5-10 (6) ☐; 11-40 (7) ☐; over 40 (8) ☐ | If NO Number of Families | Annual Fire E.C. Rate | Year of Constr. Year Code

CONSTRUCTION — Frame (1) ☐ | Brick, Stone or Masonry Veneer (2) ☐ | Brick, Stone or Masonry (3) ☐ | Frame with Aluminum or Plastic Siding (5) ☐ | Fire Resistive (4) ☐ | Mobile Homes enclosed Foundation (6) ☐ | Mobile Homes Not enclosed Foundation (7) ☐ | Modular Homes rated as Frame (9) ☐ | Specifically Rated—Not Fire Resistive (8) ☐

PROTECTION — Code | Not more than feet from hydrant | Not more than miles from Fire Dept. | Southern: Inside City limits ☐ | Inside Protected Suburb ☐ | Inside Fire District ☐ | Fire District or Town ( )

ZONE Code | **PREMIUM GR. NO.** | **DEDUCTIBLE:** Type Code Size Code | Section I $ | Other $

STATISTICAL REPORTING INFORMATION	Codes No. Type Classif. Cov. E Cov. F	Premium: Prepaid;	If paid in Installments;	Payable at: Inception	Each Anniversary
Snowmobiles	/ / — — / / / /	$	$	$	$
Watercraft	/ / (2) / / / / / /	$	$	$	$
Outboard Motor	/ / (1) / / / / / /	$	$	$	$
ALL OTHER PREMIUMS (except Scheduled Personal Property)		$	$	$	$

(a) The **residence premises** is not seasonal; (b) no **business** pursuits are conducted on the **residence premises**; (c) the **residence premises** is the only premises where you maintain a residence other than business or farm properties; (d) the **insured** has no full time **residence employee(s)**; (e) the **insured** has no outboard motor(s) or watercraft otherwise excluded under this policy for which coverage is desired. Exception, if any, to (a), (b), (c), (d) or (e)*.

*Absence of an entry means "no exceptions".

THIS DECLARATIONS PAGE, WITH POLICY JACKET, HOMEOWNERS POLICY FORM, AND ENDORSEMENTS IF ANY, ISSUED TO FORM A PART THEREOF, COMPLETES THE ABOVE NUMBERED HOMEOWNERS POLICY.

Source: Insurance Information Institute, 110 William Street, New York, NY 10038.

Appendix 2 Standard Fire Policy

STANDARD FIRE INSURANCE POLICY for Alabama, Alaska, Arizona, Arkansas, Colorado, Connecticut, Delaware, District of Columbia, Florida, Georgia, Hawaii, Idaho, Illinois, Indiana, Iowa, Kansas, Kentucky, Louisiana, Maine, Maryland, Michigan, Mississippi, Missouri, Montana, Nebraska, Nevada, New Hampshire, New Jersey, New Mexico, New York, North Carolina, North Dakota, Ohio, Oklahoma, Oregon, Pennsylvania, Rhode Island, South Carolina, South Dakota, Tennessee, Utah, Vermont, Virginia, Washington, West Virginia, Wisconsin and Wyoming.

No.

NONASSESSABLE

STANDARD FIRE POLICY

Insured's Name and Mailing Address

Policy Term: INCEPTION (Mo. Day Year) EXPIRATION (Mo. Day Year) YEARS

$ ______ Div. on Exp. Pol. ______ Renewal of

It is important that the written portions of all policies covering the same property read exactly alike. If they do not, they should be made uniform at once.

INSURANCE IS PROVIDED AGAINST ONLY THOSE PERILS AND FOR ONLY THOSE COVERAGES INDICATED BELOW BY A PREMIUM CHARGE AND AGAINST OTHER PERILS AND FOR OTHER COVERAGES ONLY WHEN ENDORSED HEREON OR ADDED HERETO.

Item No.	DESCRIPTION AND LOCATION OF PROPERTY COVERED Show address (No., Street, City, County, State, Zip Code), construction, type of roof and occupancy of building(s) covered or containing property covered. If occupied as a dwelling state if building is a seasonal or farm dwelling. If commercial state exact nature of product (and whether manufacturer, wholesaler or retailer) or the service or activity involved.	Protection Class	Dwelling Business Only			
			No. of Families	Feet From Hydrant	Miles From Fire Dept.	Zone
1.						

Item No.	PERIL(S) INSURED AGAINST AND COVERAGE(S) PROVIDED (INSERT NAME OF EACH)	Per Cent of Co-Insurance Applicable	Deductible Amount	Amount of Insurance	Rate	Prepaid or Installment Premium Due At Inception	Installment Premium Due At Each Anniversary
1.	FIRE AND LIGHTNING			$		$	$
	EXTENDED COVERAGE			X X X X X X X			

Special provision applicable only in State of Mississippi—**Total Insurance**—See form attached—
Item 1, $; Item 2, $; Item 3, $

TOTAL(S) $ $

Special provision applicable only in State of So. Carolina—**Valuation Clause**—See form attached—
Item , $; Item , $; Item , $

TOTAL PREMIUM FOR POLICY TERM PAID IN INSTALLMENTS $

Subject to Form No(s). INSERT FORM NUMBER(S) AND EDITION DATE(S) **attached hereto.**

Mortgage Clause: Subject to the provisions of the mortgage clause attached hereto, loss, if any, on building items, shall be payable to:

INSERT NAME(S) OR MORTGAGEE(S) AND MAILING ADDRESS(ES)

COUNTERSIGNATURE DATE	AGENCY AT	AGENT

IN CONSIDERATION OF THE PROVISIONS AND STIPULATIONS HEREIN OR ADDED HERETO AND OF the premium above specified, this Company, for the term of *years specified above* from *inception date shown above* At Noon (Standard Time) to *expiration date shown above* At Noon (Standard Time) at location of property involved, to an amount not exceeding the amount(s) above specified, does insure *the insured named above* and legal representatives, to the extent of the actual cash value of the property at the time of loss, but not exceeding the amount which it would cost to repair or replace the property with material of like kind and quality within a reasonable time after such loss, without allowance for any increased cost of repair or reconstruction by reason of any ordinance or law regulating construction or repair, and without compensation for loss resulting from interruption of business or manufacture, nor in any event for more than the interest of the insured, against all **DIRECT LOSS BY FIRE, LIGHTNING AND BY REMOVAL FROM PREMISES ENDANGERED BY THE PERILS INSURED AGAINST IN THIS POLICY, EXCEPT AS HEREINAFTER PROVIDED,** to the property described herein while located or contained as described in this policy, or pro rata for five days at each proper place to which any of the property shall necessarily be removed for preservation from the perils insured against in this policy, but not elsewhere.

Assignment of this policy shall not be valid except with the written consent of this Company.

This policy is made and accepted subject to the foregoing provisions and stipulations and those hereinafter stated, which are hereby made a part of this policy, together with such other provisions, stipulations and agreements as may be added hereto, as provided in this policy.

TA8-3

Appendix 2 (*concluded*)

Concealment, fraud. This entire policy shall be void if, whether before or after a loss, the insured has wilfully concealed or misrepresented any material fact or circumstance concerning this insurance or the subject thereof, or the interest of the insured therein, or in case of any fraud or false swearing by the insured relating thereto.

Uninsurable and excepted property. This policy shall not cover accounts, bills, currency, deeds, evidences of debt, money or securities; nor, unless specifically named hereon in writing, bullion or manuscripts.

Perils not included. This Company shall not be liable for loss by fire or other perils insured against in this policy caused, directly or indirectly, by: (a) enemy attack by armed forces, including action taken by military, naval or air forces in resisting an actual or an immediately impending enemy attack; (b) invasion; (c) insurrection; (d) rebellion; (e) revolution; (f) civil war; (g) usurped power; (h) order of any civil authority except acts of destruction at the time of and for the purpose of preventing the spread of fire, provided that such fire did not originate from any of the perils excluded by this policy; (i) neglect of the insured to use all reasonable means to save and preserve the property at and after a loss, or when the property is endangered by fire in neighboring premises; (j) nor shall this Company be liable for loss by theft.

Other Insurance. Other insurance may be prohibited or the amount of insurance may be limited by endorsement attached hereto.

Conditions suspending or restricting insurance. Unless otherwise provided in writing added hereto this Company shall not be liable for loss occurring
(a) while the hazard is increased by any means within the control or knowledge of the insured; or
(b) while a described building, whether intended for occupancy by owner or tenant, is vacant or unoccupied beyond a period of sixty consecutive days; or
(c) as a result of explosion or riot, unless fire ensue, and in that event for loss by fire only.

Other perils or subjects. Any other peril to be insured against or subject of insurance to be covered in this policy shall be by endorsement in writing hereon or added hereto.

Added provisions. The extent of the application of insurance under this policy and of the contribution to be made by this Company in case of loss, and any other provision or agreement not inconsistent with the provisions of this policy, may be provided for in writing added hereto, but no provision may be waived except such as by the terms of this policy is subject to change.

Waiver provisions. No permission affecting this insurance shall exist, or waiver of any provision be valid, unless granted herein or expressed in writing added hereto. No provision, stipulation or forfeiture shall be held to be waived by any requirement or proceeding on the part of this Company relating to appraisal or to any examination provided for herein.

Cancellation of policy. This policy shall be cancelled at any time at the request of the insured, in which case this Company shall, upon demand and surrender of this policy, refund the excess of paid premium above the customary short rates for the expired time. This policy may be cancelled at any time by this Company by giving to the insured a five days' written notice of cancellation with or without tender of the excess of paid premium above the pro rata premium for the expired time, which excess, if not tendered, shall be refunded on demand. Notice of cancellation shall state that said excess premium (if not tendered) will be refunded on demand.

Mortgagee interests and obligations. If loss hereunder is made payable, in whole or in part, to a designated mortgagee not named herein as the insured, such interest in this policy may be cancelled by giving to such mortgagee a ten days' written notice of cancellation.

If the insured fails to render proof of loss such mortgagee, upon notice, shall render proof of loss in the form herein specified within sixty (60) days thereafter and shall be subject to the provisions hereof relating to appraisal and time of payment and of bringing suit. If this Company shall claim that no liability existed as to the mortgagor or owner, it shall, to the extent of payment of loss to the mortgagee, be subrogated to all the mortgagee's rights of recovery, but without impairing mortgagee's right to sue; or it may pay off the mortgage debt and require an assignment thereof and of the mortgage. Other provisions relating to the interests and obligations of such mortgagee may be added hereto by agreement in writing.

Pro rata liability. This Company shall not be liable for a greater proportion of any loss than the amount hereby insured shall bear to the whole insurance covering the property against the peril involved, whether collectible or not.

Requirements in case loss occurs. The insured shall give immediate written notice to this Company of any loss, protect the property from further damage, forthwith separate the damaged and undamaged personal property, put it in the best possible order, furnish a complete inventory of the destroyed, damaged and undamaged property, showing in detail quantities, costs, actual cash value and amount of loss claimed; **and within sixty days after the loss, unless such time is extended in writing by this Company, the insured shall render to this Company a proof of loss,** signed and sworn to by the insured, stating the knowledge and belief of the insured as to the following: the time and origin of the loss, the interest of the insured and of all others in the property, the actual cash value of each item thereof and the amount of loss thereto, all encumbrances thereon, all other contracts of insurance, whether valid or not, covering any of said property, any changes in the title, use, occupation, location, possession or exposures of said property since the issuing of this policy, by whom and for what purpose any building herein described and the several parts thereof were occupied at the time of loss and whether or not it then stood on leased ground, and shall furnish a copy of all the descriptions and schedules in all policies and, if required, verified plans and specifications of any building, fixtures or machinery destroyed or damaged. The insured, as often as may be reasonably required, shall exhibit to any person designated by this Company all that remains of any property herein described, and submit to examinations under oath by any person named by this Company, and subscribe the same; and, as often as may be reasonably required, shall produce for examination all books of account, bills, invoices and other vouchers, or certified copies thereof if originals be lost, at such reasonable time and place as may be designated by this Company or its representative, and shall permit extracts and copies thereof to be made.

Appraisal. In case the insured and this Company shall fail to agree as to the actual cash value or the amount of loss, then, on the written demand of either, each shall select a competent and disinterested appraiser and notify the other of the appraiser selected within twenty days of such demand. The appraisers shall first select a competent and disinterested umpire; and failing for fifteen days to agree upon such umpire, then, on request of the insured or this Company, such umpire shall be selected by a judge of a court of record in the state in which the property covered is located. The appraisers shall then appraise the loss, stating separately actual cash value and loss to each item; and, failing to agree, shall submit their differences, only, to the umpire. An award in writing, so itemized, of any two when filed with this Company shall determine the amount of actual cash value and loss. Each appraiser shall be paid by the party selecting him and the expenses of appraisal and umpire shall be paid by the parties equally.

Company's options. It shall be optional with this Company to take all, or any part, of the property at the agreed or appraised value, and also to repair, rebuild or replace the property destroyed or damaged with other of like kind and quality within a reasonable time, on giving notice of its intention so to do within thirty days after the receipt of the proof of loss herein required.

Abandonment. There can be no abandonment to this Company of any property.

When loss payable. The amount of loss for which this Company may be liable shall be payable sixty days after proof of loss, as herein provided, is received by this Company and ascertainment of the loss is made either by agreement between the insured and this Company expressed in writing or by the filing with this Company of an award as herein provided.

Suit. No suit or action on this policy for the recovery of any claim shall be sustainable in any court of law or equity unless all the requirements of this policy shall have been complied with, and unless commenced within twelve months next after inception of the loss.

Subrogation. This Company may require from the insured an assignment of all right of recovery against any party for loss to the extent that payment therefor is made by this Company.

IN WITNESS WHEREOF, this Company has executed and attested these presents; but this policy shall not be valid unless countersigned by the duly authorized Agent of this Company at the agency hereinbefore mentioned.

Source: *Policy Kit for Students of Insurance,* Alliance of American Insurers, 20 N. Wacker Drive, Chicago, IL 60606.

Appendix 3 Homeowners 3 Policy

Homeowners 3
Special Form
Ed. 7-77

AGREEMENT

We will provide the insurance described in this policy in return for the premium and compliance with all applicable provisions of this policy.

DEFINITIONS

Throughout this policy, "you" and "your" refer to the "named insured" shown in the Declarations and the spouse if a resident of the same household, and "we", "us" and "our" refer to the Company providing this insurance. In addition, certain words and phrases are defined as follows:

1. "bodily injury" means bodily harm, sickness or disease, including required care, loss of services and death resulting therefrom.

2. "business" includes trade, profession or occupation.

3. "insured" means you and the following residents of your household:

a. your relatives;

b. any other person under the age of 21 who is in the care of any person named above.

Under Section II, **"insured"** also means:

c. with respect to animals or watercraft to which this policy applies, any person or organization legally responsible for these animals or watercraft which are owned by you or any person included in 3a or 3b. A person or organization using or having custody of these animals or watercraft in the course of any **business,** or without permission of the owner is not an **insured;**

d. with respect to any vehicle to which this policy applies, any person while engaged in your employment or the employment of any person included in 3a or 3b.

4. "insured location" means:

a. the **residence premises;**

b. the part of any other premises, other structures, and grounds, used by you as a residence and which is shown in the Declarations or which is acquired by you during the policy period for your use as a residence;

c. any premises used by you in connection with the premises included in 4a or 4b;

d. any part of a premises not owned by any **insured** but where any **insured** is temporarily residing;

e. vacant land owned by or rented to any **insured** other than farm land;

f. land owned by or rented to any **insured** on which a one or two family dwelling is being constructed as a residence for any **insured;**

g. individual or family cemetery plots or burial vaults of any **insured;**

h. any part of a premises occasionally rented to any **insured** for other than **business** purposes.

5. "motor vehicle" means:

a. a motorized land vehicle designed for travel on public roads or subject to motor vehicle registration. A motorized land vehicle in dead storage on an **insured location** is not a **motor vehicle.**

b. a trailer or semi-trailer designed for travel on public roads and subject to motor vehicle registration. A boat, camp, home or utility trailer not being towed by or carried on a vehicle included in 5a is not a **motor vehicle;**

c. a motorized golf cart, snowmobile, or other motorized land vehicle owned by any **insured** and designed for recreational use off public roads, while off an **insured location.** A motorized golf cart while used for golfing purposes is not a **motor vehicle;**

d. any vehicle while being towed by or carried on a vehicle included in 5a, 5b or 5c.

6. "property damage" means physical injury to or destruction of tangible property, including loss of use of this property.

Appendix 3 (*continued*)

7. **"residence employee"** means an employee of any **insured** who performs duties in connection with the maintenance or use of the **residence premises,** including household or domestic services, or who performs duties elsewhere of a similar nature not in connection with the **business** of any **insured.**

8. **"residence premises"** means the one or two family dwelling, other structures, and grounds or that part of any other building where you reside and which is shown as the "residence premises" in the Declarations.

SECTION I—COVERAGES

COVERAGE A DWELLING

We cover:

a. the dwelling on the **residence premises** shown in the Declarations used principally as a private residence, including structures attached to the dwelling; and

b. materials and supplies located on or adjacent to the **residence premises** for use in the construction, alteration or repair of the dwelling or other structures on the **residence premises.**

COVERAGE B OTHER STRUCTURES

We cover other structures on the **residence premises,** separated from the dwelling by clear space. Structures connected to the dwelling by only a fence, utility line, or similar connection are considered to be other structures.

We do not cover other structures:

a. used in whole or in part for **business** purposes; or

b. rented or held for rental to any person not a tenant of the dwelling, unless used solely as a private garage.

COVERAGE C PERSONAL PROPERTY

We cover personal property owned or used by any **insured** while it is anywhere in the world. At your request, we will cover personal property owned by others while the property is on the part of the **residence premises** occupied by any **insured.** In addition, we will cover at your request, personal property owned by a guest or a **residence employee,** while the property is in any residence occupied by any **insured.**

Our limit of liability for personal property usually situated at any **insured's** residence, other than the **residence premises,** is 10% of the limit of liability for Coverage C, or $1000, whichever is greater. Personal property in a newly acquired principal residence is not subject to this limitation for the 30 days immediately after you begin to move the property there.

Special Limits of Liability. These limits do not increase the Coverage C limit of liability. The special limit for each following numbered category is the total limit for each occurrence for all property in that numbered category.

1. $100 on money, bank notes, bullion, gold other than goldware, silver other than silverware, platinum, coins and medals.
2. $500 on securities, accounts, deeds, evidences of debt, letters of credit, notes other than bank notes, manuscripts, passports, tickets and stamps.
3. $500 on watercraft, including their trailers, furnishings, equipment and outboard motors.
4. $500 on trailers not used with watercraft.
5. $500 on grave markers.
6. $500 for loss by theft of jewelry, watches, furs, precious and semi-precious stones.
7. $1000 for loss by theft of silverware, silver-plated ware, goldware, gold-plated ware and pewterware.
8. $1000 for loss by theft of guns.

Property Not Covered. We do not cover:

1. articles separately described and specifically insured in this or any other insurance;
2. animals, birds or fish;
3. motorized land vehicles except those used to service an **insured's** residence which are not licensed for road use;
4. any device or instrument, including any accessories or antennas, for the transmitting, recording, receiving or reproduction of sound which is operated by power from the electrical system of a **motor vehicle,** or any tape, wire, record, disc or other medium for use with any such device or instrument while any of this property is in or upon a **motor vehicle;**

Appendix 3 (*continued*)

5. aircraft and parts;
6. property of roomers, boarders and other tenants, except property of roomers and boarders related to any **insured;**
7. property contained in an apartment regularly rented or held for rental to others by any **insured;**
8. property rented or held for rental to others away from the **residence premises;**
9. **business** property in storage or held as a sample or for sale or delivery after sale;
10. **business** property pertaining to a **business** actually conducted on the **residence premises;**
11. **business** property away from the **residence premises.**

COVERAGE D LOSS OF USE

The limit of liability for Coverage D is the total limit for all the following coverages.

1. Additional Living Expense. If a loss covered under this Section makes the **residence premises** uninhabitable, we cover any necessary increase in living expenses incurred by you so that your household can maintain its normal standard of living. Payment shall be for the shortest time required to repair or replace the premises or, if you permanently relocate, the shortest time required for your household to settle elsewhere. This period of time is not limited by expiration of this policy.

2. Fair Rental Value. If a loss covered under this Section makes that part of the **residence premises** rented to others or held for rental by you uninhabitable, we cover its fair rental value. Payment shall be for the shortest time required to repair or replace the part of the premises rented or held for rental. This period of time is not limited by expiration of this policy. Fair rental value shall not include any expense that does not continue while that part of the **residence premises** rented or held for rental is uninhabitable.

3. Prohibited Use. If a civil authority prohibits you from use of the **residence premises** as a result of direct damage to neighboring premises by a Peril Insured Against in this policy, we cover any resulting Additional Living Expense and Fair Rental Value loss for a period not exceeding two weeks during which use is prohibited.

We do not cover loss or expense due to cancellation of a lease or agreement.

ADDITIONAL COVERAGES

1. Debris Removal. We will pay the reasonable expense incurred by you in the removal of debris of covered property provided coverage is afforded for the peril causing the loss. Debris removal expense is included in the limit of liability applying to the damaged property. When the amount payable for the actual damage to the property plus the expense for debris removal exceeds the limit of liability for the damaged property, an additional 5% of that limit of liability will be available to cover debris removal expense.

2. Reasonable Repairs. We will pay the reasonable cost incurred by you for necessary repairs made solely to protect covered property from further damage provided coverage is afforded for the peril causing the loss. This coverage does not increase the limit of liability applying to the property being repaired.

3. Trees, Shrubs and Other Plants. We cover trees, shrubs, plants or lawns, on the **residence premises,** for loss caused by the following Perils Insured Against: Fire or lightning, Explosion, Riot or civil commotion, Aircraft, Vehicles not owned or operated by a resident of the **residence premises,** Vandalism or malicious mischief or Theft. The limit of liability for this coverage shall not exceed 5% of the limit of liability that applies to the dwelling for all trees, shrubs, plants and lawns nor more than $500 for any one tree, shrub or plant. We do not cover property grown for **business** purposes.

4. Fire Department Service Charge. We will pay up to $250 for your liability assumed by contract or agreement for fire department charges incurred when the fire department is called to save or protect covered property from a Peril Insured Against. No deductible applies to this coverage.

5. Property Removed. Covered property while being removed from a premises endangered by a Peril Insured Against and for not more than 30 days while removed is covered for direct loss from any cause. This coverage does not change the limit of liability applying to the property being removed.

Appendix 3 (*continued*)

6. Credit Card, Forgery and Counterfeit Money. We will pay up to $500 for:

a. the legal obligation of any **insured** to pay because of the theft or unauthorized use of credit cards issued to or registered in any **insured's** name.

We do not cover use by a resident of your household, a person who has been entrusted with the credit card, or any person if any **insured** has not complied with all terms and conditions under which the credit card is issued.

b. loss to any **insured** caused by forgery or alteration of any check or negotiable instrument; and

c. loss to any **insured** through acceptance in good faith of counterfeit United States or Canadian paper currency.

We do not cover loss arising out of **business** pursuits or dishonesty of any **insured.**

No deductible applies to this coverage.

Defense:

a. We may make any investigation and settle any claim or suit that we decide is appropriate. Our obligation to defend any claim or suit ends when the amount we pay for the loss equals our limit of liability.

b. If a claim is made or a suit is brought against any **insured** for liability under the Credit Card coverage, we will provide a defense at our expense by counsel of our choice.

c. We have the option to defend at our expense any **insured** or any **insured's** bank against any suit for the enforcement of payment under the Forgery coverage.

SECTION I—PERILS INSURED AGAINST

Coverage A Dwelling and Coverage B Other Structures

We insure for all risks of physical loss to the property described in Coverages A and B except:

1. losses excluded under Section I—Exclusions;
2. freezing of a plumbing, heating or air conditioning system or of a household appliance, or by discharge, leakage or overflow from within the system or appliance caused by freezing, while the dwelling is vacant, unoccupied or being constructed unless you have used reasonable care to:
   a. maintain heat in the building; or
   b. shut off the water supply and drain the system and appliances of water;
3. freezing, thawing, pressure or weight of water or ice, whether driven by wind or not, to a fence, pavement, patio, swimming pool, foundation, retaining wall, bulkhead, pier, wharf or dock;
4. theft in or to a dwelling under construction, or of materials and supplies for use in the construction until the dwelling is completed and occupied;
5. vandalism and malicious mischief or breakage of glass and safety glazing materials if the dwelling has been vacant for more than 30 consecutive days immediately before the loss. A dwelling being constructed is not considered vacant;
6. continuous or repeated seepage or leakage of water or steam over a period of time from within a plumbing, heating or air conditioning system or from within a household appliance;
7. wear and tear; marring; deterioration; inherent vice; latent defect; mechanical breakdown; rust; mold; wet or dry rot; contamination; smog; smoke from agricultural smudging or industrial operations; settling, cracking, shrinking, bulging, or expansion of pavements, patios, foundations, walls, floors, roofs or ceilings; birds, vermin, rodents, insects or domestic animals. If any of these cause water to escape from a plumbing, heating or air conditioning system or household appliance, we cover loss caused by the water. We also cover the cost of tearing out and replacing any part of a building necessary to repair the system or appliance. We do not cover loss to the system or appliance from which this water escaped.

Under items 2 thru 7, any ensuing loss not excluded is covered.

Coverage C Personal Property

We insure for direct loss to property described in Coverage C caused by:

1. **Fire or lightning.**
2. **Windstorm or hail.**

This peril does not include loss to the property contained in a building caused by rain, snow, sleet, sand or dust unless the direct force of wind or hail damages the building causing an opening in a roof or wall and the rain, snow, sleet, sand or dust enters through this opening.

Appendix 3 (*continued*)

This peril includes loss to watercraft and their trailers, furnishings, equipment, and outboard motors, only while inside a fully enclosed building.

3. Explosion.

4. Riot or civil commotion.

5. Aircraft, including self-propelled missiles and spacecraft.

6. Vehicles.

7. Smoke, meaning sudden and accidental damage from smoke.

This peril does not include loss caused by smoke from agricultural smudging or industrial operations.

8. Vandalism or malicious mischief.

9. Theft, including attempted theft and loss of property from a known location when it is likely that the property has been stolen.

This peril does not include loss caused by theft:

a. committed by any **insured;**

b. in or to a dwelling under construction, or of materials and supplies for use in the construction until the dwelling is completed and occupied; or

c. from any part of a **residence premises** rented by an **insured** to other than an **insured.**

This peril does not include loss caused by theft that occurs away from the **residence premises** of:

a. property while at any other residence owned, rented to, or occupied by any **insured,** except while any **insured** is temporarily residing there. Property of a student who is an **insured** is covered while at a residence away from home if the student has been there at any time during the 45 days immediately before the loss;

b. unattended property in or on any **motor vehicle** or trailer, other than a public conveyance, unless there is forcible entry into the vehicle while all its doors, windows and other openings are closed and locked and there are visible marks of the forcible entry; or the vehicle is stolen and not recovered within 30 days.

Property is not unattended when any **insured** has entrusted the keys of the vehicle to a custodian.

c. watercraft, including its furnishings, equipment and outboard motors. Other property in or on any private watercraft is covered if the loss results from forcible entry into a securely locked compartment and there are visible marks of the forcible entry; or

d. trailers and campers.

10. Falling objects.

This peril does not include loss to property contained in a building unless the roof or an exterior wall of the building is first damaged by a falling object. Damage to the falling object itself is not included.

11. Weight of ice, snow or sleet which causes damage to property contained in a building.

12. Collapse of a building or any part of a building.

This peril does not include settling, cracking, shrinking, bulging or expansion.

13. Accidental discharge or overflow of water or steam from within a plumbing, heating or air conditioning system or from within a household appliance.

This peril does not include loss:

a. to the appliance from which the water or steam escaped;

b. caused by or resulting from freezing;

c. on the **residence premises** caused by accidental discharge or overflow which occurs off the **residence premises.**

14. Sudden and accidental tearing asunder, cracking, burning or bulging of a steam or hot water heating system, an air conditioning system, or an appliance for heating water.

We do not cover loss caused by or resulting from freezing under this peril.

15. Freezing of a plumbing, heating or air conditioning system or of a household appliance.

This peril does not include loss on the **residence premises** while the dwelling is unoccupied, unless you have used reasonable care to:

a. maintain heat in the building; or

b. shut off the water supply and drain the system and appliances of water.

16. Sudden and accidental damage from artificially generated electrical current.

This peril does not include loss to a tube, transistor or similar electronic component.

Appendix 3 (*continued*)

SECTION I—EXCLUSIONS

We do not cover loss resulting directly or indirectly from:

1. Ordinance or Law, meaning enforcement of any ordinance or law regulating the construction, repair, or demolition of a building or other structure, unless specifically provided under this policy.

2. Earth Movement. Direct loss by fire, explosion, theft, or breakage of glass or safety glazing materials resulting from earth movement is covered.

3. Water Damage, meaning:

a. flood, surface water, waves, tidal water, overflow of a body of water, or spray from any of these, whether or not driven by wind;

b. water which backs up through sewers or drains; or

c. water below the surface of the ground, including water which exerts pressure on, or seeps or leaks through a building, sidewalk, driveway, foundation, swimming pool or other structure.

Direct loss by fire, explosion or theft resulting from water damage is covered.

4. Power Interruption, meaning the interruption of power or other utility service if the interruption takes place away from the **residence premises.** If a Peril Insured Against ensues on the **residence premises,** we will pay only for loss caused by the ensuing peril.

5. Neglect, meaning neglect of the **insured** to use all reasonable means to save and preserve property at and after the time of a loss, or when property is endangered by a Peril Insured Against.

6. War, including undeclared war, civil war, insurrection, rebellion, revolution, warlike act by a military force or military personnel, destruction or seizure or use for a military purpose, and including any consequence of any of these. Discharge of a nuclear weapon shall be deemed a warlike act even if accidental.

7. Nuclear Hazard, to the extent set forth in the Nuclear Hazard Clause of Section I—Conditions.

SECTION I—CONDITIONS

1. Insurable Interest and Limit of Liability. Even if more than one person has an insurable interest in the property covered, we shall not be liable:

a. to the **insured** for an amount greater than the **insured's** interest; nor

b. for more than the applicable limit of liability.

2. Your Duties After Loss. In case of a loss to which this insurance may apply, you shall see that the following duties are performed:

a. give immediate notice to us or our agent, and in case of theft also to the police. In case of loss under the Credit Card coverage also notify the credit card company;

b. protect the property from further damage, make reasonable and necessary repairs required to protect the property, and keep an accurate record of repair expenditures;

c. prepare an inventory of damaged personal property showing in detail, the quantity, description, actual cash value and amount of loss. Attach to the inventory all bills, receipts and related documents that substantiate the figures in the inventory;

d. exhibit the damaged property as often as we reasonably require and submit to examination under oath;

e. submit to us, within 60 days after we request, your signed, sworn statement of loss which sets forth, to the best of your knowledge and belief:

(1) the time and cause of loss;

(2) interest of the **insured** and all others in the property involved and all encumbrances on the property;

(3) other insurance which may cover the loss;

(4) changes in title or occupancy of the property during the term of the policy;

Appendix 3 (*continued*)

(5) specifications of any damaged building and detailed estimates for repair of the damage;

(6) an inventory of damaged personal property described in 2c;

(7) receipts for additional living expenses incurred and records supporting the fair rental value loss;

(8) evidence or affidavit supporting a claim under the Credit Card, Forgery and Counterfeit Money coverage, stating the amount and cause of loss.

3. Loss Settlement. Covered property losses are settled as follows:

a. Personal property and structures that are not buildings at actual cash value at the time of loss but not exceeding the amount necessary to repair or replace;

b. Carpeting, domestic appliances, awnings, outdoor antennas and outdoor equipment, whether or not attached to buildings, at actual cash value at the time of loss but not exceeding the amount necessary to repair or replace;

c. Buildings under Coverage A or B at replacement cost without deduction for depreciation, subject to the following:

(1) If at the time of loss the amount of insurance in this policy on the damaged building is 80% or more of the full replacement cost of the building immediately prior to the loss, we will pay the cost of repair or replacement, without deduction for depreciation, but not exceeding the smallest of the following amounts:

(a) the limit of liability under this policy applying to the building;

(b) the replacement cost of that part of the building damaged for equivalent construction and use on the same premises; or

(c) the amount actually and necessarily spent to repair or replace the damaged building.

(2) If at the time of loss the amount of insurance in this policy on the damaged building is less than 80% of the full replacement cost of the building immediately prior to the loss, we will pay the larger of the following amounts, but not exceeding the limit of liability under this policy applying to the building:

(a) the actual cash value of that part of the building damaged; or

(b) that proportion of the cost to repair or replace, without deduction for depreciation, of that part of the building damaged, which the total amount of insurance in this policy on the damaged building bears to 80% of the replacement cost of the building.

(3) In determining the amount of insurance required to equal 80% of the full replacement cost of the building immediately prior to the loss, you shall disregard the value of excavations, foundations, piers and other supports which are below the undersurface of the lowest basement floor or, where there is no basement, which are below the surface of the ground inside the foundation walls, and underground flues, pipes, wiring and drains.

(4) When the cost to repair or replace the damage is more than $1000 or more than 5% of the amount of insurance in this policy on the building, whichever is less, we will pay no more than the actual cash value of the damage until actual repair or replacement is completed.

(5) You may disregard the replacement cost loss settlement provisions and make claim under this policy for loss or damage to buildings on an actual cash value basis and then make claim within 180 days after loss for any additional liability on a replacement cost basis.

4. Loss to a Pair or Set. In case of loss to a pair or set we may elect to:

a. repair or replace any part to restore the pair or set to its value before the loss; or

b. pay the difference between actual cash value of the property before and after the loss.

5. Glass Replacement. Loss for damage to glass caused by a Peril Insured Against shall be settled on the basis of replacement with safety glazing materials when required by ordinance or law.

Appendix 3 (*continued*)

6. Appraisal. If you and we fail to agree on the amount of loss, either one can demand that the amount of the loss be set by appraisal. If either makes a written demand for appraisal, each shall select a competent, independent appraiser and notify the other of the appraiser's identity within 20 days of receipt of the written demand. The two appraisers shall then select a competent, impartial umpire. If the two appraisers are unable to agree upon an umpire within 15 days, you or we can ask a judge of a court of record in the state where the **residence premises** is located to select an umpire. The appraisers shall then set the amount of the loss. If the appraisers submit a written report of an agreement to us, the amount agreed upon shall be the amount of the loss. If the appraisers fail to agree within a reasonable time, they shall submit their differences to the umpire. Written agreement signed by any two of these three shall set the amount of the loss. Each appraiser shall be paid by the party selecting that appraiser. Other expenses of the appraisal and the compensation of the umpire shall be paid equally by you and us.

7. Other Insurance. If a loss covered by this policy is also covered by other insurance, we will pay only the proportion of the loss that the limit of liability that applies under this policy bears to the total amount of insurance covering the loss.

8. Suit Against Us. No action shall be brought unless there has been compliance with the policy provisions and the action is started within one year after the occurrence causing loss or damage.

9. Our Option. If we give you written notice within 30 days after we receive your signed, sworn statement of loss, we may repair or replace any part of the property damaged with equivalent property.

10. Loss Payment. We will adjust all losses with you. We will pay you unless some other person is named in the policy to receive payment. Payment for loss will be made within 30 days after we reach agreement with you, entry of a final judgment, or the filing of an appraisal award with us.

11. Abandonment of Property. We need not accept any property abandoned by any **insured.**

12. Mortgage Clause.

The word "mortgagee" includes trustee.

If a mortgagee is named in this policy, any loss payable under Coverage A or B shall be paid to the mortgagee and you, as interests appear. If more than one mortgagee is named, the order of payment shall be the same as the order or precedence of the mortgages.

If we deny your claim, that denial shall not apply to a valid claim of the mortgagee, if the mortgagee:

a. notifies us of any change in ownership, occupancy or substantial change in risk of which the mortgagee is aware;

b. pays any premium due under this policy on demand if you have neglected to pay the premium;

c. submits a signed, sworn statement of loss within 60 days after receiving notice from us of your failure to do so. Policy conditions relating to Appraisal, Suit Against Us and Loss Payment apply to the mortgagee.

If the policy is cancelled by us, the mortgagee shall be notified at least 10 days before the date cancellation takes effect.

If we pay the mortgagee for any loss and deny payment to you:

a. we are subrogated to all the rights of the mortgagee granted under the mortgage on the property; or

b. at our option, we may pay to the mortgagee the whole principal on the mortgage plus any accrued interest. In this event, we shall receive a full assignment and transfer of the mortgage and all securities held as collateral to the mortgage debt.

Subrogation shall not impair the right of the mortgagee to recover the full amount of the mortgagee's claim.

13. No Benefit to Bailee. We will not recognize any assignment or grant any coverage for the benefit of any person or organization holding, storing or transporting property for a fee regardless of any other provision of this policy.

14. Nuclear Hazard Clause.

a. "Nuclear Hazard" means any nuclear reaction, radiation, or radioactive contamination, all whether controlled or uncontrolled or however caused, or any consequence of any of these.

b. Loss caused by the nuclear hazard shall not be considered loss caused by fire, explosion, or smoke, whether these perils are specifically named in or otherwise included within the Perils Insured Against in Section I.

c. This policy does not apply under Section I to loss caused directly or indirectly by nuclear hazard, except that direct loss by fire resulting from the nuclear hazard is covered.

Appendix 3 (*continued*)

SECTION II—LIABILITY COVERAGES

COVERAGE E PERSONAL LIABILITY

If a claim is made or a suit is brought against any **insured** for damages because of **bodily injury** or **property damage** to which this coverage applies, we will:

a. pay up to our limit of liability for the damages for which the **insured** is legally liable; and

b. provide a defense at our expense by counsel of our choice. We may make any investigation and settle any claim or suit that we decide is appropriate. Our obligation to defend any claim or suit ends when the amount we pay for damages resulting from the occurrence equals our limit of liability.

COVERAGE F MEDICAL PAYMENTS TO OTHERS

We will pay the necessary medical expenses incurred or medically ascertained within three years from the date of an accident causing **bodily injury.** Medical expenses means reasonable charges for medical, surgical, x-ray, dental, ambulance, hospital, professional nursing, prosthetic devices and funeral services. This coverage does not apply to you or regular residents of your household other than **residence employees.** As to others, this coverage applies only:

a. to a person on the **insured location** with the permission of any **insured;** or

b. to a person off the **insured location,** if the **bodily injury:**

(1) arises out of a condition in the **insured location** or the ways immediately adjoining;

(2) is caused by the activities of any **insured;**

(3) is caused by a **residence employee** in the course of the **residence employee's** employment by any **insured;** or

(4) is caused by an animal owned by or in the care of any **insured.**

SECTION II—EXCLUSIONS

1. Coverage E—Personal Liability and Coverage F—Medical Payments to Others do not apply to **bodily injury** or **property damage:**

a. which is expected or intended by the **insured;**

b. arising out of **business** pursuits of any **insured** or the rental or holding for rental of any part of any premises by any **insured.**

This exclusion does not apply to:

(1) activities which are ordinarily incident to non-**business** pursuits; or

(2) the rental or holding for rental of a residence of yours:

(a) on an occasional basis for the exclusive use as a residence;

(b) in part, unless intended for use as a residence by more than two roomers or boarders; or

(c) in part, as an office, school, studio or private garage;

c. arising out of the rendering or failing to render professional services;

d. arising out of any premises owned or rented to any **insured** which is not an **insured location;**

e. arising out of the ownership, maintenance, use, loading or unloading of:

(1) an aircraft;

(2) a **motor vehicle** owned or operated by, or rented or loaned to any **insured;** or

(3) a watercraft:

(a) owned by or rented to any **insured** if the watercraft has inboard or inboard-outdrive motor power of more than 50 horsepower or is a sailing vessel, with or without auxiliary power, 26 feet or more in overall length; or

(b) powered by one or more outboard motors with more than 25 total horsepower, owned by any **insured** at the inception of this policy. If you report in writing to us within 45 days after acquisition, an intention to insure any outboard motors acquired prior to the policy period, coverage will apply.

f. caused directly or indirectly by war, including undeclared war, civil war, insurrection, rebellion, revolution, warlike act by a military force or military personnel, destruction or seizure or use for a military purpose, and including any consequence of any of these. Discharge of a nuclear weapon shall be deemed a warlike act even if accidental.

Appendix 3 (*continued*)

Exclusion e(3) does not apply while the watercraft is stored and exclusions d and e do not apply to **bodily injury** to any **residence employee** arising out of and in the course of the **residence employee's** employment by any **insured.**

2. **Coverage E—Personal Liability,** does not apply to:

a. liability assumed under any unwritten contract or agreement, or by contract or agreement in connection with any **business** of the **insured;**

b. **property damage** to property owned by the **insured;**

c. **property damage** to property rented to, occupied or used by or in the care of the **insured.** This exclusion does not apply to **property damage** caused by fire, smoke or explosion;

d. **bodily injury** to any person eligible to receive any benefits required to be provided or voluntarily provided by the **insured** under any worker's or workmen's compensation, non-occupational disability, or occupational disease law; or

e. **bodily injury** or **property damage** for which any **insured** under this policy is also an insured under a nuclear energy liability policy or would be an insured but for its termination upon exhaustion of its limit of liability. A nuclear energy liability policy is a policy issued by Nuclear Energy Liability Insurance Association, Mutual Atomic Energy Liability Underwriters, Nuclear Insurance Association of Canada, or any of their successors.

3. **Coverage F—Medical Payments to Others,** does not apply to **bodily injury:**

a. to a **residence employee** if it occurs off the **insured location** and does not arise out of or in the course of the **residence employee's** employment by any **insured;**

b. to any person, eligible to receive any benefits required to be provided or voluntarily provided under any worker's or workmen's compensation, non-occupational disability or occupational disease law;

c. from any nuclear reaction, radiation or radioactive contamination, all whether controlled or uncontrolled or however caused, or any consequence of any of these.

SECTION II—ADDITIONAL COVERAGES

We cover the following in addition to the limits of liability:

1. **Claim Expenses.** We pay:

a. expenses incurred by us and costs taxed against any **insured** in any suit we defend;

b. premiums on bonds required in a suit defended by us, but not for bond amounts greater than the limit of liability for Coverage E. We are not obligated to apply for or furnish any bond;

c. reasonable expenses incurred by any **insured** at our request, including actual loss of earnings (but not loss of other income) up to $50 per day for assisting us in the investigation or defense of any claim or suit;

d. interest on the entire judgment which accrues after entry of the judgment and before we pay or tender, or deposit in court that part of the judgment which does not exceed the limit of liability that applies.

2. **First Aid Expenses.** We will pay expenses for first aid to others incurred by any **insured** for **bodily injury** covered under this policy. We will not pay for first aid to you or any other **insured.**

3. **Damage to Property of Others.** We will pay up to $250 per occurrence for **property damage** to property of others caused by any **insured.**

We will not pay for **property damage:**

a. to property covered under Section I of this policy;

b. caused intentionally by any **insured** who is 13 years of age or older;

c. to property owned by or rented to any **insured,** a tenant of any **insured,** or a resident in your household; or

d. arising out of:

(1) **business** pursuits;

(2) any act or omission in connection with a premises owned, rented or controlled by any **insured,** other than the **insured location;** or

(3) the ownership, maintenance, or use of a **motor vehicle,** aircraft or watercraft.

Appendix 3 (*continued*)

SECTION II—CONDITIONS

1. Limit of Liability. Regardless of the number of **insureds,** claims made or persons injured, our total liability under Coverage E stated in this policy for all damages resulting from any one occurrence shall not exceed the limit of liability for Coverage E stated in the Declarations. All **bodily injury** and **property damage** resulting from any one accident or from continuous or repeated exposure to substantially the same general conditions shall be considered to be the result of one occurrence.

Our total liability under Coverage F for all medical expense payable for **bodily injury** to one person as the result of one accident shall not exceed the limit of liability for Coverage F stated in the Declarations.

2. Severability of Insurance. This insurance applies separately to each **insured.** This condition shall not increase our limit of liability for any one occurrence.

3. Duties After Loss. In case of an accident or occurrence, the **insured** shall perform the following duties that apply. You shall cooperate with us in seeing that these duties are performed:

a. give written notice to us or our agent as soon as practicable, which sets forth:

(1) the identity of the policy and **insured;**

(2) reasonably available information on the time, place and circumstances of the accident or occurrence; and

(3) names and addresses of any claimants and available witnesses;

b. forward to us every notice, demand, summons or other process relating to the accident or occurrence;

c. at our request, assist in:

(1) making settlement;

(2) the enforcement of any right of contribution or indemnity against any person or organization who may be liable to any **insured;**

(3) the conduct of suits and attend hearings and trials;

(4) securing and giving evidence and obtaining the attendance of witnesses;

d. under the coverage—Damage to the Property of Others—submit to us within 60 days after the loss, a sworn statement of loss and exhibit the damaged property, if within the **insured's** control;

e. the **insured** shall not, except at the **insured's** own cost, voluntarily make any payment, assume any obligation or incur any expense other than for first aid to others at the time of the **bodily injury.**

4. Duties of an Injured Person—Coverage F—Medical Payments to Others. The injured person or someone acting on behalf of the injured person shall:

a. give us written proof of claim, under oath if required, as soon as practicable;

b. execute authorization to allow us to obtain copies of medical reports and records; and

c. the injured person shall submit to physical examination by a physician selected by us when and as often as we reasonably require.

5. Payment of Claim—Coverage F—Medical Payments to Others. Payment under this coverage is not an admission of liability by any **insured** or us.

6. Suit Against Us. No action shall be brought against us unless there has been compliance with the policy provisions.

No one shall have any right to join us as a party to any action against any **insured.** Further, no action with respect to Coverage E shall be brought against us until the obligation of the **insured** has been determined by final judgment or agreement signed by us.

7. Bankruptcy of any Insured. Bankruptcy or insolvency of any **insured** shall not relieve us of any of our obligations under this policy.

8. Other Insurance—Coverage E—Personal Liability. This insurance is excess over any other valid and collectible insurance except insurance written specifically to cover as excess over the limits of liability that apply in this policy.

Appendix 3 (*concluded*)

SECTION I AND SECTION II—CONDITIONS

1. **Policy Period.** This policy applies only to loss under Section I or **bodily injury** or **property damage** under Section II, which occurs during the policy period.

2. **Concealment or Fraud.** We do not provide coverage for any **insured** who has intentionally concealed or misrepresented any material fact or circumstance relating to this insurance.

3. **Liberalization Clause.** If we adopt any revision which would broaden the coverage under this policy without additional premium within 60 days prior to or during the policy period, the broadened coverage will immediately apply to this policy.

4. **Waiver or Change of Policy Provisions.** A waiver or change of any provision of this policy must be in writing by us to be valid. Our request for an appraisal or examination shall not waive any of our rights.

5. **Cancellation.**

a. You may cancel this policy at any time by returning it to us or by notifying us in writing of the date cancellation is to take effect.

b. We may cancel this policy only for the reasons stated in this condition by notifying you in writing of the date cancellation takes effect. This cancellation notice may be delivered to you, or mailed to you at your mailing address shown in the Declarations. Proof of mailing shall be sufficient proof of notice:

(1) When you have not paid the premium, whether payable to us or to our agent or under any finance or credit plan, we may cancel at any time by notifying you at least 10 days before the date cancellation takes effect.

(2) When this policy has been in effect for less than 60 days and is not a renewal with us, we may cancel for any reason by notifying you at least 10 days before the date cancellation takes effect.

(3) When this policy has been in effect for 60 days or more, or at any time if it is a renewal with us, we may cancel if there has been a material misrepresentation of fact which if known to us would have caused us not to issue the policy or if the risk has changed substantially since the policy was issued. This can be done by notifying you at least 30 days before the date cancellation takes effect.

(4) When this policy is written for a period longer than one year, we may cancel for any reason at anniversary by notifying you at least 30 days before the date cancellation takes effect.

c. When this policy is cancelled, the premium for the period from the date of cancellation to the expiration date will be refunded. When you request cancellation, the return premium will be based on our short rate table. When we cancel, the return premium will be pro rata.

d. If the return premium is not refunded with the notice of cancellation or when this policy is returned to us, we will refund it within a reasonable time after the date cancellation takes effect.

6. **Non-Renewal.** We may elect not to renew this policy. We may do so by delivery to you, or mailing to you at your mailing address shown in the Declarations, written notice at least 30 days before the expiration date of this policy. Proof of mailing shall be sufficient proof of notice.

7. **Assignment.** Assignment of this policy shall not be valid unless we give our written consent.

8. **Subrogation.** Any **insured** may waive in writing before a loss all rights of recovery against any person. If not waived, we may require an assignment of rights of recovery for a loss to the extent that payment is made by us.

If an assignment is sought, any **insured** shall sign and deliver all related papers and cooperate with us in any reasonable manner.

Subrogation does not apply under Section II to Medical Payments to Others or Damage to Property of Others.

9. **Death.** If any person named in the Declarations or the spouse, if a resident of the same household, dies:

a. we insure the legal representative of the deceased but only with respect to the premises and property of the deceased covered under the policy at the time of death;

b. **insured** includes:

(1) any member of your household who is an **insured** at the time of your death, but only while a resident of the **residence premises;** and

(2) with respect to your property, the person having proper temporary custody of the property until appointment and qualification of a legal representative.

Appendix 4 Personal Auto Policy

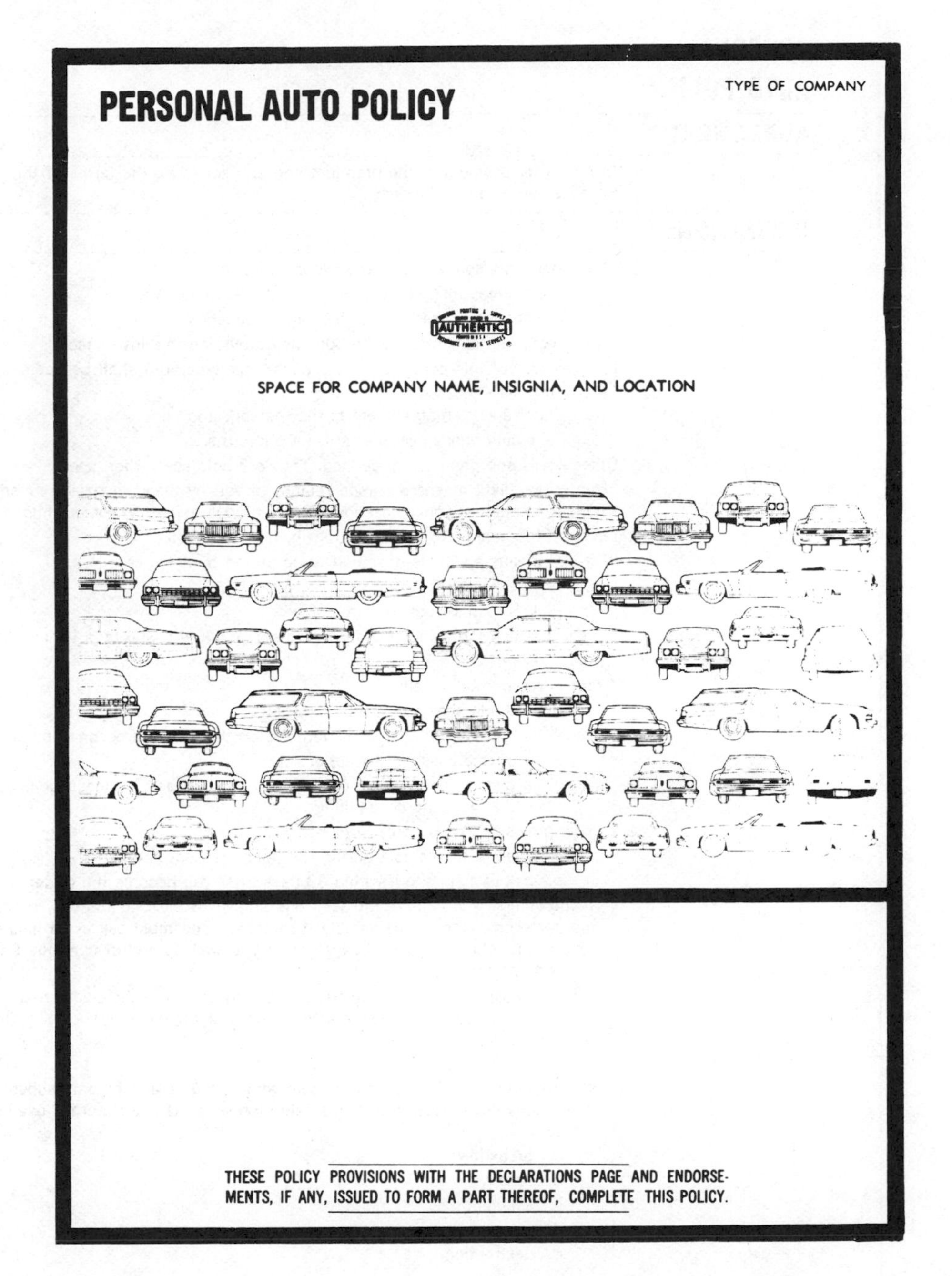

PERSONAL AUTO POLICY

TYPE OF COMPANY

SPACE FOR COMPANY NAME, INSIGNIA, AND LOCATION

THESE POLICY PROVISIONS WITH THE DECLARATIONS PAGE AND ENDORSEMENTS, IF ANY, ISSUED TO FORM A PART THEREOF, COMPLETE THIS POLICY.

Appendix 4 (*continued*)

PERSONAL AUTO POLICY

AGREEMENT

In return for payment of the premium and subject to all the terms of this policy, we agree with you as follows:

DEFINITIONS

Throughout this policy, "you" and "your" refer to:

1. The "named insured" shown in the Declarations; and
2. The spouse if a resident of the same household.

"We", "us" and "our" refer to the Company providing this insurance.

For purposes of this policy, a private passenger type auto shall be deemed to be owned by a person if leased:

1. Under a written agreement to that person; and
2. For a continuous period of at least 6 months.

Other words and phrases are defined. They are boldfaced when used.

"Family member" means a person related to you by blood, marriage or adoption who is a resident of your household. This includes a ward or foster child.

"Occupying" means in, upon, getting in, on, out or off.

"Trailer" means a vehicle designed to be pulled by a:

1. Private passenger auto; or
2. Pickup, panel truck, or van.

It also means a farm wagon or farm implement while towed by a vehicle listed in 1. or 2. above.

"Your covered auto" means:

1. Any vehicle shown in the Declarations.
2. Any of the following types of vehicles on the date you become the owner:
   a. a private passenger auto; or
   b. a pickup, panel truck or van, not used in any business or occupation other than farming or ranching.

   This provision applies only if you:
   a. acquire the vehicle during the policy period; and
   b. ask us to insure it within 30 days after you become the owner.

   If the vehicle you acquire replaces one shown in the Declarations, it will have the same coverage as the vehicle it replaced. You must ask us to insure a replacement vehicle within 30 days only if you wish to add or continue Coverage for Damage to Your Auto.

   If the vehicle you acquire is in addition to any shown in the Declarations, it will have the broadest coverage we now provide for any vehicle shown in the Declarations.
3. Any **trailer** you own.
4. Any auto or **trailer** you do not own while used as a temporary substitute for any other vehicle described in this definition which is out of normal use because of its:
   a. breakdown;
   b. repair;
   c. servicing;
   d. loss; or
   e. destruction.

Appendix 4 (*continued*)

PART A—LIABILITY COVERAGE

INSURING AGREEMENT

We will pay damages for bodily injury or property damage for which any **covered person** becomes legally responsible because of an auto accident. We will settle or defend, as we consider appropriate, any claim or suit asking for these damages. In addition to our limit of liability, we will pay all defense costs we incur. Our duty to settle or defend ends when our limit of liability for this coverage has been exhausted.

"Covered person" as used in this Part means:

1. You or any **family member** for the ownership, maintenance or use of any auto or **trailer.**
2. Any person using **your covered auto.**
3. For **your covered auto,** any person or organization but only with respect to legal responsibility for acts or omissions of a person for whom coverage is afforded under this Part.
4. For any auto or **trailer,** other than **your covered auto,** any person or organization but only with respect to legal responsibility for acts or omissions of you or any **family member** for whom coverage is afforded under this Part. This provision applies only if the person or organization does not own or hire the auto or **trailer.**

SUPPLEMENTARY PAYMENTS

In addition to our limit of liability, we will pay on behalf of a **covered person:**

1. Up to $250 for the cost of bail bonds required because of an accident, including related traffic law violations. The accident must result in bodily injury or property damage covered under this policy.
2. Premiums on appeal bonds and bonds to release attachments in any suit we defend.
3. Interest accruing after a judgment is entered in any suit we defend. Our duty to pay interest ends when we offer to pay that part of the judgment which does not exceed our limit of liability for this coverage.
4. Up to $50 a day for loss of earnings, but not other income, because of attendance at hearings or trials at our request.
5. Other reasonable expenses incurred at our request.

EXCLUSIONS

A. We do not provide Liability Coverage for any person:

1. Who intentionally causes bodily injury or property damage.
2. For damage to property owned or being transported by that person.
3. For damage to property:
   a. rented to;
   b. used by; or
   c. in the care of;

   that person.

   This exclusion does not apply to damage to:

   a. a residence or private garage; or
   b. any of the following type vehicles not owned by or furnished or available for the regular use of you or any **family member:**
      (1) private passenger autos;
      (2) **trailers;** or
      (3) pickups, panel trucks, or vans.
4. For bodily injury to an employee of that person during the course of employment. This exclusion does not apply to bodily injury to a domestic employee unless workers' compensation benefits are required or available for that domestic employee.

Appendix 4 (*continued*)

5. For that person's liability arising out of the ownership or operation of a vehicle while it is being used to carry persons or property for a fee. This exclusion does not apply to a share-the-expense car pool.
6. While employed or otherwise engaged in the business or occupation of:
   a. selling;
   b. repairing;
   c. servicing;
   d. storing; or
   e. parking;

   vehicles designed for use mainly on public highways. This includes road testing and delivery. This exclusion does not apply to the ownership, maintenance or use of **your covered auto** by:
   a. you;
   b. any **family member;** or
   c. any partner, agent or employee of you or any **family member.**
7. Maintaining or using any vehicle while that person is employed or otherwise engaged in any business or occupation not described in Exclusion 6. This exclusion does not apply to the maintenance or use of a:
   a. private passenger auto;
   b. pickup, panel truck or van that you own; or
   c. **trailer** used with a vehicle described in a. or b. above.
8. Using a vehicle without a reasonable belief that that person is entitled to do so.
9. For bodily injury or property damage for which that person:
   a. is an insured under a nuclear energy liability policy; or
   b. would be an insured under a nuclear energy liability policy but for its termination upon exhaustion of its limit of liability.

   A nuclear energy liability policy is a policy issued by any of the following or their successors:
   a. Nuclear Energy Liability Insurance Association;
   b. Mutual Atomic Energy Liability Underwriters; or
   c. Nuclear Insurance Association of Canada.

B. We do not provide Liability Coverage for the ownership, maintenance or use of:
1. Any motorized vehicle having less than four wheels.
2. Any vehicle, other than **your covered auto,** which is:
   a. owned by you; or
   b. furnished or available for your regular use.
3. Any vehicle, other than **your covered auto,** which is:
   a. owned by any **family member;** or
   b. furnished or available for the regular use of any **family member.**

   However, this exclusion does not apply to your maintenance or use of any vehicle which is:
   a. owned by a **family member;** or
   b. furnished or available for the regular use of a **family member.**

LIMIT OF LIABILITY

The limit of liability shown in the Declarations for this coverage is our maximum limit of liability for all damages resulting from any one auto accident. This is the most we will pay regardless of the number of:
1. **Covered persons;**
2. Claims made;
3. Vehicles or premiums shown in the Declarations; or

Appendix 4 (*continued*)

4. Vehicles involved in the auto accident.

We will apply the limit of liability to provide any separate limits required by law for bodily injury and property damage liability. However, this provision will not change our total limit of liability.

OUT OF STATE COVERAGE

If an auto accident to which this policy applies occurs in any state or province other than the one in which **your covered auto** is principally garaged, we will interpret your policy for that accident as follows:

If the state or province has:

1. A financial responsibility or similar law specifying limits of liability for bodily injury or property damage higher than the limit shown in the Declarations, your policy will provide the higher specified limit.
2. A compulsory insurance or similar law requiring a nonresident to maintain insurance whenever the nonresident uses a vehicle in that state or province, your policy will provide at least the required minimum amounts and types of coverage.

No one will be entitled to duplicate payments for the same elements of loss.

FINANCIAL RESPONSIBILITY REQUIRED

When this policy is certified as future proof of financial responsibility, this policy shall comply with the law to the extent required.

OTHER INSURANCE

If there is other applicable liability insurance we will pay only our share of the loss. Our share is the proportion that our limit of liability bears to the total of all applicable limits. However, any insurance we provide for a vehicle you do not own shall be excess over any other collectible insurance.

PART B—MEDICAL PAYMENTS COVERAGE

INSURING AGREEMENT

We will pay reasonable expenses incurred for necessary medical and funeral services because of bodily injury:

1. Caused by accident; and
2. Sustained by a **covered person.**

We will pay only those expenses incurred within 3 years from the date of the accident.

"Covered person" as used in this Part means:

1. You or any **family member:**
   a. while **occupying;** or
   b. as a pedestrian when struck by;

   a motor vehicle designed for use mainly on public roads or a trailer of any type.
2. Any other person while **occupying your covered auto.**

EXCLUSIONS

We do not provide Medical Payments Coverage for any person for bodily injury:

1. Sustained while **occupying** any motorized vehicle having less than four wheels.
2. Sustained while **occupying your covered auto** when it is being used to carry persons or property for a fee. This exclusion does not apply to a share-the-expense car pool.
3. Sustained while **occupying** any vehicle located for use as a residence or premises.
4. Occurring during the course of employment if workers' compensation benefits are required or available for the bodily injury.
5. Sustained while **occupying** or, when struck by, any vehicle (other than **your covered auto**) which is:
   a. owned by you; or
   b. furnished or available for your regular use.

Appendix 4 (*continued*)

6. Sustained while **occupying** or, when struck by, any vehicle (other than **your covered auto**) which is:
   a. owned by any **family member;** or
   b. furnished or available for the regular use of any **family member.**

However, this exclusion does not apply to you.

7. Sustained while **occupying** a vehicle without a reasonable belief that that person is entitled to do so.
8. Sustained while **occupying** a vehicle when it is being used in the business or occupation of a **covered person.** This exclusion does not apply to bodily injury sustained while **occupying** a:
   a. private passenger auto;
   b. pickup, panel truck, or van that you own; or
   c. **trailer** used with a vehicle described in a. or b. above.
9. Caused by or as a consequence of:
   a. discharge of a nuclear weapon (even if accidental);
   b. war (declared or undeclared);
   c. civil war;
   d. insurrection; or
   e. rebellion or revolution.
10. From or as a consequence of the following, whether controlled or uncontrolled or however caused:
   a. nuclear reaction;
   b. radiation; or
   c. radioactive contamination.

LIMIT OF LIABILITY

The limit of liability shown in the Declarations for this coverage is our maximum limit of liability for each person injured in any one accident. This is the most we will pay regardless of the number of:

1. **Covered persons;**
2. Claims made;
3. Vehicles or premiums shown in the Declarations; or
4. Vehicles involved in the accident.

Any amounts otherwise payable for expenses under this coverage shall be reduced by any amounts paid or payable for the same expenses under Part A or Part C.

No payment will be made unless the injured person or that person's legal representative agrees in writing that any payment shall be applied toward any settlement or judgment that person receives under Part A or Part C.

OTHER INSURANCE

If there is other applicable auto medical payments insurance we will pay only our share of the loss. Our share is the proportion that our limit of liability bears to the total of all applicable limits. However, any insurance we provide with respect to a vehicle you do not own shall be excess over any other collectible auto insurance providing payments for medical or funeral expenses.

PART C—UNINSURED MOTORISTS COVERAGE

INSURING AGREEMENT

We will pay damages which a **covered person** is legally entitled to recover from the owner or operator of an **uninsured motor vehicle** because of bodily injury:

1. Sustained by a **covered person;** and
2. Caused by an accident.

The owner's or operator's liability for these damages must arise out of the ownership, maintenance or use of the **uninsured motor vehicle.**

Any judgment for damages arising out of a suit brought without our written consent is not binding on us.

Appendix 4 (*continued*)

"Covered person" as used in this Part means:

1. You or any **family member.**
2. Any other person **occupying your covered auto.**
3. Any person for damages that person is entitled to recover because of bodily injury to which this coverage applies sustained by a person described in 1. or 2. above.

"Uninsured motor vehicle" means a land motor vehicle or trailer of any type:

1. To which no bodily injury liability bond or policy applies at the time of the accident.
2. To which a bodily injury liability bond or policy applies at the time of the accident. In this case its limit for bodily injury liability must be less than the minimum limit for bodily injury liability specified by the financial responsibility law of the state in which **your covered auto** is principally garaged.
3. Which is a hit and run vehicle whose operator or owner cannot be identified and which hits:
   a. you or any **family member;**
   b. a vehicle which you or any **family member** are **occupying;** or
   c. **your covered auto.**
4. To which a bodily injury liability bond or policy applies at the time of the accident but the bonding or insuring company:
   a. denies coverage; or
   b. is or becomes insolvent.

However, **"uninsured motor vehicle"** does not include any vehicle or equipment:

1. Owned by or furnished or available for the regular use of you or any **family member.**
2. Owned or operated by a self-insurer under any applicable motor vehicle law.
3. Owned by any governmental unit or agency.
4. Operated on rails or crawler treads.
5. Designed mainly for use off public roads while not on public roads.
6. While located for use as a residence or premises.

EXCLUSIONS

A. We do not provide Uninsured Motorists Coverage for bodily injury sustained by any person:

1. While **occupying,** or when struck by, any motor vehicle owned by you or any **family member** which is not insured for this coverage under this policy. This includes a trailer of any type used with that vehicle.
2. If that person or the legal representative settles the bodily injury claim without our consent.
3. While **occupying your covered auto** when it is being used to carry persons or property for a fee. This exclusion does not apply to a share-the-expense car pool.
4. Using a vehicle without a reasonable belief that that person is entitled to do so.

B. This coverage shall not apply directly or indirectly to benefit any insurer or self-insurer under any of the following or similar law:

1. workers' compensation law; or
2. disability benefits law.

LIMIT OF LIABILITY

The limit of liability shown in the Declarations for this coverage is our maximum limit of liability for all damages resulting from any one accident. This is the most we will pay regardless of the number of:

1. **Covered persons;**

Appendix 4 (*continued*)

2. Claims made;
3. Vehicles or premiums shown in the Declarations; or
4. Vehicles involved in the accident.

Any amounts otherwise payable for damages under this coverage shall be reduced by all sums:

1. Paid because of the bodily injury by or on behalf of persons or organizations who may be legally responsible. This includes all sums paid under Part A; and
2. Paid or payable because of the bodily injury under any of the following or similar law:
   a. workers' compensation law; or
   b. disability benefits law.

Any payment under this coverage will reduce any amount that person is entitled to recover for the same damages under Part A.

OTHER INSURANCE

If there is other applicable similar insurance we will pay only our share of the loss. Our share is the proportion that our limit of liability bears to the total of all applicable limits. However, any insurance we provide with respect to a vehicle you do not own shall be excess over any other collectible insurance.

ARBITRATION

If we and a **covered person** do not agree:

1. Whether that person is legally entitled to recover damages under this Part; or
2. As to the amount of damages;

either party may make a written demand for arbitration. In this event, each party will select an arbitrator. The two arbitrators will select a third. If they cannot agree within 30 days, either may request that selection be made by a judge of a court having jurisdiction. Each party will:

1. Pay the expenses it incurs; and
2. Bear the expenses of the third arbitrator equally.

Unless both parties agree otherwise, arbitration will take place in the county in which the **covered person** lives. Local rules of law as to procedure and evidence will apply. A decision agreed to by two of the arbitrators will be binding as to:

1. Whether the **covered person** is legally entitled to recover damages; and
2. The amount of damages. This applies only if the amount does not exceed the minimum limit for bodily injury liability specified by the financial responsibility law of the state in which **your covered auto** is principally garaged. If the amount exceeds that limit, either party may demand the right to a trial. This demand must be made within 60 days of the arbitrators' decision. If this demand is not made, the amount of damages agreed to by the arbitrators will be binding.

PART D—COVERAGE FOR DAMAGE TO YOUR AUTO

INSURING AGREEMENT

We will pay for direct and accidental loss to **your covered auto,** including its equipment, minus any applicable deductible shown in the Declarations. However, we will pay for loss caused by **collision** only if the Declarations indicate that Collision Coverage is provided.

"Collision" means the upset, or collision with another object of **your covered auto.** However, loss caused by the following are not considered "collision":

1. Missiles or falling objects;
2. Fire;
3. Theft or larceny;
4. Explosion or earthquake;
5. Windstorm;
6. Hail, water or flood;
7. Malicious mischief or vandalism;
8. Riot or civil commotion;
9. Contact with bird or animal; or
10. Breakage of glass.

If breakage of glass is caused by a **collision,** you may elect to have it considered a loss caused by **collision.**

Appendix 4 (*continued*)

TRANSPORTATION EXPENSES

In addition, we will pay up to $10 per day, to a maximum of $300, for transportation expenses incurred by you. This applies only in the event of the total theft of **your covered auto.** We will pay only transportation expenses incurred during the period:

1. Beginning 48 hours after the theft; and
2. Ending when **your covered auto** is returned to use or we pay for its loss.

EXCLUSIONS

We will not pay for:

1. Loss to **your covered auto** which occurs while it is used to carry persons or property for a fee. This exclusion does not apply to a share-the-expense car pool.
2. Damage due and confined to:
   a. wear and tear;
   b. freezing;
   c. mechanical or electrical breakdown or failure; or
   d. road damage to tires.

   This exclusion does not apply if the damage results from the total theft of **your covered auto.**
3. Loss due to or as a consequence of:
   a. radioactive contamination;
   b. discharge of any nuclear weapon (even if accidental);
   c. war (declared or undeclared);
   d. civil war;
   e. insurrection; or
   f. rebellion or revolution.
4. Loss to equipment designed for the reproduction of sound. This exclusion does not apply if the equipment is permanently installed in **your covered auto.**
5. Loss to tapes, records or other devices for use with equipment designed for the reproduction of sound.
6. Loss to a camper body or **trailer** not shown in the Declarations. This exclusion does not apply to a camper body or **trailer** you:
   a. acquire during the policy period; and
   b. ask us to insure within 30 days after you become the owner.
7. Loss to any vehicle while used as a temporary substitute for a vehicle you own which is out of normal use because of its:
   a. breakdown;
   b. repair;
   c. servicing;
   d. loss; or
   e. destruction.
8. Loss to:
   a. TV antennas;
   b. awnings or cabanas; or
   c. equipment designed to create additional living facilities.
9. Loss to any of the following or their accessories:
   a. citizens band radio;
   b. two-way mobile radio;
   c. telephone; or
   d. scanning monitor receiver.

   This exclusion does not apply if the equipment is permanently installed in the opening of the dash or console of the auto. This opening must be normally used by the auto manufacturer for the installation of a radio.

Appendix 4 (*continued*)

10. Loss to any custom furnishings or equipment in or upon any pickup, panel truck or van. Custom furnishings or equipment include but are not limited to:
    a. special carpeting and insulation, furniture, bars or television receivers;
    b. facilities for cooking and sleeping;
    c. height-extending roofs; or
    d. custom murals, paintings or other decals or graphics.

LIMIT OF LIABILITY

Our limit of liability for loss will be the lesser of the:
1. Actual cash value of the stolen or damaged property; or
2. Amount necessary to repair or replace the property.

PAYMENT OF LOSS

We may pay for loss in money or repair or replace the damaged or stolen property. We may, at our expense, return any stolen property to:
1. You; or
2. The address shown in this policy.

If we return stolen property we will pay for any damage resulting from the theft. We may keep all or part of the property at an agreed or appraised value.

NO BENEFIT TO BAILEE

This insurance shall not directly or indirectly benefit any carrier or other bailee for hire.

OTHER INSURANCE

If other insurance also covers the loss we will pay only our share of the loss. Our share is the proportion that our limit of liability bears to the total of all applicable limits.

APPRAISAL

If we and you do not agree on the amount of loss, either may demand an appraisal of the loss. In this event, each party will select a competent appraiser. The two appraisers will select an umpire. The appraisers will state separately the actual cash value and the amount of loss. If they fail to agree, they will submit their differences to the umpire. A decision agreed to by any two will be binding. Each party will:
1. Pay its chosen appraiser; and
2. Bear the expenses of the appraisal and umpire equally.

We do not waive any of our rights under this policy by agreeing to an appraisal.

PART E—DUTIES AFTER AN ACCIDENT OR LOSS

GENERAL DUTIES

We must be notified promptly of how, when and where the accident or loss happened. Notice should also include the names and addresses of any injured persons and of any witnesses.

A person seeking any coverage must:
1. Cooperate with us in the investigation, settlement or defense of any claim or suit.
2. Promptly send us copies of any notices or legal papers received in connection with the accident or loss.
3. Submit, as often as we reasonably require, to physical exams by physicians we select. We will pay for these exams.
4. Authorize us to obtain:
    a. medical reports; and
    b. other pertinent records.
5. Submit a proof of loss when required by us.

ADDITIONAL DUTIES FOR UNINSURED MOTORISTS COVERAGE

A person seeking Uninsured Motorists Coverage must also:
1. Promptly notify the police if a hit and run driver is involved.
2. Promptly send us copies of the legal papers if a suit is brought.

Appendix 4 (*continued*)

ADDITIONAL DUTIES FOR COVERAGE FOR DAMAGE TO YOUR AUTO

A person seeking Coverage for Damage to Your Auto must also:

1. Take reasonable steps after loss to protect **your covered auto** and its equipment from further loss. We will pay reasonable expenses incurred to do this.
2. Promptly notify the police if **your covered auto** is stolen.
3. Permit us to inspect and appraise the damaged property before its repair or disposal.

PART F—GENERAL PROVISIONS

BANKRUPTCY

Bankruptcy or insolvency of the **covered person** shall not relieve us of any obligations under this policy.

CHANGES

This policy contains all the agreements between you and us. Its terms may not be changed or waived except by endorsement issued by us. If a change requires a premium adjustment, we will adjust the premium as of the effective date of change.

We may revise this policy form to provide more coverage without additional premium charge. If we do this your policy will automatically provide the additional coverage as of the date the revision is effective in your state.

LEGAL ACTION AGAINST US

No legal action may be brought against us until there has been full compliance with all the terms of this policy. In addition, under Part A, no legal action may be brought against us until:

1. We agree in writing that the **covered person** has an obligation to pay; or
2. The amount of that obligation has been finally determined by judgment after trial.

No person or organization has any right under this policy to bring us into any action to determine the liability of a **covered person.**

OUR RIGHT TO RECOVER PAYMENT

A. If we make a payment under this policy and the person to or for whom payment was made has a right to recover damages from another we shall be subrogated to that right. That person shall do:

1. Whatever is necessary to enable us to exercise our rights; and
2. Nothing after loss to prejudice them.

However, our rights in this paragraph do not apply under Part D, against any person using **your covered auto** with a reasonable belief that that person is entitled to do so.

B. If we make a payment under this policy and the person to or for whom payment is made recovers damages from another, that person shall:

1. Hold in trust for us the proceeds of the recovery; and
2. Reimburse us to the extent of our payment.

POLICY PERIOD AND TERRITORY

This policy applies only to accidents and losses which occur:

1. During the policy period as shown in the Declarations; and
2. Within the policy territory.

The policy territory is:

1. The United States of America, its territories or possessions;
2. Puerto Rico; or
3. Canada.

This policy also applies to loss to, or accidents involving, **your covered auto** while being transported between their ports.

TERMINATION

Cancellation. This policy may be cancelled during the policy period as follows:

1. The named insured shown in the Declarations may cancel by:
   a. returning this policy to us; or
   b. giving us advance written notice of the date cancellation is to take effect.

Appendix 4 (*continued*)

2. We may cancel by mailing to the named insured shown in the Declarations at the address shown in this policy:
   a. at least 10 days notice:
      (1) if cancellation is for nonpayment of premium; or
      (2) if notice is mailed during the first 60 days this policy is in effect and this is not a renewal or continuation policy; or
   b. at least 20 days notice in all other cases.

3. After this policy is in effect for 60 days, or if this is a renewal or continuation policy, we will cancel only:
   a. for nonpayment of premium; or
   b. if your driver's license or that of:
      (1) any driver who lives with you; or
      (2) any driver who customarily uses **your covered auto;**

   has been suspended or revoked. This must have occurred:
      (1) during the policy period; or
      (2) since the last anniversary of the original effective date if the policy period is other than 1 year.

Nonrenewal. If we decide not to renew or continue this policy, we will mail notice to the named insured shown in the Declarations at the address shown in this policy. Notice will be mailed at least 20 days before the end of the policy period. If the policy period is other than 1 year, we will have the right not to renew or continue it only at each anniversary of its original effective date.

Automatic Termination. If we offer to renew or continue and you or your representative do not accept, this policy will automatically terminate at the end of the current policy period. Failure to pay the required renewal or continuation premium when due shall mean that you have not accepted our offer.

If you obtain other insurance on **your covered auto,** any similar insurance provided by this policy will terminate as to that auto on the effective date of the other insurance.

Other Termination Provisions.

1. If the law in effect in your state at the time this policy is issued, renewed or continued:
   a. requires a longer notice period;
   b. requires a special form of or procedure for giving notice; or
   c. modifies any of the stated termination reasons;

   we will comply with those requirements.

2. We may deliver any notice instead of mailing it. Proof of mailing of any notice shall be sufficient proof of notice.

3. If this policy is cancelled, you may be entitled to a premium refund. If so, we will send you the refund. The premium refund, if any, will be computed according to our manuals. However, making or offering to make the refund is not a condition of cancellation.

4. The effective date of cancellation stated in the notice shall become the end of the policy period.

TRANSFER OF YOUR INTEREST IN THIS POLICY

Your rights and duties under this policy may not be assigned without our written consent. However, if a named insured shown in the Declarations dies, coverage will be provided for:

1. The surviving spouse if resident in the same household at the time of death. Coverage applies to the spouse as if a named insured shown in the Declarations; or

2. The legal representative of the deceased person as if a named insured shown

Appendix 4 (*concluded*)

in the Declarations. This applies only with respect to the representative's legal responsibility to maintain or use **your covered auto.**

Coverage will only be provided until the end of the policy period.

TWO OR MORE AUTO POLICIES If this policy and any other auto insurance policy issued to you by us apply to the same accident, the maximum limit of our liability under all the policies shall not exceed the highest applicable limit of liability under any one policy.

In Witness Whereof, we have caused this policy to be executed and attested, and, if required by state law, this policy shall not be valid unless countersigned by our authorized representative.

← INSERT SIGNATURES AND TITLES OF PROPER OFFICERS →

Source: Insurance Services Office, copyright © 1979.

Appendix 5 Whole Life Policy

THE COUNCIL LIFE INSURANCE COMPANY

The Council Life Insurance Company agrees to pay the benefits provided in this policy, subject to its terms and conditions. Executed at New York, New York on the Date of Issue.

David Olson

Secretary

Barbara Sloan

President

Life Policy — Participating

Amount payable at death of Insured $10,000.

Premiums payable to age 90.

Schedule of benefits and premiums page 2.

Right to Examine Policy—Please examine this policy carefully. The Owner may return the policy for any reason within ten days after receiving it. If returned, the policy will be considered void from the beginning and any premium paid will be refunded.

A GUIDE TO THE PROVISIONS OF THIS POLICY

Accidental Death Benefit	12
Beneficiaries	7
Cash Value, Extended Term and Paid-Up Insurance	5
Change of Policy	6
Contract	3
Dividends	4
Loans	6
Ownership	3
Premiums and Reinstatement	4
Specification	2
Waiver of Premium Right	11

Endorsements Made At Issue Appear After "General Provisions." Additional Benefits, If Any, Are Provided By Rider.

Appendix 5 (*continued*)

Specifications

Plan and Additional Benefits	Amount	Premium	Years Payable
Whole Life (Premiums payable to age 90)	$10,000	$229.50	55
Waiver of Premium (To age 65)		4.30	30
Accidental Death (To age 70)	10,000	7.80	35

A premium is payable on the policy date and every 12 policy months thereafter. The first premium is $241.60.

TABLE OF GUARANTEED VALUES

END OF POLICY YEAR	CASH OR LOAN VALUE	PAID-UP INSURANCE	EXTENDED TERM INSURANCE YEARS	EXTENDED TERM INSURANCE DAYS
1	$ 14	$ 30	0	152
2	174	450	4	182
3	338	860	8	65
4	506	1,250	10	344
5	676	1,640	12	360
6	879	2,070	14	335
7	1,084	2,500	16	147
8	1,293	2,910	17	207
9	1,504	3,300	18	177
10	1,719	3,690	19	78
11	1,908	4,000	19	209
12	2,099	4,300	19	306
13	2,294	4,590	20	8
14	2,490	4,870	20	47
15	2,690	5,140	20	65
16	2,891	5,410	20	66
17	3,095	5,660	20	52
18	3,301	5,910	20	27
19	3,508	6,150	19	358
20	3,718	6,390	19	317
AGE 60	4,620	7,200	18	111
AGE 65	5,504	7,860	16	147

Paid-up additions and dividend accumulations increase the cash values; indebtedness decreases them.
The percentage referred to in section 5.6 is 83.000%.

Direct Beneficiary Helen M. Benson, wife of the insured

Owner Thomas A. Benson, the insured

Insured Thomas A. Benson
Policy Date May 1, 1978
Date of Issue May 1, 1978

Age and Sex 35 Male
Policy Number 000/00

Appendix 5 (*continued*)

SECTION 1. THE CONTRACT

1.1 LIFE INSURANCE BENEFIT

The Council Life Insurance Company agrees, subject to the terms and conditions of this policy, to pay the Amount shown on page 2 to the beneficiary upon receipt at its Home Office of proof of the death of the Insured.

1.2 INCONTESTABILITY

This policy shall be incontestable after it has been in force during the lifetime of the Insured for two years from the Date of Issue.

1.3 SUICIDE

If within two years from the Date of Issue the Insured dies by suicide, the amount payable by the Company shall be limited to the premiums paid.

1.4 DATES

The contestable and suicide periods commence with the Date of Issue. Policy months, years and anniversaries are computed from the Policy Date. Both dates are shown on page 2 of this policy.

1.5 MISSTATEMENT OF AGE

If the age of the Insured has been misstated, the amount payable shall be the amount which the premiums paid would have purchased at the correct age.

1.6 GENERAL

This policy and the application, a copy of which is attached when the policy is issued, constitute the entire contract. All statements in the application are representations and not warranties. No statement shall void this policy or be used in defense of a claim under it unless contained in the application.

Only an officer of the Company is authorized to alter this policy or to waive any of the Company's rights or requirements.

All payments by the Company under this policy are payable at its Home Office.

SECTION 2. OWNERSHIP

2.1 THE OWNER

The Owner is as shown on page 2, or his successor or transferee. All policy rights and privileges may be exercised by the Owner without the consent of any beneficiary. Such rights and privileges may be exercised only during the lifetime of the Insured and thereafter to the extent permitted by Sections 8 and 9.

2.2 TRANSFER OF OWNERSHIP

The Owner may transfer the ownership of this policy by filing written evidence of transfer satisfactory to the Company at its Home Office and, unless waived by the Company, submitting the policy for endorsement to show the transfer.

2.3 COLLATERAL ASSIGNMENT

The Owner may assign this policy as collateral security. The Company assumes no responsibility for the validity or effect of any collateral assignment of this policy. The Company shall not be charged with notice of any assignment unless the assignment is in writing and filed at its Home Office before payment is made.

The interest of any beneficiary shall be subordinate to any collateral assignment made either before or after the beneficiary designation.

A collateral assignee is not an Owner and a collateral assignment is not a transfer of ownership.

Appendix 5 (*continued*)

SECTION 3. PREMIUMS AND REINSTATEMENT

3.1 PREMIUMS

(a) Payment. All premiums after the first are payable at the Home Office or to an authorized agent. A receipt signed by an officer of the Company will be provided upon request.

(b) Frequency. Premiums may be paid annually, semiannually, or quarterly at the published rates for this policy. A change to any such frequency shall be effective upon acceptance by the Company of the premium for the changed frequency. Premiums may be paid on any other frequency approved by the Company.

(c) Default. If a premium is not paid on or before its due date, this policy shall terminate on the due date except as provided in Sections 3.1(d), 5.3 and 5.4.

(d) Grace Period. A grace period of 31 days shall be allowed for payment of a premium not paid on its due date. The policy shall continue in full force during this period. If the Insured dies during the grace period, the overdue premium shall be paid from the proceeds of the policy.

(e) Premium Refund at Death. The portion of any premium paid which applies to a period beyond the policy month in which the Insured died shall be refunded as part of the proceeds of this policy.

3.2 REINSTATEMENT

If the policy has not been surrendered for its cash value, it may be reinstated within five years after the due date of the unpaid premium provided the following conditions are satisfied:

(a) Within 31 days following expiration of the grace period, reinstatement may be made without evidence of insurability during the lifetime of the Insured by payment of the overdue premium.

(b) After 31 days following expiration of the grace period, reinstatement is subject to:

(i) receipt of evidence of insurability of the Insured satisfactory to the Company;

(ii) payment of all overdue premiums with interest from the due date of each at the rate of 6% compounded annually; or any lower rate established by the Company.

Any policy indebtedness existing on the due date of the unpaid premium, together with interest from that date, must be repaid or reinstated.

SECTION 4. DIVIDENDS

4.1 ANNUAL DIVIDENDS

This policy shall share in the divisible surplus, if any, of the Company. This policy's share shall be determined annually and credited as a dividend. Payment of the first dividend is contingent upon payment of the premium or premiums for the second policy year and shall be credited proportionately as each premium is paid. Thereafter, each dividend shall be payable on the policy anniversary.

4.2 USE OF DIVIDENDS

As directed by the Owner, dividends may be paid in cash or applied under one of the following:

(a) Paid-Up Additions. Dividends may be applied to purchase fully paid-up additional insurance. Paid-up additions will also share in the divisible surplus.

(b) Dividend Accumulations. Dividends may be left to accumulate at interest. Interest is credited at a rate of 3% compounded annually, or any higher rate established by the Company.

(c) Premium Payment. Dividends may be applied toward payment of any premium due within one year, if the balance of the premium is paid. If the balance is not paid, or if this policy is in force as paid-up insurance, the dividend will be applied to purchase paid-up additions.

If no direction is given by the Owner, dividends will be applied to purchase paid-up additions.

4.3 USE OF ADDITIONS AND ACCUMULATIONS

Paid-up additions and dividend accumulations increase the policy's cash value and loan value and are payable as part of the policy proceeds. Additions may be surrendered and accumulations withdrawn unless required under the Loan, Extended Term Insurance, or Paid-up Insurance provisions.

4.4 DIVIDEND AT DEATH

A dividend for the period from the beginning of the policy year to the end of the policy month in which the Insured dies shall be paid as part of the policy proceeds.

Appendix 5 (*continued*)

SECTION 5. CASH VALUE, EXTENDED TERM AND PAID-UP INSURANCE

5.1 CASH VALUE

The cash value, when all premiums due have been paid, shall be the reserve on this policy less the deduction described in Section 5.5, plus the reserve for any paid-up additions and the amount of any dividend accumulations.

The cash value within three months after the due date of any unpaid premium shall be the cash value on the due date reduced by any subsequent surrender of paid-up additions or withdrawal of dividend accumulations. The cash value at any time after such three months shall be the reserve on the form of insurance then in force, plus the reserve for any paid-up additions and the amount of any dividend accumulations.

If this policy is surrendered within 31 days after a policy anniversary, the cash value shall be not less than the cash value on that anniversary.

5.2 CASH SURRENDER

The Owner may surrender this policy for its cash value less any indebtedness. The policy shall terminate upon receipt at the Home Office of this policy and a written surrender of all claims. Receipt of the policy may be waived by the Company.

The Company may defer paying the cash value for a period not exceeding six months from the date of surrender. If payment is deferred 30 days or more, interest shall be paid on the cash value less any indebtedness at the rate of 3% compounded annually from the date of surrender to the date of payment.

5.3 EXTENDED TERM INSURANCE

If any premium remains unpaid at the end of the grace period, this policy shall continue in force as nonparticipating extended term insurance. The amount of insurance shall be the amount of this policy, plus any paid-up additions and dividend accumulations, less any indebtedness. The term insurance shall begin as of the due date of the unpaid premium and its duration shall be determined by applying the cash value less any indebtedness as a net single premium at the attained age of the Insured. If the term insurance would extend to or beyond attained age 100, paid-up insurance under Section 5.4 below will be provided instead.

5.4 PAID-UP INSURANCE

In lieu of extended term insurance this policy may be continued in force as participating paid-up life insurance. Paid-up insurance may be requested by written notice filed at the Home Office before, or within three months after, the due date of the unpaid premium. The insurance will be for the amount that the cash value will purchase as a net single premium at the attained age of the Insured. Any indebtedness shall remain outstanding.

5.5 TABLE OF GUARANTEED VALUES

The cash values, paid-up insurance, and extended term insurance shown on page 2 are for the end of the policy year indicated. These values are based on the assumption that premiums have been paid for the number of years stated and are exclusive of any paid-up additions, dividend accumulations, or indebtedness. During the policy year allowance shall be made for any portion of a year's premium paid and for the time elapsed in that year. Values for policy years not shown are calculated on the same basis as this table and will be furnished on request. All values are equal to or greater than those required by the State in which this policy is delivered.

In determining cash values a deduction is made from the reserve. During the first five policy years, the deduction for each $1,000 of Amount is $9 plus $.15 for each year of the Insured's issue age. After the fifth policy year, the deduction decreases yearly by one-fifth of the initial deduction until there is no deduction in the tenth and subsequent policy years. If the premium paying period is less than ten years, there is no deduction in the last two policy years of the premium paying period or thereafter.

5.6 RESERVES AND NET PREMIUMS

Reserves, net premiums and present values are determined in accordance with the Commissioners 1958 Standard Ordinary Mortality Table and 3% interest, except that for the first five years of any extended term insurance, the Commissioners 1958 Extended Term Insurance Table is used. All reserves are based on continuous payment of premiums and immediate payment of claims. Net annual premiums are the same in each policy year, except that if premiums are payable for more than 20 years, the net annual premium in the 21st and subsequent policy years is determined by applying the percentage shown on page 2 to the net annual premium for the 20th policy year. On the Policy Date, the present value of all future guaranteed benefits equals the present value of all future net annual premiums. The reserve at the end of any policy year is the excess of the present value of all future guaranteed benefits over the present value of all future net annual premiums. The reserve is exclusive of any additional benefits.

Appendix 5 (*continued*)

SECTION 6. LOANS

6.1 POLICY LOAN

The Owner may obtain a policy loan by assignment of this policy to the Company. The amount of the loan, plus any existing indebtedness, shall not exceed the loan value. No loan shall be granted if the policy is in force as extended term insurance. The Company may defer making a loan for six months unless the loan is to be used to pay premiums on policies issued by the Company.

6.2 PREMIUM LOAN

A premium loan shall be granted to pay an overdue premium if the premium loan option is in effect. If the loan value, less any indebtedness, is insufficient to pay the overdue premium, a premium will be paid for any other frequency permitted by this policy for which the loan value less any indebtedness is sufficient. The premium loan option may be elected or revoked by written notice filed at the Home Office.

6.3 LOAN VALUE

The loan value is the largest amount which, with accrued interest, does not exceed the cash value either on the next premium due date or at the end of one year from the date of the loan.

6.4 LOAN INTEREST

Interest is payable at the rate of 8% compounded annually, or at any lower rate established by the Company for any period during which the loan is outstanding.

The Company shall provide at least 30 days written notice to the Owner (or any other party designated by the Owner to receive notice under this policy) and any assignee recorded at the Home Office of any increase in interest rate on loans outstanding 40 or more days prior to the effective date of the increase.

Interest accrues on a daily basis from the date of the loan on policy loans and from the premium due date on premium loans, and is compounded annually. Interest unpaid on a loan anniversary is added to and becomes part of the loan principal and bears interest on the same terms.

6.5 INDEBTEDNESS

Indebtedness consists of unpaid policy and premium loans on the policy including accrued interest. Indebtedness may be repaid at any time. Any unpaid indebtedness will be deducted from the policy proceeds.

If indebtedness equals or exceeds the cash value, this policy shall terminate. Termination shall occur 31 days after a notice has been mailed to the address of record of the Owner and of any assignee recorded at the Home Office.

SECTION 7. CHANGE OF POLICY

7 CHANGE OF PLAN

The Owner may change this policy to any permanent life or endowment plan offered by the Company on the Date of Issue of this policy. The change may be made upon payment of any cost and subject to the conditions determined by the Company. For a change made after the first year to a plan having a higher reserve, the cost shall not exceed the difference in cash values or the difference in reserves, whichever is greater, plus 3½% of such difference.

Appendix 5 (*continued*)

SECTION 8. BENEFICIARIES

8.1 DESIGNATION AND CHANGE OF BENEFICIARIES

(a) By Owner. The Owner may designate and change direct and contingent beneficiaries and further payees of death proceeds:

(1) during the lifetime of the Insured.

(2) during the 60 days following the date of death of the Insured, if the Insured immediately before his death was not the Owner. Any such designation of direct beneficiary may not be changed. If the Owner is the direct beneficiary and elects a payment plan, any such designation of contingent beneficiaries and further payees may be changed.

(b) By Direct Beneficiary. The direct beneficiary may designate and change contingent beneficiaries and further payees if:

(1) the direct beneficiary is the Owner.

(2) at any time after the death of the Insured, no contingent beneficiary or further payee is living, and no designation is made by the Owner under Section 8.1 (a) (2).

(3) the direct beneficiary elects a payment plan after the death of the Insured, in which case the interest in the share of such direct beneficiary or any other payee designated by the Owner shall terminate.

(c) By Spouse (Marital Deduction Provision). Notwithstanding any provision of Section 8 or 9 of this policy to the contrary, if the Insured immediately before death was the Owner and if the direct beneficiary is the spouse of the Insured and survives the Insured, such direct beneficiary shall have the power to appoint all amounts payable under the policy either to the executors or administrators of the direct beneficiary's estate or to such other contingent beneficiaries and further payees as he may designate. The exercise of that power shall revoke any then existing designation of contingent beneficiaries and further payees and any election of a payment plan applying to them.

(d) Effective Date. Any designation or change of beneficiary shall be made by the filing and recording at the Home Office of a written request satisfactory to the Company. Unless waived by the Company, the request must be endorsed on the policy. Upon the recording, the request will take effect as of the date it was signed. The Company will not be held responsible for any payment or other action taken by it before the recording of the request.

8.2 SUCCESSION IN INTEREST OF BENEFICIARIES

(a) Direct Beneficiaries. The proceeds of this policy shall be payable in equal shares to the direct beneficiaries who survive to receive payment. The unpaid share of any direct beneficiary who dies while receiving payment shall be payable in equal shares to the direct beneficiaries who survive to receive payment.

(b) Contingent Beneficiaries. At the death of the last surviving direct beneficiary, payments due or to become due shall be payable in equal shares to the contingent beneficiaries who survive to receive payment. The unpaid share of any contingent beneficiary who dies while receiving payment shall be payable in equal shares to the contingent beneficiaries who survive to receive payment.

(c) Further Payees. At the death of the last to survive of the direct and contingent beneficiaries, the proceeds, or the withdrawal value of any payments due or to become due if a payment plan is in effect, shall be paid in one sum:

(1) in equal shares to the further payees who survive to receive payment; or

(2) if no further payees survive to receive payment, to the executors or administrators of the last to survive of the direct and contingent beneficiaries.

(d) Estate of Owner. If no direct or contingent beneficiaries or further payees survive the Insured, the proceeds shall be paid to the Owner or the executors or administrators of the Owner.

8.3 GENERAL

(a) Transfer of Ownership. A transfer of ownership will not change the interest of any beneficiary.

(b) Claims of Creditors. So far as permitted by law, no amount payable under this policy shall be subject to the claims of creditors of the payee.

(c) Succession under Payment Plans. A direct or contingent beneficiary succeeding to an interest in a payment plan shall continue under such plan subject to its terms, with the rights of transfer between plans and of withdrawal under plans as provided in this policy.

Appendix 5 (*continued*)

SECTION 9. PAYMENT OF POLICY BENEFITS

9.1 PAYMENT

Payment of policy benefits upon surrender or maturity will be made in cash or under one of the payment plans described in Section 9.2, if elected.

If policy benefits become payable by reason of the Insured's death, payment will be made under any payment plan then in effect. If no election of a payment plan is in effect, the proceeds will be held under the Interest Income Plan (Option A) with interest accumulating from the date of death until an election or cash withdrawal is made.

9.2 PAYMENT PLANS

(a) Interest Income Plan (Option A). The proceeds will earn interest which may be received in monthly payments or accumulated. The first interest payment is due one month after the plan becomes effective. Withdrawal of accumulated interest as well as full or partial proceeds may be made at any time.

(b) Installment Income Plans. Monthly installment income payments will be made as provided by the plan elected. The first payment is due on the date the plan becomes effective.

(1) Specified Period (Option B). Monthly installment income payments will be made providing for payment of the proceeds with interest over a specified period of one to 30 years. Withdrawal of the present value of any unpaid installments may be made at any time.

(2) Specified Amount (Option D). Monthly installment income payments will be made for a specified amount of not less than $5 per $1,000 of proceeds. Payments will continue until the entire proceeds with interest are paid, with the final payment not exceeding the unpaid balance. Withdrawal of the unpaid balance may be made at any time.

(c) Life Income Plans. Monthly life income payments will be made as provided by the plan elected. The first payment is due on the date the plan becomes effective. Proof of date of birth satisfactory to the Company must be furnished for any individual upon whose life income payments depend.

(1) Single Life Income (Option C). Monthly payments will be made for the selected certain period, if any, and thereafter during the remaining lifetime of the individual upon whose life income payments depend. The selections available are:

(i) no certain period,
(ii) a certain period of 10 or 20 years, or
(iii) a refund certain period such that the sum of the income payments during the certain period will be equal to the proceeds applied under the plan, with the final payment not exceeding the unpaid balance.

(2) Joint and Survivor Life Income (Option E). Monthly payments will be made for a 10 year certain period and thereafter during the joint lifetime of the two individuals upon whose lives income payments depend and continuing during the remaining lifetime of the survivor.

(3) Withdrawal. Withdrawal of the present value of any unpaid income payments which were to be made during a certain period may be made at any time after the death of all individuals upon whose lives income payments depend.

(d) Payment Frequency. In lieu of monthly payments a quarterly, semiannual or annual frequency may be selected.

9.3 PAYMENT PLAN RATES

(a) Interest Income and Installment Income Plans. Proceeds under the Interest Income and Installment Income plans will earn interest at rates declared annually by the Company, but not less than a rate of 3% compounded annually. Interest in excess of 3% will increase payments, except that for the Installment Income Specified Amount Plan (Option D), excess interest will be applied to lengthen the period during which payments are made.

The present value for withdrawal purposes will be based on a rate of 3% compounded annually.

The Company may from time to time also make available higher guaranteed interest rates under the Interest Income and Installment Income plans, with certain conditions on withdrawal as then published by the Company for those plans.

(b) Life Income Plans. Life Income Plan payments will be based on rates declared by the Company. These rates will provide not less than 104% of the income provided by the Company's Immediate Annuities being offered on the date the plan becomes effective. The rates are based on the sex and age nearest birthday of any individual upon whose life income payments depend, and adjusted for any certain period and the immediate payment of the first income payment. In no event will payments under these rates be less than the minimums described in Section 9.3(c).

(c) Minimum Income Payments. Minimum monthly income payments for the Installment Income Plans (Options B and D) and the Life Income Plans (Options C and E) are shown in the Minimum Income Table. The minimum Life Income payments are determined as of the date the payment plan becomes effective and depend on the age nearest birthday adjusted for policy duration.

The adjusted age is equal to the age nearest birthday decreased by one year if more than 25 years have elapsed since the Policy Date, two years if more than 35 years have elapsed, three years if more than 40 years have elapsed, four years if more than 45 years have elapsed or five years if more than 50 years have elapsed.

Appendix 5 (*continued*)

9.4 ELECTION OF PAYMENT PLANS

(a) Effective Date. Election of payment plans for death proceeds made by the Owner and filed at the Home Office during the Insured's lifetime will be effective on the date of death of the Insured. All other elections of payment plans will be effective when filed at the Home Office, or later if specified.

(b) Death Proceeds. Payment plans for death proceeds may be elected:

(1) by the Owner during the lifetime of the Insured.

(2) by the Owner during the 60 days following the date of death of the Insured, if the Insured immediately before his death was not the Owner. Any such election may not be changed by the Owner.

(3) by a direct or contingent beneficiary to whom such proceeds become payable, if no election is then in effect and no election is made by the Owner under Section 9.4(b) (2).

(c) Surrender or Maturity Proceeds. Payment plans for surrender or maturity proceeds may be elected by the Owner for himself as direct beneficiary.

(d) Transfers Between Payment Plans. A direct or contingent beneficiary receiving payment under a payment plan with the right to withdraw may elect to transfer the withdrawal value to any other payment plan then available.

(e) Life Income Plan Limitations. An individual beneficiary may receive payments under a Life Income Plan only if the payments depend upon his life. A corporation may receive payments under a Life Income Plan only if the payments depend upon the life of the Insured, or a surviving spouse or dependent of the Insured.

(f) Minimum Amounts. Proceeds of less than $5,000 may not be applied without the Company's approval under any payment plan except the Interest Income Plan (Option A) with interest accumulated. The Company retains the right to change the payment frequency or pay the withdrawal value if payments under a payment plan are or become less than $25.

9.5 INCREASE OF MONTHLY INCOME

The direct beneficiary who is to receive the proceeds of this policy under a payment plan may increase the total monthly income by payment of an annuity premium to the Company. The premium, after deduction of charges not exceeding 2% and any applicable premium tax, shall be applied under the payment plan at the same rates as the policy proceeds. The net amount so applied may not exceed twice the proceeds payable under this policy.

MINIMUM INCOME TABLE

Minimum Monthly Income Payments Per $1,000 Proceeds

INSTALLMENT INCOME PLANS (Options B and D)

PERIOD (YEARS)	MONTHLY PAYMENT	PERIOD (YEARS)	MONTHLY PAYMENT	PERIOD (YEARS)	MONTHLY PAYMENT
1	$84.50	11	$8.86	21	$5.32
2	42.87	12	8.24	22	5.15
3	29.00	13	7.71	23	4.99
4	22.07	14	7.26	24	4.84
5	17.91	15	6.87	25	4.71
6	15.14	16	6.53	26	4.59
7	13.17	17	6.23	27	4.48
8	11.69	18	5.96	28	4.37
9	10.54	19	5.73	29	4.27
10	9.62	20	5.51	30	4.18

Appendix 5 (*continued*)

MINIMUM INCOME TABLE

Minimum Monthly Income Payments Per $1,000 Proceeds

LIFE INCOME PLANS

SINGLE LIFE MONTHLY PAYMENTS (Option C)					
ADJUSTED AGE		CERTAIN PERIOD			
MALE	FEMALE	NONE	10 YEARS	20 YEARS	REFUND
50	55	$ 4.62	$4.56	$4.34	$4.36
51	56	4.72	4.65	4.40	4.44
52	57	4.83	4.75	4.46	4.52
53	58	4.94	4.85	4.53	4.61
54	59	5.07	4.96	4.59	4.69
55	60	5.20	5.07	4.66	4.79
56	61	5.33	5.19	4.72	4.88
57	62	5.48	5.31	4.78	4.99
58	63	5.64	5.43	4.84	5.09
59	64	5.80	5.57	4.90	5.20
60	65	5.98	5.70	4.96	5.32
61	66	6.16	5.85	5.02	5.44
62	67	6.36	5.99	5.07	5.57
63	68	6.57	6.14	5.13	5.71
64	69	6.79	6.30	5.17	5.85
65	70	7.03	6.45	5.22	6.00
66	71	7.28	6.62	5.26	6.15
67	72	7.54	6.78	5.30	6.31
68	73	7.83	6.95	5.33	6.48
69	74	8.13	7.11	5.36	6.66
70	75	8.45	7.28	5.39	6.85
71	76	8.79	7.45	5.41	7.05
72	77	9.16	7.62	5.43	7.26
73	78	9.55	7.79	5.45	7.48
74	79	9.96	7.95	5.46	7.71
75	80	10.41	8.11	5.48	7.95

JOINT AND SURVIVOR MONTHLY PAYMENTS (Option E)

ADJUSTED AGE **JOINT PAYEE ADJUSTED AGE**

MALE		45	50	55	60	65	70	75
	FEMALE	50	55	60	65	70	75	80
45	50	$3.68	$3.80	$3.90	$3.97	$4.02	$4.06	$4.10
50	55	3.80	3.97	4.13	4.25	4.34	4.41	4.46
55	60	3.90	4.13	4.35	4.56	4.72	4.84	4.92
60	65	3.97	4.25	4.56	4.86	5.13	5.33	5.48
65	70	4.02	4.34	4.72	5.13	5.51	5.85	6.10
70	75	4.06	4.41	4.84	5.33	5.85	6.33	6.73
75	80	4.10	4.46	4.92	5.48	6.10	6.73	7.28

Appendix 5 (*continued*)

WAIVER OF PREMIUM BENEFIT

1. THE BENEFIT

If total disability of the Insured commences before the policy anniversary nearest his 60th birthday, the Company will waive the payment of premiums becoming due during total disability of the Insured.

If total disability of the Insured commences on or after the policy anniversary nearest his 60th birthday but before the policy anniversary nearest his 65th birthday, the Company will waive the payment of premiums becoming due during total disability of the Insured and before the policy anniversary nearest his 65th birthday.

The Company will refund that portion of any premium paid which applies to a period of total disability beyond the policy month in which the disability began.

The premium for this benefit is shown on page 2.

2. DEFINITION OF TOTAL DISABILITY

Total disability means disability which:

(a) resulted from bodily injury or disease;
(b) began after the Date of Issue of this policy and before the policy anniversary nearest the Insured's 65th birthday;
(c) has existed continuously for at least six months; and
(d) prevents the Insured from engaging in an occupation. During the first 24 months of disability, occupation means the occupation of the Insured at the time such disability began; thereafter it means any occupation for which he is reasonably fitted by education, training or experience, with due regard to his vocation and earnings prior to disability.

The total and irrecoverable loss of the sight of both eyes, or of speech or hearing, or of the use of both hands, or of both feet, or of one hand and one foot, shall be considered total disability, even if the Insured shall engage in an occupation.

3. PROOF OF DISABILITY

Before any premium is waived, proof of total disability must be received by the Company at its Home Office:

(a) during the lifetime of the Insured;
(b) during the continuance of total disability; and
(c) not later than one year after the policy anniversary nearest the Insured's 65th birthday.

Premiums will be waived although proof of total disability was not given within the time specified, if it is shown that it was given as soon as reasonably possible, but not later than one year after recovery.

4. PROOF OF CONTINUANCE OF DISABILITY

Proof of the continuance of total disability may be required once a year. If such proof is not furnished, no further premiums shall be waived. Further proof of continuance of disability will no longer be required if, on the policy anniversary nearest the Insured's 65th birthday, the Insured is then and has been totally and continuously disabled for five or more years.

5. PREMIUMS

Any premium becoming due during disability and before receipt of proof of total disability is payable and should be paid. Any such premiums paid shall be refunded by the Company upon acceptance of proof of total disability. If such premiums are not paid, this benefit shall be allowed if total disability is shown to have begun before the end of the grace period of the first unpaid premium.

If on any policy anniversary following the date of disablement the Insured continues to be disabled and this benefit has not terminated, an annual premium will be waived.

6. TERMINATION

This benefit shall be in effect while this policy is in force, but shall terminate on the policy anniversary nearest the Insured's 65th birthday unless the Insured is then totally disabled and such disability occurred prior to the policy anniversary nearest the Insured's 60th birthday. It may also be terminated within 31 days of a premium due date upon receipt at the Home Office of the Owner's written request.

Appendix 5 (*continued*)

ACCIDENTAL DEATH BENEFIT

1. THE BENEFIT

The Company agrees to pay an Accidental Death Benefit upon receipt at its Home Office of proof that the death of the Insured resulted, directly and independently of all other causes, from accidental bodily injury, provided that death occurred while this benefit was in effect.

2. PREMIUM AND AMOUNT OF BENEFIT

The premium for and the amount of this benefit are shown on page 2. This benefit shall be payable as part of the policy proceeds.

3. RISKS NOT ASSUMED

This benefit shall not be payable for death of the Insured resulting from suicide, for death resulting from or contributed to by bodily or mental infirmity or disease, or for any other death which did not result, directly and independently of all other causes, from accidental bodily injury.

Even though death resulted directly and independently of all other causes from accidental bodily injury, this benefit shall not be payable if the death of the Insured resulted from:

(a) Any act or incident of war. The word "war" includes any war, declared or undeclared, and armed aggression resisted by the armed forces of any country or combination of countries.

(b) Riding in any kind of aircraft, unless the Insured was riding solely as a passenger in an aircraft not operated by or for the Armed Forces, or descent from any kind of aircraft while in flight. An Insured who had any duties whatsoever at any time on the flight or any leg of the flight with respect to any purpose of the flight or to the aircraft or who was participating in training shall not be considered a passenger.

4. TERMINATION

This benefit shall be in effect while this policy is in force other than under the Extended Term Insurance or Paid-up Insurance provisions, but shall terminate on the policy anniversary nearest the Insured's 70th birthday. It may also be terminated within 31 days of a premium due date upon receipt at the Home Office of the Owner's written request.

David Olson
Secretary
THE COUNCIL LIFE INSURANCE COMPANY

RECEIPT FOR PAYMENT AND CONDITIONAL LIFE INSURANCE AGREEMENT

When premium is paid at the time of application, complete this Agreement and give to the Applicant. No other Agreement will be recognized by the Company. If premium is not paid—do not detach.

THOMAS A. BENSON $10,000 LIFE POLICY - PARTICIPATING
Name of Proposed Insured — Face Amount — Plan

Received of THOMAS A. BENSON
the sum of $ 241.60 for the policy applied for in the application to THE COUNCIL INSURANCE COMPANY (CL) with the same date and number as this receipt. Checks, drafts, and money orders are accepted subject to collection.

NEW YORK, NEW YORK MAY 1 19 78. J. R. WASHINGTON Agent.
Place and Date

CONDITIONAL LIFE INSURANCE AGREEMENT

I. No Insurance Ever in Force. No insurance shall be in force at any time if the proposed insured is not an acceptable risk on the Underwriting Date for the policy applied for according to CL's rules and standards. No insurance shall be in force under an Additional Benefit for which the proposed insured is not an acceptable risk.

II. Conditional Life Insurance. If the proposed insured is an acceptable risk on the Underwriting Date, the insurance shall be in force subject to the following maximum amounts if the proposed insured dies before the policy is issued:

Life Insurance			Accidental Death Benefit	
Age at Issue	Policies Issued at Standard Premiums	Policies Issued at Higher Premiums	Age at Issue	Maximum Amount
0-24	$ 500.000	$250,000	0-14	$ 25,000
25-45	1,000,u00	500,000	15-19	50,000
46-55	800,000	400,000	20-24	75,000
56-65	400,000	200,000	25-60	150,000
66-70	200,000	100,000	Over 60	-0-
Over 70	-0-	-0-		

Reduction in Maximum Amounts. The maximum amounts set forth in the preceding table shall be reduced by any existing CL insurance on the life of the proposed insured with an Issue Date within 90 days of the date of this Agreement or by any pending prepaid applications for CL insurance on the life of the proposed insured with an Underwriting Date within 90 days of the date of this Agreement.

Termination of Conditional Life Insurance. If the proposed insured is an acceptable risk for the policy applied for according to CL's rules and standards only at a premium higher than the premium paid, any insurance under this Agreement shall terminate on the date stated in a notice mailed by CL to the applicant unless by such date the applicant accepts delivery of the policy and pays the additional premium required.

Underwriting Date. The Underwriting Date is the date of page 2 (90-2) of the application or the date of the medical examination [if required, otherwise the date of the nonmedical, page 4 (90-4)], whichever is the later.

III. Premium Adjustment. If the proposed insured is an acceptable risk for the policy applied for only at a premium higher than the premium paid and dies before paying the additional premium required, that additional premium shall be subtracted from the insurance benefit payable to the beneficiary.

IV. Premium Refund. Any premium paid for any insurance or Additional Benefit not issued or issued at a higher premium but not accepted by the applicant shall be returned to the applicant.

NOT A "BINDER"—NO INSURANCE WHERE SECTION I APPLIES—NO AGENT MAY MODIFY.

Appendix 5 (*continued*)

PART I — Life Insurance Application To *The COUNCIL Life Insurance Company*

IMPORTANT NOTICE—This application is subject to approval by the Company's Home Office. Be sure all questions in all parts of the application are answered completely and accurately, since the application is the basis of the insurance contract and will become part of any policy issued.

1. Insured's Full Name (Please Print-Give title as Mr., Dr., Rev., etc.)	Mo., Day, Yr. of Birth	Ins. Age	Sex	Place of Birth	Social Security No.
MR. THOMAS A. BENSON Single ☐ Married ☑ Widowed ☐ Divorced ☐ Separated ☐	APRIL 6, 1943	35	M	BOSTON, MASS.	000-00-0000

2. Addresses last 5 yrs.		Number Street City State	Zip Code	County	Yrs.
Mail to ☐ Home:	Present	217 E. 62 STREET NEW YORK, N.Y.	10017	NEW YORK	6
	Former				
☑ Business:	Present	PEPPER, GRINSTEAD, & CRAWCH 55 E. 49th ST	10017	NEW YORK	7
	Former				

3. Occupation	Title	Describe Exact Duties	Yrs.
Present	ATTORNEY	REPRESENTS CLIENTS IN LEGAL MATTERS	7
Former			

4. a) Employer
   b) Any change contemplated? Yes ☐ (Explain in Remarks) No ☑

5. Have you ever	Yes	No
a) been rejected, deferred or discharged by the Armed Forces for medical reasons or applied for a government disability rating?	☐	☑
b) applied for insurance or for reinstatement which was declined, postponed, modified or rated?	☐	☑
c) used LSD, heroin, cocaine or methadone?	☐	☑
6. a) In the past 3 years have you		
(i) had your driver's license suspended or revoked or been convicted of more than one speeding violation?	☐	✓
(ii) operated, been a crew member of, or had any duties aboard any kind of aircraft?	☐	✓
(iii) engaged in underwater diving below 40 feet, parachuting, or motor vehicle racing?	☐	✓
b) In the future, do you intend to engage in any activities mentioned in (ii) and (iii) of a) above? (If "Yes" to 5a or any of 6, complete Supplemental Form 3375)	☐	✓
7. Have you smoked one or more cigarettes within the past 12 months?	✓	☐
8. Are other insurance applications pending or contemplated?	☐	✓
9. Do you intend to go to any foreign country?	✓	☐
10. Will coverage applied for replace or change any life insurance or annuities? (If "Yes", submit Replacement Form)	☐	✓

11. Total Life Insurance in force $ 35,000 None ☐

12. Face Amount $ 10,000 Plan WL
Accidental Death ☑ Waiver of Premium ☐
Purchase Option—Regular ☐ Preferred ☐ PEP ☐ GOR ☐
_____ units of Wife's Term—name: _____
$_____ initial amount Decreasing Term, _____ Years
(Joint ☐) (Mot. Pro. ☐) (Straight Line ☐)
Children's Term ☐ Other: _____

13. Auto. Prem. Loan provision operative if available? Yes ☐ No ☑

14. Dividend Option
Additions (for other than Term policies) ☐ Deposits ☐
Reduce premium, if applicable, otherwise cash ☑
Supplemental Protection (Keyman only) ☐
1 Year Term—any balance to Deposits ☐ Additions ☐ Reduce prem. (cash if mo.) ☐

15. Beneficiary—for children's, wife's or joint insurance as provided in contract; for other insurance as follows, subject to policy's beneficiary provisions:

	(Name)	(Relationship to Insured)	
1st	HELEN M. BENSON	WIFE	if living, if not
2nd	DAVID A. BENSON	SON	if living, if not
3rd			if living, if not

the executors or administrators of: Insured ☑ Other (use Remarks) ☐
(Joint beneficiaries will receive equally or survivor, unless otherwise specified.)

16. Flexible Plan settlement (personal beneficiary only) ☐

17. Rights—During Insured's lifetime all rights belong to
Insured ☑ Other:
Trustee ☐ (attach Trust)
(After Insured's death as provided in contract on wife's insurance.)

18. Premium—Frequency ANNUAL Amt. Paid $241.60 None ☐
Have you received a Conditional Receipt? Yes ☑ No ☐

REMARKS (Include details (company, date, amt., etc.) for all "Yes" answers to questions 4b, 5b, 5c, 8, 9 and 10)

Q9: PLANS VACATION IN SWITZERLAND

I agree that: (1) No one but the Company's President, a Vice-President or Secretary has authority to accept information not contained in the application, to modify or enlarge any contract, or to waive any requirement. (2) Except as otherwise provided in any conditional receipt issued, any policy issued shall take effect upon its delivery and payment of the first premium during the lifetime of each person to be insured. Due dates of later premiums shall be as specified in the policy.

Dated at NEW YORK, N.Y. on MAY 1 1978 Signature of Insured Thomas A. Benson

Signature of Applicant (if other than Insured) who agrees to be bound by the representations and agreements in this and any other part of this application _____
(Name) (Relationship) (Complete address of Applicant)

Countersigned by Ed Hatay
Field Underwriter (Licensed Resident Agent)

Appendix 5 (*concluded*)

PART 1A **Statements Forming Part Of Application To** *The COUNCIL Life Insurance Company*
[Complete this Part if any Non-Medical or Family Insurance is Applied For]

1. Name of Insured THOMAS A. BENSON Ins. Age 35 Height 6 ft. 1 in. Weight 185 lbs.

2. If Family, Children's, Wife's or Joint Insurance desired, other family members proposed for insurance:

Wife (include maiden name)	Ins. Age	Mo., Day, Yr. of Birth	Height ft. in.	Weight lbs.	Life in Force $	Place of Birth

Children	Sex	Ins. Age	Mo., Day, Yr. of Birth	Children	Sex	Ins. Age	Mo., Day, Yr. of Birth

3. Has any eligible dependent (a) been omitted from 2? Yes ☐ No ☐ (b) applied for insurance or for reinstatement which was declined, postponed, modified or rated or had a policy cancelled or renewal refused? Yes ☐ No ☐ (Give name, date, company in 8)

4. Have you or anyone else proposed for insurance, so far as you know, ever been treated for or had indication of (underline applicable item) — Yes / No
   - a) high blood pressure? (If "Yes", list drugs prescribed and dates taken.) ☐ ☑
   - b) chest pain, heart attack, rheumatic fever, heart murmur, irregular pulse or other disorder of the heart or blood vessels? ☐ ☑
   - c) cancer, tumor, cyst, or any disorder of the thyroid, skin, or lymph glands? ☐ ☑
   - d) diabetes or anemia or other blood disorder? ☐ ☑
   - e) sugar, albumin, blood or pus in the urine, or venereal disease? ☐ ☑
   - f) any disorder of the kidney, bladder, prostate, breast or reproductive organs? ☐ ☑
   - g) ulcer, intestinal bleeding, hepatitis, colitis, or other disorder of the stomach, intestine, spleen, pancreas, liver or gall bladder? ☐ ☑
   - h) asthma, tuberculosis, bronchitis, emphysema or other disorder of the lungs? ☐ ☑
   - i) fainting, convulsions, migraine headache, paralysis, epilepsy or any mental or nervous disorder? ☐ ☑
   - j) arthritis, gout, amputation, sciatica, back pain or other disorder of the muscles, bones or joints? ☐ ☑
   - k) disorder of the eyes, ears, nose, throat or sinuses? ☐ ☑
   - l) varicose veins, hemorrhoids, hernia or rectal disorder? ☐ ☑
   - m) alcoholism or drug habit? ☐ ☑

5. Have you or anyone else proposed for insurance, so far as you know, (underline applicable item) — Yes / No
   - a) consulted or been examined or treated by any physician or practitioner in the past 5 years? ☑ ☐
   - b) had, or been advised to have, an x-ray, cardiogram, blood or other diagnostic test in the past 5 years? ☑ ☐
   - c) been a patient in a hospital, clinic, or other medical facility in the past 5 years? ☐ ☑
   - d) ever had a surgical operation performed or advised? ☑ ☐
   - e) ever made claim for disability or applied for compensation or retirement based on accident or sickness? ☐ ☑

6. Are you or any other person proposed for insurance, so far as you know, in impaired physical or mental health, or under any kind of medication? ☐ ☑

7. Weight change in last 6 months of adults proposed for insurance: N.A.
   Name Gain Loss Cause

8. Details of all "Yes" answers. For any checkup or routine examination, indicate what symptoms, if any, prompted it and include results of the examination and any special tests. Include clinic number if applicable.

Question No.	Name of Person	Illness & Treatment	No. of Attacks	Dates: Onset-Recovery	Doctor, Clinic or Hospital and Complete Address
5a	THOMAS A. BENSON	ANNUAL CHECKUP	—	—	LIFE EXTENSION INSTITUTE
5b	THOMAS A. BENSON	ROUTINE OF ANNUAL CHECKUP	—	—	"
5d	THOMAS A. BENSON	TONSILLECTOMY-AGE 5	1	JUNE 1949	BOSTON HOSPITAL
					2 PITTS STREET, BOSTON, MASS.

So far as may be lawful, I waive for myself and all persons claiming an interest in any insurance issued on this application, all provisions of law forbidding any physician or other person who has attended or examined, or who may attend or examine, me or any other person covered by such insurance, from disclosing any knowledge or information which he thereby acquired.

I represent the statements and answers in this and in any other part of this application to be true and complete to the best of my knowledge and belief, and offer them to the Company for the purpose of inducing it to issue the policy or policies and to accept the payment of premiums thereunder. I also agree that payment of the first premium (if after this date) shall be a representation by me that such statements and answers would be the same if made at the time of such payment.

Dated at NEW YORK, N.Y. on MAY 1 1978 Signature of Insured Thomas A. Benson

Witnessed by Ed Hatley Signature of Wife (if insured) ______

Field Underwriter (Licensed Resident Agent)

AUTHORIZATION

For purposes of determining my eligibility for insurance, I hereby authorize any physician, practitioner, hospital, clinic, institution, insurance company, Medical Information Bureau, or other organization or person that has records or knowledge of me or my health to give any such information to the Council Life Insurance Company.

If application is made to The Council Life Insurance Company for insurance on any member of my family, this authorization also applies to such member. A photostatic copy of this authorization shall be as valid as the original.

Signed on MAY 1, 1978 Thomas A. Benson
Signature of Insured

Note: There are no "standard" life insurance policies, and the contracts vary in wording and appearance from company to company. Sometimes there are also significant differences in policy provisions. This policy is generally representative of contracts issued in the United States.

Source: Education and Community Services, American Council of Life Insurance, 1850 K St., N.W., Washington, D.C. 20006

Appendix 6: Major Medical and Disability (Recovery) Income Policies

RESERVED FOR COMPANY NAME, ADDRESS AND/OR LOGOTYPE.

INSURED ____________ POLICY NUMBER ____________

EFFECTIVE DATE ____________

POLICY TERM ____________ TERM PREMIUM ____________

MAJOR MEDICAL EXPENSE POLICY

We agree to pay the benefits provided by this Policy, subject to its provisions, conditions, definitions and exclusions.

This Policy is issued in consideration of the application, a copy of which is attached to and made a part of this Policy, and payment in advance of the required premium. This payment will maintain the Policy in force for the initial Policy Term which begins on the Effective Date.

POLICY CONTINUABLE SUBJECT TO THE COMPANY'S RIGHT TO REFUSE TO CONTINUE THIS POLICY AND THE COMPANY'S RIGHT TO CHANGE THE TABLE OF RATES

You may continue this Policy in force for further specified terms by payment of the premium in advance or during the Grace Period. However, we may refuse to continue this Policy as of any renewal date but only if we are then refusing to continue all policies with the same form number as this Policy issued to residents of the state in which you reside. If we take this action you will be notified in writing not less than 31 days before the next renewal date of your policy. Any such refusal to renew shall be without prejudice to any claim originating while this Policy is in force.

On each renewal date the premium due then and thereafter may change in amount by reason of an increase in age of an Insured Person.

We may change, on a class basis, the table of rates applicable to premiums due on and after each renewal date of your Policy. Any such change will apply to all policies with the same form number as this Policy issued to residents of the state in which you then reside. We will give you written notice of any such change in the table of rates not less than 31 days before the next renewal date of your Policy.

Our acceptance of the proper renewal premium shall constitute our consent to renew this Policy. Unless renewed as herein provided, this Policy shall, except as provided in the Grace Period, terminate at the expiration of the period for which premium has been paid. All periods of insurance shall begin and end at 12:01 A.M., Standard Time, at your residence.

NOTICE OF TEN DAY RIGHT TO EXAMINE POLICY

Please examine this Policy carefully. If for any reason you are not satisfied, you may at any time within 10 days after receipt of this Policy return it to us at our Home Office or to any of our branch offices or to the agent through whom it was purchased. If the Policy is so returned, it shall be deemed void from its Effective Date and any premium paid will be refunded.

IN WITNESS WHEREOF the has caused this Policy to be signed by its President and Secretary, but it shall not be binding upon the Company unless there is attached hereto an application countersigned by a duly authorized representative of the Company.

Appendix 6 (*continued*)

GENERAL DEFINITIONS

As used in this Policy:

"You", "Your", "Yours" or "Yourself", means the person named in the Schedule as Insured.

"We", "our", or "us" means Lumbermens Mutual Casualty Company.

"Insured Person" in addition to you, also means:
(a) any person initially named in the application and for whom coverage has not been excluded by specific rider;

(b) any person added and covered under this Policy by amendment in accordance with the section entitled "Eligibility For And Termination of Coverage"; provided that any such person shall be an Insured Person only so long as the Policy is in force for such person.

"Injury" means bodily injury caused by an accident occurring while this Policy is in force as to the Insured Person whose injury is the basis of claim and includes all injuries resulting from such accident and all complications arising therefrom.

"Sickness" means sickness or disease which first manifests itself while this Policy is in force as to the Insured Person whose sickness is the basis of claim and includes all complications arising therefrom and all related conditions and recurrences thereof.

"Hospital" means an institution operated pursuant to law which (a) is primarily and continuously engaged in providing or operating, either on its premises or in facilities controlled by the hospital and under the supervision of a staff of duly licensed physicians, medical and diagnostic facilities (except an accredited institution for the treatment of chronic diseases) for the medical care and treatment of sick or injured persons on an in-patient basis for which a charge is made, and (b) provides 24 hour nursing service by or under the supervision of registered graduate professional nurses (R.N.'s).

The term "Hospital" does not include (a) Convalescent homes, convalescent, rest or nursing facilities; or (b) facilities primarily affording custodial, educational or rehabilitory care; (c) facilities for the aged, drug addicts or alcoholics.

"Convalescent Nursing Home" means an institution operated pursuant to law which (a) is primarily engaged in providing, in addition to room and board accommodations, skilled nursing care under the supervision of a duly licensed physician (b) provides continuous 24 hours a day nursing service by or under the supervision of a duly licensed physician (c) maintains a daily medical record of each patient.

The term "Convalescent Nursing Home" does not include (a) any home, facility or part thereof used primarily for rest (b) a home or facility for the aged or for the care of drug addicts or alcoholics (c) a home or facility primarily used for the care and treatment of mental diseases, disorders or custodial or educational care.

"Physician" means a duly licensed physician. "Physician" shall not include any person who is a parent, spouse, brother, sister or child of the Insured Person.

"Nurse" means a registered graduate professional nurse (R.N.) or a licensed practical nurse (L.P.N.), other than a parent, spouse, brother, sister or child of the Insured Person.

"Home Health Care Agency" means a hospital or other agency possessing a valid operating certificate issued in accordance with the public health laws of the state in which it operates, authorizing such agency to provide home health care services.

"Intensive Care or Cardiac Care Unit" means a designated ward, unit or area within a hospital for which a specified extra daily surcharge is made and which is staffed and equipped to provide, on a continuous basis, specialized or intensive care or services not regularly provided within such hospital.

"Congenital Anomaly" means a disorder which is present at birth of a child (or children), such birth occurring while this Policy is in force, and shall be considered a "Sickness".

"Mental illness" means neurosis, psychoneurosis, psychopathy, psychosis or personality disorder.

Appendix 6 (*continued*)

MAJOR MEDICAL BENEFITS

We will pay benefits, in excess of the Deductible Amount, equal to 100% of the Daily Hospital Room and Board Amount shown in the Schedule and 80% of all other Covered Expenses but not more than the Maximum Benefit, provided such expenses are incurred within a Benefit Period as the result of any one injury or any one sickness of an Insured Person.

If, during a Benefit Period, the Other Coverage Deductible exceeds the Basic Deductible, the Company's liability during such Benefit Period shall be the amount which would have been payable under this Policy in the absence of Other Coverage, but the total amount of benefits payable under this Policy and under Other Coverage shall in no event exceed in the aggregate more than 100% of the amount of Covered Expenses actually incurred during such Benefit Period.

DEDUCTIBLE AMOUNT

The Deductible Amount for an injury or sickness shall be the greater of: (a) the amount of Covered Expenses equal to the Basic Deductible shown in the Schedule; or (b) the amount of the Other Coverage Deductible, as defined below.

"Other Coverage Deductible" means the total amount of benefits for Covered Expenses for which an Insured Person is eligible under Other Coverage for said injury or sickness.

"Other Coverage" means all health care coverage, whether on a service or expense incurred basis, provided by any other insurance or welfare plan or prepayment arrangement or any federal, state or other governmental plan or law. The amount of benefit provided on a service basis shall be the amount the service rendered would normally have cost if provided on a cash basis.

DEDUCTIBLE PERIOD

Covered Expenses equal to the Basic Deductible must be incurred within the Deductible Period shown in the Schedule. The first Covered Expense used toward satisfying the Deductible Amount must be incurred while this Policy is in force with respect to the Insured Person whose injury or sickness is the basis of claim.

BENEFIT PERIOD

A Benefit Period shall be a five year period beginning on the day on which the first Covered Expense is applied against the Deductible Amount in connection with an injury or sickness of an Insured Person. However, if the Insured Person for whom the Benefit Period was established is confined as a resident in-patient in a hospital at the end of the five year period, the Benefit Period will be extended to include any further period during which such Insured Person is continuously confined.

After a Benefit Period has expired and subject to the Maximum Benefit provision, new Benefit Periods for the same injury or sickness may be established in the same manner as the first Benefit Period, but charges incurred during a previous Benefit Period may not be applied toward a new Deductible Amount.

MAXIMUM BENEFIT

The maximum payable for each injury or sickness of an Insured Person whether benefits are payable during one Benefit Period or more than one Benefit Period, shall not exceed the Maximum Benefit shown in the Schedule unless increased in accordance with the following paragraph.

Whenever benefits are paid for an injury or sickness on behalf of an Insured Person on the basis of an Other Coverage Deductible that exceeds the applicable Basic Deductible (see the provision titled "Deductible Amount"), the Maximum Benefit for such injury or sickness as respects such Insured Person shall be increased by $5.00 for each $1.00 by which the Other Coverage Deductible exceeds the Basic Deductible, not to exceed $25,000 in the aggregate for any one injury or sickness.

COMMON ACCIDENT—TWO OR MORE INSURED PERSONS

If Covered Expenses are incurred on behalf of two or more Insured Persons as a result of sustaining injury in the same accident, the benefits as respects such common accident will be payable on the same basis as those payable for any other injury or sickness, except that as respects the first Benefit Period: (1) the Covered Expenses will be combined and treated as if incurred by one Insured Person and the Basic Deductible shall apply only once; (2) the Deductible Amount will be the greater of the Basic Deductible, or the amount of Covered Charges for which benefits are provided under Other Coverage for all such Insured Persons, and (3) the Maximum Benefit provision will apply to each Insured Person separately, but any increase in the Maximum Benefit for an injury or sickness will be apportioned among such Insured Persons in proportion to the amount of such benefits provided for each such Insured Person under Other Coverage.

PRIVILEGE OF CHANGING BASIC DEDUCTIBLE

You have the right to change the Basic Deductible from the amount shown in the Schedule or from any amount to which the original Basic Deductible shall have been changed, to any amount which was available to you when the Policy was issued, subject to the following conditions:

(a) If it is desired to reduce the Basic Deductible, the reduction must be made effective on a Policy anniversary. It will be granted subject to payment in advance of the required additional premium and to evidence of insurability satisfactory to us; and if all or part of the time limits in the Policy provision entitled "Time Limit On Certain Defenses" shall have expired, they will again become effective (as to the amount of the reduction in the Basic Deductible only) for a period of two years beginning on the date the reduction becomes effective.

(b) The Basic Deductible may be increased upon the establishment of a Benefit Period in which case the increased Basic Deductible will be applicable to that Benefit Period and the premiums for the Policy will be appropriately reduced retroactively for a period of one year, or for the period since the beginning of the last previously established Benefit Period if shorter.

Appendix 6 (*continued*)

MENTAL ILLNESS

Expenses incurred for the care and treatment of mental illness of an Insured Person while hospital confined will be considered Covered Expenses if they otherwise meet the requirement of Covered Expenses except that:

(a) The Maximum Benefit for Mental Illness as shown in the Schedule is the aggregate amount payable, subject to (b) below, during the lifetime of this Policy as respects such Insured Person.

(b) Whenever benefits are payable for such Insured Person on the basis of a Deductible Amount that is greater than the Basic Deductible, the Maximum Benefit for such Insured Person shall be increased by $5.00 for each $1.00 by which such Deductible Amount exceeds the Basic Deductible. The aggregate increase in this Maximum Benefit during the lifetime of this Policy for such Insured Person shall not exceed $2,500.

As respects this section, Covered Expenses shall include charges incurred for treatment by personal attendance of a legally qualified psychiatrist or psychologist, whether such treatment be rendered in or out of the hospital, up to a maximum of $25.00 per visit; charges incurred for such treatment in excess of one visit per week shall not be considered Covered Expenses.

COVERED EXPENSES

Covered Expenses shall include charges for the following medical services, supplies and treatment furnished to the extent prescribed as necessary by the attending physician, but not to exceed the usual and customary charges in the locality where rendered or provided.

PART A

1. Hospital room and board for resident in-patient confinement therein, but not more than the Daily Room and Board Amount shown in the Schedule, except that while such confinement is within an "intensive care" or "cardiac care" unit, such charges will be allowed up to twice the rate of Daily Room and Board Amount shown in the Schedule.
2. Medical and surgical services and supplies provided by a hospital.

PART B

1. Local professional ambulance service to or from a hospital.
2. Diagnosis and medical or surgical treatment by a physician.
3. Anesthetics and the administration thereof by a physician or professional anesthetist.
4. Dental treatment when required as a result of injury to natural teeth (including their replacement) within six months after the accident; or for setting of a fractured jaw; or for dental treatment of tumors.
5. Services of a registered graduate professional nurse (R.N.) for private duty nursing while hospital confined.
6. Services of a nurse for private duty nursing outside the hospital for a maximum period of 60 consecutive days, provided such services are acquired within 5 days following a period of hospital confinement of not less than 7 days.
7. X-ray examinations, microscopic or laboratory or pathological tests, electrocardiographs, electroencephalographs and other diagnostic tests.
8. X-ray or radioactive therapy, chemotherapy, physiotherapy treatments or hemodialysis.
9. Services of a Home Health Care Agency for care or treatment provided within the home of the Insured Person.
10. Any of the following when properly identified and ordered in writing by a physician: drugs or medicines dispensed by a licensed pharmacist or physician; blood or blood plasma; casts, splints, trusses, braces or crutches, the initial purchase of artificial limbs or eyes; oxygen and the rental of equipment for the administration thereof; rental of iron lung, wheelchair or hospital-type bed, or other durable medical or surgical equipment.
11. Convalescent Nursing Home room and board and routine care provided confinement as a resident in-patient begins within 14 days following confinement in a hospital of at least 3 consecutive days and that such confinement is due to the same or related cause or causes as such preceding hospital confinement. Three days of confinement in a Convalescent Nursing Home will be allowed for each day the Insured Person was hospital confined as an in-patient, not to exceed 100 days during any one Benefit Period.

Charges shall be considered as being incurred when the services for which they are charged are actually rendered or the supplies for which they are charged are actually purchased for current use.

EXPENSES NOT COVERED

We will not pay benefits for any charges incurred as a result of:

1. injury or sickness for which benefits are payable under any Workmens Compensation or Occupational Disease Act or Law;
2. suicide or any attempt thereat, or intentionally self-inflicted injury;
3. war, declared or undeclared, or any act thereof;
4. mental illness, except as set forth in the Policy provision entitled "Mental Illness";
5. service in the Armed Forces of any country or international authority (we will return the pro-rata unearned premium for any period of such service);
6. prenatal or postnatal care or delivery in connection with normal pregnancies and pregnancies terminating in abortion, miscarriage or surgical delivery. Complications incident to pregnancy, including non-elective caesarean section, which in all other respects fall within the definition of Covered Expenses will be deemed Covered Expenses;
7. dental treatment on or to the teeth or gums or for dental prosthesis except as set forth in item 4 of Covered Expenses;
8. cosmetic surgery except when required as a result of injury or because of a congenital anomaly in a child of an Insured Person born while this Policy is in force;
9. eye refractions, or the purchase of eye glasses or hearing aids or the fitting thereof;
10. care or treatment for which the Insured Person is not required to pay because of federal, state or other governmental legislation;

Charges for any of the foregoing exceptions and limitations shall not be considered Covered Expenses nor may they be applied to the satisfaction of the Deductible Amount.

Appendix 6 (*continued*)

ELIGIBILITY FOR AND TERMINATION OF COVERAGE

Persons eligible for inclusion as Insured Persons, provided they are insurable in accordance with our general underwriting standards, are, in addition to you; (a) your spouse; and (b) your unmarried, dependent children (including step-children, legally adopted children and foster children) under 19 years of age.

Any person who is or becomes eligible for inclusion as an Insured Person after the Policy Effective Date, shall be added by amendment and become an Insured Person upon proper written application by you, the furnishing of evidence of such person's eligibility and the payment of the additional premium.

A child born to an Insured Person while this Policy is in force shall be included automatically without payment of additional premium for a period of 31 days from the date of such birth, or until the next renewal date, whichever is the greater. Thereafter, upon receipt by us of written notice of the child's birth and payment of additional premium for such child on or before such renewal date, or within the Grace Period, the child shall continue to be covered as an Insured Person under this Policy.

Insurance with respect to any Insured Person shall automatically expire upon termination of this Policy and with respect to (a) your spouse, if an Insured Person, shall automatically terminate on the renewal date of this Policy next following the date such spouse ceases to be your spouse and (b) any child who is an Insured Person shall automatically terminate on the renewal date of this Policy next following the 19th birthday anniversary or upon his prior marriage. If on the date on which coverage of an unmarried dependent child would terminate because of attainment of age 19, such person is incapable of self-sustaining employment by reason of mental retardation or physical handicap and is dependent upon you for support, then coverage of such person will continue under this Policy provided due proof of such incapacity is received by us within thirty-one days of such date. Such person will continue to be eligible for coverage while this Policy is in force so long as he remains an unmarried dependent so incapacitated, subject to the timely payment of the appropriate adult premium for such person in effect on each premium due date.

On termination of coverage for any Insured Person, the renewal premium will be the applicable premium for the coverage continuing in force. However, if we accept a premium for a subsequent term which would not have been payable except for such person, the coverage provided for such person will continue in force until the end of the term for which such premium has been accepted. Any such termination of coverage shall be without prejudice to any claim originating prior thereto.

If you die while this Policy is in force, your spouse, if then an Insured Person, shall thereafter be considered the Insured for all purposes, except that the coverages and terms thereof which applied to your spouse immediately before your death shall govern the insurance which continues for your spouse. If on any premium due date, there is no person then occupying the status of Insured, this Policy shall cease to be in force as of such premium due date.

WAIVER OF PREMIUM DURING TOTAL DISABILITY OF THE INSURED

We will waive the payment of any premium which becomes due during a period in which you are totally disabled, provided you are an insured Person, and that such disability (1) commences prior to your 65th birthday and while this Policy is in force and (2) continues without interruption for six months. In such event, any premiums due and paid during such six months will be refunded. Premiums will be waived during the continuance of total disability while you are living and the Policy is renewed in accordance with the renewal provision. In the event of your death, no further premiums will be waived, except as provided in the following paragraph.

Waiver of any premium will continue the Policy in force as if such premium had been paid and, when the first premium falling due at the termination of the period for which premiums were waived becomes payable, you shall have the right to resume payment of premiums.

If after your death your spouse becomes the Insured pursuant to the provision entitled "Eligibility For And Termination of Coverage", this waiver of premium provision shall be applicable in accordance with its terms to your spouse as the Insured in the event of total disability commencing after becoming the Insured but before attaining 65 years of age. The premium to be waived shall be the premium according to the mode of premium payment in effect when total disability began.

"Total disability", for the purpose of this provision means disability resulting from injury or sickness which prevents you from engaging in any gainful occupation for which you are or become qualified by reason of education, training or experience. However, the entire and irrecoverable loss of the sight of both eyes, or the loss of any two extremities by actual severance through or above the wrist or ankle joints, shall be accepted as constituting total disability.

No premiums shall be waived under this provision by reason of any disability which shall result from war, declared or undeclared, or any act thereof, or which shall commence while the Insured is in the Armed Forces of any country or international authority.

CONVERSION PRIVILEGE

If coverage under this Policy with respect to an Insured Person terminates for any reason other than your failure to pay required premiums when due, such person will be entitled to have issued to him without evidence of insurability a Policy of insurance (hereinafter called the Converted Policy) subject to the following conditions:

(a) If the coverage for such person is terminating for any reason except for non-payment of premium, the Converted Policy shall be on a form then in use by us which most nearly offers the same coverage as that being terminated under this Policy.

(b) Proper written application for the Converted Policy and the payment of the first premium therefor must be made to us within 31 days from the date on which such person's coverage under this Policy terminates.
The effective date of the Converted Policy will be the date of the termination of such person's coverage under this Policy. The first premium for the Converted Policy will be that applicable on such Policy's effective date to the class of risk to which such person belongs and to the form and amount of insurance provided.

(c) If this Policy excludes or limits coverage with respect to such person at the time such person's coverage terminates hereunder, said exclusion or limitation will also apply to such person under the Converted Policy.

(d) No payment shall be made under the Converted Policy for expenses for which we are required to make payment under this Policy.

(e) We will not be required to issue a Converted Policy if such issuance would result in over-insurance or duplication of benefits according to our then published underwriting standards.

Appendix 6 (*continued*)

POLICY PROVISIONS

ENTIRE CONTRACT; CHANGES: This Policy, including the copy of application, the endorsements and the other attached papers, if any, constitutes the entire contract of insurance. No change in this Policy shall be valid until approved by one of our executive officers and unless such approval be endorsed hereon or attached hereto. No agent has authority to change this Policy or to waive any of its provisions.

TIME LIMIT ON CERTAIN DEFENSES: (a) After two years from the date a person becomes covered under this Policy no misstatements, except fraudulent misstatements, made by you in the application for such person's coverage shall be used to void the Policy or to deny a claim with respect to such person for loss incurred after the expiration of such two year period. (b) No claim for loss incurred after two years from the date a person becomes covered under this Policy shall be reduced or denied on the ground that a disease or physical condition not excluded from such person's coverage by name or specific description effective on the date of loss had existed prior to the effective date of such person's coverage under this Policy.

GRACE PERIOD: A Grace Period of thirty-one days will be granted for the payment of each premium falling due after the first premium, during which Grace Period the Policy shall continue in force.

REINSTATEMENT: If any renewal premium be not paid within the time granted you for payment, a subsequent acceptance of premium by us or by any agent duly authorized by us to accept such premium, without requiring in connection therewith an application for reinstatement, shall reinstate the Policy; provided, however, that if we or such agent requires an application for reinstatement and issues a conditional receipt for the premium tendered, the Policy will be reinstated upon our approval of such application or, lacking such approval, upon the forty-fifth day following the date of such conditional receipt unless we have previously notified you in writing of our disapproval of such application. The reinstated Policy shall cover only loss resulting from such accidental injury as may be sustained after the date of reinstatement and loss due to such sickness as may begin more than ten days after the date of reinstatement. In all other respects both you and we shall have the same rights thereunder as each had under the Policy immediately before the due date of the defaulted premium, subject to any provisions endorsed hereon or attached hereto in connection with the reinstatement.

NOTICE OF CLAIM: Written notice of claim must be given to us within twenty days (thirty days in Mississippi; sixty days in Kentucky) after the occurrence or commencement of any loss covered by the Policy, or as soon thereafter as is reasonably possible Notice given by you or on your behalf to us at our Home Office in Long Grove, Illinois, or to any of our authorized agents, with information sufficient to identify you shall be deemed notice to us.

CLAIM FORMS: Upon receipt of a notice of claim, we will furnish to the claimant such forms as are usually furnished for filing proofs of loss. If such forms are not furnished within fifteen days after the giving of such notice the claimant shall be deemed to have complied with the requirements of this Policy as to proof of loss upon submitting, within the time fixed in the Policy for filing proofs of loss, written proof covering the occurrence, the character and the extent of the loss for which claim is made.

PROOFS OF LOSS: Written proof of loss must be furnished to us at our said office in case of claim for loss for which this Policy provides any periodic payment contingent upon continuing loss within ninety days after the termination of the period for which we are liable and in case of claim for any other loss within ninety days after the date of such loss. Failure to furnish such proof within the time required shall not invalidate nor reduce any claim if it was not reasonably possible to give proof within such time, provided such proof is furnished as soon as reasonably possible and in no event, except in the absence of legal capacity, later than one year from the time proof is otherwise required.

TIME OF PAYMENT OF CLAIMS: Benefits payable under this Policy for any loss other than loss for which this Policy provides any periodic payment will be paid immediately upon receipt of due written proof of such loss. Subject to due written proof of loss, all accrued indemnities for loss for which this Policy provides periodic payment will be paid monthly during the continuance of the period for which we are liable and any balance remaining unpaid upon the termination of liability will be paid immediately upon receipt of due written proof.

PAYMENT OF CLAIMS: All benefits under this Policy will be payable to you. Any accured benefits unpaid at your death will be paid to your estate.

If any benefits of this Policy shall be payable to your estate, or to a person who is a minor or otherwise not competent to give a valid release, we may pay such indemnity, up to an amount not exceeding $1,000, to any of your relatives by blood or connection by marriage who deem to be equitably entitled thereto. Any payment made by us in good faith pursuant to this provision shall fully discharge us to the extent of such payment.

PHYSICAL EXAMINATIONS: We shall have the right and opportunity at our own expense to examine an Insured Person when and as often as it may reasonably require during the pendency of a claim hereunder.

LEGAL ACTIONS: No action at law or in equity shall be brought to recover on this Policy prior to the expiration of sixty days after written proof of loss has been furnished in accordance with the requirements of this Policy. No such action shall be brought after the expiration of three years (six years in Kansas and South Carolina) after the time written proof of loss is required to be furnished.

MISSTATEMENT OF AGE: If your age has been misstated, all amounts payable under this Policy shall be such as the premium paid for the coverage would have purchased at the correct age.

CONFORMITY WITH STATE STATUTES: Any provision of this Policy which, on its effective date, is in conflict with the statutes of the state in which you reside on such date is hereby amended to conform to the minimum requirements of such statutes.

ASSIGNMENT: No assignment of interest under this Policy shall be binding upon us unless and until the original or a duplicate thereof is received at our Home Office, which does not assume any responsibility for the validity thereof.

MUTUAL POLICY CONDITIONS: This is a perpetual mutual corporation, owned by and operated for the benefit of its members. This is a non-assessable, participating Policy under which the Board of Directors in its discretion may determine and pay unabsorbed premium deposit refunds (dividends) to you.

Source: *Policy Kit for Students of Insurance,* Alliance of American Insurers, 20 N. Wacker Drive, Chicago, IL 60606.

Appendix 6 (*continued*)

recovery income policy
Insured
Policy Number
Effective Date
Policy Term
Term Premium

RESERVED FOR COMPANY NAME, ADDRESS AND/OR LOGOTYPE.

HEREBY INSURES the person named as the Insured in the Schedule and agrees to pay for loss resulting from injury or sickness, as hereinafter defined and specifically provided, subject to the provisions, conditions, definitions and exclusions herein contained.

CONSIDERATION: This Policy is issued in consideration of the statements contained in the application, a copy of which is attached hereto and the payment in advance of the first Term Premium for the Policy Term specified in the Schedule, to commence on the Effective Date specified in the Schedule. During the continuance of this Policy each renewal premium shall be due on the first day of the term to which such premium applies, except as provided in the grace period provision. Each policy term shall begin and end at 12:01 A.M., Standard Time, at the place where the Insured then resides.

GUARANTEED RENEWABLE TO AGE 65
COMPANY HAS RIGHT TO CHANGE PREMIUM RATE

This Policy is guaranteed renewable until the Policy anniversary date on or next following the Insured's 65th birthday if maintained in force by timely payment of the premiums. The Policy will expire on such Policy anniversary date unless renewed in accordance with the provision captioned "Conditionally Renewable From Age 65 To 72 While Employed Company Has Right To Change Premium Rate".

The Company has the right to change, at any time, its table of premium rates applicable on a class basis to premiums for all policies of the same form as this policy issued to persons of the same occupational classification in the state of residence of the Insured. In the event of such a change, the original classification and insuring age of the Insured will be used in determining the premium from said table. The Company agrees to give the Insured thirty days written notice of its intention to change the premium rates.

CONDITIONALLY RENEWABLE FROM AGE 65 TO 72 WHILE EMPLOYED
COMPANY HAS RIGHT TO CHANGE PREMIUM RATE

The Insured has the right, by the timely payment of the required premiums, to continue this Policy from term to term beyond the Policy anniversary date on or next following his 65th birthday for as long as he is actively and regularly employed full time, but not beyond the Policy anniversary date on or next following the Insured's 72nd birthday. During such continuance the Company may, from time to time, require proof that the Insured continues to be actively and regularly employed full time. If the Insured ceases to be so employed, other than by reason of total disability, this Policy will terminate as of the date of cessation of employment, and the Company will refund the pro-rata portion of any premium paid for any period beyond such termination date. The termination shall be without prejudice to any claim originating while this Policy is in force.

Premiums payable during this period will be based on the Company's table of premium rates applicable to all policies of this form which insure persons who have attained age 65 and who are of the same rating classification. The Company has the right to change, at any time during this period, its table of rates applicable on a class basis to premiums for all policies of the same form as this policy. The Company agrees to give the Insured thirty days written notice of its intention to change the premium rates. If the Company accepts a premium which covers any period after the policy anniversary date on or next following the Insured's 72nd birthday, this Policy will continue in force until the end of the period for which premiums have been accepted.

NOTICE OF TEN DAY RIGHT TO EXAMINE POLICY

The Insured may return this Policy within 10 days after its receipt if, upon examination, he is not satisfied with it for any reason. If this Policy is so returned, it shall be deemed void from its Effective Date, and any premium paid will be refunded.

IN WITNESS WHEREOF the has caused this Policy to be signed by its President and Secretary, but it shall not be binding upon the Company unless there is attached hereto an application countersigned by a duly authorized representative of the Company.

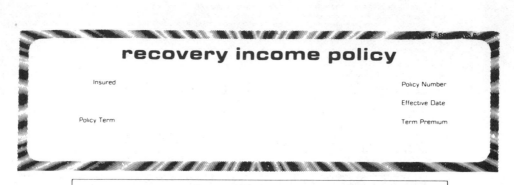

Appendix 6 (*continued*)

GENERAL DEFINITIONS

As used in this Policy:

"Injury" means accidental bodily injury sustained while this Policy is in force and causes loss or disability beginning while this Policy is in force.

"Sickness" means disease or sickness which first manifests itself while this Policy is in force and causes loss or disability beginning while this Policy is in force.

"Physician" means a legally qualified physician other than the Insured.

"Elimination Period" means the number of days at the beginning of a period of disability for which monthly benefits are not payable.

"Actively and regularly employed full time" means actively at work for not less than 30 working hours per week on a regular and continuing scheduled basis.

"Total disability" means (a) during the first 60 months of any period of continuous total disability, complete inability of the Insured to engage in any and every duty pertaining to his regular occupation or employment and (b) thereafter during the continuance of such period of total disability, means complete inability of the Insured to engage in any gainful occupation or employment in which he might reasonably be expected to engage because of education, training or experience, and with due regard to his vocation and earnings at the beginning of disability.

BENEFIT PROVISIONS

PART I TOTAL DISABILITY BENEFIT

If injury, within 180 days after the date of accident, or sickness shall result in continuous total disability and shall require the regular care of a physician, the Company will pay, upon receipt of due proof of such disability and subject to the Elimination Period specified in the Schedule, the Monthly Benefit Amount For Total Disability specified in the Schedule, (one-thirtieth of such amount for each day of any period less than one month) for the period of such continuous total disability but not exceeding the applicable Maximum Benefit Period specified in the Schedule.

If the period of total disability results from injury and (a) commences before the Insured's 64th birthday, the Maximum Benefit Period will be as stated in the Schedule, but in no event shall total disability benefits be payable beyond the Insured's 65th birthday unless the Maximum Benefit specified in the Schedule is Lifetime; or (b) commences on or after the Insured's 64th birthday, the Maximum Benefit Period will be twelve months.

If the period of total disability results from sickness and (a) commences before the Insured's 64th birthday, the Maximum Benefit Period will be as stated in the Schedule but in no event shall total disability benefits be payable beyond the Insured's 65th birthday; or (b) commences on or after the Insured's 64th birthday, the Maximum Benefit Period will be twelve months.

CONCURRENT DISABILITIES: During any period in which the Insured is totally disabled as the result of more than one sickness or more than one accident or both sickness and accident, benefits will be considered the same as if the disability resulted from one cause.

CERTAIN DISABILITIES CONSIDERED AS RESULTING FROM SICKNESS: Any period of total disability which is caused or contributed to by (1) disease or medical or surgical treatment therefor (2) infection other than a pyogenic infection sustained through an accidental cut or wound, or (3) hernia of any kind, however caused, shall be considered as resulting from sickness.

Any period of total disability which results from injury and commences while this Policy is in force but more than 180 days after the date of the accident causing the injury shall, for the purposes of this Policy, be covered under the sickness benefits of this Policy.

RECURRING DISABILITIES: Total disability commencing while this Policy is in force and resulting from or contributed to by any cause which is the same as or related to any cause of any prior period of total disability for which a benefit under this Part I is paid will be considered one period of disability for the purposes of applying the Elimination Period, the Maximum Benefit Period and the applicable Monthly Benefit Amount, unless the Insured has engaged on a full time basis in an occupation or employment for wage or profit for a continuous period of at least six months between such periods of total disability.

Appendix 6 (*continued*)

PART II TRANSPLANT DONOR BENEFIT

If, while this Policy is in force and commencing more than twelve months after the Effective Date shown in the Schedule, the Insured is totally and continuously disabled as the result of a transplant of a part of his body to the body of another person, the Company will pay, subject to the Elimination Period for sickness specified in the Schedule, a monthly benefit as specified in Part I of this Policy for a Maximum Benefit Period of six months. Loss resulting from such transplant is payable only under this Part II.

PART III WAIVER OF PREMIUM—PREMIUM REFUND

The Company will waive the payment of any premium which becomes due prior to the Insured's 65th birthday during a period of any total disability for which benefits are payable under this Policy and if such total disability has continued without interruption for at least 90 days or for the applicable Elimination Period, if longer. The Company will refund any premium which became due and was paid during such total disability. If such total disability continues beyond the period for which benefits are payable under this Policy, the Company will continue to waive the payment of all premiums which thereafter become due during the continuance of such total disability, provided the Insured furnishes the Company with due written proof of the continuance of such total disability within 31 days of the due date of each such premium. After the termination of the period of total disability during which premiums have been waived, this policy will continue in force until the next premium due date, at which time the Insured will have the right to resume the payment of premiums.

EXCLUSIONS

This Policy does not cover loss caused by or resulting from (1) declared or undeclared war or any act thereof, or (2) intentionally self-inflicted injury; or (3) injury sustained or sickness which first manifests itself while the Insured is on active duty (other than active duty for a period of training not exceeding two months) as a member of the Armed Services.

GENERAL PROVISIONS

ENTIRE CONTRACT; CHANGES: This Policy, including the endorsements and the other attached papers, if any, constitutes the entire contract of insurance. No change in this Policy shall be valid until approved by an executive officer of the Company and unless such approval be endorsed hereon or attached hereto. No agent has authority to change this Policy or to waive any of its provisions.

INCONTESTABLE: (a) After this policy has been in force for a period of two years during the lifetime of the Insured it shall become incontestable as to the statements contained in the application. (b) No claim for loss incurred or disability as defined in this Policy commencing after two years from the effective date of this Policy shall be reduced or denied on the ground that a disease or physical condition not excluded from coverage by name or specific description effective on the date of loss had existed prior to the effective date of coverage of this Policy.

GRACE PERIOD: A grace period of thirty-one days will be granted for the payment of each premium falling due after the first premium, during which grace period the Policy shall continue in force.

REINSTATEMENT: If any renewal premium be not paid within the time granted the Insured for payment, a subsequent acceptance of premium by the Company or by any agent duly authorized by the Company to accept such premium, without requiring in connection therewith an application for reinstatement, shall reinstate the Policy; provided, however, that if the Company or such agent requires an application for reinstatement and issues a conditional receipt for the premium tendered, the Policy will be reinstated upon approval of such application by the Company or, lacking such approval, upon the forty-fifth day following the date of such conditional receipt unless the Company has previously notified the Insured in writing of its disapproval of such application. The reinstated Policy shall cover only loss resulting from such accidental injury as may be sustained after the date of reinstatement and loss due to such sickness as may begin more than ten days after the date of reinstatement. In all other respects the Insured and Company shall have the same rights thereunder as they had under the Policy immediately before the due date of the defaulted premium, subject to any provisions endorsed hereon or attached hereto in connection with the reinstatement.

NOTICE OF CLAIM: Written notice of claim must be given to the Company within twenty days (thirty days in Mississippi; sixty days in Kentucky) after the occurrence or commencement of any loss covered by the Policy, or as soon thereafter as is reasonably possible. Notice given by or on behalf of the Insured or the beneficiary to the Company at its Home Office in Long Grove, Illinois, or to any authorized agent of the Company, with information sufficient to identify the Insured, shall be deemed notice to the Company.

CLAIM FORMS: The Company, upon receipt of a notice of claim, will furnish to the claimant such forms as are usually furnished by it for filing proofs of loss. If such forms are not furnished within fifteen days after the giving of such notice the claimant shall be deemed to have complied with the requirements of this Policy as to proof of loss upon submitting, within the time fixed in the Policy for filing proofs of loss, written proof covering the occurrence, the character and the extent of the loss for which claim is made.

PROOFS OF LOSS: Written proof of loss must be furnished to the Company at its said office in case of claim for loss for which this Policy provides any periodic payment contingent upon continuing loss within ninety days after the termination of the period for which the Company is liable and in case of claim for any other loss within ninety days after the date of such loss. Failure to furnish such proof within the time required shall not invalidate nor reduce any claim if it was not reasonably possible to give proof within such time, provided such proof is furnished as soon as reasonably possible and in no event, except in the absence of legal capacity, later than one year from the time proof is otherwise required.

TIME OF PAYMENT OF CLAIMS: Benefits payable under this Policy for any loss other than loss for which this Policy provides any periodic payment will be paid immediately upon receipt of due written proof of such loss. Subject to due written proof of loss, all accrued indemnities for loss for which this Policy provides periodic payment will be paid monthly during the continuance of the period for which the Company is liable and any balance remaining unpaid upon the termination of liability will be paid immediately upon receipt of due written proof.

Appendix 6 (*concluded*)

PAYMENT OF CLAIMS: All benefits under this policy will be payable to the Insured. Any accrued benefits unpaid at the Insured's death will be paid to the estate of the Insured.

If any benefits of this policy shall be payable to the estate of the Insured, or to an Insured who is a minor or otherwise not competent to give a valid release, the Company may pay such indemnity, up to an amount not exceeding $1,000, to any relative by blood or connection by marriage of the Insured who is deemed by the Company to be equitably entitled thereto. Any payment made by the Company in good faith pursuant to this provision shall fully discharge the Company to the extent of such payment.

PHYSICAL EXAMINATIONS: The Company at its own expense shall have the right and opportunity to examine the person of the Insured when and as often as it may reasonably require during the pendency of a claim hereunder.

LEGAL ACTION: No action at law or in equity shall be brought to recover on this Policy prior to the expiration of sixty days after written proof of loss has been furnished in accordance with the requirements of this Policy. No such action shall be brought after the expiration of three years (six years in Kansas and South Carolina) after the time written proof of loss is required to be furnished.

MISSTATEMENT OF AGE: If the age of the Insured has been misstated, all amounts payable under this Policy shall be such as the premium paid for the coverage would have purchased at the correct age.

If, because of misstatement of the Insured's age, the Company shall accept any premium which falls due on a date when, according to the correct age, this Policy would not have been issued or the coverage under this Policy would have ceased, then the liability of the Company shall be limited to the refund of all premiums paid for the period not covered by this Policy.

CONFORMITY WITH STATE STATUTES: Any provision of this Policy which, on its effective date, is in conflict with the statutes of the state in which the Insured resides on such date is hereby amended to conform to the minimum requirements of such statutes.

ASSIGNMENT: No assignment of interest under this Policy shall be binding upon the Company unless and until the original or a duplicate thereof is received at the Home Office of the Company, which does not assume any responsibility for the validity thereof.

SUSPENSION DURING MILITARY SERVICE: If the Insured becomes a member of the armed forces of any country or military authority on full time active duty, he may elect to suspend this Policy. Upon receipt of written notice by the Company that the Insured has elected to suspend this Policy, the Company will refund that portion of the premium which would have provided coverage for the period following the date such notice was received by the Company.

If, within five years from the date on which this Policy was so suspended, the Insured terminates his full-time active duty, the Policy will be reinstated without evidence of insurability, on receipt by the Company of (a) written election of reinstatement and (b) payment of the pro-rata unearned premium covering the period from the termination of such active duty to the next premium due date.

If the Insured does not terminate his full-time active duty within five years from the date on which this Policy was suspended, or if he does not reinstate this Policy within 90 days following termination of his full-time active duty, he may reinstate this Policy then only in accordance with the Reinstatement provision.

INCREASED BENEFITS: If the last premium due prior to commencement of any disability for which monthly benefits are payable under Part I of this Policy was paid on an annual basis, such monthly benefits shall be increased ten percent.

MUTUAL POLICY CONDITIONS: This is a perpetual mutual corporation, owned by and operated for the benefit of its members. This is a non-assessable, participating Policy under which the Board of Directors in its discretion may determine and pay unabsorbed premium deposit refunds (dividends) to the Insured.

Source: *Policy Kit for Students of Insurance,* Alliance of American Insurers, 20 N. Wacker Drive, Chicago, IL 60606.

Appendix 7 A Mathematical Note*

Because authors of most textbooks in business subjects these days believe they must include some mathematics either in the text or an appendix, this mathematical note is offered here. The author believes the reader will find it extremely useful for one purpose or another.

Every budding econometrician knows of the very basic relationship:

$$\ln\{\lim_{\delta\to\infty}\left\{[(X')^{-1}-(X^{-1})']!+\frac{1}{\delta}\right\}\delta] + (\sin^2 q+\cos^2 q) = \sum_{n=0}^{\infty}\frac{\cosh p\sqrt{1-\tanh^2 p}}{2^n} \quad (1)$$

where

ln is the natural logarithm

$\lim\limits_{\delta\to\infty}$ is the limit as δ approaches infinity

$\sin^2 q$ is the sine squared of q

$\cos^2 q$ is the cosine squared of q

$\sum\limits_{n=0}^{\infty}$ is the summation as n goes from 0 to infinity

cosh p is the hyperbolic cosine of p

$\tanh^2 p$ is the hyperbolic tangent squared of p

If one recalls that the inverse of the transpose is the transpose of the inverse, one can unburden himself/herself of a multidimensional space by noting:

$$(X')^{-1}-(X^{-1})'=0 \quad (2)$$

If one notes with a little more degree of difficulty that:

$$0!=1 \quad (3)$$

then equations (2) and (3) can be combined to obtain:

$$[(X')^{-1}-(X^{-1})']!=1 \quad (4)$$

At this point the mathematics becomes more difficult. If one inserts equation (4) into (1), equation (5) is obtained:

$$\ln[\lim_{\delta\to\infty}\left(1+\frac{1}{\delta}\right)\delta] + (\sin^2 q+\cos^2 q) = \sum_{n=0}^{\infty}\frac{\cosh p\sqrt{1-\tanh^2 p}}{2^n} \quad (5)$$

---

* The author first published this mathematical note in *The Journal of Risk and Insurance* as THE EDITOR'S PAGE while serving as its editor. Reproduction is by permission of the Journal.

After much research, it has been determined that:

$$e = \lim_{\delta \to \infty} \left(1 + \frac{1}{\delta}\right)^{\delta} \tag{6}$$

and

$$1 = \cosh p \sqrt{1 - \tanh^2 p} \tag{7}$$

By using equations (6) and (7) with (5), any student of economics and finance (insurance) can readily confirm that:

$$\ln e + (\sin^2 q + \cos^2 q) = \sum_{n=0}^{\infty} \frac{1}{2^n} \tag{8}$$

At this point one may be stumped, but with much trepidation, this roadblock can be overcome as follows:

$$1 = \sin^2 q + \cos^2 q \tag{9}$$

and further that

$$2 = \sum_{n=0}^{\infty} \frac{1}{2^n} \tag{10}$$

noting that

$$1 = \ln e \tag{11}$$

Now one arrives at an extremely difficult equation to interpret by substituting equations (9), (10), and (11) into (8).

$$1 + 1 = 2 \tag{12}$$

Because this equation is so difficult to understand for the young econometrician, equation (1) is preferred because of its clarity.

Index

A

Abandonment, 119, 539
Absolute liability, 61–62, 539
Accident, 290, 539
Accidental bodily injury, 290
Accidental death and dismemberment (AD&D) benefits, 320
Accidental death rider, 261
Accidental loss, 35
Accidental means, 290
Accounts receivable insurance, 235
Accrued benefit cost method, 336
Accumulated at interest dividends, 275
Actual cash value, 125, 127, 539
  and duplicate coverages, 128
  in health insurance, 127–28
  in liability insurance, 127
  in life insurance, 127–28
  and replacement cost, 126, 128
  in valued policies, 128
Actuarial cost methods, for funding retirement plans, 336–40, 539
Actuarial equity, 440
Additional living expense form, 182
Add-on no-fault benefits, 213, 539
Adhesion, contract of, 87, 539
Adjustable life policy, 259
Adjustment income, 47–48, 519
Administrative law, 495
Administrative services only (ASO) contract, 47, 315, 323
Admitted assets, 467, 539
Advance-premium mutuals, 411
Adverse selection, 304, 440
Aetna group, 434
Affiliated FM Insurance Company, 412
Affirmative warranty, 88, 539
Age Discrimination in Employment Act (ADEA) (1967), 319, 322, 344
Agency by ratification, 96, 539
Agent(s)
  brokers as, 97, 424
  choosing of, 528–29
  creation of agency relationship, 96
  feelings of, on deductibles, 135
  general, 423
  licensing of, 506
  local, 424
  power and authority of, 96–97
Agent(s)—*Cont.*
  special, 424–25
  surplus-line, 424, 506–7, 549
Aggregate level cost basis, 337–38
Aid to Families with Dependent Children (AFDC), 368
Aid to the Permanently and Totally Disabled (APTD), 368
Aircraft liability insurance, 237
Aleatory contract, 86–87, 539
All-risk contracts, 108, 539
Allen, Zachariah, 412
Alliance of American Insurers, 430, 433
Allocated funding instruments, 341, 539
American agency system, 421, 539
American Arbitration Association, 212
American Association of Insurance Services, 432
American Bar Association, 212–13
American Bureau of Shipping, 430
American Federation of Labor, 215
American Hull Insurance Syndicate, 430
American Institute of Certified Public Accountants, 486
American Insurance Association, 212–13, 430, 433
American Lloyds, 407
American Management Association, 43
American Medical Association, and national health insurance, 393
American Risk and Insurance Association, 365, 433
American Trial Lawyers Association, 213
Amount limit, coinsurance, 225, 539
Annual policies, 112
Annual reports, 505
Annual transit form, 192
Annuities, 262
  classification of, 262–64
  principle of, 262
Annuity certain, 263, 539
Annuity due, 263, 539
Annuity exclusion rule, 350, 352–53
Anticancellation laws, 493
Apparent authority, 97, 539
Appeal bond, 232, 539
Appleton rule, 503
Application, for insurance, 82–83
Apportionment clause, 132
Appraisal, need for after loss, 118–19
Arbitration, of claim, 427
Armstrong investigation (1905), 492
Assault, 60, 539
Assessment companies, 88 n
Assets, of insurers, 467–69
Assigned risk plans, 507–8
Assignment, 111–12, 539
  in homeowners insurance, 145–46
  in life insurance, 273 n, 279
Associated Factory Mutual Fire Insurance Companies, 412, 430
Association of Motorcycle Insurers, 430
Assumption-of-risk doctrine, 214, 539
Attained age basis, 337
Attractive nuisance, 66, 539
Auto insurance plans (AIPs), 209; *see* Personal auto policy (PAP) *and* Business auto insurance (BAP)
Auto rating, 208
Automatically convertible term life insurance, 251, 539
Automobile accidents, compensating victims of, 211–13
Automobile insurance; *see* Business auto insurance (BAP) *and* Personal auto policy (PAP)
Automobile liability insurance, 207,
  business, 209–11
  and common law of negligence, 70–71
  compensation of victims, 211–13
  personal, 207–8, 209
Average index monthly earnings form (AIME), 539
  computation of, 371, 373–74
Average monthly wage (AMW), 377, 394–95
Average rate of return, 534
Average value method, 471, 539
Averages, law of, 33–34
Aviation insurance, 136, 236–37
Aviation restrictions, 279

B

Bail bond, 232, 539
Bailee, 53
Bailee forms, 194–95
Balloon note, 257 n

Bank burglary and robbery policy, 226, 539
Bankers blanket bond, 230, 539
Bankruptcy clause, 130, 539
Banks, crime insurance coverage for, 226–27
Basic policy, automobile, 209, 539
Basic transportation policy, 192, 539
Basis rate, fire insurance, 455, 539
Battery, 60, 540
Bend points, 375
Beneficiary, 93, 540
  change of, 279
  in life insurance, 273–74, 279–80
Benefit-of-any insurance clause, 160, 540
Benefit computation years, 373, 540
Best, Alfred M., Inc., 531
Best's Insurance Reports, 407, 531
Betterments, 543
Bicycle floater, 193
Bid bond, 233, 540
Bilateral contracts, 88, 540
Binders, 83–84
Black Tom Island, New York, explosion of powder magazine on, 67
Blanket bonds
  for financial institutions, 229–30
  general, 229
Blanket coverage, 129, 540
Blanket crime policy, 231–32, 540
Blanket expense coverage, 286
Blanket health insurance, 314, 540
Blanket position bond, 229, 540
Blanket rating, 451, 540, 545
Block of business, 473, 540
Blue Cross/Blue Shield plans, 287, 290, 322, 408, 413–14
Blue Goose, Order of the, 433
Blue Shield Medical-Care Plans Association, 413
Boiler and machinery insurance, 234–35
Bona fide contracts, 88
Bonding, 227–28
  fidelity bond coverages, 228–32
  nature of, 228
  surety bond coverages, 232–33
Bottomry contracts, 13, 540
Branch office, 422, 540
Breach of duty, injury resulting from, 67
Breadth-of-benefit provisions, 287
Broad-form CGL endorsement, 204, 205
Broad-form personal theft policy, 223–24
Broad-form storekeepers policy, 231, 540
Brokers, 424, 540
  as agents, 97
  licensing of, 506
Builder's risk marine insurance policy, 189
  Burglary, 223, 540
  Burglary special coverage form, 226
  Business, crime insurance coverage for, 224–27
Business auto insurance (BAP); *see also* Personal auto policy (PAP)
  commercial and public vehicle coverage, 210
  garage insurance, 210–11
  liability coverage, 209–11
  nonownership coverage, 210
  private passenger coverage, 209
  types of coverage, 209–10
Business firm
  life and health exposures for, 49–52
  property exposures for, 53–54
Business-interruption insurance, 184–85
Business liability exposures, 74
Business liability forms, 201–2
Business methods, regulation of, 506–8
Business overhead expense health policies, 288
Businessowners program, 239–40, 540
Butterfield v. *Forrester* (1809), 69

C

Cafeteria plan of employee benefits, 318–19
Capital-stock accounts, regulation of, 504
Captive insurers, 401, 425
Cardozo, Benjamin N., 68
Carpool, coverage of, 161–62, 163
Case law, 58
Cash values, for life insurance, 248–50
Castrophe risks reinsurance, 445–46, 540
Casualty Insurance Fraud Association, 430
Ceded, 444, 540
Cession, 444, 540
Challenger, 225 n
Chance of loss, 21–22, 540
Change clause, 99
Charter, regulation by, 496
Civil law, 58–59, 540
Claims administration, 425
  arbitration, 427
  checking coverage, 425–26
  difficulties encountered by adjuster, 427
Claims administration—*Cont.*
  examples of loss-adjustment problems, 427–29
  investigation of claim, 426
  mechanics of loss adjustment, 425–27
  preparing proof of loss, 426
  salvage, 426
  subrogation, 426–27
  time limit for paying, 121
Claims chiseling, 425
Claims-made basis, 540
Claims-occurence basis, 540
Class rating, 451, 540, 545
Clayton Act, 499
Close corporation
  exposure, 51–52
  insurance, 526
Code, 57
Coinsurance amount limit, 133, 540
Coinsurance clause, 132–35, 540
Coinsurance percentage, 133, 225
Coinsurance plan, 446, 540
College Retirement Equities Fund (CREF), 265
Collison, coverage of, under automobile insurance, 155, 540
Combination safe depository policy, 226–27, 540
Combined ratio, 480, 540
Combustibility, 454
Commercial blanket bond, 229, 540
Commercial property form, 240–41, 540
Commissioners reserve valuation method (CRVM), 476, 540
Common employment doctrine, 214, 540
Common law, 58, 540–41
Commutative contracts, 86–87, 541
Company fleets, 434
Comparative negligence, 69, 541
Competition, and regulation, 492–93
Complete Life, 255 n
Completion bond, 233, 541
Comprehensive dishonesty, disappearance and destruction (3D) policy, 230–31, 541
Comprehensive general liability (CGL), 201–2
Comprehensive glass insurance, 234
Comprehensive personal liability policy, 200
Compulsory automobile insurance, 211
Compulsory government insurance, 11
Compulsory nonoccupational health insurance, 11
Computation base years, 373, 541

Concealment, 90, 541
Conditional contracts, 88, 541
Conditional or installment sales floater, 194
Conditions, 106
Consequential losses, 110, 183, 541
Constructive total loss clause, 191, 541
Consumer-type cooperative insurers, 408
Consumers Products Safety Act (1972), 431
Consumers Union, 212–13
Continent business-interruption insurance, 185, 541
Continuous-premium whole life insurance, 253–55, 541
Contractors' equipment floater, 194
Contract, insurance; *see* Insurance contract
Contractual liability form, 202–3
Contributory negligence defense, 69, 214, 541
Conventional annuities, 264, 541
Conversion, 61, 541
Convertible deductible, 541
Convertible term life insurance, 251, 541
Cooperative organizations, 431–32, 434
Cooperative ratemaking bureaus, 450
Coordination-of-benefits clauses, 91, 131, 314, 541
Corporation, insurance coverage, for loss of owner in, 51–52
Corridor deductible, 321, 541
Cost-comparison methods, 534–35
Cost-of-living rider, 261
Coverage period
  in automobile insurance, 160–61
  in homeowners insurance, 147
  in standard fire policy, 175
Craft clause, in marine insurance, 191
Credit insurance, 35, 111, 235
Creditors, rights of, in life insurance, 280–81
Crime coverages
  for business, 224–27
  federal program for, 227, 336
  for individuals, 223–24
Criminal law, 58, 541
Crop insurance, 186–87, 366
Cross-purchase plan, 526, 541
Cumulative and participating deductible, 541

D

Damageability, 454
Davies v. *Mann* (1842), 69
Dean's analytic system, 455, 541
Death benefits, exclusion from gross estate, 256 n
Debit agent, 260, 541
Declarations, 106
Decrease-in-benefits provision, 294
Decreasing term, 251, 541
Deductibles, 135
  types of, 136
Defamation, 60, 541
Defective products, liability in regards to, 59
Deferment clause, 277
Deferred annuity, 263, 541
Deferred profit-sharing plans, 346, 541
Defined benefit plan, 332–33, 541
Defined contribution plans, 332, 333, 541
Delay clause, in marine insurance, 191
Delayed benefit policy, 521
Demolition insurance, 183
Departmentalization, 419–21
Deposit administration plans, 342
Deposit term life insurance, 259
Depositors forgery bond, 230, 541
Depository bonds, 233, 541
Differences in conditions insurance (DIC), 187, 541
Direct-reporting system, 422–23, 541
Direct response, purchase of health insurance by, 289–90
Direct-selling systems, 423
Disability, definition of, in health insurance coverage, 290–92
Disability income rider, 261
Disability insurance, 128
  and health insurance, 286
  proving definite loss in, 35
  temporary plans, 390–92
  waiting periods in, 136
Disappearing deductible, 541
Disclosure, 354
Divided coverage, 129, 541
Dividends, 484–85
  policy options, 274–75, 541
  regulation of, 504
Doing business authorization, 505
Domestic animals, and liability without fault, 61–62
Domestic shipments, coverage of, under inland marine insurance, 191–93
Double dipping, 91
Double indemnity riders, 261, 290
Dramshop, 206 n
Dramshop hazard, 74
Dramshop liability policy, 206
Dread disease insurance, 286, 287

E

Earned premiums, 480, 542
Earned surplus, of life insurers, 482–84
Earnings form, as type of business-interruption insurance, 184, 185, 542
Earthquake insurance, 136, 186
Economic productivity, basic contingencies to, 247
Economic Recovery Tax Act (ERTA) (1981), 247, 274, 359, 388, 522
Education, insurance coverage for provision of, 49, 521
Embezzlement, 223, 542
Emergency fund, 49, 521
Employee benefit plan exposure, 52
Employee benefit plans, 301; *see also* Group insurance *and* Retirement plans
  decisions in establishing, 316
    contributory/noncontributory, 316–18
    specifying coverages, 318–23
  reasons for using, 302
Employee Retirement Income Security Act (ERISA) (1974), 247, 317, 326, 331
Employee Stock Ownership Plans (ESOP), 355–56
  estate tax advantages of, 356–57
Employees, insurance for loss of key, 50, 525
Employers, liability of, 217
Endorsements, 106, 139–40
Endowment insurance, 252
  premiums, 252
  uses of, 252, 254
Entire-contract statute, 90–91, 542
Entitlements, 368, 542
Entity plan, 526, 542
Entry age normal basis, 337
Equal Employment Opportunity Commission (EEOC), coverage guidelines of, 314
Equitable remedies, 98, 542
Estoppel, 98–99, 542
Excess aggregate insurance, 206, 542
Excess liability forms, 206–7
Excess liability insurance, 206, 542
Excess-line brokers/agents, 424, 506–7, 549
Excess loss, 445–46
Excess plan, 345, 542

Exclusions, 106
Exclusive agency system, 421–22, 542
Executor fund, 518–19
Expense ratio, 480
Expenses
coverage of, by health insurance, 286
regulation of insurers', 503
Experience rating, 452–53, 542
Explosion clause, 190
Expressed authority, 96, 542, 548
Extended coverage endorsement (EC), 180–81
Extra-expense insurance, 185–86, 542
Extra-expense losses, 53, 110
Extra risk, 209, 542

F

Factory Insurance Association (FIA), 412
Factory mutuals, 412
Facultative reinsurance, 445, 542
FAIR (Fair Access to Insurance Requirements) plan, 16, 493
Fair trade laws, 499
False imprisonment, 60, 542
Family
life and health exposures for, 47–49, 522–23
property exposures for, 52–53
Family auto policy (FAP), 155, 165–66; *see also* Personal auto policy (PAP)
Family forgery bonds, 230, 542
Family income insurance, 251, 256–57, 542
Family income period, 256–57
Family maintenance policy, 257
Family period income, 48, 519–20
Family policy, 257–58
Farmers' personal liability policy, 200
Favored institution, 257, 542
Federal Bankruptcy Act, 280–81
Federal crime program, 227
Federal Crop Insurance Corporation (FCIC), 186–87, 414
Federal Deposit Insurance Corporation (FDIC), 414
Federal Economic Recovery Tax Act (1981), 47
Federal insurers, 414–15
Federal Mutual Implement and Hardware Company v. *Fairfax Equipment Company,* 99 n
Federal no-fault insurance plan, 213
Federal-official bonds, 233, 542
Federal Savings and Loan Insurance Corporation (FSLIC), 414
Federal Trade Commission (FTC), 499
Federal Trade Commission Act, 499
Federal Unemployment Tax Act, 388
Fidelity bonds, 227, 542
blanket bonds for financial institutions, 229–30
blanket crime policy, 231–32
broad-form storekeepers policy, 231
coverage of, 228
forgery insurance, 230
general blanket bonds, 229
individual and schedule bonds, 228–29
3D policy, 230–31
Fiduciary, responsibilities of, under ERISA, 353
Fiduciary bond, 232
Final expenses, coverage of, 47
Financial institutions, blanket bonds for, 229–30
Financial planning, and insurance, 15
Financial reporting, 485–86
Financial responsibility laws, 211
Fire, 542
Fire insurance
background on, 173–74
standard policy, 174–76, 553–54
allied lines, 186–87
coverage period, 175
differences in conditions, 187
forms
covering additional losses, 182–86
increasing perils covered, 180–82
providing commercial coverages, 178–80
used with, 176–78
hazards that exclude or suspend cover, 175–76
locations covered, 175
losses covered, 175
perils covered, 132 n, 175
persons covered, 175
pricing procedures, 454–55
property covered, 175
tailored forms, 187
underwriting procedures, 453–54
Firearms, keeping of, and liability without fault, 62
First-class mail floater, 192–93
Fitness for a particular purpose, 72, 542
Flat amount formula, 344, 542
Flat amount unit benefit formula, 345, 542
Flat percentage formula, 344, 542
Flexible compensation, 318, 542
Flexible standard valuation and nonforfeiture laws, 477–78
Flood insurance, 366
Forgery, 223, 542
Forgery insurance, 230
4–40 rule, 347–48, 542
Franchise deductible, 136, 542
Franchise health insurance, 314
Franchise life insurance, 312
Franklin, Benjamin, 173
Fraternal insurance, 412, 542
Free-of-capture and seizure clause (FC&S), 190, 542
Free-of-particular-average clause, 190, 543
Full-interest admitted form (FIA), 189, 543
Full preliminary term reserve plan, 475
Fully funded plan, 331, 332, 543
Fully insured, 370, 543
Fumigation clause, 190
Funded ratio, 335
Funding instrument, 341, 543
Funding standard account, 334, 543

G

Garage liability insurance, 210–11, 543
Garagekeepers' legal liability insurance, 211, 543
General agency system, 422, 543
General agent, 423, 543
General average clause, 191, 543
General blanket bonds, 229
General crime exclusions, 224, 543
General Insurance Guaranty Fund, 413
General policy provisions, for life insurance, 273, 543
General property form (GPF), 178–79, 543
Gompers, Samuel, 214–15
Good Samaritan act, 65
Good-faith contracts, 88, 543
Government insurance, 11, 414–15
Grace period, 278
Graded 5–15 vesting rule, 347–48, 543
Green Tree Mutual, 411
Gross-earnings form, 184, 543
Group credit health insurance, 314–15
Group credit insurance, 308, 312
Group deferred annuities, 341–42
Group dental insurance, 322
Group health insurance, 313
administrative service only (ASO), 315
blanket policies, 314
cost of, 315
credit policies, 314–15

Group health insurance—*Cont.*
decisions in establishing, 316–23
definition of, 313
differences in from individual health, 313–14
franchise, 314
funding benefits through trust, 315–16
state regulation, 313
types of coverages, 314
wholesale, 314
Group insurance
features of
cost of insurance, 303
payment of cost, 302–3
selection of benefit levels, 303
principles of, 304
apportioning insurance, 304–5
common purpose, 304
group size, 304
participation rates, 304
role of, in employee benefit plans, 301
Group life insurance, 260, 543
decisions in establishing, 316–23
standard provisions, 306
mandatory, 306–7
optional, 307–8
state regulation
benefit levels, 305–6
eligible groups, 305
group specifications, 305
limits on insurance provided, 306
sharing of cost, 305
types of coverage, 308
credit plans, 312
dependents' coverage, 308
permanent plans, 308–9, 310, 311–12
wholesale or franchise, 312
Group ordinary, 309
regulations applicable to, 309–10
Group permanent life insurance, 341
Group property and liability insurance, 323
attitudes and objectives, 323–24
legal climate, 324–25
limitations, 324
Group survivor income benefit insurance (SIBI), 310
rationale for and reaction to, 310–11
retired lives reserve, 311–12
Guaranteed insurability agreements, 258
Guaranteed investment contracts (GICs), 342
Guest statutes, in automobile liability, 71
Gybbons, William, 87

H

Hail insurance, 186–87, 415
Hale, Matthew, 491
Hartford group, 434
Hartford Steam Boiler Inspection and Insurance Company, 234–35, 430–31
Hazard(s), 25, 543
exclusion or suspension of
in automobile insurance, 161–62, 163
in homeowners insurance, 147–48
in standard fire policy, 175–76
types of, 25
Health and Human Services, Department of, insurance coverage of, 414
Health insurance, 10, 11, 285
actual cash value of, 127–28
attempts by insurers to reduce costs, 285
choosing among coverages, 517–19
contract, 289
differences between group health and individual health, 304
group; *see* Group health insurance
guideposts for buying, 289–95
cancellation, 293
change of occupation, 293–94
costs of, 294–95
definition of accident, 290
dimensions of disability coverage, 290–92
exclusions, 290
insurer, 289–90
lump-sum provisions, 292
medical expenses, 294
renewal, 293
waiver of premium, 292–93
as indemnity contract, 91
industry of, 285
proximate cause in, 109–10
restoration and nonreduction of amounts of insurance in, 130
settlement options in, 120
types of coverages, 285
basis of loss payments, 286–87
breadth-of-benefit provisions, 287
losses, 286
nature of the peril, 285–86
underwriting standards, 288
Health Insurance Association of America (HIAA), model bills of, 313
Health maintenance organization (HMO) plans, 287, 290, 322–23, 413, 414
Hedging, 30, 543
Herbert, A. P., 63
HMO Act (1973), 414
Hold harmless agreements, 30, 543
Homeowners policies, 139, 555–66
assignments, 145–46
endorsements available in, 139–40
hazards that exclude or suspend coverage in, 147–48
limitations on amount of recovery in, 148
locations covered, 146–47
perils covered in, 141–43
period of coverage, 147
persons covered in, 145
planning for, 291
policy declarations page, 552
policyowner's duties after loss, 148
property covered in, 143
readable forms of, 139
settlement options, 150
time limits for suits and claims payment, 150–51
types of losses covered in, 143–45
House confinement, 291
Hull insurance, 236–37

I

I-CAP (Inner-City Capital) Investment Program), 15–16
Ignitability, 454
Illinois Insurance Exchange (IIE), 407
Immediate annuity, 263, 543
Immediate notice, 115, 543
Immediate participation guarantee plan, 342
Implied authority, 96, 543
Implied warranty, breach of, 72
Improvements, 543
Imputed negligence, 64, 543
Inchmaree clause, in marine insurance, 190, 543
Incidental contracts, 202, 543
Incontestability clause, 277
Incorporated proprietary insurers, 408
Incorporation, 31, 543
Increasing term, 251, 543
Indemnity, 543
and insurance, 15, 33
principle of, 91–94
Independent agency companies, 421, 543
Index-linked policies, 259
Indexing year, 372–73, 543
Individual case approach, to loss reserves, 471, 543
Individual policy pension trust, 341, 544

Individual Practice Association (IPA), 323
Individual Retirement Account (IRA), 354
  estate tax advantages of, 356–57
Industrial life insurance, 260, 544
Industrial property form, 240–41, 544
Industrial Risk Insurers, 430
Inflation, effect of, on insurance needs, 523
Inflation guard endorsement, 139, 544
Initial deductible, 321, 544
Inland marine insurance, 191, 544
  bailee forms, 194–95
  coverage of domestic shipments under, 191–93
  coverage of instrumentalities of transportation and communication, 193
  and domestic shipments, 191–93
  instrumentalities of transporation and communication, 193
  property floater policies, 193–94
  yacht and motorboat insurance, 195
Inner-City Capital Investment Program (I-CAP), 15–16
Insolvency clause, 130, 544
Installments-for-a-fixed-period, 275, 544
Installments-of-a-fixed-amount, 276, 544
Insurable interest, 544
  determining amount of, 125
  principle of, 92
    in life insurance, 92–94
    in property insurance, 92
Insurance, 32–33
  costs of, 532–35
  large-loss principle, 33–34, 514
  pricing of, 46–47, 450–53
    of fire insurance, 454–55
    of life insurance, 458–62
  principles of buying commercially, 514–17
Insurance code, 58
Insurance Company of North America (INA), 173
Insurance contract, 9, 81–82, 541
  adhesion, 87
  agents
    creations of agency relationship, 96
    power and authority of, 96–97
  application, 82–83
  approval of forms, 506
  binder, 83–84
  brokers as agents, 97
  competent parties, 85–86
Insurance contract—*Cont.*
  conditional, 88
  consideration, 86
  declarations page, 552
  defined, 81–82
  as either bilateral or unilateral, 88
  as either commutative or aleatory, 86–87
  essential elements of, 84–86
  legal purpose of, 86
  liability imposed by, 71–72
  offer and acceptance of, 84–85
  as personal contract, 91
  principle of indemnity in, 91–94
  readibility of, 139, 268
  remedies, 98
    estoppel, 98–99
    reformation, 100
    rescission, 99–100
    waiver, 98–99
  responsibility of principles, 97
  standardization of, 526–28
  utmost good faith, 88–91
Insurance coverage
  defining hazards that suspend or exclude coverage, 114–15
  defining locations covered, 112
  defining losses covered, 110
  defining perils covered, 107–110
  defining persons covered, 110–11
  defining property covered, 110
  defining time of coverage, 112–14
  graduation of, 514–16
  planning
    for integrated coverage, 516–17
    for business needs, 524–26
    for personal needs, 517–24
  procedure for analysis of, 107
  settlement options, 119–20
  time limit
    for bringing suits, 120
    for paying claims, 121
Insurance Crime Prevention Institute (ICPI), 430
Insurance exposure, criteria of, 34–37
Insurance Facts, 433
Insurance Institute for Highway Safety, 430
Insurance policies, 544
  actual cash value of, 125, 127–28
  amount of insurable interest, 125
  cancellation of, 113–14
  coinsurance clauses in, 132–35
  conditions, 106
  declarations, 106
  deductible clauses in, 135–36
Insurance policies—*Cont.*
  effect of policy period, 113
  endorsements, 106
  exclusions, 106
  face amount of, 128–29
  hour of inception of, 113
  insuring agreements, 106
  other-insurance clauses in, 131–32
  policy limits in, 129–30
  restoration and nonreduction of amounts of insurance, 130
  riders, 106
  term of, 112–13
Insurance Services Office (ISO), 237, 432
Insured, 8 9, 544
Insured plan, 341–42, 544
Insurer, 8, 544
  agency forces, 422–23
  agency systems, 421–22
  assets of, 467–69
  brokers, 424
  buyers and consultants, 425
  claims administration, 425–29
  company fleets, 434
  consumer-type cooperative, 408–13
  cooperative organizations, 431–32
  departmentalization of, 419–21
  direct-selling systems, 423
  earned surplus of property-liability, 479–82
  general agent, 423
  governmental, 414–15
  incorporated proprietary, 408
  liquidation of, 505–6
  local agents, 424
  loss control, 429
  management organization of, 419
  mass merchandising, 423
  motives for forming private, 401
  producers' cooperatives, 413–14
  profitability of life, 482
  and public relations, 433
  regulation of investments, 469–70
  reserves of property and liability, 470–79
  selection of, 530–35
  services provided to policyowner by, 532
  similarities and differences in, 401–2
  solicitors, 424
  special agents, 424–25
  surplus or excess-line brokers/agents, 424
  taxation of, 507–8

Insurer—*Cont.*
  underwriting associations, 433
  unincorporated proprietary, 402–7
Insuring agreements, 106
Integrated deductible, 321, 544
Integrated insurance planning, 516–17
Interest-only option, 275, 276, 544
Internal Revenue Service, treatment of interest by, 256–60
Inventory, preparation of, after loss, 117
Investment Company Act (1940), 500
Investment year approach, 342, 544, 545
IRC 501 (c) 9 trust, funding benefits through, 315–16
Irrevocable beneficiary, 273–74, 544

J

Jewelers' block policy, 194, 544
Joint-and-last-survivor annuity, 262, 544
  option of, 276, 544
  taxation of, 358–59
Joint life policy, 258
Judgment rating, 451, 544
Judicial bonds, 232
Judicial risk, 110, 544
Juridicial risk, 544
Jury, role of, in negligence cases, 70
Juvenile endowment, 521
Juvenile life insurance forms, 260

K

Kaiser Foundation HMO, 393
Kemper group, 434
Keogh plan, 354–55
  estate tax advantages of, 356–57
Key employee life and health insurance, 50, 525
Keynes, John Maynard, 33 n
Key rate, 455, 544

L

Labels clause, 191
Labor-Management Reporting and Disclosure Act (1959), 326
Larceny, 223, 544, 549
Large-loss principle, 33–34, 514
Last clear chance doctrine, 69, 544
Law
  classifications of, 58
  and dual liability exposures, 72–73
  and legal liability, 58–64
  and liability arising from negligence, 64–65, 67, 68–71
  and liability imposed by contract, 71–72

Law—*Cont.*
  nature of, 57–58
  and the reasonable man concept, 63–64
  sine qua non and proximate cause, 68
  sources of, 57–58
  and the standard of care owed by owners and tenants concept, 65–67
  and tort liability hazards, 73–74
Leasehold interest, 182, 544
Leasehold interest policy, attachment of, to standard fire policy, 182–83
Legal insurance, prepaid group, 325–26
Legal remedies, 98, 544
Level-premium group permanent plan, 309, 544
Level-premium life insurance plan, 251
Liability, as imposed by contract, 71–72
Liability without fault, 61–62, 544
Liability insurance, 199
  actual cash value of, 127
  automobile, 207
    business, 209–11
    compensating victims of accidents, 211–13
    personal, 207–8, 209
  basic business liability forms, 201–2
  claims, 428
  coverage, 11
  endorsements and separate policies, 202–7
  general liability program, 199–200
  inclusion of related costs in policy limits, 128 n
  limits in, 129–30
  personal liability forms, 200
  and physical damage, 120–21
  professional liability forms, 200–201
  restoration and nonreduction of amounts of insurance in, 130
  workers' compensation and employers' liability, 213–17
License bond, 233
Licensing, 504–5
  of brokers and agents, 506
  of surplus-line agents and brokers, 506–7
Life, sight or limb, loss of coverage of, by health insurance, 286
Life annuities, 263, 544
Life income option, 276, 544
Life income period-certain annuity, 263, 544

Life insurance
  actual cash value of, 127–28
  annuities, 262
    classification of, 262–64
    principle, 262
    special policies, 264–67
  cash values, 248–50
  choosing among coverages, 517–19
  classes of, 260
    group, 260
    industrial, 260
    ordinary, 260
  classifications of policies, 247–50
  cost comparisons of, 533–35
  determining amount needed, 517–21
  disability riders in, 136
  exposures
    for business firm, 49–52
    for family, 47–49
  group; *see* Group life insurance
  loss-adjustment problems in, 429
  origin of, 13–14
  as participating, 274 n
  policy dividends, 247–48
  principle of insurable interest in, 92–94
  proximate cause in, 109–10
  recent trends in, 267–68
  regulation of, 267–68, 267–68
  restoration and nonreduction of amounts of insurance in, 130
  riders, 261
    accidental death, 261
    cost-of-living, 261
    disability income, 261
    payor-benefit, 261
    waiver of premium, 261
  role of, in personal financial planning, 247
  as savings medium, 248
  settlement options in, 120
  types of
    adjustable life, 259
    deposit term, 259
    endowment, 252
    family, 257–58
    family income, 256–57
    family maintenance, 257
    guaranteed insurability agreements, 258
    index-linked, 259
    joint life, 258
    juvenile forms, 260
    modified life, 260
    mortgage protection, 257
    multiple-protection, 257

Life insurance—*Cont.*
types of—*Cont.*
preferred risk, 258
survivorship, 260
term, 250–52
universal, 255–56
variable, 259
whole life, 252–55
Life insurance contract
assignment, 279
beneficiary designations, 273–74
change of beneficiary, 279
creditor's rights in, 280–81
decisions to be made by policyowner, 273–77
deduction of indebtedness and premium refund, 279
ownership, 274
permissible provisions, 278–79
aviation, 279
suicide, 279
war, 279
policy options, 274
dividend, 274–75
nonforfeiture, 274
settlement, 275–76
provisions required by state law, 277
deferment, 277
grace, 278
incontestability, 277
loan values, 277–78
misstatement of age and sex, 277
nonforfeiture, 277
reinstatement, 278
third-party rights in, 279–80
Life Insurance Fact Book, 433
Life Insurance Medical Research Fund, 430
Life insurers
earned surplus of, 482–84
policy dividends, 484–85
profitability of, 482–84
regulation of investments, 469–70
Limit of liability rule, 129–30, 544
Limited-form personal theft policy, 224
Limited health policy, 287
Limited-pay life insurance, 254, 544
Line limits, 444, 544
in life insurance, 444
in property and liability insurance, 444
Linton, M. Albert, 534
Liquidation of insurers, 505–6
Liquidity, 531, 544
Litigation bonds, 232
Livestock floater, 194
Lloyd, Edward, 402
Lloyd's of London, 13, 14, 189, 288, 402–3
American Lloyds, 407
annual subscribers, 403
defense insurance against take over battle, 406
financial strength of, 405
functions of, 403–4
kinds of policies written by, 405–6
leadership of, 404 n
membership classes, 403
mini-name memberships, 404 n
nature of, 403
operations of, 404–5
standard policy of, 527
Lloyds Associations, 407
Loan values, of life insurance, 277–78
Local agents, 424, 544
Locations
coverage of
in automobile insurance, 160
in homeowners insurance, 146–47
in standard fire policy, 175
determining coverage of, 112
Loss(es), 25–26
chance of, 21–22, 540
control, 429–31
coverage of
in automobile insurance, 158–59
in standard fire policy, 175
determining coverage of, 110
frequency, 21, 544
identifying and evaluating exposure to, 44–45
of income protection, 11
policyowner's duties after, 115–19
predictability, 22–24
ratio, 480
ratio method, 472, 545
reserves, 471–72
types of, covered in homeowners insurance, 143–45
Lost-instrument bonds, 233, 545
Loss-severity figures, 21, 545
Loss-unit concept, 516, 545
Lump-sum benefits, 292
Lunn Gas and Electric Company v. *Meriden Fire Insurance Company,* 109

M

M&C form, 201–3
McCarran-Ferguson Act (1945), 498
Machinery clause, in marine insurance, 191
Major medical and disability income policies, 594–602
Major medical insurance, 128
Malicious mischief endorsement, 181
Malicious prosecution, 60, 545
Malpractice, 73
need for policyholder's written consent for settlement, 120
Management organization, 419
Managerial controls, use of, to reduce risk, 31
Mandatory securities valuation reserve (MSVR), 483–84
Manual rating, 451–52
Manufacturers' and contractors (M&C) form, 201–3
Manufacturers Mutual Fire Insurance Company of Rhode Island, 412
Manufacturers output policy, 240–41, 545
Marine insurance
origin of, 14
settlement claims in, 428
types of, 187–88
Market-basket plan of employee benefits, 318–19
Market-value clause, 185, 545
Martin, Richard, 87
Mass merchandising, in insurance, 423
Mathematical note, 604–5
Medicaid, 367–69
Medical expenses, insurance coverage of, 49, 294
Medicare, 382–85
Memorandum clause, 190–91, 545
Mentally incompetent, contracts made by, 85–86
Mercantile open-stock burglary policy, 224–25
Mercantile robbery policy, 225
Mercantile safe-burglary policy, 225
Mercantile theft insurance, coverage for shoplifting, 35
Merchantability, 72, 545
Merit rating, 452–53, 545
Merritt Committee investigation (1910), 492
Metropolitan Life Insurance Company, 430
MGIC Investment Corporation, 236
MGM Grand Hotel fire, 53–54
Minimum distribution allowance (MDA), 349
determining, 351–52
Mining equipment floater, 194
Minors, contracts made by, 85
Misrepresentation, 507
Misstatement of age and sex clause, 277

Mistakes, 545
  conditions under which privileged, 61
Mobile homes, insurance for, 140–41
Modification rating, 452, 545
Modified life insurance policy, 260
Modified no-fault insurance plan, 213, 545
Money and securities broad-form policy, 225
Moral hazard, 25, 448
Mortgage and property improvement loan, insurance programs, 415
Mortgage or rent fund, 48, 519
Mortgage protection policies, 257
Motor vehicle coverage, 524; *see also* Business auto insurance (BAP) *and* Personal auto policy (PAP)
Motorboat insurance, 195
Multiple-limit insurance, 173
Multiple-line insurance, 10, 237, 240–41, 545
Multiple-location forms, 179–80, 545
Multiple-protection policies, 257
Municipal Bond Insurance Association (MBIA), 236
Mutual companies, 408, 410, 545
  advance-premium, 411
  factory, 412
  fraternal, 412
  perpetual, 411
  pure assessment, 410–11
    advance-premium, 411
    perpetual, 411
  savings bank life insurance, 412–13
Mutual fund insurance, 236
Mutual savings banks, establishment of insurance departments by, 412–13

N

Name schedule bond, 228, 545
Named nonowner, 207, 545
National Association of Independent Insurers, 430
National Association of Insurance Commissioners (NAIC), 494, 495–96
  approval of over life insurance solicitation, 267–68
  model laws of, 278, 313, 477–78, 498–99
National Association of Mutual Insurance Companies, 430
National Board of Fire Underwriters, 429, 430
National Cargo Bureau, 430
National Commission on State Workmen's Compensation Laws, 217
National Council on Compensation Insurance, 430
National Council of Senior Citizens, 212–13
National Credit Union Administration, insurance of credit union accounts, 415
National health insurance (NHI), 11, 392
  basic principles for, 392
  basic proposals for, 392–93
  solutions to problem, 393–94
National Safety Council, 430
Nationwide group, 434
Negligence, 62, 545
  defenses in, 68–70
  imputed, 64
  liability arising from, 64–65, 67, 68–70
  planning for coverage of, 524
  presumed, 63–64
  statutory modifications of common law of, 70–71
Nehru, Jawaharlal, 27
Net payment cost method, 534
Net valuation premiums, 472–73
New money approach, 342
New York Insurance Exchange (NYIE), 407
No-benefit-to-bailee clause, 160
No-fault insurance, 212–13
  and automobile liability, 70
  federal plan for, 213
  and the shifting of financial loss, 7
No-filing laws, 499
Nonadmitted assets, 467, 545
Nonautomobile personal property coverage planning for, 523–24
Nonforfeiture clause, 277, 545
Nonforfeiture policy options, 274, 545
Normal cost, 336, 545
Notice of accident, 116, 545
Notice of claim or suit, 116, 545
Notice as soon as practicable, 115, 545
Nuclear accident or hazard exclusion from coverage in homeowners insurance, 148
  liability of, 26
Numbers, law of large, 33–34, 514

O

OASDHI; *see* Old Age Survivors, Disability and Health Insurance (OASDHI)
Obsolescence, penalty for, 126
Occupation, change of, and health insurance coverage, 293–94
Occupational Safety and Health Act (1970) (OSHA), 215, 217, 431
Occupational sickness, coverage of, by group health insurance, 313
Occurence, 545
Ocean marine insurance, 545
  clauses modifying coverage, 190–91
  franchise deductible in, 136
  insuring clause, 189–90
  nature of interest covered, 188
  primary coverage of, 132
  property covered, 189
  term of policy, 188
  treatment of insurance coverage, 189
  valuation of interest, 188
Office burglary and robbery policy, 226, 545
Office personal property form, 240–41, 545
Official bonds, 233
Offset plan, 345, 545
Old-Age Survivors, Disability and Health Insurance (OASDHI), 368, 369; *see also* Social security
  amounts payable for benefits, 371–77
    adjust for cost-of-living increases, 377
    allocate percentage of PIA to beneficiary, 375
    apply primary insurance amount formula, 374–75
    computing AIME, 373–74
    index the covered earnings, 371–73
    redistribute benefits if total exceeds maximum family benefit, 375–77
  conditions suspending benefits, 371
  losses
    children's benefits, 380
    disability benefits, 379–80
    lump-sum death benefit, 382
    medicare benefits, 382–85
    retirement benefits, 379–80
    survivor benefits, 380–82
  losses covered, 379–85
  perils covered under, 369
  persons covered under, 369–71
Older age health policies, 288, 545
165-line form, 174, 545
Open contracts, 188, 545
Open-cargo policy, 189
Open-rating laws, 499
Optional perils policy, attachment of, to standard fire policy, 182
Ordinary life insurance, 253–55, 260, 545, 548

Other-insurance clauses, 131, 545
  purpose of, 6
  types of, 131–32
Other-than-collision (OTC) 155–56, 545
Overseas Investment Group, 415
Overseas Private Investment Corporation (OPIC), 415
Owner of business insurance for loss of, 50–52
Owners, 93, 545–46
  standard of care owed by, 65–67
Owners', landlords' and tenants' (OL&T) form, 201–2, 203

P

Paid-in surplus accounts, regulation of, 504
Paid-up additions, use of dividends to buy, 275
Paid-up policy, 253–55
Pair-or-set clause, 119–20
Palsgraf v. *Long Island Railroad,* 68
Parcel-post form, use of, with inland marine insurance, 192
Parol evidence rule, 99, 546
Partially amortized mortgage loan, 257 n
partnership insurance, 50–51, 526
Pascal, 5
Paul, Samuel, 496–97
Paul v. *Virginia,* 496–98, 500
Pay-Related Stock Ownership Plans (PAYSOP), 355–57
Paymaster robbery policy, 225–26
Payment development method, 472, 546
Payor-benefit rider, 261
Pension Benefit Guaranty Corporation (PBGC), 343
Pension termination insurance, 11
Per risk reinsurance, 445–46, 546
Percentage unit benefit formula, 345, 546
Performance bond, 233, 546
Peril(s)
  coverage of
    in automobile insurance, 155–57
    in health insurance, 285–86
    in homeowners insurance, 140, 141–43
    in standard fire policy, 175
  defining coverage of, 107–10
  definition of, 24
  determining extent of coverage against, 108–9
  interpreting coverage of, 108
Permit bond, 233
Perpetual mutuals, 411, 546
Personal articles floater, 193, 546
Personal auto policy (PAP), 155, 567–79
  buying behavior, 514
  compensation of victims, 211–13
  coverage period of, 160–61
  hazards excluded or suspended in, 161–62, 163
  liability coverages, 207–9
  limitations on amount of recovery, 163
  locations covered in, 160
  no-benefit-to-bailee clause, 160
  nonownership coverage, 207–8
  perils covered in, 155–57
  persons covered, 159, 160
  policyowner's duties after loss, 163
  property covered in, 157–58
  related vehicles, 209
  settlement options, 163–64
  time limits for suits and claims payment, 164–65
  types of losses covered in, 158–59
  variations in, and family and special policies, 165–66
Personal effects floater, 193, 546
Personal injury liability policy, 204
Personal liability exposures, 73–74, 73–74
Personal liability forms, 200
Personal property floater, 193–94, 546
Personal property replacement-cost endorsement, 139, 546
Personal theft policy, 223–24
Persons
  coverage of
    in automobile insurance, 159, 160
    in homeowners insurance, 145
    in standard fire policy, 175
  determining coverage of, 110–11
Philadelphia Contributorship for the Insurance of Houses from Loss by Fire, 173
Physical damage or loss insurance, 10–11
Physical hazard, 25
Physicians' and surgeons' equipment floater, 194
Plan termination insurance (PTI), 353, 546
Poisson, Simeon Denis, 33
Policy dividends, 247–48, 546
Policy face amount, 128–29, 546
Policy limits, 129–30, 546
Policy proof of interest form (PPI), 189, 546
Policy reserve, 472–74
  computation of, 474–77
  nature of, 472–74
  overconservatism in computation of, 477
  regulation of, 503–4
Policyowner, 9, 546
  duties of, after loss, 115
    appraisal, 118–19
    assistance and cooperation, 118
    in automobile accident, 163
    evidence, 117
    in homeowner loss, 148
    inventory, 117
    notice of loss, 115–16, 148
    proof of loss, 117–18
    protection of property, 116
  services provided, by insurer, 352
Port-risk only marine insurance, 189
Position schedule bond, 228, 546
Power Squadron, 430
Preferred risk, 258, 442, 546
Premium, 450, 546
  for annuities, 262–63
  origin of term, 13
  tax on, 507–8
Prepaid legal insurance, 325
  regulation of, 325–26
Presumed negligence, 63–64, 546
Presumptive agency, 96, 546
Price-Anderson Act, 26
Primary insurance amount (PIA) formula, 371, 546
  allocation of percentage of, to each beneficiary, 375
  application of, 374–75
  calculation of, 373
  computation of, 377–79
Principals, responsibility of, 97
Priority coverage, 129
Private insurance, 10–11
Privilege, as defense against intentional torts, 61
Privity of contract principle, 72, 546
Pro rata liability clause, 131, 546
Probability
  law of, 33–34
  theory of, 5
Producers' cooperatives, 408, 413–14
Products
  liability, 59, 62, 72–74, 204
  regulation of, 506
Professional liability, 73
Professional liability forms, 200–201

Profit-sharing plans, income taxation of benefits of, 349–53
Profitability
of life insurers, 482–84
of property and liability insurers, 481–82
profits and commissions insurance, 185, 546
Projected benefit cost method, 336–40
Promissory warranty, 88, 546
Property
coverage of
in automobile insurance, 157–58
in homeowners insurance, 143
in standard fire policy, 175
determining coverage of, 110
exposures
for business firm, 53–54
for family, 52–53
loss of actual, 52
loss of use of, and extra expenses related to, 53
protection of, after loss, 116
Property floater policies, 193–94
Property insurance
indemnity principle in, 91–92
principle of insurable interest in, 92
proximate cause in, 109
restoration and nonreduction of amounts of insurance in, 130
Property insurance contract, 91, 546
Property liability insurance, 10–11
for business needs, 524–25
cost comparisons of, 532–33
group, 323–25
loss-adjustment problems in, 428–29
planning for, 523–24
Property liability insurers
earned surplus of, 479–82
regulation of investments, 469
Proportional reinsurance, 445–46, 546
Prospective experience rating, 452–53, 546
Prospective method, 474
Protection and indemnity clause (P&I), 191, 546
Proximate cause
breach of duty as, 67
doctrine of, 109–10
rule, 68, 546
Prudential Insurance Company of America, 507
Public and institutional property (PIP) form, 240–41, 546
Public interest
changing concept of, 491–92
effect of, on insurance business, 491
Public Law 15, 498
developments after, 498–99
federal regulatory issues, 499–500
Public official bonds, 233, 546
Public relations, 433
Punitive damages, 59, 127, 546
Pure assessment mutuals, 410–11, 546
Pure no-fault insurance plan, 213, 546
Pure risk, 43

Q–R

Qualified pension plans, 349–53
Quota share reinsurance, 445–46, 546
Radioactive contamination assumption endorsement, attachment of, to standard fire policy, 181–82
Radioactivecontaminationpolicy,194
Radiumfloater,194
Raininsurance,186
Ratemaking
organizations,432
principlesof,450–51
regulationof,501–3
typesof,451–53
Rating,9
lawson,498–99
Readability, of insurance policy, 139, 268
Reasonable man concept, 62–63
Rebating, 507
Reciprocal insurance exchanges, 408–10, 546–47
Recovery amount, limitations on, in automobile insurance, 163
Reductio ad absurdum, 36
Reformation, of contract, 100, 547
Refund annuity, 263, 547
Registered-mail and express forms, use of, with inland marine insurance, 192
Regulation
of business methods, 506–8
and competition, 492-93
financial, 501–6
goals of, 494
history of, in United States, 496–501
methods of, 494
administrative control, 495
judicial control, 495
legislative control, 494
objectives of, 491–94
product, 506–7
Regulation—*Cont.*
reasons for, 493–94
self, 496
state versus federal, 500–501
Reimbursement form, 286–87, 547
Reinstatement of lapsed policy, 278
Reinsurance, 443, 444
proportional/nonproportional, 445–46
reasons for, 447
types of, 444–45, 446–47
Release-of-attachment bonds, 547
Remedies, 98
Renewable and convertible termlife insurance, 251, 547
Renewable term life insurance, 250–51, 547
Rent fund, insurance coverage of, 48, 519
Rent insurance, attachment of, to standard fire policy, 182
Reparations, 211, 547
Replacement cost, 126
Replacement cost insurance
attachment of, to standard fire policy, 183–84
exception to actual cash value in, 128
Replacement option, 119
Replacement problem, 507, 547
Representations, in insurance contracts, 89–90, 547
Res ipsa loquitor, 63–64, 547
Rescission, 99–100, 547
Reserves; *see* Policy reserve
Residence theft, 547
Residual disability benefits, 291, 547
Residual market, 547
Respondentia, 13, 547
Retention, 443–44
Retirement plans
accrued benefit cost method of funding, 336
advantages of funding, 340
basic decisions in establishing, 343
benefit levels, 344–47
eligibility
for benefits, 344
of coverage, 343–44
funding of benefits, 348–49
income taxation of benefits, 349–53
types of benefits, 347–48
disclosure, 354
Employee Stock Ownership Plans (ESOP) as, 355–56
fiduciary responsibilities, 353

Retirement plans—*Cont.*
funding agencies, 340–42
funding issues, 331
concept of fully funded plan, 332
defined benefit plans, 332–33
defined contribution plans, 332, 333
funded ratio, 335
maximum standards, 335
minimum standards, 335
problems of meeting minimum standards, 333–35
individual retirement account as, 354
insured plans, 341–42
needs to be covered by, 49, 521–22
Pay-Related Stock Ownership Plan (PAYSOP) as, 355–56
plan termination insurance, 353
projected benefit cost method of funding, 336
Self-Employment (Keogh) Retirement plan as, 354–55
and the Tax Equity and Fiscal Responsibility Act, 357–58
tax-sheltered annuity (TSA) as, 355
termination of, 343
trust fund plans, 340
Retrocession, 444, 547
Retrospective experience rating, 452–53, 547
Retrospective method, 474, 547
Revenue Act (1978), 318–19
Reverse competition, 503
Revocable beneficiary, 273, 547
Riders, 106, 261, 547
Risk, 22, 24, 547
assumption of, as defense in a negligence action, 69
degree of, 23–24
insurance as device for handling, 32–37
methods of handling, 27–28, 29–32
social cost of, 26–27
Risk and Insurance Management Society, Inc. (RIMS), 43 212–13
Risk analysis
life and health exposures
for business firm, 49–52
for family, 47–49
property exposures
for business firm, 53–54
for family, 52–53
Risk management
achieving goal of, 44–46
objectives of, 44
Risk management—*Cont.*
process of, 44
types of risk, 43–44
Risk manager, 43
duties of, 29, 46–47
Risk premium reinsurance, 446, 547
Robbery, 223, 547
Roosevelt, Franklin D., 500
Ross v. *Odom* (1968), 316
Rule of 45, 347–48,547
Running-down clause, 190, 547
Rush v. *Commercial Realty Company,* 70

S

Safe-deposit-box insurance coverage, 224
Sales organizations, 421–23
Salesperson's floater, 194
Salvage, 119, 163, 426, 547
Savings bank life insurance, 412–13
Schedule rating, 452, 547
Scheduled expense coverage, 286, 547
Scheduled personal property endorsement, 139, 547
Scheduled property floater, 193, 547
Second-injury funds, 217, 507
Securities and Exchange Commission (SEC), 500
Securities Act (1933), 500
Securities Investor Protection Corporation (SIPC), 415
Segregated accounts, 342
Self-Employment (Keogh) Retirement Plan, 354–55
estate tax advantages of, 356–57
Self-insurance, 513–14
definition of, 32
and use of sinking funds, 28–29
Self-regulation, 496
Sentry Group, 434
Separate accounts, 342
Service forms, 286–87, 547
Service incurred health insurance plan, 287
Settlement options, 119, 547
abandonment and salvage, 119
in automobile insurance, 163
in health insurance, 120
in homeowners insurance, 150
in life insurance, 120, 275–76
pair-or-set clause, 119–20
relations with third parties, 120
replacement option, 119
Shared appreciation mortgage loan, 257 n
Sherman Antitrust Act, 498, 499, 500
Short-rate or term policies, 112, 547
Sickness insurance, 285–86
proving definite loss in, 35
Sidetract agreements, 202, 547–48
Simplified employee pension (SEP), 354, 548
Sine qua non rule, 68
Sinking funds, 28–29
Sister-ship clause, 190, 548
Sliding rate scale, 134, 548
Smoke, 548
Social insurance; *see also* Disability insurance; Old Age Survivors Disability and Health Insurance; Social security; *and* Workers' compensation
definition of, 365, 548
kinds of, in United States, 366, 367
nature of system, 365–67
need for, 366–67
Social security, 11
average monthly wage calculation for primary insurance amount, 394–95
current financial status of, 387
history of, 385–86
and politics, 385
reasons for problems, 387–88
and the shifting of financial loss, 7
Society of Actuaries, 478
Sole proprietorship insurance, 50, 525–26
Solicitors, 424, 548
Solution, 255 n
Solvency, 531, 548
Source Book of Health Insurance Data, 433
South-Eastern Underwriters Association case, 497–98, 500
Special agents, 424–25, 548
Special auto policy (SAP), 155, 165–66; *see also* Personal auto policy (PAP)
Special damages, 548
Special multi-peril program, 237, 238–39, 548
Special-purpose life insurance policies, 256–60
Special-risk health policies, 288, 548
Specific coverage, 548
Specified perils contract, 108, 548
Speculative risk, 43
Spendthrift trust clause, 281, 548
Split-funded plan, 340, 548
Split-life insurance policy, 264, 265, 267,

548
Spouse, lifetime income needed for surviving, 48, 520–21
Sprinkler-leakage insurance, 186
Stability of statistical frequencies, 33 n
Standard of care, 65–67, 73
Standard fire insurance policy; *see* Fire insurance
Standard policy, 258
Standard risk, 442, 548
Stare decisis, doctrine of, 58
State
  insurance departments of, 415, 496
  regulation by, versus federal, 500–501
  standardization of insurance policies by, 527–28
State Farm group, 434
Statutes of limitations, 150 n
Statutory law, 57–58, 548
Statutory modification, of insurance contracts, 90–91
Stimulated authority, 96, 548
Stock company, 408, 548
Stop loss, 445–46
Stop-loss reinsurance, 446, 548
Storekeepers burglary and robbery policy, 226, 548
Storekeepers' liability policy, 205–6
Straight deductible, 136, 548, 548
Straight life insurance, 253–55, 548
Straight term life insurance, 250, 548
Strict liability, 61–62
Strikes, riots and civil commotion clause (SR&CC), 190, 548
Students' bonds, 233, 548
Subcontracting, 30
Subject, 9, 93, 548
Subject-owner-beneficiary rule, 93, 548
Sublimits, as type of policy limits, 129
Subrogation, 94–95, 160, 426–27, 548
Subscriber's agreement, 409
Substandard health policies, 288, 548
Substandard risk, 442, 548
Sue-and-labor clause, 128 n, 191, 548
Suicide, coverage of, 278–79, 290
Suits, time limit for bringing, 120
Supplemental cost, 336, 548
Supplemental liability, 336, 548
Supplemental security income (SSI) program, 368
Supply bond, 232–33, 549
Surety bonds, 30–31, 227, 549
  contract bonds, 232–33
  judicial bonds, 232
Surety bonds—*Cont.*
  license (or permit) bonds, 233
  miscellaneous bonds, 233
  official bonds, 233
Suretyship coverage, 11
Surplus accounts, 483–84
  regulation of, 504
Surplus line agent/broker, 424, 549
  licensing of, 506–7
Surplus lines license, 406
Surplus share reinsurance, 445–46, 549
Surrender cost method, 533–34
Survival and wrongful death, common law statutes regarding, 71
Survivorship benefit, 249–50, 549
Survivorship life insurance policy, 260
Swine Flu Vaccine Program (1976), 26–27

T

T-life, 256 n
Taft-Hartley Act (1947), 326
Tax Equity and Fiscal Responsibility Act (TEFRA) (1982), 257–58, 322, 382, 388
Tax-free rollovers, 354
Tax Reform Act (1969), 317
Tax Reform Act (1976), 356
Tax Reform Act Stock Ownership Plans (TRASOP), 356
Tax-sheltered annuity (TSA), 355
Tax shelters, purchase of single-premium deferred annuities as, 263
Taxation
  of insurance companies, 507–8
  of interest, 256–60
Technical eligibility, 380
Temporary disability income benefit plans, 390
  benefits under, 391
  eligibility for, 391
  financing of, 391
  future of, 391–92
10-year vesting rule, 347–48, 549
Tenants, standard of care owed by, 65–67
Term insurance, 250, 549
  buying of, and investing difference, 254
  forms, 250–51
  premiums, 251
  uses of, 251–54
Term policies, 112, 549
Theft, 223, 549
Theft extension endorsement, 140, 549
Third parties
  clarification of relationship of, to insurers, 120
  coverages, 9, 549
  rights of, in life insurance, 279–81
Three-year cost recovery rule, 350
Time limits for suits and claims payment, in automobile insurance, 164–65
Time policy, 188, 189, 549
Title insurance, 236
Tort liability hazards, 73–74
Torts, 59, 549
  intentional, 59–61, 59–62
  liability hazards of, 73–74
  liability without fault, 61–62
  negligence, 62, 63–65, 67, 68–71
Total-loss only marine insurance, 189
Total taxable amount (TTA), 349, 351
Traditional net cost method, 533
Travel-accident policy, 293
Treaty reinsurance, 445, 549
Trespass, 549
  to personal property, 60–61
  to real property, 60
Trip transit form, use of, with inland marine insurance, 192
Trust fund plan, 340
Tuition form, 185, 549
Twisting, 507, 549

U

Ultra vires act, 82, 86
Umbrella liability insurance, 206, 549
Unallocated funding instruments, 341, 549
Unauthorized Insurers Service of Process Act (UISPA), 505
Underwriter, 402, 440–41
Underwriters' Laboratories, Inc., 29, 442
Underwriting, 9, 439, 549
  conflict between production and, 448
  department of, 441
  of fire insurance, 453–54
  governmental pressures on, 450
  of health insurance, 288
  of life insurance, 456–58
  and moral hazards, 448
  postselection process, 443
  preselection process, 441–42
  profit, 479–81
  profitable distribution of exposures, 440
  reinsurance, 444–45, 446–47
  retention, 443–44
  selection process, 439–40
  special problems in, 447–48, 450

Underwriting associations, 433
Unearned premium reserve, 470–71, 480, 549
Unemployment compensation, 388–89
  benefits, 389
  coverage provisions, 389
  criteria for, 36–37
  eligibility for benefits, 389–90
  financing of, 390
Unfair discrimination, 507–8
Uniform Individual Accident and Sickness Policy Provisions Act, 289
Uniform Insurers Liquidation Act, 505–6
Uniform Reciprocal Licensing Act (URLA), 505
Unilateral contracts, 88, 549
Uninsured motorists coverage, 159, 212, 549
Unit purchase plan, 309
Universal life insurance, 255–56, 265 n, 549
Universal mercantile system, 455–56, 549
Unsatisfied-judgment funds, 211
Usufruct interest, 178 n
Utmost good faith, contracts of, 88

V

Valuable papers and records insurance, 235–36
Valued form, 286–87, 549
Valued policies, 128, 428
Vandalism endorsement, 181
Variable annuity, 264–65, 549
Variable life insurance, 259
Variable rate mortage loan, 257 n
Vesting, 347–48, 549
Veterans Administration (VA), life insurance of, 414
Voluntary government insurance, 11
Voluntary reserves, 472
Voyage policy, 188, 189, 549

W

Waiting periods, in disability coverage, 136, 549
Waiver, 98–99, 549
Waiver of premium, 261
  in disability insurance, 292–93
  in group health insurance, 307
  in medical expense coverage, 293
War clauses, 37, 147–48, 279, 366
Warehouse-to-warehouse clause, 191, 549
Warranties, insurance, 88–89, 549; *see also* Products, liability
Water damage insurance, 186
Watercraft endorsement, 140, 549
Wedding presents floater, 193
Welfare and Pension Plans Disclosure Act, 326
Well drilling equipment floater, 194
Whole life insurance, 252–53, 580–93
  premiums, 253
  uses of, 253–55
Wholesale health insurance, 314
Wholesale life insurance, 312
Workers' compensation, 11, 15
  benefits under, 215–16
  coverage under, 215, 313
  directions of laws, 217
  historical development of, 214–15
  medical benefits, 216
  policy, 216–17
  rehabilitation services, 216
  as required by law, 515
  second-injury funds, 217
  survivorship benefits, 216
Written premiums, 480, 549

Y

Yacht insurance, 195
Yacht Safety Bureau, 430
Yearly renewable term (YRT), 251, 549
Yearly renewable term (YRT) plan, 446, 549

This book has been set VideoComp, in 9 and 8 point Roma, leaded 2 points. Part numbers are 14 point Souvenir Demi-Bold and part titles are 20 point Souvenir Demi-Bold. Chapter titles are 24 point Souvenir Demi-Bold. The size of the type page is 36½ by 48½ picas.

Suggestions for Further Study

In a genuinely prestigious *Who's Who* listing, one famous biographee reported that he acquired much of his university education during free time after completing his course assignments. He selectively explored broadly based literature outside his specialized fields so that he could profit from enlightened and superior knowledge and understanding about the world and about living.

Most textbooks offer suggestions for further study. However, these offerings are generally limited to additional works in the same discipline. To follow these suggestions could make the student increasingly narrow—not a desirable result. Suggestions for further study proffered in this text have a different objective. Because this text contains all that is conceivably needed for a basic course, the student may reread the relevant chapter(s) one or more times to pick up information that escaped notice or understanding in the earlier readings. Although other insurance books patently have much to offer, students can better use their limited time to read books in other fields.

The suggestions presented here are designed to entice and motivate students to broaden their education by reading carefully chosen books beyond insurance to understand why all of life should be molded into a whole—not compartmentalized with the career component occupying the largest compartment. A brief description of each suggested work is included to facilitate selection among them.

Wallace Stevens, Pulitzer prize winner, worked for the Hartford Accident and Indemnity Insurance Company for 39 years and was vice president during the last 21 years of his life. He wrote poetry during his free time and became one of the most revered and influential poets of his time. Some of his earlier poems are included in *Harmonium* (1923). Later he published *Owl's Clover* (1936), *The Man with the Blue Guitar* (1937), *Parts of a World* (1942), *Notes toward a Supreme Fiction* (1942), *Transport to Summer* (1947), *Ideas of Order* (1953) and *Collected Poems of Wallace Stevens* (Knopf, 1954). Stevens also wrote prose essays: *Three Academic Pieces* (1947) and *The Necessary Angel* (Random House, 1965). Stevens was concerned with creating some shape or order in a slovenly world of chaos as expressed in his *Harmonium.* (His best known poem, "Sunday Morning," is included in this volume.) In his *Notes toward a Supreme Fiction*, Stevens expands on the poet's role in creating the fiction necessary to transform and harmonize the world. In poems such as "The Man with the Blue Guitar" and "Anecdote of the Jar" as well as in the collected essays of *The Necessary Angel*, Stevens develops his ideas about the means of knowledge, about the contrast between reality and appearance, and on imagination as giving an aesthetic insight and order to life. Throughout most of his works, Stevens' view of the beauties and ironies of modern life is marked by intellectual comedy and the belief that "the poem is the cry of its occasion, part of the res [thing] itself and not about it."